16 0141008

D0271235

WITHDRAWN

The Macrophage

Two week loan

Please return on or before the last date stamped below.
Charges are made for late return.

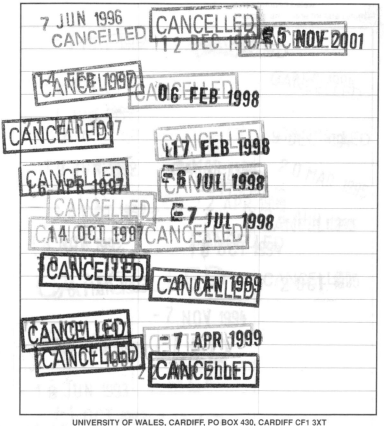

7 JUN 1996
CANCELLED
CANCELLED
25 NOV 2001
CANCELLED
06 FEB 1998
CANCELLED
17 FEB 1998
CANCELLED
6 JUL 1998
CANCELLED
14 OCT 1997
7 JUL 1998
CANCELLED
CANCELLED
CANCELLED
CANCELLED
7 APR 1999
CANCELLED
CANCELLED

UNIVERSITY OF WALES, CARDIFF, PO BOX 430, CARDIFF CF1 3XT

LF 114/0895

The Natural Immune System

The Macrophage

Edited by
CLAIRE E. LEWIS
and
JAMES O'D. McGEE

Nuffield Department of Pathology and Bacteriology
University of Oxford

OXFORD UNIVERSITY PRESS
Oxford New York Tokyo

616.079
M

Oxford University Press, Walton Street, Oxford OX2 6DP

Oxford is a trade mark of Oxford University Press

Published in the United States
by Oxford University Press, New York

© Oxford University Press, 1992

All rights reserved. No part of this publication may be reproduced,
stored in a retrieval system, or transmitted, in any form or by any means,
electronic, mechanical, photocopying, recording, or otherwise, without
the prior permission of Oxford University Press

This book is sold subject to the condition that it shall not, by way
of trade or otherwise, be lent, re-sold, hired out, or otherwise circulated
without the publisher's prior consent in any form of binding or cover
other than that in which it is published and without a similar condition
including this condition being imposed on the subsequent purchaser

A catalogue record for this book is available from the British Library

Library of Congress Cataloging in Publication Data
The Macrophage: the natural immune system/edited by Claire E. Lewis
and James O'D. McGee.
Includes bibliographical references and index.
1. Macrophages.   2. Natural immunity.   I. Lewis, Claire E.
II. McGee, James O'D.
[DNLM: 1. Bacterial Infections—immunology.   2. Hematopoiesis—
immunology.   3. Immunity, Natural.   4. Macrophages—immunology.
5. Macrophages—physiology.   6. Parasitic Diseases—immunology.
7. Virus Diseases—immunology.   WH 650 M17393]
QR185.8.M3M316   1991   616.07'9—dc20   91-24023
ISBN 0-19-963235-9
ISBN 0-19-963234-0 (pbk)

Photoset by Rowland Phototypesetting Ltd
Bury St Edmunds, Suffolk
Printed in Great Britain by
Information Press, Eynsham, Oxon

- 7 APR 1992

Foreword

SIAMON GORDON
Glaxo Professor of Cellular Pathology, University of Oxford

The macrophage is a remarkably versatile cell. Its ancient origins are shrouded in the evolution of multicellular organisms, but its specialized recognition receptors and professional phagocytic capacities are undisputed, as are the bewildering array of cytokines and low molecular weight secretory products used by the cell to perform its major role in natural and acquired host defence. The macrophage collaborates with B- and T-lymphocytes and their products in inducing responses to antigen and invading micro-organisms and, in developing potent antimicrobial cytotoxic mechanisms, is able to mediate destruction of tissues in its local environment, as well as of altered host cells. Study of its life history continues to reveal the complexity of the widespread distribution of macrophages throughout the body and its unique contribution, as a migratory leucocyte, in tissue development and the nervous system. The macrophages, normally resident at major portals of entry to the body, initiate and assemble local and systemic responses to injury and, together with newly recruited haemopoietic cells including monocytes, orchestrate the infinitely complex processes of inflammation and repair which underlie much of pathology.

Many of these cellular properties have been widely discussed. The present volume provides an up to date review of current knowledge in major topics, several of which have been neglected previously, in spite of their theoretical and practical importance. The field is set in context by a general, wide-ranging introduction by Auger and Ross which encompasses the heterogeneity of forms and functions displayed by the macrophage as it adapts to its microenvironment. The complex biochemical signalling systems involved in immunologically specific and non-specific activation of macrophage effector functions are next discussed by Adams and Hamilton. Macrophages are an important component of the haemopoietic stroma, as described by Crocker and Milon, and the recent progress in our understanding of intercellular adhesion and cytokine regulation of haemopoiesis is placed in perspective. The role of macrophages in antiviral resistance was not fully appreciated until the recent impact of HIV drew attention to its contribution to AIDS pathogenesis. Gendelman and Morahan review general aspects of macrophage determinants of viral infection, as well as of its role in lentivirus biology within the host. Other major classes of pathogenic agents which interact with macrophages are considered by Speert and Sadick respectively, who describe the uptake, killing, and evasion strategies employed by bacteria and intracellular parasites.

There are still many unsolved issues relating to the contribution of macrophages to humoral and cellular immunity. Antigen presentation and autoimmunity are discussed by Pollack and Etzioni, who also draw attention to primary immunodeficiency syndromes in man in which macrophages may be involved. Rees and Parry bravely tackle the vexed question of macrophages in tumour immunity. The role of macrophages in less obviously chronic inflammatory responses to injury of blood vessel walls, especially atherosclerosis, has become more widely studied in recent years as reviewed by Parums. Finally, the highly specialized properties of microglia, macrophages within the parenchyma of the nervous system, are summarized by Perry and Lawson.

This menu provides a feast for the macrophage specialist, as well as all scientists and clinicians with an interest in the processes which regulate tissue homeostasis in health and disease.

Acknowledgements

We would like to thank the following individuals for the support, advice and/ or forbearance in the production of this book: Mrs Anne McGee, Dr Frances Lannon, Dr Louise Muntz, Dr Johann Lorenzen, Dr Colette O'Sullivan, Ms Linda Bromley, Dr Nancy Hogg, and Professor Siamon Gordon.

We are also indebted both to Dr Jan Orenstein for providing us with a most interesting front cover illustration, and to Professor Siamon Gordon for writing an excellent foreword to set the scene for these collected works.

Claire Lewis is also pleased to have the opportunity to thank Dr John Morris of the Department of Human Anatomy, Oxford University who, during her doctoral work, provided a superb and highly stimulating scientific and editorial training. Without his guidance the production of this book would not have been possible.

The idea for this book (as one of a series entitled *The natural immune system*) was conceived during various stimulating discussions between the editors and representatives of the Science and Medical Division of the Oxford University Press. We thank these individuals for this contribution, and are pleased to acknowledge their help and encouragement in the production of this volume.

The continuing support of the Cancer Research Campaign, UK, is also gratefully acknowledged by the editors.

Oxford   C.E.L.
August 1991   J.O'D.M.

Contents

9   Macrophages in cardiovascular disease   359
D.V. PARUMS

10   Macrophages in the central nervous system   391
V.H. PERRY AND L.J. LAWSON

Contributors

D.O. Adams Departments of Pathology and Microbiology–Immunology, Duke University, Durham, North Carolina 27710, USA.

M.J. Auger Department of Clinical and Laboratory Haematology, Western General Hospital, Edinburgh EH4 2XU, UK.

P.R. Crocker The Pasteur Institute, 28, rue de Dr Roux, 75724 Paris Cedex 15, France.

A. Etzioni Division of Clinical Immunology, Department of Paediatrics, Rambam Medical Centre, Haifa 31096, *and* The Faculty of Medicine, Technion–Israel Institute of Technology, Haifa 31096, Israel.

H. E. Gendelman HIV-Immunopathogenesis Program, Department of Cellular Immunology, Walter Reed Army Institute of Research, 9620 Medical Centre Drive, Suite 200, Rockville, Maryland, 20850, USA *and* The Henry M. Jackson Foundation for the Advancement of Military Medicine, Rockville, Maryland, 20850, USA.

T.A. Hamilton Research Institute, Cleveland Clinic Research Foundation, Cleveland, Ohio 44195, USA.

L.J. Lawson Department of Pharmacology, University of Oxford, Mansfield Road, Oxford, UK.

G. Milon The Pasteur Institute, 28 rue du Dr Roux, 75724 Paris Cedex 15, France.

P.S. Morahan Medical College of Pennsylvania, Department of Microbiology and Immunology, Philadelphia, Pennsylvania, 19129, USA.

D.V. Parums Nuffield Department of Pathology and Bacteriology, University of Oxford, John Radcliffe Hospital, Headington, Oxford OX3 9DU UK.

H. Parry Institute for Cancer Studies, Department of Experimental and Clinical Microbiology, Beech Hill Road, University of Sheffield, Sheffield S10 2RX, UK.

V. H. Perry Department of Pharmacology, University of Oxford, Mansfield Road, Oxford, UK.

S. Pollack Division of Clinical Immunology, Department of Medicine, Rambam Medical Centre, Haifa 31096, Israel *and* The Faculty of Medicine, Technion–Israel Institute of Technology, Haifa 31096, Israel.

R.C. Rees Institute for Cancer Studies, Department of Experimental and Clinical Microbiology, Beech Hill Road, University of Sheffield, Sheffield S10 2RX, UK.

J.A. Ross Lister Research Laboratories, Department of Surgery, University of Edinburgh, Royal Infirmary, Edinburgh, EH3 9YW, UK.

M.D. Sadick Division of Infectious Diseases, University of California San Francisco Medical Center, Department of Medicine, 505 Parnassus Avenue, San Francisco, California 94143-0120, USA.

D.P. Speert Departments of Paediatrics and Microbiology, and the Canadian Bacterial Diseases Network, University of British Columbia *and* the Division of Infectious Diseases, British Columbia's Children's Hospital, Vancouver, British Columbia, Canada.

Abbreviations

ADCC	antibody-dependent cellular cytotoxicity
ADE	antibody-dependent enhancement
AIDS	acquired immunodeficiency syndrome
APC	antigen-presenting cell
ATP	adenosinetriphosphate
BCG	bacillus Calmette–Guérin
BSA	bovine serum albumin
CAEV	caprine arthritis encephalitis virus
CD	cluster of differentiation
CFU	colony-forming unit
CR	complement receptor
CSF	colony-stimulating factor
DAF	decay accelerating factor
DAG	diacylglycerol
DC	dendritic cell
EGF	epidermal growth factor
EpC	epithelial cells
EPO	erythropoietin
FIM	factor increasing monocytopoiesis
GM-CSF	granulocyte macrophage colony-stimulating factor
HBGF	heparin-binding growth factor
HIV	human immunodeficiency virus
HLA	human leucocyte antigen
HSV	herpes simplex virus
ICAM	intercellular adhesion molecule
LAD	leucocyte adhesion deficiency
LBP	lipopolysaccharide-binding protein
LC	Langerhans cell
LCA	leucocyte common antigen
LDL	low density lipoprotein
LDV	lactate dehydrogenase-elevating virus
LFA	leucocyte function antigen

LPS	lipopolysaccharide
LT	leucotriene
MCP	membrane cofactor protein
M-CSF	macrophage colony-stimulating factor
MAF	macrophage-activating factor
MDF	muramyl dipeptide
MFR	mannosyl-fucosyl receptor
MHC	major histocompatibility complex
MIP	macrophage inflammatory protein
MMF	macrophage fusion factor
MnGC	multinucleated giant cells
MPS	mononuclear phagocyte system (*see also* RES)
MTC	macrophage-mediated cell cytotoxicity
NGF	nerve growth factor
NK cell	natural killer cell
NK activity	natural killer activity
PA	peroxidase activity
PAF	platelet-activating factor
PDGF	platelet-derived growth factor
PG	prostaglandin
RBMM	resident bone marrow macrophage
RES	reticuloendothelial system (*see also* MPS)
ROI	reactive oxygen intermediate
SCF	stem cell factor
SCR	short consensus repeat
TAM	tumour-associated macrophages
TGF	transforming growth factor
TNF	tumour necrosis factor
VLA	very late antigen
VLDL	very low density lipoprotein

1 The biology of the macrophage

M.J. AUGER AND J.A. ROSS

1   Introduction

The macrophage is the major differentiated cell of the mononuclear phagocyte system. This system comprises bone marrow monoblasts and promonocytes, peripheral blood monocytes, and tissue macrophages.
Macrophages are widely distributed throughout the body, displaying great
structural and functional heterogeneity. They are to be found in lymphoid
organs, the liver, lungs, gastrointestinal tract, central nervous system,
serous cavities, bone, synovium, and skin; they participate in a wide range of
physiological and pathological processes.

The term 'macrophage' was first used more than 100 years ago by Elie
Metchnikoff in Messina, to describe the large mononuclear phagocytic cells
he observed in tissues (1). In 1924, Aschoff assigned these cells to the
reticuloendothelial system (RES), a broad system of cells which included
reticular cells, endothelial cells, fibroblasts, histiocytes, and monocytes (2).
However, because the RES included cells of non-macrophage lineage it did
not constitute a true system, so in 1969 it was agreed to replace this term with
the current title, mononuclear phagocyte system (MPS), on the basis that
macrophages shared important functional characteristics *in vivo* and were
derived from monocytes (3), whereas endothelial cells and fibroblasts were
not. Phylogenetically, the mononuclear phagocyte is a primitive cell type
with related cells being found in early life forms, and some single-cell
protozoa exhibiting features similar to the mammalian macrophage. Ontogenetically, the macrophage originates in the yolk sac (4), but in adult man
arises from the bone marrow (5).

2   Macrophage origin and kinetics

Macrophages originate in the bone marrow (Figure 1.1). In man the bone
marrow contains resident macrophages, as well as their precursors; monocytes, promonocytes, and monoblasts. There is considerable evidence to
suggest that monocytes and neutrophils share a common progenitor cell in
the bone marrow (6). This common progenitor is called the colony-forming
unit, granulocyte-macrophage (CFU-GM) because of its ability to give rise
to colonies of monocytes and neutrophils in semi-solid marrow cultures. It is
likely that a progenitor cell becomes committed to either monocytic or
granulocytic differentiation at a level of maturity preceding the promonocyte and promyelocyte stage. However, the human promyelocytic
leukaemia cell line HL-60 differentiates to monocytes and macrophages in
the presence of certain phorbol esters but to neutrophils in the presence of
dimethyl sulphoxide, suggesting that cells may switch at a later point (7).

The monoblast is the least mature cell of the mononuclear phagocyte
system. This immaturity is reflected in the morphology and ultrastructure

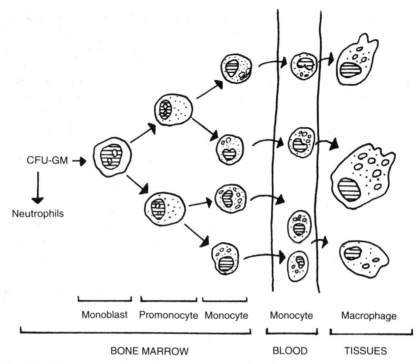

Fig. 1.1   The mononuclear phagocyte system, showing the origin of macrophages in the bone marrow.

(see Section 5). The monoblast is positive for lysozyme and non-specific esterase, although these enzymes are only present in relatively small amounts. All monoblasts have receptors for IgG and are able to phagocytose red blood cells coated with IgG, but not C3b, and only rarely ingest opsonized bacteria (8). Division of a monoblast gives rise to two promonocytes, the latter cell type being the direct precursor of the monocyte. Promonocytes stain for lysozyme and non-specific esterase, and in addition have peroxidase positive granules. The majority of promonocytes have IgG Fc receptors, C3b receptors, ingest IgG-coated red blood cells and opsonized bacteria, but relatively few C3b-coated red cells (8,9), (Figure 1.2). Unlike monoblasts, they appear to pinocytose greatly. It is believed that each dividing promonocyte gives rise to two monocytes. The cycle of monoblastic division in mice has been calculated to be 11.9 h and 16.2 h for promonocytes.

Newly formed monocytes probably remain in the bone marrow for less than 24 h before entering the peripheral blood, where they are distributed between circulating and marginating pools (10,11). Studies in mice have shown that monocytes have a half-time in the circulation of 17.4 h under normal circumstances (12), giving an average transit time in the circulation of 25 h. A longer monocyte half-time has been reported in man and may be up to 70 h (13). In the normal adult human, the relative peripheral blood monocyte count is generally between 1 and 6 per cent of the total white blood cell count and rarely exceeds 10 per cent. The absolute monocyte count in the adult therefore ranges between 300 and 700 cells per microlitre of blood. The migration of peripheral blood monocytes into extravascular tissues to become macrophages involves adherence to the endothelium, migration between endothelial cells, and subsequently through sub-endothelial structures. Adherence of monocytes (see Section 8) to endo-thelium involves high molecular weight glycoproteins, such as LFA-1 (lymphocyte function-associated antigen 1, CD11a/CD18), which interacts with ICAM-1 (intercellular adhesion molecule-1, CD54) present on vascu-lar endothelial cells (14,15). Cytokines such an interleukin-1 (IL-1) and interferon-gamma (IFNγ) increase the expression of ICAM-1 by endothelial cells and can therefore facilitate monocyte margination and migration to sites of inflammation (15). The proportion of monocytes migrating to various organs is apparently random and corresponds roughly with the size of the organ. Having arrived at their target organ, monocytes differentiate

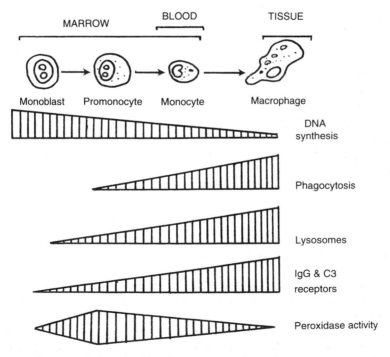

Fig. 1.2 Characteristics of cells of the mononuclear phagocyte system, showing the development of phagocyte activity, lysosomes, IgG and C3 receptors, and peroxidase activity.

Table 1.1   Distribution of mononuclear phagocytes

Bone marrow
  Monoblasts
  Promonocytes
  Monocytes
  Macrophages

Peripheral blood
  Monocytes

Tissues
  Liver (Kupffer cells)
  Lung (alveolar macrophages)
  Connective tissue (histiocytes)
  Spleen (red pulp macrophages)
  Lymph nodes
  Thymus
  Bone (osteoclasts)
  Synovium (type A cells)
  Mucosa associated lymphoid tissue
  Gastrointestinal tract
  Genitourinary tract
  Endocrine organs
  Central nervous system (microglia)
  Skin (histiocyte/Langerhans' cells)

Serous cavities
  Pleural macrophages
  Peritoneal macrophages

Inflammatory tissues
  Epithelioid cells
  Exudate macrophages
  Multinucleate giant cells

(Adapted from references 17, 99, 166.)

into macrophages (12). Once monocytes leave the circulation they do not return, but remain in the tissues as macrophages for several months.

In addition to the bone marrow, mononuclear phagocytes are to be found in a variety of locations throughout the body (Table 1.1). Although more than 95 per cent of tissue macrophages derive from monocytes, recent evidence has come to light which suggests that the remaining 5 per cent of macrophages derive from the local division of mononuclear phagocytes in the tissues. The latter are not resident macrophages, but have arrived in the tissues and body cavities from the bone marrow within the previous 24 hours, before completion of cell division (5). Macrophages in tissues and body cavities are not a constant population of cells, but are regularly being renewed by the influx of monocytes.

The ultimate fate of tissue macrophages is uncertain. The number of macrophages that die must be considerable, because the total monocyte production in the mouse is approximately 1.5×10^6 cells per 24 hours, and all of these cells will eventually leave the bone marrow and become tissue macrophages (5). Macrophages from liver, lung, and gut are known to migrate to nearby draining lymph nodes, but the lymph efferent from these nodes does not contain macrophages or monocytes, making it probable that macrophages die in lymph nodes. It is also conceivable that cell death occurs in tissues and body cavities. Mononuclear phagocytes have different kinetics during inflammatory episodes. During an acute inflammatory reaction the number of circulating monocytes increases due to an enhanced bone marrow production (16). However, the time spent in the circulation is shorter than under normal conditions, due to an efflux of monocytes from the circulation into inflammatory exudates (16). Except for the relatively small share taken by local production during acute inflammation, most of the increase in the number of macrophages in the inflammatory exudate is brought about by this influx of monocytes (17).

3 Humoral control of monocytopoiesis

Despite a great deal of information from *in vitro* studies, relatively little is known about the humoral control of monocytopoiesis *in vivo*. However, macrophages themselves appear to synthesize and secrete at least two haematopoietic growth factors, macrophage colony-stimulating factor (M-CSF) and granulocyte macrophage colony-stimulating factor (GM-CSF), which stimulate the production and function of mononuclear phagocytes (18). M-CSF and GM-CSF production by macrophages is stimulated by exposure to external stimuli, such as phagocytosable particles and endotoxin (19). Macrophages also produce and release cytokines that induce non-haematopoietic cells to elaborate M-CSF and GM-CSF. Thus, the release of interleukin-1 (IL-1) and tumour necrosis factor (TNF) from macrophages can induce fibroblasts and endothelial cells to produce M-CSF and GM-CSF, which in turn stimulate the production of mononuclear phagocytes (20–22), (Figure 1.3). Similarly, GM-CSF can stimulate TNF synthesis by mononuclear phagocytes (23). Receptors for G-CSF and GM-CSF are known to be present on mononuclear phagocytes (24).

Mononuclear phagocyte production and activity can also be influenced by certain products of T-lymphocytes, such as GM-CSF and interleukin 3 (IL-3), and these factors are probably important in the delayed hypersensitivity reaction (23). Serum collected during an inflammatory reaction contains a factor that stimulates monocytopoiesis in the bone marrow of

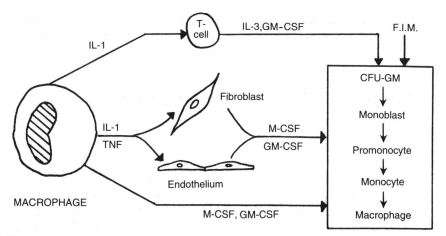

Fig. 1.3 The humoral regulation of monocytopoiesis (F.I.M., factor inducing monocytopoiesis).

mice and rabbits, yet has no M-CSF or IL-1 activity. This has been called 'factor increasing monocytopoiesis' (FIM), (25,26). GM-CSF and IL-3 are probably important in regulating monocytopoiesis during inflammatory responses, but M-CSF is felt to be a more likely candidate for regulation of monocytopoiesis in the steady state (24). Even less is understood about the humoral inhibitors of monocytopoiesis. The best studied candidates are prostanglandins of the E series, which are produced by mononuclear phagocytes (27,28) and interferons α, β, and γ (29).

4   Terminology

- *Mononuclear phagocytes:* includes monoblasts, promonocytes, monocytes, and macrophages.

- *Resident macrophages:* macrophages occurring in specific sites in normal, non-inflamed tissues. However, they may also be observed in small numbers in an inflammatory exudate. They are sometimes called 'normal macrophages'.

- *Exudate macrophages:* macrophages occurring in an exudate and identifiable on the basis of peroxidase activity, immunophenotype, and cell kinetics. They derive from monocytes and have many of the characteristics of the latter. Exudate macrophages are felt to be the precursors of resident macrophages.

- *Elicited macrophages:* macrophages attracted to a given site because of a particular stimulus. An elicited population of macrophages in heterogeneous both developmentally and functionally.

● *Activated macrophages:* macrophages exhibiting an increase in one or more functional activities, or the appearance of a new functional activity. Both resident and exudate macrophages can be activated (5).

5   Morphology of mononuclear phagocytes

5.1   Light microscopy

5.1.1   Macrophages

Macrophages are generally large, irregularly shaped cells measuring 25–50 mm in diameter (Figure 1.4). They often have an eccentrically placed, round or kidney-shaped nucleus with one or two prominent nucleoli and finely dispersed nuclear chromatin. There is often a clearly defined juxtanuclear Golgi complex in an abundant cytoplasm. The cytoplasm contains fine granules and multiple large, azurophilic granules. Cytoplasmic vacuoles are frequently seen near the cell periphery, reflecting the active pinocytosis of macrophages. Characteristically, the surface of these cells appears ruffled (30). Phase contrast microscopy reveals large cells with a propensity to adhere to and spread on glass surfaces, leaving cell organelles concentrated within the central region of the cell and with an intense ruffling of the membrane borders (30).

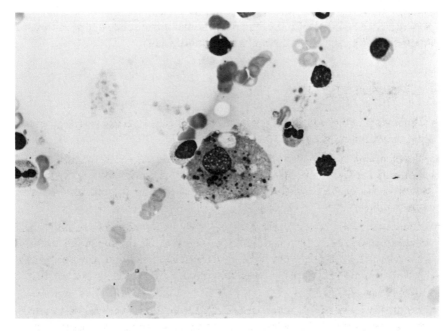

Fig. 1.4   Light micrograph of a human bone marrow macrophage (×1000).

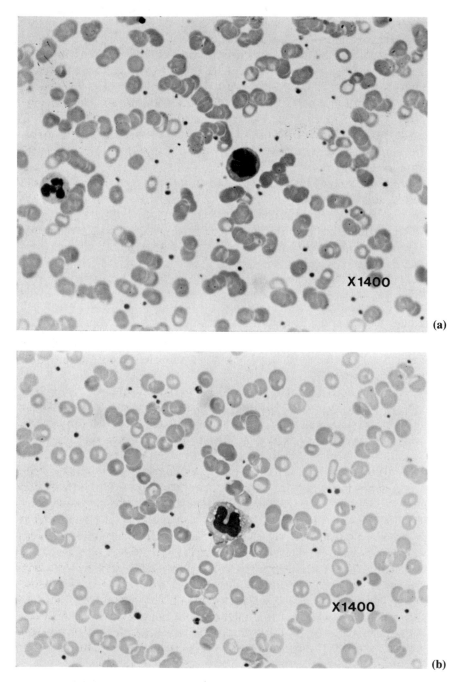

Fig. 1.5 Light micrographs of human peripheral blood monocytes. (a) Monocyte and neutrophil are present; (b) a monocyte with a typically kidney-shaped nucleus.

5.1.2 Monocytes and their precursors

Monocytes appear on stained blood films as smaller cells (12–15 μm in diameter) with an eccentrically placed nucleus occupying at least 50 per cent of the cell area (Figure 1.5). The nucleus may be kidney-shaped, round or irregular with a fine chromatin pattern. The cytoplasm contains both fine granules and large azurophilic granules, as well as clear cytoplasmic vacuoles (31). Phase contrast microscopy reveals gentle undulating movements of the cytoplasm and a prominent ruffled plasma membrane (30).

The bone marrow precursors of peripheral blood monocytes are the promonocytes and monoblasts. Promonocytes are intermediate between monoblasts and monocytes, measure 12–18 μm in diameter and are characterized by the appearance of several immature and mature azurophilic granules and deeply indented and irregularly shaped nuclei. The monoblast is indistinguishable from the myeloblast by light microscopy and is present in very small numbers in normal bone marrow specimens (31).

5.2 Ultrastructure

5.2.1 Macrophages

Macrophage ultrastructure varies with their location, degree of activation, and the procedures employed during their isolation and preparation for microscopy. However, certain general features of macrophage ultrastructure may be outlined.

Electron microscopy demonstrates an eccentric nucleus of variable shape, with chromatin disposed in fine clumps. Clear spaces between membrane-fixed chromatin clumps mark the site of nuclear pores. The cytoplasm contains scattered strands of rough endoplasmic reticulum, a well-developed Golgi complex in a juxtanuclear position, variable numbers of vesicles, vacuoles and pinocytic vesicles, large mitochondria, and electron-dense, membrane-bound lysosomes that can be seen fusing with phagosomes to form secondary lysosomes. Within the secondary lysosomes ingested cellular, bacterial, and non-cellular material can be seen in various stages of degradation and digestion (Figure 1.6). The surfaces of macrophages and monocytes are covered in ruffles and microvilli, and small surface blebs. Microtubules and microfilaments are prominent in macrophages and form a well-organized, three-dimensional cytoskeleton which surrounds the nucleus and extends throughout the cytoplasm to the cell periphery. Actin microfilaments immediately beneath the cell membrane are responsible for the prominent ruffling, locomotion, and pseudopod formation, as well as influencing endocytotic events (32–34) and establishing the polarity of migration in response to chemotactic stimuli.

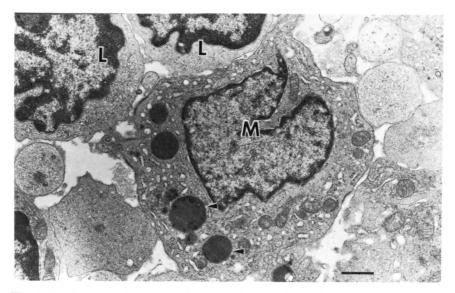

Fig. 1.6 Electron micrograph of a dermal macrophage (M) in contact with two lymphocytes (L) during a delayed type hypersensitivity reaction in skin. Membrane-bound secondary lysosomes (phagosomes) (▶) containing material of various electron densities are present in the cytoplasm. Bar = 1µm.

5.2.2   Monocytes and their precursors

The monocyte nucleus generally contains one or two small nucleoli surrounded by nucleolar-associated chromatin. The cytoplasm is relatively abundant and contains scattered rough endoplasmic reticulum and a prominent Golgi apparatus which is frequently located in the area of nuclear indentation. Small vesicles are scattered throughout the cytoplasm, but are often particularly numerous in the Golgi region and near the cell surface, where they represent pinocytotic vacuoles. Small mitochondria are abundant in the cytoplasm and inconspicuous bundles of fibrils are often seen in a perinuclear position. Cytoplasmic granules measuring from 0.05 to 0.2 µm in diameter are seen, which are dense, homogeneous, and surrounded by a limiting membrane (Figure 1.7). It is not possible on ultrastructural examination alone to recognize distinct subpopulations of monocyte granules, but ultrastructural cytochemical studies suggest such subpopulations may exist (35).

Marrow promonocytes are the first clearly identifiable members of the mononuclear phagocyte system. They are characterized by the presence of distinctive cytoplasmic granules, which are quite different from granulocyte granules. Promonocytes contain a moderate-sized nucleus with one or more nucleoli and sometimes slight peripheral chromatin condensation. A well-developed Golgi apparatus, plentiful ribosomes, and moderate numbers of

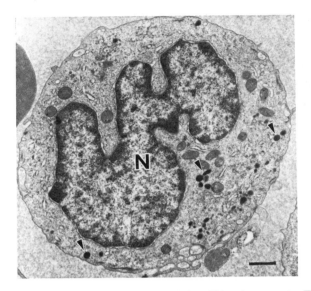

Fig. 1.7 Electron micrograph of a human peripheral blood monocyte. The cell has a lobulated nucleus (N) and the cytoplasm contains populations of dense granules (▶). Bar = 1μm.

mitochondria are seen. The maturation sequence from promonocytes through to later monocyte forms consists of increasing nuclear chromatin condensation, reduced numbers of ribosomes, and a reduction in the amount of rough endoplasmic reticulum. In more mature cells the nucleus assumes a kidney—or horseshoe—shape and nucleoli are less frequent.

6 Histochemistry of mononuclear phagocytes

Various hydrolytic enzymes have been isolated from macrophages and monocytes, including acid phosphatase, β-glucuronidase, *N*-acetyl-glucosaminidase, lysozyme, α-naphthyl butyrate esterase, and peroxidase. Monocytes also stain weakly for polysaccharides in the periodic acid-Schiff (PAS) reaction and for lipids in the Sudan black B reaction. Macrophages are generally PAS-negative, but following phagocytosis they may show globular PAS-positive intracytoplasmic deposits. They may also contain Sudan black positive material, haemosiderin, and other substances (36). Non-specific esterase is an enzyme on the external surface of the plasma membrane of macrophages and monocytes (37). It is the most commonly used cytochemical marker for monocytes. The reaction with non-specific esterase is fluoride-sensitive. Acid phosphatase is contained in the primary lysosomes of monocytes and macrophages. Several isoenzymes of acid phosphatase exist in macrophages. A granular cytoplasmic staining for 5'-nucleotidase is evident in most macrophages (38).

Human bone marrow promonocytes and blood monocytes contain granules that comprise two functionally distinct populations (35,39). One population contains acid phosphatase, aryl sulphatase, and peroxidase; these granules are modified primary lysosomes and are analogous to the azurophilic granules of the neutrophil. The content of the other population of monocyte granules is unknown, but they lack alkaline phosphatase and hence are not strictly analogous to the specific granules of neutrophils. The lysosome granules have a digestive function, whereas the function of the second population is unknown.

7   Composition and metabolism

The composition and metabolism of mononuclear phagocytes alter during differentiation. Concurrent with the transition from monocyte to macrophage there is an increase in number of mitochondria, activity of mitochondrial enzymes, and rate of cellular respiration (40). Both glucose oxidation and lactate production increase with cellular maturation. There is also an increase in both the number of lysosomes and in lysosomal enzymes. Even in an apparent resting state, however, macrophages are extremely active metabolically. For example, they are estimated to turn over the equivalent of their entire plasma membrane every 30 minutes (41). Aerobic glycolysis provides the energy required by mammalian monocytes (42). The mature macrophage employs both glycolysis and oxidative phosphorylation in the generation of energy, although the predominant source of energy depends on the origin of the macrophage. The adenosinetriphosphate (ATP) generated by glycolysis is stored in a large pool of creatine phosphate, which provides the immediate source of energy for mobility-dependent function (43). Even under anaerobic conditions, however, most macrophages are effective phagocytes. This anaerobic phagocytic capability is obviously advantageous to cells that are required to function in granulomas or abscess cavities remote from oxygenated blood. However, the human pulmonary alveolar macrophage is incapable of phagocytosis under severely anaerobic conditions and requires a partial pressure of oxygen greater than 25 mmHg for phagocytosis and energy production (44,45).

The basal metabolism of macrophages can be significantly affected by receptor–ligand interactions (46), which often result in a 'respiratory burst' with the metabolism of large quantities of glucose by way of the hexose monophosphate shunt, and an increased oxygen consumption. This respiratory burst results in altered activity of the membrane-bound oxidase complex and the reduction of molecular oxygen to superoxide (47). The superoxide thus generated is rapidly converted to hydrogen peroxide and hydroxyl radicals, which provide most of the microbicidal oxidative activity both within the phagosome and in the extracellular environment. The molecular oxygen is reduced ultimately to water, but the superoxide anion, hydrogen peroxide, and hydroxyl radicals are referred to as the reactive oxygen intermediates (ROI). The magnitude of the respiratory burst decreases markedly when monocytes mature into macrophages (48). Resident macrophages, for example, have only a weak respiratory burst, though this may be increased several-fold when they are activated *in vivo*. An increased respiratory burst can be induced *in vitro* by exposure to recombinant interferon-γ (49) and migration inhibitory factor (MIF), (50).

$$O_2 \rightarrow \quad O_2^{2-} \rightarrow \quad\quad H_2O_2 \rightarrow \quad\quad OH^- \rightarrow \quad\quad H_2O$$

Oxygen   Superoxide anion   Hydrogen peroxide   Hydroxyl radical   Water

A second consequence of receptor–ligand interaction is the release of arachidonic acid from cellular stores of phospholipids by phospholipase A2, and its subsequent conversion via either lipooxygenases or cyclooxygenases to a series of leucotrienes or prostaglandins, respectively (51).

Lysosomal enzymes involved in degradation of phagocytosed material are synthesized in the endoplasmic reticulum and packaged by the Golgi apparatus into structures called primary lysosomes (52). These primary lysosomes may fuse with phagocytic or pinocytic vacuoles (phagosomes) containing ingested materials. These structures are termed secondary lysosomes (phagolysosomes).

As discussed more fully in Chapter 2 of this volume, activation of macrophages refers to a state of enhanced cellular metabolism, mobility, lysosomal enzyme activity and cytocidal capacity (53). Macrophage activation is usually accompanied by increased elaboration of important products of mononuclear phagocytes, including lysosomal neutral proteases, acid hydrolases, complement components, enzyme inhibitors, binding proteins, interleukin—1 (IL-1), tumour necrosis factor (TNF), and factors promoting haematopoiesis. Most forms of activation, however, include down-regulation of certain physiological characteristics, as well as up-regulation of others (46).

Transmembrane signal transduction has been studied in mononuclear phagocytes. For example, it has been suggested that chemo-attractant oligopeptides binding to the appropriate receptor on the mononuclear phagocyte surface activate a phospholipase—possibly phospholipase C. This then degrades phosphotidyl inositol and releases arachidonic acid. Phosphatidyl inositol, phosphatidyl inositol-4-phosphate, and phosphatidyl inositol-4,5-biphosphate are converted into diacyl glycerol and the corresponding phosphoinosides—all of which can mobilize intracellular calcium stores. Calcium, together with arachidonate and diacyl glycerol, can activate protein kinase C (54,55). In addition, conditions that lead to the activation of the respiratory burst may translocate protein kinase C from the cytosol to the cell membrane (56); this will influence the substrates it phosphorylates and, therefore, determine which biological response will be triggered by the chemo-attractants (for example, chemotactic as distinct from secretory).

8   Macrophage surface receptors

Receptors on the surface of the macrophage determine the control of activities, such as growth, differentiation, activation, recognition, endocytosis, migration, and secretion. Numerous ligands have been reported as binding to the surface of the macrophage. These are listed in full in Table 1.2 and a selected number discussed below. Subsequent chapters will cover this topic in greater depth.

Table 1.2   Surface receptors of monocytes and macrophages

Fc receptors
   IgG_{2a}, IgG_{2b}/IgG_1, IgG_3, IgA, IgE

Complement receptors
   C3b, C3b, C3bi, C5a, C1q

Cytokine receptors
   MIF, MAF, LIF, CF, MFF, IL-1, IL-2, IL-3, IL-4
   $IFN\alpha$, $IFN\beta$, $IFN\gamma$
   Colony-stimulating factors (GM-CSF, M-CSF/CSF-1)

Receptors for peptides and small molecules
   H_1, H_2, 5HT
   1,2,5-Dihydroxy vitamin D3
   N-Formulated peptides
   Enkephalins/endorphins
   Substance P
   Arg-vasopressin

Hormone receptors
   Insulin
   Glucocorticosteroids
   Angiotensin

Transferrin and lactoferrin receptors

Lipoprotein lipid receptors
   Anionic low density lipoproteins
   PGE_2, LTB_4, LTC_4, LTD_4, PAG
   Apolipoproteins B and E (chylomicron remnants, VLDL)

Table 1.2   (*continued*)

Receptors for coagulants and anticoagulants
  Fibrinogen/fibrin
  Coagulation factor VII
  α1-Antithrombin
  Heparin

Fibronectin receptors

Laminin receptors

Mannosyl, fucosyl, galactosyl residue,
AGE receptors

α_2-Macroglobulin-proteinase complex receptors

Others
  Cholinergic agonists
  α1-Adrenergic agonists
  β2-Adrenergic agonists

AGE, advanced glycosylation end-products; GM, granulocyte macrophage; CSF, colony-stimulating factor; VLDL = very low density lipoprotein; PG, prostaglandin; LT, leucotriene; Ig, immunoglobulin; C, complement; MIF, macrophage inhibitory factor; MAF, macrophage-activating factor; LIF, leucocyte migration inhibition factor; MFF, macrophage fusion factor; IL, interleukin; H, histamine; 5HT, 5-hydroxytryptamine.
  It is important to remember that there may be overlap among cytokines and 'factors', which may comprise several active molecular species, for example, MAF activity is partly due to IFNγ.
  (Adapted from references 93–99.)

8.1   Fc and complement receptors

The first macrophage receptors to be identified were those for the Fc region of the IgG molecule (57) and for the cleavage product of the third component of complement (C3) (58). The attachment of the Fc portions of Ig molecules to the surface of the macrophage via Fc receptors may trigger various functions, such as endocytosis, the generation of transmembrane signals, resulting in the reorganization of cytoskeletal microfilaments at the site of attachment facilitating phagocytosis, and the secretion of potent mediators. Among these Fc receptors are those for IgG: FcGRI (CD64) with high affinity for monomeric IgG, and other receptors, FcGRII (CDw32) and FcGRIII (CD16) which have only low affinity for monomeric IgG but can effectively bind immune complexes by multiple receptor-ligand interactions (59). Macrophages also possess the low affinity receptor for IgE, FcERIIb (CD23), following IL-4 induction, and a role for CD23 in host defence mechanisms against IgE-inducing parasites has been suggested. Unlike other Fc receptors which have been sequenced, CD23 is not a

Table 1.3 Selected macrophage surface molecules related to known superfamilies

Superfamily	Molecule	MW (kDa)
Integrin		
LFA-1	(CD11a/CD18)	180,95
CR3	(CD11b/CD18)	170,95
CR4-2	(CD11c/CD18)	150,95
VLA-4	(CD49d/CD29)	150,130
VNR	(CD51/CD61)	140,110
VN/FNR	(CD51/CD-)	140,
SCRs		
CR1	(CD35)	160–250
DAF	(CD55)	70
MCP	(CD46)	45–70
Immunoglobulin		
FcGRI	(CD64)	75
FcGRII	(CDw32)	40
FcGRIII	(CD16)	50–65
MHC Class I		45
MHC Class II		27–33
β_2-Microglobulin		12
CSF-1R		150
ICAM-1	(CD54)	92
CD4		59
Cytokine receptor		
IL-2R		55
IL-3R		
IL-4R		
IL-6R		
GM-CSFR		80, (glycoprotein, 130)
Lectin-like		
B-Glucan		
FcERIIb (CD23)		45
MFR		175
AGE-R		90

LFA, leucocyte function antigen; CR, complement receptor; VLA, very late antigen; VN, vitronectin; FN, fibronectin; SCR, short consensus repeat; DAF, decay accelerating factor; MCP, membrane-cofactor protein; MHC, major histocompatibility complex; CSF, colony-stimulating factor; ICAM, intercellular adhesion molecule; CD, cluster of differentiation; IL, interleukin; GM, granulocyte macrophage; AGE, advanced glycosylation endproduct; MFR, mannosyl fucosyl receptor.

member of the Ig superfamily (Table 1.3) but belongs to a primitive superfamily of invertebrate and vertebrate lectins (60,61). The gene for CD23 has recently been assigned to chromosome 19.

Complement receptors on the macrophage are involved in the binding and ingestion of opsonized particles. CR1 (CD35) recognizes C3b and CR3, the Mac-1 molecule (CD11b/CD18) recognizes C3bi; the ligand for CR4 is still unclear but may also be C3bi. CR3 is an α/β heterodimeric glycoprotein, non-covalently linked and a member of the integrin supergene family of adhesion molecules as is CR4 (CD11c/CD18). CR1 is a member of a group of proteins, including the complement proteins, C1r, C1s, C2, Factor H, C4-binding protein, Factor B, MCP (CD46) and decay accelerating factor: DAF (CD55), having structural elements called short consensus repeats (SCRs). Complement regulatory proteins accelerate the decay of C3 convertases or act as cofactors for proteolytic cleavage thereby limiting the activity of C3 convertases. In this way they inhibit complement activation on autologous tissues (62). CR1 (CD35), MCP (CD46), and DAF (CD55) are membrane-bound, whereas C4-binding protein and Factor H operate in the extracellular fluid.

8.2   Cytokine receptors

Macrophages, in addition to elaborating many cytokines, possess receptors for such cytokines (Tables 1.2 and 1.3). There is a structural relationship between cytokine receptors with most showing homology with either the cytokine receptor family (IL-2R, IL-3R, IL-4R, GM-CSFR) or with the Ig superfamily. A clearly defined second messenger system has yet to be unequivocally implicated in the intracellular signalling induced by receptor activation by cytokines. Phosphorylation of proteins has been one of the earliest changes detected in cells stimulated by IL-2, IL-3, TNFα, and CSF-1, implying regulation through alterations in protein kinase activity. Some cytokine receptors may be coupled to G-proteins as interaction with ligand induces increased binding and hydrolysis of GTP in the cell membrane.

A wide variety of biological effects are generated by the interaction of ligands with their receptors. Individual cytokines or combinations of cytokines interacting with specific receptors modulate the function of macrophages (Table 1.4). A number of pleiotropic cytokines, including IFNγ (63), IFNα (64), TNFα (65), IL-2 (66), IL-4 (67), M-CSF (68), and GM-CSF (68) have been involved in the activation of macrophages (see Chapter 2). Many of the functions carried out by macrophages, including the destruction of intracellular parasites and the destruction of some malignant cells *in vitro*, are enhanced by this activation (Table 1.5). IFNγ, for example, has been found to be a major constituent of macrophage-activating factor (MAF) and also up-regulates class II expression. It has also

Table 1.4 Effects of cytokines on macrophages

Cytokine	Source	Action on macrophages
IL-1	Macrophages, others	Release of IL-1, TNF, CSF
TNFα	Macrophages, others	Release of IL-1, PAF, PGE$_2$, chemotaxis
IL-3	T-cells	Growth and differentiation
IL-4	CD4$^+$ T-cells NK cells	Fusion, increased MHC II expression, antigen presentation, induction of FcE receptor
M-CSF	Fibroblasts, macrophages	Growth and differentiation, urokinase induction
GM-CSF	T-cells, macrophages endothelium	Growth, differentiation, and ?activation
IFNα	Leucocytes	Antiviral and activation
IFNβ	Fibroblasts	Antiviral and activation
IFNγ	T-cells NK cells	Antiviral and activation (e.g., enhanced MHC II expression, respiratory burst, down-regulation of MFR)
TGFβ	Platelets, macrophages	Chemotaxis, growth factor release, macrophage deactivation

IL, interleukin; M-CSF, macrophage colony-stimulating factor; GM-CSF, granulocyte-macrophage colony stimulating factor; TNF, tumour necrosis factor; TGF, transforming growth factor; PAF, platelet-activating factor; PGE, prostaglandin E, MFR, mannosyl-fucosyl receptor, NK, natural killer cell.
(Adapted from references 93–9.)

been reported that binding of TNFα, IL-4, GM-CSF or IL-2 to receptors on the macrophage promotes MAF activity.

Granulocyte macrophage colony-stimulating factor (GM-CSF) stimulates proliferation of monocyte precursors, and platelet-activating factor (PAF) stimulates chemotaxis and bactericidal activity. Macrophage CSF (M-CSF) induces proliferation of monocyte/macrophage progenitor cells and can also activate some functions of mature cells (68,69). The c-*fms* proto-oncogene encodes the CSF-1 (M-CSF) receptor (70). Recently, IL-3 has been reported as having macrophage-activating properties, in a murine system, which are distinct from those of IFNγ and IL-4. IL-3 has MAF activity and can regulate the expression of Class II major histocompatibility complex

Table 1.5   Major alterations of macrophages induced by (or during) activation

Increased
  Size
  Increased phagocytosis for C3b- and IgG-coated particles
  Secretion of collagenase, elastase, plasminogen activator
  Prostaglandin release
  Rate of spreading
  Adherence to glass
  Rate of fluid phase pinocytosis
  Cellular ATP
  Plasmalemmal alkaline phosphodiesterase
  Glucose consumption
  O_2 consumption
  O_2 release
  H_2O_2 release
  Microbicidal activity
  Tumouricidal and tumouristatic ability
  Expression of Class II molecules

Decreased
  Mannose-fucose receptor sites
  Leukotriene production
  Plasmalemmal 5'-nucleotidase
  Secretion of apolipoprotein E

Ig, immunoglobulin; C, complement; ATP, adenosinetriphosphate.
  (Adapted from references 93–9.)

(MHC) molecules and the cellular interaction molecule LFA-1 (71) and induces IL-1 mRNA expression, although IL-1 bioactivity was only demonstrated after the addition of sub-optimal amounts of LPS (72).

Macrophages express IL-4 receptors and the function of this cell type can be modulated by this cytokine. Among the most recently described (73,74) is the influence of IL-4 on macrophage production of other cytokines such as IL-1, TNFα, and IL-6 with possible implications for control of, for example, the acute phase protein response (see Section 11.1).

8.3   Macrophage lipoprotein receptors

The macrophage has specific receptors which allow them to take up and digest cholesterol-containing lipoproteins: low-density lipoproteins (LDLs). These receptor-mediated mechanisms differ from those in other cell types, such as fibroblasts and smooth muscle cells. There are several types of lipoprotein receptors on macrophages: the LDL receptor recognizes apolipoprotein E and apolipoprotein B-100 and is regulated by intracellular cholesterol levels; the β-VLDL receptor which is less responsive to cellular cholesterol levels; and 'scavenger' receptors. Modified (acetylated) LDLs are recognized by scavenger receptors. The macrophage scavenger receptors, which have been implicated in the pathogenesis of atherosclerosis (see Chapter 9), have an unusually broad binding specificity. Ligands include modified LDL and some polyanions. The scavenger receptor type I has three principal extracellular domains that could participate in ligand binding: two fibrous coiled-coil domains (α-helical coiled-coil domain IV and collagen-like domain V), and the 110-amino acid, cysteine-rich, C-terminal domain VI. Kodama and co-workers (75) have cloned complementary DNAs, encoding a second scavenger receptor which they have termed type II. This receptor is identical to the type I receptor, except that the cysteine-rich domain is replaced by a six-residue C terminus. Despite this truncation, the type II receptor mediates endocytosis of chemically modified LDL with high affinity and specificity, similar to that of the type I receptor. Therefore, one or both of the extracellular fibrous domains are responsible for the unusual ligand-binding specificity of the receptor.

8.4   AGE receptors

Proteins of the extracellular matrix undergo multiple reactions with glucose to form advanced glycosylation endproducts (AGEs), which are highly active in protein cross-linking. A macrophage/monocyte receptor for AGE moieties, which have been implicated in tissue damage associated with ageing and diabetes, mediates the uptake of AGE-modified proteins by a process that also induces IL-1 and TNFα secretion. Postulating that cytokines might regulate this AGE-receptor system, Vlassara and co-workers (76) evaluated the effect of cachectin/TNFα, IL-1, and IFNγ on AGE-protein processing. TNFα induced a several-fold enhancement of binding, endocytosis, and degradation of AGE-modified bovine serum albumin (BSA) by both murine peritoneal macrophages and human blood monocytes *in vitro*, and also enhanced the rate of disappearance of AGE-modified red blood cells *in vivo*. These data suggest that TNFα, in addition to influencing tissue regeneration and remodelling, may also normally regulate the disposal of tissue-damaging AGE-proteins through an autocrine mechanism.

8.5   Lectin-like receptors

Macrophages express a variety of lectin-like (Tables 1.2 and 1.3) proteins which are specific for oligosaccharides terminating in fucose, mannose, galactose, and sialic acid. Sugar-specific recognition is an important determinant of cell-to-cell interaction, and the mannose receptor (77) has a role in receptor-mediated endocytosis and mediates phagocytosis independently of Fc and C3 receptors.

8.6 Adhesion receptors and migration

There is considerable overlap in the categorization of adhesion receptors on the cell surface and published information on monocyte migration lags behind studies of the neutrophil. Monocytes are more difficult to isolate in sufficient numbers to study their adhesive interactions. Monocytes share a number of adhesion molecules (Tables 1.3 and 1.6) with both neutrophils, for example, CD11b/CD18 (CR3), the PADGEM/GMP140 (CD62) ligand, and with lymphocytes, for example, CD11a/CD18 (LFA-1) and CD49d/CD29 (VLA-4). This could indicate that similar mechanisms of migration are utilized by these cell types. Inflammatory mediators, including LPS, IFNγ, IL-1, and TNFα, cause strong induction of ICAM-1 (CD54) in a wide variety of tissues and greatly increase the binding of monocytes and lymphocytes through their cell surface LFA-1. This contributes to the infiltration of mononuclear cells into sites of inflammation, for example, in delayed-type hypersensitivity reactions in skin (78). LFA-1 (CD11a/CD18) is a member of the integrin family of cell adhesion molecules which comprise α and β subunits. Three subfamilies are distinguished by their β subunits; the β1 (CD29), β2 (CD18), and β3 (CD61) integrins. LFA-1 belongs to the β2 family and is most closely related to two other integrins Mac-1 (CD11b/CD18) and p150,95 (CD11c/CD18). These two are particularly important in adhesion of myeloid cells to ligands which become insoluble during activation of the complement and clotting cascades (79) and in binding to other cells. The importance of the β2 family of leucocyte integrins is illustrated in individuals lacking the common β2 subunit and whose phagocytes are unable to traverse the endothelium at sites of infection. This is a congenital

Table 1.6 Recognized cluster of differentiation antigens present on the monocyte/macrophage series

Cluster	Main cellular reactivity	Recognized membrane component
CD4	T-subset (M)	Class II/HIV receptor, gp59
CD9	Pre-B, M, Plt	p24
CD11a	Leucocytes	LFA-1, gp180/95
CD11b	M, G, NK	C3bi receptor, gp155/95
CD11c	M, G, NK, B subset	gp150, 95
CDw12	M, G, Plt	(p90–120)
CD13	M, G	Aminopeptidase N, gp150
CD14	M, (G), LC	gp55
CD15	G, (M)	3-FAL, X-hapten

Table 1.6   (*continued*)

CD16	NK, G, M	FcRIII, gp50–65
CD17	G, M, Plt	Latosylceramide
CD18	Leucocytes broad	β-Chain to CD11, b, c
CD19	B (some M leukaemias)	gp95
CD23	B-subset, act.M, Eo	FcERII, gp45–50
CD25	Activated B, T, M	IL-2R β-chain, gp55
CD29	Broad	VLA-b, integrin β-chain, Plt.GPIIa
CD31	Plt, M, G, B, (T)	gp140, Plt.GPIIIa
CDw32	M, G, B	FcRII, gp40
CD33	M, Prog., AML	gp67
CD34	Prog.	gp105–120
CD35	G, M, B	CR1
CD36	M, Plt, (B)	gp90, Plt.GPIV
CD37	B, (T, M)	gp40–52
CD43	T, G, M, brain	Leukosialin, gp95
CD44	Leucocytes, brain, RBC	Pgp-1, gp80–95, Hermes-1
CD45	Leucocytes	LCA, T200
CD45RA	T-subset, B, G, M	Restricted LCA, gp220, exon A
CD45RB	T-subset, B, G, M	Restricted LCA, gp200, exon B
CD45RO	T-subset, B, G, M	Restricted LCA, gp180, exons spliced out
CD46	Leucocytes	MCF, gp66/56
CD47	Broad	gp47–52, N-linked glycan
CD48	Leucocytes	gp41, PI-linked
CDw49d	M, T, B (LC), Thy	VLA-a4 chain, gp150
CDw50	Leucocytes	gp148/108
CDw52	Leucocytes	Campath-1, gp21–28
CD53	Leucocytes	gp32–40
CD54	Broad, activation	ICAM-1
CD55	Broad	DAF
CD58	Leucocytes, epithelium	LFA-3, gp40–65
CD59	Broad	gp18–20
CD63	Plt activ., M, (G, T, B)	gp53
CD64	M	FcRI, gp75
CDw65	G, M	Ceramide-dodecasaccharide 4c
CD68	M	gp110
CD71	Prol., M	Transferrin receptor
CD74	B, M	Class II associated invariant chain, gp41/35/33
CDw78	B, (M)	–

(brackets denote reactivity with a subset of cells); M, monocyte/macrophage; T, T-cell; B, B-cell; G, granulocyte; Thy, thymocyte; Plt, platelet; LC, Langerhans' cell; NK, natural killer cell; LCA, leucocyte common antigen; MCF, membrane cofactor protein; DAF, decay accelerating factor Eo, eosinophil; Prog., progenitor cell; Prol., proliferating cell; AML, acute myeloid leukaemia; RBC, red blood cell. Adapted from Knapp, W. (*et al.* (ed.) (1989). *Leucocyte typing, IV*. Oxford University Press.)

leucocyte adhesion deficiency (LAD) in which the patients are prone to recurring infections—it is often fatal in childhood unless corrected by bone marrow transplantation.

VLA-4 (CD49d/CD29) is an unusual β1 integrin expressed on monocytes, resting lymphocytes, and neural crest-derived cells, functioning as both a cell and a matrix receptor (80). It binds to a region of fibronectin distinct from the binding site of VLA-5 (81) and also binds to the cell receptor VCAM-1 (82). The complexities of the integrin family are described in a recent review of adhesion molecules (83).

As well as the integrins, macrophages possess adhesion molecules belonging to the Ig superfamily and are also capable of binding to molecules of the selectin family. The selectins described thus far (Mel-14/LAM-1, ELAM-1, PADGEM) help regulate leucocyte binding to endothelium at inflammatory sites. One of the selectins mentioned above, called PADGEM, GMP-140, or CD62, is contained within the Weibel–Palade bodies of endothelial cells and α-granules of platelets and quickly appears on the surface of these cells after stimulation by products of the clotting cascade where it mediates adhesion of monocytes and neutrophils (84).

Of the Ig superfamily, a number of molecular species are present on the macrophage membrane and include LFA-3 (CD58), ICAM-1 (CD54), and MHC Class I and II. MHC Class I and II molecules are the ligands for CD8 and CD4, respectively. CD54 is the ligand for LFA-1 and CD58 is the ligand for CD2, another member of the Ig superfamily, which is present on T-cells. Thus, the molecules in the Ig superfamily are important in macrophage/T-cell interactions. Members of the Ig superfamily share the Ig domain which comprises 90–100 amino acids arranged in a sandwich of two sheets of anti-parallel β-strands usually joined by a disulphide bond. ICAM-1, in contrast to the MHC and Ig molecules, has unpaired domains.

8.7 Surface antigens

A large number of cell surface molecules are present on the surface of monocytes and macrophages and are largely the means by which this cell type interacts with its environment. Some of these are growth factor receptors, others recognition or adhesion molecules important in cellular interactions, others are enzymes or receptors for specific ligands important in the role of the macrophage. During differentiation and/or activation, this mosaic of antigens is constantly changing in a way which is orchestrated by genetic programming in response to signals from the extracellular environment. Many of these antigens, such as MHC Class I and II, are not lineage-specific but are also found on other cell types. MHC Class II molecules, products of the HLA-DR, -DP, and -DQ loci, are expressed disco-ordinately by monocytes (85) with DR molecules expressed at a high surface density. All peripheral monocytes can be induced to express HLA-DQ and -DP molecules in the presence of IFNγ (86).

A large number of other molecules are present which are more restricted in their cell-specific expression and are obviously important in the cellular interactions involving macrophages. Through the production of monoclonal antibodies and the vehicle of international workshops on human leucocyte differentiation antigens, a plethora of information on cell surface regulatory molecules has been generated. Some surface antigens (Table 1.6) have relatively well-defined functions, whereas little is known of the functions of others. Although most receptors described above are also cell surface structures this section concentrates on antigens primarily identified by the availability of monoclonal antibodies rather than by function. The following selection is by no means exhaustive and many more remain to be described or ascribed a function.

The CD14 molecule is one of the most characteristic surface antigens of the monocyte lineage and comprises 356 amino acids anchored to the plasma membrane by a phosphoinositol linkage (87). It is expressed at high density and is an excellent marker of monocytes and tissue macrophages but is also present at lower density on a proportion of neurophils (heterogeneous expression), Langerhans cells, follicular dendritic cells, histiocytes and high endothelial venules. Antibodies against the CD14 molecule induce oxidative burst formation but little is known of the function of the intact protein on the macrophage surface. A soluble form of this molecule, which also has a molecular weight 53 kDa, identical to the surface-linked form, is present in urine (88). The CD14 gene is located on the long arm of chromosome 5 (5q32) in a region containing a cluster of genes encoding growth factors and receptors (GM-CSF, IL-3, IL-5, ECGF, CSF-1, CSF-1R, and PDGFR) (89), and their functions may possibly be related. This chromosomal region is deleted in a number of acute myeloid leukaemias and pre-leukaemic conditions. A number of suggestions for the function of this molecule have included the involvement of CD14 in delivering a stimulatory signal to alloreactive T-cells and in the process of phagocytosis (90).

The CD68 antigen is a specific marker of monocytes and macrophages. Antibodies against this antigen label macrophages and other members of the mononuclear phagocyte lineage in routinely processed tissue sections and have been used to stain a range of lymphoid, histiocytic, and myelomonocytic proliferations (91). The antigen recognized is present in intracellular granules but may exist in the extracellular environment. This may provide some clue regarding its function.

The CD33 molecule is restricted to myeloid cells and is at least expressed on some multipotent progenitor cells (CFU-GEMM) and early erythroid progenitors (BFU-E). Virtually all granulocyte-macrophage progenitor cells (CFU-GM) are identified by CD33 antibodies. It is presumed that the function of this molecule relates specifically to the function of cells of the myelomonocytic lineage (92). Binding of antibodies against this molecule has been detected in sections of the spleen, testis, placenta, liver (Kupffer cells), lung (alveolar macrophages) and in the dermis of skin. Langerhans cells in the epidermis also possess surface CD33 at low density.

9   Macrophage heterogeneity

The seeding of monocytes to different tissues where they remain as macrophages is apparently random as there is no evidence that the tissue destination is pre-programmed. Resident macrophages are widely distributed in the absence of any inflammatory signal and display regional heterogeneity. Functional, morphological, and phenotypic heterogeneity may reflect the local environment of the macrophage and involvement in various physiological or pathological processes.

9.1   Alveolar macrophages

Macrophages are a major cellular component of the lung with a lifespan, suggested by bone marrow transplant studies, of approximately three months (100). Several functionally and biochemically distinct subpopulations of alveolar macrophage have been demonstrated in normal human and pathological (sarcoid) lung tissue (101). The most characteristic ultrastructural feature of alveolar macrophages is the abundance of membrane-bound cytoplasmic inclusions (102) containing proteolytic enzymes. Analysis of the tissue distribution of a novel monocyte subpopulation, forming about 13 per cent of circulating monocytes (103), revealed large numbers of these CD14+, CD16+ cells in the alveolar space. Alveolar macrophages may represent a self-replicating population as they proliferate readily to colony-stimulating factors *in vitro* and maintain their numbers after bone marrow ablation (104). Macrophages in the lung are involved in local defence against a variety of pathogenic and particulate entrants via the airway and play an early role in inflammation and the control of infection. Alveolar and recruited macrophages have a central role in chronic granulomatous conditions, such as sarcoidosis (Section 11.8), silicosis, and asbestosis; and in infections, such as tuberculosis and *Legionella*.

9.2   Kupffer cells

The resident macrophages of the liver are involved in the clearance of particulate and soluble substances and express Fc and other receptors, such as the mannosyl-fucosyl receptor (MFR), CD14, and CD33. It is believed that the response of Kupffer cells to lipopolysaccharide (LPS) and other gut-derived stimuli may be important in their interactions with hepatocytes (105). Indeed, these cells may be at least partially reponsible for regulating the acute phase response in injury and malignancy by producing IL-6 which appears to deliver the final signal to hepatocytes to trigger the altered metabolism associated with the acute phase response (see Section 11.1). Large numbers of monocytes are recruited to the liver following uptake of micro-organisms by Kupffer cells and contribute to the immune response against the invaders. With regard to the role of liver macrophages in malignancy a recent study has demonstrated that although the macrophage population of the liver is heterogeneous with respect to endocytic and lysosomal enzyme activity, all liver macrophages in the rat can be activated to a tumouricidal state by the intravenous injection of liposomal muramyl dipeptide (MDP), (106).

9.3   Spleen

The spleen contains a heterogeneous population of macrophages and related cells. Differences reported in phenotype and appearance (107) probably reflect the different functions they undertake: trapping and processing of foreign antigens in the marginal zone, specialized interactions with T- and B-cells in the lymphoid areas, and phagocytosis/degradation of red blood cells in the red pulp.

9.4   Bone marrow

Macrophages play an integral role in the support of haemopoiesis. Bone marrow and the fetal liver contain a network of mature macrophages which ramify through the stroma. These stromal macrophages make intimate contact with a 'nest' of surrounding developing haemopoietic cells (108) which can be isolated intact. The stromal macrophages appear to be essential for maintaining the growth and differentiation of haemopoietic precursors *in vitro* and possess adhesion molecules for maintaining contact with developing haemopoietic cells (109).

9.5   Intestine

The gut lamina propria in both the large and small intestine contains a large population of macrophages. They are also present in the specialized gut-associated lymphoid tissue with a well-defined structure, such as the tonsils and the Peyers' patches (110).

9.6   Other sites

Macrophages are present in many other areas of the body, such as the subendothelium of the greater arteries. Morphological, histochemical, and ultrastructural results have shown that these are mainly metabolically quiescent, resident macrophages, their number being regulated by influences depending on endothelium and intimal factors. The major signal for human subendothelial macrophage accumulation appears to be intimal deposition of lipids (see also Chapter 9). Many macrophages also penetrate the blood–brain barrier under normal circumstances, first entering the nervous system during embryonic development, and then taking the form of microglial cells, whose function is unknown; this will be discussed later in Chapter 10. Macrophages, other than the microglia, are common inhabitants of the choroid plexus and leptomeninges. An interesting aspect of the macrophage and microglia phenotype is the presence of CD4 molecules on their surface which make them susceptible to invasion by the human immunodeficiency virus (HIV) with a possible bearing on the transport of the virus across the blood–brain barrier and the development of encephalopathy reported in AIDS. The control of expression of CD4 on monocytes, macrophages, and microglia in rats has been investigated by Perry and Gordon (111).

9.7   Relationship to Langerhans cells and other 'professional' antigen-presenting cells

There are two conflicting views concerning the relationship between macrophages and 'professional' antigen-presenting cells (APCs), such as dendritic cells (DCs) in lymph nodes and Langerhans cells (LCs) (Figure 1.8) in

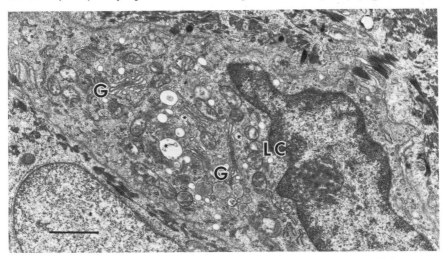

Fig. 1.8 Electron micrograph of part of an epidermal Langerhans cell (LC) between keratinocytes in the skin. The Langerhans cell has a well-developed Golgi (G) and distinctive tennis-raquet-shaped Birbeck granules (∗) in the cytoplasm. Scale bar = 1μm.

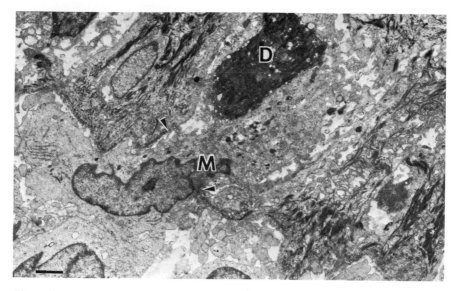

Fig. 1.9   A macrophage (M) breaching the basal lamina (▶) of the skin to engulf a dead keratinocyte (D) during a secondary contact allergic response to dinitro-chlorobenzene. Scale bar = 2μm.

the epithelium of skin. Some studies, based on the reactivity of monoclonal antibodies (112), would indicate that precursors of human LCs express myeloid antigens upon entry into the epidermis losing many of these surface molecules in residence. However, these myeloid antigens are expressed on the LCs in disease states (113,114). Others argue that the different functional attributes of APCs, for example, that they are at least a thousand-fold more effective at presenting antigen than macrophages but are poorly phagocytic by comparison, and their different tissue distributions from early stages of ontogeny, indicate that they are derived from separate cell lineages (115). Classical tissue macrophages are present in the dermis of skin often invading the epidermis during inflammatory responses (Figure 1.9).

9.8   Giant cells

Epithelioid cells (EpCs) and their fusion products, the multinucleated giant cells (MnGCs) are members of the mononuclear phagocyte system. They are considered to be a terminal stage of development of the macrophage system and, in contrast to other macrophages, are poorly phagocytic but exhibit increased lysosomal and respiratory enzyme activity (116). EpC and MnGC cells have reduced numbers of cell surface Ig and complement receptors (117) and are common in granulomatous lesions. The histogenesis of the multinucleated cells that characterize myeloma cast nephropathy

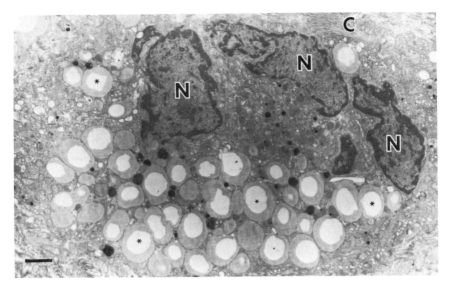

Fig. 1.10 Multiple nuclei (N) of a multinucleated giant cell within connective tissue collagen (C) from a patient with Xanthoma. Large lipid-containing vacuoles (∗) occupy much of the cytoplasm. Scale bar = 2μm.

('myeloma kidney') has long been a subject of debate. Recent studies have implicated monocyte/macrophage-derived cells rather than tubular epithelial cells as the progenitors of these multinucleated cells. Alpers *et al.* (118) claim to have confirmed the macrophage origin of the multinucleated cells in this form of renal injury. Giant cells containing lipid vacuoles (Figure 1.10) are common in xanthoma and lipid storage diseases.

10 Macrophage functions

10.1 Phagocytosis and destruction of micro-organisms

10.1.1 Recognition and phagocytosis

Mononuclear phagocytes and neutrophils provide a defence against microbial invasion. The neutrophil, in general, is a more efficient phagocyte, except when the particle is large in relation to the cell or when the particle load is great (40). Under these circumstances mononuclear phagocytes are more effective than neutrophls. Macrophages thus represent a major defence against invasion of the host by a wide variety of micro-organisms, including bacteria, viruses, fungi, and protozoa. Macrophages move toward the microbial particles guided by a gradient of chemotactic molecules emanating from them (see Section 10.2), (119). Engulfment then occurs, beginning with the macrophage advancing pseudopodia over regions of the micro-organism that express recognition molecules, opsonins, which bind to specific sites on both invading micro-organisms and macrophages. Opsonins are of various types, but those most studied are IgG and fragments of the third component of complement. Receptors that bind specifically to the Fc domain of various subclasses of IgG and to several isotypes of C3 are present on the macrophage surface (see Section 8.1), (46). Many micro-organisms are capable of activating the complement cascade and generating complement fragments that coat the organism and opsonize it. Furthermore, the macrophage itself is an important source of complement components and macrophage-derived complement factors can opsonize micro-organisms for subsequent destruction in the absence of other sources. After binding with the appropriate ligand, initiation of the process of internalization and microbial destruction occurs (120). Adsorption can also occur without opsonization if the micro-organisms possess surface determinants that can be recognized directly by the macrophage; an example is the interaction of the macrophage mannose-fucose receptor with carbohydrate residues (121).

The protrusive pseudopodial movement underlying phagocytosis represents events within only a localized region of membrane and peripheral cytoplasm (122,123). Granule movements then become prominent at the base of the forming phagocytic vacuole and exocytosis of granule contents into the phagosomal vacuole is thought to occur (124). The pseudopodial actin cytoskeleton plays a major role in phagocytosis (125).

Fc receptor-mediated phagocytosis results in the release of large amounts of oxygen and arachidonic acid metabolites by macrophages (48,126). In contrast, ligation of C3 receptors fails to release either arachidonic or oxygen metabolites from mononuclear phagocytes (127,128). Macrophages also have receptors for C5a. Occupancy of this receptor induces secretion of IL-1 and initiates chemotactic phenomena (129). Particle ingestion by mononuclear phagocytes may occur over a broad pH range and is accompanied by enhanced glucose oxidation similar to that which occurs with phagocytosis by neutrophils (130).

Although many micro-organisms are phagocytosed and destroyed with comparable ease by macrophages, there are certain pathogens that parasitize macrophages and replicate within them. When the macrophage is activated, these intracellular pathogens may be inhibited or destroyed. *Listeria, Salmonella, Brucella, Mycobacteria, Chlamydia, Rickettsia, Leishmania, Toxoplasma, Trypanosoma,* and *Legionella pneumophilia* have been found capable of invading and inhabiting non-activated macrophages (120). *Mycobacterium tuberculosis* may release certain substances, such as sulpholipids, that interfere with fusion of primary lysosomes with phagosomes and thereby avoid exposure to the lysosomal enzymes of the macrophage (131). *Leishmania* and *Mycobacterium lepraemurium* survive within secondary lysosomes despite exposure to lysosomal enzymes;

this may be due to the resistance of the microbial cell wall to the macrophages' degradative enzymes (120). The human immunodeficiency virus (HIV) has also been shown to infect and replicate within monocytes and macrophages. Infection with HIV occurs by binding of the virus to the CD4 molecule which, as mentioned previously, is present at a low density on monocytes and macrophages (132).

10.1.2 Microbicidal mechanisms

The production and intracellular release of reactive oxygen intermediate species are a major microbidical mechanism employed by monocytes and macrophages (see Section 7). As monocytes mature into macrophages there is evidence of decreased microbicidal activity. This may be due to a reduction in the respiratory burst or by the decreased content of granule peroxidase as monocytes mature into macrophages (96,133). In addition to oxygen-dependent cytotoxic systems, phagocytes are equipped with oxygen-independent means of killing micro-organisms. A variety of granule-associated proteins in macrophages have been shown to possess antimicrobial activity. These include elastase, collagenases, lipases, deoxy-ribonucleases, polysaccharidases, sulphatases, phosphatases, and the defensins (134). The latter are a group of small cationic proteins that have distinct antimicrobial properties and have been isolated from rabbit alveolar macrophages and human peripheral blood neutrophils (134). The primary lysosomes fuse with phagocytic vacuoles (phagosomes) containing ingested materials, to form secondary lysosomes or phagolysosomes (52). The mechanism of fusion of the primary lysosome and the phagosome is not known, but it is clear that formation of the secondary lysosome is necessary for degradation of the ingested material (135). Mononuclear phagocytes are also capable of interferon production, which may aid in protection against viral infection (136). Monocyte cationic proteins, other than peroxidase, have been shown to have fungicidal activity (137). Macrophages activated by cytokines, such as IFNγ, TNFα, or IL-1, have greater microbicidal capacities than non-activated cells (138).

There are differences in the mechanisms by which blood monocytes and tissue macrophages kill some microbes. For example, human monocytes kill *Candida albicans* readily, whereas macrophages do not. Macrophages will, however, kill *Candida pseudotropicalis* as this organism does not require peroxidase activity in order to be destroyed (137,139).

The relatively long lifespan of the macrophage and its sustained bio-synthetic capacity permit the continued production of antimicrobial proteins and continued microbicidal activity.

10.2   Chemotaxis

Chemotaxis refers to the directed movement of cells along a concentration gradient of a 'chemotactic factor' (140). Leucocyte responses to chemotactic stimuli are vital for host defence, and in the past 10 years, a great deal of insight has been gained into the mechanisms of chemotaxis in mononuclear phagocytes. Chemotactic factors, or chemoattractants, initiate a leucocyte response after binding to specific receptors on the cell surface. Specific receptors have been characterized for a number of chemoattractants including N-formylated peptides, C5a and leucotriene B4 (LTB4), (140). N-Formylated peptide receptors are internalized following chemoattractant binding. The mononuclear phagocytes involved must bear receptors for chemoattractants which can be up- or down-regulated, and the binding of chemoattractants must activate certain transduction pathways for cell activation, resulting in such abilities as attachment to the endothelial cell surface, proper orientation of the cell, shape change due to cytoskeletal rearrangement, and movement across the endothelial cell layer towards the inflammatory focus (diapedesis) (140).

In 1975, Schiffmann discovered the synthetic chemotactic peptide N-formylmethionylleucylphenylalanine (FMLP) (141) and described its receptor on leucocytes one year later. This is the most extensively studied chemoattractant receptor (142,143). Phagocytes have been shown to express surface receptors for FMLP and in addition to initiating locomotion, the FMLP receptor has been linked to respiratory burst activation and lysosomal enzyme degranulation (144). A high density of receptors is located along the cell's leading edge, presumably to optimize detection of low concentrations of chemoattractants. The FMLP receptor appears to exist in two different affinity states on macrophages, high and low affinity, which are regulated by a guanine-binding protein (145). In addition to FMLP, intracellular receptor pools exist for the complement chemotactic factor CR3 (or iC3b), which co-purifies with specific granules in neutrophils (146). Another mediator of phagocyte chemotaxis is C5a (147). Recently it has been shown that IFNγ stimulates monocyte chemotaxis (148) although this chemotactic effect is turned off with prolonged exposure to IFNγ.

Once receptors are occupied and the cell responds to a stimulus, there is some adaptation and chemotactic activity is decreased in the face of the same concentration of chemoattractant. Multiple controls exist for termination of chemoattractant signalling. The agonist can be hydrolysed externally or internalized and degraded within the cell. Elevation of intracellular cAMP levels also attenuates the chemoattractant-induced activation of leucocytes, perhaps through inhibitors of calcium influx or subsequent responses (149).

Although specific receptors are present for the various chemoattractants, they appear to utilize a common mechanism for stimulating phosphoinositide hydrolysis. Binding of the chemoattractant to the receptor activates the protein kinase C pathway of the mononuclear phagocyte (54,55). Temporal studies show rapid (<5 s) increases in phosphoinositide metabolism and cytosolic calcium levels, followed by changes in physiological functions, e.g., shape change, degranulation, and superoxide production (149). However, the ability of macrophages to participate in the inflammatory response is also regulated by another second messenger system involving cAMP. Prostaglandins E_1 and E_2 and histamine elevate cAMP concentrations in leucocytes through receptor-mediated activation of adenylate cyclase (150). The increased cAMP levels attenuate chemoattractant-induced macrophage activation. Chemoattractants also increase cellular cAMP levels, by a calcium-mediated inhibition of cAMP degradation. This may serve as an autoregulatory action in chemoattractant-induced leucocyte activation (149,151).

Mononuclear phagocytes must attach to a surface before moving in response to the sensing of the FMLP and other receptors. In recent years, much interest has focused on the leucocyte-endothelial cell interaction. Endothelial cell adhesiveness for neutrophils can be markedly enhanced by pretreatment with endotoxin, phorbol esters, and IL-1 (152). The increased adhesion appears to involve the LFA-1/MAC-1/p150,95 (CD 11/18) complex on phagocytes, as well as one or more inducible factors on the endothelial cell surface important to migration, for example, ICAM 1 (14,15). After attachment to endothelium, mononuclear phagocytes move across the endothelial cell layer towards the inflammatory focus. Chemotactic disorders of phagocytes can lead to dramatic and often life-threatening host defence problems (140).

10.3   Antigen processing and presentation

Several different types of cells may take up antigen when it enters the body. The APC for regulatory T-cells may be a MHC Class II-expressing dendritic cell, B-cell, or 'professional' phagocyte, the macrophage, which can phagocytose antigen with or without the help of Fc receptors. Indeed, one of the major functions of the macrophage is to assist in initiating and facilitating cell-mediated immune responses against pathogens. After uptake, antigen is processed inside the cell and in the case of protein antigens, peptides are generated and recycled to the cell surface in association with glycoproteins encoded by the Class II (HLA-DR, -DP, -DQ) genes of the major histocompability complex.

However, intracellular processing of antigen may allow the appearance of peptides on the cell surface in association with, not only Class II, but also Class I molecules for recognition by the appropriate MHC Class II- (CD4-

expressing T-cell) or Class I- (CD8- expressing T-cell) restricted antigen-specific T-cells.

There appear to be fundamental differences not only in the processing of endogenous and exogenous antigens but also in the processing for Class I-restricted presentation and Class II-restricted presentation. Most endogenous proteins are degraded by non-lysosomal proteolytic mechanisms. The cytosolic ubiquitin-dependent system is the best characterized and depends on proteins being initially conjugated to ubiquitin before degradation by specific proteases. For exogenous protein there is evidence that the proteins are enclosed in endosomal vesicles containing proteases which later fuse with Golgi-derived endosomes containing acidic proteases. Transport of the phagocytosed and degraded antigens, and processed peptides derived from these molecules, into the endoplasmic reticulum appears to be essential for the effective processing and the presentation of peptides on the surface of cells.

10.3.1   Processing for Class I-restricted antigen presentation

The primary requirement for presentation in the context of Class I molecules is cytoplasmic localization of the antigen, as described above. Synthesis of new Class I molecules does not appear to be necessary. Recent reports have suggested (153,154) that processed cytoplasmic antigens associate with Class I molecules before their release from the endoplasmic reticulum. The macrophage in this instance, by expressing the antigen in the context of Class I molecules, may be targeted by Class I-restricted cytotoxic T-cells and destroyed.

10.3.2   Processing for Class II-restricted antigen presentation

It appears that antigens endocytosed and degraded in endosomes intersect the biosynthetic pathway of Class II molecules (155) and this is necessary for presentation in the context of these MHC molecules. In contrast, endocytosed antigen cannot be presented in the context of Class I molecules (156,157). The epitope recognized by responding T-cells appears to be created when a peptide fragment associated with the MHC molecule. It has also been suggested that for some exogenous antigens the invariant chain (CD74), associated with Class II molecules, is necessary for processing and presentation to occur.

In summary, the following criteria must be fulfilled for the macrophage to be capable of presenting antigen to T-cells for the initiation of an immune response. The cell must be able to:

(1) internalize antigen, for example by phagocytosis, to allow processing to occur;

(2) process antigen by proteolysis, the primary mode of antigen degradation;

(3) transcribe the products of MHC Class II (and/or Class I) genes and express these at the cell surface in sufficient quantity;

(4) associate the processed peptide fragments, several amino acids long, with the MHC molecules and express these on the cell surface; and

(5) provide the necessary regulatory signals in the form of cytokines to responding cells.

10.3.3   T-cell activation

T-cell interaction with the Class II/peptide conformation is required, but is not sufficient alone for T-cell activation to occur. T-cell activation requires a second signal—the presence of IL-1 which stimulates T-cell growth and differentiation by inducing receptors for IL-2 and by stimulating IL-2 production. This may also require other macrophage/T-cell interactions through cell surface adhesion molecules. Various experimental approaches have demonstrated that the type of response generated by presenting cell and T-cell interaction can be radically altered by blocking cell surface receptors other than those of Class II (158).

10.4   Secretion

It has become increasingly apparent that mononuclear phagocytes, in addition to their phagocytic and immunomodulatory properties, have an extensive secretory capability that includes secretion not only of enzymes but of many other biologically active substances (Table 1.7). Over 100 substances have been reported to be secreted by mononuclear phagocytes, with molecular mass ranging from 32 kDa (superoxide anions) to 440000 kDa (fibronectin), and biological activity ranging from induction of cell growth to cell death (138). Secretion includes both release of constituents of these cells into the external milieu and also discharge of these materials into the phagocytic vacuole. These two processes are thought to be related. Three points concerning the diversity of macrophage secretory products are worth noting.

1. A single macrophage product can have diverse activities.
2. A single activity can reflect the action of many macrophage products.
3. Few, if any macrophage secretory products arise solely from macrophages (138).

Macrophage secretion involves synthesis on the rough endoplasmic reticulum, co-translational glycosylation and translocation into the lumen of the endoplasmic reticulum, transport to the Golgi and vesicle transport to the plasma membrane. After an intracellular triggering event causes the translocation of secretory vesicles to the inner surface of the plasma mem-

Table 1.7   Secretory products of mononuclear phagocytes

Enzymes

Lysozyme
Lysosomal acid hydrolases
  proteases
  lipases
  (deoxy)ribonuclease
  phosphatases
  glycosidases
  sulphatases
Neutral proteases
  collagenase
  elastase
  myelinase
  angiotensin convertase
  plasminogen activator
  cytolytic proteinase
Lipases
  lipoprotein lipase
  phospholipase A2
Arginase

Enzyme & cytokine inhibitors
Protease inhibitors
  α_2-macroglobulin
  α_1-antitrypsin inhibitor
  plasminogen activator inhibitor
  collagenase inhibitor
Phospholipase inhibitor
IL-1 inhibitors

Complement components
Classical pathway
  C1, C4, C2, C3, C5
Alternative pathway
  factor B, factor D, properdin
Active fragments
  C3a, C3b, C5a, Bb
Inhibitors
  C3b inactivator, β-1H

Reactive oxygen intermediates
Superoxide

Hydrogen peroxide
Hydroxyl radical
Arachidonic acid intermediates
Cyclo-oxygenase products:
  PGE_2, prostacyclin, thromboxane
Lipo-oxygenase products
  hydroxyeicosotetranoic acids
  leucotrienes
  Platelet-activating factors

Coagulation factors
Tissue factor
Prothrombin activator
Coagulation factors II, VII, IX, X, XIII
Plasminogen activator
Plasminogen activator inhibitors

Cytokines
IL-1, IL-6, IL-8
TNFα
IFNα, IFNβ
Platelet-derived growth factors
Fibroblast growth factor
Transforming growth factor β
GM-CSF
M-CSF
Erythropoietin
Factor inducing monocytopoiesis
Angiogenesis factor

Others
Thrombospondin
Fibronectin
Lipronectin
Lipocortin
Transcobalamin II
Transferrin
Ferritin
Haptoglobin
Glutathione
Uric acid
Apolipoprotein E
Neopterin

(Adapted from references 96, 135–8.)

brane, repulsive forces are overcome enabling contact of the two opposing membranes. Fusion of the secretory vesicle membrane and the plasma membrane then occurs with re-establishment of the membrane bilayer structure, thereby maintaining the integrity of the cell while expelling vesicle contents to the external milieu (135).

Some secretory products, such as lysozyme (159), complement components and apolipoprotein E are synthesized and secreted continuously (constitutive secretion), whereas others are only released upon appropriate stimulation (regulated or induced secretion) (135,160). Stimulation of synthesis could occur at the level of transcription/translation or at the level of vesicle packaging, processing, transport or membrane fusion. Different proteins may be controlled by one or both of these broad mechanisms (135).

10.4.1 Enzymes

Lysozyme mediates digestion of the cell walls of some bacteria and is a well documented secretory product of macrophages (159,161). However, the efficacy of this enzyme as an antibacterial agent is uncertain as relatively few bacteria are susceptible to hydrolysis by lysozyme. Furthermore, naturally occurring substrates for lysozyme, other than bacterial cell wall polysaccharides, have yet to be elucidated. Lysozyme is secreted constitutively and essentially all populations of monocytes and macrophages produce and secrete large amounts (159). Lysozyme secretion is more marked in macrophages and monocytes than monoblasts and promonocytes (162).

Lysosomal acid hydrolases are released by macrophages in response to numerous appropriate exogenous stimuli (163). These enzymes were once regarded solely as intracellular digestive enzymes, but are now known to be secreted actively into the extracellular fluid in response to engagement of macrophage receptors for Fc, complement or cytokines, or after exposure to bacterial products (164,165). Acid hydrolases can degrade collagen, basement membrane, and other components of connective tissue. They can also hydrolyse complement, immunoglobulins, and kinins (166). The enzymes include proteases, lipases, (deoxy) ribonucleases, phosphatases, glycosidases, and sulphatases (138) which are active at low pH.

Neutral proteases include collagenase, elastase, angiotensin convertase, plasminogen activator, and cysteine protease (138,167–169). These are active at a neutral pH and their secretion is closely and differentially regulated during activation (160). Elastase and collagenase have no clear-cut independent antibacterial activity, although they may react synergistically with other enzymes (134). Although resident macrophages are poor secretors of most proteases, inflammatory macrophages secrete substantial amounts. In the case of collagenase and plasminogen activator, unstimulated macrophages have very low levels of intracellular enzyme, suggesting appropriate signals induce both synthesis and secretion of these products. Release of neutral proteases is regulated in two steps—an initial priming signal and a subsequent signal which triggers actual release/ secretion of the product in question (160). Priming for neutral protease secretion can be induced by cytokines, endotoxin, and proteases themselves. Secretion by primed macrophages can be triggered by acetylated proteins, endotoxin, or a phagocytic challenge (160,170). Secretion of this set of neutral proteases can be shut off by binding of α_2-macroglobulin-protease complexes to their specific receptor (170). This effect in most readily observed in fully activated macrophages where protease secretion is highest.

Lipases such as lipoprotein lipase and phospholipase A2, are also secreted by macrophages (138).

10.4.2   Enzyme inhibitors

Secretion of proteases can also be dramatically reduced by binding of α_2-macroglobulin-protease complexes to their surface receptor (170), with subsequent internalization and degradation of the enzyme molecules. As well as the large α_2-macroglobulin molecule, which inhibits not only plasmin but also plasminogen activator, colleagenase, elastase, and kallikrein, macrophages secrete inhibitors of plasmin of low and intermediate molecular weight (120). α1-Antitrypsin inhibitor, plasminogen activator inhibitors, collagenase inhibitor, as well as a phospholipase inhibitor and inhibitors of IL-1, have also been found in macrophages (138).

10.4.3   Complement components

Macrophages secrete numerous components of the complement system, including members of both classical and alternative pathways. These include C1, C4, C2, C3, C5, factor B, factor D, properdin, C3b inactivator, and β-IH (171,172). Furthermore, active fragments generated by macrophage proteases, such as C3a, C3b, C5a, and Bb, are secreted (173). Elevated complement secretion can be induced in various populations of macrophages by host infection with *Listeria* monocytogenes or Bacillus Calmette-Guérin (BCG). Cholinergic and adrenergic receptor agonists stimulate synthesis and secretion following *in vitro* exposure (174). In addition to synthesizing and secreting numerous complement components, macrophages can bind and degrade activated complement through at least two types of complement receptor. After interaction with receptors on the macrophage surface, complement may affect the migratory, endocytic, and secretory behaviour of the cells. For example, C3a and C5a stimulate macrophage migration, but a product of the alternative pathway (Bb) suppresses migration and promotes cell spreading (120).

10.4.4   Reactive oxygen intermediates

When exposed to certain stimuli, phagocytes undergo marked changes in the way they handle oxygen. Their rates of oxygen uptake increase greatly and they begin to produce reactive oxygen intermediates (ROI), such as superoxide, hydrogen peroxide and hydroxyl groups (47), (see Section 7). Because of the sharp increase in oxygen uptake, this series of changes has come to be known as the 'respiratory burst', although its purpose is to generate cytotoxic agents rather than to produce energy (47). Secretion of ROI is incompletely understood at the molecular level. Engagement of Fc receptors, complement receptors, receptors for mannose terminal glyco-proteins, or exposure to the phorbol ester, PMA, can stimulate an oxidative burst (175,176). Induction of the secretion of ROI does not correlate precisely with induction of tumoricidal function (46), neither is phagocytosis necessarily accompanied by a respiratory burst. Generation of ROI by external stimuli requires the activation of a NADPH oxidase, and the rapidity of enzyme activation (within seconds in some instances) essentially rules out its *de novo* synthesis (177). It has therefore been suggested that macrophage activation may lead to modification of existing oxidase mole-cules rather than to generation of new ones.

10.4.5   Arachidonic acid intermediates

Macrophages are a major source of these products and their release con-stitutes an important aspect of their function (178). For example, pros-taglandins of the E series can play an autoregulatory role by limiting certain aspects of tumour cytolysis by macrophages (178). The biochemical path-ways involved in the synthesis of the various arachidonic acid products are well known (179). Arachidonic acid metabolites include prostacyclin, thromboxane, prostaglandin E_2, and leucotriene B4 (51). The enzymes responsible for metabolism of arachidonic acid are targets for regulation of arachidonic acid metabolism. For example, availability of arachidonic acid for metabolism depends on phospholipase A2, which cleaves arachidonic acid from its stored form in the cell's pool of neutral phospholipid. Levels of cyclo-oxygenase and lipooxygenase control the pattern of metabolism for the released arachidonic acid.

10.4.6   Coagulation factors

Mononuclear phagocytes have been known for some time to synthesize coagulation factors. Different 'procoagulant' factors have been described in cells from different species, different anatomical sites, stimulated by dif-ferent agonists under different conditions either *in vitro* or *in vivo*. Peripheral blood monocytes have been studied much more extensively than tissue macrophages due to the relative ease of access. The procoagulant which has been most consistently found in human mononuclear phagocyte populations is tissue factor, which is expressed on the cell surface (180). Active tissue factor, in the presence of adequate phospholipid, greatly enhances the ability of factor VII to activate the extrinsic coagulation cascade (181). Stimulation of monocytes by a variety of agents including endotoxin, immune complexes, complement component C5a, and inflammation-inducing particles, strongly increases tissue factor synthesis by the cell in a dose- and time-dependent manner (182). Unstimulated monocytes express little if any tissue factor, but after stimulation tissue factor is expressed within two hours (180). Little is known concerning the biosynthesis and intracellular transport of tissue factor, although it seems likely that changes in intracellular concentrations of calcium, cyclic nucleotides, and arachidonic acid metabolites, as well as transmethylation reactions are of importance and modulate the integrated response which leads to altered gene expression, *de novo* synthesis of apoprotein III (the protein component of tissue factor) and the intracellular transport of this by a vesicular route to the cell membrane, where it is inserted (182). Other procoagulants synthesized by monocytes are described, including a prothrombin activator (183) and coagulation factors II, VII, IX, X, and XIII (184).

Human monocytes have been found to synthesize a plasminogen activator (185). A recent study suggested that the nature of the plasminogen activator produced by human monocytes depends on the differentiation of the cell, with mature, differentiated macrophages producing urokinase and granulocyte/macrophage progenitors producing tissue-type plasminogen activator (186). Urokinase receptors have been found on the surface of monocytes and a monocytoid cell line and linked to cell motility and growth (187). It has been suggested that urokinase binding to monocyte membranes may represent a mechanism whereby monocytes develop migratory properties. A rapid plasminogen activator inhibitor, called minactivin, is also produced by monocytes (188).

10.4.7   Cytokine secretion

Following recognition of antigen, both T- and B-cells become susceptible to activation by cytokines. Cells of the macrophage lineage are responsible for the secretion of many cytokines and assist in the control and fine tuning of the immune response. The identification of different cytokines generally began with the description of a biological action and the isolation of peptide(s) that mediated this action. It soon emerged that one cytokine might be responsible for many different actions, depending on such criteria as target cell, local concentration, and the combination of other cytokines present, and also that many cytokines have overlapping activities. For largely historical reasons several groupings of cytokines have emerged, including the tumour necrosis factor (TNF), transforming growth factor (TGF), colony-stimulating factor (CSF), interferon (IFN), and interleukin (IL) families (Table 1.8). The criteria for designation as an IL (production by leucocytes, known primary structure, and action during immune responses) are so broad that many of the cytokines described above could now be termed interleukins.

TNF was first identified in serum from mice primed with BCG and challenged with endotoxin. On transfer to tumour-bearing animals there

Table 1.8 Cytokines secreted by macrophages

Cytokine	Other names	Stimuli for production	Biological action
IFNα	viral IFN, Type I IFN	Viruses, bacteria	Antiviral; antimitotic; MHC Class II (+), NK activity (+); decreased c-*myc* expression
M-CSF	MGF, CSF-1, MGI-1M	LPS, IL-1	Macrophage colonies; antiviral, induces PGE$_2$, plasminogen activator, IL-1, IFNγ, TNFα
GM-CSF	MGI-1GM, CSF-2, NIF-T, pluripoietin-α	LPS, IL-1, TNF, retroviral infection	Granulocyte, eosinophil, macrophage colonies, radioprotection, protection from bacterial and parasitic infections; enhances neutrophil and eosinophil functions; PGE$_2$, IL-1, TNF, and O$_2$ induction
G-CSF	MGI-2, DF, CSF-β	LPS, IL-1	Granulocyte colonies; terminal differentiation of myeloid cells; enhancement of neutrophil function
TNFα	cachectin, TNF	LPS and other microbial agents, IL-2, GM-CSF, IL-1	Necrosis of tumours; endotoxic shock-like syndrome; cachexia; fever; IL-1; acute phase protein response; antiparasitic; *in vitro* induction of ICAM-1, IL-1, GM-CSF, IL-6; up-regulation of MHC I and II expression

Table 1.8 Cytokines secreted by macrophages

Cytokine	Other names	Stimuli for production	Biological action
IL-1	BAF, ETAF, LAF	Microbial products, TNF, GM-CSF, IL-2, antigen presentation	Immunoregulation (induction of IL-2, IL-4, IL-6, TNF); fever; acute phase protein response; hypotension; slow wave sleep; induction of collagenase and PGE$_2$, bone and cartilage resorption in culture
IL-6	BSF-2, IFNβ2, HSF	IL-1, TNF, PDGF	Proliferation of myeloma cell lines, haemopoietic cells (GM-CSF and IL-3-like action); induces IL-2R in T-cells; induces Ig production in B-cells; induces acute phase protein production by hepatocytes; fever
TGFβ	–	–	Inhibition of IL-2 effects; role in fibrosis and wound healing *in vivo*; anti-proliferative effects on hepatocytes, epithelial cells, T- and B-cells; influences integrin expression and differentiation; inhibits proliferative actions of EGF, PDGF, IL-2, and FGF

	Basic FGF, HBGF, MDGF		Endothelial cell chemotaxis and growth; IFNγ induction; angiogenesis *in vivo*; myoblast and cortical neurone growth
PDGF	PDGF I, PDGF II	Activated by thrombin, coagulation, LPS, lectins, zymosan	Induction of IL-1, IL-1R, IFNγ, IFNβ, PGE_2, LDL-receptor, *c-myc*, *c-fos*, amino acid transport; neutrophil activation; intracellular actin reorganization; augments synthesis of collagen; chemotaxis and proliferation of mesenchymal cells
EGF	β-Urogastrone	—	Proliferation and differentiation of basal layer in epithelia; angiogenic; wound healing

Note: The above are only a selection of the activities associated with individual cytokines.

IFN, interferon; MGI, macrophage/granulocyte inducer; MGF, macrophage/granulocyte factor; CSF, colony-stimulating factor; NIF-T, neutrophil inhibiting factor, T-cell-derived; G, granulocyte; M, macrophage; ICAM, intercellular adhesion molecule; BAF, B-cell activating factor; ETAF, epidermal cell-derived T-cell activating factor; LAF, lymphocyte-activating factor; BSF-2, B-cell stimulatory factor; HSF, hepatocyte-stimulating factor; TGF, transforming growth factor; FGF, fibroblast growth factor; HBGF, heparin-binding growth factor; MGDF, macrophage-derived growth factor; PDGF, platelet-derived growth factor; EGF, epidermal growth factor.

was evidence of tumour necrosis. TNFα, produced by macrophages, was later shown to be identical to cachectin, which is responsible for wasting in neoplastic and parasitic diseases. The genes encoding both TNFα (189) and TNFβ (produced predominantly by lymphocytes) have been cloned, sequenced and assigned to chromosome 6 near the MHC loci. The stimuli for production are LPS and other microbial agents, IL-2, GM-CSF, and IL-1. TNFs are involved in the necrosis of tumours, endotoxic shock-like syndrome, cachexia, fever, the acute phase protein response, and may have some antiparasitic effects *in vivo*. TNFα has been shown to have cytostatic and cytotoxic effects *in vitro* against a variety of human tumours and to be involved in the induction of IL-1, GM-CSF, IL-6, and ICAM-1 (CD54) production (190).

Macrophages are known to produce IFNα in response to viruses, bacteria, and tumour or foreign cells (191). The biological actions of IFNα include antiviral and antimitotic effects, up-regulation of MHC Class II expression, and an increase in natural killer (NK) cell activity.

Following stimulation by LPS or IL-1, cells of the monocyte/macrophage series produce M-CSF, GM-CSF, and G-CSF (192), (see Section 3). M-CSF induces the formation of monocyte precursor colonies and also induces production of PGE_2, plasminogen activator, IL-1, IFNγ and TNFα. GM-CSF induces the formation of granulocyte, eosinophil, and monocyte colonies, is involved in radioprotection of marrow, fighting bacterial and parasitic infections by enhancing eosinophil and neutrophil function, and influences IL-1 and TNFα production. G-CSF promotes the formation of granulocyte colonies, the terminal differentiation of myeloid cells and enhances mature neutrophil function.

Monocytes, together with many other cells, produce IL-1, which is involved in immunoregulation, influencing IL-2, IL-4, IL-6, IL-1, and TNFα production. IL-1 represents a family of polypeptides with a wide range of biological activities including augmentation of cellular immune responses (T-, B-, and NK cells), proliferation of fibroblasts, chemotaxis of monocytes, neutrophils, and lymphocytes; stimulation of prostaglandin E_2, increased numbers of peripheral blood neutrophils, and neutrophil activation (193). IL-1 plays a role in fever, the acute phase protein response, hypotension, and slow wave sleep, the production of collagenase from mesenchymal cells and influences bone and cartilage resorption. IL-1 is known to synergize with IFN and IL-2 in enhancing tumour killing NK cells and stimulates myeloid progenitor cells to proliferate in long-term bone marrow cultures (194).

Cells of the monocyte/macrophage series are the main source of IL-6, although this cytokine is also produced by activated T-cells and fibroblasts. Cardiac myxoma cells and cervical adenocarcinoma cell lines, and recently (195) some human B-cell lines have also been shown to produce IL-6 (195). There is evidence that IL-1 and TNFα induce the up-regulation of IL-6 production (196). Platelet-derived growth factor (PDGF) is also a stimulus and autocrine production has been reported in some cell lines. IL-6 (197) is the cytokine primarily involved in delivering the final signal for an alteration in the regulation of protein synthesis to hepatocytes (see Section 11.1) during the acute phase protein response. Macrophages express IL-4 receptors and IL-4 has been shown to down-regulate IL-6 production (73). IL-6 induces the proiiferation of immature and mature T-cells (198), as well as the expression of the IL-2 receptor on these cells. Proliferation of haemopoietic cells due to the IL-3- and GM-CSF-like action of IL-6 has also been reported and IL-6 acts on B lymphocytes as a differentiation factor, inducing Ig secretion, and as both a positive and negative regulator of growth acting through IL-6 receptors on these cells.

Human monocytes, together with lymphocytes, hepatocytes, endothelial cells, and dermal fibroblasts, also secrete a novel neutrophil-activating peptide (NAP, previously termed MONAP, MDNCF, NAF, LYNAP, 1B-ENAP or NCF), now known as IL-8 (for general references see 199). This cytokine stimulates the chemotaxis of both neutrophils and T-cells, and inhibits IFNγ release by human NK cells *in vitro* (199–201). The expression of the IL-8 gene in monocytes is regulated by known inflammatory agents, such as LPS, PGE$_2$, IL-1, TNFγ and IFNγ (202).

TGF-β types 1,2 and 3 are also produced by macrophages (203) and has myriad properties (204) including immunosuppressive actions, such as inhibition of all known IL-2 effects including IL2-R expression. TGF-β is chcmotactic for monocytes and plays a role in fibrosis and wound healing with increased gene expression of collagen I, III, and IV and induction of osteoblasts proliferation, fibroblast chemotaxis, and production of col-lagenase. There are also general cellular effects (205,206) and TGFβ appears to deliver and anti-proliferative message for hepatocytes, epithelial cells, keratinocytes, T- and B-cells. TGFβ also influences the expression of integrins and cell adhesion/cytoskeleton interactions and inhibits some actions of other cytokines, such as epidermal growth factor (EGF), PDGF, IL-2, and fibroblast growth factor (FGF).

Heparin-binding growth factors (HBGF) of the basic type (FGF) are produced by macrophages and play a role in angiogenesis and in neuron, myoblast, and endothelial cell growth (207). PDGF and EGF are also produced by monocytes and both have numerous effects. PDGF is involved in vasoconstriction, wound healing, and vascular permeability (209). EGF is involved in the proliferation and differentiation of basal cell layers in epithelia and in wound healing (209). Macrophage inflammatory protein-2 (MIP-2) is also a heparin-binding protein and is a member of a large family of proteins having the ability to modulate the inflammatory response. The murine MIP-2 and its human homologues have recently been cloned (210).

10.5   Tumour cell control

Macrophages infiltrate tumours (often in large numbers) and lysis of tumour cells by monocytes and macrophages is thought to be a mechanism of host defence against tumours (211,212). Cultured human monocytes have been reported to kill tumour cells when activated with cytokines and endotoxin (213). Several modes of tumour cell control by macrophages have been reported (Figure 1.11).

10.5.1   *Inhibition of tumour cell division*

Inhibition of tumour cell division may occur by mediators secreted by macrophages which act on all proliferating cells present. These mediators are largely uncharacterized, but include prostaglandins, IL-1, and TNFα. This inhibition is not thought to require cell contact and occurs rapidly (214).

10.5.2   *Macrophage-mediated tumour cytotoxicity*

Macrophage-mediated tumour cytotoxicity (MTC) is a contact dependent, non-phagocytic process which occurs very slowly over 1 to 3 days. It is selective for neoplastic cells and is independent of antibody production. After recognition of the neoplastic cells, binding to macrophages occurs followed by the secretion of toxic substances, which result in the eventual lysis of the bound tumour cells. TNFα and a novel serine protease are the major candidates for the toxic mediators. Reactive oxygen intermediates can probably potentiate MTC (94).

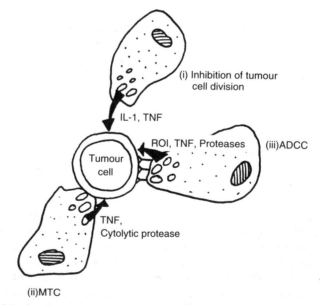

Fig. 1.11   Mechanisms of tumour cell control by macrophages.

10.5.3 *Antibody-dependent cellular cytotoxicity*

Antibody-dependent cellular cytotoxicity (ADCC) is a process whereby macrophages are able to lyse antibody-coated tumour cells (46,94). The classical form of ADCC by macrophages is rapid and mediated by polyclonal antisera. However, in experimental systems in both mice and men, monoclonal antibodies against tumour cells direct and enhance macrophage cytotoxicity (214–216). The Fab portions of the Ig molecule bind to antigen on the surface of tumour cells and the Fc portion binds to surface receptors on the macrophage. After binding, lysis occurs. Secretion of lytic mediators by macrophages occurs upon occupancy and cross-linking of the Fc receptor. Reactive oxygen intermediates, especially hydrogen peroxide, play a major role in cytolysis, but other mediators may also be important, such as complement components, neutral protease, and TNFα. ADCC may occur rapidly over 5 to 6 h, or slowly over 1 to 2 days. Cytokines, such as recombinant human M-CSF (217) may enhance monocyte differentiation into macrophages with increased antitumour ADCC.

Though TNFα appears to be an important mediator of the cytotoxicity of human mononuclear phagocytes *in vitro*, and IFNγ can increase this cytotoxicity by sensitizing tumour cells to the lytic action of TNFα (218), phase 1 trials in patients with various types of cancer given recombinant TNFα systemically have shown response rates of less than 5 per cent (219). However, direct injection into the tumour has given more encouraging results (220).

As well as macrophages exerting some control over tumour cells, some tumour cell types can interfere with mononuclear phagocyte function. Reduced monocyte chemotaxis and phagocytosis are well recognized in subjects with malignant disease (221). The mechanisms whereby the tumour suppresses the antitumour activity of the macrophage are of great interest and probably involve both suppressor T-cells and substances derived from tumour cells themselves.

11 Introduction to the role of mononuclear phagocytes in health and disease

11.1 The acute phase protein response

The acute phase protein response results from disturbances to homeostasis due to neoplastic growth, tissue injury, infection or immunological disorders. It comprises fever, tachycardia, shock, and changes in concentration of circulating proteins, such as C-reactive protein, serum amyloid-A, and fibrinogen. In 1951, it was shown by Miller and co-workers (222) that the liver is the major organ for the synthesis of the acute phase proteins. As this altered protein turnover in the liver is related to trauma in other parts of the body the existence of mediators, probably released by leucocytes which control the acute phase protein response, was proposed. The monocyte/macrophage was later (223) shown to be central to this response and several monocyte products are important in the control of the acute phase protein response: IL-1, TNFα, and IL-6. IL-1 may induce fever by triggering the release of prostaglandin E acting on the hypothalamus to reset the hypothalamic thermoregulatory receptor. IL-1 and TNFα also mediate the accelerated catabolism of muscle protein and negative nitrogen balance, which result in the myalgia and the impaired physical performance in acute infection and malignancy.

Increased circulating levels of TNFα and IL-6 have been observed in tumour-bearing rodents (224,225), and repeated injection of TNFα (226) or the transplantion of transfected cells secreting TNFα (227) has been shown to induce a syndrome similar to that of cancer cachexia. TNFα has previously been proposed as a key mediator of catabolism in cancer patients but the results of current studies suggest that IL-6 rather than TNFα may be important in delivering the signal to hepatocytes for altered protein metabolism. It has recently been shown (228) that IL-6 is elevated in the serum of weight-losing patients with advanced colon cancer, and that this relates to profound changes in hepatic protein metabolism (fixed hepatic protein synthesis was suppressed and acute phase protein production increased). Recently, IL-6 (229) induced transcriptional activation of a set of human acute phase proteins (230,231) and nuclear transcription factors which interact with the C-reactive protein promoter (232) have been described.

The mechanisms which lead to enhanced cytokine release in cancer patients are poorly understood, as too are the complex factors which control cytokine release in normal individuals. Recent work suggests a close correlation between increased monocyte cytokine release and depressed T-cell function in a group of patients with advanced colon cancer (authors, unpublished results). Several interesting areas have just begun to be explored which may relate to cachexia, for example, the observation that IL-4 (74) can down-regulate IL-1 and TNFα gene expression in monocytes from individuals with no disease, and down-regulate the production of IL-6 by human peripheral blood mononuclear cells (73). Both IL-1 and TNFα have been shown to be capable of inducing IL-6 production (196,233) and may play a role in any regulatory imbalance in cachectic patients. Furthermore, the involvement of a cytokine responsive regulatory sequence has been shown to be important for the induction of IL-6 gene expression by IL-1 and TNFα (234).

11.2   Haematopoiesis

The growth of committed haematopoietic progenitor cells *in vitro* requires factors that may be derived from macrophages, mesenchymal cells, and

T-lymphocytes. These factors may only act locally within the bone marrow and not be detected in plasma (18). GM-CSF is secreted by normal human macrophages and monocytes and highly purified natural or recombinant human GM-CSF stimulates granulocyte/macrophage and eosinophil colony formation *in vitro*. In addition to its effect on progenitor differentiation, GM-CSF also induces a variety of functional changes in mature macrophages and neutrophils. For example, it has been shown that GM-CSF stimulates the oxidative metabolism and Fc-dependent phagocytic activity of peritoneal macrophages (235).

Macrophage synthesis of G-CSF appears to depend on induction with endotoxin and this may be an important factor in inducing increased haematopoiesis during stress (236). Furthermore, macrophages produce both IL-1 and TNFα in response to endotoxin. These monokines may induce circulating T-lymphocytes to produce both GM-CSF and IL-3 which stimulate haematopoiesis (236). Monocyte-derived IL-1 and/or TNFα may also induce fixed bone marrow stromal cell populations (endothelial and fibroblasts) to produce GM-CSF and G-CSF as well (see Section 3). Basal haematopoiesis, on the other hand, is probably maintained by local production of growth factors by fixed stromal cells (endothelial cells, fibroblasts, and perhaps macrophages).

Mononuclear phagocytes also appear to participate in the regulation of early erythroid development. GM-CSF, in the presence of erythropoietin induces the formation of colonies derived from early erythroid burst-forming units (BFU-E) and from mixed colony-forming units that comprise granulocytes, erythroid cells, macrophages, and megakaryocytes (CFU-GEMM). Cultured macrophages have recently been found to express the erythropoietin gene and it has been postulated that a subpopulation of resident, bone marrow macrophages may be responsible for producing erythropoietin under adult steady state conditions. The kidney may only function as an erythropoietin producing organ under conditions of erythropoietic stress (237).

11.3   Haemostasis

A host response to infection, tumours or injury may be to activate the coagulation system within the circulation, resulting in disseminated intravascular coagulation. One of the most severe examples of this occurs in meningococcal septicaemia (234–8), although it occurs less severely but more commonly with solid tumours (239). Monocytes and macrophages synthesize and express tissue factor and possibly other coagulation factors (see Section 10.4.6). Mononuclear cells taken from the peripheral blood of patients with tumours of the breast (240) and lung (241), inflammatory bowel disease (242), and meningococcal septicaemia (243) synthesize increased amounts of tissue factor *in vitro*, and a strong positive correlation has been found between the generation of monocyte tissue factor *in vitro* and *in vivo* blood coagulation in patients with certain solid tumours (240,241) and inflammatory bowel disease (242).

IL-1 and TNFα can induce tissue factor synthesis and expression by endothelial cells lining blood vessels, thereby having a potentially important role in thrombogenesis. Furthermore, they have been shown to down-regulate the activity of the protein C pathway on endothelial cells, thereby reducing natural anticoagulant mechanisms and further supporting thrombogenesis (24,245).

11.4   The destruction of micro-organisms

Mononuclear phagocytes play a prominent role in the defence against a variety of infectious agents, including bacteria, viruses, protozoa, and parasites. Following attraction in increased numbers to an infected focus by a variety of substances (see Section 10.2), including bacterial components and endotoxins, complement components, immune complexes, and collagen fragments (166), they remain there under the influence of a migration inhibition factor released by T-cells (246). After arriving at the infected focus the mononuclear cells phagocytose the infectious agent (see Section 10.1). Once ingested, the organism may be killed by both oxygen-dependent and oxygen-independent mechanisms. It is clear that not all organisms are killed by the same mechanism. Oxygen-dependent mechanisms include the production and intracellular release of reactive oxygen species, such as superoxide, hydrogen peroxide, and hydroxyl ions derived from the respiratory burst. Indeed, the ability of murine macrophages to kill or inhibit the intracellular replication of the protozoa *Toxoplasma gondii* and *Trypanosoma cruzi* correlates closely with their oxidative capacity, as judged by release of hydrogen peroxide (48). Oxidized halogens have been shown to destroy many bacterial components including nucleotides and redox enzymes, at a very rapid rate, but kill bacteria even more quickly (47). Superoxide and hydrogen peroxide are only weakly microbicidal and the peroxidase-H_2O_2-halide system appears to be important, which results in the oxidized halogens.

Some organisms are killed by oxygen-independent mechanisms, when there is acidification of the phagocytic vacuole itself to a pH of 4.5–5 after lysosomal fusion (165). This acidification occurs within 15 minutes. However, killing of organisms is probably not due to acidification of the phagocytic vacuole alone, but is also likely to be related to the pH optima of lysosomal acid hydrolases which themselves kill some species.

Certain micro-organisms are able to escape the potent microbidical activity of mononuclear phagocytes. *Mycobacterium tuberculosis* may release substances that interfere with the fusion of primary lysosomes with phagosomes. *Leishmania* and *M. lepraemurium* survive within secondary lysosomes due to the resistance of the microbial cell wall to the macrophages' degradative enzymes (see Section 10.1).

11.5 The disposal of damaged or senescent cells

Macrophages phagocytose aged erythrocytes during their circulation through the spleen. The mechanism whereby macrophages recognize senescent cells is unknown. Senescent red cells are sequestered in the spleen and their destruction presumably occurs because of a subtle abnormality detected by splenic macrophages. However, the relevant abnormalities are uncertain. Furthermore, splenectomy does not enhance red cell survival in otherwise normal individuals. Hypotheses have ranged from ageing cells progressively losing sialic acid, cation and water, red cell membrane surface, altered membrane lipid, and proteins, through to the concept that as the normal erythrocyte ages its membrane non-specifically binds increasing quantities of Ig until it may be coated sufficiently in order to be recognized by the macrophage Fc receptors and phagocytosed (247). It is possible that aged leucocytes and platelets are removed by similar mechanisms (166). Once ingested by macrophages, the erythrocyte is degraded to liberate iron from haem, which is then stored in protein complexes and transferred to developing erythroblasts (248).

11.6 Wound healing, tissue repair, and remodelling

Macrophages are rapidly recruited to wounds after injury, where they can synthesize and secrete collagenase and elastase, helping to debride the wound (167,168). Macrophages also participate in wound healing and tissue remodelling by releasing substances that induce fibroblast proliferation and neovascularization and in remodelling bone through resorption by osteoclasts (138,249).

11.7 Atherogenesis

The nature of the role of the macrophage in atherogenesis is uncertain. Some evidence points to an important role for the macrophage in plaque development, whilst equally convincing evidence suggests they act as a defence against plaque progression (250). Macrophages are usually present in small numbers in human atheromatous plaques, but in certain experimental models it is the predominant cell type. This leads to difficulties in extrapolating between the two situations. Macrophages may become loaded with lipid and cholesterol and when they die this may become deposited in the blood vessel wall (251). In addition, it has been suggested that monocyte-derived 'foam' cells may leave the artery wall and whilst re-entering the circulation may cause endothelial injury. The latter could then result in platelet adhesion and aggregation, as well as allowing lipid influx (252). Conversely, macrophages may be equally important as scavenger cells in removing excess cholesterol and other fatty substances from intimal lesions. The lipases, collagenase, and elastase they synthesize and secrete may accelerate plaque regression (253). Whether macrophages in atherosclerotic plaques are primarily important in plaque progression or regression is the subject of current investigations (see Chapter 9).

11.8   Autoimmunity

The macrophage plays a role in many autoimmune diseases in humans. Only a few will be mentioned here as this topic is discussed extensively in Chapter 7. In rheumatoid arthritis, macrophages and other 'professional' APCs are the first cells to be involved, processing and presenting antigen to antigen-specific T-cells. The initial stimulus for the disease remains unknown but may be due to a single virus or several viruses, possibly possessing epitopes cross-reactive with self antigens, which are the object of the immune response. A majority of patients with rheumatoid arthritis have HLA-DR4- and/or HLA-DR1- expressing cells but these two haplotypes are not the only genetic components of the disease. The immune response gradually becomes organized in the perivascular areas of the synovial membrane with the accumulation of T-cells leading to the proliferation of B-cells within a network of new blood vessels and synovial cell proliferation. Macrophages appear to be responsible for the angiogenesis (254), and thus the development of a network of new blood vessels in the synovial membrane essential to the evolution of rheumatoid synovitis. Cytokines originating from macrophages (255) within the rheumatoid synovial membrane have been demonstrated to be at much higher levels than those secreted by lymphocytes. Thus macrophages, by their production of cytokines, may orchestrate the disease process with the alteration in endothelial cell adhesion and the subsequent influx of neutrophils. Eventually, severe inflammation and synovial hyperplasia results in an invasive advance that effects cartilage, tendons, and subchondral bone.

In Hashimoto's spontaneous and experimental autoimmune thyroiditis, the thyroid gland is diffusely infiltrated by lymphocytes, which may aggregate to form secondary lymphoid follicles, as well as plasma cells and macrophages (256). The role of macrophages is not clear but they may have a role in the initial processing and presentation of the self antigen involved. The serum of patients with Hashimoto's disease usually contains antibodies to thyroglobulin.

Macrophages play a central role in sarcoidosis which is a multisystem disorder of unknown aetiology manifesting as inflammation of the alveolar structures followed by the development of granulomas. Autoantibodies reactive with T-cells are often present. The active sarcoid granuloma consists of a tightly packed central follicle of macrophages, epitheloid cells, and multinucleated giant cells surrounded by a perimeter of lymphocytes, monocytes, and fibroblasts (257). It has been suggested that the central follicle of the granulomata contains activated macrophages whose primary function is the secretion of cytokines rather than phagocytosis. Although the lungs are the primary organ affected, granulomas are often present at other sites.

11.9 Diseases of the central nervous system

A role for the macrophage both in the induction and effector phases of multiple sclerosis (MS) has been suggested. Inappropriate induction of antigen-specific helper T-cells resulting in altered regulation of the immune response is postulated to be one of the factors in the mechanism of autoimmune disease. In MS once autoreactive T-cells have been presented with the relevant antigen and received the appropriate cytokine stimuli they become activated and cross into the central nervous system (CNS) across the blood–brain barrier (258). Subsequent proliferation of these autoreactive T-cells may occur following presentation by indigenous macrophages, microglia or possibly astrocytes. Damage to the CNS and oedema follow the release of cytokines and macrophages, which are known to strip myelin from nerve sheaths, play a role in the subsequent demyelination.

12 Summary

The macrophage is the major differentiated cell of a phylogenetically primitive system of cells termed the mononuclear phagocyte system. In the adult human, macrophages originate in the bone marrow but become widely distributed throughout the body, being particularly prominent in the lymph nodes and spleen, liver, lungs, gastrointestinal tract, serous cavities, bone, synovium, skin, and CNS. Once thought of as solely phagocytic, it is now known that they have many important and diverse functions. They have a prominent role in defence against many infectious agents and following attraction to an infected focus by chemoattractants, they remain there under the influence of a migration inhibition factor released by T-cells. After arrival at the infected focus the macrophage may phagocytose and kill infectious agents by a variety of mechanisms. Macrophages also play an important role in inducing and regulating the immune response, by taking up protein antigens and generating immunogenic fragments from them which may be used to activate T-cells. Macrophages are frequently found to infiltrate tumours and they may form an important mechanism of host defence against the tumour cell, either inhibiting tumour cell division or killing the cells following secretion of soluble mediators. Macrophages are known to secrete a large number of other substances *in vitro*, although the physiological significance is sometimes uncertain. However, some appear to have a role in the induction of the acute phase response, regulation of haematopoiesis, cleansing and healing of injured tissue, regulation of haemostasis, as well as a possible role in the pathogenesis of atherosclerosis, autoimmune and CNS diseases. The more that is learned of macrophage biology, the more remarkable and fundamental this group of cells appear to be.

Acknowledgements

The authors would like to thank A. Ross, MRC Human Genetics Unit, and J. Spencer, Department of Dermatology, Royal Infirmary, Edinburgh for help with the electron micrographs. Work in the author's (JAR) laboratory is supported by the Melville Trust for the Care and Cure of Cancer and by the Cancer Research Campaign.

References

1 Karnovsky, M.L. (1981). Metchinkoff in Messina: a century of studies on phagocytosis. *N. Eng. J. Med.*, **304**, 1178–80.

2 Aschoff, L. (1924). Das reticulo–endotheliale system. *Ergeb. Inn. Med. Kinderheilkd.*, **26**, 1–118.

3 Furth, R. van, Cohn, Z.A., Hirsch, J.G., Humphry, J.H., Spector, W.G., and Langevoort, H.L. (1972). The mononuclear phagocyte system: a new classification of macrophages, monocytes and their precursor cells. *Bull. WHO.*, **46**, 845–52.

4 Moore, M.A.S. and Metcalf, D. (1970). Ontogeny of the Haemopoietic system: Yolk sac origin of *in vivo* and *in vitro* colony forming cells in the developing mouse embryo. *Br. J. Haematol.*, **18**, 279–96.

5 Furth, R. van (1989). Origin and turnover of monocytes and macrophages. *Curr. Top. Pathol.*, **79**, 125–50.

6 Metcalf, D. (1971). Transformation of granulocytes to macrophages in bone marrow colonies *in vitro*. *J. Cell Physiol.*, **77**, 277–80.

7 Koeffler, H.P. and Golde, D.W. (1980). Human myeloid leukaemia cell lines: A review. *Blood*, **56**, 344–50.

8 Furth, R. van, Diesselhoff-den Dulk, M.M.C., Raeburn, J.A., van Zwet, Th.L., Crofton, R., and Blussé van Oud Alblas, A. (1980). Characteristics, origin and kinetics of human and murine mononuclear phagocytes. In *Mononuclear phagocytes. Functional aspects* (ed. R van Furth). Martinus Nijhoff, The Hague, Boston, London.

9 Furth, R. van and Diesselhoff-den Dulk, M.M.C. (1970). The kinetics of promoncytes and monocytes in the bone marrow. *J. Exp. Med.*, **132**, 813–28.

10 Meuret, G. and Hoffmann, G. (1973). Monocyte kinetic studies in normal and disease states. *Br. J. Haematol.*, **24**, 275–85.

11 Furth, R. van and Sluiter, W. (1986) Distribution of blood monocytes between a marginating and a circulating pool. *J. Exp. Med.*, **163**, 474–9.

12 Furth, R. van and Cohn, Z.A. (1968). The origin and kinetics of mononuclear phagocytes. *J. Exp. Med.*, **128**, 415–35.

13 Whitelaw, D.M. (1966). The intravascular lifespan of monocytes. *Blood*, **28**, 445–64.

14 Rothlein, R., Dustin, M.L., Marlin, S.D., and Springer, T.A. (1986). A human intercellular adhesion molecule (ICAM-1) distinct from LFA-1. *J. Immunol.*, **137**, 1270–4.

15 Dustin, M.L., Rothlein, R., Bhan, A.K., Dinarello, C.A., and Springer, T.A. (1986). Induction by IL-1 and interferon-γ: Tissue distribution, biochemistry and function of a natural adherence molecule (ICAM-1). *J. Immunol.*, **137**, 245–54.

16 Furth, R. van, Diesselhoff-den Dulk, M.M.C., and Mattie, H. (1973). Quantitative study on the production and kinetics of mononuclear

phagocytes during an acute inflammatory reaction. *J. Exp. Med.*, **138**, 1314–30.

17 Furth, R. van. (1988). Phagocytic cells: development and distribution of mononuclear phagocytes in normal steady state and inflammation. In *Inflammation: Basic principles and clinical correlates* (ed. J.I. Gallin, I.M. Goldstein, and R. Snyderman). Raven, New York.

18 Jones, A.L. and Millar, J.L. (1989). Growth factors in haemopoiesis. In *Clinical haematology: A plastic Anaemia* (ed. E.C. Gordon-Smith). Bailliere Tindall, London.

19 Thorens, B., Mermod, J.J., and Vassalli, P. (1987). Phagocytosis and inflammatory stimuli induce GM-CSF mRNA in macrophages through post transcriptional regulation. *Cell*, **48**, 671–9.

20 Broudy, V.C., Kaushansky, K., Segal, G.M., Harlan, J.M., and Adamson, J.W. (1986). Tumour necrosis factor type alpha stimulates human endothelial cells to produce granulocyte/macrophage colony-stimulating factor. *Proc. Natl. Acad. Sci. U.S.A.*, **83**, 7467–71.

21 Munker, R., Gasson, J., Ogawa, M., and Koeffler, H.P. (1986). Recombinant human tumour necrosis factor induces production of granulocyte-monocyte colony stimulating factor. *Nature*, **323**, 79–82.

22 Bagby, G.C. Jr., Dinarello, C.A. Wallace, P., Wagner, C., Hefeneider, S., and McCall, E. (1986). Interleukin 1 stimulates granulocyte macrophage colony-stimulating activity release by vascular endothelial cells. *J. Clin. Invest.*, **78**, 1316–23.

23 Cannistra, S.A., Rambaldi, A. Spriggs, D.R., Herrmann, F., Kufe, D., and Griffin, J.D. (1987). Human granulocyte-macrophage colony stimulating factor induces expression of the tumour necrosis factor gene by the U937 cell line and by normal human monocytes. *J. Clin. Invest.*, **79**, 1720–8.

24 Golde, D.W. and Groopman, J.E. (1990). Production, upright distribution and fate of monocytes and macrophages. In *Haematology* (4th edn), (ed. W.J. Williams, E. Beutler, A.J. Erslev, and M.A. Lichtman). McGraw-Hill, New York.

25 Waarde, D. van, Hulsing-Hesselink, E., Sandkuyl, L.A., and van Furth, R. (1977). Humoral regulation of monocytopoiesis during the early phase of an inflammatory reaction caused by particulate substances. *Blood*, **50**, 141–53.

26 Shum, D.T. and Galsworthy, S.B. (1982). Stimulation of monocyte production by an endogenous mediator induced by a component from *Listeria* monocytogenes. *Immunology*, **46**, 343–51.

27 Pelus, L.M. Broxmeyer, H.E. Kurland. J.I., and Moore, M.A.S. (1979). Regulation of macrophage and granulocyte proliferation: Specificities of prostaglandin E and lactoferrin. *J. Exp. Med.*, **150**, 277–92.

28 Kurland, J.I., Bockman, R.S., Broxmeyer, H.E., and Moore, M.A.S.

(1978). Limitation of excessive myelopoiesis by the intrinsic modulation of macrophage-derived prostaglandin E. *Science*, **199**, 522–5.

29 Trinchieri, G. and Perussia, B. (1983). Immune interferon: A pleitropic lymphokine with multiple effects. *Immunol Today*, **6**, 131–6.

30 Douglas, S.D. and Hassan, N.F. (1990). Morphology of monocytes and macrophages. In *Haematology* (*4th edn*), (ed. W.J. Williams, E. Beutler, A.J. Erslev, and M.A. Lichtman). McGraw-Hill, New York.

31 Goldman, J.M. (1989). Granulocytes, monocytes and their benign disorders. In *Postgraduate haematology* (ed. A.V. Hoffbrand and S.M. Lewis). Heinemann, Oxford.

32 Hartwig, J.H. and Shelvin, P.A. (1986). The architecture of actin filaments and the ultrastructural location of actin binding protein in the periphery of lung macrophages. *J. Cell Biol.*, **103**, 1007–20.

33 Stossel, T.P. (1981). Actin filaments and secretion. The macrophage model. *Meth. Cell Biol.*, **23**, 215–30.

34 Stossel, T.P. (1988). The mechanical responses of white blood cells. In *Inflammation: Basic principles and clinical correlates*. (ed. J.I., Gallin, I.M. Goldstein, and R. Snyderman). Raven, New York.

35 Hayhoe, F.G.J. and Quaglino, D. (1988). *Haematological cytochemistry* (2nd edn). Churchill Livingstone, Edinburgh.

36 Schmalzl, F. and Braunsteiner, H. (1970). The cytochemistry of monocytes and macrophages. *Ser. Haemat.*, **3**, 93–131.

37 Yam, L.T., Li, C.Y., and Crosby, W.H. (1971). Cytochemical identification of monocytes and granulocytes. *Am. J. Clin. Pathol.*, **55**, 283–90.

38 Ginsel, L.A., Onderwater, J.J.M., De Water, R., Block, J., and Daems, W.T. (1983). 5'-nucleotidase activity in mouse peritoneal macrophages. *Histochemistry*, **79**, 295–309.

39 Nichols, B.A. and Bainton, D.F. (1973). Differentiation of human monocytes in bone marrow and blood: Sequential formation of two granule populations. *Lab. Invest.*, **29**, 27–40.

40 Cohn, Z.A. (1968). The structure and function of monocytes and macrophages. *Adv. Immunol.*, **9**, 163–214.

41 Steinman, R.M., Mellman, J.S., Muller, W.A., and Cohn, Z.A. (1983). Endocytosis and the recycling of plasma membrane. *J. Cell Biol.*, **96**, 1–27.

42 Oren, R., Franham, A.E., Saito, K., Milofsky, E., and Karnovsky, M.L. (1963). Metabolic patterns in three types of phagocytosing cells. *J. Cell Biol.*, **17**, 487–501.

43 Loike, J.P., Kozler, V.F., and Silverstein, S.C. (1979). Increased ATP and creatine phosphate turnover in phagocytosing mouse peritoneal macrophages. *J. Biol. Chem.*, **254**, 9558–64.

44 Cohen, A.B. and Cline, M.J. (1971). The human alveolar macro-

phage: isolation, cultivation *in vitro*, and studies of morphologic and functional characteristics. *J. Clin. Invest.*, **50**, 1390–8.

45 Hocking, W.G. and Golde, D.W. (1979). The pulmonary alveolar macrophage. *N. Eng. J. Med.*, **301**, 580 and 639.

46 Adams, D.O. and Hamilton, T.A. (1984). The cell biology of macrophage activation. *Ann. Rev. Immunol.*, **2**, 283–318.

47 Babior, B.M. (1984). The respiratory burst of phagocytes. *J. Clin. Invest.*, **73**, 599–601.

48 Klebanoff, S.J. (1988). Phagocytic cells: products of oxygen metabolism. In *Inflammation: Basic principles and clinical correlates* (ed. J.I. Gallin, I.M. Goldstein, and R. Snyderman). Raven, New York.

49 Nathan, C.F., Murray, H.W., Wiebe, M.E., and Rubin, B.Y. (1983). Identification of interferon-γ as the lymphokine that activates human macrophage oxidative metabolism and antimicrobial activity. *J. Exp. Med.*, **158**, 670–89.

50 Nathan, C.F., *et al.* (1984). Activation of human macrophages: comparison of other cytokines with interferon-gamma. *J. Exp. Med.*, **160**, 600–5.

51 Pawlowski, N.A., Kaplan, G., Hamill, A.L., Cohn, Z.A., and Scott, W.A. (1983). Arachidonic acid metabolism by human monocytes. Studies with platelet-depleted cultures. *J. Exp. Med.*, **158**, 393–412.

52 Nichols, B.A., Bainton, D.F., and Farquhar, M.G. (1971). Differentiation of monocytes. Origin, nature and fate of their azurophil granules. *J. Cell Biol.*, **50**, 198–515.

53 North, R.J. (1978). The concept of the activated macrophage. *J. Immunol.*, **121**, 806–9.

54 Nishizuka, Y. (1984). The role of protein kinase C in cell surface signal transduction and tumour promotion. *Nature*, **308**, 693–8.

55 McPhail, L.C., Wolfson, M., and Snyderman, R. (1984). Protein kinase C (PKC) and neutrophil activation. PKC becomes tightly membrane associated when cells are stimulated with phorbol myristate acetate (PMA). *Fed. Proc.*, **43**, 974–86.

56 Myers, M.A., McPhail, L.C., and Snyderman, R. (1984). Protein kinase C activity in human lymphocytes and monocytes: Phorbol myristate acetate stimulation shifts activity from cytosol to membrane components. *Clin. Res.*, **32**, 353A.

57 Berken, A. and Benacerref, B. (1966). Properties of antibodies cytophilic for macrophages. *J. Exp. Med.*, **123**, 119–44.

58 Lay, W.H. and Nussenzweig, V. (1968). Receptors for complement on leucocytes. *J. Exp. Med.*, **128**, 991–1009.

59 Unkeless, J.C., Sciglione, E., and Freedman, V.H. (1988). Structure and function of human and murine receptors for IgG. *Ann. Rev. Immunol.*, **6**, 251–81.

60 Kikutani, H. Inui, S., Sato, R., Barsumian, E.L., Owaki, H.,

Yamasaki, K., Kaisho, T., Uchibayashi, N., *et al.* (1986). Molecular structure of the human lymphocyte receptor for immunoglobulin E. *Cell*, **47**, 657–65.

61 Kinet, J-P. (1989). Antibody-cell interactions: Fc receptors. *Cell*, **57**, 351–4.

62 Hourcade, D., Holers, V.M., and Atkinson, J.P. (1989). The regulators of complement activation (RCA) gene cluster. *Adv. Immunol.*, **45**, 381.

63 Gonwa, T.A., Frost, J.P., and Karr, R.W. (1986). Human monocytes have the capability of expressing HLA-DQ and HLA-DP molecules upon stimulation with interferon-gamma. *J. Immunol.*, **137**, 519–24.

64 Dinarello, C.A. and Mier, J.W. (1987). Lymphokines. *N. Eng. J. Med.*, **317**, 940–5.

65 Talmadge, J.E., *et al.* (1988). Immunomodulatory properties of recombinant murine and human tumour necrosis factor. *Cancer Res.*, **48**, 544–50.

66 Malkovsky, M. (1987). Recombinant IL-2 directly augments the cytotoxicity of human monocytes. *Nature*, **325**, 262–5.

67 Paul, W.E. and Ohara, J. (1987). B-cell stimulatory factor-1/Interleukin-4. *Ann. Rev. Immunol.*, **5**, 429–59.

68 Metcalf, D. (1989). The molecular control of cell division, differentiation commitment and maturation in haemopoietic cells. *Nature*, **339**, 27–30.

69 Nakamura, M., *et al.* (1989). Expression of a novel 3.5-kb macrophage colony-stimulating factor transcript in human myeloma cells. *J. Immunol.*, **143**, 3543–7.

70 Rettenmier, C.W., Roussel, M.F., and Sherr, C.J. (1988). The colony-stimulating factor 1 (CSF-1) receptor (c-*fms* proto-oncogene product) and its ligand. *J. Cell Sci.*, **9**, (Suppl.), 27–44.

71 Frendl, G. and Beller, D.I. (1990). Regulation of macrophage activation by IL-3. I. IL-3 functions as a macrophage-activating factor with unique properties, inducing Ia and lymphocyte function associated antigen-1 but not cytotoxicity. *J. Immunol.*, **144**, 3392–9.

72 Frendl, G., Fenton, M.J., and Beller, D.I. (1990). Regulation of macrophage activation by IL-3. II. IL-3 and lipopolysaccharide act synergistically in the regulation of IL-1 expression. *J. Immunol.*, **144**, 3400–10.

73 Lee, J.D., Swisher, S.G., Minehart, E.H., McBride, W.H., and Economou, J.S. (1990). Interleukin-4 downregulates interleukin-6 production in human peripheral blood mononuclear cells. *J. Leuc. Biol.*, **47**, 475–9.

74 Essner, R., Rhoades, K., McBride, W.H., Morton, D.L., and Economou, J.S. (1989). IL-4 down regulates IL-1 and TNF gene expression in human monocytes. *J. Immunol.*, **142**, 3857–61.

75 Kodama, T., Freeman, M., Rohrer, L., Zabrecky, J., Matsudaira, P., and Krieger, M. (1990). Type I macrophage scavenger receptor contains alpha-helical and collagen-like coiled coils. *Nature*, **343**, 531–5.

76 Vlassara, H., Moldawer, L., and Chan, B. (1989). Macrophage/monocyte receptor for nonenzymatically glycosylated protein is upregulated by cachectin/tumor necrosis factor. *J. Clin. Invest.*, **84**, 1813–20.

77 Ezekowitz, R.A.B. and Stahl, P.D. (1988). The structure and function of vertebrate mannose lectin-like proteins. *J. Cell Sci.*, **9**, (Suppl.), 121–33.

78 Vejlsgaard, G.L., Ralfkaier, E., Avnstrop, C., Czajkowski, M., Marlin, S.D., and Rothlein, R. (1989). Kinetics and characterisation of intercellular adhesion molecule-1 (ICAM-1) expression on keratinocytes in various inflammatory skin lesions and malignant cutaneous lymphoma. *J. Am. Acad. Dermat.* **20**, 782–90.

79 Kishimoto, T.K., Larson, R.S., Corbi, A.L., Dustin, M.L., Staunton, D.E., and Springer, T.A. (1989). The Leucocyte Integrins. *Adv. Immunol.*, **46**, 149–82.

80 Hemler, M.E. (1990). VLA proteins in the integrin family: structures, functions and their role on leucocytes. *Ann. Rev. Immunol.*, **8**, 365–400.

81 Guan, J-L. and Hynes, R.O. (1990). Lymphoid cells recognise an alternatively spliced segment of fibronectin via the integrin receptor $\alpha_4\beta_1$. *Cell*, **60**, 53–61.

82 Elics, M.J., *et al.* (1990). VCAM-1 on activated endothelium interacts with the leucocyte integrin VLA-4 at a site distinct from the VLA-4/fibronectin binding site. *Cell*, **60**, 577–84.

83 Springer, T.A. (1990). Adhesion receptors of the immune system. *Nature*, **346**, 425–34.

84 Johnston, G.I., Cook. R.G., and McEver, R.P. (1989). Cloning of GMP140, a granule membrane protein of platelets and endothelium: sequence similarity to proteins involved in cell adhesion and inflammation. *Cell*, **56**, 1033–44.

85 Guy, K., Ritchie, A.S., and van Heyningen, V. (1984). Anomalous expression of MHC Class II antigens on human monocytes. *Disease Markers*, **2**, 283–5.

86 Gonwa, T.A., Frost, J.P., and Karr, R.W. (1986). All human monocytes have the capability of expressing HLA-DQ and HLA-DP molecules on stimulation with interferon-gamma. *J. Immunol.*, **137**, 519–24.

87 Haziot, A., Chen, S., Ferrero, E., Low, M.G., Silber, R., and Goyart, S.M. (1988). The monocyte differentiation antigen, CD14, is anchored to the cell membrane by a phosphatidylinositol linkage. *J. Immunol.*, **141**, 547–52.

88 Bazil, V., *et al.* (1987). Biochemical characterisation of a soluble form

of the 53 kDa monocyte surface antigen. *Eur. J. Immunol.*, **16**, 1583–9.

89 Goyart, S.M., Ferrero, E., Rettig, W.J., Yenamandra, A.K., Obata, F., and Le Beau, M.M. (1988). The CD14 monocyte differentiation antigen maps to a region encoding growth factor receptors and receptors. *Science*, **239**, 497–500.

90 Schneider, E.M., Lorenz, I., Kogler, G., and Wernet, P. (1989). Modulation of monocyte function by CD14-specific antibodies *in vitro*. In *Leucocyte typing*, Vol. IV (ed. W. Knapp *et al.*), pp. 794–5. Oxford University Press.

91 Warnke, R.A., *et al.* (1989). Diagnosis of myelomonocytic and macrophage neoplasms in routinely processed tissue biopsies with monoclonal antibody KP1. *Am. J. Path.*, **135**, 1089–95.

92 Peiper, S.C., *et al.* (1989). Report on the CD33 cluster workshop: biochemical and genetic characterization of gp67. In *Leucocyte typing*, Vol. IV (ed. W. Knapp *et al.*), pp. 814–16. Oxford University Press.

93 Fogelman, A.M., Van Lenten, B.J., Warden, C., Haberland, M.E., and Edwards, P.A. (1988). Macrophage liproprotein receptors. *J. Cell Sci.*, **9**, (Suppl.), 135–49.

94 Adams, D.O. and Hamilton, T.A. (1988). Phagocytic cells. Cytotoxic activities of macrophages. In *Inflammation. Basic principles and clinical correlates* (ed. J.I. Galin, I.M. Goldstein, and R. Snyderman), pp. 471–92. Raven, New York.

95 Werb, Z. and Goldstein, I.M. (1987). Phagocytic cells: Chemotactic and effector functions of macrophages and granulocytes. In *Basic and clinical immunology* (6th edn), (ed. D.P. Stites, J.D. Stoba, and J.V. Wells), pp. 96–113. Appleton and Lange, Norwalk.

96 Papadimitriou, J.M. and Ashman, R.B. (1989). Macrophages: Current views on their differentiation, structure and function. *Ultrastruct. Path.*, **13**, 343–72.

97 Gordon, S., Perry, H., Rabinowitz, S., Lap-Ping, C., and Rosen, H. (1988). Plasma membrane receptors of the mononuclear phagocyte system. *J. Cell Sci.*, **9**, (Suppl.), 1–26.

98 Law, S.K.A. (1988). C3 receptors on macrophages. *J. Cell Sci.*, **9**, (Suppl.), 67–97.

99 Gordon, S., Keshav, S., and Chung, L.P. (1988). Mononuclear phagocytes: tissue distribution and functional heterogeneity. *Current Opinion in Immunology*, **1**, 26–35.

100 Thomas, E.D., Ramberg, R.E., Sale, G.E., Sparkes, R.S., and Golde, D.W. (1976). Direct evidence for a bone marrow origin of the alveolar macrophage in man. *Science*, **192**, 1016–18.

101 Sandron, D., Reynolds, H.Y., Laval, A.M., Venet, A., Israel-Biet, D., and Chretein, J. (1986). Human alveolar macrophage subpopulations isolated on discontinuous albumin gradients: cytological data in normals and sarcoid patients. *Eur. J. Resp. Dis.*, **68**, 177–85.

102 Nakstad, B., Lyberg, T., Skjorten, F., and Boye, N.P. (1989) Subpopulations of human alveolar macrophages: an ultrastructural study. *Ultrastruct. Path.*, **13**, 1–13.
103 Passlick, B., Flieger, D., and Loms Ziegler-Heitbrock, H.W. (1989). Identification and characteristics of a novel monocyte population in human peripheral blood. *Blood*, **74**, 2527–34.
104 Tarling, J.D., Lin, H-S., and Hsu, S. (1987). Self renewal of pulmonary alveolar macrophages. *J. Leuc. Biol.*, **42**, 443–6.
105 Fuller, G.M., Bunzel, R.J., Woloski, B.M., and Nham, S-U. (1987). Isolation of hepatocyte stimulating factor from human monocytes. *Biochem. Biophys. Res. Commun.*, **144**, 1003–9.
106 Daemen, T., Veninga, A., Roerdink, F.H., and Scherphof, G.L. (1989). Endocytic and tumoricidal heterogeneity of rat liver macrophage populations. *Cell Cancer Ther.*, **5**, 157–167.
107 Buckley, P.J., Smith, M.R., Braverman, M.F., and Dickson, S.A. (1987). Human spleen contains phenotypic subsets of macrophages and dendritic cells that occupy discrete microanatomic locations. *Am. J. Path.*, **128**, 505–20.
108 Crocker, P.R. and Gordon, S. (1985). Isolation and characterisation of resident stromal macrophages and haemopoietic cell clusters from mouse bone marrow. *J. Exp. Med.*, **162**, 993–1014.
109 Crocker, P.R., Morris, L., and Gordon, S. (1988). Novel cell surface adhesion receptors involved in interactions between stromal macrophages and haemopoietic cells. *J. Cell Sci.*, **9**, (Suppl.), 185–206.
110 Hume, D.A., Allan, W., Hogan, P.G., and Doe, W.F. (1987). Immunohistochemical characterization of macrophages in the liver and gastrointestinal tract: expression of CD4, HLA-Dr, OKM1 and the mature macrophage marker 25F9 in normal and diseased tissue. *J. Leuc. Biol.*, **42**, 474–84.
111 Perry, V. H. and Gordon, S. (1987). Modulation of CD4 antigens on macrophages and microglia in rat brain. *J. Exp. Med.*, **166**, 1138–43.
112 Murphy, G.F., Messadi, D., Fonferko, E., and Hancock, W.W. (1986). Phenotypic transformation of macrophages to Langerhans cells in the skin. *Am. J. Path.*, **123**, 401–6.
113 Groh, V., *et al.* (1988). The phenotypic spectrum of Histiocytosis X cells. *J. Invest. Derm.*, **90**, 441–7.
114 Franklin, W.A., *et al.* (1986). Immunohistological analysis of human mononuclear phagocytes and dendritic cells by using monoclonal antibodies. *Lab. Invest.*, **54**, 322–35.
115 Romani, N., *et al.* (1989). Cultured human Langerhans cells resemble lymphoid dendritic cells in phenotype and function. *J. Invest. Derm.*, **93**, 600–9.
116 Williams, G.T. and Williams, W.J. (1983). Granulomatous inflammation—a review. *Clin. Path.*, **36**, 723–33.

117 Papadimitriou, J.M. and van Bruggen, I. (1986). Evidence that multi-nucleate giant cells are examples of mononuclear phagocyte differentiation. *J., Path.*, **148**, 149–57.
118 Alpers, C.E., Magil, A.B., and Gown, A.M. (1989). Macrophage origin of the multinucleated cells of myeloma cast nephropathy *Am. J. Clin. Path.*, **92**, 662–5.
119 Metchnikoff, E. (1905). *Immunity in infective disease.* Cambridge University Press.
120 Nathan, C.F., Murray, H.W., and Cohn, Z.A. (1980). The macrophage as an effector cell. *N. Eng. J. Med.*, **303**, 622–6.
121 Sung, S.S., Nelson, R.S., and Silverstein, S.C. (1983). Yeast mannans inhibit binding and phagocytosis of zymosan by mouse peritoneal macrophages. *J. Cell Biol.*, **96**, 160–6.
122 Griffin, F.M. Jr., Griffin, J.A., Leider, J.E., and Silverstein, S.C. (1975). Studies on the mechanism of phagocytosis. I. Requirements for circumferential attachment of particle-bound ligands to specific receptors on the macrophage plasma membrane. *J. Exp. Med.*, **142**, 1263–82.
123 Griffin, F.M., Griffin, J.A., and Silverstein, S.C. (1976). Studies on the mechanism of phagocytosis. II. The interaction of macrophages with anti-immunoglobulin IgG-coated bone marrow derived lymphocytes. *J. Exp. Med.*, **144**, 788–809.
124 Hirsch, J. G. (1962). Cinemicrophotographic observations on granule lysis in polymorphonuclear leucocytes during phagocytosis. *J. Exp. Med.*, **116**, 827–33.
125 Stossel, T.P. (1988) The mechanical responses of white blood cells. In *Inflammation: Basic principles and clinical correlates* (ed. J.I. Gallin, I.M. Goldstein, and R. Snyderman). Raven, New York.
126 Rouzer, C.A., Scott, W.A., Kempe, J., and Cohn, Z.A. (1980). Prostaglandin synthesis by macrophages requires a specific receptor–ligand interaction. *Proc. Natl. Acad. Sci. U.S.A.*, **77**, 4279–82.
127 Aderem, A.A., Wright, S.D., Silverstein, S.C., and Cohn, Z.A. (1985). Ligated complement receptors do not activate the arachidonic acid cascade in resident peritoneal macrophages. *J. Exp. Med.*, **161**, 617–22.
128 Wright, S.D. and Silverstein, S.C. (1983). Receptors for C3b and C3bi promote phagocytosis but not the release of toxic oxygen from human monocytes. *J. Exp. Med.*, **158**, 2016–23.
129 Goodman, M.G., Chenoweth, D.E., and Weigle, W.O. (1982). Induction of interleukin 1 secretion and enhancement of humoral immunity by binding of human C5a to macrophage surface C5a receptors. *J. Exp. Med.*, **156**, 912–17.
130 Cline M.J., Lehrer, R.I., Territo, M.C., and Golde, D.W. (1978).

Monocytes and macrophages: Functions and diseases. *Ann. Intern. Med.*, **88**, 78–88.

131 Shurin, S.B. and Stossel, T.P. (1978). Complement (C3)-activated phagocytosis by lung macrophages. *J. Immunol.*, **120**, 1305–12.

132 Eales, L.-J. and Parkin, J.M. (1988). Current concepts in the immuno-pathogenesis of AIDS and HIV infection. *Br. Med. Bull.*, **44**, 38–55.

133 Nakagawara, A., Nathan, C.F., and Cohn, Z.A. (1981). Hydrogen peroxide metabolism in human monocytes during differentiation *in vitro*. *J. Clin. Invest.*, **68**, 1243–52.

134 Elsbach, P. and Weiss, J. (1988). Phagocytic cells: Oxygen-independent antimicrobial systems. In *Inflammation: Basic principles and clinical correlates.* (ed. J.I. Gallin, I.M. Goldstein, and R. Snyderman). Raven, New York.

135 Henson, P.M., Henson, J.E., Fittschen, C., Kimani, G., Bratton, D.L., and Riches, D.W.H. (1988). Phagocytic cells: Degranulation and secretion. In *Inflammation: Basic principles and clinical correlates.* (ed. J.I. Gallin, I.M. Goldstein, and R. Snyderman). Raven, New York.

136 Smith, T.J. and Wagner, R.R. (1967). Rabbit macrophage interferons. I. Conditions for biosynthesis by virus-infected and uninfected cells. *J. Exp. Med.*, **125**, 559–77.

137 Lehrer, R.I. (1975). The fungicidal mechanisms of human monocytes. I. Evidence for myeloperoxidase-linked and myeloperoxidase-independent candidacidal mechanisms. *J. Clin. Invest.*, **55**, 338–46.

138 Nathan, C.F. (1987) Secretory products of macrophages. *J. Clin. Invest.*, **79**, 319–26.

139 Lehrer, R.I. and Cline, M.J. (1969) Leucocyte myeloperoxidase deficiency and disseminated candidiasis: The role of myeloperoxidase in resistance to Candida infection. *J. Clin. Invest.*, **48**, 1478–88.

140 Brown, C.C. and Gallin, J.I. (1988) Chemotactic disorders. In *Haematology/oncology clinics of North America. Phagocytic defects, Vol. I, Abnormalities outside of the respiratory burst* (ed. J.T. Curnutte). W.B. Saunders, Philadelphia.

141 Schiffmann, E., Corcoran, B., and Wahl, S. (1975). *N*-Formyl-methionyl peptides as chemoattractants for leucocytes. *Proc. Natl. Acad. Sci. U.S.A.*, **72**, 1059–62.

142 Snyderman, R. and Fudman, E.G. (1980). Demonstration of a chemotactic factor receptor on macrophages. *J. Immunol.*, **124**, 2754–7.

143 Pike, M.C., Fischer, D.G., Koren, H.S., and Snyderman, R. (1980). Development of specific receptors for *N*-formylated chemotactic peptides in a human monocyte cell line stimulated with lymphokines. *J. Exp. Med.*, **152**, 31–40.

144 Snyderman, R. and Pike, M.C. (1984). Chemoattractant receptors on phagocytic cells. *Ann. Rev. Immunol.*, **2**, 257–81.

145 Snyderman, R., Pike, M.C., Edge, S, and Lane, B. (1984). A chemotactic receptor on macrophages exists in two affinity states regulated by guanine nucleotides. *J. Cell Biol.*, **98**, 444–8.

146 Fearon, D.T. and Collins, L.A. (1983). Increased expression of C3b receptors on polymorphonuclear leucocytes induced by chemotactic factors and by purification procedures. *J. Immunol.*, **130**, 370–5.

147 Snyderman, R., Phillips, J.K., and Mergenhagen, S.E. (1971). Biological activity of complement in vivo. Role of C5 in accumulation of polymorphonuclear leucocytes in inflammatory exudates. *J. Exp. Med.*, **134**, 1131–43.

148 Sechler, J. and Gallin, J.I. (1987). Recombinant gamma interferon is a chemoattractant for human monocytes. *Fed. Proc.*, **46** (Abstract 5523).

149 Snyderman, R. and Uhing, R.J. (1988). Phagocytic cells: Stimulus–response coupling mechanisms. In *Inflammation: Basic principles and clinical correlates* (ed. J.I. Gallin, I.M. Goldstein, and R. Snyderman). Raven, New York.

150 Takenawa, T., Ishitoya, J., and Nagai, Y. (1986). Inhibitory effect of prostaglandin E2, forskolin and dibutyryl cAMP on arachidonic acid release and inositol phospholipid metabolism in guinea pig neutrophils. *J. Biol. Chem.*, **261**, 1092–8.

151 Gallin, J.I., Sandler, J.A., Clyman, R.I., Manganiello, V.C., and Vaughan, M. (1978). Agents that increase cyclic AMP inhibit accumulation of cAMP and depress human monocyte locomotion. *J. Immunol.*, **120**, 492–6.

152 Schleimer, R. and Rutledge, B. (1986). Cultured human vasular endothelial cells acquire adhesiveness for neutrophils after stimulation with interleukin 1, endotoxin and tumour-promoting phorbol esters. *J. Immunol.*, **136**, 649–54.

153 Nuchtern, J.G., Bonifacino, J.S., Biddison, W.E., and Klausner, R.D. (1989). Brefeldin A implicates egress from the endoplasmic reticulum in Class I-restricted antigen presentation. *Nature*, **339**, 223–6.

154 Yewdell, J.W. and Bennik, J.R. (1989). Brefeldin A specifically inhibits presentation of protein antigens to cytotoxic T lymphocytes. *Science*, **244**, 1072–5.

155 Cresswell, P. (1985). Intracellular Class II HLA antigens are accessible to transferrin-neuraminadase conjugates internalised by receptor-mediated endocytosis. *Proc. Natl. Acad. Sci. U.S.A.*, **82**, 8188–92.

156 Morrison, L.A., Lukacher, A.E., Braciale, V.L., Fan, D.P., and Braciale, T.J. (1986). Differences in antigen presentation to MHC Class I- and Class II-restricted influenza virus-specific cytolytic T lymphocyte clones. *J. Exp. Med.*, **163**, 903–21.

157 Moore, M.W., Carbone, F.R., and Bevan, M.J. (1988). Introduction

of soluble protein into the Class I pathway of antigen processing and presentation. *Cell*, **54**, 777–85.

158 Qin, S., Cobbold, S., Benjamin, R. and Waldmann, H. (1989). Induction of classical tolerance in the adult. *J. Exp. Med.*, **169**, 779–94.

159 Gordon, S., Todd, J., and Cohn, Z.A. (1974) *In vitro* synthesis and secretion of lysozyme by mononuclear phagocytes. *J. Exp. Med.*, **139**, 1228–48.

160 Gordon, S. (1978). Regulation of enzyme secretion by mononuclear phagocytes: Studies with macrophage plasminogen activator and lysozyme. *Fed. Proc.*, **37**, 2754–8.

161 Osserman, E.F. (1975). Lysozyme. *N. Eng. J. Med.*, **292**, 424–5.

162 Cohn, Z.A. and Benson, B.A. (1965). The differentiation of mononuclear phagocytes: Morphology, cytochemistry and biochemistry. *J. Exp. Med.*, **121**, 153–70.

163 Page, R.C., Davies, P., and Allison, A.C. (1978). The macrophage as a secretory cell. *In. Trev. Cytol.*, **52**, 119–57.

164 Pantalone, R.M. and Page, R.C. (1975). Lymphokine-induced production and release of lysosomal enzymes by macrophages. *Proc. Natl. Acad. Sci. U.S.A.*, **72**, 2091–4.

165 Gabig, T.G. and Babior, B.M. (1981). The killing of pathogens by phagocytes. *Ann. Rev. Med.*, **32**, 313–26.

166 Lasser, A. (1983). The mononuclear phagocyte system: a review. *Hum. Pathol.*, **14**, 108–26.

167 Werb, Z. and Gordon, S. (1975). Secretion of a specific collagenase by stimulated macrophages. *J. Exp. Med.*, **142**, 346–60.

168 Werb, Z. and Gordon, S. (1975). Elastase secretion by stimulated macrophages: characterization and regulation. *J. Exp. Med.*, **142**, 361–77.

169 Siverstein, E., Friedland, J., and Setton, C. (1979). Angiotensin converting enzyme: induction in rabbit alveolar macrophages and human monocytes in culture. *Adv. Exp. Med. Biol.*, **121**, 149–56.

170 Johnson, W.J., Pizzo, S.V., Imber, M.J., and Adams, D.O. (1982). Receptors for maleylated proteins regulate secretion of neutral proteases by murine macrophages. *Science*, **218**, 574–6.

171 Whaley, K. (1980). Biosynthesis of the complement components and the regulatory proteins of the alternative complement pathway by human peripheral blood monocytes. *J. Exp. Med.*, **51**, 501–16.

172 Strunk, R.C., Whitehead, A.S., and Cole, F.S. (1985). Pretranslational regulation of the synthesis of the third component of complement in human mononuclear phagocytes by the lipid A portion of lipopolysaccharide. *J. Clin. Invest.*, **76**, 985–90.

173 Brade, V. and Bentley, C. (1980). Synthesis and release of complement components by macrophages. In *Mononuclear phagocytes: Functional aspects* (ed.) van Furth R., Martinus Nijhoff, Boston.

174 Whaley, K., Lappin, D., and Barkas, T. (1981). C2 synthesis by human monocytes is modulated by a nicotinic cholinergic receptor. *Nature*, **293**, 580–3.

175 Johnston, R.B. (1981). Enhancement of phagocytosis-associated oxidase metabolism as a manifestation of macrophage activation. *Lymphokines*, **3**, 33–56.

176 Nathan, C.F. and Root, R.K. (1977). Hydrogen peroxide release from mouse peritoneal macrophages. Dependence on sequential activation and triggering. *J. Exp. Med.*, **146**, 1648–2.

177 McPhail, L.C. and Snyderman, R. (1983). Activation of the respiratory burst enzyme in human polymorphonuclear leucocytes by chemoattractants and other soluble stimuli: Evidence that the same oxidase is activated by different transductional mechanisms. *J. Clin. Invest.*, **72**, 192–200.

178 Bonney, R.J. and Davies, P. (1984). Possible autoregulatory functions of the secretory products of mononuclear phagocytes. *Contemp. Top. Immunobiol*, **14**, 199–23.

179 Sammuelsson, B., Goldyne, M., Granstrom, E., Hamberg, M., Hammarstrom, S., and Malmsten, C. (1978). Prostaglandins and thromboxanes. *Ann. Rev. Biochem.*, **47**, 977–1029.

180 Prydz, H. and Allison, A. (1978). Tissue thromboplastin activity of isolated human monocytes. *Thromb. Haemostas.*, **39**, 582–91.

181 Nemerson, Y. (1966). The reaction between bovine brain tissue factor and factor VII and X. *Biochemistry*, **5**, 601–8.

182 Edwards, R.L. and Rickles, F.R. (1984). Macrophage procoagulants. In *Progress in haemostasis and thrombosis*, (Vol. 7), (ed. T.H. Spaet). Grune and Stratton, New York.

183 Hogg, N. (1983). Human monocytes have prothrombin cleaving activity. *Clin. Exp. Immunol.*, **53**, 725–30.

184 Van Dam-Mieras, M.C.E., Muller, A.D., van Deijk, W.A., and Hemker, H.C. (1985). Clotting factors secreted by monocytes and macrophages: analytical considerations. *Thromb. Res.*, **37**, 9–19.

185 Stephens, R.W. and Golder, J.P. (1984). Novel properties of human monocyte plasminogen activator. *Eur. J. Biochem.*, **139**, 253–8.

186 Wilson, E.L. and Francis, G.E. (1987). Differentiation-linked secretion of urokinase and tissue plasminogen activator by normal human haemopoietic cells. *J. Exp. Med.*, **165**, 1609–23.

187 Stoppelli, M.P., Corti, A., Soffientini, A., Cassani, G., Blasi, F., and Assoian, R.K. (1985). Differentiation-enhanced binding of the aminoterminal fragment of human urokinase plasminogen activator to a specific receptor on U937 monocytes. *Proc. Natl. Acad. Sci. USA*, **82**, 4939–43.

188 Stephens, R.W., *et al.* (1985). Minactivin expression in human monocyte and macrophage populations. *Blood*, **66**, 333–7.

189 Shirai, T., Yamaguchi, H., Ito, H., Todd, C.W., and Wallace, R.B. (1985). Cloning and expression in *Escherichia coli* of the gene for tumour necrosis factor. *Nature*, **313**, 803–6.
190 Cerami, A. and Beutler, B. (1988). The role of cachectin/TNF in endotoxic shock and cachexia. *Immunol. Today*, **9**, 28–31.
191 Pestka, S., Langer, J.A., Zoon, K.C., and Samuel, C.E. (1987). Interferons and their actions. *Ann. Rev. Biochem.*, **56**, 727–77.
192 Metcalf, D. (1987). The molecular control of normal and leukaemic granulocytes and macrophages. *Proc. Roy. Soc. (Biol.)*, **230**, 389–423.
193 Dinarello, C.A. (1985). An update on human interleukin-1: from molecular biology to clinical relevance. *J. Clin. Immunol.*, **5**, 287–97.
194 Fibbe, W.E., *et al.* (1987). Interleukin-1 (IL-1) stimulates myeloid progenitor cells to proliferate in long term bone marrow cultures. *Blood (Suppl. 1)*, **70**, 172a.
195 Hutchins, D., Cohen, B.B., and Steel, C.M. (1990). Production and regulation of interleukin 6 in human B lymphoid cells. *Eur. J. Immunol.*, **20**, 961–8.
196 Zhang, Y., Lin, J-X., Yip, Y.K., and Vilcek, J. (1989(. Stimulation of Interleukin-6 mRNA levels by tumour necrosis factor and Inter-leukin-1. *Ann. N. Y. Acad. Sci.*, **557**, 548–9.
197 Heinrich, P.C. (1990). Interleukin-6 and the acute phase protein response. *Biochem. J.*, **265**, 621–36.
198 Matsuda, T., *et al.* (1989). IL-6/BSF2 in normal and abnormal regu-lation of immune responses. *Ann. N. Y. Acad. Sci.*, **557**, 466–76.
199 Mielk, V., *et al.* (1990). Detection of neutrophil-activating peptide NAP/IL-8. *J. Immunol.*, **144**, 153–61.
200 Lewis, C.E., McCracken, D., Ling, R., Richards, P.S., McCarthy, S.P., and McGee, J.O'D. (1991). Analysis of cytokine release at the single cell level: use of the reverse haemolytic plaque assay. *Immunol. Rev.*, **119**, 23–39.
201 Larsen, C.G., Anderson, A.O., Appela, E., Oppenheim, J.J., and Matsushima, K. (1989). The neutrophil-activating protein (NAP-1) is also chemotactic for T lymphocytes. *Science*, **243**, 1464–6.
202 Kunkel, S.L., *et al.* (1990). In *Cytokines and lipocortins in inflamma-tion and differentiation* (ed. Melli and Parente). Wiley–Liss, New York.
203 Assoian, R.K., *et al.* (1987). Expression and secretion of type beta transforming growth factor by activated human macrophages. *Proc. Natl. Acad. Sci. U.S.A.*, **84**, 6020–4.
204 Chieftez, S., *et al.* (1987). The transforming growth factor-beta system, a complex pattern of cross-reactive ligands and receptors. *Cell*, **48**, 409–15.
205 Massague, J. (1987). The TGF-beta family of growth and differenti-ation factors. *Cell*, **49**, 437–8.

206 Ignotz, R.A. and Massague, J. (1987). Cell adhesion protein receptors as targets for transforming growth factor-beta action. *Cell*, **51**, 189–97.

207 Lobb, R.R., Harper, J.W., and Fett, J.W. (1986). Purification of heparin-binding growth factors. *Ann. Biochem.*, **154**, 1–14.

208 Ross, R. (1987). Platelet-derived growth factor. *Ann. Rev. Med.*, **38**, 71–9.

209 Carpenter, G. (1987). Receptors for epidermal growth factor and other polypeptide mitogens. *Ann. Rev. Biochem.*, **56**, 881–914.

210 Tekamp-Olson, P., *et al.* (1990). Cloning and characterisation of cDNAs for murine macrophage inflammatory protein 2 and its human homologues. *J. Exp. Med.*, **172**, 911–19.

211 Wood, G.W. and Gollahon, K.A. (1977). Detection and quantitation of macrophage infiltration into primary tumours with the use of cell surface markers. *J.N.C.I.*, **59**, 1081–7.

212 Eccles, S.A. and Alexander, P. (1974). Macrophage content of tumours in relation to metastatic spread and host immune reaction. *Nature*, **250**, 667–9.

213 Grabstein, K.H., *et al.* (1986). Induction of macrophage tumoricidal activity by granulocyte-macrophage colony stimulating factor. *Science*, **232**, 506–8.

214 Steplewski, Z., Lubeck, M.D., and Koprowski, H. (1983). Human macrophages armed with murine immunoglobulin G2a antibodies to tumours destroy human cancer cells. *Science*, **221**, 865–7.

215 Adams, D.O., Hall, T., Steplewski, Z., and Koprowski, H. (1984). Tumours undergoing rejection induced by monoclonal antibodies of the IgG2a isotype contain increased numbers of macrophages activated for a distinctive form of antibody-dependent cytolysis. *Proc. Natl. Acad. Sci. U.S.A.*, **81**, 3506–10.

216 Johnson, W.J., Steplewski, Z., Matthews, T.J., Hamilton, T.A., Koprowski, H., and Adams, D.O. (1986). Cytolytic interactions between murine macrophages, tumour cells, and monoclonal antibodies: Characterization of lytic conditions and requirements for effector activation. *J. Immunol.*, **136**, 4704–13.

217 Munn, D.H., Garnick, M.B., and Cheung, N-K.V. (1990). Effects of parenteral recombinant human macrophage colony-stimulating factor on monocyte number, phenotype, and antitumour cytotoxicity in nonhuman primates. *Blood*, **75**, 2042–8.

218 Feinman, R., Henriksen - De Stephano, D., Tsujimoto, M., and Vilcek, J. (1987). Tumour necrosis factor is an important mediator of tumour cell killing by human monocytes. *J. Immunol.*, **138**, 635–40.

219 Blick, M., Sherwin, S.A., Rosenblum, M. and Gutterman, J. (1987). Phase I study of recombinant tumour necrosis factor in cancer patients. *Cancer Res.*, **47**, 2986–9.

220 Taguchi, T. (1987). Clinical studies on recombinant human tumour necrosis factor. *Immunobiology*, **175**, 37.

221 Sokol, R.J. and Hudson, G. (1983). Disordered function of mononuclear phagocytes in malignant disease. *J. Clin. Path.*, **36**, 316–23.

222 Miller, L.L., Bly, C.G., Watson, M.L., and Bale, W.F. (1951). The dominant role of the liver in plasma protein synthesis. *J. Exp. Med.*, **94**, 431–53.

223 Sipe, J.D., Vogel, S.N., Ryan, J.L., McAdam, K.P.W.J., and Rosenstreigh, D.L. (1979). Detection of a mediator derived from endotoxin stimulated macrophages that induces the acute phase serum amyloid A response in mice. *J. Exp. Med.*, **150**, 597–606.

224 Jablons, D.M., McIntosh, J.K., Mule, J.J., Nordan, R.P., Rudikoff, S., and Lotze, M. (1989). Induction of interferon-b$_2$/Interleukin-6 by cytokine administration and detection of circulating Il-6 in the tumour bearing state. *Ann. N.Y. Acad. Sci.*, **557**, 157–61.

225 Stovroff, M.C., Fraker, D.L., and Norton, J.A. (1989). Cachectin activity in the serum of cachectic tumour-bearing rats. *Arch. Surg.*, **124**, 94–9.

226 Tracey, K.J., Wei, H.E., and Manogue, K.R. (1988). Cachectin/tumour necrosis factor induces cachexia, anaemia and inflammation. *J. Exp. Med.*, **167**, 1211–27.

227 Oliff, A., *et al.* (1987). Tumours secreting human TNF/cachectin induce cachexia in mice. *Cell*, **50**, 555–63.

228 Fearon, K.C.H., McMillan, D.C., Preston, T., Winstanley, F.P., Cruckshank, A.M., and Shenkin, A. (1991). Elevated circulating Interleukin-6 is associated with an acute phase response but reduced fixed hepatic protein synthesis in patients with cancer. *Ann. Surg.*, **213**, 26–31.

229 Tamm, I. (1989). IL-6: Current research and new questions. *Ann. N.Y. Acad. Sci.*, **557**, 478–89.

230 Morrone, G., *et al.* (1988). Recombinant Interleukin-6 regulates the transcriptional activation of a set of human acute phase genes. *J. Biol. Chem.*, **263**, 12554–8.

231 Poli, V., Oliviero, S., Morrone, G., and Cortese, R. (1989). Characterisation of an IL-6-responsive element (IL6RE) present on liver-specific genes and identification of the cognate IL-6-dependent DNA-binding protein (IL6DBP). *Ann. N.Y. Acad. Sci.*, **557**, 297–309.

232 Majello, B., Arcone, R., Toniatto, C., and Ciliberto, G. (1990). Constitutive and IL-6-induced nuclear factors that interact with the human C-reactive protein promoter. *EMBO J.*, **9**, 457–65.

233 Jirik, F.R., *et al.* (1989). Bacterial lipopolysaccharide and inflammatory mediators augment IL-6 secretion by human endothelial cells. *J. Immunol.*, **142**, 144–7.

234 Shimizu, H., Mitomt, K., Watanabe, T., Okamoto, S., and Yamamoto. (1990). Involvement of a NK-kB-like transcription factor in the activation of the Interleukin-6 gene by inflammatory lymphokines. *Mol. Cell. Biol.*, **10**, 561–8.

235 Coleman, D.L., Chodakewitz, J.A., Bartiss, A.H. and Mellors, J.W. (1988). Granulocyte-macrophage colony-stimulating factor enhances selective effector functions of tissue-derived macrophages. *Blood*, **72**, 573–78.

236 Sieff, C.A. (1987). Haematopoietic growth factors. *J. Clin. Invest.*, **79**, 1549–57.

237 Rich, I.N. (1988). The macrophage as a production site for haematopoietic regulator molecules: sensing and responding to normal and pathophysiological signals. *Anticancer Res.*, **8**, 1015–40.

238 Dennis, L.H., Cohen, R.J., and Schachner, S.H. (1968) Consumptive coagulopathy in fulminant meningococcaemia. *J.A.M.A.*, **205**, 183–5.

239 Auger, M.J. and Mackie, M.J. (1988). Haemostasis in malignant disease. *J. Roy. Coll. Phys. Lond.*, **22**, 74–9.

240 Auger, M.J. and Mackie, M.J. (1987). Monocyte procoagulant activity in breast cancer. *Thromb. Res.*, **47**, 77–84.

241 Edwards, R.L., Rickles, F.R., and Cronlund, M. (1981). Abnormalities of blood coagulation in patients with cancer. Mononuclear cell tissue factor generation. *J. Lab. Clin. Med.*, **98**, 917–28.

242 Edwards, R.L., *et al.* (1987). Activation of blood coagulation in Crohn's disease. Increased plasma fibrinopeptide A levels and enhanced generation of monocyte tissue factor activity. *Gastroenterology*, **92**, 329–37.

243 Osterud, B. and Flaegstad, T. (1983). Increased tissue thromboplastin activity in monocytes of patients with meningococcal infection: related to an unfavourable prognosis. *Thromb. Haemostas.*, **49**, 5–7.

244 Bevilacqua, M.P., Pober, J.S., Majeau, G.R., Cotran, R.S., and Gimrone, M.A. (1984). Interleukin 1 induces biosynthesis and cell surface expression of procoagulant activity in human vascular endothelial cells. *J. Exp. Med.*, **160**, 618–21.

245 Nawroth, P.P. and Stern, D.M. (1986). Modulation of endothelial cell haemostatic properties by tumour necrosis factor. *J. Exp. Med.*, **163**, 740–5.

246 Rocklin, R.E., Benzden, K., and Greineder, D. (1980). Mediators of immunity: lymphokines and monokines. *Adv. Immunol.*, **29**, 55–136.

247 Kay, M.M.B. (1975). Mechanism of removal of senescent cells by human macrophages in situ. *Proc. Natl. Acad. Sci. U.S.A.*, **72**, 3521–3525.

248 Hershko, C. (1977). Storage iron regulation. In *Progress in haematology*, Vol. X (ed. E.B. Brown). Grune and Stratton, New York.

249 Knighton, D.R. and Fiegel, V.D. (1989). The macrophages: effector

cell wound repair. In *Perspectives in shock research: Metabolism, immunology, mediators, and models*. (ed. Passmore). Alan R. Liss, New York.

250 Wissler, R.W., Vesselinovitch, D., and Davis, H.R. (1987). Cellular components of the progressive atherosclerotic process. In *Atherosclerosis. Biology and clinical science* (ed. A.G. Olsson). Churchill Livingstone, Edinburgh.

251 Stary, H.C. (1983). Macrophages in coronary artery and aortic intima and in atherosclerotic lesions of children and young adults up to age 29. In *Atherosclerosis*, Vol. VI (ed. G. Schettler, A.M. Gotto, G. Middelhoff, A.S. Habenicht, and K.R. Jurutka). Springer, Berlin.

252 Gerrity, R.G. (1981). The role of the monocyte in atherogenesis. I. Transition of blood borne monocytes into foam cells in fatty lesions. *Am. J. Path.*, **103**, 181–90.

253 Wissler, R.W. (1984). The pathobiology of the atherosclerotic plaque in the mid-1980s. In *Regression of atherosclerotic lesions* (ed. M.R. Malinow and V.H. Blaton). Plenum, New York.

254 Koch, A.E., Polverini, P.J., and Leibovich, S.J. (1986). Stimulation of neovascularisation by human rheumatoid synovial tissue macrophages. *Arth. Rheum.*, **29**, 471–9.

255 Harris, E.D. (1990). Rheumatoid arthritis: Pathophysiology and implications for therapy. *N. Eng. J. Med.*, **322**, 1277–89.

256 Charriere, J. (1989). Immune mechanisms in autoimmune thyroiditis. *Adv. Immunol.*, **46**, 263–334.

257 Thomas, P.D. and Hunninghake, G.W. (1987). Current concepts of the pathogenesis of sarcoidosis. *Am. Rev. Resp. Dis.*, **135**, 747–60.

258 Hafler, D.A. and Weiner, H.L. (1988). T-cells in multiple sclerosis and inflammatory central nervous system diseases. *Immunol. Rev.*, **100**, 307–33.

2 Molecular basis of macrophage activation: diversity and its origins

D.O. ADAMS AND T.A. HAMILTON

1 Introduction

The contemporary era of macrophage activation began in the 1960s with the dissection of acquired cellular resistance to facultative or obligate intracellular parasites by George Mackaness and his colleagues (1). They found that such resistance required orchestration by sensitized lymphocytes, subsequently found to be T-cells, but was actually effected by large, 'angry' macrophages, which were termed 'activated'. The concept of macrophage activation was subsequently broadened when a number of workers, including Hibbs and Remington, and Evans and Alexander, observed that macrophages activated for non-specific host resistance to parasites quite effectively and selectively destroyed neoplastic cells in culture. Thus, activation can be viewed, by some workers, as acquisition of competence for enhanced microbicidal or tumouricidal function.

Acquisition of the competence to destroy neoplastic cells selectively in the absence of antibody (macrophage-mediated tumour cytotoxicity—MTC) was studied by a number of workers including Hibbs, Meltzer, and Russell (1). These scientists and their colleagues observed that the induction of such a function was the result of a multistep cascade of events (Figure 2.1). Although macrophages resident in tissues were relatively resistant to such induction, immature mononuclear phagocytes taken from sites of inflammation responded readily to inductive signals and were, therefore, termed 'responsive' macrophages. Treatment of these macrophages with macrophage-activating factor (MAF), subsequently found to be interferon-gamma (IFNγ), induced a state which was termed 'primed'. Primed macrophages, although not cytolytic themselves, readily became so when pulsed with traces (i.e. ng/ml) of bacterial lipopolysaccharide (LPS). These cytolytic macrophages were termed 'fully activated'. Subsequent studies found that MTC depended upon two cellular capacities: (1) the ability to capture and then bind vigorously neoplastic but not non-neoplastic cells; and (2) the ability to secrete cytolytic factors including a novel cytolytic proteinase (CP) and tumour necrosis factor (TNFα), (1,2). It was found that neither resident nor responsive macrophages would bind tumour cells but that macrophages primed or activated, either *in vivo* or *in vitro*, bound tumour cells but did not secrete the lytic mediators. Secretion of these lytic mediators was found to require a triggering signal, such as LPS, thus providing some evidence for the role of the priming and triggering signals in inducing the complete function of cytolysis. Further studies indicated that macrophages could lyse tumour cells in two additional circumstances: (1) a rapid antibody-dependent form of cytolysis (antibody-dependent cellular cytotoxicity—ADCC), completed within a few hours after cellular contact and effective against a limited panel of tumour cells; and (2) a slower version of ADCC, requiring 1 to 2 days for completion and effective against all neoplastic targets tested (1–3). Of interest, the slow version of ADCC showed a

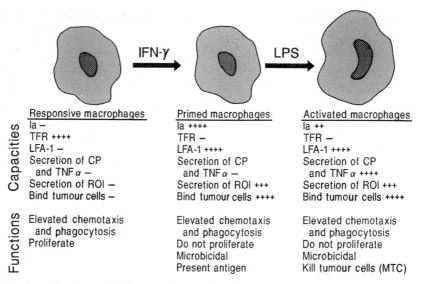

	Responsive macrophages	Primed macrophages	Activated macrophages
Capacities	Ia –	Ia ++++	Ia ++
	TFR ++++	TFR –	TFR –
	LFA-1 –	LFA-1 ++++	LFA-1 ++++
	Secretion of CP and TNFα –	Secretion of CP and TNFα –	Secretion of CP and TNFα ++++
	Secretion of ROI –	Secretion of ROI +++	Secretion of ROI +++
	Bind tumour cells –	Bind tumour cells ++++	Bind tumour cells ++++
Functions	Elevated chemotaxis and phagocytosis	Elevated chemotaxis and phagocytosis	Elevated chemotaxis and phagocytosis
	Proliferate	Do not proliferate	Do not proliferate
		Microbicidal	Microbicidal
		Present antigen	Kill tumour cells (MTC)

Fig. 2.1 A basic model of macrophage activation for macrophage-mediated tumour cytotoxicity. Shown are responsive, primed, and activated macrophages and two major signals, IFNγ and LPS, which respectively prime and trigger cytolysis. Also shown are a few selected, objective markers of each stage plus certain functions which are turned on or turned off in each of the three stages. (Reproduced from reference 124.)

distinct preference for antibody isotype and was relevant to several models of tumour rejection *in vivo*. Acquisition of competence for rapid and slow ADCC was found to be distinct, *in vivo* and *in vitro*, both from one another and from acquisition of competence for MTC. Competence for rapid ADCC was observed in certain responsive, primed, or fully activated macrophages, which had a high capacity for release of reactive oxygen intermediates (ROI); competence for the slow variant of ADCC was observed in responsive or primed macrophages.

Analysis of the development of activation was facilitated when operationally defined stages of activation were characterized using a library of objective markers (1). These quantitative and readily applicable markers characterized macrophages respectively in the resident, responsive, primed, and fully activated stages of development (Figure 2.1). Interestingly, macrophages in each of the several stages of development were marked by profound changes in expression of membranous and secreted proteins and, over the spectrum of the four stages of development, such changes were found to include both enhanced and diminished expression of these proteins (1,4). In many cases, changes in specific protein expression correlated precisely with changes in ability to execute a complex function. For example, the ability of macrophages to present antigen to T-cells is stringently dependent upon cell surface expression of Class II MHC (immune-associated or Ia) molecules. Such molecules are minimally expressed in resident and responsive macrophages, highly expressed in primed macrophages, and modestly expressed in fully activated macrophages. Correspondingly, macrophage competence to present antigen to T-cells is minimal in the first two stages of development, maximal in the primed state, and diminished in the fully activated state. Similarly, close correlations were made between expression of proteins requisite for binding of tumour cells, such as leucocyte function antigen-1 (LFA1), and secretion of lytic mediators, such as TNFα and the cytolytic serine proteinase. From such studies, a comprehensive definition of macrophage activation emerged.

Macrophage activation can be defined as acquisition of competence to complete a complex function (1). Such a function is a complex action, task, or role, usually quantified by determining in a physiological assay the rate or extent of completion of a defined task. Examples of complex functions include chemotaxis, phagocytosis, processing and presentation of antigen, lysis of an intracellular parasite, and destruction of a tumour cell in any one of the three ways described above. Competence to complete a complex function is dependent, in turn, upon acquisition of the requisite capacities. A capacity is a single attribute of the macrophage (i.e. property, ability, or characteristic), usually quantified biochemically or immunologically as a specific feature of the cell's composition or metabolism. Examples of capacities include the number of Fc receptors for a given isotype of immunoglobulin, affinity of a given population of receptors for a given chemotactic agent, number of Ia molecules present on the cell surface, number of molecules of interleukin-1 (IL-1) secreted, content of a particular acid hydrolase within the macrophage, and the amount of a given species of activated oxygen intermediate produced. Capacities thus basically represent the complete expression of separate and independently regulated gene products, and functions represent the end result of operative interactions of such gene products. In sum, macrophage activation represents in very large part the enhanced and suppressed expression of various genes encoding for proteins cardinal to the function being activated.

As understanding of the fundamental biology and significance of macrophage activation has grown, so has our appreciation of the complexity and breadth of activation (Figure 2.2). It is now apparent that the natural physiology of these cells is to lie relatively dormant in the tissues until they contact appropriate inductive signals. These signals then induce activation. Of particular note is the potential of macrophages for being activated in numerous different ways; each way represents the enhancement of one or more functions and the suppression of others. Macrophages should thus be viewed as pleuripotent cells which can be modulated in the tissues in a large number of ways. Indeed, the number of discrete states of activation may

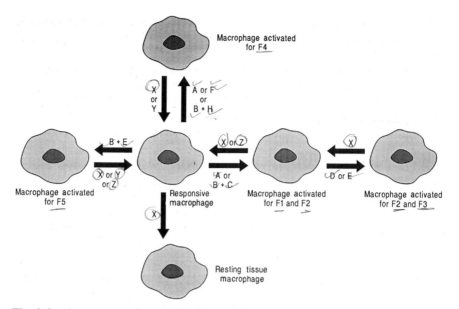

Fig. 2.2 A more complex model of macrophage activation. In this model, responsive macrophages can be activated along four basic pathways. Application of various combinations of inductive signals (A–H) leads to four distinct forms of activation. In each of these forms of activation the macrophages are selectively activated for one or more of functions (F1–F5). Counteracting these inductive signals are suppressive signals X, Y, and Z. Various combinations of X, Y, or Z bring macrophages back to the responsive state. The responsive macrophages in turn can be pushed back to the resting tissue macrophage by suppressive signal X. (Reproduced from reference 124.)

range between 100 and 1000 (*vide infoca*). Of importance is the fact that activation is not permanent. Macrophage activation is regulated not only by many inductive signals but by many suppressive signals. When macrophages have been activated, cessation of inductive signals plus application of suppressive signals returns the cells to the basal state.

The complexity of macrophage activation can begin to be appreciated when one considers the complex signals capable of inducing activation in whole or in part. Although IFNγ is a major macrophage-activating factor and can induce multiple forms of resistance to intracellular parasitism, resistance to certain micro-organisms requires additional signals, such as one of the interleukins or a colony-stimulating factor (6). Furthermore, various lymphokines can interact synergistically, and the lymphokines participating in such interactions vary, depending upon the form of acquired resistance being analysed. These complexities are clearly echoed at the level of gene expression. Depending upon the particular gene as well as the type of macrophage, two lymphokines may have similar, disparate, co-operative/ synergistic, or even antagonistic effects.

Over the past five years, the molecular mechanisms underlying and responsible for macrophage activation have come under intense scrutiny. In particular, the model of activation for tumour cytolysis, induced by sequential exposure to IFNγ and LPS, has been extensively studied (7–9). At multiple levels, the second messengers coupled to the receptors ligating inductive and suppressive signals have been identified. It has been established that enhanced or suppressed expression of membranous or secreted proteins generally reflects alterations in levels of specific mRNA, which in turn frequently, although not invariably, reflect alterations in transcription of the relevant gene. Second messengers have been found to produce a number of tertiary changes, including covalent modifications of proteins and binding of nuclear transcription factors to appropriate regulatory regions of the genes they control. From these, a general (albeit obvious) paradigm has emerged: extracellular signal → ligation of specific receptor → transmembranous signalling → generation of second messenger → covalent modification of proteins → and enhanced binding of nuclear regulatory factors → altered transcription of specific genes → altered levels of specific mRNA → translation of specific mRNA → processing of translated protein → membranous insertion–secretion of completed and modified protein.

Receptors, such as those for the Fc portions of activated immunoglobulins or for chemotactic *N*-formylated peptides, initiate a variety of rapidly expressed, macrophage responses (8). These responses, including chemotaxis, ingestion, secretion of neutral proteases and lysosomal enzymes, and release of metabolites of arachidonate, are initiated by the formation of second messenger systems coupled to these receptors. Many of these rapidly acting regulatory systems, although outside the scope of this chapter, have recently been reviewed (10–14).

The purpose of this chapter is to review what is currently known of the specific elements of the above general paradigm pertinent to macrophage activation. A question of particular interest is how the relatively limited number of second messengers and nuclear proteins currently identified in macrophages account for the great diversity in the forms of macrophage activation.

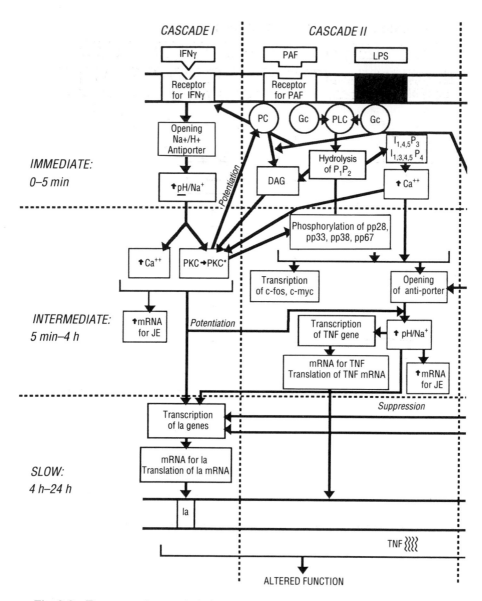

Fig. 2.3 Four cascades regulating two forms of macrophage activation—activation for tumour cytolysis and activation for presentation of antigen (see **Fig. 2.1**). The first two cascades (cascades I and II) are inductive. Cascade III is amphipathic, whereas cascade IV is suppressive. The cascades begin at the top of the figure with application of extracellular ligands which include IFNγ in cascade I; platelet-activating factor (PAF) and LPS in cascade II; LPS and maleyated (mal-BSA) in cascade III; and PAF, prostaglandin E$_2$ (PGE$_2$), and the fast form of α$_2$-macroglobulin (α$_2$-M) in cascade IV. These respectively act upon membranous receptors or binding sites to initiate a variety of intracellular events. In the immediate time frame of 0–5 min, rapid second messengers are induced. A second messenger, in this time frame, for cascade III has not been identified. PC, phosphatidylcholine; PLC, phospholipase C;

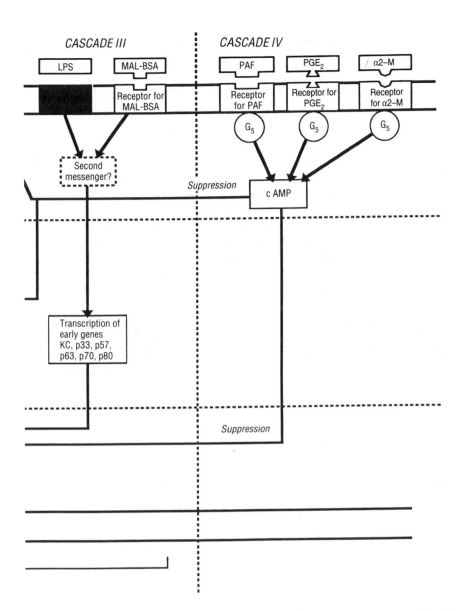

cAMP, cyclic AMP; GS, suppressive guanidine-binding nuclear proteins; and DAG, diacylglycerol. In the intermediate time frame of 5 min to 4 h, delayed second messenger effects and certain gene effects occur, which include transcription and stabilization of mRNA. PKC, protein kinase C; PKC*, the enhanced functional form of PKC; TNFα, tumour necrosis factor α; JE, one of the 'competence' genes. In the slow time frame of 4–24 h, other genomic events including transcription of Ia genes is observed. The end result of these cascades is either surface expression of proteins, such as Ia, or secretion of proteins, such as TNFα. The combined alterations in expression of membranous and secreted proteins lead to altered functions. Note that several arrows show potential interactions between several of the cascades. (Adapted from reference 9.)

2   Molecular mechanisms regulating macrophage activation

2.1   Overview

From the above, macrophage activation can be seen to be a complex process which one would anticipate to be regulated by a large number of extracellular signals. The principal emphasis in analysing macrophage activation over the past decade has been elucidation of those signals which induce activation for enhanced microbicidal or tumouricidal function and for other complex functions, such as presentation of antigen to T-cells. More recently, attention has also been focused on regulation of major gene products of macrophages. In particular, increasing emphasis is being placed on defining the mechanisms by which extracellular stimuli or inhibitors alter both gene expression and the complex functions listed above. Certain of these events have been integrated into an overview model (Figure 2.3).

2.2   Second messengers initiated by cytokines

The list of cytokines now recognized to regulate macrophage function is impressive and includes interferon, interleukins, colony-stimulating factors, growth factors, and small inflammatory proteins (5,6,15–17) (Table 2.1). Of these, the second messengers initiated by IFNγ, IL-1, CSF-1 have been the most extensively studied.

IFNγ acts upon macrophages via a high affinity surface receptor (15). The cDNA encoding the receptor has been isolated and the amino acid sequence of the receptor deduced (18–24). It has an extracellular (*N*-terminal) domain, a single membrane-spanning domain, and a very large cytoplasmic domain of over 200 amino acids. The murine and human receptors have approximately 53 per cent homology of constituent peptides and these sequences are randomly distributed throughout. The receptors do not exhibit homologies with known proteins, including protein kinases. Transfection studies with both murine and human cDNAs indicate that such transfection confers high-affinity ligand binding but not effective transductional mechanisms, suggesting that the latter activity requires an additional, species-specific transducing element.

Ligation of the receptor for IFNγ has recently been defined to produce at least one rapidly acting second messenger (25–27). Addition of IFNγ to macrophages results, within a few seconds, in a marked rises in intracellular pH (pH$_i$) accompanied by a concomitant influx of Na$^+$ ions. Both the change in pH$_i$ and increased [Na$^+$]$_i$ are inhibited by amiloride and several of its analogues, such as MBA and MCA, suggesting that the exchange was mediated via the Na$^+$/H$^+$ exchanger or antiport, IFNγ has also been shown to produce a delayed cytosolic alkalinization in a pre-B-cell line (28).

Table 2.1   Selected extracellular ligands and macrophage activation*

Ligand	Macrophage activation	Macrophage suppression
Cytokines		
IFNα	+	+
IFNβ	+	
IFNγ	+	
TNFα	+	+
IL-1	+	
IL-2	+	
IL-4	+	
IL-6	+	
Colony-stimulating factors		
CSF-1		−
GM-CSF	+	
Growth factors		
TGFβ	+	−
FGF		
Low MW cytokines		
MCP-1	+	
Other molecules		
LPS	+	+
mal-BSA	+	+
PAF		
PGE₂		+
Dethamexasone		+
Serotonin		+

*See reference numbers 1, 4–6, 15–17; +, positive effect; −, negative effect.

Although inhibitor studies have variously indicated evidence for and against a role of protein kinase C (PKC) in the inductive effects of IFNγ upon macrophages, direct evidence that IFNγ leads to alterations in hydrolysis of PIP_2, formation of diacylglycerol (DAG), or elevation of intracellular $[Ca^{++}]$ has not been forthcoming (7,8). Delayed effects of IFNγ upon macrophages include: (1) an enhanced pumping of Ca^{2+} ions from the cytosol into the extracellular space not accompanied by rises in $[Ca^{2+}]_i$; and (2) a change in the potential of protein kinase C for phosphorylation (29–31). The enhanced potential of PKC induced by IFNγ is only manifested in cells exposed to an appropriate stimulant of PKC such as LPS (see below) or phorbol myristate acetate (PMA). To date, the enhanced exchange of Na^+/H^+ induced by IFNγ has been most closely linked to the functional effects of IFNγ. Specifically, increased transcription of Class II MHC genes in tissue macrophages, enhanced mRNA levels for the cytokine gene JE (a murine homologue of macrophage chemotactic protein (MCP-1)), and priming for tumour cytolysis have been linked to such ionic exchange (25–27). It should be emphasized that the receptor for IFNγ may well be pleiotropically coupled within many cells. Convincing studies indicate that ligation of this receptor may initiate at least two quite distinct intracellular pathways (7,8). If so, the activation of Na⁺/H⁺ exchange may represent only part of the identification of the rapid messengers initiated by IFNγ.

IL-1 also acts upon a high affinity surface receptor as do IL-4, Il-6, and GM-CSF (15). Each of these, like the receptor for IFNγ, has an extracellular domain, a single membrane-spanning domain, and a cytoplasmic tail without sequence homologies to any known proteins, such as protein kinases. The external domains of receptors for IL-1 and IL-6, indicate that these genes are members of the immunoglobulin superfamily. The receptor for IL-2 is quite distinct, comprising two proteins (an α and a β subunit), both of which are required for formation of the high-affinity receptor complex. Several lines of evidence indicate that many of these receptors are coupled to other proteins necessary for production of second messengers. Of the interleukins currently known to influence macrophages, the transductional effects induced by IL-1 in a variety of cells have been the best studied to date (32–34). Activation of a guanine nucleotide binding protein (G protein), elevations in cyclic AMP (cAMP), cytosolic alkalinization coupled to an influx of Na⁺ ions, translocation of PKC to the membrane, activation of a serine/threonine kinase(s), hydrolysis of polyphosphoinositides, and production of diacylglycerol by breakdown of phosphatidylcholine in the absence of phosphatidylinositol turnover have all been observed in response to IL-1. To date there is no consensus as to the mechanism or mechanisms of transduction initiated by IL-1, or which of these events, if any, are critical to the subsequent genomic and functional effects of IL-1. Recently, it has been suggested that the high affinity receptor for IL-2 can transmit a signal which activates tyrosine protein phosphorylation via a tyrosine kinase (35).

A cDNA clone encoding an integral membrane protein of 406 amino acids has recently been isolated which binds TNFα as well as TNFβ (15,36). The predicted amino acid sequence defines a protein which has features typical of an integral membrane protein, comprising an extracellular domain rich in cysteines, a transmembranous segment making a single helical span, and a cytoplasmic domain rich in serines. Although no homology was detected between the cytoplasmic domain and any other protein, considerable homologies were observed between the extracellular domain and five other proteins including the nerve growth factor (NGF) receptor. The transductional mechanism by which this receptor acts remains undefined. It has been suggested that a 200 kDa protein distinct from the receptor may be also required for signal transduction (37). Intracellular events observed after ligation of the receptor include: increases in membrane fluidity; influx of calcium into the cytosol; activation of phospholipase A2; serine phosphorylation of a 26 kDa cytosolic protein; translocation of PKC from the cytosol to the membrane, and enhancement of cAMP levels (38–40). Again, it remains to be established which of these events if any are cardinal to the pleiotrophic effects of TNFα upon various cells including macrophages.

The high affinity surface receptor for CSF-1 is a tyrosine kinase which in fact has been shown to be the product of the *C-fms* oncogene (15,41,42). Thus, the CSF-1 receptor, like the receptors for insulin, epidermal growth factor (EGF), platelet-derived growth factor (PDGF), and insulin-like growth factor 1 (IGF-1), is a tyrosine kinase and can initiate Na^+/H^+ exchange, Ca^{2+} influx, activation of phospholipase $C\gamma$, and stimulation of glucose and amino acid transport. Of these, particular emphasis has been placed upon phosphorylation of several substrates by the tyrosine kinase portion of the receptor.

2.3 Bacterial endotoxin and other inductive signals

Bacterial endotoxin has been recognized as a prototypic macrophage activating signal for many years and, as such, has come under intense scrutiny. In recent years, considerable information has been accumulated as to the exact mechanism(s) by which this complex molecule exerts its pleiotropic effects on many cells including macrophages (43,44). For most, if not all, of the functions of LPS, the active chemical moeity is the lipid A component; a membrane active lipid that has a quite distinct structure including replacement of the typical *sn*-1,2-diacylglycerol moiety with 2,3-diacylglucosamine. Over the past decade, the covalent structure of lipid A has been precisely elucidated, but the critical chemical component of lipid A that makes it immunostimulatory has not been identified. The molecular basis of the interaction of lipid A with cellular membranes, where it is known to bind in a complex, two-step process and initiate activities within the cells, remains elusive. Earlier models posited the intercalation of lipid A into the lipid component of the membranous bilayer (7,8). Although a specific receptor for LPS or lipid A has been diligently sought, conclusive evidence has not been presented. Dissaccharide precursor of lipid A that is not fully acetylated (lipid A_{IVA}) can induce some of the functional activities of lipid A (43). In fact, saturable, 'specific' binding of lipid A_{IVA} to macrophages and macrophage-like tumour cells has been reported. Interestingly, acetylated low density lipoproteins (LDL) compete with lipid$_{IVA}$ for such binding (43). Of particular relevance has been recent reports from Morrison and others of membranous proteins of several molecular weights to which LPS and lipid A bind (45,46). A number of other cellular proteins also bind lipid A. LPS, complexed to the 60 kDa serum glycoprotein lipopolysaccharide-binding protein (LBP), can bind to the 55 kDa membrane glycoprotein

CD14 and directly to the CD11/CD18 complex (see ref. 47). At present, potential candidates for the cellular target of LPS include several membranous proteins of various sizes, one or more of the family of scavenger receptors which recognize acetylated LDL and similar compounds, and other membranous and cell-associated proteins (43). Given the pleiotropic effects of LPS on multiple cell types, it is still reasonable to consider whether LPS may not bind to and act through a variety of cell-associated proteins.

One of the signalling pathways initiated by LPS in macrophages is clearly the breakdown of polyphosphoinositides. Stimulation of macrophages with small concentrations of LPS (for example, in the range of ng/ml) can lead to the hydrolysis of phosphatidyl-inositol-4,5-bisphosphate (PIP^2), the formation of multiple breakdown products of this compound including inositol-1,4,5-phosphate, and the tetra-*kis*-1,3,4,5-inositol phosphate as well as the formation of diaclyglycerol (48). These two inositol isomers have been linked to increased levels of $[Ca^{2+}]_i$, respectively from intracellular and extracellular stores, and LPS has been shown to produce a rapid and sustained elevation in $[Ca^{2+}]_i$, dependent in part upon an extracellular supply of calcium. LPS also stimulates protein kinase C and enhanced phosphorylation of a characteristic substrate set of proteins including proteins identified by one-and two-dimensional gel electrophoresis as being of 68, 33, and 28 kDa (49). Rigorous evidence for phosphorylation via protein kinase C has been provided by performance of partial digests of the phosphoproteins with two distinct proteolytic enzymes and electrophoretic analysis of the subsequent phosphopeptides. The nature and function of these phosphoprotein substrates remains to be established. A 68 kDa protein has recently been described as a target protein for LPS which appears quite similar to the 87 kDa protein which is a major substrate for protein kinase C in a variety of cells (50,51). In addition, myristoylation of the 68 kD protein enhances the rate of phosphorylation via PKC. This altered phosphorylation has been linked to macrophage priming for release of metabolites of arachidonic acid by LPS (52).

The effects of LPS on polyphosphoinositide hydrolysis can be mimicked in macrophages by platelet-activating factor (PAF)—a potent bioether (53). A high affinity receptor on macrophages for PAF has recently been described (51). Ligation of this receptor causes rapid breakdown of polyphosphoinositides, rapid and extensive elevations in $[Ca^{2+}]_i$, formation of diacylglycerol, and phosphorylation via protein kinase C. In fact, the pattern of phosphorylation induced by PAF qualitatively resembled almost precisely that induced by LPS. The effects of PAF and LPS are, however, quantitatively quite distinct. The hydrolysis of polyphosphoinositides initiated by PAF is quite rapid, rising to a peak within a few minutes and then rapidly subsiding to basal levels. That induced by LPS, by contrast, requires up to 5 to 10 min for maximal activity and persists for much longer periods of time, up to 1 to 2 h. These quantitative differences in the induction of signal transduction are reflected in genomic and functional effects (*see below*).

The breakdown of polyphosphoinositides, initiated either by LPS or PAF, produces other second messengers. First, these two agonists cause more extensive generation of DAG by several-fold than can be accounted for by the hydrolysis of PIP_2; in fact, DAG from this source is estimated to be only 10 to 20 per cent of the total amount of DAG produced by LPS or PAF (54–56). Current evidence indicates that this additional DAG comes from the breakdown of phosphatidylcholine. Secondly, LPS and PAF produce a delayed activation of the sodium/hydrogen antiport (26). It is well established in many cells that the antiport can be activated by stimulation of PKC and this has been observed in macrophages. PAF, at 5–10 min, and LPS, at 10–20 min, initiate influx of Na^+ ions into macrophages and an increase of pH_i. The PAF-induced changes not only occur more rapidly but wane more rapidly, whereas those induced by LPS occur later and persist for longer.

LPS also initiates a quite distinct set of transductional events. These are characterized by the rapid appearance (in less than 30 min) of gene products, specific mRNA for many of which increases rapidly and also falls rapidly (57,58). The protein products of these have been characterized by one- and two-dimensional gel electrophoresis and also by cDNA cloning. At least one member of the family has been identified as 'KC', a cytokine which appears to be the murine homologue of GRO or MSH-1 (59). By analogy to genes appearing early in the process of viral infections, these genes have been termed immediate early genes (also sometimes called 'competence' genes). Appearance of immediate early mRNA transcripts can be ascribed in most cases to enhanced transcription of the relevant genes (9). From the general biology of transcription, as well as the time course of induction, one could reasonably postulate that initiation of this pathway requires a rapidly transduced intracellular signalling mechanism. At present, however, this rapid second messenger remains to be identified. It is clear, however, that these events initiated by LPS are not attributable to the breakdown of polyphosphoinositides (9). First, they are not initiated by PAF. Secondly, they are not mimicked by PMA and/or ionophores which increase $[Ca^{2+}]_i$, such as A23187. Thirdly, ligands such as maleylated-bovine serum albumin (mal-BSA), do not initiate polyphosphoinositide turnover but do initiate these events. Finally, this pathway of events is clearly marked by expression of the gene KC, whereas the expression of JE (*see below*) is clearly linked to the turnover of polyphosphoinositides. In sum, the induction of certain immediate early genes by LPS appears to be a cascade of transductional and functional events quite distinct from that which includes the breakdown of polyphosphoinositides initiated by LPS and PAF.

The receptor mediating the induction of these immediate early genes has aroused considerable interest. Maleylated-BSA has been traditionally thought to be taken up by the scavenger receptor, which recognizes acetylated LDL (60,61). Recent evidence indicates that this receptor is actually one of a family of such receptors. A critical line of evidence for this conclusion comes from the recent cloning of two of these receptors; both have distinct structural differences but bind acetylated LDL (62,63). Haberland, Fogelman, and coworkers have shown that malondialdehyde-treated LDL is cleared via a receptor distinct from that which clears mal-BSA (61). Finally, oxidized LDL is cleared by a receptor distinct from that taking up acetylated LDL (63). From these data, it now appears quite likely that there is a family of at least two (and probably more) receptors which can scavenge polyanionic molecules. Those effects of LPS, which are mimicked by mal-BSA, appear to be mediated via a lower affinity receptor which clears both mal-BSA and α-casein, rather than the high affinity receptor which clears malondialdehyde-LDL (65).

2.4   Suppressive signals

Increased attention is now being paid to agonists which suppress rather than induce various forms of macrophage activation. It has long been established that PGE_2 is a potent suppressor of macrophage function because this compound, via a surface receptor, can lead to elevated levels of cAMP. The molecular basis of the effects of elevated cAMP, in addition to the stimulation of protein kinase A have, however, remained obscure. Recently, it has been found that at least one effect of cAMP is to suppress the activation of Na^+/H^+ exchange induced by IFNγ (66). Other studies indicate that this suppressive effect is not confined to IFNγ but is also seen with other agonists of Na^+/H^+ exchange in macrophages (67). A second pathway has recently been elucidated for the action of $α_2$-macroglobulin-protease complexes. It has been established for some time that these complexes suppress a number of functions of mononuclear phagocytes (68). Recent evidence indicates that these complexes initiate the release of PGE_2 from macrophages which then, as described above, acts via cAMP to suppress Na^+/H^+ exchange (69).

One potent mechanism of suppressing gene expression is mediated by the stimulation of immediate early genes (9). This family of genes includes known nuclear regulatory proteins and it is likely that members of this group of genes suppress as well as initiate transcription. It has been clearly shown that mal-BSA, clearing via the lower affinity receptor for mal-BSA, can suppress the transcription of Class II MHC genes initiated by IFNγ (70). This suppressive effect can be blocked by the co-administration of an inhibitor of protein synthesis, such as cycloheximide. TNFα, itself a weak inducer of Class II MHC gene expression, can suppress IFNγ-mediated initiation of transcription of these genes, although the mechanism of this effect remains to be established (71).

2.5 Interactions between second messenger systems

Several of the second messenger systems described above have been shown to interact with one another. Pre-treatment of macrophages can potentiate second messengers initiated by LPS in several ways. First, IFNγ has been found to produce a change in the activity of PKC. Thus, IFNγ does not initiate phosphorylation via PKC but pre-treatment of macrophages with IFNγ potentiates phosphorylation via PKC, when stimulated by LPS, PAF or PMA (29–31). This potentiation has been ascribed to a change in the turnover of PKC, and several lines of evidence indicate that it does not result from an increased number of enzyme molecules, suggesting possible covalent modification of the enzyme itself. Secondly, IFNγ potentiates the generation of DAG as described above (56). Whether this effect is related to or distinct from, the change in the potential of PKC remains to be fully clarified. As a likely consequence of these two changes, pre-treatment of macrophages with IFNγ potentiates the activation of Na$^+$/H$^+$ exchange induced by either LPS or PAF by making the shift of PH$_i$ into the alkaline more rapid and by raising the degree of alkalinization (26). IFNγ also decreases the concentration of LPS required to initiate induction of immediate early genes quite substantially (57). The molecular mechanism by which this occurs is not yet known.

As noted above, PGE$_2$, acting via elevations in AMP can dampen responses to both IFNγ and to LPS by suppressing activation of Na$^+$/H$^+$ exchange (66). Whether or not other transductional mechanisms initiated by these or other agonists are also inhibited, such as breakdown of polyphosphoinositides, remains to be established.

LPS has recently been found to have an interesting counter-suppressive effect (72). Specifically, LPS blocks the PGE$_2$-mediated enhancement of AMP activities, possibly by activating phosphodiesterases that accelerate degradation of cAMP. In any event, this counter-suppressive mechanism could help to explain why inductive effects of LPS, both at the level of transductional mechanisms as well as functional effects, persist for considerable periods of time.

2.6 Gene regulation and macrophage activation

The genes analyzed to date in macrophage activation, the signals which control these, and the level or levels of regulation of these genes have recently been reviewed (4). By the quantification of transcription, mRNA levels, and production of protein, regulation has been observed at the levels of transcription, post-transcription (for example, stability of specific mRNA), translation, and post-translation. The changes for a few genes, at whatever levels of regulation, have been initially mapped to one or more second messenger systems described above. The complexities of gene regulation *vis-à-vis* different stimuli in macrophage activation are considered at length in the following section. In terms of specific molecular mechanisms regulating gene activity in mononuclear phagocytes, a clear picture is emerging in terms of Class II MHC genes and taking shape for the TNFα gene.

Class II MHC genes are stringently regulated by inductive and suppressive signals in macrophages (1,5,73). The principal inductive signal in macrophages is IFNγ, whereas a number of agents, such as LPS and PGE$_2$, suppress transcription. Control is extended principally, although not exclusively, at the level of transcription (4). The sequences of upstream and intragenomic regulatory control regions in Class II MHC genes have been defined for both murine and human genes (74,75) (Figure 2.4). Although the critical regulatory regions of the genes vary depending upon the cell type, the cardinal region in macrophages is the promoter region lying within the 160 nucleotides upstream of the initiation start site (69). Lying within this region are three highly conserved regions termed X, Y, and W (H or Z) boxes. X and Y boxes comprise 14 highly conserved nucleotides separated by a 20 bp (base pair) divergent sequence. The X box is unique to Class II MHC genes but the Y box contains an inverted CCAAT sequence found in many other promoters. Approximately 15–25 nucleotides 5' of the X box is a conserved heptamer the Z, H, or W box.

In transgenic mice and a wide variety of cells and cell lines as well as in the functional significance of these conserved regions has been analysed (78,79). This broad region of the promoter is essential for both basal and IFNγ-induced transcription. Considerable attention has been focused on the role of both X and Y boxes in conferring full expression of Class II MHC genes in response to IFNγ in a variety of cells. In macrophages, transfection of macrophage-like cell lines with mutated promoter constructs has indicated the presence of X, Y, and W boxes is necessary for full expression of these

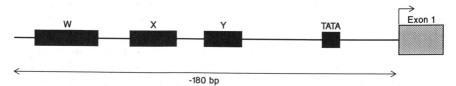

Fig. 2.4 A schematic illustration of the promoter region of Class II MHC genes in macrophages. Immediately preceeding the transcription start sites is a TATA box and then highly conserved regions termed Y, X, and W. (Adapted from reference (74).)

genes after treatment with IFNγ. Transgenic mice bearing mutated genes in which either the X or Y boxes were entirely deleted indicated the presence of both X and Y elements was critical for accurate and efficient transcription of the gene but that deletion of the Y box appeared to abrogate completely IFNγ-induced transcription. Nuclear extracts from a variety of cells and cell lines contain proteins binding to elements lying within the promoter (76,77,79–81). To date, several proteins binding to the reversed CCAAT element within the Y box have been identified in various forms of macrophage. It is perhaps worth emphasizing, however, that the regulation of Class II MHC genes is quite distinct between macrophages and macrophage-like cell lines. Recently, a Y box-binding protein has been identified in primary tissue macrophages (81). This protein, termed nuclear factor Yγ or NFYγ, does not bind to the inverted CCAAT sequence but rather to the sequence immediately downstream. Induction of binding of NFYγ correlates with induction of transcription by IFNγ. Induction of NFYγ binding is inhibited by amiloride (as noted above to be an inhibitor of Na^+/H^+ exchange) under the same conditions where IFNγ-mediated induction of transcription is suppressed. PGE_2 inhibits concomitantly Na^+/H^+ exchange, binding of NFYγ, and transcription. Suppression of transcription induced by mal-BSA is, however, mediated by a distinct mechanism which requires the synthesis of new proteins (70). To date, the specific molecular basis of this suppression has not been identified.

The structure of the gene encoding TNFα has been elucidated (15,83,84). The TNF locus, lying on chromosome 6 in man and chromosome 17 in mice, is located at the boundary between the clusters of Class III and I genes of the MHC and contains the closely linked genes TNFα and TNFβ. The two genes are transcribed with the same polarity and about 1000 base pairs (bp's) separate the 3′ end of TNFα from the start site of TNFβ transcription. TNFβ, produced by mitogen-stimulated lymphocytes, is transcriptionally silent in macrophages. The primary transcript of TNFα is approximately 2600 bases and contains three introns. The promoter of the gene contains several motifs found to be regulatory in other genes, in addition to the usual TATA element (Figure 2.5). In the murine TNFα promoter, Shakov and coworkers have identified four sequences with homology to the NFϰB recognition motif, a potential SP-1 binding site, and a sequence with some homology to the Y box found in the promoters of MHC Class II genes (83,84). Also of interest, the 3′ untranslated sequence of TNFα contains the motif TTATTTAT, which has been found in the 3′ untranslated regions of a number of cytokines and is thought to regulate protein production either by directing degradation of mRNA or by controlling efficiency of translation.

Recent studies have begun to map the critical regions of the 5′ end of the gene to identify *cis*-acting elements actually relevant to gene activation (15). Studies to date have used 5′ deletions of the TNFα promoter and have

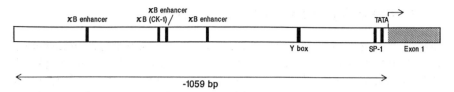

Fig. 2.5 The promoter region of the TNFα gene. Immediately 5′ to the transcription initiation site lies a TATA box followed by a binding site for SP-1, four binding sites for NFκB or NFκB-like molecules, and a homologue of the Y box observed in Class II MHC genes. (Adapted with permission from reference 33, and revised according to personal communication from Dr S.A. Nedospasov.)

identified two broad regions of deletion which decrease LPS-mediated induction (83, 84). The first of these contains the recognition site for NFκB and the other contains the sequence with homology to the Y box of Class II MHC genes. Gel retardation assays have revealed that LPS induces the formation of DNA protein complexes mapping to motifs with homology to NFκB, and a complex with the motif having homology to the Y box. Subsequent analyses have indicated that binding to more than one and perhaps all of the four elements with similarities to NFκB may be important. The molecular mechanisms linking second messengers initiated by LPS and the binding of these nuclear proteins, however, remain to be resolved.

The role of post-transcriptional events in regulating the protein products of various genes in macrophage activation has not been given great attention with one striking exception (4). Beutler, Cerami, and co-workers have extensively analysed the regulation of TNFα secretion (85–87). LPS potently stimulates transcription of these genes approximately three-fold, but these workers found a subsequent 100-fold increase in cellular mRNA specific for TNFα. Furthermore, specific mRNA for TNFα may not be translated until the cells are appropriately stimulated by IFNγ. Overall, LPS can lead to a 10 000-fold increase in the amount of TNFα protein synthesized and secreted. Although the molecular mechanisms of these post-transcriptional events have not been clearly identified, recent evidence has drawn attention to the above-mentioned TTATTTAT element in the 3′ portion of the TNFα gene which can markedly enhance translational efficiency (86). The second messengers initiated by LPS to effect regulatory control at these levels are not yet identified. Studies with several inhibitors do indicate, however, that the second messengers initiated by LPS are bifurcated and act differently upon stability/accumulation of specific message and derepression of translation (75).

3 Complexity in macrophage activation

The comprehensive tissue distribution and broad spectrum of homeostatic and defensive functions of the mononuclear phagocyte system (MPS) strongly suggest that the functional status of these cells is likely to be complex, and this indeed appears to be the case. Complexity is reflected clearly in terms of functional diversity both within the cells of a given tissue and between cell populations from various tissues (88). Very little evidence if any, however, supports the proposition that the heterogeneity of macrophages results from any distinct functional lineages of these cells, analogous to the differentiation-determined subsets of lymphocytes (1,89). Rather, such differences appear to reflect differences in the state or type of activation. These differences probably derive in turn from a number of sources, including time of residence of the cells within the tissue, lack of synchrony in the response of cells to stimulation, and variations in the distribution/quantity of inductive/suppressive stimuli within the tissue (4,90). The basic view of a highly diverse MPS is clearly supported by striking behavioural distinctions observed between macrophages resident in different tissues sites (for example, monocytes in the circulation, alveolar macrophages, Kupffer cells, microglia in the brain, osteoclasts in bone, and macrophages in the spleen, etc.). Although rigorous comparisons of such populations have yet to be systematically performed, well-documented qualitative and quantitative differences in response patterns between such populations have been made (91). In sum, differences between macrophage populations obtained from and in different tissue sites probably arise largely from differences in the relevant stimuli present in the particular micro-environment of those cells.

Analysis of macrophage activation for tumouricidal or microbicidal function has clearly demonstrated that functional potential can be acquired in a stepwise fashion and that discrete stages of activity can be distinguished from one another on the basis of objective biochemical or functional markers (Figure 2.1). Historically, the number of distinct macrophage functional states has been perceived to be relatively limited. In this view, many, different extracellular stimuli modulate a broad spectrum of functional changes but act coincidentally or in parallel. Macrophage activation is, in fact, largely a consequence of alterations in expression of specific genes (see above). Thus, each functional stage may be distinguished from other similar but non-identical stages by the precise pattern of gene products expressed or not expressed. The argument that the numerous genes comprising the functional repertoire of macrophages are not regulated co-ordinately or *en banc* by a single stimulus but rather are regulated independently is presented below. Thus, the potential number of discrete states of macrophage activation which can be characterized by distinct differences in function can be large.

UWCC LIBRARY

One can then attempt to estimate the number of such states. As the number of secretory gene products from macrophages alone is over 100 (see Chapter 1) and because membranous and intracellular proteins are also involved in the functions of these cells, one can reasonably postulate that well over 100 inducible genes are necessary for execution of the many macrophage functions. If these genes are independently regulated, the potential number of discrete gene combinations would thus be 2^{100} or 1.27×10^{30}. Obviously, all of these potential differences in gene expression are not likely to be observed. Furthermore, of those observed, all are unlikely to be functionally significant, because of redundancy in effector molecules and because some gene alterations may not be relevant to the particular functions being analysed. If only 10 discrete macrophage genes were important to activation, one would estimate the number of different states of activation could be 2^{10} or 1024. Although such calculations obviously take one into the realm of the biologically absurd, it is not difficult, after performing such calculations, to envisage that the states of activation could be at least in the hundreds.

This estimate fits well with the known biology of the cells. The number of states of activation for the destruction of tumour cells, for example, is at least 4 (2,3,4) (Table 2.2). Activation for the destruction of various parasitic organisms, such as schistosomes and *Leishmania*, is also complex. When ones considers induction for microbicidal activity alone, it is apparent that activation for destruction of *Leishmania* is distinct from that for schistosomes (Table 2.3). Activation of Leishmanicidal function may be further subdivided by its response to the potential suppressant transforming growth factor β (TGF-β) (Table 2.4). Finally, activation of macrophages for resistance to such parasites, as opposed to destruction, is quite distinct and is also complex in its own right. As the number of different homeostatic and defensive functions carried out by macrophages in the body is minimally 20–30, one can estimate a minimum number of more than 100 biological states of activation. As will be discussed in detail below, when a given panel of

Table 2.2 Competence of various forms of macrophage to mediate four types of tumour cell destruction

	Resident Macrophage	Responsive Macrophage	Primed Macrophage	Activated Macrophage
MTC	−	−	−	++++
Fast ADCC	−	−	−	++++
Slow ADCC	−	++++ or −	++++ or −	−
Cytostasis	−	−	−	++++

(Adapted from reference 1.)

Table 2.3   Kill of two micro-organisms by activated macrophages

Activating agent	Micro-organism	
	Schistosomes	*Leishmania*
IFNγ + other lymphokines	+	+
GM-CSF	+	−

(Adapted from C.A. Nacy, personal communication, and reference 6.)

genes is examined thoroughly, a large number of discrete states of activation, if defined in terms of the pattern of genes turned on and turned off, can be discerned. From a biological perspective, therefore, one can also reasonably estimate the number of states of activation to number minimally in the hundreds.

Regardless of the precise amount of diversity in activation, one major source of diversity in macrophage activation will doubtless be the number of different inductive and suppressive stimuli which macrophages encounter in the tissues, the amounts of these stimuli, and the temporal sequences in which they are presented. Each extracellular signal is entirely capable, in turn, of generating multiple intracellular signals, which can induce a variety of effects depending upon a number of factors including duration and spatial localization of the second messenger, intracellular substrates (for example, nuclear binding proteins regulated), and complexity of the regulatory region of the gene under consideration. Diversity in the regulation of gene expression can be thus considered to result from two sources: (1) complexity in the extracellular environment of the macrophages (i.e. the number and/or relative quantity and/or sequence of presentation of different stimuli); and (2) complexity in the intracellular environment of the macrophages (i.e. the molecular processes through which cellular responses to extracellular stimulation are mediated).

The complexity of extracellular regulatory signals can be gauged by examination of Table 2.1. Certain signals are inductive or suppressive and others are amphipathic. Perhaps the most potent single stimulus of macrophage inflammatory gene expression is LPS. Many of the products of LPS stimulation are also capable of inducing further response either in the same cell or in surrounding cells (for example, autocrine or paracrine effects) (5,92). For example, LPS induces the expression of a large number of cytokines including TNFα, IL-1α, IL-1β, IL-6, M-CSF, GM-CSF, and IFNα/β (92–97). Each of these can in turn increase the magnitude of their own expression or expand the character of the response to include greater functional diversity or both. In addition to its own products, the MPS is

Table 2.4   Kill of *Leishmania* by activated macrophages

Activating agent	Potential suppressant	Kill
IFNγ	0	+
IFNγ	TGFβ	−
IFNγ + IL-2 or IL-4	0	+
IFNγ + IL-2 or Il-4	TGFβ	+

(Adapted from personal communication from C.A. Nacy, personal communication and reference 6.)

highly responsive to multiple secretory products of the T-cell, such as IFNγ, IL-2, and IL-4 (1). Similar scenarios for each of these signals can be envisaged. All of these agents are well known to have multiple effects on macrophages when acting alone. Diversity in the response of mononuclear phagocytes can be further enhanced when such agents act in combination (98–109). For example, multiple stimuli (i.e. IFNγ, IFNα,β, M-CSF, and GM-CSF) synergize with LPS to enhance the synthesis and secretion of TNFα (102,103,105,107). Numerous recent reports substantiate the cooperative action of the interferons and IL-2 on production of a variety of cytokines including IP-10, TNFα, IL-1α and IL-1β (96,98,104). These combined effects are, however, not always parallel or co-operative, but can also be markedly antagonistic (94,99,101,110). Perhaps the most thoroughly studied example is the suppression of IFNγ-driven Class II MHC expression by LPS or PGE_2 (70,110). In addition, IFNγ antagonizes the LPS-driven expression of a gene of unknown function termed D7 in murine peritoneal macrophages (111). PGE_2 and other agents that elevate cAMP selectively suppress mRNA for JE and TNFα and enhance mRNA for IL-1β (112–114).

The magnitude of diversity in macrophage activation will be limited not only by the complexity of environmental stimuli but by the freedom with which expression of any inducible gene can vary with respect to other genes responsive to the same inducer. That is, the complexity produced by different stimuli would be less if the spectrum of cellular responses to external stimuli were limited (i.e. if the expression of many genes was closely coupled in response to one stimulus). Co-ordinate expression of genes, in point of fact, does not appear to be the case in the vast majority of situations. Different genes in various cell populations stimulated by a single agent are almost invariably regulated independently when analysed with care (see, for example, Table 2.2). This view is consistent with contemporary views of the regulatory regions of genes, which contain multiple, independent (as well as co-operative) regulatory regions—the modular or cassette model of gene regulation (115). As one example, the long-terminal repeat (LTR) of the HIV-1 virus contains at least five conserved nucleotide sequences which could bind potentially and transcription factors SP-1, NFϰβ, HSV-1, ICP-O, and adenovirus EIA (116,117). For induction of the IFNβ gene in fibroblasts, Maniatis and colleagues initially observed that induction required the attachment of one new protein and the detachment of two proteins in order to initiate transcription (118). Current evidence indicates the binding of as many as four new proteins leads to transcription, and that eight distinct binding regions have been identified in a stretch of 80 nucleotides. Furthermore, different surface-active stimuli, acting via different second messenger systems, may initiate different nuclear binding events to initiate transcription. The induction of c-*fos*, for example, may be either mediated by protein kinase C or protein kinase A (119). In direct support of this concept are many observations in multiple experimental systems that the expression of a particular gene in response to a single stimulus may be readily distinguished from expression of other genes. In macrophages, LPS, for example, initiates the production of specific mRNA transcripts- for TNFα, IL-1α, IL-1β, JE, and KC, but that expression of the mRNAs for TNFα and JE are differentially sensitive to the secondary action of agents which elevate intracellular cAMP (112). Similarly, mRNA production for IL-1 and TNFα are differentially regulated by inhibition of PKC (120). Also, IFNγ-mediated expression of Class II MHC antigens and of LFA-1 can be distinguished by virtue of differential sensitivity to altered intracellular Ca^{2+} levels (121). These results further indicate that multiple signalling pathways operate in response to one extracellular signal and that these can be independently linked to different genes. This concept can even be extended to include the effects of several stimuli working in combination. When IFNγ and IL-2 are used together, the mechanisms through which they induce the expression of IP-10 mRNA can be clearly distinguished from those involved in expression of TNFα mRNA by several criteria (98). In sum, one surface-active agent can clearly initiate activation of multiple genes which are not only regulated independently but which require distinct transductional mechanisms and nuclear binding proteins for induction.

Of equal interest is the fact that when multiple stimuli induce expression of a single gene, the intracellular signalling mechanism responsible may be specific to the stimulus (Table 2.5). For example, several gene products inducible with LPS in murine peritoneal macrophages (i.e. C7, D8, D3) are also responsive to other stimuli, in particular IFNγ or IFNβ (122). When examined under a variety of experimental circumstances, it becomes clear that distinct pathways mediate an apparently common response (i.e. the expression of a single gene). For example, while the LPS-induced expression of D8 is entirely suppressed by co-treatment with dexamethasone, the IFNβ-induced expression of D8 is insensitive to this treatment (122, 123). In addition, the induction of IL-1β by LPS in human monocytes is sensitive to calmodulin antagonists, whereas that by IL-2 is not (97).

To summarize, multiple extracellular stimuli can regulate expression of a

Table 2.5 Modulation of eight selected genes in macrophages by several inductive and suppressive stimuli

Stimulation conditions	Gene expression[a]							
	TNFα	IL-1α	IL-1β	JE	KC	IP-10	D7	D8
LPS	+	+	+	+	+	+	+	+
LPS + cAMP	−	+	+++	−	+	+	+	+
LPS + DEX	−	+	+	+	+	−	+	−
IFNγ	−	−	−	+/−[b]	−	+	−	−
IFNγ + LPS	+	+	+	+	+	+	−	+
IFNγ + DEX	−	−	−	−	−	−	−	−
IFNγ + IL-2	+	+	+	−	−	+	−	−
IFNβ	−	−	−	−	−	+	−	+
IFNβ + DEX	−	−	−	−	−	−	−	−

[a] Results are based upon Northern blot measurements of mRNAs in murine peritoneal macrophages. (Data are from references 59, 98, 102, 111–14, 122, 123, and unpublished observations.)
[b] May be + or − depending on several variables including source of IFNγ and mouse strain.

given gene, albeit by quite distinct routes (Figure 2.6). Conversely, one gene can be regulated by multiple extracellular signals, each of them again acting by diverse intracellular mechanisms. Much of this diversity of gene response patterns can be traced to two fundamental phenomena. First, the ultimate response to a single surface stimulus may be mediated by the generation of more than one intracellular signalling pathway; concomitantly, expression of any particular gene is controlled independently from the expression of others. Secondly, expression of any single gene can be responsive to multiple extracellular stimuli, and the intracellular signalling pathways induced by each extracellular stimulus are likely to be mechanistically distinct. Through the synergistic combination of these two concepts, the behaviour of individual genes acquires great freedom with respect to all other genes.

4   Summary

This chapter has presented arguments that the activation of mononuclear phagocytes and its primary constituent base (i.e. the regulation of gene expression) are quite complex. Complexity is established at two broad levels: (1) the inductive and suppressive signals presented to the macrophage; and (2) the molecular mechanism regulating the genes affected.

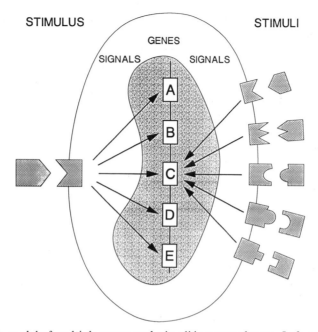

Fig. 2.6 A model of multiple genes and stimuli in macrophages. *Left*, one stimulus activates five distinct genes. *Right*, five different stimuli can act on one gene.

Regulation of activation by extracellular signals is complex, because multiple signals induce activation and because individual signals can be inductive or suppressive of a given form of activation. Two or more signals may interact with one another depending on the precise gene and form of activation, and these interactions may be antagonistic, independent, co-operative, or even necessary. At the gene level, it is apparent that one signal can induce the expression (and repression) of multiple genes. Similarly, multiple signals can induce (and repress) a single gene. Phenomenological observations on cells in general, and on macrophages in particular, indicate that the regulation of each gene is most likely to be separate and independent from that of others and that true co-ordinate expression of genes is very seldom, if ever, observed when scrutinized closely. This view is consistent with current observations on the precise molecular mechanisms regulating genes in terms of multiplicity of nuclear binding proteins affecting the same gene, the multiplicity of messengers regulating the same gene, and the multiplicity of regulatory regions within the promoters of various genes.

As one considers the specific molecular bases of complexity, it is apparent that each of the multiple extracellular signals affecting a given gene may well induce multiple intracellular signal cascades. One gene may be initiated by several distinct nuclear binding proteins and these may bind to different regions of the gene's promoter. One can thus propose a combinatorial model explaining complexity of gene regulation in macrophages. The possible number of combinations of regulated genes would be: [number of second messengers] × [number of nuclear transcriptional factors] × [number of different binding sites for transcription factors for a given gene]. If one postulated only 10 second messengers, 20 transcription factors, and 10 nuclear binding sites, one would achieve 2000 combinatorial possibilities— far more than sufficient to account for the number of biological states of activation postulated here to actually occur. This reductionist model obviously simplifies the situation greatly. It does not take into account temporal, quantitative, spatial, or qualitative differences between second messengers generated. It also does not take into account variations in substrates for these second messengers either in various parts of the cell or between cells, nor the interactions between various second messengers. It does not take into account combination function of transcription factors (for example, the products of c-*fos* and c-*jun*), or that multiple transcription factors regulating the same gene. What this calculation does tell us is that even with the data now available in a very simplified model, one can reasonably anticipate that the molecular mechanisms responsible for diversity are more than sufficient to account for the likely number of different states of activation.

The number of states of activation has been estimated by several means (i.e. biological estimates, estimates of number of gene combinations possible, and estimates of combinatorial complexity models) to be in the range of two to three orders of magnitude (i.e. several hundred).

If this model is proven to be correct upon rigorous examination, this complexity would be of obvious advantage to the host, as it would provide great opportunity for diversity in activation. This is consonant with the fact that these cells exhibit a very wide array of defensive and homeostatic functions (1–5). From a teleological point of view, such close regulation would be highly efficient because it would focus the cell's limited protein and metabolic repertoire in defined paths. Also from a teleological point of view, such diversity could provide exquisite selectivity in terms of function. As noted above, there is biological precedence for this in the wide variety of states of activation actually already observed (for example, with regard to destruction of intracellular parasites). Finally, from the teleological point of view, diversity would provide great redundancy, and therefore back-up and safety to the system.

The biological evidence already at hand indicates that there is indeed considerable diversity of activation in the mononuclear phagocyte family. This chapter argues that such diversity is much larger than had previously been speculated. This possibility must now come under rigorous biological scrutiny, with particular reference to highly critical studies in intact animals. It is already interesting at this point in the evaluation of the model to ask if the degree of diversity in macrophage activation will ever begin to approach the diversity observed in the more traditional elements (for example, T- and B-cells) of the immune system. It is also interesting to speculate as to whether or not there may be enhanced exon shuffling in macrophages as is observed in other immune effector and regulatory elements.

At present, this model has three biological implications. First, it is an eminently testable hypothesis. It is hoped that the present model will serve as a heuristic force to promote the most rigorous experimental scrutiny. Secondly, the model may well have broader biological use as a way of examining gene diversity, expression, and regulation in an essentially non-dividing eukaryotic cell population. Thirdly, the model may well point to improved therapeutic modalities because one could begin to anticipate very discrete therapeutic agents aimed at suppressing or initiating one specific form of macrophage activation.

Acknowledgements

This work was supported in part by USPHS Grants CA29589, CA16784, EO2922, CA39621, and HL29589.

References

1 Adams, D.O. and Hamilton, T.A. (1984). The cell biology of macrophage activation. *Ann. Rev. Immunol.*, **2**, 283–318.
2 Somers, S.D. Johnson, W.J., and Adams, D.O. (1986). Destruction of tumor cells by macrophages: Mechanisms of recognition and lysis and their regulation. In *Basic and clinical tumor immunology* (ed. R. Herberman), pp. 69–122.
3 Hamilton, T.A. and Adams, D.O. (1987). Mechanisms of macrophage-mediated tumor injury. In *Tumor immunology— Mechanisms, diagnosis, therapy* (ed. W. den Otter and E.T. Rueitenberg), pp. 89–127. Elsevier, Amsterdam.
4 Adams, D.O. and Koerner, T.J. (1988). Gene regulation in macrophage development and activation. *Year Immunol.*, **4**, 159–80.
5 Adams, D.O. and Hamilton, T.A. (1988). Macrophages as destructive cells in host defense. In *Inflammation: Basic principles and clinical correlates* (ed. J.I. Gallin, I.M. Goldstein and R. Snyderman), pp. 471–92. Raven Press, New York.
6 Nacy, C.A., Green, S.J., Lciby, D.A., Fortier, A.H., Nelson, B.Λ., Karter, D.C. *et al.* (1991). Macrophages, cytokines, and *Leishmania*. In *Mononuclear phagocytes in cell biology* (ed. G.L. Lopez Berenstein and J. Klostergaard), CRC Press, New York. (In press.)
7 Adams, D.O. and Hamilton, T.Λ. (1987). Molecular bases of signal transduction in macrophage activation induced by IFNγ and by second signals. *Immunol. Rev.*, **97**, 5–28.
8 Hamilton, T.A. and Adams, D.O. (1987). Molecular mechanisms of signal transduction in macrophage activation. *Immunol. Today*, **8**, 151–8.
9 Adams, D.O., Johnson, S.P., and Uhing, R.J. (1990). Early gene expression in the activation of mononuclear phagocytes. In *Current topics in membranes and transport*, Vol. 35 (ed. S. Grinstein and O.D. Rothstein), pp. 587–601. Academic Press, New York.
10 Uhing, R.J., Cowlen, M., and Adams, D.O. (1990). Mechanisms regulating the release of arachidonate metabolites in mononuclear phagocytes. In *Current topics in membranes and transport*, Vol. 35 (ed. S. Grinstein and O.D. Rotstein), pp. 349–74. Academic Press, New York.
11 Prescott, S.M., Zimmerman, G.A., and McIntyre, T.M. (1990). Platelet-activating factor. *J. Biol. Chem.*, **265**, 17 381–4.
12 Snyderman, R. and Uhing, R.J. (1988). Phagocytic cells: Stimulus-response coupling mechanisms. In *Inflammation. Basic principles and clinical correlates* (ed. J.I. Gallin, I.M. Goldstein, and R. Snyderman), pp. 309–24. Raven, New York.

13 Kinet, J.-P. (1989). Antibody–cell interactions: Fc receptors. *Cell*, **57**, 351–4.
14 Riches, D.W.H., Channon, J.Y., Leslie, C.C., and Henson, P.M. (1988) Receptor-mediated signal transduction in mononuclear phagocytes. *Prog. Allergy*, **65**, 122.
15 Arai, K., Lee, F., Miyajima, A., Miyataka, S., Narai, N., and Yokota, T. (1990). Cytokines: coordinators of immune and inflammatory responses. *Ann. Rev. Biochem.*, **59**, 783–836.
16 Gillis, S. (1989). T-cell-derived lymphokines. In *Fundamental immunology* (2nd edn), (ed. W.E. Paul), pp. 621–38. Raven, New York.
17 Durum, S.K. and Oppenheim, J.J. (1989). Macrophage-derived mediators: Interleukin-1 tumor necrosis factor, interleukin-6, interferon, and related cytokines. In *Fundamental Immunology* (2nd edn), (ed. W.E. Paul), pp. 639–62. Raven, New York.
18 Kumar, C.S., *et al.* (1989). Molecular characterization of the murine interferon-gamma receptor cDNA. *J. Biol. Chem.*, **264**, 17 939–46.
19 Cofano, F., Moore, S.K., Tanaka, S., Yuhki, N., Landolfo, S., and Apella, E. (1990). Affinity purification, peptide analysis, and cDNA sequence of the mouse IFNγ receptor. *J. Biol. Chem.*, **265**, 4064–71.
20 Hemmi, S., Peghini, P., Metzler, M., Merlin, G., Dembic, Z., and Aguet, M. (1989). Cloning of murine IFNγ receptor cDNA: expression in human cells mediates high affinity binding but is not sufficient to confer sensitivity to murine IFNγ. *Proc. Natl. Acad. Sci. U.S.A.*, **86**, 9901–5.
21 Munro, S. and Maniatis, T. (1989). Expression cloning of the murine IFNγ receptor cDNA. *Proc. Natl. Acad. Sci. U.S.A.*, **86**, 9248–52.
22 Gray, P.W. *et al.* (1989). Cloning and expression of the cDNA for the murine IFNγ receptor. *Proc. Natl. Acad. Sci. U.S.A.*, **86**, 8497–8501.
23 Aguet, M., Dembeck, Z., and Merlin, G. (1988). Molecular cloning and expression of the human IFNγ receptor. *Cell*, **55**, 273–80.
24 Jung, V., Jones, C., Kurmar, C.S., Stefanos, S., O'Connell, S., and Pestka, S. (1990). Expression and reconstitution of a biologically active human IFNγ receptor in hamster cells. *J. Biol. Chem.*, **265**, 1827–30.
25 Prpic, V. *et al.* (1989). Role of Na^+/H^+ Exchange by Interferon-γ in enhanced expression of JE and I-Aβ genes. *Science*, **244**, 469–71.
26 Prpic, V., Yu, S.F., Uhing, R.J., and Adams, D.O. LPS and PAF activate the Na^+/H^+ antiporter and induce the immediate early gene JE in murine peritoneal macrophages. (Manuscript in preparation.)
27 Prpic, V., Yu, S.F., and Adams, D.O. (1989). (Unpublished observations)
28 Smith, L.L., Stanton, T.H., Calalb, M.B. and Bomsztyk, K. (1988). Recombinant murine IFNγ-induced differentiation of pre-B lymphocytes as associated with Na^+/H^+ exchange-dependent and -independent cytoplasmic alkalinization. *J. Biol. Chem.*, **63**, 7359–63.

29 Somers, S.D., Weiel, J., Hamilton, T., and Adams, D.O. (1986). Phorbol esters and calcium ionophore can prime murine peritoneal macrophages for tumor cell destruction. *J. Immunol.*, **136**, 4199–4205.

30 Hamilton, T.A., Becton, D.A., Somers, S.D., and Adams, D.O. (1985). Interferon gamma modulates protein kinase C activity in murine peritoneal macrophages. *J. Biol. Chem.*, **260**, 1378–81.

31 Becton, D.L., Hamilton, T.A., and Adams, D.O. (1985). Characterization of protein kinase C activity in interferon gamma treated murine peritoneal macrophages. *J. Cell. Physiol.*, **125**, 485–91.

32 Dinarello, C.A. and Savage, S. (1989). Interleukin-1 and its receptor. *Crit. Rev. Immunol.*, **9**, 1–20.

33 Dinarello, C.A. (1989). Interleukin-1 and its biologically related cytokines. *Adv. Immunol.*, **44**, 153–205.

34 Dower, S.K., Qwarnstorm, E.E., Page, R.C., Blanton, R.A., Kupper, T.S., Raines *et al.* (1990). Biology of the interleukin-1 receptor. *Invest. Dermat.*, **94**, 68S–73S.

35 Saltzman, E.M., Luhoskyj S.M., and Casnellie, J.E. (1989). The 75 000 dalton interleukin-2 receptor translates a signal for the activation of a tyrosine protein kinase. *J. Biol. Chem.*, **264**, 1979–83.

36 Smith, C.A. *et al.* (1990). A receptor for tumor necrosis factor defines an unusual family of cellular and viral proteins. *Science*, **48**, 1019–23.

37 Yonehara, S., Ishii, A., and Yonehara, M. (1989). A cell-killing monoclonal antibody (anti-fas) to a cell surface antigen co-downregulates with the receptor of tumor necrosis factor uses. *J. Exp. Med.*, **169**, 1747–56.

38 Schütze, S., Nottrott, S., Pfizenmaier, K., and Krönke, M. (1990). Tumor necrosis factor signal transduction. Cell-type specific activation and transligation of protein kinase C. *J. Immunol.*, **144**, 2604–8.

39 Schütze, S., Surrich, P., Pfizenmaier, K., and Krönke, M. (1989). Tumor necrosis factor signal transduction. Tissue-specific serine phosphorylation of a 26 KdA cytosolic protein. *J. Biol. Chem.*, **264**, 3562–7.

40 Zhang, Y., Lin, J.-X. Yip, Y.K., and J. Vilcek. (1988). Enhancement of cAMP levels and of protein kinase activity by tumor necrosis factor and interleukin-1 in human fibroblasts: Role in the induction of interleukin-6. *Proc. Natl. Acad. Sci. U.S.A.*, **85**, 6802–5.

41 Sherr, C.J. (1990). Regulation of mononuclear phagocyte proliferation by colony-stimulating factor-1. *Int. J. Cell Cloning*, **8** (Suppl. 1), 46–62.

42 DiPersio, J.F., Golde, D.W., and Gasson, J.D. (1990). GM-CSF receptor structure and transmembrane signalling. *Int. J. Cell Cloning*, **8** (Suppl. 1), 63–75.

43 Raetz, C.R.H. (1990). Biochemistry of endotoxins. *Ann. Rev. Biochem.*, **59**, 129–70.

44 Morrison, D.C. (1989). The case of specific lipopolysaccharide receptors expressed on mammalian cells. *Microbial Pathogen.*, **7**, 389–98.

45 Lei, M.-G. and Morrison, D.C. (1988). Specific endotoxic lipopolysaccharide-binding proteins on murine splenocytes. I. Detection of lipopolysaccharide-binding sites on splenocytes and splenocyte subpopulations. *J. Immunol.*, **141**, 996–1005.

46 Adams, D. O. (1991). LPS-initiated signal transduction pathways in macrophages. In: *Bacterial endotoxic lipopolysaccharides*, (ed. D. C. Morrison and J. L. Ryan), Vol. 1 of Molecular Biochemistry and Cellular Biology. CRC Press.

47 Wright, S.D., Ramos, R.A., Tobias, P.S., Ulevitch, R.J., and Mathison, J.C. (1990). CD14, a receptor for complexes of lipopolysaccharide (LPS) and LPS binding protein. *Science*, **249**, 1431–3.

48 Prpic, V., *et al.* (1987). The effects of bacterial endotoxin on the hydrolysis of phosphatidylinositol-4,5-bisphosphate in murine peritoneal macrophages. *J. Immunol.*, **139**, 526–33.

49 Weiel, J., Hamilton, T., and Adams, D.O. (1986). LPS induces altered phosphate labelling of proteins in murine peritoneal macrophages. *J. Immunol.*, **136**, 3012–18.

50 Aderem, A.A., Albert, K.A., Keum, M.M., Wang, J.K.T., Greengard, P., and Cohn, Z.A. (1988). Stimulus-dependent myristoylation of a major substrate of protein kinase C. *Nature*, **332**, 362–4.

51 Rosen, A., Nairn, A.C., Greengard, P., Cohn, Z.A., and Aderem, A.A. (1989). Bacterial lipopolysaccharide regulates the phosphorylation of the 68K protein kinase C substrate in macrophages. *J. Biol. Chem.*, **264**, 9118–21.

52 Aderem, A.A. (1988). Murine myristoylation as an intermediate step during signal transduction in macrophages: Its role in arachidonic acid metabolism and in response to IFNγ. *J. Cell Sci.*, **9** (Suppl.), 151–67.

53 Prpic, V., *et al.* (1988). Biochemical and functional responses stimulated by platelet activating factor in murine peritoneal macrophages. *J. Cell. Biol.*, **107**, 363–72.

54 Uhing, R.J., Prpic, V., Hollenbach, P.W., and Adams, D.O. (1989). Involvement of protein kinase C in platelet activating factor-stimulated diacylglycerol accumulation in murine peritoneal macrophages. *J. Biol. Chem.*, **264**, 9224–30.

55 Sebaldt, R.J., Adams, D.O., and Uhing, R.J. Quantification of phospholipid precursor contributions to stimulated diglycerides in mononuclear phagocytes. Manuscript submitted to *J. Biol. Chem.*

56 Sebaldt, R.J., Prpic, V., Hollenbach, P.W., Adams, D.O., and Uhing, R.J. (1990). Interferon-gamma potentiates the accumulation of diacylglycerol in murine macrophages. *J. Immunol.*, **145**, 684–9.

57 Hamilton, T.A., Somers, S.D., Jansen, M.M., and Adams, D.O. (1986). Effects of bacterial lipopolysaccharide on protein synthesis in murine peritoneal macrophages: Relationship to activation for macrophage tumoricidal function. *J. Cell. Physiol.*, **128**, 9–17.

58 Johnston, P.A., Jansen, M.M., Somers, S.D., Adams, D.O., and Hamilton, T.A. (1987). Maleyl-BSA and fucoidan induce expression of a set of early proteins in murine mononuclear phagocytes. *J. Immunol.*, **138**, 1551–8.
59 Introna, M., Bast, R. C., Hamilton, T.A., Tannenbaum, C.S., and Adams, D.O. (1987). The effect of LPS on expression of the early competence genes JE and KC in murine peritoneal macrophages. *J. Immunol.*, **138**, 3891–6.
60 Brown, M.S. and Goldstein, J.L. (1983). Lipoprotein metabolism in the macrophage: Implications for cholesterol deposition in atherosclerosis. *Ann. Rev. Biochem.*, **52**, 233–61.
61 Fogelman, A.M., Van Lenten, B.J., Wardin, C., Haberland, M.E., and Edwards, P.A. (1988). Macrophage lipoprotein receptors. *J. Cell Sci.*, **9** (Suppl.), 135–49.
62 Kodama, T., Freeman, M., Rohrer, L., Zabrecky, J., Matsudaira, P., and Krieger, M. (1990). Type 1 macrophage scavenger receptor contains α-helical and collagen-like coiled cells. *Nature*, **343**, 531–5.
63 Rohrer, L., Freeman, M., Kodama, T., Pinman, M., and Kriger, M. (1990). Coiled-coil fibrous domains mediate ligand binding by macrophage scavenger receptor type II. *Nature*, **343**, 570–2.
64 Sparrow, C.P., Parthasarathy, F.S., and Steinberg, D. (1989). A macrophage receptor that recognizes oxidized low density lipoprotein but not acetylated low density lipoprotein. *J. Biol. Chem.*, **264**, 2599–2604.
65 Haberland, M.E., Tannenbaum, C.S., Williams, R.E., Adams, D.O., and Hamilton, T.A. (1989). Role of maleyl-albumin receptor in activation of murine peritoneal macrophages *in vitro*. *J. Immunol.*, **142**, 855–62.
66 Figueiredo, F. *et al.* (1990). Activation of the cAMP cascade inhibits an early event involved in murine macrophage Ia expression. *J. Biol. Chem.* **265**, 12317–23.
67 Cowlen, M.S., Prpic, V., Figueiredo, F., Okonogi, K., Yu, S.F., Uhing, R.J. *et al.* (1990). Regulation of interferon-γ and platelet-activating factor-stimulated Na+/H+ antiport activity and gene expression by cAMP in murine peritoneal macrophages. *FASEB Proc.*, **4**(4), PA5050 (Abstr.).
68 Hoffman, M., Pizzo, S.V., and Reinberg, J.B. (1987). The effect of α_2-macroglobulin "fast" forms on peritoneal macrophage Ia expression. *J. Immunol.*, **139**, 1885–90.
69 Uhing, R.J., Martensen, C.H., Rubinstein, D.S., Hollenbach, P.W., and Pizzo, S.V. Exposure of macrophages to α_2-macroglobulin "fast" forms results in the rapid secretion of eicosanoids. *Biochim. Biophys. Acta*, (In Press.)

70 Hamilton, T.A., Gainey, P.V., and Adams, D.O. (1987). Maleylated-BSA suppresses IFNγ-mediated Ia expression in murine peritoneal macrophages. *J. Immunol.*, **138**, 4063–8.

71 Melhus, O., Koerner, T.J., and Adams, D.O. (1991). Effects of TNFα on the expression of Class II MHC molecules in macrophages induced by IFNγ: Evidence for suppression at the level of transcription. *J. Leuc. Biol.*, **49**, 21–8.

72 Okonogi, K., Gettys, T.W., Uhing, R.J., Tarry, W., Adams, D.O., and Prpic, V. (1991). Inhibition of PGE_2-stimulated cAMP accumulation by lipopolysaccharide (LPS) in macrophages. *J. Biol. Chem.*, **266**, 10305–12.

73 Unanue, E.R. and Allen, P.M. (1987). The basis for the immuno-regulatory role of macrophages in other accessory cells. *Science*, **36**, 551–7.

74 Sullivan, K.E., Calliman, A.F., Nakanishi, M., Tsang, S.Y., Wang, Y. and Peterlin, B.M. (1990). A model for the transcriptional regulation of MH class II genes. *Immunol. Today*, **8**, 289–96.

75 Flavell, R., Allen, H., Burkly, L.C., Sherman, D.H., Waneck, G.L., and Wider, G. (1986). Molecular biology of the H-2 histocompatibility complex. *Science*, **437**, 443.

76 Duran, B., Marfing, C., Le-Meur, M., Benoist C., and Mathis, D. (1987). Conserved major histocompatibility complex class II boxes—x and y—are transcriptional control elements and specifically bind nuclear proteins. *Proc. Natl. Acad. Sci. U.S.A.*, **84**, 6249–53.

77 Tsang, S.Y., Nakanishi, M., and Peterlin, B.M. (1990). Patient analysis of the DRA promoter: *Cis*-acting sequences and *trans*-acting factors. *Mol. Cell. Biol.*, **10**, 711–19.

78 Van Ewijk, W. *et al.* (1988). Compartmentization of MHII class II gene expression in transgenic mice. *Cell*, **53**, 357–70.

79 Finn, P.W., Kara, C.J., Douhan, III, J.D., Tranvan, T. Volsum, V., and Glemshire, L. (1990). IFN-gamma regulates binding of two nuclear protein complexes in a macrophage cell line. *Proc. Natl. Acad. Sci. U.S.A.*, **87**, 914–18.

80 Didier, D.K., Schiffenbauer, J., Woulfe, S.L., Cacheis, M., and Schwartz, B.D. (1988). Characterization of the cDNA encoding a protein binding to the major histocompatibility complex class II Y box. *Proc. Natl. Acad. Sci. U.S.A.*, **85**, 7322–6.

81 Bolleknes, A.J., Staub, A., Benoist, C., and Mathis, B. (1987). A multiplicity of CCAAT box-binding protein. *Cell*, **50**, 863–72.

82 Shackleford, R., Ting, J.Y-P., Adams, D.O., and Johnson, S. Induction of a novel nuclear binding protein to the promoter of Class II MHC genes by IFN-γ and its regulation by second messengers in murine tissue macrophages. (MS in prep.)

83 Shakkhof, A.N., Collart, M.A., Vassalli, P., Nedospasov, S.A., and

Jongeneel, C.V. (1990). $\varkappa$B-type enhancers are involved in the lipopolysaccharide-mediated transcriptional activation of the tumor necrosis factor alpha gene in primary macrophages. *J. Exp. Med.*, **171**, 35–46.

84 Collart, M.A., Baeuerle, P., and Vassalli, P. (1990). Regulation of tumor necrosis factor alpha transcription in macrophages: Involvement of four $\varkappa$B-like motifs and of constitutive and inducible forms of NF-$\varkappa$-B. *Mol. Cell. Biol.* **10**, 1498–1506.

85 Beutler, B., Krochin, N., Milsark, I.W., Luedke, C., and Sarami, A. (1986). Control of cachectin (tumor necrosis factor) synthesis: Mechanisms of endotoxin resistance. *Science*, **32**, 977–80.

86 Han, J., Brown, T., and Beutler, B. (1990). Endotoxin-responsive sequences control cachetin-tumor necrosis factor biosynthesis at the translational level. *J. Exp. Med.*, **171**, 465–75.

87 Han, J., Thompson, P., and Beutler, B. (1990). Dexomethasone and pentoxifylline inhibit endotoxin-induced cachetin-tumor necrosis factor synthesis at separate points in the signaling pathway. *J. Exp. Med.*, **172**, 391–4.

88 Walker, W.S. (1976). Functional heterogeneity of macrophages, In *Immunobiology of the macrophage* (ed. D.S. Nelson), pp. 91–110, Academic Press, New York.

89 Hamilton, T.A. (1988). Molecular mechanisms in the activation of mononuclear phagocytes. In *Immunopharmacology* (ed. T. J. Rogers and S. C. Gilman), (pp. 213–52). Telford Press, New Jersey.

90 Hamilton, T.A., Ohmori, Y., Narumi, S., and Tannenbaum, C.S. Regulation of diversity in macrophage activation. In *Mononuclear phagocytes in cell biology*, (ed. G. Lopez-Berestein and J. Klostergaard). CRC Press, New York. (In Press.)

91 Thomasson, M.J., Barna, B.P., Rankin, D., Wiedemann, H.D., and Ahmad, M. (1989). Differential effect of GM-CSF on human monocytes and alveolar macrophages. *Cancer Res.*, **49**, 4086–9.

92 Nathan, C.F. (1987). Secretory products of macrophages. *J. Clin. Invest.*, **79**, 319–26.

93 Grabstein, K.H., (1986). Induction of macrophage tumoricidal activity by granulocyte-macrophage colony stimulating factor. *Science*, **232**, 506–8.

94 Aderka, D., Le, J. and Vilcek, J. (1989). IL-6 inhibits lipopolysaccharide-induced tumor necrosis factor production in cultured human monocytes, U937 cells, and in mice. *J. Immunol.*, **143**, 3517–23.

95 Mace, K.F., Ehrke, M.J., Hori, K., Maccubin, D.L., and Mihich, E. (1988). Role of tumor necrosis factor inmacrophage activation and tumoricidal activity. *Cancer Res.*, **48**, 5427–32.

96 Numerof, R.P., Aronson, F.R., and Mier, J.W. (1988). IL-2 stimu-

lates the production of IL-1α and IL-1β by human peripheral blood mononuclear cells. *J. Immunol.*, **141**, 4250–7.

97 Kovacs, E.J., Brock, B., Varesio, L., and Young, H.A. (1989). IL-2 induction of IL-1β mRNA expression in monocytes. Regulation by agents that block second messenger pathways. *J. Immunol.*, **143**, 3532–7.

98 Narumi, S., Finke, J.H., and Hamilton, T.A. (1990). Interferon-γ and interleukin-2 synergize to induce selective monokine expression in murine peritoneal macrophages. *J. Biol. Chem.*, **265**, 7036-41.

99 Hart, P.H., Vitti, G.F., Burgess, D.R., Whitty, G.A., Piccoli, D.S., and Hamilton, J.A. (1989). Potential antiinflammatory effects of interleukin-4: Suppression of human monocyte tumor necrosis α, interleukin-1, and prostaglandin E_2. *Proc. Natl. Acad. Sci. USA*, **86**, 3803–7.

100 Hart, P.H., Burgess, D.R. and Vitti, G.F., and Hamilton, J.A. (1989). Interleukin-4 stimulates human monocytes to produce tissue-type plasminogen activator. *Blood*, **74**, 1222–5.

101 Cao, H., Wolff, R.G., Meltzer, M.S., and Crawford, R.M. (1989). Differential regulation of class II MHC determinants on macrophages by IFN-γ and IL-4. *J. Immunol.*, **143**, 3524–31.

102 Koerner, T.J., Adams, D.O., and Hamilton, T.A. (1987). Regulation of tumor necrosis factor (TNF) expression: interferon gamma enhances the accummulation of mRNA for TNF induced by lipopolysaccharide in murine peritoneal macrophages. *Cell. Immunol.*, **109**, 437–46.

103 Nedwin, G.E., Sverdersky, L.P., Bringman, T.S., Palladino, M.A., Jr., and Goeddel, D.V. (1985). Effect of interleukin-2, interferon-γ, and mitogens on the production of tumor necrosis factors α and β. *J. Immunol.*, **135**, 2492–7.

104 Jirik, F.R., *et al.* (1989). Bacterial lipopolysaccharide and inflammatory mediators augment IL-6 secretion by human endothelial cells. *J. Immunol.*, **142**, 144–7.

105 Burchett, S.K., Weaver, W.M., Westall, J.A., Larsen, A., Kronheim, S., and Wilson, C.B. (1988). Regulation of tumor necrosis factor/cachetin and IL-1 secretion in human mononuclear phagocytes. *J. Immunol.*, **140**, 3473–81.

106 Hermann, F., *et al.* (1989). Functional consequences of monocyte IL-2 receptor expression. Induction of IL-1β secretion by IFNγ and IL-2. *J. Immunol.*, **142**, 139–43.

107 Arend, W.P., Gordon, D.F., Wood, W.M., Janson, R.W., Joslin, F.G., and Jameel, S. (1989). IL-1β production in cultured human monocytes is regulation at multiple levels. *J. Immunol.*, **143**, 118–26.

108 Warren, M.K. and Ralph, P. (1986). Macrophage growth factor CSF-1 stimulates human monocyte production of interferon, tumor

necrosis factor, and colony stimulating activity. *J. Immunol.*, **137**, 2281–5.

109 Ghezzi, P. and Dinarello, C.A. (1988). IL-1 induces IL-1 III. Specific inhibition of IL-1 production by IFNγ. *J. Immunol.*, **140**, 4238–44.

110 Steeg, P.S., Johnson, H.M., and Oppenheim, J.J. (1982). Regulation of murine macrophage I-A antigen expression by an immune interferon-like lymphokine: inhibitory effect of endotoxins. *J. Immunol.*, **129**, 2402–10.

111 Tannenbaum, C.S., Koerner, T.J., Jansen, M.M., and Hamilton, T.A. (1988). Characterization of lipopolysaccharide-induced macrophage gene expression. *J. Immunol.*, **140**, 3640–5.

112 Tannenbaum, C.S., and Hamilton, T.A. (1989). Lipopolysaccharide-induced gene expression in murine peritoneal macrophages is selectively suppressed by agents which elevate intracellular cAMP. *J. Immunol.*, **142**, 1274–80.

113 Kunkel, S.L., Wiggins, R.C., Chensue, S.W., and Larrcik, J. (1986). Regulation of macrophage tumor necrosis factor production by prostaglandin E_2. *Biochem. Biophys. Res. Comm.*, **137**, 404–10.

114 Ohmori, Y., Strassman, G., and Hamilton, T.A. (1990). cAMP differentially regulates expression of mRNAs encoding interleukin-1α and interleukin-1β in murine peritoneal macrophages. *J. Immunol.*, **145**, 3333–9.

115 Dynan, W.S. (1989). Modularity in promoters and enhancers. *Cell*, **58**, 1 4.

116 Greene, W.C. (1990). Regulation of HIV-1 expression. *Ann. Rev. Immunol.*, **8**, 453–75.

117 Zinn, K. and Maniatis, T. (1987). Detection of factors that interact with the human β-interferon regulatory region *in vivo* by DNAase-1 footprinting. *Cell*, **45**, 611–18.

118 Fan, C.M. and Maniatis, T. (1989). Two different virus-inducible elements are required for human β-interferon gene regulation. *Embo. J.*, **8**, 101–10.

119 Verma, I.M. and Sassone-Corsi, P. (1987). Protooncogene *fos*: Complex but versatile regulation. *Cell*, **51**, 513–14.

120 Kovacs, E.J., Radzioch, D., Young, H.A., and Varesco, L. (1988). Differential inhibition of IL-1 and TNFα expression by agents which block second messenger pathways in murine macrophages. *J. Immunol.*, **141**, 3131–5.

121 Strassmann, G., Somers, S.D., Springer, T.A., Adams, D.O., and Hamilton, T.A. (1986). Biochemical models of interferon gamma-mediated macrophage activation: independent regulation of lymphocyte function associated antigen (LFA)-1 and I-A antigen expression on murine peritoneal macrophages. *Cell. Immunol.*, **97**, 110–20.

122 Hamilton, T.A., Bredon, N., Ohmori, Y., and Tannenbaum, C.S.

(1989). IFNγ and IFNβ independently stimulate the expression of lipopolysaccharide-inducible genes in murine peritoneal macrophages. *J. Immunol.*, **142**, 2325–31.

123 Narumi, S. and Hamilton, T.A. (1990). Dexamethasone selectively regulates LPS-inducible gene expression in murine peritoneal macrophages. 101.

124 Adams, Dolph (1991). Macrophage activation. In *Encyclopedia of immunology*, (ed. I. M. Roitt and P. J. Delves). W. B. Saunders Co., Philadelphia. (In press.)

3 Macrophages in the control of haematopoiesis

P.R. CROCKER AND G. MILON

1   Introduction

Haematopoiesis is a complex physiological process which involves the simultaneous growth and differentiation of eight distinct cell lineages, all of which are derived from a single cell, the self-renewing pluripotent stem cell. The function of the haematopoietic system is to maintain homoeostasis by continuously providing the body with erythrocytes for oxygen delivery, platelets to maintain the integrity of the circulatory system, granulocytes and monocytes to combat invading microbes, and lymphocytes to provide a second, more specific defence against disease. It is a highly dynamic and flexible system which must be able to adapt appropriately to the varying and continuing demands of the organism.

The haematopoietic system comprises two essential compartments: Firstly, a stem cell compartment which, in a hierarchical fashion, gives rise progressively to lineage-restricted progenitors and ultimately the mature blood cells, and secondly, the haematopoietic stroma which consists of a variety of cell types and extracellular matrix components which, together, provide a specialized micro-environment required for the self-renewal, growth, and differentiation of stem cells.

The macrophage has long been recognized as a potentially important cell in the regulation of haematopoiesis (1). It is unique within the haematopoietic system in being both derived from haematopoietic stem cells and a prominent member of the micro-environment. It establishes intimate physical associations with developing haematopoietic cells and is thus strategically positioned to function as a regulatory cell through close-range interactions. The best known macrophage association is with developing erythroblasts, to create a distinct anatomical unit, the erythroblastic island. The pioneering studies of Bessis and colleagues gave rise to the concept that macrophages function as 'nurse' cells for erythropoiesis in the bone marrow by providing essential nutrients during erythroblast development (1). In more recent years the concept of the macrophage as a nurse cell has gained direct support from the finding that mononuclear phagocytes are important secretory cells, being potentially capable of producing a wide range of cytokines which can contribute to haematopoietic regulation.

The development of methods to cultivate haematopoietic cells in semi-solid medium (2) has provided an experimental basis for the identification, purification, and molecular cloning of those molecules which are required for haematopoietic cell survival, growth, and differentiation. Originally known as the colony-stimulating factors (2), this expanding family of haematopoietic regulatory factors comprises at least 13 distinct glycoproteins or cytokines (Tables 3.1 and 3.2). The cloning and expression of haematopoietic growth factor cDNAs have provided large quantities of pure, recombinant material for experimental purposes. This has been essential in order to define precisely the biological activities of each factor,

Table 3.1 Production of haematopoietic regulatory factors by macrophages

Regulatory molecule	Regulation	Target cells	Effect	References
M-CSF	LPS, adhesion, TNFα, IL-4	G, M	G, D	57
GM-CSF	LPS, TNFα, adhesion	G, M, eo, meg	G, D	15,17
G-CSF	LPS, GM-CSF, multi-CSF	G, M, (G, D); stem (P)	G, D, P	15,17
Erythropoietin	low O$_2$?	E	G, D	95
IL-1	LPS, IL-1, TNFα, M-CSF, GM-CSF, IFNγ	Stem	P	15,21
TNFα	LPS, TNFα, IL-1, IFNγ	G, M, E(I); stem, mo(P)	P, I	34
IL-6	LPS, TNFα, IL-1	T, G, M(G); meg, B(D); stem(P)	G, D, P	15
Activin		E	D	43
LIF?		Stem	P	100
MIP-1α	LPS, constitutive?	G, M(P); stem(I)	P, I	39
MIP-1β	LPS	G, M	P	39
MIP-2	LPS	G, M	P	39
TGF-β	LPS, constitutive	M; stem	I	43
IFNα	LPS	M	I	15
PGE$_2$	LPS, IL-1	M	I	27

Abbreviations used for target cells: G, granulocyte; M, macrophage; eo, eosinophil; meg, megakaryocyte; E, erythrocyte; mo, monocyte; B and T; B- and T-lymphocytes. Letters in brackets correspond to selective effects on the target cells. Abbreviations used for the effect on target cells: G, growth; D, differentiation; P, potentiation; I, inhibition of growth.

either alone or in combination with others, on different target cells within or outside the haematopoietic tissue. It has also permitted the production of highly specific monoclonal and polyclonal antisera which can be used to demonstrate the activity of a particular factor, in complex biological mixtures, by its selective neutralization. Further supporting evidence for a role of a particular factor in haematopoiesis is provided by the demonstration that the *in vitro* effects are reproduced when the factor is injected *in vivo*. This appears to be the case with the majority of haematopoietic growth factors tested to date (3).

Despite the spectacular advances in our understanding of the biochemistry and genetics of haematopoietic regulatory molecules and of the cells which make them, there remains much to be learnt in our understanding of the actual role of these substances in the *in vivo* regulation of steady state blood cell formation. Haematopoiesis is found only in specialized micro-environments, these being principally the bone marrow in the adult, and the yolk sac, fetal liver, and spleen during development. The closest *in vitro* approximations of the *in vivo* micro-environment are the long-term bone marrow cultures originally developed by Dexter and co-workers for myeloid and erythroid production and subsequently modified by Witte and Whitlock for B lymphopoiesis (4,5). In both cases, maintenance of self-renewing stem cells and the growth and differentiation of progenitors into mature blood cells depend on the development in the culture dishes of an adherent stroma, consisting of fibroblast-like cells, endothelial cells, and macrophages. No exogenous growth factors are required (apart from ill-defined serum factors), but direct stromal cell–haematopoietic cell interactions are necessary to maintain long-term haematopoietic activity. In the absence of direct physical contact, the haematopoietic progenitors rapidly die. The apparent absence, from these cultures, of many of the factors which support the survival, growth and differentiation of isolated progenitor cells has raised the question of which of the factors identified in the *in vitro* assays are relevant to the *in vivo* situation (5).

In this chapter we will discuss the various ways in which macrophages may contribute to the control of haematopoiesis. We will also speculate as to how macrophage-derived products may contribute to the complex cytokine networks, the existence of which has been suggested by *in vitro* studies. We will also consider the nature of the cellular interactions which occur between macrophages and developing haematopoietic cells *in vivo*. Finally, we will

Table 3.2 Haematopoietic regulatory molecules secreted by cells other than macrophages

Regulatory molecule	Producer cells	Target cells	Effect	References
Multi-CSF/IL-3	T-cell	G, M, meg, mast; stem	G	16
IL-4	T-cell	G, M, B, T, mast	G, P	16
IL-5	T-cell	B, eo	G, D	16
IL-7	Fibroblastoid	B, T	G	15,16
IL-9	T-cell	T, E	G, D	96
IL-11	Fibroblastoid	B, meg	P	97
SCF (*kit* ligand)	Fibroblastoid, others?	Stem	G, P	47,98

See Table 3.1 for abbreviations used for target cells and effects.

discuss the contribution of macrophages to haematopoiesis in certain pathological conditions.

2   Macrophages and haematopoiesis: general aspects

2.1   Macrophage distribution and heterogeneity

Mononuclear phagocytes are present in most tissues of the adult, especially in the haematopoietic and lymphoid organs and in connective tissues (6). Bone marrow-derived blood monocytes are the immediate precursors of the majority of tissue macrophages (Figure 3.1; see also Chapter 1). Having entered tissue compartments, macrophages may be capable of a limited number of divisions before undergoing terminal differentiation. Certain populations, such as alveolar macrophages, appear to be capable of self-maintenance due to extensive local proliferation and turnover (7). The lifespan of tissue macrophages is generally not known, but studies of bone marrow chimeras and repopulation kinetics following macrophage depletion indicate a turnover time in the order of weeks to months.

Macrophages are capable of remarkable diversity and phenotypic heterogeneity. In the absence of overt inflammation, resident macrophages in different tissues or even within the same tissue can display considerable

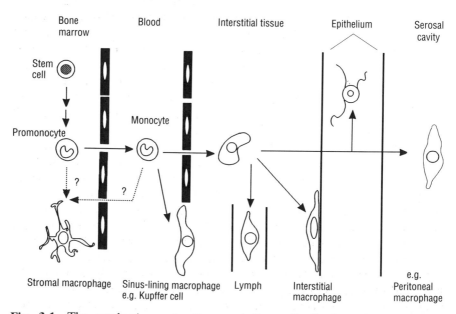

Fig. 3.1 The production, migration, and tissue distribution of mononuclear phagocytes in the steady state.

phenotypic heterogeneity as detected *in situ*, either by immunocytochemistry using monoclonal antibodies to macrophage-restricted markers, or, more recently, by hybridization using labelled DNA probes complementary to specific mRNA products. It is reasonable to speculate that such heterogeneity reflects adaptive functional differentiation of macrophage subpopulations at different sites. The mechanisms which give rise to resident tissue macrophage heterogeneity are unknown but at least a part of this may be related to the variable lifespans of different macrophage subpopulations which in turn may be influenced by the anatomical location in which the developing macrophage finds itself. For instance, the type of extracellular matrix, the relative concentration of plasma components, the degree of phagocytic activity, and local cell-to-cell signalling and secretion of cytokines may all play a role in determining the differentiation programme.

Much of our understanding as to the mechanisms which give rise to macrophage heterogeneity has come from *in vitro* studies using macrophages or monocytes which can be readily obtained in large numbers. These studies have demonstrated the remarkable plasticity of the macrophage genome in response to diverse external stimuli, but there remains much to be learnt of how the myriad of environmental factors is able to act in an orchestrated fashion to produce a macrophage which is adapted for 'steady state' homeostatic types of function as opposed to a cell which is activated to kill invading micro-organisms or resolve inflammatory lesions.

The above considerations are important when the role of macrophages in the control of haematopoiesis is considered. The majority of haematopoietic regulatory factors are produced and act over a short distance within the local micro-environment. In the absence of overt inflammation or immune activation it is probable that the only macrophage populations which are *capable* of playing a role in the regulation of haematopoiesis are those actually within the haematopoietic tissues, namely resident bone marrow macrophages (RBMM). As discussed in Section 2.3, RBMM display a complex cell surface phenotype that distinguishes them from monocytes and other tissue macrophage populations and presumably reflects a differentiation programme that is adapted for haematopoietic tissues (Table 3.3). RBMM are fragile cells which cannot be obtained in the quantity and purity required to carry out precise biochemical analysis. Thus, our detailed knowledge of the regulation and production of regulatory molecules by macrophages is currently limited to macrophage-like cell lines or to those populations which can be isolated in a pure form, such as blood monocyte-derived macrophages in the human or peritoneal cavity macrophages in rodent models. Results obtained with these systems need not necessarily apply to the functions of resident macrophages in haematopoietic tissues, but, instead, may provide an experimental model which can later be tested with the appropriate macrophage populations using the sensitive qualitative approaches currently available.

Table 3.3 Phenotype of resident bone marrow macrophages in human and mouse: comparison with other mononuclear phagocytes

Antigen/receptor/function	Blood monocytes Human		Cultured macrophage Human		Resident bone marrow macrophage				Resident peritoneal macrophage Mouse	
					Human		Mouse			
	+ve	0–3+	+ve	0–3+	% +ve	0–3+	% +ve	0–3+	% +ve	0–3+
CD2	0	0	0	0	0	0	0	0	0	0
CD4	21	+	40	+	100	++	0	0	0	0
CD11a α-subunit LFA1	100	++	100	++	96	++	ND	–	ND	–
CD11b α-subunit Mac-1	83	+++	100	++	31	+	0	0	100	++
CD11c α-subunit p150/95	90	++	100	++	74	++	ND	–	ND	–
CD13 Aminopeptidase	81	+	100	++	52	+	ND	–	ND	–
CD14 LPS binding protein receptor	71	+++	60	++	61	+	ND	–	ND	–
CD16 FcRIII	5	+	95	++	96	++	ND	–	ND	–
CD25 IL-2 receptor	0	0	3	+	17	+	ND	–	ND	–
CD31 GPIIa	93	++	75	++	100	+++	ND	–	ND	–
CD32 FcRII	90	+	100	++	100	++	100	+++	100	+
CD35 C3B receptor	69	++	43	++	0	0	0	0	90	++
CD36 Thrombospondin receptor	72	+	38	+	31	+	ND	–	ND	–
FcRI	ND	–	ND	–	100	++	100	+++	25–40	+
Class II MHC	99	++	98	++	100	++	20–60	++	5–20	+
Transferrin receptor	ND	–	74	+	0	0	ND	–	ND	–
Mannosyl-fucosyl receptor	ND	–	ND	–	ND	–	100	++	100	++
M-CSF receptor	ND	–	ND	–	ND	–	5	+	80	+
Sheep erythrocyte receptor/ sialoadhesin	ND	–	ND	–	ND	+++	50–90	+++	0–5	+
Erythroblast receptor	0	0	ND	–	100	++	100	+++	0–5	+

For further details see references 12 and 99.
ND: Not determined.

One of the difficulties in extrapolating the results obtained with 'model' systems to events that may actually occur *in vivo* is that terminally differentiated macrophages within the haematopoietic micro-environment may have lost the capacity to express certain genes which can be readily induced in macrophages used in the *in vitro* model systems. For example, Kupffer cells (resident liver macrophages) lack the capacity to secrete reactive oxygen intermediates in response to exposure to interferon-gamma (IFNγ), yet appear fully capable of upregulating the expression of MHC Class II molecules in response to the same stimulus (8). Similarly, human monocytes undergo extensive phenotypic changes during *in vitro* culture and this can be influenced by the type of substrate, the presence or not of cytokines, such as M-CSF and IFNγ, and the type of serum used to supplement the culture medium.

2.2 Distribution and properties of macrophages in haematopoietic tissues

The widespread distribution of macrophages in haematopoietic tissues has been observed in several mammalian species, where they make up an important part of the haematopoietic microenvironment. Isolation studies in the mouse indicated that at least 1 per cent of the nucleated cells in femoral bone marrow are resident macrophages which, *in situ*, establish a three-dimensional network of plasma membrane processes (Figure 3.2). The RBMM population is morphologically and phenotypically distinct from the developing monocytes which are in a state of rapid turnover (9). The resident macrophages are thought to be 'fixed' in the marrow where they constitute part of the reticuloendothelial system (10). Although mitotic figures have been observed *in situ* (11), uptake of tritiated thymidine has not been seen following their isolation (12). It is probable that RBMM are non-replicating 'end cells' whose continual repopulation depends on monocytes which are derived either from local marrow monocyte pools or from those circulating in the blood (Figure 3.1).

Resident macrophages of haematopoietic tissues can be recognized by various criteria, such as morphology and ultrastructure, the presence of phagocytic inclusions (see Figure 3.5), reactivity for intense lysosomal acid phosphatase, and labelling by specific monoclonal antibodies. By all approaches, RBMM are seen to be distributed evenly throughout the haematopoietic compartments. A small proportion is present within the sinusoids where they may contribute to the uptake of effete erythrocytes or blood-borne debris.

Phenotypic analysis of isolated RBMM has been carried out in two species, human and mouse (Table 3.3). These studies clearly show that in addition to morphological differences between monocytes and other macrophage populations, many differences in cell surface phenotype also

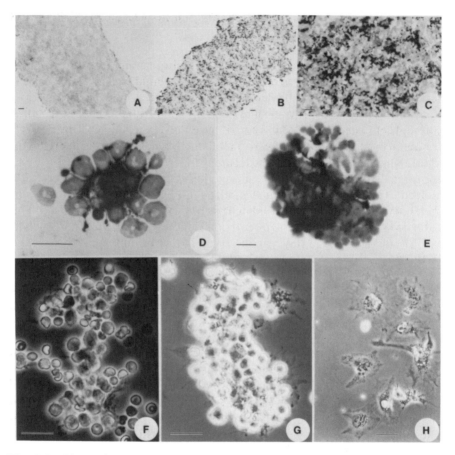

Fig. 3.2 Photomicrographs of resident bone marrow macrophages *in situ* (A–C) and following isolation (D–H). (A–C), cryostat sections of mouse femoral bone marrow were fixed with acetone and stained by the immunperoxidase method with either (A) no first antibody or (B,C) with the monoclonal antibody, SER-4 (Section 4). This antibody can be seen to specifically label the plasma membrane processes of resident bone marrow macrophages, thereby revealing the arborising, three-dimensional network of stromal macrophages. (Scale bars = 25 µm.) (D,E), clusters of bone marrow cells were prepared from femoral marrow plugs by collagenase digestion and separated from single cells by velocity sedimentation. Cytocentrifuge smears were stained by immunoperoxidase with monoclonal antibody, F4/80. In (D), a single, stained macrophage is at the centre of an erythroblastic island. In (E), a larger cluster containing several macrophages reveals extensive macrophage plasma membrane associations with haematopoietic cells (Scale bars = 10µm.) (F–H), phase contrast micrographs of adherent haematopoietic clusters and macrophages following attachment to a glass substrate. (F) well-spread macrophage(s) mostly in contact with erythroid cells; (G), a similar cluster associated with myeloid cells; (H), purified resident bone marrow macrophages following stripping of the attached haematopoietic cells in the absence of divalent cations. (Scale bars = 10 µm.) (Further information provided in reference 12.)

exist. The most striking difference is the ability of bone marrow macrophages, but not monocytes or macrophages from other tissues, to avidly bind haematopoietic cells. In the human this is largely an erythroid interaction but in the mouse there are also prominent associations with developing myeloid cells (Figures 3.2 and 3.5). The properties and possible significance of these specialized cellular associations are discussed below (Section 4).

3   Control of haematopoiesis by soluble regulatory factors

3.1   Steady state versus induced haematopoiesis

The cytokines that control blood cell production have been the subject of several comprehensive reviews in recent years and the reader is referred to these for detailed information on their molecular biology, biochemistry, receptors, and actions (2,4,13–17).

Apart from the colony-stimulating factors (CSFs) and erythropoietin which were discovered and characterized on the basis of their haematopoietic growth activities, many of the other cytokines were originally discovered in unrelated biological assays. Only subsequently were they found to be active within the developing haematopoietic system (Table 3.1 and 3.2). The different factors can be subdivided on the basis of their biological effects on haematopoietic progenitors as follows:

(1) those such as the CSFs, IL-3 (multi-CSF), GM-CSF, G-CSF, M-CSF, which act directly on progenitor cells to promote their survival, growth and differentiation into mature blood cells;

(2) those typified by IL-1 and IL-6 which have weak or no intrinsic growth stimulating activity but which act in synergy with certain other growth factors to promote growth and differentiation;

(3) those such as IL-1 and TNFα which stimulate proliferation indirectly by inducing growth factor production by other cells; and

(4) those such as TGFβ, MIP-1α, and IFNα which act as selective inhibitors of proliferation.

Many cytokines are pleiotropic with multiple biological properties. They can frequently stimulate both positive and negative effects depending on the type of target cell and the biological response under study (15). There is also considerable redundancy, with molecularly unrelated cytokines exhibiting overlapping biological spectra. It could be argued that this allows fine tuning of immunological, inflammatory, and haematological responses, but it is also possible that only a limited number of the total available cytokines is used at one time, depending on the requirements of the host and, more importantly the tissue compartments examined. We will first consider non-steady state haematopoiesis.

A high level of production of many cytokines by macrophages *in vitro* has been shown to depend on the presence of various exogenous stimuli. These include bacterial components, such as lipopolysaccharide (LPS), other cytokines, or non-specific factors, such as adherence and phagocytosis by macrophages. As activation is also required for cytokine production by T-cells (16), it is probable that this type of regulation has evolved to allow the rapid, orchestrated production of the appropriate haematopoietic cell populations during inflammatory and immunological reactions. The release of haematopoietic factors by diverse cell types, existence of autocrine secretion and the multitude of diverse regulatory pathways would give rise to a rapid amplification of cytokine production via complex networks. In addition to their ability to regulate the growth of haematopoietic cells, many cytokines also have potent effects on 'end cell' function, such as the stimulation of macrophage and granulocyte microbicidal activity (18). Under certain circumstances, particularly in acute short-term inflammatory reactions, this latter activity may be more important than the capacity to regulate the growth of progenitor populations. However, if the causative agent of the inflammatory response persists, the continued production of cytokines by activated T-cells and macrophages may modify haematopoietic responses through alterations in the growth and differentiation of progenitor cells (discussed further in Section 5). The most clear-cut example of this is observed for bone marrow production of eosinophils stimulated by IL-5. Following infection of mice by helminth parasites, such as *Nippostrongylus brasiliensis* and *Schistosoma mansoni*, activated T-cells release IL-5 into the circulation, leading to massive eosinophilia and associated pathologies. Injection of a monoclonal antibody against IL-5 was able to block the bone marrow eosinophilic response, thus demonstrating the critical role of this molecule under non-steady state conditions (19).

In the absence of inflammation or immune activation, it is possible that only a limited repertoire of regulatory cytokines is displayed by stromal cells of the steady state haematopoietic micro-environment. In long-term bone marrow cultures or stroma which have been depleted of haematopoietic cells, many investigators have demonstrated that M-CSF, IL-6, IL-7, and TGFβ are constitutively produced whereas GM-CSF, G-CSF and IL-11 require addition of inducing agents, such as LPS, IL-1 or TNFα (15). One of the most potent stem cell growth factors, IL-3 cannot be detected in these cultures even after stimulation, thereby questioning its relevance for the early stages of steady-state haematopoiesis. IL-3 is specifically made by activated T-cells, as are certain other haematopoietic regulators, IL-4, IL-5, and IL-9 (Table 3.2). These molecules are likely to be important in haematopoiesis during immunological reactions, but are apparently not required during steady state haematopoiesis because nude and scid mice which lack mature T-cells do not exhibit defective renewal of blood cells.

3.2 Production of haematopoietic regulatory factors by macrophages

In general, macrophages are cells with an extremely diverse secretory repertoire (20) (see Chapter 1) so it is not surprising that many of the cytokines which have been shown to play a role in the regulation of haematopoiesis can also be produced by monocytes and/or tissue macrophages under appropriate circumstances (Tables 3.2 and 3.3). However, none of these is exclusively made by macrophages and in many cases, particularly under steady state conditions, macrophages are likely to make a relatively minor contribution when compared to other cells of the haematopoietic micro-environment, such as endothelial cells and fibroblasts. Of the list of factors presented in Table 3.1, three of them, IL-1, TNFα, and the macrophage inflammatory protein (MIP) family, are thought to be made principally by macrophages. These molecules are unrelated in terms of molecular structure, yet appear to be able to mediate broadly similar biological effects within the haematopoietic system. None are directly able to stimulate growth but act synergistically in the presence of other factors, and all have the ability to mediate either positive or negative regulatory effects on haematopoietic progenitors of different cell lineages. The possible role of these three cytokines in the control of haematopoiesis is discussed below.

3.2.1 *Interleukin-1 as a central regulator of haematopoiesis*

Interleukin-1 (IL-1) exists in two forms, IL-1α and IL-1β, which in the human are only 26 per cent homologous yet bind to the same receptor and elicit shared biological responses (21). Details of the molecular biology, biochemistry, unusual secretion pathway, and cellular targets of IL-α,-β have been recently reviewed and will not be discussed here (15,21).

Although originally defined as a product of stimulated monocytes/macrophages, it is now known that other cells are able to synthesize and secrete IL-1. These include endothelial cells, T-cells, B-cells, astrocytes and fibroblasts, keratinocytes, and thymic epithelial cells (15). For the latter two cell types, IL-1 seems to be a constitutive secretory product (22).

Like the majority of cytokines, IL-1 is strongly induced *in vitro* by diverse exogenous and endogenous agents, including LPS, M-CSF, TNFα, IL-1 itself, and IFNγ. Experiments with isolated progenitor cells, long-term bone marrow cultures, and following injection into mice have shown that IL-1 can function as a key regulatory molecule in haematopoiesis (23).

As already mentioned, IL-1 has no intrinsic growth factor activity, but is able to influence progenitor cell growth and differentiation in two distinct ways, either by inducing the production of growth factors/inhibitors by other cells or by acting as a synergistic factor for progenitor development in the presence of other growth factors (Figure 3.2). Thus, IL-1 can stimulate the production of GM-CSF, G-CSF, M-CSF, IL-6, and TNFα by endothelial cells and fibroblasts and can stimulate CSF release by haematopoietic progenitors themselves (24). IL-1 has also been shown to stimulate macrophages for further production of IL-1, thereby suggesting the existence of autocrine regulation (23).

IL-1 is also able to promote myeloid cell production via stimulation of stem cells in the presence of the IL-3, GM-CSF, G-CSF, and M-CSF. This activity was originally ascribed to 'hemopoietin-1' which was subsequently shown to be identical to IL-1α (23). The effects of IL-1 on progenitors may be indirect, being mediated via accessory cell release of other stem cell potentiators such as IL-6 or other cytokines (23,25).

The mechanism by which IL-1 is able to augment the production of the various haematopoietic growth regulators is thought to be at the level of posttranscriptional control (26). Many of the mRNA transcripts for the cytokines express AU rich sequences at their 3′ non-translated regions which have been shown to greatly reduce the half-life of a normally stable message, such as that for globin (15). In the presence of IL-1 the half-life of cytokine mRNA transcripts is prolonged to greater than 24 h and this effect has been proposed to account for the haematopoietic activities of IL-1, including (1) induction of growth factors, (2) synergy with other factors, (3) priming, and (4) autoinduction (26).

In addition to its ability to induce the production of growth factors and potentiate their effects on early progenitors, IL-1 can also be shown to stimulate the release of suppressive factors. For myelopoiesis, the overall effect of injected IL-1 appears to be stimulatory (23), but this is counterbalanced to some extent by induction of PGE_2-mediated myelosuppression (27). There is also growing evidence that macrophage-derived IL-1 can inhibit erythropoiesis via induction of TNFα secretion (28). Transfer of small numbers of unstimulated peritoneal macrophages either into normal mice or into mice infected with an anaemia-inducing strain of Friend virus had an inhibitory effect on erythropoiesis as assessed by the decreased numbers of CFU-E recovered from the spleen. The effect was reproduced with macrophage supernatants and could be inhibited specifically by addition of anti-IL-1 antisera or pre-treatment of the mice with anti-TNFα antisera, IL-1 has also been shown to block the IL-7-dependent proliferation of early B-cell progenitors, prevent long-term B lymphopoiesis in long-term cultures, and stimulate the release of uncharacterized growth inhibitory factors from stromal cells (15).

The production of IL-1 by macrophages and/or other cells of the haematopoietic micro-environment could thus be instrumental in regulating haematopoiesis, both under steady state conditions and during inflammatory responses. Although production of IL-1 by macrophages only reaches high levels following stimulation by factors such as LPS, it is plausible that there is low-level constitutive secretion *in vivo* which can be enhanced during periods of haematopoietic stress. Moreover, negative control of high-level IL-1 could be mediated by soluble IL-1 inhibitor which is also produced by macrophages and inhibits the action of IL-1 by antagonizing binding to the membrane IL-1 receptor of target cells (29).

A continual stimulus for basal low-level secretion of IL-1 by macrophages could be provided by constitutively produced inducing agents such as M-CSF, which is also readily detectable in the plasma. Other IL-1 inducers may exist in the haematopoietic micro-environment, such as cytokines (for example, GM-CSF), non-specific stimuli like phagocytosis and substrate interactions (30), and via coupling of receptors and ligands which mediate cellular adhesion (22). In this context it should be emphasized that constitutive and induced production of IL-1 has been demonstrated for thymic epithelial cells, which, like resident bone marrow macrophages, bind avidly to proliferating cells.

Even in the absence of secretion, IL-1 may become associated with the macrophage plasma membrane in a biologically active form, as has been demonstrated with macrophages during lymphocyte activation and hepatocyte acute phase protein synthesis (31). Little is known of how IL-1 is

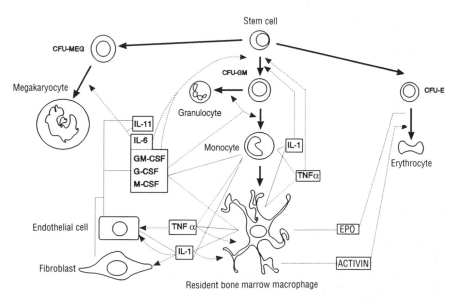

Fig. 3.3 The stimulating network which may exist in the control of haematopoiesis by soluble factors derived from mononuclear phagocytes. (For further details see Tables 3.1 and 3.2.)

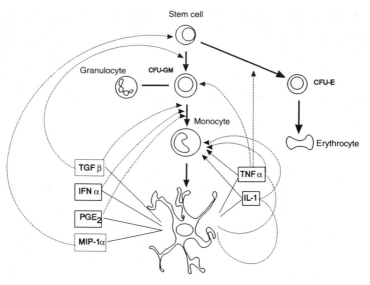

Fig. 3.4 The inhibitory network which may exist in the control of haematopoiesis by soluble factors derived from mononuclear phagocytes. (For further details see Tables 3.1 and 3.2.)

targeted to the cell membrane because it lacks a signal peptide and is therefore secreted by an unusual mechanism (32).

To conclude, from the networks shown in Figures 3.3 and 3.4, the net result of raising the levels of IL-1 would be to enhance myelopoiesis at the expense of erythropoiesis, a situation which has been observed following injection of mice with IL-1 (33) and which is observed in certain forms of chronic inflammation (see Section 5 for further discussion). In acute inflammatory responses, enhanced local production of IL-1 by macrophages, either within or outside the haematopoietic micro-environment could act as a trigger to dramatically up-regulate production of granulocytes and monocytes via stromal cell production of CSFs (Figure 3.3). The co-ordinated interplay between molecules, such as IL-1, TNFα, CSF, and inhibitory factors, could provide a mechanism for the fine-tuning of haematopoietic regulation.

3.2.2   *The role of TNFα in haematopoiesis*

TNFα was originally discovered as an endotoxin-induced serum factor able to trigger the haemorrhagic necrosis of tumours *in vivo* (34). Under the name 'cachectin', the same molecule was characterized as a macrophage product which could suppress lipoprotein lipase activity, being the presumptive cause of cachexia in certain parasitic diseases (34). Subsequent studies employing recombinant TNFα have shown that, like IL-1, TNFα is a multifunctional pleiotropic cytokine with complex biological effects, many of which are shared by IL-1 (20,35). Although other cells, such as T-cells and NK cells, can produce TNFα, macrophages are probably the most important source *in vivo* (34). Like IL-1, TNFα appears to act in concert with other factors rather than on its own and is capable of exerting both positive and negative effects within the haematopoietic system. Positive effects of TNFα could be mediated indirectly by inducing the secretion of M-CSF, GM-CSF, G-CSF, and IL-1 by endothelial cells, fibroblasts, and macrophages, as demonstrated *in vitro* (15). The same factors are present in the serum after injections of TNFα (35).

In colony assays, TNFα is generally found to inhibit growth of bone marrow progenitors for granulocyte-macrophages and erythroid cells (15). Some of the suppressive effects may be due to release of inhibitory factors by accessory cells in the cultures or due to down-regulation of growth factor receptors, as demonstrated with mouse cells for the M-CSF receptor (36). However, using a population of purified human CD34+ cells, which is enriched in stem cells, TNFα was found to act in a direct manner to strongly potentiate their growth in the presence of multi-CSF/IL-3 and GM-CSF (37).

Experiments *in vivo* have also demonstrated a complex role for TNFα in haematopoietic regulation (35). Erythropoiesis was found to be specifically inhibited with reduced haematocrit and a lowered number of early and late erythroid progenitor cells. Interestingly, the circulating monocyte number was increased over that of control mice, consistent with the *in vitro* observation that TNFα and M-CSF synergize for mononuclear phagocyte proliferation (38).

It remains to be shown whether TNFα actually plays a role during steady state haematopoiesis. Like IL-1, TNFα can exist in a biologically active form as a membrane-associated molecule and could thus act at a short distance during cellular interactions of resident bone marrow macrophages with haematopoietic cells.

3.2.3   The macrophage inflammatory protein (MIP) family and stem cell inhibition

The macrophage inflammatory proteins, MIP-1α, MIP-1β, and MIP-2 were initially characterized as homologous macrophage-derived heparin-binding proteins (6000–8000 kDa) which cause local acute inflammation when injected into the footpads of mice (39). The proinflammatory action of MIPs appears to be due to a combined effect of inducing chemotaxis and respiratory burst of neutrophils. In LPS-stimulated macrophage-like cell lines, MIP-1, and MIP-2 are major secretory products, comprising approximately 2 per cent and 0.5 per cent respectively of the total secreted proteins (39).

Subsequent studies of the activities of these three proteins on bone marrow cells showed them to have no growth activity alone but to be able to augment the growth of granulocyte-macrophage progenitors in the presence of sub-optimal levels of CSFs (40). Using purified human CD34+ bone marrow cells as a source of early progenitors it was subsequently shown that MIP-1β and MIP-2 retained their potentiating effect, whereas MIP-1α was inhibitory for colony formation (40).

The selective growth inhibitory activity of MIP-1α for early progenitors may be the most important property of this family of molecules in haematopoietic regulation. MIP-1α was recently purified independently on the basis of its ability to inhibit stem cell entry into cell cycle and block the *in vitro* growth of very early progenitor cells in response to IL-1 and M-CSF (41). As this biological activity was originally discovered as a putative product of mononuclear phagocytes from normal bone marrow cells, it seems likely that MIP-1α is secreted in a constitutive manner by primary macrophages and macrophage-like cell lines (41).

Stem cells are normally quiescent, non-proliferating cells which only enter cell cycle following haematopoietic stress such as that which can be induced experimentally by the injection of such cytotoxic drugs as 5-fluorouracil or hydroxyurea. Under these conditions, bone marrow cells with the properties of macrophages release a factor which stimulates stem cells to enter into cell cycle (42). The molecular nature of this stimulatory factor is currently not known, but IL-1 is one of a number of candidates.

The regulation of stem cell growth may be an important macrophage function in the control of haematopoiesis. In addition to MIP-1α, macrophages are able to secrete TGFβ which has been shown to selectively inhibit the proliferation of very early progenitor cells *in vitro* and *in vivo* (43). An important area for future research will be to determine whether secretion of these inhibitory agents is a property of the resident bone marrow macrophages or whether developing monocytes or other cells of the haematopoietic micro-environment also have this capacity. It will also be of interest to determine whether MIP-1α secretion is limited to certain macrophage subpopulations and whether macrophages outside the bone marrow release significant quantities, especially during inflammatory reactions. The MIPs are small proteins compared to the other cytokines and if released into the blood stream they would be expected to enter the haematopoietic tissues and affect haematopoiesis. The discovery that MIP-1α can modify the behaviour of both primitive stem cells and fully differentiated granulocytes is yet another example of how pleiotropic cytokines can mediate diverse effects within the haematopoietic system.

3.3   Insights from genetic mutations into the *in vivo* role of haemopoietic regulatory factors

Given the vast amount of information now available concerning the ability of cytokines to modify haematopoietic cell behaviour *in vitro*, it is important to interpret these data in the context of the haematopoietic system as it exists *in vivo*, with the eventual goal of piecing together the events which actually occur within the animal both under steady state and non-steady state conditions. This is of great importance if the role of the macrophage in haematopoiesis is to be fully understood, because, as discussed above, it is a cell which has great *potential* but in reality we know very little of its *actual* functions.

One of the most powerful approaches to dissecting complex physiological processes involves the application of modern tools of molecular biology to introduce, mutate, or delete specific genes or combinations of genes and determine the resulting phenotype. Within the haematopoietic system as a whole, this approach is still in its infancy, but in forthcoming years it is anticipated that this approach may give great insight into the specific functions of the various candidate regulatory molecules. To date, transgenetic experiments have created lines of mice which carry multiple copies of haematopoietic growth factor genes, such as GM-CSF (44) and IL-5 (45). These mice produce high levels of macrophages and eosinophils respectively, thus showing that elevated concentrations of these factors *in vivo* mirror their previously-established *in vitro* properties, a conclusion which has been similarly reached in many cases following injection of large quantities of purified growth factor. Arguably, a more powerful genetic approach to establishing the role of haematopoietic growth factors, especially under steady state conditions, is gene ablation or mutation by site-directed mutagenesis. This approach has only recently become feasible using totipotential embryonic stem cells which can be cultured *in vitro*, selected for the desired genotype, and re-introduced *in utero*. As yet, genetic ablation studies have not been described for haematopoietic regulatory factors. However, naturally occurring mutations of the haematopoietic system have recently been characterized at the molecular level and these have given valuable insight into the regulation of haematopoiesis.

3.3.1 The white-spotting and steel loci

The white-spotting (W) and steel (Sl) loci were identified in mice as independent mutations which result in a similar phenotype, that is, altered coat colour, defects in gonadal development, and varying degrees of macrocytic anaemia related to alterations in haematopoietic stem cell behaviour (46). The gene product of the W locus was identified as the protooncogene *c-kit*, a transmembrane tyrosine kinase receptor which was expressed in haematopoietic tissues as well as others affected by the mutation. Recently, the gene product of the Sl locus was identified as a new haematopoietic growth factor, stem cell factor (SCF), which when added to *in vitro* bone marrow cultures affects several lineages, but shows particularly striking effects on erythroid development (47). As had been predicted from the similar phenotypes associated with the two loci, SCF encoded at the Sl locus is the ligand for the c-*kit* tyrosine kinase receptor encoded at the W locus (47). This is the first example in the haematopoietic system where a growth factor and a receptor have been shown to play an indispensable role in the maintenance of haematopoiesis under steady state conditions. It is also of great interest that SCF can naturally exist as a classic transmembrane protein, as there is much circumstantial evidence to suggest that this receptor-ligand pair operates *in vivo* through close-range cellular interactions (46).

3.3.2   The osteopetrosis locus

The osteopetrotic mouse provides another example of a naturally occurring mutation (op) which affects the haematopoietic system. These mice lack the capacity to generate osteoclasts which are required for bone degradation and its subsequent remodelling (48). They are also reported to have a defective mononuclear phagocyte system, consistent with the evidence demonstrating that a common progenitor is shared between monocytes/ macrophages and osteoclasts (49). When compared to normal litter mates (op/+, +/+) the haematological system of osteopetrotic (op/op) mice was found to differ as follows: op/op mice had very few mononuclear phagocytes in the peritoneal cavity and severely reduced numbers of monocytes in the peripheral blood. Whereas the thymus appeared normal, the bone marrow was hypocellular and the spleen, where cellularity was not increased, contained around twice the CFU-S number and 10 times more late progenitors for mononuclear phagocytes. The op locus maps to chromosome 3 and has been recently shown to lie in the coding sequence of the M-CSF gene. Recent data have shown that fibroblasts from op/op mutant mice are unable to synthesize M-CSF due to the presence of a single base pair insertion in the coding region of M-CSF, resulting in a stop codon 21 base pairs downstream of the translation start site (50,51).

It will be important to analyse precisely the hypocellularity of the bone marrow and determine whether bone marrow stromal fibroblasts and macrophages are affected in terms of their density and haematopoietic activities. Although preliminary results point to a decreased number of bone marrow stromal macrophages (52) further studies are necessary to establish which functions of M-CSF and its receptor, c-*fms*, are affected. Like c-*kit*, c-*fms* is a tyrosine kinase receptor. Following ligation by M-CSF, c-*fms* mediates diverse effects on the physiology of mononuclear phagocytes, including not only growth and differentiation, but also complex end-cell functional activities which could be important in inflammatory and immunological reactions (53). In addition, the finding that the placenta contains high levels of M-CSF and c-*fms* suggests that this receptor-ligand interaction may also be important during fetal development (53).

It is remarkable that these two sets of naturally occurring mutations of the haematopoietic system, both of which result in clear-cut perturbation of steady state haematopoiesis, involve a homologous receptor-coupling system. Precise control over cellular differentiation events seems to be a recurring feature of the tyrosine kinase family of receptors as also shown by the elegant studies on eye development in Drosophila which is in part controlled by the tyrosine kinase receptor, sevenless, and its ligand, bride-of-sevenless (54).

4   Interactions between macrophages and haematopoietic cells

4.1   Importance of adhesion in the haematopoietic system

In addition to the control of haematopoiesis via secreted haematopoietic regulatory factors, there is good evidence that cell-to-cell contact-mediated interactions between stromal cells and haematopoietic progenitors play a critical role, especially during steady state haematopoiesis (5). In long-term bone marrow cultures which support myelopoiesis or B lymphopoiesis, cell contact between progenitor cells and stromal cells is necessary for the sustained growth and renewal of pluripotential stem cells (5,29). These cultures contain a mixture of different cell types, including fibroblastoid cells and their derivatives (for example adipocytes), endothelial cells, 'blanket cells', and macrophages, all of which can be identified in haematopoietic tissues. The stromal cells secrete an extracellular matrix which is rich in collagens, fibronectin, laminin, and glycosaminoglycans (4, 5). Cell lines can be cloned from primary haematopoietic tissue which retain the ability to support the growth and differentiation of haematopoietic progenitors. These cell lines have the properties of fibroblastoid or endothelial-like cells and secrete a complex extracellular matrix (29).

The finding that cloned stromal cells support haematopoietic cell growth in an adherence-dependent fashion suggests that cellular interactions between progenitors and stromal cells play a key role in haematopoietic regulation. Adhesion is mediated by, as yet uncharacterized, receptors and ligands, although a recent study with a stromal cell line which supports B lymphopoiesis showed that certain monoclonal antibodies which were directed to stromal cells were able to block lymphocyte progenitor adhesion and growth. The antigen recognized was subsequently shown to be CD44, a receptor for hyaluronic acid (55). Stem cells have also been shown to express a putative 110 kDa lectin-like receptor with specificity for mannosylated and galactosylated glycoconjugates and it has been proposed that this receptor is important for stem cell homing and localization in the bone marrow (56).

In addition to adhesion molecules and lectin-like interactions, the adhesion to stroma and the subsequent growth of progenitors may be enhanced by receptor-ligand interactions between plasma membrane or extracellular matrix-anchored growth factors and the corresponding receptors expressed by progenitor cells. The full-length predicted sequences of the haematopoietic growth factors M-CSF and SCF (*kit* ligand) contain classic transmembrane domains (47, 57). In the absence of proteolytic cleavage, they are stably expressed within the plasma membrane where they retain haematopoietic growth activity (58). Soluble growth factors, such as GM-CSF, may also be rendered insoluble by being specifically targeted to the extracellular matrix, as has recently been demonstrated for LIF (59). GM-CSF could be extracted from glycosaminoglycans derived from haematopoietic tissue (60) and addition of the haematopoietic growth factors GM-CSF and multi-CSF to purified heparan sulphate led to their incorporation and retention of biological activity (61).

Components of the extracellular matrix may also interact directly with receptors expressed on the surface of immature haematopoietic cells, as shown for fibronectin, haemonectin, and thrombospondin (56, 62). The regulated loss of adhesion receptors during differentiation may be important in allowing maturing haematopoietic cells to leave the bone marrow and enter the circulation.

4.2   Cellular interactions between macrophages and haematopoietic cells

4.2.1   The erythroblastic islet

Within the haematopoietic system the best-known cellular interaction of macrophages is with developing erythroblasts, to create a distinctive anatomical unit, the erythroblastic islet (Figures s 3.2 and 3.5). With the exception of primitive erythropoiesis in the yolk sac of the fetus, erythroid development *in vivo* is invariably found in close association with central macrophages (1). This is particularly striking in the fetal liver where macrophage production precedes erythroblast development and where

Fig. 3.5 (A), electron micrograph of an isolated erythroblastic island derived from the spleen of an anaemic mouse. The central macrophage (M) is surrounded by developing erythroblasts (E) and contains a recently ingested erythroblast nucleus (▶) together with a nucleus in a more advanced stage of digestion) (→). (B), immunoelectron micrograph of an isolated cluster showing a resident bone marrow macrophage (M) attached to two developing granulocytes (G). The cluster was stained by immunoperoxidase with the monoclonal antibody, SER-4, (anti-sialoadhesin) and then sectioned to reveal the distribution of the receptor within the cluster. Sialoadhesin was found to be concentrated at the points of cell contact between macrophages and granulocytes (▶), indicating the possibility of specific receptor-ligand interactions.

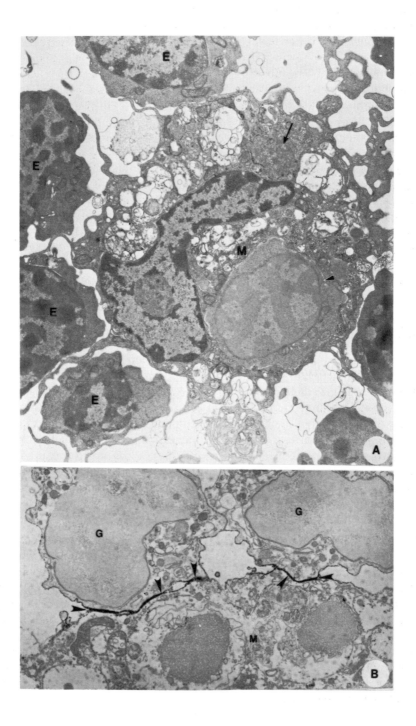

erythroblasts surrounding individual macrophages are synchronized in their developmental stages. Similar structures develop in long-term cultures of mouse bone marrow 2–3 days after the addition of anaemic mouse serum, and time-lapse video has shown that erythroblasts remain attached to macrophages up until enucleation (4). In the adult bone marrow, erythroid developmental stages in erythroblastic islets are less homogenous, but synchronous structures can be re-established during episodes of stimulated erythropoiesis, when they can even be found within sinusoids (63). The association of macrophages with erythroid cells is relatively long term, being initiated at around the CFU-E stage and persisting up until enucleation (4), this corresponding to approximately four rounds of cell division or approximately 48 hours.

Despite much speculation since the pioneering studies of Bessis and colleagues (1), there is still no clear-cut evidence for a critical function for the central macrophage of erythroblastic islets apart from the phagocytosis of the expelled nuclei and the presumed turnover of the iron and other metabolites that arise from their breakdown. However, the original suggestion that macrophages could act as trophic cells by providing a local supply of erythropoietin (EPO) has gained direct support from the studies of Rich and colleagues who demonstrated that macrophage cultures express EPO mRNA by *in situ* hybridization and secrete biologically active EPO, especially when cultured at low oxygen tension (64). The significance of this in erythropoiesis is unclear, however, as EPO can be readily detected in normal plasma and, in long-term bone marrow cultures, addition of EPO is required to stimulate late-stage erythrocyte development (4, 5). Moreover, the kidney, which is the well-known source of EPO during erythropoietic stress, is also active under steady state conditions when mRNA can be detected using a sensitive nuclease protection assay (65). The cells in kidney which produce EPO have been shown by *in situ* hybridization to be peritubular endothelial-like cells and not macrophages which are abundant in the kidney (66,67). Moreover, the ability of injected recombinant EPO to correct the anaemia of chronic renal failure in virtually all cases, suggests that the kidney, rather than haematopoietic tissues, is normally the limiting source of EPO (68).

Besides EPO, other factors can promote late-stage erythroid development and can be produced by macrophages. These include activin, a member of the TGFβ family (43), and tissue inhibitor of metalloproteinase (TIMP) (69).

Other possible functions of the central macrophage of the erythroblastic islet may be related to the cellular organization of the haematopoietic microenvironment. It has been suggested, for example, that the central macrophage, which is mobile in long-term cultures, acts as a vehicle to transport all of its maturing reticulocyte from haematopoietic areas to the wall of the venous sinus, ready for delivery into the circulation (4).

4.2.2 Macrophage–myeloid cell interactions

In addition to erythroid cells, macrophages in haematopoietic tissues also establish intimate associations with late-stage developing myeloid cells, notably monocytes, granulocytes, and eosinophils. In the mouse, these associations can be readily observed under steady state conditions by immunocytochemistry of bone marrow sections using macrophage-specific monoclonal antibodies (70). However, they become even more pronounced following selective stimulation of the myeloid series. Macrophage-associated monocytes can be observed following infection of mice with BCG (see Section 5.1), neutrophils following subcutaneous injection of calcium phosphate precipitated talc and eosinophils following infection of mice with the helminth parasite *Mesocestoides corti* (P.R.C., unpublished observations). The cellular associations with macrophages are particularly striking in the last two examples, as there is virtually no erythropoiesis observable in the bone marrow, and the resident macrophages are exclusively present in 'myeloid islets'.

Valuable insights into the kinetics of macrophage–myeloid interactions have been obtained from time-lapse video studies of long-term mouse bone marrow cultures (4). Essentially two types of macrophage-myeloid associations were observed. First, during the development of the 'cobblestone' regions of granulopoiesis, macrophages and myeloid precursors migrate under 'blanket cells' where the macrophages become 'fixed'. Division of myeloid cells takes place almost exclusively in these regions and there is transient, dynamic cell-to-cell contact formation between the proliferating myelocytes and the stromal macrophages. A second type of myeloid association is also seen in these cultures in which macrophages outside of the cobblestone areas are seen to form relatively stable associations (hours to days) with mature, post-mitotic granulocytes.

Isolation of haematopoietic clusters from mouse bone marrow has also revealed the relatively stable association of resident macrophages with developing myelocytes (12). As the great majority of the attached cells take up tritiated thymidine, it is likely that the associations observed *in vivo* correspond mainly to the former 'cobblestone' type described above. It is possible that the second type of association reflects an inherent artefact of the long-term cultures, that unidirectional release of mature progeny across the endothelial barrier cannot occur as it does *in vivo*, resulting in long-term associations with macrophages which would not be established in the bone marrow. Although the biological significance of these cellular associations is presently unknown, it is of considerable interest that a macrophage-specific cell interaction molecule, sialoadhesin, is selectively concentrated at regions of cell-to-cell contact with myeloid, but not erythroid cells (discussed in Section 4.3).

4.2.3   Other cellular associations of resident bone marrow macrophages

Besides erythroid and myeloid cells, resident macrophages in cross-sections of mouse bone marrow can frequently be seen to establish intimate and extensive plasma membrane contact with mature megakaryocytes (P.R.C., unpublished observations). A wide variety of cytokines, characterized and uncharacterized, have been shown to affect different aspects of mega-karyocyte growth and differentiation *in vitro*, such as the cloning efficiency, number of cells per colony, the nuclear ploidy, and cytoplasmic maturation (71). Macrophages may be an important source of IL-6 which, together with IL-3, has been shown to promote growth and differentiation of murine megakaryocyte progenitors *in vitro* (72). Furthermore, injection of IL-6 in cynomolgus monkeys led to greatly elevated platelet production (73).

The bone marrow of mammals is the major site of B-lymphopoiesis and up to 24 per cent of bone marrow cells can be identified as developing B-cells by their expression of the B220 isoform of CD45 (74). However, isolation of macrophage–haematopoietic clusters and studies of long-term bone marrow cultures supporting B-lymphopoiesis have shown that macrophages do not establish extensive cellular associations with immature cytoplasmic μ+ B-cells. In long-term cultures, this appears to be the exclusive property of fibroblastoid-type stromal cells (75), consistent with the observation made *in situ* that developing B-cells are predominantly localized to subendosteal regions where fibroblastoid cell processes are also found (74). Interestingly, it was observed in the latter study that bone marrow macrophages were in contact with, and appeared to be in the process of phagocytozing B220+ B-cells. It was suggested that the macrophage network might provide a mechanism for recognizing and rapidly disposing of defective or potentially autoreactive B lineage cells.

Stem cells in the bone marrow are also concentrated subendosteally and in long-term *in vitro* systems immature progenitors have been shown to adhere selectively to non-macrophage stromal cells (76). The physical attachment of resident bone marrow macrophages to haematopoietic cells appears to be rather restricted to erythroid and myeloid cells which are in a relatively late stage of their differentiation programme. The nature of the macrophage receptors involved in these cellular interactions is discussed below.

4.3   Adhesion receptors involved in macrophage–haematopoietic cell interactions

4.3.1   The erythroblast receptor, EbR

Using murine-resident tissue macrophages, isolated from adult bone mar-row or fetal liver and stripped of their attached haematopoietic cells, two distinct receptors have been defined which are able to mediate adhesion to haematopoietic cells (77) (Figures 3.2 and 3.5). High avidity adhesion of immature haematopoietic cells to stromal macrophages is largely dependent on the presence of divalent cations, calcium being preferred to magnesium (78). This receptor, designated the erythroblast receptor (EbR), was originally characterized with stripped fetal liver macrophages to which fetal erythroblasts had been re-added. EbR is likely to be a cell-surface protein because expression was lost when macrophages were treated with trypsin whereas the ligand expressed on erythroblasts was resistant. Following further cultivation *in vitro*, EbR activity was re-expressed and this could be

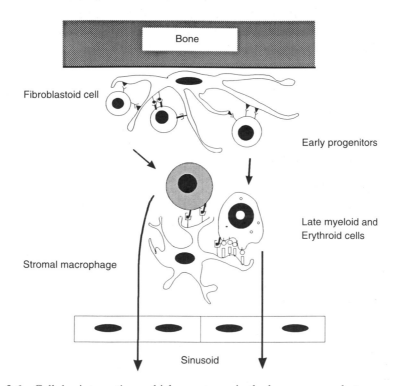

Fig. 3.6   Cellular interactions which may occur in the bone marrow between early haematopoietic progenitors and fibroblastoid stromal cells and then between late-stage progenitors and resident stromal macrophages. Interactions between fibroblastoid stromal cells and early progenitors may be mediated by various receptors and ligands including CD44, lectin-like receptors, proteoglycans, M-CSF and its receptor, and SCF and its receptor. Macrophages interact with late-stage erythroid and myeloid cells, adhesion being mediated by the erythroblast receptor (EbR) in both cases. Sialoadhesin is selectively concentrated at contact points of macrophages with myeloid cells where it mediates specialized cellular interactions. Close-range cellular interactions are essential for maintenance of steady state haematopoiesis.

inhibited in the presence of cycloheximide, thereby showing that the receptor is synthesized by macrophages. The biochemical nature of EbR is currently unknown but inhibition experiments with anti-fibronectin receptor antibodies and RGD-containing peptides showed that EbR is unlikely to be a fibronectin receptor (78).

Subsequent studies with fetal liver macrophages using adult bone marrow cells as a cellular ligand have shown similar divalent cation-dependent binding characteristics. Bone marrow cells, which had been separated into fractions differing in density, bound to stripped macrophages at similar levels, suggesting that the EbR ligand is expressed equally on the majority of adult haematopoietic cells, including erythroid, myeloid, and B-lymphoid lineages (PRC, unpublished observations). In contrast, circulating erythrocytes were weakly bound by EbR indicating that the ligand is lost during maturation of erythroblasts to reticulocytes (78).

When fetal erythroblasts or adult bone marrow cells were added to adult RBMM, the majority of binding was divalent cation-dependent, but low levels of binding were still seen in the complete absence of divalent cations. It is now known that this cation-independent binding of haematopoietic cells is mediated by a second, distinct receptor, called sialoadhesin. The properties and possible signifance of this receptor are discussed below.

4.3.2   Sialoadhesin

Sialoadhesin was originally discovered as a receptor expressed by RBMM, but not monocytes or peritoneal macrophages, which mediated divalent cation-independent binding of unopsonized sheep erythrocytes in the absence of phagocytosis. Although originally called SER (sheep erythrocyte receptor) it has recently been renamed 'sialoadhesin' because it is now established that the purified receptor behaves as a lectin-like cell interaction molecule which specifically recognizes sialic acid present in certain cell glycoconjugates (79a). A monoclonal antibody to sialoadhesin, SER-4, was selected by its ability to block binding of sheep erythrocytes and was found to immunoprecipitate a plasma membrane glycoprotein with an apparent molecular weight of 185 000 (70). By immunocytochemistry, expression of sialoadhesin was macrophage-restricted and present at high levels on subpopulations of these cells in lymph nodes and haematopoietic tissues, consistent with the proposed role of this receptor in cell-to-cell binding functions of macrophages.

Evidence that sialoadhesin binds *in vivo* to a specific cell-associated ligand was obtained in recent immunoelectron microscopic experiments in which it was found that the receptor was highly concentrated at the contact points between resident macrophages and myelomonocytic cells but not at contact points with erythroid cells attached to the same macrophage (Figure 3.5B) (79b). Concentration of receptors and ligands at points of cell-to-cell contact is frequently observed with cell adhesion molecules and also with molecules whose function is not necessarily related to adhesion, but rather to cellular signalling. On T-cells, for example, the accessory molecule CD4 has been shown to become concentrated along with the T-cell receptor at the contact points formed with antigen-presenting cells (80). This 'capping' is thought to be an important part of the initial process leading to T-cell activation and is due, at least in part, to the mutual co-capping of CD4 with its ligand, MHC Class II molecules, on antigen-presenting cells.

The selectivity of sialoadhesin localization at contact points with myeloid, rather than erythroid, cells is interesting because it suggests that its function as a cell interaction molecule is orientated towards late stage myelopoiesis rather than erythropoiesis. This idea is also consistent with studies on its developmental expression in haematopoietic tissues. The fact that no sialoadhesin was detectable on embryonic day 14 fetal liver macrophages by immunocytochemistry accords well with the results of the cellular-binding studies described above. Expression of sialoadhesin was first detected in fetal liver, spleen, and bone marrow between embryonic day 18 and birth, a period which corresponds to the onset of intensive myeloid development.

The selective 'capping' of sialoadhesin at the cell contact sites of adult RBMM with myeloid cells is explained most simply by postulating that, compared to erythroblasts, developing myeloid cells express on their surface a higher amount of the ligand recognized by sialoadhesin. Following cell-to-cell contact mediated by EbR, lateral diffusion of sialoadhesin within the plane of the macrophage plasma membrane would lead to a high concentration of sialoadhesin at regions of contact with myeloid cells.

Sialoadhesin has been purified in sufficient quantity to begin characterization of the nature of cellular ligands that are recognized. Using, as a model system, human erythrocytes which had been modified to contain sialic acid as either NeuAcα2$\rightarrow$3Galβ1$\rightarrow$3GalNAc or as NeuAcα2$\rightarrow$6Galβ1$\rightarrow$4GlcNAc, sialoadhesin exhibited a clear preference for the former, suggesting that on native human erythrocytes, the receptor recognized sialic acid present in O-linked oligosaccharides on glycoproteins. This conclusion was supported by the findings that: (a) human glycophorin was a potent inhibitor of haemagglutination; and (b) sialoadhesin bound specifically to glycophorins on Western blots of erythrocyte membrane proteins. Sialoadhesin was also found to bind avidly to sialic acid carried by certain gangliosides of defined structure. In rank order, sialoadhesin recognized: $G_{T1b} > G_{D1a} > G_{M3} > G_{Q1b} > G_{M2} > G_{D1b} > G_{D3}$; G_{M1} was not recognized (79*a*).

From these studies, it can be concluded that either sialoglycoproteins or glycolipids could potentially carry the carbohydrate structures which are naturally recognized by sialoadhesin on developing myeloid cells. The importance of this type of cellular recognition has been demonstrated following the recent discovery of carbohydrate ligands recognized by the LECCAM family of adhesion receptors (81,82). The three members of this family have a similar overall structure, including carbohydrate-binding domains, and all have been shown to recognize carbohydrate (82). LECAM-1 (gp90MEL), the lymphocyte homing receptor, recognizes a sialylated ligand on high endothelial cells of peripheral lymph nodes venules. ELAM-1, an inducible endothelial leucocyte adhesion molecule which is involved in site-specific binding of leucocytes to inflammatory lesions has been shown to bind specifically sialyl-Lewis$_x$ tetrasaccharide, Neu5Acα2→3Galβ1→4(Fucα1-3)GlcNAc. PADGEM (GMP140), which mediates binding of activated platelets to neutrophils and monocytes, recognizes the unsialylated Lewis$_x$ tetrasaccharide, Galβ1→4(Fucα1-3)GlcNAc (82).

Although the biological functions of sialoadhesin remain to be established, the results obtained to date support a model of selective carbohydrate-mediated interaction between resident bone marrow macrophages and developing myelomonocytic cells. Sialoglycoconjugates exhibit enormous structural diversity as a result of up to 30 modifications of sialic acid which can be linked in different positions in a variety of oligosaccharides (83). The interaction of sialoglycoconjugates expressed by developing myeloid cells with sialoadhesin expressed by stromal macrophages could provide precise positional information to the rapidly differentiating haematopoietic cells. A receptor-ligand interaction of this type could thereby influence the terminal stages of differentiation or affect egress into the blood stream. From cellular binding experiments, however, it appears unlikely that sialoadhesin functions as a high avidity cell interaction molecule. It seems more probable that adhesion *per se* is mediated by EbR and this promotes the binding of sialoadhesin with its ligand once close membrane-to-membrane contact has been established. A similar interplay between different classes of cell-interaction molecules has been shown to exist within the immune system, where the important role of cell adhesion molecules is now well established (81).

5   Macrophages and haematopoiesis in the non-steady state

5.1   Production and recruitment of monocytes in response to intracellular infection: an *in vivo* study

5.1.1   Introductory remarks

During the past two decades many aspects of the host immune response against pathogens have been elucidated from *in vitro* studies, with specific functions being assigned to discrete cell populations. However, it remains an important goal to improve our understanding of the spatial and temporal events which take place *in vivo*. The immune system is a dispersed complex of lymphoid units connected to both haematopoietic tissues and to non-lymphoid tissues where exogenous micro-organisms like bacteria or parasites exert their pathogenicity.

Amongst these micro-organisms, intracellular pathogens, such as *Listeria*, *Mycobacteria*, and *Leishmania* species, owe much of their virulence to their ability to rapidly enter and survive within mononuclear phagocytes which are resident in most tissues of the body. In a currently accepted scheme, pathogen-reactive T-cells are activated and expand in the lymphoid organs which drain the infected sites. The programme of differentiation which is initiated following specific T-cell recognition of infected cells not only controls the lymphocyte proliferation but also their ability to be mobilised from these lymphoid organs and enter infected tissues. Having entered an infected tissue, lymphocytes may initiate the development of granulomas which are complex functional units mainly composed of macrophages which have been recruited from haematopoietic tissues. The establishment of granulomas has been shown to be critical in experimental murine infections for complete clearance of *Listeria monocytogenes*, and for control of *Mycobacterium* sp., *Leishmania donovani* (84) and *Leishmania mexicana amazonensis*. The nature of T-cells involved in this host response may be varied. For example, in the liver of mice infected with *Listeria monocytogenes* the development of protective granulomas was found to depend on the transfer of CD8+ T-cells (85). In other sets of experiments using mice infected with *L. donovani* (84) it has been shown that the replication of the parasite in the liver was reduced only if both CD4+ and CD8+ T-cells enter the mantle of the developing granuloma.

Such protective responses require co-ordinated interactions between the haematopoietic system on the one hand and recruited lymphocytes and macrophages in the infected tissue on the other. As a crucial function of activated T-cells is their mobilization at the infected sites and recruitment of monocytes/macrophages, it is important to consider where and how these immigrant macrophages are transiently over-produced. Experimental infection with BCG provides one of the few examples in which the interplay between lymphocytes and macrophages has been shown to result in control over the haematopoietic system. In this case the net outcome is a transient production of activated monocytes which are required for controlling bacterial growth.

5.1.2 Murine infection initiated by bacillus Calmette–Guérin (BCG)

Following intravenous infection of mice by viable BCG (10^7 units), the bacteria enter mononuclear phagocytes in many different tissues, including the bone marrow. During an analysis of the ability of the immune response of different strains of mice to control bacterial growth in the liver, it was noticed that C57Bl/6 mice were relatively resistant between day 12–21 and this was associated with an early and transiently increased production of monocytes and a simultaneous decreased production of erythrocytes in the bone marrow (86,87). In contrast, the more susceptible C3H/He mice showed no haematopoietic changes and fewer liver granulomas were detected, despite the fact that the level of bone marrow infection was similar to that of C57Bl/6 mice. The transient anaemia observed in C57Bl/6 mice was found to be associated with a decreased population size of EPO-responsive cells and an increased concentration of EPO in the serum but the erythrocyte lifespan was normal (86). These changes may be due to the T-cell dependent release of TNFα which, when injected into mice, has been shown to induce an anaemia with similar characteristics (88), (see Section 5.2).

Upon further analysis of these two strains of mice, it was found that the early transient haematopoietic changes observed in C57Bl/6 bone marrow were the results of (7) the transient homing of a high number of BCG-reactive CD4 T-cells in the infected bone marrow (89), and (2) their ability, once activated, to locally release IL-3. Activation could result from interaction with BCG-infected resident bone marrow macrophages which express MHC Class II molecules (Figure 3.5). As the number of early progenitors of macrophages remained unchanged, one interpretation of the results is that

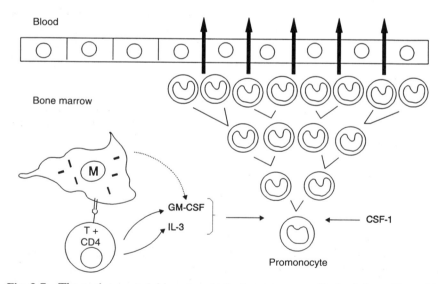

Fig. 3.7   The early events taking place in the bone marrow of mice infected i.v. with 10^7 viable BCG. BCG enter and multiply within resident bone marrow macrophages (M). BCG-reactive CD4+ T-cells, which have homed to the infected bone marrow, are activated and release IL-3 and GM-CSF. Both growth factors are able to synergize with CSF-1 to enhance the proliferation of monocytes which are subsequently thought to aid in granuloma formation and host resistance in infected tissues.

IL-3 and GM-CSF selectively amplify promonocytes, either alone or in synergy with CSF-1, thus leading to a rapid expansion of the bone marrow monocyte population (Figure 3.7).

Part of this hypothesis was confirmed by demonstrating that anti-IL-3 (10 μg given at day 1 and 3 after BCG infection in C57Bl/6 mice) completely prevents the transient over-production of monocytes measured at day 4 and 5. The possible involvement of GM-CSF in monocyte production is more complex as both T-cells and infected or non-infected mononuclear phagocytes may be a source. Indeed, more anti-GM-CSF antibody (100 μg at day 1 and 3) was found to be necessary to inhibit the transient increased production of monocytes measured at days 4 and 5. Once produced, these monocytes could rapidly transit through blood, become localized in infected tissues, such as liver, and then become activated for enhanced microbicidal activity by cytokines released from activated T-cells or even infected macrophages (90).

In the context of the role of macrophages in haematopoietic control over granuloma formation, it is important to refer to two recent observations. The maintenance/turnover of granulomas in the liver of mice intravenously infected with BCG was found to be strictly dependent on local TNFα production, as injection of anti-TNFα at day 7 or 14 into BCG-infected mice interfered dramatically with the development of granulomas and subsequent mycobacterial elimination (90). It is tempting to speculate that once recruited into the liver, those monocytes which have been over-produced in the bone marrow between day 3 and 5, are not only cells highly responsive to the activating effect of cytokines, such as IFNγ, but are also capable of further local proliferation under the synergistic effect of TNFα and M-CSF. In supporting this view, it has been shown recently that peritoneal exudate macrophages (a population enriched in recruited macrophages) may be stimulated *in vitro*, by both TNFα and CSF-1 to undergo further proliferation and differentiation towards giant cell formation (36,38).

5.2 Does the anaemia of chronic disease result from systemic TNFα release?

The anaemia of chronic inflammatory disease is often characterized by a slight reduction in the lifespan of red blood cells, disturbed iron metabolism, and reduced red blood cell production (91). What might be the role of macrophage-derived products in this disorder? In a recent report, administration for seven days of sub-lethal quantities of human TNFα to rats led to a progressive decline in the number of circulating erythrocytes (91). When compared to the similar chronic administration of IL-1α, or salmonella LPS, it appears that only TNFα and LPS produce anaemia by: (1) decreasing erythropoiesis; (2) reducing the lifespan of erythrocytes; and (3) lowering the incorporation of plasma iron into newly synthesized erythrocytes (92).

Thus, it was concluded that the LPS-induced anaemia is primarily mediated through TNFα and not IL-1 release, as IL-1α administration did not lead to a net reduction in red blood cell mass.

As discussed earlier (Section 3), TNFα is thought to be primarily a product of activated macrophages. In chronic infections, such as malaria or visceral leishmaniasis, the mononuclear phagocyte system is greatly expanded (93) and continuously exposed to activation signals, produced either from the parasites themselves or from activated T-cells. This may result in the chronic, long-term production of TNFα, thereby contributing to the anaemia associated with these diseases. Experimental support for this possibility has been demonstrated in a mouse model of malaria with *Plasmodium berghei* in which administration of anti-TNFα antibodies was able to partially prevent the anaemia (94).

6   Summary

Mononuclear phagocytes are versatile, heterogeneous cells which potentially have the capacity to exert major controls over the haematopoietic system. Under non-steady state conditions macrophages within or outside of the haematopoietic system are an important potential source of cytokines which may exert both short- and long-term changes on haematopoietic cell self-renewal, growth, and differentiation. Under steady state conditions their close proximity to developing haematopoietic cells within the haematopoietic microenvironment provides an ideal system to control cell growth, differentiation, and movement. The precise physiological role of the resident bone marrow macrophage in the control of haematopoiesis remains an enigma, but analysis of their secretory capacity and characterization of the specific receptors and ligands which mediate specialized cellular interactions between this cell type and haematopoetic cells may ultimately provide insights into their functions in steady state haematopoiesis.

References

1 Bessis, M. and Breton-Gorius, J. (1962). Iron metabolism in the bone marrow as seen by electron microscopy: a critical review. *Blood*, **19**, 635–63.

2 Metcalf, D. (1984). *The hemopoietic colony stimulating factors.* Elsevier – North Holland.

3 Steward, W.P., Scarffe, J.H., Dexter, T.M., and Testa, N.G. (1990). Clinical application of haematopoietic growth factors. In *Colony stimulating factors. Molecular and cellular biology* (ed. T.M. Dexter, J.M. Garland, and N.G. Testa). Marcel Dekker, New York and Basel.

4 Allen, T.D., Dexter, T.M., and Simmons, P.J. (1990). Marrow biology and stem cells. In *Colony stimulating factors. Molecular and cellular biology* (ed. T.M. Dexter, J.M. Garland and N.G. Testa). Marcel Dekker, New York and Basel.

5 Dexter, T.M., *et al.* (1990). Stromal cells in haemopoiesis. *Molecular Control of Haemopoiesis*, Ciba Foundation Symposium, No. 148, pp. 76–86. Wiley, London.

6 Gordon, S. (1986). Biology of the macrophage. *J. Cell Sci.*, **4** (Suppl.), 267–86.

7 Chen, B.D.M., Mueller, M., and Olencki T. (1988). Interleukin 3 (IL-3) stimulates the clonal growth of pulmonary alveolar macrophages of the mouse: role if IL-3 in the regulation of macrophage production outside the bone marrow. *Blood*, **72**, 685–90.

8 Lepay, D.A., Nathan, C.F., Steinman, R.M., Murray, H.W., and Cohn, Z.A. (1985). Murine Kupffer cells: mononuclear phagocytes deficient in the generation of reactive oxygen intermediates. *J. Exp. Med.*, **161**, 1079–86.

9 Van Furth, R. (1989). Origin and turnover of monocytes and macrophages. *Curr. Top. Pathol.*, **79**, 125–50.

10 Florey, H.W. and Gowans, J.L. (1962). In *General pathology* (3rd edn). (ed. H. Florey). Lloyd-Luke, London.

11 Westen, H. and Bainton, D.F. (1979). Association of alkaline-phosphatase-positive reticulum cells in bone marrow with granulocytic precursors. *J. Exp. Med.*, **150**, 919–37.

12 Crocker, P.R. and Gordon, S. (1985). Isolation and characterization of resident stromal macrophages and hematopoietic cell clusters from mouse bone marrow. *J. Exp. Med.*, **162**, 993–1014.

13 Metcalf, D. (1989). The molecular control of cell division, differentiation commitment and maturation in haemopoietic cells. *Nature*, **339**, 27–30.

14 *Molecular control of haemopoiesis* (1990). Ciba Foundation Symposium, No. 148. John Wiley, London.

15 Arai, K.-I., Lee, F., Miyajima, A., Miyatake, S., Arai, N., and Yokota, T. (1990). Cytokines: coordinators of immune and inflammatory responses. *Ann. Rev. Biochem.*, **59**, 783–836.
16 Kelso, A. and Metcalf, D. (1990). T lymphocyte-derived colony stimulating factors. *Adv. Immunol.*, **48**, 69–105.
17 Nicola, N.A. (1989). Hemopoietic cell growth factors and their receptors. *Ann. Rev. Biochem.*, **58**, 45–77.
18 Hoover, D.L. and Meltzer, M.S. (1989). Lymphokines as monocyte activators. In *Human Monocytes* (ed. M. Zembala and G.L. Asherson). Academic Press, London.
19 Rennick, D.M., Thompsonsnipes, L., Coffman, R.L., Seymour, B.W.P., Jackson, J.D., and Hudak, S. (1990). *In vivo* administration of antibody to interleukin-5 inhibits increased generation of eosinophils and their progenitors in bone marrow of parasitized mice. *Blood*, **76**, 312–16.
20 Nathan, C.F. (1987). Secretory products of macrophages. *J. Clin. Invest.*, **79**, 319–26.
21 Mizel, S.B. (1989). The interleukins. *FASEB J.*, **3**, 2379–88.
22 Le, P.T., Vollger, L.W., Haynes, B.F., and Singer, K.H. (1990). Ligand binding to the LFA-3 cell adhesion molecule induces IL-1 production by human thymic epithelial cells. *J. Immunol.*, **144**, 4541–47.
23 Moore, M.A.S., Muench, M.O., Warren, D.J., and Laver, J. (1990). Cytokine networks involved in the regulation of haemopoietic stem cell proliferation and differentiation. *Molecular control of haemopoiesis*. Ciba Foundation Symposium, No. 148, pp. 43–58. Wiley, London.
24 Bot, F.J., Schipper, P., Broeders, L., Delwel, R., Kaushansky, K., and Lowenburg, B. (1990). Interleukin-1-alpha also induces granulocyte-macrophage colony-stimulating factor in immature normal bone marrow cells. *Blood*, **76**, 307–11.
25 Schaafsma, M.R., *et al.*, (1989). Interleukin-6 is not involved in the interleukin-1 induced production of colony stimulating factors by human bone marrow stromal cells and fibroblasts. *Blood*, **74**, 2619–23.
26 Bagby, G.C. Jr. (1989). Interleukin-1 and hematopoiesis. *Blood Rev.*, **3**, 152–61.
27 Pelus, L.M. (1989). Blockage of prostaglandin biosynthesis in intact mice dramatically augments the expression of committed myeloid progenitor cells (colony-forming units-granulocyte, macrophage) after acute administration of recombinant human IL-1 alpha. *J. Immunol.*, **143**, 4171–9.
28 Furmanski, P. and Johnson, C.S. (1990). Macrophage control of normal and leukemic erythropoiesis—identification of the macrophage-derived erythroid suppressing activity as interleukin-1 and the mediator of its *in vivo* action as tumor necrosis factor. *Blood*, **75**, 2328–34.

29 Dorshkind, K. (1990). Regulation of hemopoiesis by bone marrow stromal cells and their products. *Ann. Rev. Immunol.*, **8**, 111–37.

30 Thorens, M.B., Mermod, J.-J., and Vassalli, P. (1987). Phagocytosis and inflammatory stimuli induce GM-CSF mRNA in macrophages through post-transcript regulation. *Cell*, **48**, 671–9.

31 Beuscher, H.U., Fallon, R.J., and Colten, H.R. (1987). Macrophage membrane interleukin 1 regulates the expression of acute phase proteins in human hepatoma Hep 3B cells. *J. Immunol.*, **139**, 1896–1901.

32 Rubartelli, A. Cozzolino, F., Talio, M., and Sitia, R. (1990). A novel secretory pathway for interleukin-1B, a protein lacking a signal sequence. *Embo J.*, **9**, 1503–10.

33 Johnson, C.S., Keckler, D.J., Topper, M.I., Braunschweiger, P.G., and Furmanski, P. (1989). *In vivo* hematopoietic effects of recombinant interleukin-1 alpha in mice: stimulation of granulocytic, monocytic, megakaryocytic, and early erythroid progenitors, suppression of late-stage erythropoiesis, and reversal of erythroid suppression with erythropoietin. *Blood*, **73**, 678–83.

34 Sherry, B. and Cerami, A. (1988). Cathectin/tumor necrosis factor exerts endocrine, paracrine, and autocrine control inflammatory responses. *J. Cell Biol.*, **107**, 1269–77.

35 Kaushansky, K., Broudy, V.C., Harlan, J.M., and Adamson, J.W. (1988). Tumor necrosis factor-alpha and tumor necrosis factor-beta (lymphotoxin) stimulate the production of granulocyte-macrophage colony-stimulating factor, macrophage colony-stimulating factor, and IL-1 *in vivo*. *J. Immunol.*, **141**, 3410–15.

36 Chen, B.D.M. and Mueller, M. (1990). Recombinant tumor necrosis factor enhances the proliferative responsiveness of murine peripheral macrophages to colony stimulating factor but inhibits their proliferative responsiveness to granulocyte-macrophage colony stimulating factor. *Blood*, **75**, 1627–32.

37 Caux, C., Saeland, S., Favre, C., Duvert, V., Mannoni, P., and Banchereau, J. (1990). Tumor necrosis factor-alpha strongly potentiates interleukin-3 and granulocyte-macrophage colony-stimulating factor-induced proliferation of human CD34+ hematopoietic progenitor cells. *Blood*, **75**, 2292–8.

38 Branch, D.R., Turner, A.R., and Guilbert, L.J. (1989). Synergistic stimulation of macrophage proliferation by the monokines tumor necrosis factor-alpha and colony-stimulating factor 1. *Blood*, **73**, 307–11.

39 Wolpe, S.D. and Cerami, A. (1989). Macrophage inflammatory proteins 1 and 2: members of a novel superfamily of cytokines. *FASEB J.*, **3**, 2565–73.

40 Broxmeyer, H.E. *et al.*, (1990). Enhancing and suppressing effects of

recombinant murine macrophage inflammatory proteins on colony formation *in vitro* by bone marrow myeloid progenitor cells. *Blood*, **76**, 1110–16.

41 Graham, G.J., *et al.*, (1990). Identification and characterization of an inhibitor of haemopoietic stem cell proliferation. *Nature*, **344**, 442–4.

42 Wright, E.G., Ali, A.M., Riches, A.C., and Lord, B.I. (1982). Stimulation of hemopoietic stem cell proliferation: characteristics of the stimulator producing cells. *Leuk. Res.*, **6**, 531–9.

43 Massagué, J. (1990). The transforming growth factor-β family. *Ann. Rev. Cell Biol.*, **6**, 597–641.

44 Lang, R.A., *et al.* (1987). Transgenic mice expressing a hemopoietic growth factor gene (GM-CSF) develop accumulations of macrophages, blindness, and a fatal syndrome of tissue damage. *Cell*, **51**, 675–86.

45 Dent, L.A., Strath, M., Mellor, A.L., and Sanderson, C.J. (1990). Eosinophilia in transgenic mice expressing interleukin 5. *J. Exp. Med.*, **172**, 1425–32.

46 Russell, E.S. (1979). Hereditary anemias of the mouse: A review for geneticists. *Adv. Gen.*, **20**, 357–9.

47 Witte, O.N. (1990). Steel locus defines new multipotent growth factor. *Cell*, **63**, 5–6.

48 Wiktor-Jedrzejczak, W., Ahmed, A., Szczylik, C., and Skelly, R.R. (1982). Hematological characterization of congenital osteopetrosis in op/op mouse. *J. Exp. Med.*, **156**, 1516–27.

49 Udagawa, N., *et al.* (1990). Origin of osteoclasts—Mature monocytes and macrophages are capable of differentiating into osteoclasts under a suitable microenvironment prepared by bone marrow-derived stromal cells. *Proc. Natl Acad. Sci. U.S.A.*, **87**, 7260–4.

50 Yoshida, H., *et al.* (1990). The murine mutation osteopetrosis is in the coding region of the macrophage colony stimulating factor gene. *Nature*, **345**, 442–4.

51 Wiktor-Jedrzejczak, W., *et al.* (1990). Total absence of colony-stimulating factor 1 in the macrophage-deficient osteopetrotic (Op Op) Mouse. *Proc. Natl Acad. Sci. U.S.A.*, **87**, 4828–32.

52 Felix, R., Cecchini, M.G., Hofstetter, W., Elford, P.R., Stutzer, A., and Fleisch, H. (1990). Impairment of macrophage colony-stimulating factor production and lack of resident bone marrow macrophages in the osteopetrotic op op mouse. *J. Bone Min. Res.*, **5**, 781–9.

53 Sherr, C.J., Kato, J.Y., Borzillo, G., Downing, J.R., and Roussel, M.F. (1990). Signal-response coupling mediated by the transduced colony-stimulating factor-1 receptor and its oncogenic *fms*-variants in naive cells. *Molecular Control of Haemopoiesis*, Ciba Foundation Symposium, No. 148, pp. 96–104. Wiley, London.

54 Pawson, T. and Bernstein, A. (1990). Receptor tyrosine kinases:

genetic evidence for their role in Drosophila and mouse development. *Trends in Genetics*, **6**, 350–6.

55 Miyake, K.M., K.L., Hayashi, S-L, Ono, S., Hamaoka, T., and Kincade, P.W. (1990). Monoclonal antibodies to Pgp-1/CD44 block lympho-hemopoiesis in long-term bone marrow cultures. *J. Exp. Med.*, **171**, 477–88.

56 Tavassoli, M. and Hardy, C. (1990). Molecular basis of homing of intravenously transplanted stem cells to the marrow. *Blood*, **76**, 1059–70.

57 Kawasaki, E.S. and Ladner, M.B. (1990). Molecular biology of macrophage colony-stimulating factor. In *Colony-stimulating factors*, molecular and cellular biology (ed. T.M. Dexter, J.M. Garland and N.G. Testa). Marcel Dekker, New York and Basel.

58 Stein, J., Borzillo, G.V., and Rettenmier, C.W. (1990). Direct stimulation of cells expressing receptors for macrophage colony-stimulating factor (CSF-1) by a plasma membrane-bound precursor of human CSF-1. *Blood*, **76**, 1308–14.

59 Rathjen, P.D., Toth, S., Willis, A., Heath, J.K., and Smith, A.G. (1990). Differentiation inhibiting activity is produced in matrix-associated and diffusible forms that are generated by alternate promoter usage. Cell, 62, 1105–14.

60 Gordon, M.Y., Riley, G.P., Watt, S.M., and Greaves, M.F. (1987). Compartmentalization of a haematopoietic growth factor (GM-CSF) by glycosaminoglycans in the bone marrow microenvironment. *Nature*, **326**, 403–5.

61 Roberts, R., Gallagher, J., Spooncer, E., Allen, T.D., Bloomfield, F., and Dexter, T.M. (1988). Heparan sulphate bound growth factors: a mechanism for stromal cell mediated haemopoiesis. *Nature*, **332**, 376–8.

62 Long, M. W. and Dixit, V.M. (1990). Thrombospondin functions as a cytoadhesion molecule for human hematopoietic progenitor cells. *Blood*, **75**, 2311–18.

63 Ben-Ishay, Z. and Yoffey, J.M. (1971). Reticular cells of erythroid islands of rat bone marrow in hypoxia and rebound. *J. Reticuloendothel. Soc.*, **10**, 482–94.

64 Vogt, C.P.S. and Rich, I.N. (1989). A role for the macrophage in normal hemopoiesis. III. *In vitro* and *in vivo* erythropoietin gene expression in macrophages detected by *in situ* hybridization. *Exp. Hematol.*, **17**, 391–7.

65 Ratcliffe, P.J., Jones, R.W., Phillips, R.E., Nicholls, L.G., and Bell, J.L. (1990). Oxygen-dependent modulation of erythropoietin mRNA levels in isolated rat kidneys studied by RNAse protection. *J. Exp. Med.*, **172**, 657–60.

66 Koury, S.T., Bondurant, M.C., and Koury, M.J. (1988). Localization

of erythropoietin synthesizing cells in murine kidneys by *in situ* hybridization. *Blood*, **71**, 524–7.

67 Hume, D.A. and Gordon, S. (1983). Mononuclear phagocyte system of the mouse defined by immunohistochemical localisation of antigen F4/80. Identification of resident macrophages in renal medullary and cortical interstitium and the juxta-glomerular complex. *J. Exp. Med.*, **157**, 1704–9.

68 Adamson, J.W. and Eschbach, J.W. (1990). The use of recombinant human erythropoietin in humans. In *Molecular control of haemopoiesis*. Ciba Foundation Symposium, No. 148, pp. 186–200. John Wiley, London.

69 Hayakawa, T., Yamashita, K., Kishi, J., and Harigaya, K. (1990). Tissue inhibitor of metalloproteinases from human bone marrow stromal cell line km 102 has erythroid-potentiating activity, suggesting its possibly bifunctional role in the hematopoietic microenvironment. *FEBS Lett.*, **268**, 125–8.

70 Crocker, P.R. and Gordon, S. (1989). Mouse macrophage hemagglutinin (sheep erythrocyte receptor) with specificity for sialylated glycoconjugates characterized by a monoclonal antibody. *J. Exp. Med.*, **169**, 1333–46.

71 Hoffman, R. (1989). Regulation of megakaryocytopoiesis. *Blood*, **74**, 1196–1212.

72 Koike, K. *et al.* (1990). Interleukin-6 enhances murine megakaryocytopoiesis in serum-free culture. *Blood*, **75**, 2286–91.

73 Asano, S., *et al.* (1990). *In vivo* effects of recombinant human interleukin-6 in primates: stimulated production of platelets. *Blood*, **75**, 1602–5.

74 Jacobsen, K. and Osmond, D.G. (1990). Microenvironmental organization and stromal cell associations of B lymphocyte precursor cells in mouse bone marrow. *Eur. J. Immunol.*, **20**, 2395–2404.

75 Kincade, P.W., Lee, G., Pietrangeli, C.E., Hayashi, S-I. and Gimble, J.M. (1989). Cells and molecules that regulate B lymphopoiesis in bone marrow. *Ann. Rev. Immunol.*, **7**, 111–43.

76 Verfaillie, C., Blakolmer, K., and McGlave, P. (1990). Purified primitive human hematopoietic progenitor cells with long-term *in vitro* repopulating capacity adhere selectively to irradiated bone marrow stroma. *J. Exp. Med.*, **172**, 509–20.

77 Crocker, P.R., Morris, L., and Gordon, S. (1988). Novel cell surface adhesion receptors involved in interactions between stromal macrophages and haematopoietic cells. *J. Cell Sci.*, **9**, (Suppl.) 185–206.

78 Morris, L. Crocker, P.R., and Gordon, S. (1988). Murine fetal liver macrophages bind developing erythroblasts by a divalent cation-dependent hemagglutinin. *J. Cell Biol.*, **106**, 649–56.

79*a* Crocker, P.R., et al. (1991). Purification and properties of Sialoadhesin, a sialic acid-binding receptor of murine tissue macrophages. *EMBO*, **10**, 1661–9.

79*b* Crocker, P.R., Werb, Z., Gordon, S., and Bainton, D.F. (1990). Utrastructural localization of a macrophage-restricted sialic acid binding hemagglutinin, SER, in macrophage-hematopoietic cell clusters. *Blood*, **76**, 1131–8.

80 Kupfer, A. and Singer, S.J. (1989). Cell biology of cytotoxic and helper T cell functions. Immunofluorescence microscopic studies of single cells and cell couples. *Ann. Rev. Immunol.*, **7**, 309–37.

81 Springer, T.A. (1990). The sensation and regulation of interactions with the extracellular environment: The cell biology of lymphocyte adhesion receptors. *Ann. Rev. Cell Biol.*, **6**, 359–402.

82 Brandley, B.K., Swiedler, S.J., and Robbins, P.W. (1990). Carbohydrate ligands of the LEC cell adhesion molecules. *Cell*, **63**, 861–3.

83 Paulson, J.C. (1989). Glycoproteins: what are the sugar chains for? *TIBS*, **14**, 272–6.

84 McElrath, M.J., Murray, H.W., and Cohn, Z.A. (1988). The dynamics of granuloma formation in experimental visceral leishmaniasis. *J. Exp. Med.*, **167**, 1927–37.

85 Mielke, M.E.A., Ehlers, S., and Hahn, H. (1988). T cell subsets in DTH, protection and granuloma formation in primary and secondary *Listeria* infection in mice: superior role of Lyt-2+ cells in acquired immunity. *Immunol. Lett.*, **19**, 211–16.

86 Marchal, G. and Milon, G. (1981). Decreased erythropoiesis: The origin of the BCG induced anaemia in mice. *Br. J. Haematol.*, **48**, 551–60.

87 Milon, G., Gheorghiu, M., Lagranderie, M., Lebastard, M., and Marchal, G. (1984). BCG-induced anaemia in mice: No direct effect of the growth of bacilli. *Ann. Immunol. (Inst. Pasteur)*, **135C**, 195–204.

88 Johnson, C.J. Chang, M-J., and Furmanski, P. (1988). *In vivo* hematopoietic effects of tumor necrosis factor-α in normal and erythroleukemic mice: Characterization and therapeutic applications. *Blood*, **2**, 1875–83.

89 Marchal, G. and Milon, G. (1986). Control of hemopoiesis in mice by sensitized L3T4+ Lyt2-lymphocytes during infection with bacillus Calmette–Guérin. *Proc. Natl. Acad. Sci. U.S.A.*, **83**, 3977–81.

90 Kindler, V. Sappino, A.P., Grau, G.E., Piguet, P-F., and Vassalli, P. (1989). The inducing role of tumor necrosis factor in the development of bactericidal granulomas during BCG infection. *Cell*, **56**, 731–40.

91 Tracey, K.J., *et al.* (1988). Cachectin/tumor necrosis factor induces cachexia, anemia, and inflammation. *J. Exp. Med.*, **167**, 1211–27.

92 Moldawer, L.L., *et al.* (1989). Cachectin/tumor necrosis factor-α alters

red blood kinetics and induces anemia *in vivo*. *FASEB J.*, **3**, 1637–43.

93 Lee, S. Crocker, P.R., and Gordon, S. (1986). Macrophage plasma membrane and secretory properties in murine malaria. *J. Exp. Med.*, **163**, 54–74.

94 Miller, K.L., Silverman, P.H., Kullgren, B., and Mahlmann, L.J. (1989). Tumor necrosis factor alpha and the anemia associated with murine malaria. *Infect. Immun.*, **57**, 1542–46.

95 Goldwasser, E., Beru, N., and Smith, D. (1990). Erythropoietin in *Colony stimulating factors. Molecular and cellular biology* (ed. T.M. Dexter, J.M. Garland, and N.G. Testa). Marcel Dekker, New York and Basel.

96 Donahue, R.E., Yang, Y-C., and Clark, S.C. (1990). Human P40 T-cell growth factor (interleukin-9) supports erythroid colony formation. *Blood.*, **75**, 2271–5.

97 Paul, S.R., *et al.* (1990). Molecular cloning of a cDNA encoding interleukin-11, a stromal cell-derived lymphopoietic and hematopoietic cytokine. *Proc. Natl. Acad. Sci. U.S.A.*, **87**, 7512–16.

98 Matsui, Y., Zsebo, K.M., and Hogan, B.L.M. (1990). Embryonic expression of a haematopoietic growth factor encoded by the Sl Locus and the ligand for c-Kit. *Nature*, **347**, 667–9.

99 Lee, S-H., *et al.* (1988). Isolation and immunocytochemical characterisation of human bone marrow stromal macrophages in hemopoietic clusters. *J. Exp. Med.*, **168**, 1193–98.

100 Leary, A.G., Wong, G.G., Clark, S.C., Smith, A.G., and Ogawa, M. (1990). Leukemia inhibitory factor differentiation-inhibiting activity human interleukin for DA cells augments proliferation of human hematopoietic stem cells. *Blood*, **75**, 1960–4.

4 Macrophages in viral infections

H.E. GENDELMAN AND P.S. MORAHAN

1 Introduction

Mononuclear phagocytes (blood monocytes, tissue macrophages, and dendritic cells) comprise the principal cellular elements in the clearance and inactivation of most viral pathogens. Paradoxically, these same cells also represent a major target cell and infectious reservoir for many viruses, notably lentiviruses. The ultimate outcome of virus–macrophage interactions is the net result of a complex series of reactions that rely upon changes in macrophage differentiation in both the steady state and during immune responses. Such changes dramatically affect the ability of macrophages to act as scavenger cell, immune effector cell, or susceptible target cell for virus replication. This chapter will discuss the various outcomes that result from interactions between the virus and the macrophage. Antiviral mechanisms (host resistance) and virus-target cell infections (pathogen virulence) will be explored in their relationships to acute and persistent infection and disease.

The cardinal feature of mononuclear phagocytes is their vigorous phagocytic ability. Thus, mononuclear phagocytes have the ability to eliminate virus from the circulation following a blood-borne infection. Their scavenger function constitutes a first line of defence that reduces the virus load until specific immune responses become available (1–11). A second line of defence comes from the ability of macrophages to restrict virus infection or replication in other cells by one of a number of antimicrobial effector cell mechanisms (4,11). For example, virus-induced antibodies result in neutralization and lysis of virus-infected target cells which is mediated, in part, by the macrophage acting as a non-specific effector cell for antibody-dependent cellular cytotoxicity (ADCC). Monocytes and macrophages can also initiate a series of immune reactions through the cytokine network that greatly increase the antiviral defence capacity of the host. Alternatively, macrophages themselves may be activated for enhanced antiviral activity by cytokines produced by virus-specific T-cells. A third line of defence comes from the capacity of monocytes, tissue macrophages, and dendritic cells to act as antigen-presenting cells (APCS) inducing specific antiviral immune responses (8–10). These APCS take up, process, and deliver viral antigens to T-cells in regional lymph nodes for initiation of specific immune responses that subsequently clear the infection.

The preceding antiviral defence mechanisms may not be sufficient to prevent a primary infection, leading to persistent virus replication and disease (12–19). In these cases, the macrophage may act as a permissive target cell for viral latency and persistence.

2   Macrophages as scavenger cells in viral infections

Initial virus–macrophage interactions are dependent upon specific and non-specific viral receptors on the macrophage plasma membrane. After binding and uptake, the ability of the virus to complete a full replication cycle depends both upon the differentiation and activation status of the macrophage and upon the requirements of the particular infecting viral strain (3,16,18,19). These two factors determine whether viral infection is abortive (no infection), latent (viral DNA or RNA genome present without evidence of replicative viral gene expression), restricted/persistent (viral genome present but viral life cycle is incomplete or very inefficient), permissive (viral life cycle goes to completion with efficient production of progeny virions), or enhanced (increased levels of virus infection, for example, mediated by antibody or complement-facilitated uptake of virions). Macrophage differentiation and activation can dramatically alter the outcome of infection by changing viral receptors and/or transcriptional or other factors that mediate efficient replication. Viral genetic factors, independent of the state of cell differentiation, can determine whether an infection is abortive or permissive. Most often, cellular and viral factors act in tandem to influence viral infection. An overview of the interactions between the virus and the macrophage is illustrated in Table 4.1.

As a first line of defence, macrophages occupy a pre-eminent position in controlling the susceptibility of animals to viral infection. The scavenger capacity allows mononuclear phagocytes to function as a principal cell responsible for the quantitative removal of viral pathogens from the infected host. Macrophages closely monitor body compartments and thereby control the entry of viruses to target organs such as the liver, spleen, and lymphatics (4,8–10). The macrophage is a vital sentry cell able to resist infection by many viruses. They adsorb, phagocytize, and destroy numerous potential pathogens and thus significantly reduce any viral inoculum delivered to the host. The macrophage ingests then inactivates virus through digestion, mediated by scores of hydrolytic cellular enzymes contained within their phagolysosomes (1,8). Uptake of virus into macrophages can occur in various ways, including phagocytosis, fusion, and viropexis. Phagocytosis occurs through both specific and non-specific viral receptors, such as those for the Fc portion of immunoglobulin (Ig), complement split products, or glycosylated proteins. Indeed, the entry of African swine fever virus into swine macrophages, the natural host cell for this virus, is mediated by saturable binding sites on the plasma membrane, whereas entry of this virus into non-permissive rabbit macrophages is mediated by non-saturable binding sites (20). The lack of specific receptors in the rabbit macrophages may be related to the absence of productive infection.

Table 4.1 Representative classes of viruses and their major mechanisms of interaction with monocytes and macrophages

Class	Nucleic acid	Virus	Virus–macrophage interactions
Retroviridae Oncovirinae	ssRNA, enveloped proviral DNA in replication cycle	Avian myoblastosis virus (AMV), avian myelocytomatosis virus (MC29), murine spleen focus-forming virus (AF-1)	Macrophage transformation correlates with induction of tumours *in vivo*. Replication in bone marrow progenitor cells
Lentivirinae	ssRNA, enveloped proviral DNA in replication cycle	Human immunodeficiency virus (HIV)	Latent, restricted, and permissive. Infects brain and spinal cord macrophages and microglia, pulmonary macrophages, follicular dendritic cells, blood monocytes, and Langerhans cells (infrequently)
	ssRNA, enveloped proviral DNA in replication cycle	Simian immunodeficiency virus (SIV)	Semi-permissive and permissive. Tropism for macrophages in brain, lung, gut, and lymph nodes. Similar macrophage–virus interactions as described with HIV
	ssRNA, enveloped proviral DNA in replication cycle	Visna-maedi virus	Latent, semi-permissive and permissive. Near 'exclusive' tropism for cells of monocyte lineage. Bone marrow promonocytes, blood monocytes and macrophages in brain, lung, and lymph node

Table 4.1 (*continued*)

Class	Nucleic acid	Virus	Virus–macrophage interactions
	ssRNA, enveloped proviral DNA in replication cycle	Caprine-arthritis encephalitis virus (CAEV)	Latent, semi-permissive and permissive near 'exclusive' tropism for cells of monocyte lineage, including blood monocytes, brain, and synovial macrophages
	ssRNA, enveloped proviral DNA in replication cycle	Feline immunodeficiency virus (FIV)	Restricted infection in peritoneal macrophages and blood monocytes
Togaviridae Pestivirus	ssRNA, enveloped positive-sense genome	Lactic dehydrogenase virus (LDV)	Replication restricted to Class II (Ia$^+$) macrophages, leading to increased incidence of autoimmunity. Association between expression of endogenous retroviruses and cytocidal replication of LDV
Alphavirus/ Flavivirus	ssRNA, enveloped positive-sense genome	Murray Valley encephalitis virus, dengue virus, West Nile virus, yellow fever virus	Associated with antibody-dependent enhancement of viral infection. Enhancement dependency on macrophages bearing Fc receptors.
Rubivirus	ssRNA, enveloped positive-sense genome	Rubella virus	Replication in monocytes and macrophages, level of virus replication dependent on cellular differentiation/activation as reported with herpes viruses

Family	Genome	Virus	Notes
Coronaviridae	ssRNA, enveloped positive-sense genome	Respiratory coronavirus (229E)	Human monocytes and macrophages, productive infection
	ssRNA, enveloped positive-sense genome	Feline infectious peritonitis virus	Monocytes are predominant if not exclusive target cells for viral infection. Antibody-dependent enhancement of infection reported
	ssRNA, enveloped positive-sense genome	Transmissible gastroenteritis coronavirus (TGEV)	Productive replication in swine alveolar macrophages
Orthomyxoviridae	ssRNA, enveloped negative-sense genome	Influenza A	Targets monocytes and T-cells, active replication depends on interactions of both cell types. Macrophage infection linked to TNFα production. Restriction at level of viral protein synthesis.
Arenaviridae	ssRNA, enveloped negative-sense genome	Junin, Lassa, Machupo, Rift Valley Fever	Permissive replication in cultured mouse peritoneal macrophages, limited cytopathicity
	ssRNA, enveloped negative-sense genome	Lymphocytic chorio-meningitis virus (LCV)	Permissive replication in cultured mouse peritoneal and splenic macrophages, (resident macrophages provide a barrier to initial viral dissemination)

Table 4.1 (*continued*)

Class	Nucleic acid	Virus	Virus–macrophage interactions
Hepadnaviridae	dsDNA, non-enveloped	Hepatitis B virus	Targets monocytes, probable reservoir during subclinical infections, related to secondary hematologic complications
Papovaviridae	dsDNA, non-enveloped	Simian virus 40	Macrophage transformation
Herpesviridae	dsDNA, enveloped	Herpes simplex virus (HSV)	Restricted replication in promonocytes, monocytes, and tissue macrophages at the level of DNA polymerase immediate early gene expression. Viral replication dependent on animal strain, age, and stage of cellular differentiation
	dsDNA, enveloped	Cytomegalovirus (CMV)	Restricted replication at level of early gene expression. In monocytes and tissue macrophages, association of virulence of murine cytomegalovirus with macrophage susceptability to infection
Iridoviridae	dsDNA, enveloped	African swine fever virus	Primary productive replication in monocytes and macrophages. Intracellular viral particles predominate late after infection. Restriction at level of DNA polymerase
Poxviridae	dsDNA, enveloped	Ectromelia virus	Permissive replication in lymph node and resident peritoneal macrophages

2.1 Macrophage-mediated clearance of virus from the circulation

Clearance abilities of mononuclear phagocytes for removal of viruses from the circulation are determined by particle size and number, and macrophage susceptibility to viral infection. The latter is influenced by genetic factors, age, and the immune status of the host (21–28). In the earliest studies, viral clearance rates from experimentally inoculated animals were assessed using the liver as the primary clearance organ. In these studies, non-pathogenic viruses injected intravenously were cleared rapidly (less than 30 minutes) by liver macrophages and then destroyed (21,22). Viral clearance rates were dependent upon particle size. Larger viruses, vaccinia and ectromelia, were cleared less rapidly than smaller viruses, vesicular stomatitis virus (VSV), Rift Valley fever (RVF) virus, influenza or Semliki Forest virus (21–25).

The ability of macrophages to clear virus from the systemic circulation is also dependent on the administered load (23). Under certain conditions (large numbers of viral particles) virions can bypass liver macrophages and directly reach hepatic cells without a preliminary cycle of inactivation in macrophages. Such infections often lead to significant morbidity with concomitant tissue pathology, and ultimately the death of the host. For example, when an inoculum of influenza exceeding the infectious dose$_{50}$ (ID_{50}) is injected into mice, infected hepatic cells are demonstrated in less than 7 hours (23). Here, the liver macrophage only partially clears the viral inoculum and a substantial viral dose reaches the primary hepatocyte targets. This leads to rapid liver damage and death. A second example is RVF virus (24). With viral inocula exceeding the ID_{50}, RVF virus is only partially cleared from blood and the residual virus induces significant hepatic infection and liver pathology.

The susceptibility of liver macrophages to viral infection can also determine liver clearance rates. Indeed, the virus may enter and replicate within the liver macrophage. This may lead to infection of adjacent hepatic cells or dissemination of virus to other cells in the body as reported in equine infectious anemia (EIA), canine distemper, yellow fever, and ectromelia viral infections (12). An interesting example is frog virus 3, whose structural proteins are toxic to liver macrophages (29–31). Infection with frog virus 3 can decrease resistance of mice to vaccinia virus, a virus that normally does not cause infection of hepatocytes (29), and can abrogate the genetic resistance of mice to mouse hepatitis virus infections (31).

Most studies on macrophage-mediated clearance of virus were performed over 20 years ago. Thus, the exact mechanisms of clearance and subsequent destruction of virus have not been elucidated at the molecular level. This role of the macrophage merits re-investigation. Such studies could establish which macrophages are the most important in clearance, the relative roles of the macrophage in comparison with other cells (polymorphonuclear leucocytes, natural killer cells), which intracellular mechanisms are responsible for viral destruction, and whether viral genomes remain latent in certain macrophage subsets.

2.2   Genetic determinants

Infection or inactivation of virus in scavenger mononuclear phagocytes involves host gentic determinants. The importance of genetic determinants to scavenger function and cell–virus susceptibility to infection was first demonstrated by Bang and Warwick (25). These investigators showed that host genetic factors determined the susceptibility of animals to disease, and that this was reflected in the susceptibility of macrophages to infection *in vitro*. In genetically susceptible mice, murine hepatitis viral infections of liver, lung, and heart macrophages resulted in cytopathic changes and tissue degeneration. In contrast, virus-infected macrophages from resistant mice did not develop any cytopathic changes. Similar results were reported for West Nile viral infections (26). Here again, little or no virus was produced by macrophages from resistant strains of mice, whereas large levels of virus (with concomitant tissue damage) were produced in tissue macrophages of genetically susceptible mice.

Lentiviral infections of macrophages and subsequent tissue pathology are also related to genetic factors (27). Macrophages and microglia in the central nervous system (CNS) are major target cells for visna-maedi virus, and naturally occurring CNS disease is very common during epizootic disease of Icelandic sheep. In experimentally inoculated Icelandic sheep, visna-maedi virus is frequently identified in macrophages. Macrophage infection in Icelandic sheep is often followed by extensive inflammatory lesions in the CNS and progressive, debilitating neurological disease. In contrast, intracerebral inoculation of visna-maedi virus into British sheep results in an abortive infection of CNS macrophages and no disease (27). In the CNS of such animals, only transient localized periventricular lymphocytic inflammatory responses and small foci of demyelination later healed by scar formation are identified.

Studies such as those described above have clearly correlated genetic resistance of the animal to resistance of the macrophage to viral infection. It is difficult to directly prove that macrophages are the sole cell responsible for this genetic resistance, even though the inherited differences in susceptibility are clearly manifested in cell culture. Indeed, there may be a synergistic effect with host immune mechanisms. Impairment of host resistance can be produced *in vivo*, whereas the genetic resistance of the macrophage is still present *in vitro*. For example, when mice genetically resistant to mouse hepatitis virus type 3 are treated with anti-interferon serum; resistance *in vivo* is reduced, whereas the resistance of the macrophage *in vitro* remains intact (32). The authors concluded that interferon (IFN) is an important host defence factor, but that other factors, such as the capacity of macrophages to restrict viral replication probably underlie the genetically determined susceptibility to viral infection. Another study, using radiation chimeras between virus resistant and susceptible cells, showed that resistance was expressed in one population of hematopoietic-derived cells which is radio-resistant and has a lifespan of between 30 and 90 days (33). The authors suggested two complementary mechanisms, a resistance gene that may operate at the level of the macrophage, and other cells capable of mounting an efficient virus-specific immune response. Establishment of the precise role of the macrophage in genetically determined antiviral resistance systems awaits further study, such as transfer of purified mononuclear phagocytes (adult or stem cells) of the genetically resistant lineage into susceptible mice, or very selective depletion of certain macrophage populations in the resistant mouse.

2.3   Age-related determinants

The age of the animal plays a pivotal role in the ability of the macrophage to contain viral infection. The studies by R.T. Johnson (28) demonstrated that changes in susceptibility of macrophages to viral infection were related to age. Age predicted the ability of the macrophages to be infected by virus and was correlated with whether viral dissemination occurred in the inoculated animal. Both immature (suckling) and adult mice inoculated intracerebrally with herpes simplex virus developed CNS infection. Virus spread was stopped only in the adult animals inoculated intraperitoneally. Virus-inoculated suckling mice showed unrestricted infection of peritoneal macrophages with coincident virus dissemination. Peritoneal macrophages of suckling mice were productively infected with virus *in vitro*, and spread virus to other cell types. Such contiguous viral spread, however, was abrogated by transfer of macrophages from adult mice to suckling mice. Furthermore, susceptibility of adult animals to viral infection was increased by transfer of macrophages from suckling mice to adult animals. Later studies confirmed the resistance patterns of macrophages from adult and neonatal mice with other viral pathogens (6,34,35).

The cell transfer studies provided direct evidence for the critical role of peritoneal macrophages in age-related resistance to herpes simplex virus. It would now be useful to perform macrophage transfer studies with the newer methodologies available for identifying and purifying macrophages from other cell types, such as natural killer (NK) cells, which are known to also play a role in antiviral resistance (15). In addition, prelabelling the transferred macrophages would allow monitoring of their location in relation to viral infection (36,37). Such studies could provide definitive evidence as to whether the tissue macrophage is the sole cell necessary for age-related antiviral resistance.

2.4   Monocyte/macrophage depletion

A close association between viral resistance in macrophages with genetic and/or age-related host factors has been established. In attempts to outline the precise role of the macrophage in resistance to viral infections, an experimental approach complementary to cell transfer, that of selective cell depletion, was employed. Macrophage populations were partially depleted *in vivo*, for example, macrophage specific antiserum, macrophage toxins, such as silica or aurothiomalate, or [89]Sr (6,11,38–45). These treatments generally increased host susceptibilities to a variety of viral infections, implicating macrophages as important cells in host resistance. It must be appreciated, however, that studies using depletion are not easily interpreted. Indeed, no system exists that selectively depletes all macrophage populations. Moreover, other elements of the immune system are also affected by these treatments. Treatment with ^{89}Sr, for example, induces severe monocytopenia but does not decrease resident macrophage populations (43). NK cells, as well as mononuclear cells, are affected by silica and ^{89}Sr treatment (40,42). Treatment with toxins, such as silica, affect the local tissue macrophages, but not monocytes (40). Experiments using a combination of selective depletion strategies may prove useful in more accurately depleting mononuclear phagocytes.

Furthermore, no genetic model of selective cell depletion, such as the nude mouse for T-cells, exists for macrophages. The nude mouse system was crucial in clarifying the role of the T-cell in immune responses. Other selective depletion systems using radiation with or without cell transfers and/or specific antibodies have proven useful for establishing the roles of B-cells and NK cells in host resistance (15). Each depletion method must be fully characterized before conclusions are made about identifying cells responsible for antiviral resistance. It is likely that continued development of the selective depletion approach, together with transfer of more highly purified cell populations and their use in pathogenesis studies, will provide definitive data on the exact role of the macrophage in host resistance.

3   Macrophages as effector cells in viral infection

In addition to the clearance of virus, the macrophage may contain or destroy viral pathogens or mediate their destruction, either non-specifically (6,11) or through interactions with other arms of the immune system. Clearance, phagocytosis, and digestion of an opsonized virus is a starting point for a complex sequence of interactions and biological antiviral activities involving all arms of the immune system. For example, mononuclear phagocytes are involved in T-, NK, and B-cell responses to viruses and their combined abilities to contain or eliminate viral pathogens.

The macrophage is also a secretory cell and produces many mediator substances, such as complement, arachidonic acid metabolites, neutral proteases including plasminogen activator, collagenase and elastase, various growth factors, and cytokines which have potential for regulating viral growth (4). These cytokines include platelet-derived growth factor, tumor necrosis factor (TNFα), colony-stimulating factors (CSFs), the interleukins, and a group of interferons (i.e. IFNα and β) which can act in concert with other virus-clearance mechanisms to abort or restrict viral infections. The cytokine network may also up- or down-regulate viral gene expression through mediating activation of mononuclear phagocytes. For example, macrophages produce IFNα, TNFα and IL-6 which may each act directly on virus-producing cells (macrophages and other cells) through cellular activation, and/or affect the ability of cells to become infected with virus through modulation of cell surface receptors, viral binding and entry or affecting intracellular antiviral mechanisms. The antiviral activity of several cytokines has been demonstrated *in vitro* (6,7), but their role *in vivo* remains to be defined. The situation *in vivo* is complicated by the fact that cytokines seldom act singly. Additive, synergistic, and antagonistic effects occur with combinations of cytokines *in vitro*. Considerable investigation will be required to understand the relative roles of cytokines in conjunction with macrophages in virus infections *in vivo*.

3.1   The role of IFN in the regulation of antiviral activity

Of all the cytokines studied, IFN is pre-eminent in its ability to induce host cell defensive mechanisms during viral infections (46–76, 78–81). IFN production during *in vivo* viral infection appears to be a critical component of host antiviral responses. The IFN system becomes operative within hours of systemic viral infection (46–47) and is likely to be a major factor in abortive viral infections. Macrophages are quite intimately related to the IFN system (47–50). Contrary to most of the other cells in the body, macrophages can be induced by a variety of microbial pathogens as well as viruses to make IFNα and β, and co-operate with T-cells in the production of IFNγ (49). Furthermore, many of the functional properties of the macrophage are under the influence of IFN.

A prominent role for IFN in host-mediated antiviral immunity is supported by experimental data on the outcome of infection following partial depletion of the IFN system (32,51,52–54). Treatment of mice with polyclonal antibody to IFNγ has shown that IFNγ is critical for host defence against herpes simplex virus, even though no detectable circulating levels of IFNγ is found during infection (53). Another model has emphasized the importance of IFN in genetic resistance to influenza viral infection, (55–57). A2G mice inoculated with influenza A virus are resistant to infection, and this is correlated with failure of virus to grow in explants of A2G peritoneal macrophages. Following inoculation of mice with anti-mouse IFN, influenza A virus replicates to high titres and produces disease in the A2G mice. This is correlated with growth of virus in peritoneal macrophages. Thus, the inoculation of some strains of mice with anti-IFN renders them susceptible to viral infection and suggests that the resistance is due to IFN. IFN-mediated resistance *in vivo* is hypothesized to occur in conjunction with macrophages, although other cells also express the genetically mediated antiviral resistance *in vitro* (32,55–58). It should be noted that resistance to viral infection is not always mediated through IFN; anti-IFN treatment of mice does not abrogate genetic resistance to flavivirus infection (59).

3.2   Genetic determinants and the host cell both determine the response of virus-infected cells to IFN

Both genetic determinants and the specific host cell have a prominent role in determining the ultimate antiviral activity of IFN. For example, genetic and host cell determinants define the IFN-mediated antiviral activities for influenza virus (55–58) and human immunodeficiency virus (HIV), (60–64). The mechanism of IFN-mediated viral restriction of influenza viral infections revolves around the Mx gene (55–58). In macrophages derived from mice bearing the Mx gene (Mx+), IFN treatment *in vitro* results in a post-translational block in viral replication following influenza infection (56). When fibroblasts obtained from Mx+ mice are treated with IFN and then infected with influenza, the block in virus replication is reported to occur at the level of transcription (57). The Mx gene-mediated block in virus replication, thus, may occur at distinct stages of the viral life cycle, dependent upon the viral target cell. Either type of IFN-mediated antiviral activity (transcriptional, post-translational) is found only in cells bearing the Mx gene (A2G mice). Viral replication is poorly inhibited by IFNα in mice lacking this gene.

IFN activity during HIV infection depends on whether the virus infects CD4+ T-cells or monocytes (60–64). IFN restricts HIV-replication *in vitro* in its major target cells, the CD4+ T-cell, and the monocyte by distinct mechanisms. In monocytes, IFN can prevent HIV infection at the level of proviral DNA if given before or at the time of the viral challenge. If cells are productively infected with HIV, IFN restricts infection by producing defective particles and ultimately by decreasing levels of viral mRNAs. In contrast, HIV-infected CD4+ T-cells treated with IFN show only a modest effect on the viral life cycle. Here, IFN-treated HIV-infected cells demonstrate an inhibition in assembly and/or release of progeny viral particles in a similar fashion to that previously reported in murine and avian retroviral systems. These results taken together clearly demonstrate that both genetic determinants and the host cell underlie specific antiviral activities of IFNα.

3.3 Viral induction of IFN and the antiviral response

There is well-established precedent that IFNα,β is induced by viral infection, and that these IFNs play a major role in restricting viral replication *in vivo* (65–75). The antiviral activity of IFNα,β is operative against a wide spectrum of viruses, and mediated through the synthesis of antiviral proteins in the IFNα,β-treated cells (46,47,65,66). Once induced, IFNα,β can restrict viral replication in infected macrophages as well as in neighbouring cells. IFNα,β synthesis is ultimately diminished by a feedback mechanism resulting from the elimination and/or restriction of the virus.

The mechanism whereby virus infection up-regulates IFN is thought to involve the derepression of genes coding for these cytokines. The relative ratios of IFNα or β produced can differ, depending upon the differentiation or activation state of the macrophage and the animal species. For example, Newcastle disease virus (NDV) increases by 90 per cent IFNβ production by resident mouse peritoneal macrophages (76). In bone marrow-derived macrophages, or in peritoneal macrophages cultured with colony-stimulating factor (CSF), the pattern is changed. There is a 6 to 20-fold increase in the amount of IFN induced by the virus, and this IFN consists of equal amounts of the IFNα and β species. Human monocytes infected by NDV produce predominantly IFNα not β.

Following herpes simplex virus (HSV) infection of freshly isolated human blood monocytes, IFN is induced and its production correlates with a highly restricted viral replication (69–73). In IFN-treated HSV-infected macrophages, the restriction by IFNα is at the level of immediate early gene expression and is postulated to be mediated by IFNα-induced cellular proteins that also result in the inhibition of monocyte differentiation (70–72). In support of this mechanism is the fact that virus-infected cells treated with anti-IFN demonstrate both enhancement in infectious virus production and monocyte-macrophage differentiation. There is, however, considerable heterogeneity apparent in the monocytes (77) that complicates the delineation of the mechanisms involved. It is uncertain in which mononuclear phagocytes IFN is produced, and whether the antiviral effect of IFN is direct or is indirectly mediated through IFN-induced inhibition of monocyte-macrophage differentiation.

In freshly isolated peritoneal macrophages or blood monocytes infected by VSV, EMC, and parainfluenza, small amounts of infectious virus are associated with high levels of induced IFNα (51,52,74,75). VSV and EMC infection of peritoneal macrophages from several mouse strains results in an abortive infection which results in productive infection only when mice are treated with anti-IFN, suggesting that endogenous IFN is responsible for the resistance of macrophages *in vivo* (78). However, cellular factors other than, or in addition to, endogenous IFN probably play a role in the resistance of macrophages to virus. Indeed, anti-IFN treatment of mice does not abrogate the resistance of peritoneal macrophages to HSV infection *in vitro* (79). Moreover, monocytes non-permissive for respiratory syncytial virus produce very low levels of IFN in response to virus infection *in vitro* (74). It is possible that non-IFN-mediated antiviral resistance may be partially explained by the formation of toxic oxygen intermediates and other related cellular factors. This is not important in the antiviral resistance against VSV (80). However, the hypothesis merits additional investigation using primary cultures of macrophages from individuals who are genetically deficient in oxidative metabolism.

IFN is an important regulatory factor in suppression of lentiviruses. The first report that IFN could restrict lentiviral replication came from studies of visna-maedi and caprine arthritis encephalitis viruses (CAEV), (67,68). Here, replication of visna-maedi or CAEV in ruminant macrophages is restricted more than 1000-fold by an IFN produced during the interaction of virus-infected macrophages and peripheral blood mononuclear cells. In this fashion, IFN can control the speed of viral infection and the maintenance of the prolonged asymptomatic period typically following lentiviral infections.

The role of IFN in HIV-induced disease is quite complex, and as yet incompletely defined. Serum levels of IFNα increase during disease onset (81) and concomitant viremia, yet IFNα treatment of HIV-infected cells cultured *in vitro* inhibits viral replication (60–64). The mechanisms underlying these apparent conflicting observations are not yet clear. Decreased numbers of IFNα receptors on infected cells during HIV disease, and increased production of cytokines *in vivo* which abrogate the action of IFN, are two mechanisms postulated. Despite the incomplete and sometimes conflicting data, these various findings, taken together, support a prominent and early role for IFN in antiviral defence and underscore the possible role of endogenous IFN in maintaining macrophage resistance to viral infection.

3.4   Non-IFN macrophage-mediated antiviral activities

As shown above, antiviral mechanisms in addition to IFN must be involved in the resistance of macrophages to certain viruses. Macrophage-mediated inhibition of HSV replication in normally permissive cells also cannot always be explained by IFN (3,6,82–85). When activated peritoneal macrophages are added to HSV-inoculated VERO, mouse embryo or hamster BK21 cells (cells normally highly permissive for virus), yields of intracellular and cell-free virus from the permissive cells are dramatically reduced (3,83). These macrophage antiviral activities are independent of IFN, or any cytotoxicity of the macrophage for the viral-permissive cell population, but require some macrophage-target cell contact (83,84). In a similar system, arginase pro-duced by activated macrophages apparently could so deplete the culture medium of arginine that the replication of HSV is aborted. The addition of arginine back into the culture media results in productive HSV infection (85). Similar cell-to-cell mechanisms and soluble factor effects have been shown to be involved in macrophage-mediated tumoricidal activities (86). *In vivo*, tumours are often infiltrated by macrophages, and adoptive transfer of macrophages retards tumour growth through the generation of toxic oxygen intermediates, cytocidal factors, or cellular proteins/enzymes that deplete or compete for nutrients required for sustained tumour growth (77,86). These or other related events may underlie non-IFN mediated macrophage resist-ance against viral infections.

4   Macrophages as antigen-presenting cells in viral infection

In addition to the non-specific scavenger and effector functions described above, mononuclear phagocytes serve a critical function in antigen presen-tation for induction of the host virus-specific antiviral response. Antigen presentation involves the expression and release of IL-1 and other cytokines from macrophages that then affect helper T-cell and B-cell responses (10). The macrophage and other APCs take up, process, and present antigen in association with the major histocompatibility complex (MHC). T-cell ac-tivation involves clustering around the APC at the antigen-MHC complex. This leads to primary or secondary immune responses for containment and/or destruction of the invading microbial pathogen. Thus, macrophages and other APCs are essential in initiating the specific immune response to eliminate virus.

Virus infection may also alter this normal APC function, by either up- or down-regulation of IL-1 (87,88). The effects of cytomegalovirus (CMV) infection have been extensively studied, because of the well-documented immunosuppression that accompanies this virus infection (88). Both decreased and increased levels of IL-1 have been reported after CMV infection *in vitro* of primary cultures of macrophages or macrophage-like cell lines (88–92). The initial reports showed decreased IL-1 production, but recently much of this decrease has been shown to be the result of mycoplasma contamination (91). A consensus appears to be developing that the major effect of CMV is up-regulation of IL-1, possibly concomitantly with production of a suppressor of IL-1 activity (89,90). Paradoxically, as CMV causes an increase in IL-1 production, a down-regulation of cell-mediated immune response occurs (87,88,93). Recently, CMV infection has been shown to diminish both MHC Class I surface expression on macrophages and lymphocyte stimulation (94). Homology between CMV and MHC Class I DNA has been demonstrated, which is suggested to be the basis for the observed binding of CMV to β_2-microglobulin and subsequent immunosuppression (88,95). A recent study of HIV infection of monocytes has also noted effects on MHC, showing decreased expression of CD4, together with increased expression of HLA-DR and decreased expression of HLA-DQ Class II antigens (96). Such seemingly opposing effects as cytokine enhancement and MHC suppression are not necessarily contradictory. Secretion of inflammatory cytokines may contribute to viral pathology, whereas aberrant expression of Class I and II antigens may favour viral persistence through escape from immune recognition. This hypothesis might explain some of the pathology of cytomegalovirus and HIV in the brain of infected individuals.

The process of antigen presentation can also lead to or accelerate disease if the invading virus directly destroys the antigen-presenting cell (APC), or if the process itself results in spread of virus from APC to previously uninfected T- or B-cells. Interactions between mononuclear phagocytes and T-cells occur during antigen presentation and result in the activation of antigen-responsive T-cell clones. These activated T-cells produce IL-2 which can act as an autocrine factor in cell proliferation and growth of virus. The spread of virus between HIV or simian immunodeficiency virus (SIV)-infected macrophages and T-cells during the course of antigen presentation provides one example (97). Although all lentiviruses can replicate in cells of the mononuclear phagocyte lineage, only the primate viruses, HIV and SIV, and the feline immunodeficiency virus 'FIV' also infect T-cells. This T-cell infection ultimately results in immunodeficiency. Recent studies suggest that the close co-operative interactions between monocytes and CD4+ T-cells during the immune response results in spread of virus between these cells (97). HIV-infected macrophages can transmit virus to T-cells more efficiently than T-cells exposed to cell-free virus. When antibodies to MHC Class II are added to the co-cultivated cells, antigen presentation is diminished along with cell-to-cell transmission of virus. The elaboration of various cytokines and subsequent cellular activation may accelerate the process of virus transfer and replication.

Lactate dehydrogenase-elevating virus (LDV) is one of the few virus infections in which macrophage infection with virus has clearly been shown to modulate specific immune responses (98–110). Although mechanisms remain to be defined (98–110), they may be related to the fact that only subpopulations of macrophages are infected (98,101–103,108). These subpopulations are thought to be Ia+ macrophages (102,107). However, subsequent studies using anti-Ia antibodies and cell sorting techniques have established no correlation between Ia antigen positivity and permissivity for LDV (103,108). Nonetheless, LDV infection has also been proposed as an example of direct destruction of APC by virus (102,106,107). The data does not exclude the possibility of cell killing mediated by immune mechanisms, continuation of cell differentiation, or changed patterns of cell trafficking *in vivo* (98). Whatever the mechanism(s), it is evident that LDV infection modulates immune responses. Both enhancement and suppression of experimental allergic encephalomyelitis have also been observed in LDV-infected mice (104,109). Stimulation of autoimmune antibodies to intracellular components, such as the Golgi, have also been described (110), as well as alterations in antigen presentation (98,105). The immunoregulatory potential of LDV in chronically infected mice may be mediated by factors that have been observed during infection, such as the high levels of IFN induced by the virus, circulating IgG1 complexes of virus and antibody, polyclonal activation, changes in cell trafficking, or altered macrophage function (98).

It is clear that many viral infections can modulate immune responses, and alteration in macrophage function is one of the major factors that has been commonly noted (87). A proposal that viruses can cause disease in the absence of morphological evidence of cell injury, by altering the ability of cells to make specialized products (13), is particularly pertinent as macrophages are resistant to productive infection by most viruses. Given the present state of confusion about the effects of viruses on the APC function of macrophages, considerable investigation is needed to define the mechanisms of virus-induced dysfunction in macrophages and their role in immunomodulation.

5   Antibody-mediated enhancement of viral growth

During many viral infections, the host humoral immune response results in the production of a variety of antibodies, but only a fraction have antiviral activities. Some antibodies have no neutralizing activities and others have clearly been demonstrated to enhance infection *in vitro* (111–131).

Antibody-dependent enhancement (ADE) of viral infection *in vitro* was first characterized with Murray Valley encephalitis virus. The studies demonstrated that virus yields were increased more than five-fold in chick embryo monolayer cultures if virus was mixed with antiviral antibody, compared with viral inoculation of cells without antibody. Halstead and colleagues (111) investigating dengue hemorrhagic fever observed that dengue viral replication in mononuclear cells was enhanced 50–100-fold by subneutralizing concentrations of antiviral antibody. They found that enhancement was dependent upon cells bearing receptors for the Fc portion of Ig (111), with virus entering cells by complexing with non-neutralizing antibodies. Although Flaviviridae (Murray Valley encephalitis, dengue, West Nile, and yellow fever viruses) are the earliest examples of ADE (112–120), the phenomenon is not confined to this family (121–124). Alpha viruses (family Togaviridae), Rhadoviridae, Bunyaviridae, Coronaviridae, Reoviridae, Herpesviridae, Poxviridae, and Lentiviridae have all been reported to demonstrate ADE *in vitro* (111,121–124).

The role of ADE in disease pathogenesis remains to be established. Up to this time there has only been loose correlation with exacerbation of clinical disease; ADE may be an explanation for the complications of dengue virus infection known as dengue haemorrhagic fever (DHF) and dengue shock syndrome (DSS), (113). Disease pathogenesis is correlated with high levels of viral infected monocytes. Such infected cells could certainly induce a cascade of events that result in haemorrhage and increased vascular permeability. Indeed, sub-neutralizing antibodies that mediate enhancement of infection in monocytes are present in human dengue immune sera. Inoculation of live virus dengue vaccines is also associated with development of enhancing antibodies to related viral strains (119).

For HIV-infected monocytes and macrophages several studies demonstrate that the Fc receptor (FcR) plays a role in ADE. For HIV infection of monocytes, three potential mechanisms for viral uptake are described including: (1) non-specific phagocytosis of virions; (2) CD4-mediated entry; and (3) receptor-mediated endocytosis of antibody-HIV complex through the FcR or complement receptors (CR1, CR3, CR4) or ADE (125–131). This latter process occurs *in vitro* and up to an order of magnitude increase in levels of virus are reported to be mediated by ADE in HIV-infected monocytes (127–130). The interaction of antibody-bound HIV and CD4 appears critical for this enhancement (130). One report further demonstrates that ADE can also alter viral tropism. Here, lymphotropic HIV particles that normally abortively infect monocytes are able to grow permissively in the presence of specific enhancing antibodies (129). Potential clinical relevance has been demonstrated by finding antibodies that mediate ADE in the blood of seropositive patients and immunized chimpanzees; however, there was no relationship between the presence or magnitude of the ADE phenomenon and clinical stage (131).

The phenomenon of ADE raises concern in vaccine development. Some antibodies may be induced by vaccines that can then enhance viral infection *in vivo* and alter protection against a later viral challenge. At this time, however, the question remains whether ADE is primarily an *in vitro* phenomenon or has any significant clinical impact.

6 Monocyte/macrophage differentiation/activation and viral strain as determinants of abortive, latent, restricted, permissive, enhanced, or cytopathic outcomes

All of the above activities of macrophages (scavenger, effector, antigen presentation, infection enhancement) are affected by the differentiation and/or activation state of the mononuclear phagocyte. Mononuclear phagocyte differentiation is defined as a process that occurs as part of normal cellular development and homeostasis and reflects permanently altered expression of genes (77). Activation, in contrast, is any process that causes reversible changes in macrophage phenotype and functions, mediated by altered expression of one gene or a co-ordinated set of genes (77). Both changes in mononuclear phagocyte homeostasis have been studied in a number of viral systems and shown to directly affect viral gene expression. How these two processes interplay in producing the well-known heterogeneity of macrophages is not yet understood.

Macrophages are clearly heterogeneous in their permissiveness for viral infection, as usually only a subpopulation is infected (6,7,79,98,146). For example, even with LDV infection, where the macrophage is the primary target, viral gene expression can be detected in only a small subpopulation of cells (98,101,108). The growth of LDV is limited to 5–20 per cent of cultured macrophages regardless of input multiplicity of infection (98,101,103). In LDV-infected mice, virus-infected cells are widely distributed in interstitial connective tissues and in every organ system, in close association with Ia+ and F4/80+ cells, with the exception of brain and spinal cord (98,107). *In vivo*, viral persistence centres around the continuous generation of additional susceptible cell populations. Macrophage differentiation may lead to the acquisition of specific viral receptors resulting in viral replication. At present, there is no marker to identify the susceptible macrophage subpopulation. It may be a transient differentiation state, with both expression of specific virus receptors as well as intracellular factors being responsible for viral permissiveness (98,100).

Fig. 4.1 Monocyte/macrophage differentiation controls the tempo of visna viral replication *in vitro*. Peripheral blood mononuclear cells from a normal sheep were inoculated with visna virus at a multiplicity of infection of 2 and cultured for 24 h in serum-free DMEM (A,C,E), or 5 per cent normal lamb sera in DMEM (B,D,F). A and B were stained with peroxidase. Note the intense staining in undifferentiated cells (A) and the lack of staining in differentiated cells (B). Samples (C and D) were processed for *in situ* hybridization using ^{35}S-labelled viral DNA probes, and (E and F) were labelled immunocytochemically with monoclonal antibodies to the visna virus glycoprotein, gp135. Note the paucity of hybridization signal and staining in undifferentiated cells (C and E respectively) and the intense signal and staining of the differentiated cells (D and F respectively).

6.1   Monocyte/macrophage differentiation regulates viral infection and determines the outcome of infection for diverse classes of viruses

In the simplest model, when blood monocytes are cultured *in vitro* they acquire some of the properties of mature macrophages. The many factors which contribute to monocyte/macrophage differentiation generally, although not always, lead to more efficient macrophage infection by diverse classes of viruses (6,7,132–142,154). Viral gene expression may be directly analysed during monocyte differentiation. Alternatively, populations of monocytes/macrophages may be studied *in vivo* using immunohistochemical or *in situ* hybridization techniques as they develop from bone marrow precursor cells and blood monocytes to become resident tissue macrophages.

For the ruminant lentivirus (visna-maedi and CAEV) infection of monocytes *in vitro*, viral gene expression is closely linked to monocyte differentiation (132–141). When ruminant monocytes are incubated in serum-free medium, to prevent their maturation to macrophages, very low levels of viral transcription occurs. Here, virus replication is severely restricted. However, when these monocytes are cultured in medium containing serum, to allow for cell differentiation, viral mRNA expression is enhanced more than 1000-fold and the viral life cycle goes to completion (permissive infection) (139), (Figure 4.1). The close correlation between monocyte maturation and viral gene expression is linked in a causal fashion to the induction of specific cellular nucleic acid-binding proteins (141). These proteins activate viral transcription during cell maturation by binding to regulatory elements in the lentivirus proviral long terminal repeat (LTR) sequence (AP-1 and AP-4 sites).

Visna-maedi virus infection *in vivo* mirrors these *in vitro* observations. Here again viral gene expression is closely linked to the maturation and differentiation of monocytes to macrophages. The virus is restricted in

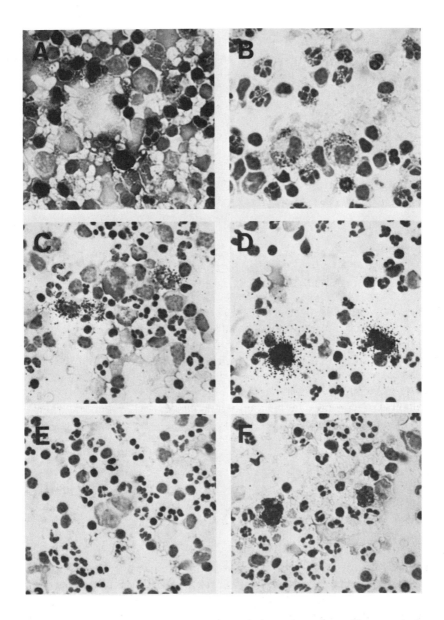

precursor monocytes and becomes permissive when the cells mature into
macrophages (173) (Plate 1). Only a subpopulation of mononuclear
phagocytes are susceptible to virus. While blood monocytes, alveolar
macrophages, microglial and dendritic cells are susceptible: liver macrophages (Kupffer cells) and connective tissue histiocytes are not (135). This
suggests additional heterogeneity of macrophage populations for susceptibility to viral infection, in that during differentiation only select populations

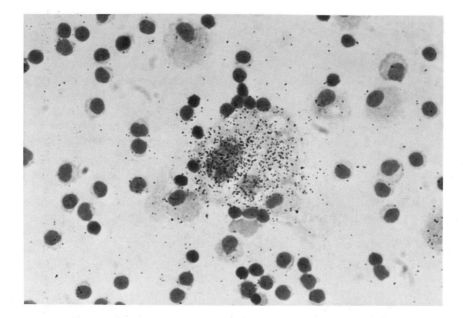

Fig. 4.2 Peripheral blood mononuclear cells from a normal sheep were infected with visna virus at a multiplicity of infection of 2 then cultivated for 5 days in 5 per cent normal lamb sera in DMEM. After 5 days of infection, the cell preparations were processed for *in situ* hybridization with an ^{35}S-labelled visna virus DNA probe. Note the selective intense signal overlying the macrophage but not the smaller surrounding T-cells.

of cells acquire the necessary viral receptors and/or cellular transcriptional factors for efficient viral replication.

Human monocytes and other mononuclear phagocytes infected with respiratory syncytial virus (RSV), parainfluenza virus-3, HIV, African swine fever, cytomegalovirus or HSV exhibit similar enhancement of replication associated with macrophage differentiation (6,7,74,142–145,154). Infection of monocytes with HSV that have been cultured for several days generally results in increases in virus production compared to infection of monocytes cultured for 1 day. It should be noted, however, that this enhanced virus replication in primary cultures of differentiated macrophages is still generally below that achieved in completely permissive cells.

Macrophage-like cell lines differentiated by treatment with phorbol esters have also been used in investigation of the relationships between cell differentiation and HSV gene expression (6,7,146–149). Generally, although not always, enhanced viral replication is observed upon cell differentiation (146). For example, a restricted viral replication leads to productive infection when U937 cells are treated with PMA and then

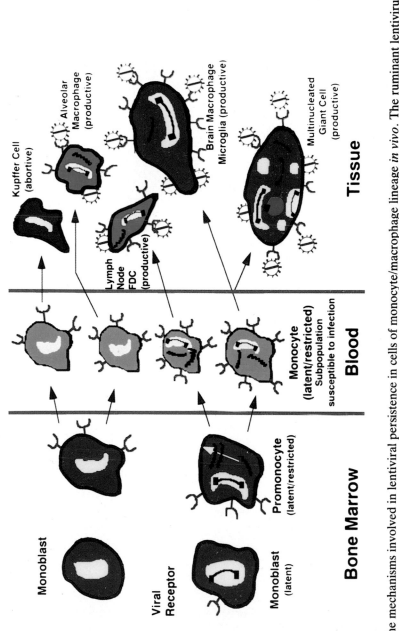

Plate 1 The mechanisms involved in lentiviral persistence in cells of monocyte/macrophage lineage *in vivo*. The ruminant lentiviruses infect progenitor monocytes in bone marrow which results in a latent or restricted infection. Only when cells leave the bone marrow and mature into blood monocytes and tissue macrophages is the viral life cycle driven to completion. Lentiviral gene expression is dependent on the stage of differentiation or activation of the macrophage.

infected with HSV. In untreated macrophages infected with HSV, immediate–early and some early viral transcripts are demonstrated, but the mRNAs for the viral DNA polymerase and the major DNA-binding protein ICP8 are absent or barely detectable and the mRNA for the late gene glycoprotein C (gC) is completely absent. The block appears not to be at viral entry or transport to the nucleus, but to occur prior to steady state accumulation of viral RNA for immediate early genes (146–148). Following PMA-treatment, more than 50 per cent of cells support a productive HSV replication and the viral life cycle goes to completion.

Although monocyte differentiation to macrophages is generally associated with increased permissiveness for viral infection, this is not the situation with all viruses (7,153). One example of macrophage differentiation linked to a down-regulation of viral gene expression is found in FIV (152) infection of peritoneal macrophages (153). Macrophages are recovered from the peritoneum of cats and are productively infected *in vitro*. However, in this instance, macrophage differentiation induced by phorbol esters was associated with restricted rather than productive levels of progeny virus (153).

6.2 Macrophage activation and up-regulation of viral gene expression

In contrast to differentiation, macrophage activation, typically induced by bacterial products (for example, LPS), or cytokines (for example, IFNs and CSFs), results in reversible changes in macrophage gene expression and phenotype. Both suppression and enhancement of infection have been observed in the interactions of activated macrophages with viruses (6,79,82–84,155–171).

During the immune response, lymphocytes secrete a number of different factors that activate macrophages and augment viral replication in either or both cells. For example, influenza infection of purified macrophages or lymphocytes is usually abortive (172–176). However, during the initiation of the immune response lymphocytes and monocytes can be productively infected. In this instance, infection requires physical association of monocytes and lymphocytes in clusters (175,176). This association between lymphocytes and monocytes results in the synthesis of influenza viral antigens by autologous lymphocytes. This facilitation of infection may play a role in generating productive viral infection *in vivo* and subsequent viral immunity.

The most extensive studies of mononuclear phagocyte cell activation and its influence on viral replication have been performed on HIV-infected macrophages (156–171). Mechanisms that augment viral expression in HIV-infected blood monocytes and macrophages occur during the immune response and likely play pivotal roles in the onset and progression of clinical disease (156–171). To this end, investigators have studied how a latent or restricted HIV infection could be up-regulated to produce infectious virus. HIV-infected cells derived from the U937 myelomonocytic cell line were developed to determine what activation factors cause productive viral replication. Additional studies have been performed on primary monocytes to validate those experimental findings. Host cell activation factors, including phorbol esters, macrophage or macrophage-granulocyte CSFs (MCSF and GMCSF), interleukins (IL-1, -3, -4, and -6) and TNFα markedly increased HIV replication in both myelomonocytic cell lines and in primary monocytes (156–171). Similar enhancement of HIV has been shown by macrophage activation mediated by bacterial products, such as LPS, detoxified endotoxin, and mycobacterial trehalose dimycolate (170,171). A major mechanism of increased HIV gene expression appears to be mediated through the induction of NF-kB, a cell activation factor (165–168,171). NF-kB binds to an upstream NF-kB binding site in the HIV-LTR and activates *in vitro* transcription from the HIV promoter.

These many examples demonstrate quite clearly that monocyte activation by cytokines can result in enhanced levels of HIV expression. In studies performed in our laboratory, monocytes cultured in MCSF prior to viral infection are 100- to 1000-fold more susceptible to virus than cells cultured in medium alone (169). Moreover, at any time following HIV infection, the frequency and absolute levels of viral DNA and/or mRNA/cell is significantly greater in cells treated with MCSF when compared to equal numbers of cells treated with media alone. The differences are directly related to the concentration of MCSF. IL-6 upregulates viral replication in both myeloid cells and monocytes and its major effects are uniquely post-transcriptional (162). Here, levels of HIV proteins and progeny virions are increased without concomitant increases in viral mRNAs. Studies of transgenic mice containing integrated but non-expressed HIV-LTR-CAT plasmid DNAs show increased LTR-directed gene expression in differentiated macrophages after exposure to a variety of cytokines including, MCSF, GMCSF, IL-1, -4, and -2 (177).

Thus, a variety of cellular activation signals can up-regulate HIV gene expression *in vitro* and alter the outcome of the virus–macrophage interactions. These observations have considerable potential clinical significance for immunotherapeutic treatment of patients. In this regard it is encouraging that, although CSFs can clearly enhance HIV infection *in vitro*, enhanced anti-HIV activity was observed when alveolar macrophages infected with HIV were cultured with GMCSF in combination with zidovudine (178).

6.3   Influences of viral strain on the outcome of macrophage–virus interactions: transformation

In addition to both differentiation and activation of the host mononuclear phagocyte, the infecting viral strain can determine the ultimate outcome of viral infection in macrophages, including viral transformation. Oncogenic retroviruses, such as avian myoblastosis virus (AMV), murine retroviruses, and avian myelocytomatosis virus (MC29) can transform macrophages (179–190). Following transformation, changes in macrophage cell-specific products are observed, but the extent varies. In the AMV-transformed macrophage, phagocytosis, cytoplasmic lipid accumulation, and acid phosphatase activity are strongly suppressed, and the morphological characteristics of cells resemble immature monocytes. However, no correlation between the numbers of transformant leukaemic cells and the stage of monocyte differentiation was observed (190). This suggests that the stage of macrophage differentiation does not affect the susceptibility to AMV infection and subsequent transformation (179–182,190).

In the MC29-transformed macrophages, the cell phenotype is unaltered and morphologic properties of the transformed cell are similar to those of mature macrophages (190). A relationship between monocyte cell transformation *in vitro* and tumorigenicity *in vivo* underlies MC29 infections in chickens (180–183,189). MC29 infected Brown Leghorn chickens result in a high incidence of tumours, predominantly endotheliomas induced by the expression of the viral *myc* gene (188). When parts of *myc* are deleted, the virus has a reduced ability to transform macrophages and induces fewer tumours (189).

6.4   Influences of viral strain on the outcome of macrophage–virus interactions: HIV cell tropism

Early reports describing *in vitro* infection of the lymphotropic HIV strain (HTLV-IIIB/LAV) in monocytes showed levels of replication just above the limits of detection by reverse transcriptase (RT) and p24 viral antigen assays (191,192). Recovery of progeny HIV from tissue macrophages or from co-cultures of patient PBMC and normal donor monocytes yielded progeny virions with abilities to infect both monocytes and T-cells (monocytotropic HIV) (193–195). Proviral DNA, mRNA, p24 antigens, and RT activity were detected in monocytes or released into culture fluids following inoculation of cultured cells with monocytotropic HIVs. Cytopathicity was demonstrated by syncytia formation. In the initial report (193), primary cultures of brain explants from patients with AIDS-associated encephalopathy were enriched for macrophages by repeated trypsin digestion of adherent cell monolayers. These macrophage-enriched monolayers produced RT activity in culture supernatants which was passed to new donor monocytes and elicited a productive HIV infection. The recovered virus was over 100-fold more efficient in infecting monocytes as compared to lymphoblasts. In these analyses the lymphotropic isolate HTLV-IIIB/LAV was conversely over 10 000 fold more effective for infection of T-cells compared to monocytes. The restricted infection of mono-

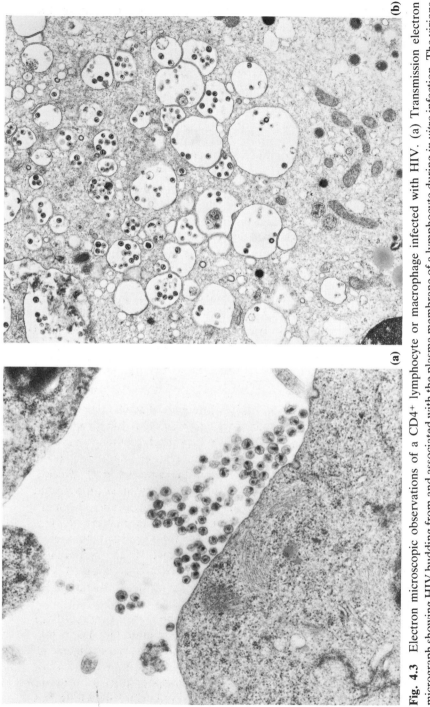
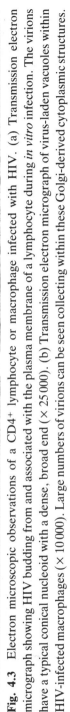

Fig. 4.3 Electron microscopic observations of a CD4⁺ lymphocyte or macrophage infected with HIV. (a) Transmission electron micrograph showing HIV budding from and associated with the plasma membrane of a lymphocyte during *in vitro* infection. The virions have a typical conical nucleoid with a dense, broad end (× 25 000). (b) Transmission electron micrograph of virus-laden vacuoles within HIV-infected macrophages (× 10 000). Large numbers of virions can be seen collecting within these Golgi-derived cytoplasmic structures.

cytes with HTLV-IIIB/LAV was shown recently to be related to the accumulation of proviral DNA. This viral DNA serves as a template for HIV mRNA and subsequent progeny viral particle production by cytokine treatment. In one report, monocytes infected with HTLV-IIIB and treated with IL-4 resulted in a productive viral infection with cytopathicity including multinucleated giant cell formation (164). This suggested that host cell transcriptional factors and not exclusively viral factors, could regulate viral-cell tropism.

Four outcomes of HIV replication can occur in monocytes that are dependent, in part, on the infecting viral strain:

(1) an abortive infection (no infection);
(2) a latent or restricted infection with lymphotropic viruses (HTLV-IIIB/LAV);
(3) a low level permissive infection with early passage isolates; and
(4) cytopathic infection with laboratory adapted strains resulting in multinucleated giant cell formation and cell death (18) (Plate 2).

During viral isolation on to monocytes, progeny HIV is continually produced at low levels for several weeks (low level permissive/persistent infection) (194,195). In such cultures, minimal cytopathology is associated with low levels of RT activity released into culture supernatants. Analysis of these infected monocytes by electron microscopy showed a predominant but not exclusive, intracellular virus accumulation (194,196) (Figure 4.3). High proportions of infected cells (over 50 per cent) were identified by FACS flow cytometry and *in situ* hybridization assays. Infection of monocytes by HIV serially passaged through monocytes revealed a gradual but progressive increase in cytopathic effects (multinucleated giant cell formation and cell lysis) and increased levels of intracellular and extracellular RT activity reflecting, in part, increases in plasma membrane virus budding. Recent investigations studied the molecular basis for these differences through the construction of recombinant full-length clones and reciprocal fragment exchanges between a monocytotropic isolate (ADA) and portions of lymphotropic HIV clones (197). Here, interactions of the viral envelope gene (*env*) product and an early event of the viral life cycle was discovered as a key determinant of viral tropism. This HIV determinant encompassed a 94 amino acid region of the surface *env* glycoprotein including the entire V3 loop was responsible for viral growth in monocytes (198,199).

In the HIV system, both the viral strain and the state of macrophage differentiation/activation clearly affect the outcome of infection. The mechanisms governing the role of the virus in the interaction are becoming clear. However, the mechanisms underlying the heterogeneity in the response of the macrophage are less clear. It is evident that a subpopulation of cells are infected. That macrophages are heterogeneous is well established (77), but the origin of this heterogeneity and the ultimate effect on viral gene expression remains to be defined at the molecular level.

7   Viral infection of macrophages and relationship to disease: studies of lentiviral pathogenesis in susceptible hosts

Lentiviruses are linked by similarities in gene structure and function, in mechanisms of replication and restriction, and in biological outcomes of viral infection that is host species-specific (200–207). Viral infection of ruminants, cats, cattle, non-human primates, and humans results in persistent infection over long time periods, often in the face of a vigorous host immune response (200–208). Disease begins slowly after a considerable time lag and progressively leads to degeneration of viral-target tissues resulting in cachexia and death. The viruses are all tropic for macrophages and their abilities to continuously replicate *in vivo* depend on their unique abilities to live symbiotically in these phagocytic cells and simultaneously circumvent host immune defences (16). The persistence of lentiviruses in macrophages is maintained through the regulation of IFNα and other cellular factors which affect viral gene expression. The development of disease is related to increased viral replication and in some instances strongly associated with the levels of infection in macrophage populations (18,19). This association of clinical disease with increased levels of viral replication in tissue macrophages is typified by the pneumonitis, encephalitis and arthritis of ruminants. Disease may result from alternations in macrophage function by the abnormal elaboration of cytokines, through aberrant communication between immune cell populations, through the multitude of secondary immune responses directed against the infected cells, or by direct viral-induced cytopathicity (16–19).

7.1   Equine infectious anaemia virus (EIAV)

Equine infectious anaemia (EIA) is a chronic, relapsing infectious disease of horses caused by a lentivirus that persists in infected animals for life (208,209). Initial exposure to a virulent EIA usually results in acute disease characterized by fever, anaemia, and anorexia. A viraemia occurs within 5 to 30 days and is secondary to extensive viral replication in peripheral blood monocytes and tissue macrophages (210–212). The hallmark of EIA is periodic recrudescence of clinical illness. During this phase of disease the animals develop a serological response to virus. Each relapse is typified by classic signs of EIA: fever, anorexia, loss of weight, anaemia, and CNS obtundation. The recurrences of acute disease usually decrease in severity and frequency within one year of infection and most horses eventually

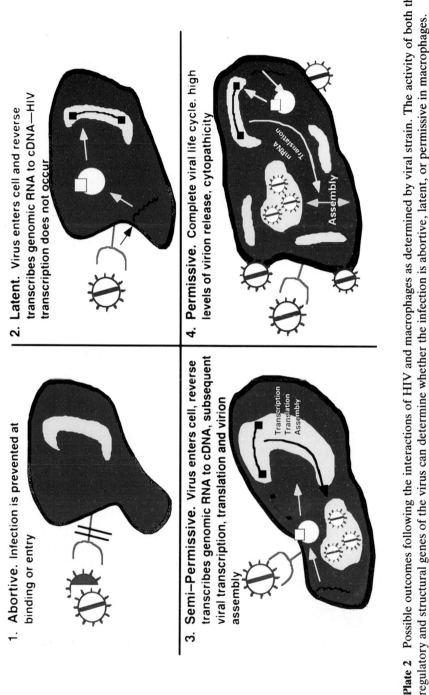

Plate 2 Possible outcomes following the interactions of HIV and macrophages as determined by viral strain. The activity of both the regulatory and structural genes of the virus can determine whether the infection is abortive, latent, or permissive in macrophages.

become asymptomatic and are unapparent carriers of the virus. The recrudescent bursts of viral replication occur in macrophages and are coupled with antigenic variation of the viral glycoproteins that underlie disease expression and viral replication (213–216). These bursts of viral replication give rise to immune complexes that are either deposited in specific tissues giving rise to immune complex disease, or are ingested and cleared by mononuclear phagocytes. Association of immune complexes with circulating red blood cells leads to haemolysis, the hallmark of this disease. The viral infected cells include spleen and liver macrophages.

7.2   EIAV–macrophage interactions

The first report of lentivirus infection in macrophages was made by immunofluorescence analyses of EIAV antigens in Kupffer macrophages of acutely infected horses (210). EIAV infection of macrophages is persistent. This persistent infection is typified by virus mutation which occurs at random and can be selected by reactivity of emerging viral strains with specific antibodies (213–216). Emergence of new, non-neutralizable virus coincides with the cyclical episodes of disease in horses. In this particular instance, continued replication of virus in monocytes and macrophages is related more to specific properties of EIAV rather than the host cell. Field strains of EIA replicate in equine monocytes *in vitro*, leading to high levels of unrestricted viral replication including budding from the cell membrane and cell death within 2–3 days. During disease, similar levels of productive viral infections can occur in tissue macrophages and result in poor clinical outcomes (16,216). For example, during subclinical disease immune complexes are cleared and EIAV is restricted in macrophages. However, when unrestricted replication occurs, mediated either by cytokines or by the emergence of pathogenic viral strains, viral replication in tissue macrophages gives rise to immune complex disease.

7.3   Visna-maedi and caprine-arthritis encephalitis virus (CAEV) of sheep and goats

Visna-maedi (in Icelandic: visna—paralysis and wastings; maedi—laboured breathing) is a pneumo-encephalitic disease of ruminants caused by a lentivirus. However, in nature, infections are usually relatively symptomless. When symptoms do develop they are gradual in onset often following an incubation period of months to years. Disease manifestations include: chronic progressive cachexia, pneumonitis, and CNS disorders (217–220). Because of the slow pathogenic process, the aetiological agent of visna-maedi was named lentivirus (Latin *lentus*, meaning slow). The concept of slow disease was first reported by Sigurdsson in 1954 (220) following his studies of scrapie, Johne's disease, and visna-maedi.

Visna-maedi was inadvertently introduced into the Icelandic sheep population through the importation of 20 chronically infected Karabul rams from Germany in 1933. The infection spread through much of Iceland and was recognized as an epizootic disease in the early 1940s. Although lentiviruses of sheep are relatively common pathogens in most parts of the world, explosive epidemics as seen in Iceland are rare. Many viral strains have been isolated from diseased animals in different countries and are related genetically and antigenically (221). The arthritis-encephalitis virus of goats, or CAEV, has genetic and biological properties distinct from those of visna-maedi. This virus has low virulence for tissue culture cells of sheep origin, replicates to high levels in synovial tissues and does not elicit neutralizing antibodies (219).

7.4   Virus–macrophage interactions in visna-maedi and CAEV infections

A common feature of both viruses is their ability to replicate in cells of monocyte/macrophage lineage, leading to active chronic inflammation and disease in viral target tissues (132–141). Lesions are characterized by proliferation and infiltration of mononuclear cells with disruption of normal tissue architecture. Histological changes are observed in the lung, brain, and spinal cord, lymph nodes and spleen, joints and mammary glands (217–219). The presence of macrophages expressing cell surface viral antigens in lungs, udder, joints, or CNS tissues provides the focus of inflammatory responses involving mononuclear cells. The many factors which contribute to macrophage activation lead to an up-regulation of viral gene expression and an increase in this inflammatory response. There is a demonstrably strong correlation between productive viral replication in macrophages and tissue pathology. Thus, continuous viral replication in macrophages sets the stage for disease by providing continuous antigenic stimulation for the inflammatory cellular immune response in viral target tissues.

During lentiviral infections of sheep and goats infected macrophages most likely play an important role as vectors of viral transmission from animal to animal as well as vehicles for dissemination and perpetrators of disease within an individual animal. Virus spread among animals is strongly associated with specific populations of virus-infected macrophages. Colostrum is an important source of transmission of visna-maedi virus to lambs and of CAEV to kids (222). A study of an infected herd of goats demonstrated that all doses that replicated virus in their blood monocytes also had infected macrophages in colostrum. This correlation of infection within macrophage populations was established by showing that infection of neonatal animals was prevented by withholding colostrum. Therefore, it is probable that these animals became infected after ingesting infected macrophages.

7.5   Human immunodeficiency virus (HIV)

The acquired immune deficiency syndrome is one of the most significant and devastating illness of the immune system ever described. HIV has already infected millions of individuals world wide and numbers are expected to climb (223). The central feature of this disease in the relentless destruction of CD4+ T-cells leading to opportunistic infections, malignancies, and death of the host. HIV also produces primary virus-induced disease in specific target tissues including the brain, lung, skin, and lymphatics. Here, the major site of virus replication is the macrophage and not the CD4+ T-cell (224–234).

7.6   HIV–macrophage interactions

Macrophages are infected at high frequencies in the brain (224–228), spinal cord (229), lymphatic tissue (230,231), and lung (232–234) and this is closely associated with disease. For example, *in situ* hybridization studies of HIV RNA transcripts in brain tissues of infected individuals demonstrate a frequency of productively infected macrophages in specific regions (15 per cent) of the CNS (224). Here, HIV-infected macrophages often induce histological changes most pronounced in the white matter but also within subcortical structures (the caudate and putamen of the basal ganglia). Histopathological alterations include a generalized myelin pallor (the most common finding) with secondary astroglial reactions. Scattered microglial nodes and multinucleated giant cells (the hallmark of HIV infection) are commonly found in and around foci of demyelination (235–237). The predominant infected cell, if not the exclusive HIV-infected cell in brain tissue during disease, is the macrophage (microglial and multinucleated giant cells) (224–228). Similarly, high numbers of HIV-infected macrophages are found in the spinal cord (229). Pathological examinations of the spinal cord demonstrate vacuolation of white matter and frequently a predominant macrophage infiltration. Although macrophages represent the predominant virus-infected cell type in both the brain and spinal cord, the histopathological outcomes are quite distinct. Patients with the most severe clinical CNS symptoms usually have the most intense pathological changes and the highest levels of HIV gene products in the brain and spinal cord in both mononucleated and multinucleated macrophages. The prominence of infected macrophages in CNS tissues, the early detection of virus in circulating monocytes, and the mechanisms of HIV-monocyte interactions, including mechanisms for evasion from immune surveillance, all support the theory that the HIV-infected monocyte traffics to the CNS and sets the stage for infection and tissue disease. The mechanisms whereby HIV-infected brain macrophages could give rise to CNS disease are outlined in Plate 3.

The lymph nodes and lungs represent other prominent sites of HIV replication in cells of macrophage lineage (230,231). Electron microscopic studies of lymph nodes from HIV-infected individuals demonstrate typical lentiviral particles associated with or budding from follicular dendritic cells in patients from all stages of clinical disease. A relationship between progressive follicular destruction, low antibody titres and the increased numbers of follicular dendritic cells bearing viral particles has been demonstrated. Similarly, HIV is isolated from macrophages in bronchoalveolar lavage fluids (232–234). In both lymph node and lung tissues the frequency of productively infected cells is less than 10 per cent.

In contrast to the high levels of productively infected macrophages in the brain, spinal chord, lymphatic, and lung tissues, the frequency of viral mRNA expressing cells in liver, skin, bone marrow, and blood is quite low (238–244). Here, monocytes and tissue macrophages are rarely infected. It is often difficult to explain disease-related histopathology in the face of a low frequency of virus-infected cells. For example, haematological abnormalities, including anaemia, leucopenia, thrombocytopenia, and myelodysplasia are common in AIDS patients and this suggests that HIV infects progenitor myeloid-monocytic cells (245–248). In fact, direct evidence of HIV infection in progenitor cells has been obtained from *in vitro* studies alone (245). Here, cultured bone marrow cells (positively selected CD34+ cells) were productively infected following exposure to HIV. The levels of viral gene expression were similar to those observed in HIV-infected monocyte/macrophages. Viral infection was non-cytopathic and virions were produced intracellularly (245). These results and others suggested that the bone marrow may function as a reservoir for HIV, differentiating into cells of monocytoid lineage and spreading virus throughout the host (245–248). However, recent studies call this theory into question. Bone marrow suspension cells from 14 patients with AIDS or AIDS-related complex were analysed and results employing fluorescence-based cell and polymerase chain reaction (PCR) amplification and sorting failed to show evidence of viral infection in the haematopoietic progenitor cells analysed *ex vivo* (249).

Levels of productive viral infection in blood are also quite low, commonly less than 0.001 per cent (240). However, unlike the bone marrow, large numbers of blood leucocytes harbour proviral DNA (241–244). The frequency of provirus in blood of HIV-seropositive individuals is less than 0.1 per cent as detected by PCR amplification of DNA or by isolation of HIV from blood cells by limiting dilution assays. The highest rates of infection are in CD4+ T-cells. Monocytes are only rarely infected in bone marrow and peripheral blood (242,243). Similar findings are observed in other subpopulations of macrophages outside the CNS: lymph nodes and lung (238).

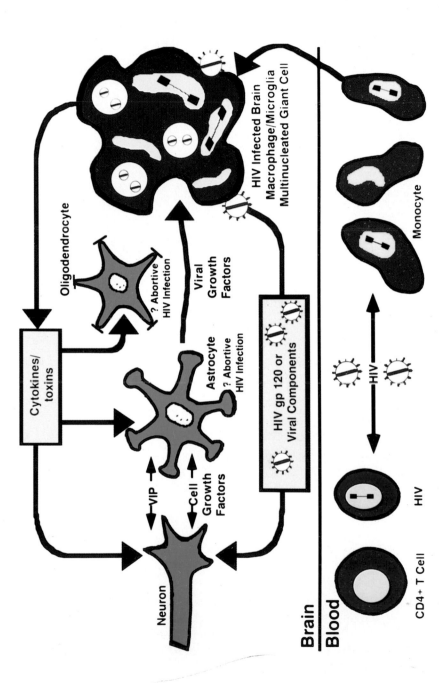

Plate 3 The progression of disease during HIV infection of the central nervous system. The macrophage is the major target cell for productive HIV infection in the brain, and may become infected through circulating HIV-infected T-cells or monocytes which traffic to the brain and set up a persistent infection in microglial cells. Neurological disease is mediated through the production of viral components or cytokines/toxins made from the infected brain macrophage.

7.7 Mononuclear phagocytes in lentiviral persistence: mechanisms for evasion of host immune surveillance during subclinical infection and disease

Lentiviruses infect monocytes and macrophages and represent a primary target cell for virus in the human host. How infection in these cells is perpetuated despite vigorous host immune responses and ultimately leads to clinical disease is not yet understood. However, some of the shared biological features of these viruses provide clues as to the role of the macrophage in viral persistence and pathogenesis. All lentiviruses share common biological, morphological, biochemical, and molecular features. Common mechanisms for viral persistence include:

(1) latent or restricted infection;

(2) permissive infection in macrophages with intravacuolar virion accumulation (196) (Figure 4.4) and reduced viral envelope glycoproteins expressed on the cell surface;

(3) restricted infection of precursor stem cells of macrophage lineage, whereby virus is maintained in cells with prolonged lifespans (16–19,193–196);

(4) virus-induction of neutralizing antibodies providing a milieu for the generation of neutralization escape mutants by immune pressure to produce altered antigenic variants (250–252);

(5) cell-to-cell spread of virus from monocytes to T-cells or monocytes to monocytes (253);

(6) restriction of viral gene expression by cytokines (for example, IFN) secreted by monocytes and/or T-cells (163);

(7) antibody-mediated enhancement in association with the Fc or complement receptors (as operative in Flaviviral infections) (127–130); and

(8) infection and replication of virus in brain macrophages and microglia in a privileged CNS sanctuary (224–229).

The generation of antigenic variants may lead to viral persistence and escape from host immune surveillance and is related specifically to the genetic properties of the virus and not the macrophage. Lentiviral replication results in the induction of antibodies to all polypeptides of the virion. Immunoprecipitation assays show that binding antibodies to the envelope glycoproteins of the virus are produced in most cases. In contrast, antibodies to viral neutralization epitopes develop slowly, weeks to months after infection or not at all, often depend on the virus strain. During the course of disease, virus populations may be recovered that are not neutralized by sera obtained early in the course of infection. This escape of virus from neutralization, often termed 'antigenic drift', is characteristic of many lentiviral infections and is one mechanism for persistent viral replication (251,252). A defined clinical role for antigenic drift in disease pathogenesis has been demonstrated for EIAV (252).

7.8   Virus–virus interactions

Viral gene expression in monocytes may be regulated by a second, super-infecting viral pathogen. Considerable interest has been generated in the interactions of other viruses, and HIV in particular, as they play major roles as opportunistic pathogens during disease and could potentially accelerate the onset of AIDS. Furthermore, and through the course of HIV infection, individuals often become co-infected with a variety of viruses. Co-infection with herpes simplex virus (HSV), cytomegalovirus (CMV) and Epstein–Barr virus (EBV), are commonly found in people with, or at risk for, AIDS. Studies examining the role of DNA viruses in the up-regulation of HIV gene expression were initially performed by examining the effects of hetero-logous viruses on expression of the HIV LTR (254). When plasmids containing the immediate early genes of heterologous DNA viruses were co-transfected into cells with plasmids containing the CAT gene linked to the HIV LTR or these cells infected directly with virus, CAT activity was increased. As HSV and CMV replicate in macrophages and dual infection of brain macrophages by HIV and CMV was reported (255), these dual infected cells could play significant roles in the progression of HIV disease possibly to resistance to or enhancement of viral infections.

8   Summary

The role played by monocytes and macrophages in resistance to virus infection, persistence, and dissemination has been reviewed. The scavenger cell function, antigen presentation, effector cell function, the state of differentiation, and activation of this cell type, and the strain of the virus are all critical in determining the outcome of virus–cell interactions. Improved treatment for viral infections will include a comprehensive understanding of these factors at the molecular, cellular, and pathogenic levels. The mechan-isms by which macrophages restrict viral replication or result in permissive infection and disease is typified by the most significant and devastating viral illness of this century, HIV.

Acknowledgements

This work is dedicated to Mr Henry H. Hoyt, Jr. and Dr Joseph Harun of Carter–Wallace Inc. Their generous support over many years made many of these studies possible. The authors wish to thank members of the HIV-Immunopathogenesis Program for their tireless work and devotion, Ms

Victoria Hunter for excellent illustrations and graphics, Drs Monte S. Meltzer, Donald Skillman, Jim Turpin, and Linixian Wu for critical review of the manuscript, and members of the Military Medical Consortium for Applied Retroviral Research for continued support and excellent patient management. Dr H.E. Gendelman is a Carter–Wallace fellow of The Johns Hopkins University School of Public Health and Hygiene in the Department of Immunology and Infectious Diseases. These studies were supported in part by the Henry M. Jackson Foundation for the Advancement of Military Medicine, Rockville, MD (HEG) and by a research grant, AI 25751, from the National Institute for Allergy and Infectious Diseases (PSM). The views expressed are not necessarily those of the Department of Defense or the United States Army.

References

1 Mims, C.A. (1964). Aspects of the pathogenesis of virus diseases. *Bacteriol. Rev.*, **28**, 30–71.

2 Lopez, C. (1983). Natural resistance mechanisms against herpes virus in health and disease. In *Immunobiology of herpes simplex virus infection* (ed. B. Rouse and C. Lopez). CRC Press, Boca Raton, Florida.

3 Morahan, P.S. (1983). Interactions of herpesviruses with mononuclear phagocytes. In *Immunobiology of herpes simplex virus infection*. (ed. B. Rouse and C. Lopez), pp. 72–89. CRC Press, Boca Raton, Florida.

4 Nathan, C.F. (1987). Secretory products of macrophages. *J. Clin. Invest.*, **79**, 319–24.

5 Mogensen, S.C. (1979). Role of macrophages in natural resistance to virus infections. *Micro. Rev.*, **43**, 1–26.

6 Morahan, P.S., Connor, J.R., and Leary, K.R. (1985). Viruses and the versatile macrophage. *Br. Med. Bull.*, **41**, 15–21.

7 Wu, L. Morahan, P.S., and Leary K. (1990). Mechanisms of intrinsic macrophage-virus interactions *in vitro*. *Micro. Path.*, **9**, 293–301.

8 Oppenheim, J.J. and Leonard, E.J. (1989). Introduction to human monocytes. In *Human monocytes* (ed. M. Zembala and G.L. Asherson). Academic Press, New York.

9 Van Furth, T., Cohn, Z.A., Hirsch, J.G., Humphry, J.H., Spector, W.G., and Langevoort, H.L., (1972). The mononuclear phagocyte system: a new classification of macrophages, monocytes and their precursor cells, *Bull. W.H.O.*, **46**, 845–55.

10 Gordon, S. (1986). Biology of the macrophage. *J. Cell. Sci.* **4**, 267–76.

11 Morahan, P.S. and Morse, S.S. (1979). Macrophage-virus interactions. In *Virus-lymphocyte interactions: Implications for disease* (ed. S. Proffitt), pp. 17–35, Elsevier, North Holland.

12 Johnson, R.T. and Griffin, D.E. (1978). Pathogenesis of viral infections. In *Handbook of clinical neurology: Infections of the nervous system* (ed. P.J. Vinken and G.W. Bruyn). North-Holland, New York.

13 Oldstone, M.B.A. (1989). Viral alteration of cell function. *Sci. American*, **Aug.**, 42–8.

14 Semenov, B.F. (1981). Viruses as nonspecific modulators of immunological reactivity. *Acta Virol.*, **25**, 122–8.

15 Morahan, P.S. and Murasko, D.M. (1988). Viral infections. In *Natural immunity in disease processes* (ed. D.S. Nelsa) pp. 557–86, Academic Press, Australia.

16 Narayan, O. and Clements, J.E. (1989). Biology and pathogenesis of lentiviruses. *J. Gen. Virol.*, **70**, 1617–1639.

17 Pauza, C.D. (1988). HIV persistence in monocytes leads to pathogenesis and AIDS. *Cell. Immunol.*, **112**, 414–24.

18 Gendelman, H.E. *et al.* (1989). The macrophage in the persistence and pathogenesis of HIV infection. *AIDS (London)*, **3**, 475–95.

19 Meltzer, M.S., Skillman, D.R., Gomatos, P.J., Kalter, D.C., and Gendelman, H.E. (1990). Role of mononuclear phagocytes in the pathogenesis of human immunodefiency virus infection. *Ann. Rev. Immunol.*, **8**, 169–94.

20 Alcami, A., Carrascosa, A.L., and Vinuela, E. (1990). Interaction of African swine fever virus with macrophages. *Virus Res.*, **17**, 93–104.

21 Brunner, K.T., Hurez, D., McCluskey, R.T., and Bencerraf, B. (1960). Blood clearance of P^{32} labelled vesicular stomatitis and Newcastle disease viruses by the reticuloendothelial system in mice. *J. Immunol.*, **85**, 99–104.

22 Mims, C.A. (1959). The response of mice to large intravenous injections of ectromelia virus. I. The fate of injected virus. *Br. J. Exp. Pathol.*, **40**, 543–50.

23 Mims, C.A. (1960). An analysis of the toxicity for mice of influenza virus. II. Intravenous toxicity. *Bri. J. Exp. Pathol.*, **41**, 593–8.

24 Mims, C.A. (1956). Rift Valley fever virus in mice. II. Adsorption and multiplication of virus. *Br. J. Exp. Pathol.*, **37**, 110–19.

25 Bang, F.B. and Warwick, A. (1960). Mouse macrophages as host cells for the mouse hepatitis virus and the genetic basis of their susceptibility. *Proc. Natl. Acad. Sci. U.S.A.*, **46**, 1065–75.

26 Theis, G. and Koprowski, H. (1961). A cellular basis for virus resistance. *Fed. Proc.* **20**, 265.

27 Kennedy, P.G.E., Narayan, O., Zink, M.C., Hess, J., Clements. J.E., and Adams, R.J. (1989). The pathogenesis of visna, a lentivirus induced immunopathologic disease of the central nervous system. In *Clinical and molecular aspects of viral illness of the nervous system* (ed. D.H. Gilden and H. Lipton). Martinus Nijhoff, Boston.

28 Johnson, R.T. (1964). The pathogenesis of herpes virus encephalitis. II. A cellular basis for the development of resistance with age. *J. Exp. Med.*, **120**, 359–79.

29 Steffan, A-M., Gendrault, J-L., and Kirn, A. (1978). Synthesis of vaccinia specified antigens in mouse hepatocytes after frog virus 3-induced damage to the sinusoidal cells. *FEMS Microbiol. Lett.*, **3**, 5–7.

30 McCuskey, R.S., (1986). *In vivo* and electron microscopic study of dynamic events occurring in hepatic sinusoids following frog virus 3 infection. In *Cells of the hepatic sinusoid*, Vol. I) (ed. A. Kirn, D.L. Knook, and E. Wisse), pp. 351–6. Marcel Dekker, New York.

31 Pereira, C.A., Steffan, A-M., and Kirn, A. (1984). Kupffer and endothelial cell damage renders A/J mice susceptible to mouse hepatitis virus type 3. *Virus Res.*, **1**, 557–63.

32 Virelizier, J-L. and Gresser, I. (1978). Role of interferon in the

pathogenesis of viral diseases of mice as demonstrated by the use of anti-interferon serum. V. Protective role in mouse hepatitis virus type 3 infection of susceptible and resistant strains of mice. *J. Immunol.*, **120**, 1616–19.

33 DuPuy, J-M., DuPuy, C., and DeCarie, D. (1984). Genetically determined resistance to mouse hepatitis virus 3 is expressed in hematopoietic donor cells in radiation chimeras. *J. Immunol.*, **133**, 1609–13.

34 Hirsch, M.S., Zisman, B., and Allison, A.C. (1970). Macrophages and age-dependent resistance to herpes simplex virus in mice. *J. Immunol.*, **104**, 1160–5.

35 Turner, G.S. and Ballard, R. (1976). Interaction of mouse peritoneal macrophages with fixed rabies virus *in vivo* and *in vitro*. *J. Gen. Virol.* **30**, 223–31.

36 Melnicoff, M.J., Morahan, P.S., Jensen, B.D., Breslin, E.W., and Horan, P.K. (1988). *In vivo* labelling of resident peritoneal macrophages. *J. Leuk. Biol.*, **43**, 387–97.

37 Rosen, H. and Gordon, S. (1990). Adoptive transfer of fluorescence-labelled cells shows that resident peritoneal macrophages are able to migrate into specialized lymphoid organs and inflammatory sites in the mouse. *Eur. J. Immunol.*, **20**, 1251–8.

38 Zisman, B., Hirsch, M.S., and Allison, A.C. (1970). Selective effects of anti-macrophage serum, silica and antilymphocyte serum on pathogenesis of herpes virus infection of young adult mice. *J. Immunol.*, **104**, 1155–9.

39 Mogensen, S.C. and Anderson, H.K. (1977). Effect of silica on the pathogenic distinction between herpes simplex virus type 1 and 2 hepatitis in mice. *Infect. Immunol.*, **17**, 274–277.

40 duBuy, H. (1975). Effect of silica on virus infections in mice and mouse tissue culture. *Infect. Immunol.*, **11**, 996–1002.

41 Schlabach, A.J., Martinez, D., Fiedl, A.K., and Tytell, A.A. (1979). Resistance of C58 mice to primary systemic herpes simplex virus infection: macrophage dependence and T-cell independence. *Infect. Immunol.*, **26**, 615–22.

42 Lopez, C., Ryshke, R., and Bennett, M. (1980). Marrow-dependent cells depleted by ^{89}Sr mediate genetic resistance to herpes simplex virus type 1 in mice. *Infect. Immunol.*, **28**, 1028–34.

43 Morahan, P.S., Coleman, P.H., Morse, S.S., and Volkman, A. (1982). Resistance to infections in mice with defects in the activities of mononuclear phagocytes and natural killer cells: effects of immunomodulators in beige mice and ^{89}Sr-treated mice. *Infect. Immunol.*, **37**, 1079–85.

44 Pinto, A.J., Stewart, D., van Rooijen, N., and Morahan, P.S. (1991). Selective depletion of liver and splenic macrophages using liposomes

encapsulating the drug dichloromethylene diphosphonate: effects on antimicrobial resistance. *J. Leuk. Biol.*, **49**, 579–86.

45 Schirmacher, P., Worsdorfer, M., Lubbe, K., Falke, D., Thoenes, W., and Dienes, H.P. (1989). HSV hepatitis in the mouse: a light and electron microscopic study with immunohistology and *in situ* hybridization. *Virchows Arch. B. Cell Pathol.*, **56**, 351–61.

46 Stanton, G.J. and Baron, S. (1984). Interferon and viral pathogenesis. In *Concepts in viral pathogenesis* (ed. A.L. Notkins and M.B.A. Oldstone). Springer, New York.

47 De Maeyer, E. and De Maeyer-Guignard, J. (1988). From an antiviral factor to a family of multifunctional cytokines. In *Interferons and other regulatory cytokines*. John Wiley, New York.

48 Bell, D.M., Roberts Jr, N.J., and Hall C.B. (1983). Different antiviral spectra of human macrophage interferon activities. *Nature*, **305**, 319–21.

49 Goldberg, M., Belkowski, M., and Bloom, B.R. (1989). Regulation of macrophage growth and antiviral activity by interferon-γ. *J. Cell. Biol.*, **109**, 1331–40.

50 Goldfeld, A.E. and Maniatis, T. (1989). Coordinate viral induction of tumor necrosis factor a and interferon b in human B cells and monocytes. *Proc. Natl. Acad. Sci. U.S.A.*, **86**, 1490–4.

51 Gresser, I., Tovey, M.G., Maury, C., and Bandu, M.T. (1976). Role of interferon in the pathogenesis of virus diseases in mice as demonstrated by the use of anti-interferon serum. II. Studies with herpes simplex, Moloney sarcoma, vesicular stomatitis, Newcastle disease, and influenza virus. *J. Exp. Med.*, **144**, 1316–24.

52 Belardelli, F., Vignaux, F., Proietti, E., and Gresser, I. (1984). Injection of mice with antibody to interferon renders peritoneal macrophages permissive for vesicular stomatitis virus and encephalomyocarditis virus. *Proc. Natl. Acad. Sci. U.S.A.*, **81**, 602–6.

53 Stanton, G.J., Jordan, C., Hart, A., Heard, H., Langford, M.P., and Baron, S. (1987). Nondetectable levels of interferon gamma is a critical host defense during the first day of herpes simplex virus infection. *Micro. Path.*, **3** , 179–83.

54 Morahan, P.S., Pinto, A.J., Stewart, D., Murasko, D.M., and Brinton, M.A. (1991). Varying role of alpha/beta interferon in the antiviral efficacy of synthetic immunomodulators against Semliki forest virus infection. *Antiviral Res.*, **15**, 241–54.

55 Horisberger, M.A., Staeheli, P., and Haller, O. (1983). Interferon induces a unique protein in mouse cells bearing a gene for resistance to influenza virus. *Proc. Natl. Acad. Sci. U.S.A.*, **80**, 1910–14.

56 Meyer, T. and Horisberger, M.A. (1984). Combined action of mouse α and β interferons in influenza virus-infected macrophages carrying the resistance gene Mx. *J. Virol.*, **49**, 709–16.

57 Krug, R.M., Shaw, M., Broni, B., Shapiro, G., and Haller, O. (1985). Inhibition of influenza viral mRNA synthesis in cells expressing the interferon-induced Mx gene product. *J. Virol.* **56**, 201–6.

58 Staeheli, P. and Haller, O. (1987). Interferon-induced Mx protein: A mediator of cellular resistance to influenza virus. In *Interferon*, Vol. 8. (eds.) Academic Press, London.

59 Brinton, M.A., Arnheiter, H., and Haller, O. (1982). Interferon independence of genetically controlled resistance to flaviviruses. *Infec. Immunol.*, **36**, 284–8.

60 Kornbluth, R.S., Oh, P.S., Munis, J.R., Cleveland, P.H., and Richman, D.D. (1989). Interferons and bacterial lipopoylsaccharide protect macrophages from productive infection by human immunodeficiency virus *in vitro*. *J. Exp. Med.*, **169**, 1137–48.

61 Kornbluth, R., Oh, P.S., Munis, J.R., Cleveland, P.H., and Richman, D.D. (1990). The role of interferons in the control of HIV replication in macrophages. *Clin. Immunol. Immunopath*, **54**, 200–19.

62 Gendelman, H.E., *et al.* (1990). Regulation of HIV replication in infected monocytes by IFNα mechanisms for viral restriction. *J. Immunol.*, **145**, 2669–76.

63 Gendelman, H.E., *et al.* (1990). Restriction of HIV replication in infected T cells and monocytes by interferon-α. *AIDS Res. Hum. Retro.*, **6**, 1045–9.

64 Yasuda, Y., *et al.* (1990). Interferon-α treatment leads to accumulation of virus particles on the surface of cells persistently infected with the human immunodeficiency virus type 1. *J. Acq. Imm. Def. Syn.*, **3**, 1046–51.

65 Bukowski, J.F. and Welsh, R.M. (1986). The role of natural killer cells and interferon in resistance to acute infection of mice with herpes simplex virus type 1. *J. Immunol.*, **136**, 3481–5.

66 Friedman, R.M. and Pitha, P.M. (1984). The effect of interferon on membrane-associated viruses. In *Interferon Mechanisms of production and action*, Vol. 3 (ed. R.M. Friedman). Elsevier, New York.

67 Narayan, O., Sheffer, D., Clements, J.E., and Tennekoon, G. (1985). Restricted replication of lentiviruses: visna viruses induce a unique interferon during interaction between lymphocytes and infected macrophages. *J. Exp. Med.*, **162**, 1954–69.

68 Zin, K.M.C. and Narayan, O. (1989). Lentivirus-induced interferon inhibits maturation and proliferation of monocytes and restricts the replication of caprine arthritis encephalitis virus. *J. Virol.*, **63**, 2578–84.

69 Zawatzky, R., Gresser, I., Demayer, E., and Kirchner, H. (1982). The role of interferon in the resistance of C57BL/6 mice to various doses of herpes simplex virus type 1. *J. Infect. Dis.*, **146**, 405–12.

70 Linnavuori, K. and Hovi, T. (1983). Restricted replication of herpes

simplex virus in human monocyte cultures: role of interferon. *Virology*, **130**, 1–9.

71   Domke-Opitz, I., Straub, P., and Kirchner, H. (1986). Effect of interferon on replication of herpes simplex virus types 1 and 2 in human macrophages. *J. Virol.*, **60**, 37–42.

72   Straub, P., Domke, I., Kirchner, H., Jacobsen, H., and Panet, A. (1986). Synthesis of herpes simplex virus proteins and nucleic acids in interferon-treated macrophages. *Virology*, **150**, 411–18.

73   Ellermann-Eriksen, S., Liberto, M.C., Iannello, D., and Mogensen, S.C. (1986). X-linkage of the early in vitro a/b response of mouse peritoneal macrophages to herpes simplex virus type 2. *J. Gen. Virol.*, **67**, 1025–33.

74   Krilov, L., Hendry, R.M., Godfrey, E., and McIntosh, K. (1987). Respiratory virus infection of peripheral blood monocytes: correlation with ageing of cells and interferon production *in vitro. J. Gen. Virol.*, **68**, 1749–60.

75   Proietti, E., Gessani, S., Belardelli, F., and Gresser, I. (1986). Mouse peritoneal cells confer an antiviral state on mouse cell monolayers: role of interferon. *J. Virol.*, **57**, 456–63.

76   Hoss, A., Zwarthoff, E.C., and Zawatzky, R. (1989). Differential expression of interferon alpha and beta induced with Newcastle disease virus in mouse macrophage cultures. *J. Gen. Virol.*, **70**, 575–89.

77   Morahan, P.S., Volkman, A., Melnicoff, M., and Dempsey, W.L. (1988). Macrophage heterogeneity. In *Macrophages and cancer* (ed. G. Heppner and A. Fulton), pp. 1–25. CRC Press, Boca Raton, Florida.

78   Vogel, S.N. and Fertsch, D. (1987). Macrophages from endotoxin-hyporesponsive (Lps/d) C3H/HeJ mice are permissive for vesicular stomatitis virus because of reduced levels of endogenous interferon: possible mechanism for natural resistance to virus infection. *J. Virol.*, **61**, 812–18.

79   Sit, M.F., Tenney, D.J., Rothstein, J.L., and Morahan, P.S. (1988). Effect of macrophage activation on resistance of mouse peritoneal macrophages to infection with herpes simplex virus types 1 and 2. *J. Gen. Virol.*, **69**, 1999–2010.

80   Rager-Zisman, B., Kunkel, M., Tanaka, Y., and Bloom, B.R. (1982). Role of macrophage oxidative metabolism in resistance to vesicular stomatitis virus infection. *Infect. Immunol.*, **36**, 1229–37.

81   Preble, O.T., *et al.* (1985). Role of interferon in AIDS. *Ann. N.Y. Acad. Sci.*, **437**, 65–72.

82   Hayashi, K., Kurata, T., Morishma, T., and Nassery, T. (1980). Analysis of the inhibitory effect of peritoneal macrophages on the spread of herpes simplex virus. *Infect. Immunol.*, **28**, 350–8.

83   Morse, S.S. and Morahan, P.S. (1981). Activated macrophages medi-

ate interferon-independent inhibition of herpes simplex virus. *Cell. Immunol.*, **58**, 72–9.

84 Morahan, P.S., Morse, S.S., and McGeorge, M.B. (1980). Macrophage extrinsic antiviral activity during herpes simplex virus infection. *J. Gen. Virol.*, **46**, 291–301.

85 Wildy, P., Gell, P.G.H., Rhodes, J., and Newton, A. (1982). Inhibition of herpes simplex virus multiplication by activated macrophages: a role for arginase? *Infect. Immunol.*, **37**, 40–5.

86 Herberman, R.B. (1977). Immunogenicity of tumor antigens. *Biochim. Biophy. Acta*, **473**, 93–119.

87 Rouse, B.T. and Horchov, D.W. (1986). Immunosuppression in viral infections. *Rev. Infect. Dis.*, **8**, 850–73.

88 Rinaldo, C.R. (1990). Immune suppression by herpesviruses. *Ann. Rev. Med.*, **41**, 331–8.

89 Lewis, M.A., Slater, J., Leverone, L.I., and Campbell, A.E. (1990). Enhancement of interleukin-1 activity by murine cytomegalovirus infection of a macrophage cell line. *Virology*, **178**, 452–60.

90 Moses, A.V. and Garnett, H.M. (1990). Effect of human cytomegalovirus on the production and biological action of interleukin-1. *J. Infect. Dis.*, **162**, 381–8.

91 Scott, D.M., Rodgers, B.C., Freeke, C., Buiter, J., and Sissons, J.G.P. (1989). Human cytomegalovirus and monocytes: limited infection and neglible immunosuppression in normal mononuclear cells infected *in vitro* with mycoplasma-free virus strains. *J. Gen. Virol*, **70**, 685–94.

92 van Bruggen, I., Price, P., Robertson, T.A., and Papadimitriou, J.M. (1989). Morphological and functional changes during cytomegalovirus replication in murine macrophages. *J. Leuk. Biol.*, **46**, 508–20.

93 Campbell, A.E., Slater, J.S., and Futch, W.S. (1989). Murine cytomegalovirus-induced suppression of antigen-specific cytotoxic T lymphocyte maturation. *Virology*, **173**, 268–75.

94 Campbell, A.E., Slater, J., Cavanaugh, V., and Stenberg, R. Cytomegalovirus infection inhibits antigen presentation to cytotoxic T lymphocytes. *Fed. Proc.*, (In press).

95 Browne, H., Smith, G., Beck, S., and Minson, T. (1990). A complex between the MHC Class I homologue encoded by human cytomegalovirus and beta-2-microglobulin. *Nature*, **347**, 770–2.

96 Mann, D.L., Gartner, S., LeSane, F., Blattner, W.A., and Popovic, M. (1990). Cell surface antigens and function of monocytes and a monoccytelike cell line before and after infection with HIV. *Clin. Immunol. Immunopath.*, **54**, 174–83.

97 Mann, D.L., Gartner, S., LeSane, F., Buchow, H., and Popovic, M. (1990). HIV-1 transmission and function of virus-infected monocytes/macrophages. *J. Immunol.*, **144**, 2152–8.

 98 Rowson, K.E.K. and Mahy, B.W.J. (1985). Lactate dehydrogenase-elevating virus. *J. Gen. Virol.*, **66**, 2297–312.
 99 Brinton-Darnell, M., Collins, J.K., and Plagemann, P.G.W. (1975). Lactate dehydrogenase-elevating virus replication, maturation, and viral RNA synthesis in primary mouse macrophage cultures. *Virology*, **65**, 187–95.
100 Lagwinska, E., Stewart, C.C., Adles, C., and Schlesinger, S. (1975). Replication of lactic dehydrogenase virus and Sindbis virus in mouse peritoneal macrophages. Induction of interferon and phenotypic mixing. *Virology*, **65**, 204–14.
101 Stueckemann, J.A., *et al.* (1982). Replication of lactate dehydrogenase-elevating virus in macrophages. 2. Mechanism of persistent infection in mice and cell culture. *J. Gen. Virol.*, **59**, 263–72.
102 Inada, T. and Mims, C.A. (1985). Ia antigens and Fc receptors of mouse peritoneal macrophages as determinants of susceptibility to lactic dehydrogenase virus. *J. Gen. Virol.*, **66**, 1469–77.
103 Kowalchyk, K. and Plagemann, P.G.W. (1985). Cell surface receptors for lactate dehydrogenase-elevating virus on subpopulation of macrophages. *Virus Res.*, **2**, 211–29.
104 Inada, T. and Mims, C.A. (1986). Infection of mice with lactic dehydrogenase virus prevents development of experimental allergic encephalomyelitis. *J. Neuroimmunol.*, **11**, 53–6.
105 Isakov, N., Feldman, M., and Segal, S. (1982). Acute infection of mice with lactic dehydrogenase virus (LDV) impairs the antigen-presenting capacity of their macrophages. *Cell. Immunol.*, **66**, 317–32.
106 Stueckemann, J.A., *et al.* (1982). Replication of lactate dehydrogenase-elevating virus in macrophages. 1. Evidence for cytocidal replication. *J. Gen. Virol.*, **59**, 245–62.
107 Inada, T. and Mims, C.A. (1985). Patterns of infection and selective loss of Ia+ cells in suckling and adult mice inoculated with lactic dehydrogenase virus. *Arch. Virol.*, **86**, 151–65.
108 Buxton, I.K., Chan, S.P.K., and Plagemann, P.G.W. (1988). Ia is not the major receptor for lactate dehydrogenase-elevating virus on macrophages from CBA and Balb/c mice. *Virus Res.*, **9**, 205–19.
109 Stroop, W.G. and Brinton, M.A. (1985). Enhancement of encephalomyeloradiculitis in mice sensitized with spinal cord tissue and infected with lactate dehydrogenase-elevating virus. *J. Neuroimmunol.*, **8**, 79–92.
110 Weiland, E., Weiland, F., and Grossman, A. (1987). Lactate dehydrogenase-elevating virus induces anti-Golgi apparatus antibodies. *J. Gen. Virol.*, **68**, 1983–91.
111 Halstead, S.B. (1983). Immune enhancement of viral infection. *Prog. Allergy*, **31**, 301–64.

112 Porterfield, J.S. (1985). Antibody enhanced viral growth in macrophages. *Immunol. Lett.*, **11**, 213–17.

113 Pang, T. (1983). Delayed-type hypersensitivity: Probable role in the pathogenesis of dengue hemorrhagic fever/dengue shock syndrome. *Rev. Infect. Dis.*, **5**, 346–52.

114 Halstead, S.B., Marchette, N.J., Chow, J.S., and Lolekha, S. (1976). Dengue virus replication enhancement in peripheral blood leukocytes from immune human beings. *Proc. Soc. Exp. Biol. Med.*, **5**, 36–139.

115 Halstead, S.B. and O'Rourke, E.J. (1977). Dengue viruses and mononuclear phagocytes. I. Infection enhancement by non-neutralizing antibody. *J. Exp. Med.*, **146**, 218–29.

116 Halstead, S.B., Porterfield, J.S., and O'Rourke, E.J. (1980). Enhancement of dengue virus infection in monocytes by flavivirus antisera. *Am. J. Trop. Med. Hyg.*, **29**, 638–42.

117 Halstead, S.B. (1980). Dengue haemorrhagic fever—a public health problem and a field for research. *Bull. W.H.O.*, **58**, 1–21.

118 Halstead, S.B. (1981). The pathogenesis of dengue: molecular epidemiology in infectious disease. *Am. J. Epidemiol.*, **114**, 632–48.

119 Eckels, K.H., Klinks, S.C., Dubois, D.R., Wahl, L.M., and Bancroft, W.H. (1985). The association of enhancing antibodies with seroconversion in humans receiving a dengue-2 live virus vaccine. *J. Immunol.*, **135**, 4201–3.

120 Brandt, W.E., McCown, J.M., Gentry, M.K., and Russell, P.K. (1982). Infection enhancement of dengue type 2 virus in the U-937 human monocyte cell line by antibodies to flavivirus cross-reactive determinants. *Infect. Immunol.*, **36**, 1036–41.

121 Ochiai, H., Kurokawa, M., Hayashi, K., and Niwayama, S. (1986). Antibody-mediated growth of infleunza A NWS virus in macrophage like cell line P388D1. *J. Virol.*, **62**, 20–6.

122 Traavik, T., Uhlin-Hansen-L., Flaegstad, T., and Christie, K.E. (1988). Antibody-mediated enhancement of BK virus infection in human monocytes and a human macrophage-like cell line. *J. Med. Virol.*, **24**, 283–97.

123 Inada, T., Chong, K.T., and Mims, C.A. (1985). Enhancing antibodies, macrophages and virulence in mouse cytomegalovirus infection. *J. Gen. Virol.*, **66**, 871–8.

124 Jolly, P.E., Huso, D.L., Sheffer, D., and Narayan, O. (1989). Modulation of lentivirus replication by antibodies: Fc portion of immunoglobulin molecule is essential for enhancement of binding, internalization, and neutralization of visna virus in macrophages. *J. Virol.*, **63**, 1811–13.

125 Gomatos, P.J., *et al.* (1990). Relative inefficiency of soluble recombinant CD4 for inhibition of infection by monocyte-tropic HIV in monocytes and T cells. *J. Immunol.*, **144**, 4183–8.

126 Robinson, W.E. Jr., Montefiori, D.C., and Mitchell, W.M. (1988). Antibody-dependent enhancement of human immunodeficiency virus type-1 infection. *Lancet*, **i**, 790–4.

127 Homsy, J., Tateno, M., and Levy, J.A. (1988). Antibody-dependent enhancement of HIV infection. *Lancet*, **i**, 1285–6.

128 Takeda, A., Tuazon, C.U., and Ennis, F.A. (1988). Antibody-enhanced infection by HIV-1 via Fc receptor mediated entry. *Science*, **242**, 580–3.

129 Homsy, J., Meyer, M., Tateno, M., Clarkson, S., and Levy, J.A. (1989). The Fc and not CD4 receptor mediates antibody enhancement of HIV infection in human cells. *Science*, **244**, 1357–60.

130 Jauault, T., Chapuis, F., Olivier, R., Parravicini, C., Bahraoui, E., and Gluckman, J.-C. (1989). HIV infection of monocytic cells: role of antibody-mediated virus binding to Fc-gamma receptors. *AIDS*, **3**, 125–33.

131 Laurence, J., Saunders, A., Early, E., and Salmon, J.E. (1990). Human immunodeficiency virus infection of monocytes: relationship to Fc-gamma receptors and antibody-dependent viral enhancement. *Immunology*, **70**, 338–43.

132 Narayan, O., Wolinsky, J.S., Clements, J.E., Strandberg, J.D., Griffin, D.E., and Cork, L. (1983). Slow virus replication: the role of macrophages in the persistence and expression of visna viruses of sheep and goats. *J. Gen. Virol.*, **59**, 345–56.

133 Narayan, O., Kennedy-Stoskopf, S., Sheffer, D., Griffin, D.E., and Clements, J.E. (1983). Activation of caprine arthritis-encephalitis virus expression during maturation of monocytes to macrophages. *Infect. Immunol.*, **41**, 67–73.

134 Anderson, L.W., Klevjer-Anderson, P., and Liggitt, H.D. (1983). Susceptibility of blood-derived monocytes and macrophages to caprine arthritis-encephalitis virus. *Infect Immunol.*, **41**, 837–40.

135 Gendelman, H.E., Narayan, O., Kennedy-Stoskopf, S., Clements, J.E., and Pezeshkpour, G. (1984). Slow virus macrophage interactions: characterization of a transformed cell line of sheep alveolar macrophages that express a marker for susceptibility to ovine-caprine lentivirus infections. *Lab. Invest.*, **51**, 547–55.

136 Peluso, R., Haase, A., Stowring, L., Edwards, M., and Ventura, P. (1985). A trojan horse mechanism for the spread of visna virus in monocytes. *Virology*, **147**, 231–6.

137 Gendelman, H.E., Narayan, O., Molineaux, Clements, J.E., and Ghotbi, Z. (1985). Slow, persistent replication of lentiviruses: Role of tissue macrophages and macrophage precursors in bone marrow. *Proc. Natl. Acad. Sci. U.S.A.*, **82**, 7086–90.

138 Geballe, A.P., Ventura, P., Strowring, L., and Haase, A.T. (1985).

Quantitative analysis of visna virus replication *in vivo*. *Virology*, **141**, 148–54.

139 Gendelman, H.E., *et al.* (1986). Tropism of sheep lentiviruses for monocytes: Susceptibility to infection and virus gene expression increase during maturation of monocytes to macrophages. *J. Virol.*, **58**, 67–74.

140 Lairmore, M.D., Akita, G., Russell, H.E., and DeMartini, J.C. (1987). Replication and cytopathic effects of ovine lentivirus strains in alveolar macrophages correlate with in vivo pathogenicity. *J. Virol.*, **61**, 4038–42.

141 Gabuzda, D.H., Hess, J.L., Small, J.A., and Clements, J.E. (1989). Regulation of the visna virus long terminal repeat in macrophages involves cellular factors that bind sequences containing AP-1 sites. *Mol. Cell. Biol.*, **9**, 2728–33.

142 Esparza, I., Gonzalez, J.C., and Vinuela E. (1988). Effect of interferon-α, interferon-γ and tumour necrosis factor on African swine fever replication in porcine monocytes and macrophages. *J. Gen. Virol.*, **69**, 2973–84.

143 Stevens, J.G. and Cook, M.L. (1971). Restriction of herpes simplex virus by macorphages: An analysis of the cell–virus interaction. *J. Exp. Med.*, **133**, 19–38.

144 Leary, K., Connor, J.R., and Morahan, P.S. (1985). Comparison of herpes simplex virus type 1 DNA replication and virus production in murine bone marrow-derived and resident peritoneal macrophages. *J. Gen. Virol.*, **66**, 1123–9.

145 Howie, S., Norval, M., Maingay, J., and McBride, W.H. (1986). Interactions between herpes simplex virus and murine bone marrow macrophages. *Arch. Virol.*, **87**, 229–39.

146 Tenney, D.J. and Morahan, P.S. (1987). Effects of differentiation of human macrophage-like U937 cells on intrinsic resistance to herpes simplex virus type 1. *J. Immun.*, **139**, 3076–83.

147 Tenney, D.J. and Morahan, P.S. Differentiation of the U937 macrophage cell line removes an early block of HSV-1 infection. *Viral Immunol.*, (Submitted).

148 Kemp, L.M., Estridge, J.K., Brennan, A., Katz, D.R., and Latchman, D.S. (1990). Mononuclear phagocytes and HSV-1 infection: increased permissivity in differentiated U937 cells is mediated by post-transcriptional regulation of viral immediate early gene expression. *J. Leuc. Biol.*, **47**, 483–9.

149 Lopez-Guerrero, J.A., Pimentel-Muinos, F.X., Fresno, M., and Alonso, M.A. (1990). Role of soluble cytokines on the restricted replication of poliovirus in the monocytic U937 cell line. *Virus Res.*, **16**, 225–30.

150 Morahan, P.S., Mama, S., Anaraki, F., and Leary, K. (1989).

Molecular localization of abortive infection of resident peritoneal macrophages by herpes simplex virus type 1. *J. Virol.*, **63**, 2300–7.

151 Albers, I., Kirchner, H., and Domke-Opitz, I. (1989). Resistance of human blood monocytes to infection with herpes simplex virus. *Virology*, **169**, 466–9.

152 Pederson, N.C., Ho, E.W., Brown, M.L., and Yamamoto, J.K. (1987). Isolation of a T-lymphotropic virus from domestic cats with an immunodeficiency-like syndrome. *Science*, **235**, 790–3.

153 Brunner, D. and Pedersen, N.C. (1989). Infection of peritoneal macrophages *in vitro* and *in vivo* with feline immunodeficiency virus. *J. Virol.*, **63**, 5483–8.

154 Sarmiento, M. and Kleinerman, E.S. (1990). Innate resistance to herpes simplex virus infection. Human lymphocyte and monocyte inhibition of viral replication. *J. Immunol.*, **144**, 1942–53.

155 Kohl, S., Loo, L.S., Drath, D.B., and Cox, P. (1989). Interleukin-2 protects neonatal mice from lethal herpes simplex virus infection: a macrophage-mediated, gamma interferon-induced mechanism. *J. Infec. Dis.*, **159**, 239–47.

156 Folks, T.M., Justement, J., Kinter, A., Dinarello, C.A., and Fauci, A.S. (1987). Cytokine-induced expression of HIV-1 in a chronically infected promonocyte cell line. *Science*, **238**, 800–2.

157 Koyangi, Y., O'Brien, W.A., Zhao, J.O., Golde, D.W., Gasson, J.C., and Chen, I.S.Y. (1988). Cytokines alter production of HIV-1 from primary mononuclear phagocytes. *Science*, **241**, 1673–5.

158 Hammer, S.M., Gillis, J.M., Groopman, J.E., and Rose, R.M. (1987). *In vitro* modification of human immunodeficiency virus infection by granulocyte-macrophage colony-stimulating factor and g interferon. *Proc. Natl. Acad. Sci. U.S.A.*, **83**, 8734–8.

159 Matsuyama, T.H., *et al.* (1989). Enhancement of HIV replication and giant cell formation by tumor necrosis factor. *AIDS Res. Hum. Retro.*, **5**, 139–46.

160 Okamoto, T., *et al.* (1989). Augmentation of human immunodeficiency virus type 1 gene expression by tumor necrosis factor alpha. *AIDS Res. Hum. Retro.*, **5**, 131–8.

161 Clouse, K.A., *et al.* (1989). Monokine regulation of human immunodeficiency virus-1 expression in a chronically infected human T cell clone. *J. Immunol.*, **142**, 431–8.

162 Poli, G., *et al.* (1990). Interleukin 6 induces human immunodeficiency virus expression in infected monocytic cells alone and in synergy with tumor necrosis factor by transcriptional and post-transcriptional mechanisms. *J. Exp. Med.*, **172**, 151–6.

163 Schrier, R.D., McCutchan, J.A., Venable, J.C., Nelson, J.A., and Wiley, C.A. (1990). T-cell-induced expression of human immunodeficiency virus in macrophages. *J. Virol.*, **64**, 3280–8.

164 Novak, R.M., Holzer, T.J., Kennedy, M.M., Heynen, C.A., and Dawson, G. (1990). The effect of interleukin 4 (BSF-1) on infection of peripheral blood monocyte-derived macrophages with HIV-1. *AIDS Res. Hum. Retro.*, **6**, 973–6.

165 Nabel, G. and Baltimore, D. (1987). An inducible transcription factor activates expression of human immunodeficiency virus in T cells. *Nature*, **326**, 711–13.

166 Jones, K., Kadonaga, J., Luciw, P., and Tijian, R. (1986). Activation of the AIDS retrovirus promotor by the cellular transcription factor, SP1. *Science*, **232**, 755–9.

167 Griffin, G.E., Leung, K., Folks, T.M., Kunkel, S., and Nabel, G.J. (1989). Activation of HIV gene expression during differentiation by induction of NF-kB. *Nature*, **339**, 70–3.

168 Osborn, L., Kunkel, S., and Nabel, G.J. (1989). Tumor necrosis factor alpha and interleukin 1 stimulate the human immunodeficiency virus enhancer by activation of the nuclear factor kB. *Proc. Natl. Acad. Sci. U.S.A.*, **86**, 2336–40.

169 Kalter, D.C., *et al.* (1991). Enhanced HIV replication in MCSF-treated monocytes. *J. Immunol.*, **146**, 298–306.

170 Masihi, K.N., Lange, W., and Rohde-Schultz, B. (1990). Exacerbation of human immunodeficiency virus infection in promonocytic cells by bacterial immunomodulators. *J. Acq. Immunodef. Synd.*, **3**, 200–5.

171 Pomerantz, R.J., Feinberg, M.B., Trono, D., and Baltimore, D. (1990). Lipopolysaccharide is a potent monocyte/macrophage-specific stimulator of human immunodeficiency virus type 1 expression. *J. Exp. Med.*, **172**, 253–61.

172 Roberts, N.J. Jr. and Domurat F. (1989). Virus-induced immunosuppression: Influenza virus. In *Virus-induced immunosuppression* (ed. S. Spector, M. Bendinelli, and H. Friedman). Plenum, New York.

173 Rodgers, R. and Mims, C.A. (1981). Interaction of influenza virus with mouse macrophages. *Infect. Immunol.*, **31**, 751–7.

174 Van Campen, H., Easterday, B.C., and Hinshaw, V.S. (1989). Virulent avian influenza A viruses: Their effect on avian lymphocytes and macrophages *in vivo* and *in vitro*. *J. Gen. Virol.*, **70**, 2887–95.

175 Mock, D.J., Domurat, F., Roberts, N.J. Jr., Walsh, E.E., Licht, M.R., and Keng, P. (1987). Macrophages are required for influenza virus infection of human lymphocytes. *J. Clin. Invest.*, **79**, 620–4.

176 Mock, D.J. and Robert, N.J. Jr (1990). Role of the monocyte-macrophage in influenza virus infection of lymphocytes: implication for HIV infection. *AIDS Res. Hum. Retro.*, **6**, 965–6.

177 Leonard, J., *et al.* (1989). The human immunodeficiency virus long terminal repeat is preferentially expressed in Langerhans' cells in transgenic mice. *AIDS Res. Hum. Retro.*, **5**, 421–30.

178 Hammer, S.M., Gillis, J.M., Pinkston, P., and Rose, R.M. (1990).

Effect of zidovudine and granulocyte-macrophage colony-stimulating factor on human immunodeficiency virus replication in alveolar macrophages. *Blood*, **75**, 1215–19.

179 Roussel, M., *et al.* (1979). Three new types of viral oncogene of cellular origin specific for haematopoietic cell transformation. *Nature*, **281**, 452–5.

180 Durban, E.M. and Boettiger, D., (1981). Differential effects of transforming avian RNA tumor viruses on avian macrophages. *Proc. Natl. Acad. Sci. U.S.A.*, **78**, 3600–4.

181 Durban, E.M. and Boettiger, D. (1981). Replicating, differentiated macrophages can serve as *in vitro* targets for transformation by avian myeloblastosis virus. *J. Virol.*, **37**, 488–92.

182 Linial, M. (1982). Two retroviruses with similar transforming genes exhibit differences in transforming potential. *Virology*, **119**, 382–91.

183 Enrietto, P.J., Hayman, M.J., Ramsay, G.M., Wyke, J.A., and Payne, L.N. (1983). Altered pathogenicity of avian myelocytomatosis (MC29) viruses with mutations in the v-*myc* gene. *Virology*, **124**, 164–72.

184 Franz, T., *et al.* (1985). Transformation of mononuclear phagocytes *in vivo* and malignant histiocytosis caused by a novel murine spleen focus-forming virus. *Nature*, **315**, 149–51.

185 Blasi, E., Mathieson, B.J., Varesio, L., Cleveland, J.L., Borchert, P.A., and Rapp, U.R. (1985). Selective immortalization of murine macrophages from fresh bone marrow by a *raf/myc* recombinant murine retrovirus. *Nature*, **318**, 667–70.

186 Graf, T., *et al.* (1986). v-*mil* Induces autocrine growth and enhanced tumorigenicity in v-*myc*-transformed avian macrophages. *Cell*, **45**, 357–64.

187 Palmieri, S. (1986). Isolation of an MH2 retrovirus mutant temperature sensitive for macrophage but not fibroblast transformation. *J. Virol.*, **58**, 134–41.

188 Baubach, W.R., Keath, E., and Cole, M.D. (1986). A mouse-c-myc retrovirus transforms established fibroblast lines *in vitro* and induces monocyte-macrophage tumors *in vivo*. *J. Virol.*, **59**, 276–83.

189 Biegalke, B.J., Heaney, M.L., Bouton, A., Parsons, J.T., and Linial, M. (1987). MC29 deletion mutants which fail to transform chicken macrophages are competent for transformation of Quail macrophages. *J. Virol.*, **61**, 2138–42.

190 Boettiger, D. and Durban, E.M. (1980). Progenitor-cell populations can be infected by RNA tumor viruses, but transformation is dependent on the expression of specific differentiated functions. *Cold Spring Harb. Symp. Quant. Biol.*, **44**, 1249–51.

191 Ho, D.D., Rota, T.R., and Hirsch, M.S. (1986). Infection of

monocyte/macrophages by human T lymphotropic virus type III. *J. Clin. Invest.*, **77**, 1712–15.

192 Nicholson, J.K.A., Cross, G.D., Callaway, C.S., and McDougal, J.S. (1986). *In vitro* infection of human monocytes with human T lymphotropic virus type III/lymphadenopathy-associated virus (HTLV-III/LAV). *J. Immunol.*, **137**, 323–9.

193 Gartner, S., Markovits, P., Markovitz, D.M., Kaplan, M.H., Gallo, R.C., and Popovic, M. (1986). The role of mononuclear phagocytes in HTLV-III/LAV infection. *Science*, **233**, 215–19.

194 Gendelman, H.E., *et al.* (1988). Efficient isolation and propagation of human immunodeficiency virus on recombinant colony stimulating factor 1-treated monocytes. *J. Exp. Med.*, **167**, 1428–41.

195 Gendelman, H.E., *et al.* (1990). Macrophage-HIV interaction: viral isolation and target cell tropism. *AIDS (London)*, **4**, 221–8.

196 Orenstein, J.M., Meltzer, M.S., Phipps, T., and Gendelman, H.E. (1988). Cytoplasmic assembly and accumulation of human immunodeficiency virus types 1 and 2 in recombinant human colony stimulating factor-1 treated human monocytes: an ultrastructural study *J. Virol.*, **62**, 2578–86.

197 Westervelt, P., Gendelman, H.E., and Ratner, L. (1990). A determinant within the HIV-1 gp120 envelope protein critical for infection of primary monocytes. In *Vaccines 91* (ed. H.S. Ginsberg and R. Chanock). Cold Spring Harbor Publications, New York.

198 O'Brien, W.A., *et al.* (1990). HIV-1 tropism for mononuclear phagocytes can be determined by regions of gp120 outside the CD4-binding domain. *Nature*, **348**, 69–73.

199 Westervelt, P., Gendelman, H.E., and Ratner, L. A determinant within the HIV-1 surface envelope glycoprotein critical for productive infection of cultured primary monocytes. *Proc. Natl. Acad. Sci. U.S.A.* (In press).

200 Desrosiers, R.C. and Letvin, N.L. (1987). Animal models for acquired immunodeficiency syndrome. *Rev. Infect. Dis.*, **9**, 438–46.

201 Rosenberg, Z.F. and Fauci, A.S. (1989). The immunopathogenesis of HIV infection. *Adv. Immunol.*, **47**, 377–429.

202 Gonda, M.A., Braun, M.J., Carter, S.G., Kost, T.A., and Bess, J.W. (1987). Characterization and molecular cloning of a bovine lentivirus related to human immunodeficiency virus. *Nature, London*, **330**, 388–91.

203 Daniel, M.D., *et al.* (1985). Isolation of T-cell tropic HTLV-III-like retrovirus from macaques. *Science*, **228**, 1201–6.

204 Kanki, P.J., *et al.* (1985). Serologic identification and characterization of a macaque T-lymphotropic retrovirus closely related to HTLV-III. *Science*, **228**, 1199–1201.

205 Letvin, N.L., *et al.* (1985). Induction of AIDS-like disease in macaque

monkeys with T-cell tropic retrovirus STLV-III. *Science*, **230**, 71–3.

206 Barre-Sinoussi, F., *et al.* (1983). Isolation of a T-lymphotropic retrovirus from a patient at risk for acquired immune deficiency syndrome (AIDS). *Science*, **220**, 868–71.

207 Clavel, F., Guetard, D., Brun-Vezinet, F., Chamaret, S., and Rey, M.A. (1986). Isolation of a new human retrovirus from West African patients with AIDS. *Science*, **233**, 343–6.

208 Konno, S. and Yamamoto, H. (1970). Pathology of equine infectious anaemia. *Cornell Vet.*, **60**, 393–449.

209 Cheevers, W.P. and McGuire, T.C. (1985). Equine infectious anemia virus: Immunopathogenesis and persistence. *Rev. Infect. Dis.*, **7**, 83–8.

210 McGuire, T.C., Crawford, T.B., and Henson, J.B. (1971). Immunofluorescent localization of equine infectious anemia virus in tissue. *Am. J. Pathol.*, **62**, 283–94.

211 Kobayashi, K. and Kono, Y. (1967). Propagation and titration of equine infectious anemia virus in horse leukocyte culture. *Natl. Inst. An. Health Q (Tokyo)*, **7**, 8–21.

212 Ushimi, C., Henson, J.B., and Gorham, J.R. (1972). Study of the one-step growth curve of equine infectious anemia virus by immunofluorescence. *Infect. Immunol.*, **5**, 890–5.

213 Montelaro, R.C., Parekh, B., Orrego, A., and Issel, C.J. (1984). Antigenic variation during persistent infection by equine infectious anemia virus, a retrovirus. *J. Biol. Chem.*, **259**, 10539–44.

214 Payne, S., Parekh, B., Montelaro, R.C., and Issel, C.J. (1984). Genomic alterations associated with persistent infections by equine infectious anaemia virus, a retrovirus. *J. Gen. Virol.*, **65**, 1395–9.

215 Carpenter, S., Evans, L.H., Sevoian, M., and Chesebro, B. (1987). Role of the host immune response in selection of equine infectious anemia virus variants. *J. Virol.*, **61**, 3783–9.

216 Montelaro, R.C., Ball, J., Rwambo, P., and Issel, C. (1989). Antigenic variation during persistent lentivirus infections and its implications for vaccine development. *Adv. Exp. Med. Biol.*, **251**, 251–72.

217 Dawson, M. (1987). Pathogenesis of maedi-visna. *Vet. Rec.*, **120**, 451–4.

218 Nathanson, N., Georgsson, G., Palsson, P.A., Najjar, J.A., Lutley, R., and Petursson, G. (1985). Experimental visna in icelandic sheep: The prototype lentiviral infection. *Rev. Infect. Dis.*, **7**, 75–82.

219 Narayan, O. and Cork, L. (1985). Lentiviral diseases of sheep and goats: Chronic pneumonia leukoencephalomyelitis and arthritis. *Rev. Infect. Dis.*, **7**, 89–98.

220 Sigurdsson, B. (1954). Observations on three slow infections of sheep, maedi, paratuberculosis, rida, a slow encephalitis of sheep with general remarks on infections which develop slowly and some of their special characteristics. *Br. Vet. J.*, **110**, 255–70; 307–22; 341–54.

221 Ruby, P., Gogolewski, D., Adams, S., McGuire, T.C., Banks, K.L., and Cheevers, W.P. (1985). Antigenic cross-reactivity between caprine arthritis-encephalitis, visna and progressive pneumonia viruses involves all virion-associated proteins and glycoproteins. *J. Gen. Virol*, **66**, 1233–40.

222 Kennedy-Stoskopf, S., Narayan, O., and Strandberg, J.D. (1985). The mammary gland as a target organ for infection with caprine arthritis encephalitis virus. *J. Comp. Pathol.*, **95**, 609–17.

223 Lifson, A.R., Rutherford, G.W., and Jaffe, H.W. (1988). The natural history of human immunodeficiency virus infection. *J. Infect. Dis.*, **158**, 1360–7.

224 Koenig, S, *et al.* (1986). Detection of AIDS virus in macrophages in brain tissue from AIDS patients with encephalopathy. *Science*, **233**, 1089–3.

225 Wiley, C.A., Schrier, R.D., Nelson, J.A., Lampert, P.W., and Oldstone, M.B.A. (1986). Cellular localization of human immunodeficiency virus infection within the brains of acquired immunodeficiency syndrome patients. *Proc. Natl. Acad. Sci. U.S.A.*, **83**, 7089–93.

226 Gartner, S., Markovits, P., Markovitz, D.M., Betts, R.F., and Popovic, M. (1986). Virus isolation and identification of HTLV-III/LAV producing cells in brain tissue from a patient with AIDS. *JAMA*, **256**, 2365–71.

227 Stoler, M.H., Eskin, T.A., Benn, S., Angerer, R.C., and Angerer, L.M. (1986). Human T-cell lymphotorpic virus type III infection of the central nervous system. A preliminary *in situ* analysis. *JAMA*, **256**, 2381–3.

228 Vazeux, R., *et al.* (1987). AIDS subacute encephalitis. Identification of HIV-infected cells. *Am. J. Pathol.*, **126**, 403–10.

229 Eilbott, D.J., *et al.* (1989). Human immunodeficiency virus type 1 in spinal cords of acquired immunodeficiency syndrome in patients with myelopathy: expression and replication in macrophages. *Proc. Natl. Acad. Sci. U.S.A.*, **86**, 3337–41.

230 Armstrong, J.A. and Horne, R. (1984). Follicular dendritic cells and virus-like particles in AIDS-related lymphadenopathy. *Lancet*, **ii**, 370–2.

231 Le Tourneau, A., Audouin, J., Diebold, J., Marche, C., Tricottet, V., and Reynes, M. (1986). LAV like particles in lymph node germinal centres in patients with the persistent lymphadenopathy syndrome and the acquired immunodeficiency syndrome-related complex. An ultrastructural study of 30 cases. *Hum. Pathol.*, **17**, 1047–53.

232 Ziza, J.-M., *et al.* (1985). Lymphadenopathy-associated virus isolated from bronchoalveolar lavage fluid in AIDS-related complex with lymphoid interstitial pneumonitis. *N. Eng. J. Med.*, **313**, 183.

233 Chayt, K.J., *et al.* (1986). Detection of HTLV-III RNA in lungs of

patients with AIDS and pulmonary involvement. *JAMA*, **256**, 2356–9.

234 Plata, F., *et al.* (1987). AIDS virus-specific cytotoxic T lymphocytes in lung disorders. *Nature*, **328**, 348–51.

235 Navia, B.A., Cho E.-S., Petito, C.K., and Price, R.W. (1986). The AIDS dementia complex. II Neuropathology. *Ann. Neurol.*, **19**, 525–35.

236 Price, R.W., Brew, B., Sidtis, H., Rosenblum, M., Scheck, A.C., and Cleary, P. (1988). The brain in AIDS: central nervous system HIV-1 infection and AIDS dementia complex. *Science*, **239**, 586–92.

237 Michaels, J., Sharer, L.R., and Epstien, L.G. (1988). Human immunodeficiency virus type 1 (HIV-1) infection of the nervous system: a review. *Immundef. Rev.*, **1**, 71–104.

238 Kalter, D.C., Gendelman, H. E., and Meltzer, M.S. (1990). Infection of human epidermal Langerhans' cells by HIV. *AIDS*, **4**, 266.

239 Schmitt, M.P., *et al.* (1990). Permissivity of primary cultures of human Kupffer cells for HIV-1. *AIDS Res. Hum. Retro.*, **6**, 987–91.

240 Harper, M.E., Marselle, L.M., Gallo, R.C., and Wong-Staal, F. (1986). Detection of lymphocytes expressing human T-lymphotropic virus type III in lymph nodes and peripheral blood from infected individuals by *in situ* hybridization. *Proc. Natl. Acad. Sci. U.S.A.*, **83**, 772–6.

241 Schnittman, S.M., *et al.* (1989). The reservoir for HIV-1 in human peripheral blood is a T cell that maintains expression of CD4. *Science*, **245**, 305–8.

242 Psallidopoulos, M.C., *et al.* (1989). Integrated proviral human immunodeficiency virus type 1 is present in CD4+ peripheral blood lymph-ocytes in healthy seropositive individuals. *J. Virol.*, **63**, 4626–31.

243 Schnittman, S.M., *et al.* (1990). Increasing viral burden in CD4+ T cells from patients with human immunodeficiency virus (HIV) infection reflects rapidly progressive immunosuppression and clinical disease. *Ann. Int. Med.*, **113**, 438–43.

244 Ho, D.D., Moudgil, T., and Alam, M. (1989). Quantitation of human immunodeficiency virus type 1 in the blood of infected persons. *N. Eng. J. Med.*, **321**, 1621–5.

245 Folks, T.M., Kessler, S.W., Orenstein, J.M., Justement, J.S., Jaffe, E.S., and Fauci, A.S. (1988). Infection and replication of HIV-1 in purified progenitor cells of normal bone marrow. *Science*, **242**, 919–21.

246 Sun, N.C., *et al.* (1989). Bone marrow examination in patients with AIDS and AIDS-related complex (ARC). *Am. J. Clin. Path.*, **92**, 589–94.

247 Watanabe, M., Ringler, D., Nakamura, M., DeLong, P.A., and Letvin, N.L. (1990). Simian immunodeficiency virus inhibits bone marrow hematopoetic progenitor cell growth. *J. Virol.*, **64**, 656–63.

248 Scadden, D.T., *et al.* (1990). Human immunodeficiency virus infection of human bone marrow stromal fibroblasts *Blood*, **76**, 317–22.

249 von Laer, D., *et al.* (1990). CD34+ hematopoietic progenitor cells are not a major reservoir of the human immunodeficiency virus. *Blood*, **76**, 1281–6.

250 Nara, P.L., *et al.* (1990). Emergency of viruses resistant to neutralization by V3-specific antibodies in experimental human immunodeficiency virus type IIIB infection of chimpanzees. *J. Virol.*, **64**, 3779–912.

251 Narayan, O., Clements, J.E., Griffin, D.E., and Wolinsky, J.S. (1981). Neutralizing antibody spectrum determines the antigenic profiles of emerging mutants of visna virus. *Infect. Immunol.*, **32**, 1045–50.

252 Clements, J.E., Gdovin, S.L., Montelaro, R.C., and Narayan, O. (1988). Antigenic variation in lentiviral diseases. *Ann. Rev. Immunol.*, **6**, 139–59.

253 Crowe, S.M., Mills, J., Kirihara, J., Boothman, J., Marshall, J.A., and McGrath, M.S. (1990). Full-length recombinant CD4 and recombinant gp120 inhibit fusion between HIV infected macrophages and uninfected CD4-expressing T-lymphoblastoid cells. *AIDS Res. Hum. Retro.*, **6**, 1031–43.

254 Gendelman, H.E., *et al.* (1986). Trans-activation of the human immunodeficiency virus long terminal repeat sequence by DNA viruses. *Proc. Natl. Acad. Sci. U.S.A.*, **83**, 9759–63.

255 Nelson, J.A., Reynolds-Kohler, C., Oldstone, M.B.A., and Wiley, C. (1988). HIV and HCMV coinfect brain cells in patients with AIDS. *Virology*, **165**, 286–90.

5 Macrophages in bacterial infection

D.P. SPEERT

1 Introduction

1.1 Role of macrophages in defence against infection

Bacterial pathogens must breach normal host defences to establish invasive infections. The macrophage stands guard at potential portals of entry to discourage such intruders and to maintain sterility of deep tissues. Despite the rich panoply of antimicrobial devices available to the macrophage, many bacterial species have developed means of resisting these normal cidal mechanisms. Some bacteria are able to persist within macrophages and some are even dependent upon this intracellular haven for their survival. This chapter will provide an overview of the macrophage's antibacterial activities and will describe some of the strategies used by intra- and extracellular pathogens to overcome these normal host defence mechanisms.

Macrophages are poised to exert their antibacterial activity at mucosal surfaces and as filtering agents within the lymphoid organs (reticuloendothelial system). The lungs are protected against inhaled infectious microorganisms by the pulmonary alveolar macrophage. As this cell type can be harvested from humans and animals without great difficulty, much of the work to be described in this chapter is derived from studies of pulmonary alveolar macrophages. These cells are unique among macrophages in their phenotypic characteristics which may derive from their oxygen-rich environment. Therefore, generalizations from the pulmonary alveolar macrophage to other macrophage phenotypes should be made with caution. Other 'free' macrophages can be found in the pleural spaces, synovial fluid, peritoneum, and at inflammatory sites.

Fixed macrophages within the liver (Kupffer cells) and the spleen provide a robust form of protection against bloodborne bacterial infection (1). Whereas the pulmonary alveolar macrophage must be prepared at times to phagocytose bacteria in the absence of opsonins, splenic and hepatic macrophages can be assisted by circulating complement and immunoglobulin (Ig). Fixed tissue macrophages are also found in the bone marrow, lamina propria of the gastrointestinal tract, lymph nodes, brain (microglia), skin (Langerhans cells), kidney, endocrine organs, and perivascular space. The antibacterial functions of macrophages in these diverse locations has not been clearly established and will not be discussed in this chapter.

Macrophages can be viewed as a dispersed secretory organ capable of augmenting the antibacterial activities of other types of leucocytes. In addition to producing interleukins (ILs) 1 and 6 and tumour necrosis factor alpha (TNFα), pulmonary alveolar macrophages secrete cytokines that recruit and activate neutrophils (for example, IL-8). These and other secretory products with defined antibacterial roles will be discussed.

1.2   The macrophage as safe haven for intracellular parasites

Pathogenic bacteria have evolved many creative means of evading normal host defenses. As macrophages and neutrophils play such a critical role in protecting the host against infection, many bacterial virulence mechanisms are directed at subjugating normal phagocytic processes. Extracellular pathogens are virulent by avoiding phagocytic recognition and/or ingestion. Intracellular pathogens, on the other hand, are able to survive within phagocytic cells and may even depend upon the environment within the macrophage for persistence and growth. Facultative intracellular parasites (such as *Salmonella typhimurium*) are those which are able to grow within or without eukaryotic cells and can be cultivated on artificial laboratory media. Obligate intracellular parasites (such as *Mycobacterium leprae*) are those which are absolutely dependent upon the intracellular niche for their growth.

Intracellular parasites may exploit other features of macrophages to enhance their virulence. The blood-brain barrier is quite effective in limiting the spread of bacteria to the central nervous system (CNS). Under certain circumstances, however, bacteria gain access to the CNS after being phago-cytosed by monocytes (2). This 'trojan horse' phenomenon has been shown for *Streptococcus suis* (2) and may play a role in the spread of infection with other bacteria and viruses, such as the human immunodeficiency virus (3).

In understanding the nature of the host–parasite relationship in intracellu-lar parasitism of macrophages, it is essential to recognize that there is a dynamic interplay between prokaryote and eukaryote. Study of bacterial features is not informative unless their effects upon the host cell are understood. Similarly, the effects of bacterial products on macrophage function are meaningful only in so far as they influence the fate of the micro-organism. An example of this dynamic interaction is seen when *Salmonella cholerasuis* and epithelial cells are co-cultivated. Contact between host and parasite causes a change in the bacterial phenotype with expression of new surface components that apparently mediate invasion (4). Other examples of this sort of dynamic interplay will be discussed later.

2   Phenotypic and genotypic differences among macrophages

2.1   Phenotypic differences among macrophages

As discussed in Chapter 1, macrophages have a wide tissue distribution. In studies using a highly specific monoclonal antibody, the relative density of macrophages has been estimated in different murine tissues (5,6). The organs with the highest density of macrophage-specific antigen are the liver, large and small bowel, bone marrow, spleen, lymph nodes, and kidney (6). The bulk of tissue macrophages appear to have developed from circulating blood monocytes under the influence of the local environment in which they come to reside (5). The marked differences among conditions within these various tissues may be largely responsible for the phenotypic diversity among macrophages. In addition to those macrophages found imbedded deep in tissues, are classes of macrophages associated with vascular endothelium, pulmonary alveoli, and serosal surfaces. It is in these locations that macrophages are poised to exert their function as scavengers of microbial pathogens. Each macrophage phenotype has unique characteristics which may serve to arm it for battle with microbes under the special conditions in which it must function.

In addition to the resident tissue macrophages, additional monocytic cells are recruited by inflammatory stimuli, such as thioglycollate broth or bacterial infection (7–9). These recruited cells are phenotypically different from the resident cells; they have alterations in expression and function of surface antigens and receptors (8), and an enhanced capacity to produce reactive oxygen intermediates (8) and kill intracellular pathogens (9).

Macrophage phenotypic characteristics can also be modulated by other local factors. Cytokines, such as interferon-gamma (IFNγ), have profound effects upon expression of receptors and other surface molecules, including HLA-DR antigens (10,11). The effects are specific, with the up-regulation of certain receptors and the suppression of the functions of others (12–15). Multiple effector functions of macrophages are enhanced by IFNγ, chief among which is the generation of reactive oxygen intermediates (16). Dexamethasone counters many of the effects of this interferon, including expression of the Ia antigen and receptors for mannosyl/fucosyl (15) and Fc (17), (see Section 3.1).

2.1.1   Phagocytic and bacteriocidal activity of different macrophage phenotypes

Evidence that circulating monocytes have an enhanced capacity to kill bacteria as compared to fixed tissue macrophages comes from studies of *Listeria monocytogenes* infections in mice (18,19). Shortly after intravenous infection, monocytes are recruited from the peripheral blood to the liver where they appear to be critically important in eliminating infective foci. Upon resolution of the infection, new monocytes are no longer recruited. Experiments such as this have suggested that there are intrinsic differences in the capacity of mononuclear phagocytes of different phenotype to phagocytose and kill bacteria.

Comparisons of phagocytic activity *in vitro* have been made among different cell types and for the same type between different animal species.

Human peripheral blood monocytes are capable of killing a diverse range of bacterial species, but they do so less efficiently than polymorphonuclear leucocytes (PMN) (20,21). The difference between these two cell types appears to be due to intrinsic differences in phagocytic rather than bacteriocidal capacity. Studies on peritoneal and pulmonary alveolar macrophages from humans, rabbits, guinea pigs, hamsters, rats, and mice demonstrate intact oxygen-dependent and -independent bacteriocidal mechanisms (22–27). Notable differences are observed among species (22,26) and between cells obtained from different sites (22,25).

Human pulmonary alveolar macrophages generate greater quantities of reactive oxygen intermediates than do monocytes upon stimulation. This difference is reflected in their superior capacity to kill *Pseudomonas aeruginosa* and *L. monocytogenes* (25). However, under the influence of IFNγ, the respiratory burst and microbicidal capacity of monocytes, but not alveolar macrophages, is enhanced (25). Pulmonary alveolar macrophages also depend upon high oxygen tension (28) and oxidative phosphorylation for metabolic energy to a greater extent than do monocytes or PMNs (27). The resting respiratory rate of human pulmonary alveolar macrophages is three times greater than that of the monocyte (29).

Human and murine peritoneal macrophages have notable similarities. Resident (unelicited) cells generate a feeble respiratory burst upon stimulation as compared to elicited (with thioglycollate in mice; by chronic peritoneal dialysis in humans) cells (23). These elicited human peritoneal cells kill opsonized *Staphylococcus epidermidis*, *Staphylococcus aureus*, and *Escherichia coli* as efficiently as do PMNs (24).

Some functional differences have been described between human umbilical cord blood monocyte-derived macrophages and those from the peripheral blood of healthy adults (30). Significant differences in susceptibility to phagocytosis have been noted among various bacterial species. Phagocytosis of *S. aureus*. *E. coli*, and Group A streptococci by cord blood monocyte-derived macrophages are normal when compared to adult cells. However, killing of *S.aureus*, and both phagocytosis and killing of Group B streptococci are impaired (30).

2.1.2 *Pulmonary alveolar macrophages and protection of the lungs against inhaled bacteria*

The respiratory tract is exposed to an enormous quantity of bacteria and other inhaled particles, some of which gain access to the lower airways. Pulmonary macrophages play a critically important role in protecting the lung against infection by these inhaled micro-organisms and stand guard as the resident phagocytic cells (29,31–35). Neutrophils are recruited to assist only when the first line of defence is overwhelmed. Pulmonary macrophages are found in the alveoli, small and large airways, interstitium of the lung, and lining the pulmonary vessels (36). The best characterized of these cells are those which can be lavaged from the lung, generally referred to as pulmonary alveolar macrophages.

The normal human tracheobronchial secretions have relatively low levels of complement and IgM, but IgG and IgA are generally present (37,38). Although the pulmonary alveolar macrophage has receptors for complement and for the Fc portion of IgG (39,40), it may be far more dependent upon non-opsonic phagocytosis than other macrophages which benefit from the full array of serum opsonins.

Receptors for a wide array of ligands are found on pulmonary alveolar macrophages permitting ingestion of a disparate range of particulate and soluble substances (29). The human pulmonary alveolar macrophage is also armed with surface-exposed 'cytophilic' IgG (41). As protein A binds to IgG in a non-immunological fashion, strains of *Staphylococcus aureus* expressing this protein are phagocytosed non-opsonically by pulmonary alveolar macrophages. In general, pulmonary alveolar macrophages phagocytose and clear Gram-positive bacteria better than Gram-negatives in the absence of serum opsonins (36). Strains of *Haemophilus influenzae* type b and encapsulated *Streptococcus pneumoniae*, which are pathogenic for humans, are relatively resistant to opsonization by normal human serum (42), a factor which may aid their virulence in pulmonary infections. Non-pathogenic bacteria, such as unencapsulated *H. influenzae*, are susceptible to phagocytosis and killing by pulmonary alveolar macrophages after opsonization with normal human serum (42). Pulmonary alveolar macrophages are unique among human phagocytic cells in their dependence upon oxygen for optimum phagocytosis (28).

Pulmonary alveolar macrophages elaborate an impressive array of secretory products and enzymes with potential antibacterial properties. In addition to lysozyme, which constitutes 25 per cent of the total protein released, these cells produce lysosomal acid hydrolases and neutral proteases (29,36). They also secrete a wide array of cytokines, biologically active lipids, reactive oxygen radicals, complement components, and free fatty acids, all with potential antibacterial activity (36).

2.1.3   *Kupffer cells and protection against blood-borne infection*

Transient bacteraemia is probably a common daily occurrence, but septicaemia is a relatively rare event. Macrophages of the reticuloendothelial system serve to filter bacteria from the blood and prevent infection except by those species of bacteria which are able to resist this normal host defence (43). The resident macrophage of the liver, the Kupffer cell, is located in the hepatic sinusoids where it is exposed to the constant flow of blood. It is thus poised to remove potential pathogens from the circulation. Splenic macrophages also play a critical role in blood stream clearance but they have not been studied as thoroughly *in vitro* as Kupffer cells. Pulmonary intravascular macrophages probably also play an important role in removing certain bacteria, after intravenous injection (44). The critical role of Kupffer cells is demonstrated in individuals with reticuloendothelial system blockade (45) or in animals whose Kupffer cells have been damaged artificially (46). Hepatic phagocytic cells have an enormous capacity to phagocytose bacteria and other particulate debris non-opsonically (47), a feature largely due to the presence of lectins of different specificities (48–51). Opsonins also play a critical role in augmenting reticuloendothelial clearance of blood-borne bacteria; disabling the complement system drastically lowers the LD_{50} for some species of bacteria (43). Opsonizing antibody also enhances the phagocytic capacity of Kupffer cells and permits the elimination of the more virulent species of bacteria (1,52). Kupffer cells and splenic macrophages appear to complement each other; the former clear complement-coated particles predominantly whereas the latter phagocytose those opsonized with IgG (43).

Upon activation, Kupffer cells have an enhanced capacity to phagocytose IgG-coated particles (47), but some controversy exists regarding their ability to generate reactive oxygen radicals (18,53). Unactivated, resident Kupffer cells or Kupffer cells activated by exposure to various cytokines appear unable to generate reactive oxygen intermediates in response to either soluble or particulate stimuli (18). However, after murine infection with *L. monocytogenes*, monocytes are recruited to the liver. These immigrant macrophages are capable of generating reactive oxygen radicals and killing intracellular parasites (19).

2.2   Genetic influences on macrophage antibacterial activities

Genetic differences in susceptibility to infection is suggested by the observation that infectious diseases occur more frequently in certain ethnic groups. Furthermore, differences in permissiveness to infection with intracellular parasites implies a genetic influence on macrophage bacteriocidal capacity. Skamene and co-workers have explored the reasons for differences in susceptibility to infection among different inbred strains of mice. Intracellular pathogens studied include *Salmonella typhimurium*, *Leishmania donovani*, and *Mycobacterium bovis* (54–59). They found that strains segregated into groups on the basis of susceptibility or resistance to all three of these pathogens, suggesting that the inheritance is under monogenic dominant control (55). The genes controlling susceptibility to each of these pathogens have been designated *Ity* (for *S. typhimurium*), *Lsh* (for *L. donovani*) and *Bcg* (for *M. bovis*); evidence now suggests that they are in fact one gene. The murine gene is on chromosome 1, and the human homologue appears to be on the long arm of chromosome 2 (57,59). The product of the *Bcg* gene has not been determined yet. Nonetheless, macrophages from animals with the *Bcg*-resistant genotype have an enhanced capacity for generation of reactive oxygen intermediates, greater surface expression of la antigen, decreased expression of 5'-nucleotidase activity, and an enhanced capacity to present antigen to T-cells (56,58,59). When animals with the *Bcg*-resistant genotype are treated with silica to poison macrophage function, they adopt the antibacterial characteristics of *Bcg*-susceptible animals (59).

The existence of differences among humans in susceptibility to infection has long been suspected. However, this is far more difficult to demonstrate than for inbred strains of mice. Tuberculosis is more prevalent in the black than in white population in the United Sates (60). This difference has been ascribed to social rather than genetic factors. However, a recent study demonstrated that under identical social and environmental conditions (nursing home or prison), black individuals have a two-fold greater likelihood than whites of developing infection with *mycobacterium tuberculosis* (60). An immunological explanation for this difference was suggested by another study in which *M. tuberculosis* replicated more rapidly in macrophages from black than from white subjects (61). When the human homologue of the *Bcg* gene is identified and cloned, it may be possible to determine more precisely what genetic factors protect against infection with intracellular pathogens.

3 Phagocytosis of micro-organisms

3.1 Macrophage receptors

Phagocytosis is a dynamic process in which bacteria are attached to the macrophage membrane in preparation for ingestion. This attachment step is mediated by specific macrophage receptors and is dependent upon the nature of the bacterial surface. A list of macrophage phagocytic receptors is given in Table 5.1. Opsonization of bacteria with complement and/or Ig permits macrophages and other phagocytic cells to recognize, by a limited number of receptors, a wide array of bacterial species with broad heterogeneity in surface characteristics. The principal macrophage phagocytic receptors recognize the breakdown products of complement component 3 (C3b and C3bi) and the Fc portion of IgG (62,63). The role(s) in antibacterial defence played by the receptors for the Fc portion of IgA (64,65) and for fibronectin (65,66) are less clear. In addition to phagocytosis via opsonic receptors, macrophages are well-equipped for non-opsonic phagocytosis (67–70). Although described as 'non-specific' phagocytosis, the involvement of specific receptors in the process has been demonstrated recently (70,71). The mannosyl/fucosyl receptor is perhaps the best characterized of these non-opsonic receptors. In addition to its role in recycling mannosylated macromolecules from the circulation (72), it appears to be involved in the ingestion of certain bacteria, fungi, and parasites (70,73,74). Other lectin-

Table 5.1 Human macrophage receptors for phagocytosis of bacteria

Receptor	Ligand	References
Opsonic receptors		
Fc-γ RI	IgG1 > IgG3 > IgG4 > > IgG2	62,77
Fc-γ RII	IgG1 > IgG2 = IgG4 > > IgG3	62,77
Fc-γ RIII	IgG1 and IgG3	62,77
Fc-α	IgA	64
Complement receptor 1	C3b	62,63,91
Complement receptor 3	C3bi	62,63,91
C1q receptor	Mannose-binding protein	169
	Lung surfactant protein A	169
CD14	LPS-binding protein	174
Non-opsonic receptors		
Mannosyl/fucosyl receptor	Mannose residues	70,72
Adhesion promoting		
receptors (CD18)	Bacterial LPS	71

like interactions have been described (75), but the specific receptors involved remain to be characterized. Binding of bacteria to macrophages via Ia antigens has also been described (76).

3.1.1 Heterogeneity of macrophage receptors

The expression and function of macrophage phagocytic receptors is influenced profoundly by local conditions. For instance, the presence of IFNγ causes Fc receptors to be up-regulated, but their capacity to mediate ingestion is diminished (14). Mannosyl/fucosyl receptor function is also grossly inhibited under the same conditions (15). Similar marked differences in macrophage phenotype are found between resident and recruited peritoneal macrophages (5). Murine Kupffer cells lack detectable complement receptor 3, as opposed to circulating monocytes and those that are freshly recruited to the liver (5). Human Fc-γ receptors also display considerable heterogeneity (77). For instance, Fc-γ RIII is found on neutrophils and tissue macrophages but not on circulating monocytes. This heterogeneity in macrophage phagocytic receptors emphasizes the unique antibacterial potential among the different phenotypes.

3.2   Opsonization

The immune system is able to eliminate potential pathogens by opsonizing them with specific IgG and phagocytosing them via Fc-γ receptors. Complement acts synergistically with Ig, enhancing the efficiency of Fc receptor-mediated phagocytosis. In the absence of specific opsonizing antibody, some strains of bacteria fix and activate complement; this process results in the deposition of C3 breakdown products (C3b and C3bi) for which receptors exist on macrophages (complement receptors 1 and 3 respectively). Bacteria can activate complement via the classical or alternative pathway in an antibody-dependent or -independent fashion. The characteristics of the bacterial surface determine the nature of complement activation, and the deposition and accessibility for ligation by macrophage receptors. For instance the carbohydrate composition of *Salmonella typhimurium* lipopolysaccharide determines the degree of complement deposition, susceptibility to phagocytosis and virulence among various strains (78). Although encapsulated *Staphylococcus aureus* activates and fixes complement to its surface, the bacteria may be resistant to *in vitro* phagocytosis; the activated complement components are deposited below the capsule and are not available for ligation by complement receptors (79). In general, encapsulated bacteria are virulent by virtue of their resistance to phagocytosis. Specific opsonizing antibodies are elicited during the immune response; these antibodies are deposited on the capsule, rendering the bacteria susceptible to phagocytosis.

3.3   The process of phagocytosis

The phagocytic process has been characterized with the aid of particles coated with monospecific ligands. This has permitted the detailed characterization of individual phagocytic receptors. Sheep erythrocytes can be coated with IgG, IgM, C3b, or C3bi. Using this system, investigators have made seminal observations about the functions of the receptors for Fc-γ and complement. From these studies has emerged the 'zipper hypothesis' of phagocytosis (80). It appears that particles must be coated circumferentially with a phagocytosis-promoting ligand in order for ingestion to occur. If an opsonin is only deposited on one pole of a particle, attachment to the macrophage membrane without subsequent ingestion is seen. Opsonization with complement alone may not be sufficient for phagocytosis to occur. Complement-coated erythrocytes will adhere to resident, unactivated macrophages, but will not be ingested without the additional influence of a second agent, such as fibronectin or a phorbol ester (81). However, complement receptors on elicited or activated macrophages are constitutively competent for ingestion (82). Macrophages from animals previously injected with lipopolysaccharide or microbe-containing immune complexes are also competent to ingest complement-coated particles (83).

Whereas the zipper hypothesis may explain the mode of entry of most extracellular pathogens into macrophages, it may not hold for pathogen-directed ingestion. Certain intracellular pathogens, such as *Legionella*

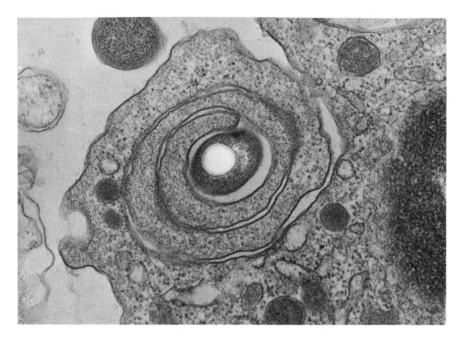

Fig. 5.1 *Coiling phagocytosis.* Human monocytes and *Legionella pneumophila* were co-incubated, fixed, and examined by electron microscopy. A single *L. pneumophila* bacterium is seen within a coiled monocyte pseudopod. This process of coiling phagocytosis is also seen when human alveolar macrophages and neutrophils ingest *L. pneumophila.* The process is not observed when the bacteria are opsonized with specific antibody to *L. pneumophila*, but phagocytosis occurs by conventional phagocytosis as depicted in *Figure 5.2.* (Reproduced from *Cell* (1984), **36**, 27–33, with the permission from Dr Marcus Horwitz and Cell Press.)

pneumophila enter macrophages via a process called 'coiling phago-cytosis' (84), (Figure 5.1). This mode of ingestion is common to human monocytes, pulmonary alveolar macrophages and PMNs, but it is not seen if the bacteria are opsonized with specific IgG (84). Extracellular pathogens, such as *Escherichia coli* or *Streptococcus pneumoniae* are ingested by a 'conventional process' (Figure 5.2), akin to the zipper mechanism described above. It is possible that coiling phagocytosis is common to other intracellular pathogens and that this mode of entry facilitates survival with mac-rophages.

The process of non-opsonic phagocytosis is complex and depends upon the physical and chemical characteristics of the bacterial surface and com-plementary macrophage receptors. In order for unopsonized bacteria to be phagocytosed, they must first make contact with the macrophage mem-brane. Hydrophilic and electrostatic forces prevent many strains of bacteria from approaching the macrophage; these bacteria may thereby be resistant

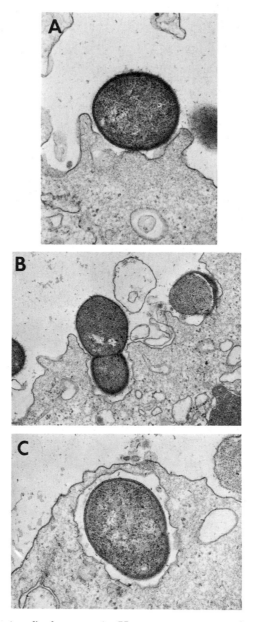

Fig. 5.2 *'Conventional' phagocytosis.* Human monocytes and a strain of *Streptococcus pneumoniae* were co-incubated, fixed, and examined by electron microscopy. A bacterium is shown entering the monocyte by the conventional process: pseudopodia extend around the bacterium (A and B), fuse, and engulf it within a phagosome (C). (Reproduced from Cell (1984), **36**, 27–33, with permission from Dr Marcus Horwitz and Cell Press.)

to non-opsonic phagocytosis (85,86). Opsonization with IgG renders them susceptible to phagocytosis; it has been suggested that this occurs by virtue of abrogation of normal repulsive forces (87). Susceptibility to non-opsonic phagocytosis is largely determined by bacterial surface structures. Pili of *Pseudomonas aeruginosa* and *E. coli* enhance phagocytosis (86,88), whereas the mucoid exopolysaccharide of *P. aeruginosa* abrogates hydrophobicity and renders such strains phagocytosis-resistant (89).

3.4   Phagocytosis of specific bacterial species

The mechanism of bacterial entry into phagocytic cells is of great interest, as the specific receptor ligated may determine the ultimate fate of the ingested microbe. For instance, when *Toxoplasma gondii* is ingested non-opsonically, it fails to trigger an oxidative burst and survives, whereas when opsonized with IgG, it is killed by reactive oxygen intermediates (90). The same may be true for bacteria. As ligation of Fc but not complement receptors triggers an oxidative burst (91) the type of opsonization may determine a micro-organism's fate. For some pathogens, establishment of intracellular parasitism requires that they be ingested without triggering fusion of phagosome and lysosome. Such is the case when unopsonized *Chlamydia psittaci* (92) and *Mycobacterium tuberculosis* (93) are ingested by macrophages. However, when they are phagocytosed after opsonization with IgG, phagosome–lysosome fusion occurs, exposing the ingested bacteria to the toxic effects of lysosomal degradative enzymes (92,94).

Complement receptors 1 and 3 are critical in phagocytosis of a wide range of bacterial species, both intracellular and extracellular pathogens. The proliferation of macrophage receptor-specific monoclonal antibodies has made it possible to identify the role of specific receptors in bacterial phagocytosis. Observations analogous to those made in phagocytosis studies with sheep erythrocytes have emerged from investigations of *Haemophilus influenzae* type b (95). In the absence of specific antibody, these bacteria are bound to macrophages via complement receptor 3 but are not ingested. The addition of anti-capsular antibody results in bacterial ingestion without enhancing macrophage binding. Both complement receptors 1 and 3 may mediate the ingestion of *Legionella pneumophila* (96), *Mycobacterium tuberculosis* (97), and *M. leprae* (98) after opsonization with nonimmune serum.

Macrophage receptors mediating nonopsonic phagocytosis have also been identified. Phagocytosis of a K12 strain of *E. coli* by human monocyte-derived macrophages was shown to be mediated in concert by all three members of the family of adhesion-promoting receptors (LFA-1, complement receptor 3 and p150,95), (71). This strain lacks type 1 pili, a surface component which also mediates non-opsonic phagocytosis by PMNs and macrophages (69). Lipopolysaccharide was identified as the bacterial ligand which was recognized by the macrophage receptors. Binding of *Mycobacterium avium*–*Mycobacterium intracellulare* to human monocyte-derived macrophages is mediated by a protein receptor which is, as yet, unidentified (99). Mannosyl/fucosyl receptors appear to play a critical role in the phagocytosis of unopsonized *Pseudomonas aeruginosa* by human monocyte-derived macrophages (70). Although bacterial piliation and hydrophobicity influence the susceptibility of *P. aeruginosa* to phagocytosis, the bacterial ligand has not been determined (86).

4   Bacteriocidal mechanisms of macrophages

Macrophages are equipped for killing ingested prey by both oxidative and nonoxidative mechanisms (Table 5.2), (100–102). Macrophage bacteriocidal power varies among different phenotypes and is clearly inferior to that of circulating PMNs (see Section 2.1). Indeed, the somewhat effete microbicidal potential of macrophages makes them an attractive niche for survival of intracellular pathogens. Much of what is known about leucocyte microbicidal action is derived from studies on PMNs. Nonetheless, some notable differences exist between macrophages and PMNs, particularly with respect to their oxidative microbicidal activity.

4.1   Oxidative microbicidal mechanisms

The critical role of the oxidative burst in defence against bacterial infection is demonstrated in patients with chronic granulomatous disease whose

Table 5.2 Macrophage antimicrobial mechanisms

Mechanism	Product	References
Oxidative		101,104
MPO-independent	Hydroxyl radical	
	Singlet oxygen	
	Superoxide anion	
	Hydrogen peroxide	
MPO-dependent	Hypochlorite	
	Singlet oxygen	
Non-oxidative		
Non-enzymatic	Defensins (macrophage cationic proteins 1 and 2)	109
Enzymatic	Lysozyme	100,117
	Other lysosomal enzymes	110–113

PMNs and macrophages lack the capacity to generate reactive oxygen intermediates (103,104). Since the initial description of superoxide production by macrophages, much has been learned about the biochemical pathways and the requisite components of the respiratory burst. Patients with chronic granulomatous disease have been invaluable in helping to unravel the intricacies of this system; defects in their cells have provided new insights into what is required for oxidative killing of ingested bacteria.

Macrophages produce superoxide anion (O_2^-) in response to stimulation by both particulate and soluble stimuli (105). Oxygen is consumed in a reaction involving the one electron reduction of oxygen to superoxide. O_2^- then enters into reactions culminating in generation of bactericidal products. Reactive oxygen intermediates can be generated by both myeloperoxidase-dependent and -independent mechanisms (104).

4.1.1   Myeloperoxidase-independent mechanisms

Macrophages, as opposed to PMNs and peripheral blood monocytes, have very low levels of myeloperoxidase (MPO) (106) and therefore rely upon the myeloperoxidase-independent mechanism predominantly. In this system, highly reactive oxygen intermediates appear to be derived from the interaction of O_2^- and hydrogen peroxide (H_2O_2). The principle toxic reactants formed are hydroxyl radical ($OH\cdot$) and singlet oxygen (101). $OH\cdot$ is formed with the aid of an iron catalyst as follows:

$$O_2^- + O_2^- + 2H^+ \rightarrow H_2O_2 + O_2$$
$$Fe^{2+} + H_2O_2 \rightarrow Fe^{3+} + OH\cdot + OH^-$$
$$Fe^{3+} + O_2^- \rightarrow Fe^{2+} + O_2$$

Net $$O_2^- + H_2O_2 \rightarrow OH\cdot + OH^- + O_2$$

4.1.2   Myeloperoxidase-dependent mechanisms

This mechanism is employed by both monocytes and PMNs to generate reactive oxygen intermediates. In this system, superoxide anion dismutates to form hydrogen peroxide.

$$O_2^- + O_2^- + 2H^+ \rightarrow H_2O_2 + O_2$$

Myeloperoxidase then catalyses the oxidation of chloride to hypochlorite anion (OCl^-):

$$H_2O_2 + Cl^- \rightarrow H_2O + OCl^-$$

from which singlet oxygen ($^1O_2$) appears to be derived:

$$OCl + H_2O_2 \rightarrow Cl^- + H_2O + {}^1O_2$$

Iodide or bromide can substitute for chloride in these reactions. However, chloride is the favoured reactant because of its presence within the phagolysosome. The hypochlorite is probably highly bacteriocidal because of its oxidizing capacity, particularly its ability to oxidize amines to chloramines. Despite the potent bacteriocidal potential of this system, its role in protection against infection may be of minimal importance; patients with myeloperoxidase deficiency do not appear to be at increased risk for serious infections (107,108).

4.2 Non-oxidative microbicidal mechanisms

A wide array of antimicrobial substances are packaged with lysosomes (109–113) and are delivered to the site of ingested bacteria upon phagosome–lysosome fusion. These substances are present constitutively and neither require macrophage activation nor stimulation of the respiratory burst to exert their bactericidal activity. Human alveolar macrophages lack certain lysosomal components found in PMNs, among which are lactoferrin, neutrophil-type elastase, bacterial permeability inducing protein, and cathepsin (109). Nonetheless, macrophages are able to kill ingested bacteria using non-oxidative mechanisms. Most information about the bactericidal activities of lysosomal constituents is derived from studies with PMNs.

4.2.1 Macrophage cationic proteins

Macrophage cationic peptides 1 and 2 have been purified from rabbit alveolar macrophages (109). These antimicrobial peptides share amino acid homology with their analogues from PMNs (the neutrophil cationic proteins) (109). They are able to kill both Gram-positive and Gram-negative bacteria and can exert their antimicrobial activity in an anaerobic environment. They function best between pH 7 and 8, conditions which exist immediately after phagocytosis (114). It appears that killing is mediated by permeabilization of bacterial inner and outer membranes (115,116).

4.2.2 Lysozyme

Although lysozyme is present in macrophages in relatively high concentration and its mechanism of bacteriolysis has been determined (117), the role of this enzyme in antibacterial defence is not firmly established. It is capable of killing *Micrococcus lysodekticus* and *Bacillus megaterium*, neither of which constitutes a significant threat to humans. The principal role of lysozyme in antimicrobial defence may be digestive rather than bactericidal (100).

4.2.3 Other lysosomal enzymes

Macrophages elaborate a wide range of enzymes (110–112) including plasminogen activator, elastase, collagenase, lipoprotein lipase, phospholipase, lysosomal acid hydrolases, arginase, RNAase, DNAase, acid phosphatase, β-*N*-acetyl glucosaminidase, cathepsin, and β-glucuronidase (118).

Although they are able to lyse bacteria (119) and to digest bacterial cell walls (120), a direct role for these enzymes in antibacterial defence has not been established clearly. Like lysozyme they may serve a primary digestive role.

5   Antibacterial secretory activities of macrophages

Macrophages produce over 100 substances with wide-ranging effects upon bacteria as well as on other organs and tissues (118) (see also Chapter 1). Many of the antimicrobial substances elaborated (such as reactive oxygen intermediates and lysozyme) are secreted and exert their effects outside the confines of the lysosomal compartment (Table 5.3).

5.1   Macrophage activation and antibacterial activities

The concept of the activated macrophage evolved from studies on animals with acquired resistance to infection (121). In these classical studies, it was demonstrated that non-specific antibacterial activity developed in animals after infection with specific pathogens. Subsequent studies demonstrated that this state of activation was derived from the effect of lymphocyte products (122), ultimately shown to be IFNγ (16). Activated macrophages are larger in size, and have a pronounced plasma membrane ruffling,

Table 5.3   Antibacterial secretory products of macrophages

Product	References
Cytokines	
IL-1	125,126
IL-6	123,124
TNF	131
Neutrophil chemotactic factor	139,140
Neutrophil activating peptide-1 (IL-8)	144
Reactive oxygen intermediates	101,104
Superoxide anion	
Hydrogen peroxide	
Hydroxyl radical	
Singlet oxygen	
Hypochlorite	
Complement components	118

enhanced capacity for spreading and attaching to solid surfaces and increased secretion of neutral proteases (7,8). In addition, these cells gain the capacity to ingest complement-coated particles via their receptors for C3b and C3bi (82) and to secrete superoxide anion in nanomolar concentrations, equivalent to PMNs (8). Activated macrophages also secrete increased quantities of lysosomal enzymes including plasminogen activator, collagenase, and elastase (8). This activation phenotype is seen in peritoneal cells that have been elicited by injection of thioglycollate broth or proteose peptone (8).

With enhanced secretion of both reactive oxygen intermediates and lysosomal enzymes, a wide range of pathogens fall prey to the antibacterial arsenal of the activated macrophage. Activation appears to be primarily effective in enhancing the bacteriocidal capacity of macrophages for intracellular pathogens. This has been demonstrated with macrophages incubated in the presence of recombinant IFNγ (see Section 6.1). Although such activated macrophages are better able to kill ingested bacteria, their capacity to dispose of extracellular pathogens, such as *Pseudomonas aeruginosa* and *Staphylococcus aureus* (Speert and Thorson, unpublished observations), may be impaired. While enhancing superoxide anion production, IFNγ impairs the capacity of human monocyte-derived macrophages to ingest particles via Fc and complement receptors (14). It also impairs their capacity to internalize both mannosylated macromolecules (15) and zymosan (Speert and Thorson, unpublished observations) via the mannosyl/fucosyl receptor.

5.2   Cytokine production

As mentioned earlier, macrophages elaborate IL-1, -6, and TNFα when activated or stimulated by other leucocyte products. These cytokines have multiple activities, both pro- and anti-inflammatory, some of which influence the ability of the host to respond to infections (123,124).

5.2.1   Interleukin-1 (IL-1)

IL-1 is an endogenous pyrogen and may raise body temperature by inducing production of prostaglandins. The salutary role of fever in control of infectious diseases has not been clearly demonstrated, although the elevation of body temperature is associated with the acute phase response and with modulation of various aspects of the immune system (125). IL-1 is produced by mononuclear phagocytes after stimulation by almost all infectious agents (126). When infused intravenously into rabbits, recombinant IL-1β acts synergistically with TNFα to induce shock (127), a manifestation of Gram-negative bacterial septicemia. IL-1 also induces the liver to elaborate acute phase reactants, products which are clearly associated with acute infection and inflammation. Effects of IL-1 on T-cells (activation and release of IL-2) and on B-cells (proliferation and enhanced antibody production) are also critical in host defence against infection. Human recombinant IL-1α enhances resistance in mice to infection with *P. aeruginosa*, *S. pneumoniae*, *S.aureus*, and *Klebsiella pneumoniae* (128,129).

5.2.2   Tumour necrosis factor alpha

TNFα, like IL-1 is induced by lipopolysaccharide, a component of Gram-negative bacterial cell membranes (130). TNFα has multiple effects both salutary and deleterious on the host (131). In addition to its role as an endogenous pyrogen, at low concentrations this cytokine amplifies super-oxide anion production by PMNs and enhances their adherence to endothelial cells. Either alone or in combination with IL-2, TNFα enhances the killing of *Mycobacterium avium* by macrophages (132). Other proinflammatory effects include enhancement of IL-1 production, (131,133). It is one of the mediators of shock in Gram-negative bacterial septicaemia (133) and its presence in the blood of patients with meningococcal septicaemia is associated with a fatal outcome (134).

Numerous recent reports have documented toxic and lethal effects of TNFα and their prevention with specific anti-TNFα antibodies and cyclo-oxygenase inhibitors (133,135–137). The quantity of TNFα produced during experimental murine listeriosis is correlated with the outcome of the infection; high levels of serum TNFα are detected in serum during a lethal infection, but none is found in animals which survive (138). Nonetheless, spleen cells from sublethally infected mice have an enhanced capacity to produce TNFα, and their listeria infection is rendered lethal by the infusion of antibody to TNFα. Thus, it appears from this model that TNFα can have both adverse and protective effects during bacterial infection, depending in part upon the quantity elaborated.

5.3   Macrophage products with direct effects upon neutrophils

Pulmonary alveolar macrophages elaborate factors which enhance pulmonary antibacterial defences by attracting or augmenting the function of neutrophils (Table 5.3). Upon stimulation with aggregated IgG, zymosan, immune complexes or bacteria, factors are released by human pulmonary alveolar macrophages which are chemotactic for human neutrophils (139,140). These substances are active in the absence of complement and may augment normal pulmonary host defences when alveolar macrophages are unable to deal effectively with an infectious challenge (141). Once present in the bronchopulmonary secretions, neutrophils are activated by a neutrophil-activating factor (142,143), a low molecular weight basic protein that enhances their capacity to produce superoxide anion and to kill *P. aeruginosa*. Neutrophil-activating peptide-1/interleukin-8 is produced by both monocytes and macrophages after stimulation by lipopolysaccharide, IL-1α, IL-1β, and TNFα (144). This cytokine is chemotactic and enhances exocytosis of vesicles and granules, expression of receptors and release of reactive oxygen intermediate by neutrophils.

6 Augmentation of macrophage antibacterial function

Although macrophages are able to ingest and kill certain bacterial species unaided by opsonins or cytokines, optimum antibacterial activity depends upon the assistance of a diverse range of substances (Table 5.4). These substances are either distributed widely (complement) or restricted to specific organs (pulmonary surfactant). Their enhancing activity is either nonspecific (complement) or limited to specific bacterial species (mannose-binding protein, LPS-binding protein).

6.1 Interferon-gamma

IFNγ dramatically enhances the capacity of macrophages to generate a respiratory burst (16). This enhanced oxidative capacity is translated into augmented bactericidal activity against a wide range of intracellular pathogens (145). Recently, IFNγ has also been shown to enhance the superoxide production of neutrophils and monocytes from patients with variant forms of chronic granulomatous disease (146,147). Although most of these patients demonstrate a capacity to generate superoxide anion while receiving IFNγ, their enhanced microbicidal activity may be out of proportion to a modest respiratory burst. It has been suggested that the partial correction of the phagocytic killing defect may be due in part to enhancement of non-oxidative killing as well.

Table 5.4 Factors that enhance macrophage antibacterial activity

Factor	References
IFNγ	16
Colony-stimulating factors	156
Macrophage CSF	
Granulocyte-macrophage CSF	
Complement	160–163
Pulmonary surfactant protein A	168,170
1,25(OH)-vitamin D$_3$	171
Mannose-binding protein	172
Lipopolysaccharide-binding protein	173

Macrophages that have been cultured in the presence of IFNγ have an enhanced capacity to kill certain bacterial intracellular pathogens. When treated with recombinant human IFNγ, human monocytes and pulmonary alveolar macrophages gain the capacity to inhibit the multiplication of *L. pneumophila* (148–150). Studies with human monocytes (150) have demonstrated that *L. pneumophila* is dependent upon iron for growth, and that IFNγ enhances monocyte antibacterial activity by down-regulating transferrin receptors and limiting access of intracellular bacteria to iron. IFNγ also enhances the capacity of murine macrophages to kill *S. typhimurium* (151). The enhancement is unaffected by the addition of reactive oxygen radical scavengers, suggesting that the killing is mediated by non-oxidative mechanisms. Thus, IFNγ enhances the macrophage antibacterial activity against two bacterial species, in both cases apparently by augmenting non-oxidative mechanisms.

The effect of IFNγ on bactericidal activity against *Mycobacteria* is determined largely by the animal species from which the macrophages are obtained (152). Whereas recombinant IFNγ enhances the cidal capacity of murine bone marrow-derived macrophages for *M. tuberculosis* (153,154), human monocyte-derived macrophages become less microbicidal after maturation in the presence of IFNγ (155).

6.2   Colony-stimulating factors

Macrophage colony-stimulating factor (M-CSF) and granulocyte-macrophage colony-stimulating factor (GM-CSF) are cytokines which enhance the capacity of macrophages to respond to bacterial infections. Both CSFs are secreted constitutively, but their levels are increased after bacterial infection or injection of lipopolysaccharide (156). They are both produced by fibroblasts, whereas GM-CSF is also elaborated by endothelial cells and T-cells, and M-CSF by monocytes and endothelial cells (156,157). Although their principal function may be that of increasing macrophage proliferation, they also can enhance secretion of other inflammatory mediators, such as superoxide anion, prostaglandin E, arachidonic acid, IL-1, plasminogen activator, IFN-γ, TNFα, and other CSFs (156). Furthermore, these CSFs enhance the phagocytic and cidal activities of macrophages (156,158,159).

6.3   Complement

Complement profoundly enhances the antibacterial activity of macrophages. The critical role of complement in clearance of bacteria from the bloodstream has been demonstrated in animals depleted of serum complement by treatment with cobra venom factor (to remove C3-C9), as well as in animals with a congenital deficiency of specific complement components (C3 and C4), (160,161). Clearance of *S. pneumoniae* is optimum in the immune animal in the presence of an intact classical complement pathway; the alternative pathway is of critical importance in enhancing clearance in the non-immune animal (160). Despite the presence of circulating specific antibody, depletion of complement by cobra venom factor produces a lethal defect in these animals.

Complement also plays an important role in enhancing clearance of certain bacterial species from the lung (162,163). By depleting complement with cobra venom factor, it was shown that clearance of *S. pneumoniae* and *P. aeruginosa* from the murine lung was compromised (162). Similar observations were made by Heidbrink et al. (163). In addition, they demonstrated that clearance of *S. aureus* was unaffected by complement depletion. The normal clearance of *S. aureus* in the complement-deficient animal could be mediated by macrophages armed with cytophilic antibody (41), (see Section 2.1).

Complement might enhance bacterial clearance by any of several mechanisms. It may serve as a source of chemotactic factors for recruitment of either neutrophils or mononuclear phagocytes to the site of infection. It might provide the necessary opsonins for enhancing phagocytosis, enabling C3-activation products to be deposited on the bacterial surface via either the classical or alternative pathway. It might facilitate the lysis of certain Gram-negative bacterial species. Finally, complement, acting in concert with Ig, has been shown to be necessary for intracellular killing of staphylococci (164).

6.4   Other factors capable of enhancing the microbicidal activity of macrophages

Fibronectin is a glycoprotein with a wide tissue distribution and with diverse effects upon phagocytic cells (165). Of particular importance in antibacterial defenses, fibronectin enhances the capacity of human monocyte-derived macrophages to ingest complement-coated particles (166) and to kill ingested bacteria (165,167).

6.4.1   Surfactant

Pulmonary alveolar macrophages function in an environment with very low levels of complement and Ig, concentrations too low to provide optimal opsonization of bacteria for phagocytosis. The alveolar spaces are bathed in surfactant which serves primarily to maintain their patency. Surfactant protein A, a component of pulmonary surfactant, has striking similarities to both complement subunit C1q and to mannose-binding protein (168) and can function as an opsonin (168). Surfactant protein A has a long collagen-like domain which mediates binding to the C1q receptor of mononuclear phagocytes (169) and can enhance phagocytosis (168). Although surfactant protein A enhances phagocytosis by both Fc and complement receptors, it cannot substitute for C1q in forming haemolytically active C1 (168). Phagocytosis but not killing of *S. aureus* by pulmonary alveolar macrophages is enhanced by surfactant protein A, and its effect is additive to that of serum (170).

6.4.2 Vitamin D

1,25(OH)-Vitamin D_3 has recently been shown to enhance the antituberculous activity of human monocyte-derived macrophages (171). These studies were performed in order to explain the observation that sunlight bolsters natural resistance to infection with *M.tuberculosis* (171). The enhancing effect of the vitamin D metabolite was demonstrated best in the presence of autologous serum and less so with heterologous serum or an artificial serum substitute.

6.4.3 Mannose-binding protein

As described above, there is considerable structural homology between surfactant protein A, C1q, and the human mannose-binding protein (168). The human mannose-binding protein, like the other two substances, acts as an opsonin; it binds to the C1q receptor (169) and enhances the phagocytosis of bacteria rich in surface mannose residues, such as *Salmonella montevideo* (172). The role of this protein in host defence remains to be determined.

6.4.4 Lipopolysaccharide-binding protein

LPS-binding protein (173) acts in a fashion analogous to the mannose-binding protein described above. It is an acute phase reactant that binds to both the LPS of Gram-negative bacteria and to a specific receptor on human monocyte-derived macrophages. It appears to bind to macrophage CD14

Table 5.5 Defects in macrophage antibacterial defence

Defect	References
Inborn abnormalities	
Chronic granulomatous disease	103,104
Leucocyte adherence defect	177,178
Secondary or acquired abnormalities	
Systemic lupus erythematosus	45
End-stage renal disease	179
Corticosteroid therapy	180
Viral infection	181

(174), the function of which is not blocked by monoclonal antibodies to complement receptors 1 or 3, or to Fc receptors 1-3 (173,174).

7   Defects in macrophage antibacterial activity

Inborn errors of bactericidal or phagocytic function restricted to the monocyte-macrophage system have not been identified (175). Nonetheless, several disease states, both inherited and acquired (Table 5.5), have an associated impairment or enhancement of macrophage function (175,176). As these disease states are associated with widespread pathophysiological abnormalities, it has been difficult to gain new insights into the normal functions of the macrophage from these conditions.

7.1   Diseases involving errors of macrophage antibacterial function

7.1.1   Chronic granulomatous disease (CGD)

CGD is a syndrome characterized by an inability of leucocytes to mount an oxidative burst upon membrane stimulation (104). The disease is predominantly of X-linked recessive inheritance and is due to an absence of a specific membrane-bound cytochrome, necessary for single electron transfer. Approximately one-third of patients have normal levels of cytochrome but lack one of several cytosolic factors essential for generating an oxidative burst. CGD is a defect of both granulocytes and of mononuclear phagocytes (176). Bacteria which are killed predominantly by reactive oxygen intermediates and which make catalase (to protect themselves against the toxic effects of bacterial hydrogen peroxide) are particularly virulent in these patients. A wide range of bacteria can infect CGD patients, but *S. aureus*, *Serratia marcescens*, other Gram-negative bacteria, and several different fungal species are particularly problematical. As mentioned above, IFNγ has been shown to correct partially the bacteriocidal defect in these patients (147), but the mechanism remains to be fully elucidated.

7.1.2   Leucocyte adherence defect (LAD)

Like CGD, this is a disease which effects both granulocytes and mononuclear phagocytes, but unlike CGD, oxidative metabolism of cells from affected individuals is normal. Leucocytes from patients with LAD lack the three glycoproteins of the adhesion-promoting CD18 family (Mac-1, LFA-1, p150,95), (175,177). These patients are prone to recurrent soft tissue infections most commonly with *S. aureus* and *P. aeruginosa* (178). Patients with LAD may be severely or moderately affected depending upon the concentration of adhesion-promoting glycoproteins on their leucocytes (177).

7.2   Secondary or acquired abnormalities of macrophage function

Abnormalities of mononuclear phagocytic bactericidal or phagocytic function may accompany an acquired non-infectious disease or may be seen during an acute viral infection.

7.2.1   Systemic lupus erythematosus (SLE)

Patients with SLE have a defect in reticuloendothelial clearance (45). Such a defect is not unexpected since these patients have elevated levels of circulating immune complexes. Clearance of sensitized erythrocytes by splenic Fc receptors is impaired in SLE; the degree of impairment is correlated with disease severity and with the level of circulating immune complexes (45). Blockade of the reticuloendothelial system by immune complexes may also interfere with clearance of bacteria opsonized with IgG and put these patients at increased risk for infection.

7.2.2   End-stage renal disease

Similar abnormalities in reticuloendothelial system Fc receptor-mediated clearance of sensitized erythrocytes occur in patients with end-stage renal disease (179). These patients are at increased risk for sepsis or pneumonia with encapsulated bacteria. Patients with markedly impaired Fc receptor-mediated clearance of IgG-sensitized erythrocytes are at the greatest risk for sepsis and pneumonia (179). Pathogens in these patients are encapsulated and include *S. pneumoniae*, *S. aureus*, *H. influenzae*, *P. aeruginosa*, and *E. coli*. This underscores the critical role played by fixed tissue macrophages in maintaining sterility of the bloodstream.

7.2.3   Corticosteroid therapy

Patients receiving prednisone develop monocytopenia and a transient defect in monocyte bacteriocidal and fungicidal activity (180).

7.2.4   Acute viral infection

Patients with acute viral infections often develop bacterial superinfection, raising the possibility of transient immunosuppression. Among macrophage antibacterial activities impaired by viral infection are chemotaxis, attachment of particles to phagocytic receptors, receptor-mediated phagocytosis, and bacterial killing mediated by phagosome-lysosome fusion (181).

8   Bacterial strategies for subversion of macrophage defences

In order for bacteria to cause disease, they must be able to circumvent the formidable array of antibacterial defences elaborated and displayed by the normal host. As the macrophage stands guard as gatekeeper, bacteria have had to develop strategies for breaching this first line of defence. With the aid of modern microbial molecular biological techniques, much has been learned in the past decade about the means by which pathogenic bacteria achieve their goal of persisting and causing disease in a hostile environment (182–188). This section provides an overview of the means by which bacteria survive, in spite of, or partly because of the presence of macrophages. However, these descriptions are brief and are only meant to provide examples which exemplify different bacterial pathogenetic strategies. More thorough overviews of bacterial virulence determinants and mechanisms of intracellular survival are provided in recent review articles (189–193).

8.1   Bacterial antiphagocytic strategies

Bacteria are able to survive and cause disease by evading one or more of the steps in the normal phagocytic/bactericidal process. Both intracellular and extracellular pathogens have developed a clever array of methods to avoid phagocytosis or to subvert normal processes once they have been phagocytosed. Extracellular pathogens often depend upon characteristics of their cell surface to avoid opsonization and phagocytosis. Intracellular pathogens, on the other hand, may require the intramacrophage environment for their survival, thereby depending upon phagocytosis for expression of virulence. Strategies deployed by bacteria to avoid normal defences are outlined in Table 5.6 and briefly described and illustrated with examples below. Although much has been discovered recently about bacterial virulence mechanisms, a great deal remains to be learned. The observations described below represent possible explanations for bacterial survival in the face of macrophage antibacterial activities. No doubt many bacterial species use multiple mechanisms to evade host phagocytic defences and may employ strategies as yet to be identified.

8.2   Avoidance of phagocytosis

Pyogenic extracellular pathogens are generally resistant to phagocytosis in the absence of serum opsonins. These bacterial species are often encapsulated (for example, *H. influenzae* type b and *S.pneumoniae*, *E. coli*, and Group A streptococci) and require specific anticapsular antibody for phagocytosis by neutrophils and macrophages (63,189,194,195). They generally do not activate or fix complement to their surfaces in the absence of specific IgG or IgM. Some bacterial species, such as encapsulated *S. aureus*, may fix complement in a cryptic subcapsular location inaccessible for ligation by complement receptors (79).

In addition to capsules, some bacteria elaborate an antiphagocytic slime

Table 5.6   Bacterial strategies to subvert macrophage defences

Strategy	Bacterial species (examples)	References
Avoidance of phagocytosis		
Antiphagocytic capsule	*Haemophilus influenzae*	
	Streptococcus pneumoniae	
	Escherichia coli	63,79,189,195
	Staphylococcus aureus	
Antiphagocytic slime	*Pseudomonas aeruginosa*	89,197
IgG bound in incorrect conformation	*Staphylococcus aureus*	205
Inhibition of chemotaxis	*Bordetella pertussis*	207
Failure to trigger respiratory burst	*Mycobacterium leprae*	209
Escape from the phagosome	*Listeria monocytogenes*	210,211
Prevention of phagosome–lysosome fusion	*Chlamydia psittaci*	92
	Mycobacterium tuberculosis	93
	Mycobacterium leprae	218
	Legionella pneumophila	217
Prevention of phagosome acidification	*Legionella pneumophila*	220
Resistance to non-oxidative killing	*Salmonella typhimurium*	221,222
Resistance to oxidative killing	*Mycobacterium leprae*	223,224
	Pseudomonas aeruginosa	225
Prevention of activation	*Mycobacterium leprae*	226

substance. This material is loosely affixed to the bacterial surface and may interfere with different macrophage antibacterial activities. Mucoid strains of *P. aeruginosa* from patients with cystic fibrosis elaborate a polyuronic acid polysaccharide which is highly viscous and interferes with leukocyte chemotaxis (196) and phagocytosis (89,197). It is antiphagocytic by virtue of its hydrophilicity (89). The antiphagocytic properties of the mucoid exopolysaccharide can be overridden by specific opsonizing antibodies (198). Macrophage-mediated anti-*Pseudomonas* activity is further compromised in patients with cystic fibrosis by virtue of fragmented immunoglobulin present in serum and bronchopulmonary secretions (199,200). Although phagocytosis of *P. aeruginosa* is enhanced by specific opsonizing antibody (201–204), IgG from patients with cystic fibrosis lacks the Fc portion, rendering it antiphagocytic; it binds to the bacterial surface but is unable to ligate Fc receptors on the macrophage (199,200).

As described above, many strains of *S. aureus* possess surface-exposed protein A which is capable of directly binding IgG via its Fc domain. This characteristic makes the organism susceptible to phagocytosis by macrophages possessing cytophilic IgG (41). However, the same bacterial feature provides an antiphagocytic defence by binding IgG in the incorrect orientation to the bacterial surface (with the Fc domain buried), rendering the bacteria resistant to phagocytosis by macrophages and neutrophils lacking cytophilic antibody (205). A direct correlation exists between the level of protein A expressed on the bacterial surface and the resistance to opsonic phagocytosis (205).

8.3   Inhibition of chemotaxis

Bordetella pertussis, the agent of whooping cough, elaborates a number of extracellular products with profound effects on the host (206). Chief among these toxins is lymphocytosis-promoting factor (pertussis toxin), a protein that impairs macrophage chemotaxis (207). The disease is characterized by destruction of respiratory ciliated epithelial cells without evidence of bacterial invasion. The microbial virulence is probably enhanced by its ability to inhibit the recruitment of phagocytic cells. Macrophage bacteriocidal capacity is further impaired by a bacterial adenylate cyclase which interferes with superoxide generation by both alveolar macrophages and neutrophils (208).

8.4   Failure to trigger a respiratory burst
upon phagocytosis

One of the principal microbicidal mechanisms of macrophages is the generation of reactive oxygen intermediates upon phagocytosis of bacteria. Some bacterial species (for example, *M. leprae*) fail to trigger a respiratory burst and are thereby able to enter macrophages without falling prey to the effects of these toxic radicals (209). This feature is dependent upon bacterial viability (209). The receptor-mediated process by which bacteria enter macrophages appears to be critical in determining their intracellular fate. As ligation of certain receptors but not others initiates the generation of reactive oxygen intermediates (91), the means by which bacteria enter macrophages may determine whether they are killed or are able to establish intracellular parasitism.

8.5   Escape from the phagosome

Once ingestion has occurred, microbicidal substances must be delivered to the phagosome in order for the bacteria to be killed. *Listeria monocytogenes* is able to survive within macrophages by escaping from the phagosome into the cytoplasm (210,211). This phenomenon is mediated by a haemolysin; mutants unable to produce this enzyme are avirulent and do not grow within eukaryotic cells (210,212,213). Once free within the cytoplasm, *Listeria* spreads from cell to cell within a 'comet' or actin (211). This process is mediated by polymerization of host actin filaments; when cytochalasin D is added to the system, the bacteria fail to spread from cell to cell (211). The key role played by the haemolysin in intracellular parasitism is demonstrated by the fact that when it is cloned into *Bacillus subtilis*, the recipient bacteria are able to survive and grow in macrophages (214). *Mycobacterium leprae* may also be able to escape from the phagosome into the cytoplasm of macrophages (215).

8.6   Prevention of phagosome–lysosome fusion

The contents of macrophage granules are delivered to bacteria-containing phagosomes by the process of phagosome–lysosome fusion. This process follows logically after ingestion of most bacteria, but some species survive because they prevent fusion. The capacity of ingested organisms to inhibit phagosome–lysosome fusion was shown in classic studies by Jones and Hirsch with *Toxoplasma gondii* (216). The viability of ingested microbes and the state of opsonization largely determine whether or not fusion occurs. For instance, unopsonized *Chlamydia psittaci* enter macrophages and survive without evidence of phagosome–lysosome fusion. On the other hand, if the chlamydia are opsonized with specific antiserum, fusion occurs shortly after ingestion (92). A similar sequence of events is seen with *L. pneumophila*, where viability and opsonization determine whether or not phagosome–lysosome fusion occurs (217).

Seminal observations regarding prevention of phagosome–lysosome fusion were made with *M. tuberculosis* (93). Viable mycobacteria were found in unfused phagosomes, whereas phagosomes containing damaged bacilli fused with lysosomes; this suggested an active role for the mycobacteria in preventing fusion and a mechanism of intracellular survival. However, if the mycobacteria were pretreated with specific antibody, fusion of phagosome and lysosome was uninhibited. Despite this fusion, the bacteria were able to survive and replicate within the macrophages (94). Thus, one must be cautious in attributing a cause and effect relationship in a process as complex and multifaceted as phagocytic killing of micro-organisms. Infection of macrophages with *M. leprae* also prevents phagosome–lysosome fusion (218). Sulphatides from *M.tuberculosis* accumulate within the macrophage secondary lysosomes and render them incapable of fusion (219).

8.7   Inhibition of phagosome acidification

Phagocytosis and killing by macrophages is usually associated with acidification of the phagosomes within which the bacteria are contained. In the case of *L.pneumophila*, however, live bacteria appear to interfere with the process of acidification (220). The pH of phagosomes containing live

Legionella is 0.8 pH units higher than those containing killed organisms. This interference with acidification is not seen with other bacteria incapable of establishing intracellular parasitism, such as *E.coli*; the pH of the phagosomes containing live or killed *E.coli* is the same (220).

8.8 Resistance to non-oxidative killing

Salmonella typhimurium is a facultative intracellular pathogen. After macrophage phagocytosis, phagosome–lysosome fusion occurs, but the bacteria are able to survive. Digestion of killed but not live bacteria occurs, suggesting that the viable bacteria are resistant to the effects of lysosomal enzymes (221). It has been suggested that these bacteria are resistant to the bactericidal effects of defensins, and that the synthesis of the bacterial protective feature is under control of a transcriptional regulatory protein (222).

8.9 Resistance to oxidative killing

Once within the phagolysosome, bacteria are exposed to the full brunt of the macrophage's oxidative attack. Some bacteria are intrinsically resistant to killing by reactive oxygen intermediates, while others are able to detoxify oxygen radicals. For instance, *M. leprae* elaborates superoxide dismutase which may interfere with the bacteriocidal effects of O_2^- (223). Glycolipids from *M. leprae* and the mucoid exopolysaccharide from *P. aeruginosa* are able to scavenge hypochlorite, thereby protecting the bacteria from the toxic effects of this potent antimicrobial factor (224,225).

8.10 Prevention of macrophage activation

As demonstrated above, *M. leprae* exhibits multiple mechanisms for evasion of normal macrophage bactericidal defences. Perhaps key to its survival and virulence, is its capacity to prevent macrophage activation, even after stimulation with IFNα (226). One of the hallmarks of lepromatous leprosy is the presence within dermal lesions of macrophages laden with a prodigious mycobacterial load with few infiltrating lymphocytes (227,228). By contrast, dermal lesions from patients with tuberculoid leprosy contain lightly parasitized macrophages with contiguous CD4+ cells, and with CD8+ cells at the periphery of the lesions (229). The immunological defect in patients with lepromatous leprosy is an inability to activate macrophages for mycobacterial killing (230). This appears not to be an intrinsic macrophage abnormality, but rather a deficiency in a macrophage activating factor/cytokine, such as IL-2 (231). IL-1 production from peripheral blood mononuclear cells of lepromatous leprosy patients is also deficient (232). The resistance of macrophages to activation can be induced by the lipoarabinomannan of *M. leprae* (233).

The dermal lesions in patients with lepromatous leprosy respond to local immunotherapy (234). Shortly after IL-2 is injected intradermally into the lesions, there is an influx of lymphocytes. This is followed by liberation of the mycobacteria from disintegrating macrophages, immigration of blood monocytes with mycobacteriocidal capacity and subsequent reduction in acid fast bacilli in the lesions. This clearly demonstrates the importance of macrophage activation and the role of cytokines in the effective eradication of intracellular parasites.

9   Summary

Macrophages play a critically important role in host defence against bacterial infection. They exert their antibacterial activities at mucosal surfaces and as filtering agents within the reticuloendothelial system. The phenotypic diversity among macrophages attests their adaptation to a wide range of environmental conditions and the special requirements for function in these diverse arenas.

Phagocytosis and bacterial killing are functions for which macrophages are well-suited. They ingest potential pathogens via an array of non-opsonic and opsonic receptors and kill their prey with the aid of reactive oxygen intermediates and non-oxidative factors. The capacity to ingest and kill bacteria is enhanced by an assortment of opsonins, cytokines, and other immunomodulators. Despite the impressive antibacterial armamentarium with which macrophages are fortified, they are impotent in the eradication of certain bacterial strains and species.

Many bacterial species are virulent because of their resistance to normal phagocytic defences. Extracellular pathogens generally resist phagocytosis except when opsonized with specific Ig. Intracellular pathogens thrive within eukaryotic cells and are able to withstand the macrophage's bacteriocidal assault. Bacteria utilize a clever array of survival strategies including avoidance of phagocytosis, failure to trigger a respiratory burst, escape from the phagosome, prevention of phagosome–lysosome fusion and resistance to either oxidative or non-oxidative killing. New therapeutic strategies are being developed to augment natural antibacterial defences and prevent these intracellular pathogens from parasitizing macrophages.

Acknowledgements

The critical suggestions of Drs John Curnutte, Brett Finlay, Siamon Gordon, Marcus Horwitz, Anne Junker, Paul Quie, David Scheifele, Samuel Silverstein, and Samuel Wright are gratefully acknowledged.

Dr Speert is a scholar of the Canadian Cystic Fibrosis Foundation. This work was supported by grants from the Canadian Cystic Fibrosis Foundation, the Medical Research Council of Canada, and the Canadian Bacterial Diseases Network Research Program.

References

1 Rogers, D.E. (1960). Host mechanisms which act to remove bacteria from the blood stream. *Bacteriol. Rev.*, **24**, 50–66.

2 Williams, A.E. and Blakemore, W.F. (1990). Pathogenesis of meningitis caused by *Streptococcus suis* type 2. *J. Infect. Dis.*, **162**, 474–81.

3 Meltzer, M.S., Skillman, D.R., Gomatos, P.J., Kalter, D.C., and Gendelman, H.E. (1990). Role of mononuclear phagocytes in the pathogenesis of human immunodeficiency virus infection. *Ann. Rev. Immunol.*, **8**, 169–94.

4 Finlay, B.B., Heffron, F., and Falkow, S. (1989). Epithelial cell surfaces induce *Salmonella* proteins required for bacterial adherence and invasion. *Science*, **243**, 940–3.

5 Gordon, S., Perry, V.H., Rabinowitz, S., Chung, L., and Rosen, H. (1988). Plasma membrane receptors of the mononuclear phagocyte system. *J. Cell Sci.*, **9**, (Suppl.), 1–26.

6 Lee, S., Starkey, P.M., and Gordon, S. (1985). Quantitative analysis of total macrophage content in adult mouse tissues: immunochemical studies with monoclonal antibody F4/80. *J. Exp. Med.*, **161**, 475–89.

7 North, R.J. (1978). The concept of the activated macrophage. *J. Immunol.*, **121**, 806–9.

8 Cohn, Z. (1978). The activation of mononuclear phagocytes: fact, fancy and future. *J. Immunol.*, **121**, 813–16.

9 North, R.J. (1970). The relative importance of blood monocytes and fixed macrophages to the expression of cell-mediated immunity to infection. *J. Exp. Med.*, **132**, 521–34.

10 Basham, T.Y. and Merigan, T.C. (1983). Recombinant interferon-gamma increases HLA-DR synthesis and expression. *J. Immunol.*, **130**, 1492–4.

11 Becker, S. (1984). Interferons as modulators of human monocyte-macrophage differentiation. I. Interferon-gamma increases HLA-DR expression and inhibits phagocytosis of zymosan. *J. Immunol.*, **132**, 1249–54.

12 Guyre, P.M., Morganelli, P.M., and Miller, R. (1983). Recombinant immune interferon increases immunoglobulin G Fc receptors on cultured human mononuclear phagocytes. *J. Clin. Invest.*, **72**, 393–97.

13 Perussia, B., Dayton, E.T., Lazarus, R., Fanning, V., and Trinchieri, G. (1983). Immune interferon induces the receptor for monomeric IgG1 on human monocytic and myeloid cells. *J. Exp. Med.*, **158**, 1092–113.

14 Wright, S.D., Detmers, P.A., Jong, M.T.C., and Meyer, C. (1986). Interferon-gamma depresses binding of ligand by C3b and C3bi receptors on cultured human monocytes, an effect reversed by fibronectin. *J. Exp. Med.*, **163**, 1245–59.

15 Mokoena, T. and Gordon, S. (1985). Human activation: modulation of mannosyl, fucosyl receptor activity *in vitro* by lymphokines, gamma and alpha interferons, and dexamethasone. *J. Clin. Invest.*, **75**, 624–31.

16 Nathan, C.F., Murray, H.W., Wiebe, M.E., and Rubin, B.Y. (1983). Identification of interferon-gamma as the lymphokine that activates human macrophage oxidative metabolism and antimicrobial activity. *J. Exp. Med.*, **158**, 670–89.

17 Warren, M.K. and Vogel, S.N. (1985). Opposing effects of glucocorticoids on interferon-gamma-induced murine macrophage Fc receptor and Ia antigen expression. *J. Immunol.*, **134**, 2462–9.

18 Lepay, D.A., Nathan, C.F., Steinman, R.M., Murray, H.W., and Cohn, Z.A. (1985). Murine Kupffer cells: mononuclear phagocytes deficient in the generation of reactive oxygen intermediates. *J. Exp. Med.*, **161**, 1079–96.

19 Lepay, D.A., Steinman, R.M., Nathan, C.F., Murray, H.W., and Cohn, Z.A. (1985). Liver macrophages in murine listeriosis: cell-mediated immunity is correlated with an influx of macrophages capable of generating reactive oxygen intermediates. *J. Exp. Med.*, **161**, 1503–12.

20 Peterson, P.K., Verhoef, J., Schmeling, D., and Quie, P.G. (1977). Kinetics of phagocytosis and bacterial killing by human polymorphonuclear leukocytes and monocytes. *J. Infect. Dis.*, **136**, 502–9.

21 Steigbigel, R.T., Lambert, L.H., and Remington, J.S. (1974). Phagocytic and bactericidal properties of normal human monocytes. *J. Clin. Invest.*, **53**, 131–42.

22 Catterall, J.R., Black, C.M., Leventhal, J.P., Rizk, N.W., Wachtel, J.S., and Remington, J.S. (1987). Nonoxidative microbicidal activity in normal human alveolar and peritoneal macrophages. *Infect. Immun.*, **55**, 1635–40.

23 Peterson, P.K., Gaziano, E., Suh, H.J., Devalon, M., Peterson, L., and Keane, W.F. (1985). Antimicrobial activities of dialysis-elicited and resident human peritoneal macrophages. *Infect. Immun.*, **49**, 212–18.

24 Verbrugh, H.A., Keane, W.F., Hoidal, J.R., Freiberg, M.R., Elliott, G.R., and Peterson, P.K. (1983). Peritoneal macrophages and opsonins: antibacterial defense in patients undergoing chronic peritoneal dialysis. *J. Infect. Dis.*, **147**, 1018–29.

25 Kemmerich, B., Rossing, T.H., and Pennington, J.E. (1987). Comparative oxidative microbicidal activity of human blood monocytes and alveolar macrophages and activation by recombinant gamma interferon. *Am. Rev. Resp. Dis.*, **136**, 266–9.

26 Nguyen, B.T., Peterson, P.K., Verbrugh, H.A., Quie, P.G., and Hoidal, J.R. (1982). Differences in phagocytosis and killing by alveolar

macrophages from humans, rabbits, rats and hamsters. *Infect. Immun.*, **36**, 504–9.

27 Oren, R., Farnham, A.E., Saito, K., Milofsky, E., and Karnovsky, M.L. (1963). Metabolic patterns in three types of phagocytizing cells. *J. Cell Biol.*, **17**, 487–501.

28 Cohen, A.B. and Cline, M.J. (1971). The human alveolar macrophage: isolation, cultivation *in vitro*, and studies of morphologic and functional characteristics. *J. Clin. Invest.*, **50**, 1390–8.

29 Fels, A. and Cohn, Z.A. (1986). The alveolar macrophage. *J. Appl. Physiol.*, **60**, 353–69.

30 Marodi, L., Leijh, P.C.J., and van Furth, R. (1984). Characteristics and functional capacities of human cord blood granulocytes and monocytes. *Ped. Res.*, **18**, 1127–31.

31 Goldstein, E., Lippert, W., and Warshauer, D. (1974). Pulmonary alveolar macrophage: defender against bacterial infection of the lung. *J. Clin. Invest.*, **54**, 519–28.

32 Hocking, W.G. and Golde, D.W. (1979). The pulmonary-alveolar macrophage (first of two parts). *N. Eng. J. Med.*, **301**, 580–7.

33 Rehm, S.R., Gross, G.N., and Pierce, A.K. (1980). Early bacterial clearance from murine lungs: species-dependent phagocytic response. *J. Clin. Invest.*, **66**, 194–9.

34 Green, G.M. and Kass, E.H. (1963). The role of the alveolar macrophage in the clearance of bacteria from the lung. *J. Exp. Med.*, **119**, 167–75.

35 Coonrod, J.D. (1989). Role of leukocytes in lung defenses. *Respiration*, **55** (Suppl. 1), 9–13.

36 Sibille, Y. and Reynolds, H.Y. (1990). Macrophages and polymorphonuclear neutrophils in lung defense and injury. *Am. Rev. Resp. Dis.*, **141**, 471–501.

37 Reynolds, H.Y. and Newball, H.H. (1974). Analysis of proteins and respiratory cells obtained from human lungs by bronchial lavage. *J. Lab. Clin. Med.*, **84**, 559–73.

38 Reynolds, H.Y. and Thompson, R.E. (1973). Pulmonary host defenses. II. Interaction of respiratory antibodies with *Pseudomonas aeruginosa* and alveolar macrophages. *J. Immunol.*, **111**, 369–80.

39 Reynolds, H.Y., Kazmierowski, J.A., and Newball, H.H. (1975). Specificity of opsonic antibodies to enhance phagocytosis of *Pseudomonas aeruginosa* by human alveolar macrophages. *J. Clin. Invest.*, **56**, 376–85.

40 Naegel, G.P., Young, K.R. Jr, and Reynolds, H.Y. (1984). Receptors for human IgG subclasses on human alveolar macrophages. *Am. Rev. Resp. Dis.*, **129**, 413–18.

41 Verbrugh, H.A., Hoidal, J.R., Nguyen, B.T., Verhoef, J., Quie, P.G., and Peterson, P.K. (1982). Human alveolar macrophage

cytophilic immunoglobulin G-mediated phagocytosis of protein A-positive staphylococci. *J. Clin. Invest.*, **69**, 63–74.

42 Jonsson, S., Musher, D.M., Chapman, A., Goree, A., and Lawrence, E.C. (1985). Phagocytosis and killing of common bacterial pathogens of the lung by human alveolar macrophages. *J. Infect. Dis.*, **152**, 4–13.

43 Frank, M.M. (1989). The role of macrophages in blood stream clearance. In *Human monocytes* (ed. M. Zembala and G.L. Asherson). Academic Press, London.

44 Bowdy, B.D., *et al.* (1990). Organ-specific disposition of group B streptococci in piglets: evidence for a direct interaction with target cells in the pulmonary circulation. *Ped. Res.*, **27**, 344–8.

45 Frank, M.M., Hamburger, M.I., Lawley, T.J., Kimberly, R.P., and Plotz, P.H. (1979). Defective reticuloendothelial system Fc-receptor function in systemic lupus erythematosus. *N. Eng. J. Med.*, **300**, 518–23.

46 Friedman, R.L. and Moon, R.J. (1977). Hepatic clearance of *Salmonella typhimurium* in silica-treated mice. *Infect. Immun.*, **16**, 1005–12.

47 Wardle, E.N. (1987). Kupffer cells and their function. *Liver*, **7**, 63–75.

48 Hubbard, A.L., Wilson, G., Ashwell, G., and Stukenbrok, H. (1979). An electron microscope autoradiographic study of the carbohydrate recognition systems in rat liver. *J. Cell Biol.*, **83**, 47–64.

49 Rumelt, S., Metzger, Z., Kariv, N., and Rosenberg, M. (1988). Clearance of *Serratia marcescens* from blood in mice: role of hydrophobic versus mannose-sensitive interactions. *Infect. Immun.*, **56**, 1167–70.

50 Leunk, R.D. and Moon, R.J. (1982). Association of type 1 pili with the ability of livers to clear *Salmonella typhimurium*. *Infect. Immun.*, **36**, 1168–74.

51 Perry, A. and Ofek, I. (1984). Inhibition of blood clearance and hepatic tissue binding of *Escherichia coli* by liver lectin-specific sugars and glycoproteins. *Infect. Immun.*, **43**, 257–62.

52 Benacerraf, B., Sebestyen, M.M., and Schlossman, S. (1959). A quantitative study of the kinetics of blood clearance of P32-labelled *Escherichia coli* and staphylococci by the reticuloendothelial system. *J. Exp. Med.*, **110**, 27–48.

53 Filice, G.A. (1988). Antimicrobial properties of Kupffer cells. *Infect. Immun.*, **56**, 1430–5.

54 Gros, P., Skamene, E., and Forget, A. (1981). Genetic control of natural resistance to *Mycobacterium bovis* (BCG) in mice. *J. Immunol.*, **127**, 2417–21.

55 Skamene, E., Gros, P., Forget, A., Kongshavn, P.A.L., St Charles, C., and Taylor, B.A. (1982). Genetic regulation of resistance to intracellular pathogens. *Nature*, **297**, 506–9.

56 Denis, M., Forget, A., Pelletier, M., and Skamene, E. (1988). Pleiotropic effects of the Bcg gene: III. Respiratory burst in Bcg-congenic macrophages. *Clin. Exp. Immunol.*, **73**, 370–5.

57 Schurr, E., Skamene, E., Forget, A., and Gros, P. (1989). Linkage analysis of the Bcg gene on mouse chromosome 1: identification of a tightly linked marker. *J. Immunol.*, **142**, 4507–13.

58 Buschman, E., Taniyama, T., Nakamura, R., and Skamene, E. (1989). Functional expression of the Bcg gene in macrophages. *Res. Immunol.*, **140**, 793–7.

59 Schurr, E., Buschman, E., Malo, D., Gros, P., and Skamene, E. (1990). Immunogenetics of mycobacterial infections; mouse-human homologies. *J. Infect. Dis.*, **161**, 634–9.

60 Stead, W.W., Senner, J.W., Reddick, W.T., and Lofgren, J.P. (1990). Racial differences in susceptibility to infection by *Mycobacterium tuberculosis*. *N. Eng. J. Med.*, **322**, 422–7.

61 Crowle, A.J. and Elkins, N. (1990). Relative permissiveness of macrophages from black and white people for virulent tubercle bacilli. *Infect. Immun.*, **58**, 632–8.

62 Silverstein, S.C., Greenberg, S., Di Virgilio, F., and Steinberg, T.H. (1989). Phagocytosis. In *Fundamental immunology*, (ed. W.E. Paul), Raven Press, New York.

63 Horwitz, M.A. (1982). Phagocytosis of microorganisms. *Rev. Infect. Dis.*, **4**, 104–23.

64 Richards, C.D. and Gauldie, J. (1985). IgA-mediated phagocytosis by mouse alveolar macrophages. *Am. Rev. Resp. Dis.*, **132**, 82–5.

65 Yang, K.D. *et al.* (1990). Effect of fibronectin on IgA-mediated uptake of type III group B streptococci by phagocytes. *J. Infect. Dis.*, **161**, 236–41.

66 Brown, E.J. and Goodwin, J.L. (1988). Fibronectin receptors on phagocytes: characterization of the arg-gly-asp binding proteins of human monocytes and polymorphonuclear leukocytes. *J. Exp. Med.*, **167**, 777–93.

67 Wood, W.B., Jr, Smith, M.R., and Watson, B. (1946). Studies on the mechanism of recovery in pneumococcal pneumonia. IV. The mechanism of phagocytosis in the absence of antibody. *J. Exp. Med.*, **84**, 387–401.

68 Sharon, N. (1984). Carbohydrates as recognition determinants in phagocytosis and in lectin-mediated killing of target cells. *Biol. Cell*, **51**, 239–46.

69 Ofek, I. and Sharon, N. (1988). Lectinophagocytosis: a molecular mechanism of recognition between cell surface sugars and lectins in the phagocytosis of bacteria. *Infect. Immun.*, **56**, 539–47.

70 Speert, D.P., Wright, S.D., Silverstein, S.C., and Mah, B. (1988). Functional characterization of macrophage receptors for *in vitro*

phagocytosis of unopsonized *Pseudomonas aeruginosa. J. Clin. Invest.*, **82**, 872–79.

71 Wright, S.D. and Jong, M.T.C. (1986). Adhesion-promoting receptors on human macrophages recognize *Escherichia coli* by binding to lipopolysaccharide. *J. Exp. Med.*, **164**, 1876–88.

72 Stahl, P., Schlesinger, P.H., Sigardson, B., Rodman, J.S., and Lee, Y.C. (1980). Receptor-mediated pinocytosis of mannose glycoconjugates by macrophages: characterization and evidence for receptor recycling. *Cell*, **19**, 207–15.

73 Kan, V.L. and Bennett, J.E. (1988). Lectin-like attachment sites on murine pulmonary alveolar macrophages bind *Aspergillus fumigatus* conidia. *J. Infect. Dis.*, **158**, 407–14.

74 Blackwell, J.M., Ezekowitz, R.A.B., Roberts, M.B., Channon, J.Y., Sim. R.B., and Gordon, S. (1985). Macrophage complement and lectin-like receptors bind *Leishmania* in the absence of serum. *J. Exp. Med.*, **162**, 324–31.

75 Ashwell, G. and Harford, J. (1982). Carbohydrate-specific receptors of the liver. *Ann. Rev. Biochem.*, **51**, 531–54.

76 Stewart, J.S., Glass, E.J., and Weir, D.M. (1982). Macrophage binding of *Staphylococcus albus* is blocked by anti l-region alloantibody. *Nature*, **298**, 852–4.

77 Unkeless, J.C. (1989). Function and heterogeneity of human Fc receptors for immunoglobulin G. *J. Clin. Invest.*, **83**, 355–61.

78 Liang-Takasaki, C., Makela, P.H., and Leive, L. (1982). Phagocytosis of bacteria by macrophages: changing the carbohydrate of lipopolysaccharide alters interaction with complement and macrophages. *J. Immunol.*, **128**, 1229–35.

79 Wilkinson, B.J., Peterson, P.K., and Quie, P.G. (1979). Cryptic peptidoglycan and the antiphagocytic effect of the *Staphylococcal aureus* capsule: model for the antiphagocytic effect of bacterial cell surface polymers. *Infect. Immun.*, **23**, 502–8.

80 Griffin, F.M., Jr., Griffin, J.A., Leider, J.E., and Silverstein, S.C. (1975). Studies on the mechanism of phagocytosis. I. Requirements for circumferential attachment of particle-bound ligands to specific receptors on the macrophage plasma membrane. *J. Exp. Med.*, **142**, 1263–82.

81 Wright, S.D. and Silverstein, S.C. (1982). Tumor-promoting phorbol esters stimulate C3b and C3b' receptor-mediated phagocytosis in cultured human monocytes. *J. Exp. Med.*, **156**, 1149–64.

82 Bianco, G., Griffin, F.M., Jr., and Silverstein, S.C. (1975). Studies of the macrophage complement receptor: alteration of receptor function upon macrophage activation. *J. Exp. Med.*, **141**, 1278–90.

83 Griffin, F.M., Jr, and Mullinax, P.J. (1990). High concentrations of bacterial lipopolysaccharide, but not microbial infection-induced in-

flammation, activate macrophage C3 receptors for phagocytosis. *J. Immunol.*, **145**, 697–701.

84   Horwitz, M.A. (1984). Phagocytosis of the legionnaires' disease bacterium (*Legionella pneumophila*) occurs by a novel mechanism: engulfment within a pseudopod coil. *Cell*, **36**, 27–33.

85   van Oss, C.J. (1978). Phagocytosis as a surface phenomenon. *Ann. Rev. Microbiol.*, **32**, 19–39.

86   Speert, D.P., Loh, B.A., Cabral, D.A., and Salit, I.E. (1986). Nonopsonic phagocytosis of nonmucoid *Pseudomonas aeruginosa* by human neutrophils and monocyte-derived macrophages is correlated with bacterial piliation and hydrophobicity. *Infect. Immun.*, **53**, 207–12.

87   van Oss, C.J. and Gillman, C.F. (1972). Phagocytosis as a surface phenomenon. II. Contact angles and phagocytosis of encapsulated bacteria before and after opsonization by specific antiserum and complement. *J. Reticuloendothel. Soc.*, **12**, 497–502.

88   Silverblatt, F.J., Dreyer, J.S., and Schauer, S. (1979). Effect of pili on susceptibility of *Escherichia coli* to phagocytosis. *Infect. Immun.*, **24**, 218–23.

89   Cabral, D.A., Loh, B.A., and Speert, D.P. (1987). Mucoid *Pseudomonas aeruginosa* resists nonopsonic phagocytosis by human neutrophils and macrophages. *Ped. Res.*, **22**, 429–31.

90   Wilson, C.B., Tsai, V., and Remington, J.S. (1980). Failure to trigger the oxidative metabolic burst by normal macrophages: possible mechanism for the survival of intracellular pathogens. *J. Exp. Med.*, **151**, 328–46.

91   Wright, S.D. and Griffin, F.M., Jr (1985). Activation of phagocytic cells' C3 receptors for phagocytosis. *J. Leuc. Biol.*, **38**, 327–39.

92   Wyrick, P.B. and Brownridge, E.A. (1978). Growth of *Chlamydia psittaci* in macrophages. *Infect. Immun.*, **19**, 1054–60.

93   Armstrong, J.A. and D'Arcy Hart, P. (1971). Response of 92 cultured macrophages to *Mycobacterium tuberculosis* with observations on fusion of lysosomes with phagosomes. *J. Exp. Med.*, **134**, 713–40.

94   Armstrong, J.A. and D'Arcy Hart, P. (1975). Phagosome-lysosome interactions in cultured macrophages infected with virulent tubercle bacilli. *J. Exp. Med.*, **142**, 1–16.

95   Noel, G.J., Katz, S., and Edelson, P.J. (1988). Complement-mediated early clearance of *Haemophilus influenzae* type b from blood is independent of serum lytic activity. *J. Infect. Dis.*, **157**, 85–90.

96   Payne, N.R. and Horwitz, M.A. (1987). Phagocytosis of *Legionella pneumophila* is mediated by human monocyte complement receptors. *J. Exp. Med.*, **166**, 1377–89.

97   Schlesinger, L.S., Bellinger-Kawahara, C.G., Payne, N.R., and Horwitz, M.A. (1990). Phagocytosis of *Mycobacterium tuberculosis* is

mediated by human monocyte complement receptors and complement component C3. *J. Immunol.*, **144**, 2771–80.

98 Schlesinger, L.S. and Horwitz, M.A. (1990). Phagocytosis of leprosy bacilli is mediated by complement receptors CR1 and CR3 on human monocytes and complement component C3 in serum. *J. Clin. Invest.*, **85**, 1304–14.

99 Catanzaro, A. and Wright, S.D. (1990). Binding of *Mycobacterium avium-Mycobacterium intracellulare* to human leukocytes. *Infect. Immun.*, **58**, 2951–6.

100 Andrew, P.W., Jackett, P.S., and Lowrie, D.B. (1985). Killing and degradation of microorganisms by macrophages. In *Mononuclear phagocytes: Physiology and pathology* (ed. R.T. Dean and W. Jessup). Elsevier, New York.

101 Shepherd, V.L. (1986). Role of the respiratory burst of phagocytes in host defense. *Sem. Resp. Infect.*, **1**, 99–106.

102 Rook, G.A.W. (1989). Intracellular killing of microorganisms. In *Human monocytes* (ed. M. Zembala and G.L. Asherson). Academic Press, London.

103 Quie, P.G., White, J.G., Holmes, B., and Good, R.A. (1967). *In vitro* bactericidal capacity of human polymorphonuclear leukocytes: diminished activity in chronic granulomatous disease of childhood. *J. Clin. Invest.*, **46**, 668–79.

104 Curnutte, J.T. and Babior, B.M. (1987). Chronic granulomatous disease. *Adv. Hum. Gen.*, **16**, 229–95.

105 Drath, D.B. and Karnovsky, M.L. (1975). Superoxide production by phagocytic leukocytes. *J. Exp. Med.*, **141**, 257–60.

106 Ward, P.A., Warren, J.S., and Johnson, K.J. (1988). Oxygen radicals, inflammation, and tissue injury. *Free Rad. Biol. Med.*, **5**, 403–8.

107 Kitahara, M., Eyre, H.J., Simonian, Y., Atkin, C.L., and Hasstedt, S.J. (1981). Hereditary myeloperoxidase deficiency. *Blood*, **57**, 888–93.

108 Parry, M.F., Root, R.K., Metcalf, J.A., Delaney, K.K., Kaplow, L.S., and Richar, W.J. (1981). Myeloperoxidase deficiency: prevalence and clinical significance. *Ann. Int. Med.*, **95**, 293–301.

109 Ganz, T., Selsted, M.E., and Lehrer, R.I. (1986). Antimicrobial activity of phagocyte granule proteins. *Sem. Resp. Infect.*, **1**, 107–17.

110 Darte, C. and Beaufay, H. (1983). Analytical subcellular fractionation of cultivated mouse resident peritoneal macrophages. *J. Exp. Med.*, **157**, 1208–28.

111 Richmond, V.L. (1974). *In vitro* hydrolase and phagocytic activities of alveolar macrophages. *J. Lab. Clin. Med.*, **83**, 757–67.

112 Cohn, Z. and Wiener, E. (1963). The particulate hydrolases of macrophages. I. Comparative enzymology, isolation and properties. *J. Exp. Med.*, **118**, 991–1008.

113 Goldstein, E. (1983). Hydrolytic enzymes of alveolar macrophages. *Rev. Infect. Dis.*, **5**, 1078–92.

114 Geisow, M.J., D'Arcy Hart, P., and Young, M.R. (1981). Temporal changes of lysosome and phagosome pH during phagolysosome formation in macrophages: studies by fluorescence spectroscopy. *J. Cell Biol.*, **89**, 645–52.

115 Lehrer, R.I., Barton, A., Daher, K.A., Harwig, S.S., Ganz, T., and Selsted, M.E. (1989). Interaction of human defensins with *Escherichia coli*: mechanism of bactericidal activity. *J. Clin. Invest.*, **84**, 553–61.

116 Sawyer, J.G., Martin, N.L., and Hancock, R.E.W. (1988). Interaction of macrophage cationic proteins with the outer membrane of *Pseudomonas aeruginosa. Infect. Immun.*, **56**, 693–8.

117 Salton, M.R.J. (1957). The properties of lysozyme and its action on microorganisms. *Bacteriol. Rev.*, **21**, 82–99.

118 Nathan, C.F. (1987). Secretory products of macrophages. *J. Clin. Invest.*, **79**, 319–26.

119 Thorne, K.J.I., Oliver, R.C., and Barrett, A.J. (1976). Lysis and killing of bacteria by lysosomal proteinases. *Infect. Immun.*, **14**, 555–63.

120 Strominger, J.L. and Ghuysen, J. (1967). Mechanisms of enzymatic bacteriolysis. *Science*, **156**, 213–21.

121 Mackaness, G.B. (1964). The immunological basis of acquired cellular resistance. *J. Exp. Med.*, **120**, 105 20.

122 Mackaness, G.B. (1969). The influence of immunologically committed lymphoid cells on macrophage activity *in vivo. J. Exp. Med.*, **129**, 973–92.

123 Bendtzen, k. (1988). Interleukin 1, interleukin 6 and tumor necrosis factor in infection, inflammation and immunity. *Immunol. Lett.*, **19**, 183–92.

124 Groopman, J.E., Molina, J., and Scadden, D.T. (1989). Hematopoietic growth factors: biology and clinical applications. *N. Engl. J. Med.*, **321**, 1449–59.

125 Dinarello, C.A., Cannon, J.G., and Wolff, S.M. (1988). New concepts on the pathogenesis of fever. *Rev. Infect. Dis.*, **10**, 168–89.

126 Dinarello, C.A. (1984). Interleukin-1 and the pathogenesis of the acute-phase response. *N. Engl. J. Med.*, **311**, 1413–18.

127 Okusawa, S., Gelfand, J.A., Ikejima, T., Connolly, R.J., and Dinarello, C.A. (1988). Interleukin 1 induces a shock-like state in rabbits. *J. Clin. Invest.*, **81**, 1162–72.

128 Ozaki, Y., Ohashi, T., Minami, A., and Nakamura, S. (1987). Enhanced resistance of mice to bacterial infection induced by recombinant human interleukin-1 alpha. *Infect. Immun.*, **55**, 1436–40.

129 Minami, A., Fujimoto, K., Ozaki, Y., and Nakamura, S. (1988).

Augmentation of host resistance to microbial infections by recombinant human interleukin-1 alpha. *Infect. Immun.*, **56**, 3116–20.

130 Michie, H.R. *et al.* (1988). Detection of circulating tumor necrosis factor after endotoxin administration. *N. Engl. J. Med.*, **318**, 1481–6.

131 Beutler, B. and Cerami, A. (1987). Cachectin: more than a tumor necrosis factor. *N. Engl. J. Med.*, **316**, 379–85.

132 Bermudez, L.E. and Young, L.S. (1988). Tumor necrosis factor, alone or in combination with IL-2, but not IFN-gamma, is associated with macrophage killing of *Mycobacterium avium* complex. *J. Immunol.*, **140**, 3006–13.

133 Tracey, K.J., Lowry, S.F., and Cerami, A. (1988). Cachectin: a hormone that triggers acute shock and chronic cachexia. *J. Infect. Dis.*, **157**, 413–20.

134 Waage, A., Halstensen, A., and Espevik, T. (1987). Association between tumour necrosis factor in serum and fatal outcome in patients with meningococcal disease. *Lancet*, **i**, 355–7.

135 Kettelhut, I.C., Fiers, W., and Goldberg, A.L. (1987). The toxic effects of tumor necrosis factor *in vivo* and their prevention by cyclooxygenase inhibitors. *Proc. Natl. Acad. Sci. U.S.A.*, **84**, 4273–7.

136 Mannel, D.N., Northoff, H., Bauss, F., and Falk, W. (1987). Tumor necrosis factor: a cytokine involved in toxic effects of endotoxin. *Rev. Infect. Dis.*, **9** (Suppl. 5), S602–6.

137 Cross, A.S., Sadoff, J.C., Kelly, N., Bernton, E., and Gemski, P. (1989). Pretreatment with recombinant murine tumor necrosis factor-alpha/cachetic and murine interleukin 1-alpha protects mice from lethal bacterial infection. *J. Exp. Med.*, **169**, 2021–7.

138 Havell, E.A. (1987) Production of tumor necrosis factor during murine listeriosis. *J. Immunol.*, **139**, 4225–31.

139 Merrill, W.W., Naegel, G.P., Matthay, R.A., and Reynolds, H.Y. (1980). Alveolar macrophage-derived chemotactic factor: kinetics of *in vitro* production and partial characterization. *J. Clin. Invest.*, **65**, 268–76.

140 Hunninghake, G.W., Gadek, J.E., Fales, H.M., and Crystal, R.G. (1980). Human alveolar macrophage-derived chemotactic factor for neutrophils: stimuli and partial characterization. *J. Clin. Invest.*, **66**, 473–83.

141 Toews, G.B., Hansen, E.J., and Streiter, R.M. (1990). Pulmonary host defenses and oropharyngeal pathogens. *Am. J. Med.*, **88** (Suppl. 5A), 5A20S–24S.

142 Pennington, J.E., Rossing, T.H., and Boerth, L.W. (1983). The effect of human alveolar macrophages on the bactericidal capacity of neutrophils. *J. Infect. Dis.*, **148**, 101–9.

143 Pennington, J.E., Rossing, T.H., Boerth, L.W., and Lee, T.H. (1985). Isolation and partial characterization of a human alveolar macrophage-

derived neutrophil-activating factor. *J. Clin. Invest.*, **75**, 1230–7.

144 Baggiolini, M., Walz, A., and Kunkel, S.L. (1989). Neutrophil- activating peptide-1/interleukin 8, a novel cytokine that activates neutrophils. *J. Clin. Invest.*, **84**, 1045–9.

145 Murray, H.W. (1988). Interferon-gamma, the activated macrophage, and host defense against microbial challenge. *Ann. Int. Med.*, **108**, 595–608.

146 Ezekowitz, R.A.B., Orkin, S.H., and Newburger, P.E. (1987). Recombinant interferon gamma augments phagocyte superoxide production and X-linked chronic granulomatous disease gene expression in X-linked variant chronic granulomatous disease. *J. Clin. Invest.*, **80**, 1009–16.

147 Ezekowitz, R.A.B., Dinauer, M.C., Jaffe, H.S., Orkin, S.H., and Newburger, P.E. (1988). Partial correction of the phagocyte defect in patients with X-linked chronic granulomatous disease by subcutaneous interferon gamma. *N. Engl. J. Med.*, **319**, 146–51.

148 Jensen, W.A., Rose, R.M., Wasserman, A.S., Kalb, T.H., Anton, K., and Remold, H.G. (1987). *In vitro* activation of the antibacterial activity of human pulmonary macrophages by recombinant gamma-interferon. *J. Infect. Dis.*, **155**, 574–7.

149 Nash, T.W., Libby, D.M., and Horwitz, M.A. (1984). Interaction between the Legionnaires' bacterium (*Legionella pneumophila*) and human alveolar macrophages: influence of antibody, lymphokines, and hydrocortisone. *J. Clin. Invest.*, **74**, 771–82.

150 Byrd, T.F. and Horwitz, M.A. (1989). Interferon gamma-activated human monocytes downregulate transferrin receptors and inhibit the intracellular multiplication of *Legionella pneumophila* by limiting the availability of iron. *J. Clin. Invest.*, **83**, 1457–65.

151 Kagaya, K., Watanabe, K., and Fukazawa, Y. (1989). Capacity of recombinant gamma interferon to activate macrophages for Salmonella-killing activity. *Infect. Immun.*, **57**, 609–15.

152 Rook, G.A.W., Steele, J., Ainsworth, M., and Champion, B.R. (1986). Activation of macrophages to inhibit proliferation of *Mycobacterium tuberculosis*: comparison of the effects of recombinant gamma-interferon on human monocytes and murine peritoneal macrophages. *Immunology*, **59**, 333–8.

153 Flesch, I. and Kaufmann, S.H.E. (1987). Mycobacterial growth inhibition by interferon-gamma activated bone marrow macrophages and differential susceptibility among strains of *Mycobacterium tuberculosis*. *J. Immunol.*, **138**, 4408–13.

154 Flesch, I.E.A. and Kaufmann, S.H.E. (1988). Attempts to characterize the mechanisms involved in mycobacterial growth inhibition by gamma-interferon activated bone marrow macrophages. *Infect. Immun.*, **56**, 1464–9.

155 Douvas, G.S., Looker, D.L., Vatter, A.E., and Crowle, A.J. (1985). Gamma interferon activates human macrophages to become tumoricidal and leishmanicidal but enhances replication of macrophage-associated mycobacteria. *Infect. Immun.*, **50**, 1–8.

156 Metcalf, D. (1987). The role of the colony-stimulating factors in resistance to acute infections. *Immunol. Cell Biol.*, **65**, 35–43.

157 Clark, S.C. and Kamen, R. (1987). The human hematopoietic colony-stimulating factors. *Science*, **236**, 1229–37.

158 Cheers, C., Hill, M., Haigh, A.M., and Stanley, E.R. (1989). Stimulation of macrophage phagocytic but not bactericidal activity by colony-stimulating factor 1. *Infect. Immun.*, **57**, 1512–16.

159 Ruef, C. and Coleman, D.L. (1990). Granulocyte-macrophage colony-stimulating factor: pleiotropic cytokine with potential clinical usefulness. *Rev. Infect. Dis.*, **12**, 41–62.

160 Hosea, S.W., Brown, E.J., and Frank, M.M. (1980). The critical role of complement in experimental pneumococcal sepsis. *J. Infect. Dis.*, **142**, 903–909.

161 Noel, G.J., Mosser, D.M., and Edelson, P.J. (1990). Role of complement in mouse macrophage binding of *Haemophilus influenzae* type b. *J. Clin. Invest.*, **85**, 208–18.

162 Gross, G.N., Rehm, S.R., and Pierce, A.K. (1978). The effect of complement depletion on lung clearance of bacteria. *J. Clin. Invest.*, **62**, 373–8.

163 Heidbrink, P.J., Toews, G.B., Gross, G.N., and Pierce, A.K. (1982). Mechanisms of complement-mediated clearance of bacteria from the murine lung. *Am. Rev. Resp. Dis.*, **125**, 517–20.

164 Leijh, P.C.J., van den Barselaar, M.T., van Zwet, T.L., Daha, M.R., and van Furth, R. (1979). Requirement of extracellular complement and immunoglobulin for intracellular killing of micro-organisms by human monocytes. *J. Clin. Invest.*, **63**, 772–84.

165 Proctor, R.A. (1987). Fibronectin: an enhancer of phagocyte function. *Rev. Infect. Dis.*, **9** (Suppl.), S412–19.

166 Wright, S.D., Craigmyle, L.S., and Silverstein, S.C. (1983). Fibronectin and serum amyloid P component stimulate C3b and C3bi-mediated phagocytosis in cultured human monocytes. *J. Exp. Med.*, **158**, 1338–43.

167 Proctor, R.A., Textor, J.A., Vann, J.M., and Mosher, D.F. (1985). Role of fibronectin in human monocyte and macrophage bactericidal activity. *Infect. Immun.*, **47**, 629–37.

168 Tenner, A.J., Robinson, S.L., Borchelt, J., and Wright, J.R. (1989). Human pulmonary surfactant protein (SP-A), a protein structurally homologous to C1q, can enhance FcR- and CR1- mediated phagocytosis. *J. Biol. Chem.*, **264**, 13923–8.

169 Malhotra, R., Thiel. S., Reid, K.B.M., and Sim R.B. (1990). Human

leukocyte C1q receptor binds other soluble proteins with collagen domains. *J. Exp. Med.*, **172**, 955–9.

170 O'Neill, S.J., Lesperance, E., and Klass, D.J. (1984). Human lung lavage surfactant enhances staphylococcal phagocytosis by alveolar macrophages. *Am. Rev. Resp. Dis.*, **130**, 1177–9.

171 Crowle, A.J., Ross, E.J., and May, M.H. (1987). Inhibition by 1,25(OH)2-vitamin D3 of the multiplication of virulent tubercle bacilli in cultured human macrophages. *Infect. Immun.*, **55**, 2945–50.

172 Kuhlman, M., Joiner, K., and Ezekowitz, R.A.B. (1989). The human mannose-binding protein functions as an opsonin. *J. Exp. Med.*, **169**, 1733–45.

173 Wright, S.D., Tobias, P.S., Ulevitch, R.J., and Ramos, R.A. (1989). Lipopolysaccharide (LPS) binding protein opsonizes LPS-bearing particles for recognition by a novel receptor on macrophages. *J. Exp. Med.*, **170**, 1231–41.

174 Wright, S.D., Ramos, R.A., Tobias, P.S., Ulevitch, R.J., and Mathison, J.C. (1990). CD14, a receptor for complexes of lipopolysaccharide (LPS) and LPS binding protein. *Science*, **249**, 1431–3.

175 Johnston, R.B. Jr. (1988). Monocytes and macrophages. *N. Engl. J. Med.*, **318**, 747–52.

176 Douglas, S.D. and Musson, R.A. (1986). Phagocytic defects-monocytes/macrophages. *Clin. Immunol. Immunopath.*, **40**, 62–8.

177 Anderson, D.C., *et al.*, (1985). The severe and moderate phenotype of heritable Mac-1, LFA-1 deficiency: their quantitative definition and relation to leukocyte dysfunction and clinical features. *J. Infect. Dis.*, **152**, 668–89.

178 Schmalstieg, F.C. (1988). Leukocyte adherence defect. *Ped. Infect. Dis. J.*, **7**, 867–72.

179 Ruiz, P., Gomez, F., and Schreiber, A.D. (1990). Impaired function of macrophage Fc-gamma receptors in end-stage renal disease. *N. Engl. J. Med.*, **322**, 717–22.

180 Rinehart, J.J., Sagone, A.L., Balcerzak, S.P., Ackerman, G.A., and LoBuglio, A.F. (1975). Effects of corticosteroid therapy on human monocyte function. *N. Engl. J. Med.*, **292**, 236–41.

181 Rouse, B.T. and Horohov, D.W. (1986). Immunosuppression in viral infections. *Rev. Infect. Dis.*, **8**, 850–73.

182 Isberg, R.R. and Falkow, S. (1985). A single genetic locus encoded by *Yersinia pseudotuberculosis* permits invasion of cultured animal cells by *Escherichia coli* K-12. *Nature*, **317**, 262–4.

183 Isberg, R.R., Voorhis, D.L., and Falkow, S. (1987). Identification of invasin: a protein that allows enteric bacteria to penetrate cultured mammalian cells. *Cell*, **50**, 769–78.

184 Cianciotto, N.P., Eisenstein, B.I., Mody, C.H., Toews, G.B., and Engleberg, N.C. (1989). A *Legionella pneumophila* gene encoding a

species-specific surface protein potentiates initiation of intracellular infection. *Infect. Immun.*, **57**, 1255–62.

185 Cianciotto, N., Eisenstein, B.I., Engleberg, N.C., and Shuman, H. (1989). Genetics and molecular pathogenesis of *Legionella pneumophila*, an intracellular parasite of macrophages. *Mol. Biol. Med.*, **6**, 409–24.

186 Horwitz, M.A. (1987). Characterization of avirulent mutant *Legionella pneumophila* that survive but do not multiply within human monocytes. *J. Exp. Med.*, **166**, 1310–28.

187 Fields, P.I., Groisman, E.A., and Heffron, F. (1989). A *Salmonella* locus that controls resistance to microbicidal proteins from phagocytic cells. *Science*, **243**, 1059–62.

188 Fields, P.I., Swanson, R.V., Haidaris C.G., and Heffron, F. (1986). Mutants of *Salmonella typhimurium* that cannot survive within the macrophage are avirulent. *Proc. Natl. Acad. Sci. U.S.A.*, **83**, 5189–93.

189 Densen, P. and Mandell, G.L. (1980). Phagocyte strategy vs. microbial tactics. *Rev. Infect. Dis.*, **2**, 817–38.

190 Edelson, P. J. (1982). Intracellular parasites and phagocytic cells: cell biology and pathophysiology. *Rev. Infect. Dis.*, **4**, 124–35.

191 Brubaker, R.R. (1985). Mechanisms of bacterial virulence. *Ann. Rev. Microbiol.*, **39**, 21–50.

192 Moulder, J.W. (1985). Comparative biology of intracellular parasitism. *Microbiol. Rev.*, **49**., 298–337.

193 Finlay, B.B. and Falkow, S. (1989). Common themes in microbial pathogenicity. *Microbiol. Rev.*, **53**, 210–30.

194 Whitnack, E., Bisno, A.L., and Beachey, E.H. (1981). Hyaluronate capsule prevents attachment of group A streptococci to mouse peritoneal macrophages. *Infect. Immun.*, **31**, 985–91.

195 Horwitz, M.A. and Silverstein, S.C. (1980). Influence of the *Escherichia coli* capsule on complement fixation and on phagocytosis and killing by human phagocytes. *J. Clin. Invest.*, **65**, 82–94.

196 Stiver, H.G., Zachidniak, K., and Speert, D.P. (1988). Inhibition of polymorphonuclear leukocyte chemotaxis by the mucoid exopolysaccharide of *Pseudomonas aeruginosa*. *Clin. Invest. Med.*, **11**, 247–52.

197 Krieg, D.P., Helmke, R.J., German, V.F., and Mangos, J.A. (1988). Resistance of mucoid *Pseudomonas aeruginosa* to nonopsonic phagocytosis by alveolar macrophages *in vitro*. *Infect. Immun.*, **56**, 3173–9.

198 Pier, G.B., *et al.* (1987). Opsonophagocytic killing antibody to *Pseudomonas aeruginosa* mucoid exopolysaccharide in older non-colonized patients with cystic fibrosis. *N. Engl. J. Med.*, **317**, 793–8.

199 Fick, R.B., Jr., Naegel, G.P., Matthay, R.A., and Reynolds, H.Y. (1981). Cystic fibrosis Pseudomonas opsonins: inhibitory nature in an *in vitro* phagocytic assay. *J. Clin. Invest.*, **68**, 899–914.

200 Fick, R.B., Jr., Naegel, G.P., Squier, S.U., Wood, R.E., Gee, J.B.L., and Reynolds, H.Y. (1984). Proteins of the cystic fibrosis respiratory tract: fragmented immunoglobulin G opsonic antibody causing defective opsonophagocytosis. *J. Clin. Invest.*, **74**, 236–48.

201 Reynolds, H.Y. (1974). Pulmonary host defenses in rabbits after immunization with *Pseudomonas* antigens: the interaction of bacteria, antibodies, macrophages and lymphocytes. *J. Infect. Dis.*, **130** (Suppl.), S134–42.

202 Reynolds, H.Y., Atkinson, J.P., Newball, H.H., and Frank, M.M. (1975). Receptors for immunoglobulin and complement human alveolar macrophages. *J. Immunol.*, **114**, 1813–19.

203 Murphey, S.A., Root, R.K., and Schreiber, A.D. (1979). The role of antibody and complement in phagocytosis by rabbit alveolar macrophages. *J. Infect. Dis.*, **140**, 896–903.

204 Reynolds, H.Y. and Thompson, R.E. (1973). Pulmonary host defenses. I. Analysis of protein and lipids in bronchial secretions and antibody responses after vaccination with *Pseudomonas aeruginosa*. *J. Immunol.*, **111**, 358–68.

205 Peterson, P.K., Verhoef, J., Sabath, L.D., and Quie, P.G. (1977). Effect of protein A on staphylococcal opsonization. *Infect. Immun.*, **15**, 760–4.

206 Weiss, A.A. and Hewlett, E.L. (1986). Virulence factors of *Bordetella pertussis*. *Ann. Rev. Microbiol.*, **40**, 661–86.

207 Meade, B.D., Kind, P.D., Ewell, J.B., McGrath, P.P., and Manclark, C.R. (1984). *In vitro* inhibition of murine macrophage migration by *Bordetella pertussis* lymphocytosis-promoting factor. *Infect. Immun.*, **45**, 718–25.

208 Confer, D.L. and Eaton, J.W. (1982). Phagocyte impotence caused by an invasive bacterial adenylate cyclase. *Science*, **217**, 948–50.

209 Holzer, T.J., Nelson, K.E., Schauf, V., Crispen, R.G., and Andersen, B.R. (1986). *Mycobacterium leprae* fails to stimulate phagocytic cell superoxide anion generation. *Infect. Immun.*, **51**, 514–20.

210 Gaillard, J., Berche, P., Mounier, J., Richard, S., and Sansonetti, P. (1987). *In vitro* model of penetration and intracellular growth of *Listeria monocytogenes* in the human enterocyte-like cell line Caco-2. *Infect. Immun.*, **55**, 2822–9.

211 Tilney, L.G. and Portnoy, D.A. (1989). Actin filaments and the growth, movement, and spread of the intracellular bacterial parasite, *Listeria monocytogenes*. *J. Cell Biol.*, **109**, 1597–1608.

212 Kuhn, M., Kathariou, S., and Goebel, W. (1988). Hemolysin supports survival but not entry of the intracellular bacterium *Listeria monocytogenes*. *Infect. Immun.*, **56**, 79–82.

213 Portnoy, D.A., Jacks, P.S., and Hinrichs, D.J. (1988). Role of

hemolysin for the intracellular growth of *Listeria monocytogenes*. *J Exp. Med.*, **167**, 1459–71.

214 Bielecki, J., Youngman, P., Connelly, P., and Portnoy, D.A. (1990). *Bacillus subtilis* expressing a haemolysin gene from *Listeria monocytogenes* can grow in mammalian cells. *Nature*, **345**, 175–6.

215 Mor, N. (1983). Intracellular location of *Mycobacterium leprae* in macrophages of normal and immune-deficient mice and effect of rifampin. *Infect. Immun.*, **42**, 802–11.

216 Jones, T.C. and Hirsch, J.G. (1972). The interaction between *Toxoplasma gondii* and mammalian cells. II. The absence of lysosomal fusion with phagocytic vacuoles containing live parasites. *J. Exp. Med.*, **136**, 1173–93.

217 Horwitz, M.A. (1983). The legionnaires' disease bacterium (*Legionella pneumophila*) inhibits phagosome-lysosome fusion in human monocytes. *J. Exp. Med.*, **158**, 2108–26.

218 Frehel, C. and Rostogi, N. (1987). *Mycobacterium leprae* surface components intervene in the early phagosome-lysosome fusion inhibition event. *Infect. Immun.*, **55**, 2916–21.

219 Goren, M.B., D'Arcy Hart, P., Young, M.R., and Armstrong, J.A. (1976). Prevention of phagosome-lysosome fusion in cultured macrophages by sulfatides of *Mycobacterium tuberculosis*. *Proc. Nat. Acad. Sci. U.S.A.*, **73**, 2510–14.

220 Horwitz, M.A. and Maxfield, F.R. (1984). *Legionella pneumophila* inhibits acidification of its phagosome in human monocytes. *J. Cell Biol.*, **99**, 1936–43.

221 Carrol, M.E.W., Jackett, P.S., Aber, V.R., and Lowrie, D.B. (1979). Phagolysosome formation, cyclic adenosine 3'.5'-monophosphate and the fate of *Salmonella typhimurium* within mouse peritoneal macrophages. *J. Gen. Microbiol.*, **110**, 421–9.

222 Groisman, E.A. and Saier, M.H. Jr (1990). Salmonella virulence: new clues to intramacrophage survival. *TIBS*, **15**, 30–3.

223 Wheeler, P.R. and Gregory, D. (1980). Superoxide dismutase, peroxidatic activity and catalase in *Mycobacterium leprae* purified from armadillo liver. *J. Gen. Microbiol.*, **121**, 457–64.

224 Neill, M.A. and Klebanoff, S.J. (1988). The effect of phenolic glycolipid-1 from *Mycobacterium leprae* on the antimicrobial activity of human macrophages. *J. Exp. Med.*, **167**, 30–42.

225 Learn, D.B., Brestel, E.P., and Seetharama, S. (1987). Hypochlorite scavenging by *Pseudomonas aeruginosa* alginate. *Infect. Immun.*, **55**, 1813–18.

226 Sibley, L.D. and Krahenbuhl, J.L. (1987). *Mycobacterium leprae*-burdened macrophages are refractory to activation by gamma interferon. *Infect. Immun.*, **55**, 446–50.

227 Kaplan, G. and Hancock, G.E. (1989). Macrophages in leprosy. In

Human monocytes (ed. M. Zembala and G.L. Asherson). Academic Press, London.

228 Birdi, T.J. and Anitia, N.H. (1989). The macrophage in leprosy: a review on the current status. *Internat. J. Leprosy*, **57**, 511–25.

229 Modlin, R.L. and Rea, T.H. (1988). Immunopathology of leprosy granulomas. *Springer Sem. Immunopathol.*, **10**, 359–74.

230 Bloom, B.R. and Mehra, V. (1984). Immunological unresponsiveness in leprosy. *Immunol. Rev.*, **80**, 5–28.

231 Kaplan, G. and Cohn, Z.A. (1985). Cell-mediated immunity in lepromatous and tuberculoid leprosy. In *Mononuclear phagocytes: characteristics, physiology and function* (ed. R. van Furth). Martinus Nijhoff, Boston.

232 Watson, S., Bullock, W., Nelson, K., Schauf, V., Gelber, R., and Jacobson, R. (1984). Interleukin 1 production by peripheral blood mononuclear cells from leprosy patients. *Infect. Immun.*, **45**, 787–9.

233 Sibley, L.D., Hunter, S.W., Brennan, P.J., and Krahenbuhl, J.L. (1988). Mycobacterial lipoarabinomannan inhibits gamma interferon-mediated activation of macrophages. *Infect. Immun.*, **56**, 1232–6.

234 Kaplan, G., *et al.* (1989). The reconstitution of cell-mediated immunity in the cutaneous lesions of lepromatous leprosy by recombinant interleukin 2. *J. Exp. Med.*, **169**, 893–907.

6 Macrophages in parasitic infection

M.D. SADICK

1   Introduction

Since the original observations of *Listeria*-resistant macrophages in convalescent mice by Mackaness nearly 30 years ago (1), it has become established that macrophages play a pivotal role in the clearance of infectious organisms. They can be found lining the submucosae (2), surrounding blood vessels or close to epithelial cells (3); thus they are often the first cells of the immune system to encounter invading pathogens. The ultimate responsibilities of macrophages are two-fold. First, they must present parasite-derived antigens to the rest of the immune system in the presence of Class II major histocompatibility complex. (MHC), as well as immuno-modulating cytokines, in a manner that will induce an appropriate (curative or protective) immune response. Secondly, they must function as effective phagocytic killer cells.

These two different roles present something of a paradox. In their normal tissue-fixed or 'resting' state, macrophages are minimally microbicidal. Matured resting macrophages have been shown *in vitro* to produce only low levels of reactive microbicidal compounds (for example, H_2O_2, •OH, or hypohalous acid) in response to ingesting parasites, such as *Trypanosoma cruzi*, *Toxoplasma gondii*, *Leishmania spp.* (4,5). As a result, these parasites are able to infect macrophages. However, once macrophages are activated they are able to generate the metabolic burst required to produce the toxic intermediate compounds which can kill invading parasites. Activation of macrophages is dependent upon the establishment of a cellular immune response in which the cytokines responsible for macrophage activation are produced (see Table 6.1). The initiation of this immune response is, in turn, dependent upon macrophages. Therefore, the competition in this scenario is between the parasite avoiding immune recognition and/or actively enhancing an immune response in which macrophage-activating cytokines are not produced, versus the macrophages effectively presenting parasite antigens and initiating an immune response in which macrophage-activating cytokines are produced.

In this chapter, the strategies that certain parasites have evolved to avoid engaging the immune system are discussed, together with the strategies employed by the immune system to fight the infection. What emerges is a picture of competition between specific immune response(s) and macrophage activation which is, in many instances, capitalized upon by parasites.

2   Evasion strategies of parasites

In order to live as a mammalian parasite, an organism must be able to survive despite the presence of a complex and potent host immune system.

Table 6.1 Cytokines with macrophage-modulating activity

Cytokine	Cell(s) of origin	Activity on macrophages	Activity on other cells
IL-2	T-cells NK cells	Induces production of TNFα	Stimulates T-cell proliferation (especially T_H1)
IL-3	T-cells	By itself: induces surface-Ia expression With IL-4: inhibits IFNγ-mediated activation	Panspecific colony-stimulating factor
IL-4	T-cells NK cells	By itself: some macrophage activation (induces short-term surface-Ia expression) With IL-3: Inhibits IFNγ-mediated activation	B-cell maturation and IgE switch factor Stimulates T_H2 cell proliferation Mast cell growth factor
IFNγ	T-cells NK cells	Induces reactive oxygen intermediates Induces reactive nitrogen intermediates Induces surface-Ia expression	Some activity as a B-cell switch factor (IgG_{2a}) Inhibits proliferative effect of IL-4 or T_H2 cells
TNFα (cachectin)	Macrophages T-cells NK cells	Induces reactive oxygen intermediates	Augments B-cell and thymocyte proliferation
TNFβ (LT)	T-cells	Induces reactive oxygen intermediates	Augments B-cell and thymocyte proliferation
GM-CSF	Fibroblasts Endothelial cells Epithelial cells T-cells	Oxygen-independent? Induction of TNFα synthesis?	Ganulocyte and macrophage colony-stimulating factor

Of paramount importance is preventing the host from establishing an immune response which would lead to activation and increased phagocytosis by macrophages. The complexity of the host immune response which results in such fine control, specificity, and enhanced potency also provides many levels at which parasites may subvert its development. Some major examples of parasite evasion strategies are given below, starting with those parasites furthest removed from macrophage involvement to those actually residing within macrophages.

2.1   Extracellular parasites

Many parasites survive extracellularly in their mammalian host. As such, they are exposed to the full arsenal of the soluble cytotoxic factors that the host is able to produce, especially antibodies and complement. Antibodies may be either directly microbicidal via complement fixation and lysis or indirectly microbicidal via macrophages (for example, complement receptor or Fc receptor-mediated uptake and killing by macrophages). Two of the major evasion mechanisms employed by parasites constantly exposed to the extracellular milieu are: (a) antigenic variation, leaving the immune response misdirected; and (b) acquisition of host cell determinants such that the immune response is unable to recognize the parasite as foreign. Examples of parasites utilizing these two mechanisms are African trypanosomes and schistosomes, respectively.

2.1.1   Trypanosoma

African *Trypanosoma spp.* are the aetiological agents for African trypanosomiasis, or sleeping sickness, and are a major cause of both human (*Trypanosoma rhodesiense* and *T. gambiense*) and cattle (*T. brucei*) disease in Africa. Injected into their mammalian hosts by tsetse flies, trypanosomes remain extracellular, bloodstream trypomastigotes throughout their mammalian phase. Although fully exposed to the host immune response, they make no attempt to avoid immune detection. Rather, they present a very immunogenic protein on their surface called the 'variant specific glycoprotein' (VSG), (6). The host immune system focuses readily on the surface glycoprotein, and eventually produces opsonizing antibodies against it. Macrophages deal effectively with the trypanosomes which contain the eliciting VSG, however, although most of the existing parasites are phagocytosed and killed, some stop synthesizing the original VSG in favour of a new VSG that comprises a new 'variable antigenic type' (VAT), (7). The trypanosomes producing the new VSG are unrecognized by the existing immune response (antibodies) and are, therefore, neither opsonized by antibody nor phagocytosed and killed by macrophages. These organisms proliferate and eventually elicit a new immune response which leads to their opsonization and destruction. Again, there are a number of survivors that produce yet another VSG, and the cycle continues. The net result is that the trypanosomes cycle through successive rounds of replication, each time with a new VAT-expressing VSG, and the host immune response cycle through successive rounds of stimulation. With each successive course of VSG expression, the host immune response appears to be increasingly suppressed and less sensitive (7). Eventually the host is unable to respond to a new VSG and parasite growth goes unchecked resulting in the final fatal wave of parasitaemia associated with untreated trypanosomiasis.

2.1.2   Schistosoma

These members of the helminth family, are a cause of disease world-wide. The species associated with human disease are *Schistosoma japonicum*, *S. mekongi*, *S. mansoni*, and *S. haematobium*. Schistosomes have a complex life cycle with freshwater snails as the required intermediate host for all species, and a vertebrae animal as the definitive host (humans for *S. japonicum*, *S. mekongi*, *S. mansoni*, and *S. haematobium*). The asexual replication cycle takes place in the snails, resulting in the production of free-swimming 'cercariae'. Using proteolytic enzymes contained within an anterior head structure, the cercariae invade through the epidermis of humans who are wading in the water. Once inside their human host, the former cercariae shed their 'ciliated epidermal plates', develop into schistosomules, and make their way to the portal vein of the liver where they mature to adult worms. During the establishment of infection, a specific immune response is generated. It is potent enough to prevent any further (super-) infection by additional schistosomes. The concommitant immunity to superinfection is antigen-specific and involves activation of macrophages by T-cell derived cytokines (8,9), (see Table 6.1). However, the initial infecting schistosomes are not killed. The most accepted reason for this survival is that the infecting worms camouflage themselves with host proteins: erythrocyte A, B, and O proteins, serum proteins, and MHC Class I and II proteins (8). Disguised as they are, they may survive in their human hosts for many years. During this time they produce many eggs, most of which are excreted into the environment, hatching in water and beginning the cycle once again. Some eggs, however, lodge in the host tissues. These eggs are not coated with host proteins and induce a strong host immune response against the egg-containing tissue that is primarily responsible for the pathogenesis of the disease.

2.2   Intracellular parasites

Intracellular parasites have evolved a different mechanism by which they are able to avoid the various soluble cytotoxic and/or opsonizing products of the host immune response. These organisms sequester themselves behind the curtain of the host cell cytoplasmic membrane, a barrier which extracellular, soluble immune products are not able to breach. However, an intracellular milieu poses its own challenges to survival. Parasites must gain entry into the host cell. This sometimes requires active entry (such as infection of erythrocytes or muscle cells) or they may take advantage of the cell's own natural phagocytic activity (such as infection of macrophages). Additionally, although an antiparasite antibody response would have little effect on their survival, they must avoid eliciting a cellular immune response that would result in activated macrophages. An example of an intracellular pathogen that spends most of its time hidden from the immune system is *Plasmodia* spp. (malaria). For those parasites that inhabit the macrophages themselves, there is an additional consideration. Intramacrophage parasites must deal with degradative conditions that exist in a parasitophorous vacuole in which the phagosome and enzyme-containing lysosomes fuse together. The major strategies utilized are escape from the phagosome into the cytoplasm (*Trypanosoma cruzi*), prevention of phagosome/lysosome fusion (*Toxoplasma gondii*)—or adaptation for survival within a fused phagolysosome (*Leishmania* spp.).

2.2.1   Plasmodia

Plasmodia spp. (*P. malaria*, *P. vivax*, *P. falciparum*, and *P. ovale*) are the aetiological agents for human malaria. Injected by feeding anopheline mosquitos into the human host as sporozoites, the *Plasmodia* spend only a short time as blood-borne organisms. They quickly invade hepatic cells and convert to merizoites, and then progress to the erythrocytic cycle, exposed to the extracellular milieu only briefly between the time they lyse one host erythrocyte and infect another. Invasion of host erythrocytes appears to be via active entry, a process which requires adenosine triphosphate (ATP) and the phosphorylation of spectrin (10). In addition to physical sequestration, there is also evidence that the merizoites may vary their surface antigens (11), further misdirecting the host immune response.

2.2.2   Trypanosoma cruzi

These are the aetiological agents for American trypanosomiasis or Chagas disease. Transmitted to the human host by triatomid insects through the insect faeces, they have both an extracellular bloodstream 'trypomastigote' form which does not replicate and an intracellular 'amastigote' form. Employing a strategy of physical sequestration similar to that of *Plasmodia*, the amastigotes may infect striated muscle or smooth muscle (heart). Additionally, both the amastigote and trypomastigote forms are highly capable of infecting macrophages (12). Their evasion strategy to avoid being killed by the degradative environment of the macrophage phagolysosome is a relatively simple one. Prior to fusion of lysosomes with the phagosome, which the *T. cruzi* occupies, the trypanosome escapes into the surrounding cytoplasm. Protected in this manner from the contents of the lysosome, the amastigotes multiply until they burst the host macrophage and infect adjacent macrophages (13).

2.2.3   Toxoplasma

Toxoplasma gondii, the aetiological agents of human toxoplasmosis, are also able to infect macrophages. Ingested as oocysts by the human host, the

T. gondii rapidly invade the host tissue as tachyzoites (dividing form) and bradyzoites (encysted form). Like *T. cruzi*, *T. gondii* may infect many different cells of the human host and be taken up by macrophages into a phagosome. But there the similarity ceases. Rather than escaping into the cytoplasm, *T. gondii* remains in the phagosome. However, it prevents the fusion of phagosome with lysosomes. Such an inhibition of fusion requires the *T. gondii* to be viable and is initiated at the time of uptake into the macrophage (14). It is an active process and appears to be the result of a parasite-directed exclusion from the phagosome membrane of a necessary protein(s) required for phagosome/lysosome fusion. In this manner, the organism is able to survive and multiply, eventually lysing the host macrophage and infecting surrounding macrophages (15).

2.2.4   Leishmania

Leishmania spp. (*L. major*, *L. donovani*, *L. donovani chagasi*, *L. mexicana*, and *L. braziliensis*) are the aetiological agents for Old and New World leishmaniasis. Unlike *Trypanosoma cruzi* or *Toxoplasma gondii*, in the mammalian host all *Leishmania* spp. are obligate intramacrophage parasites. Injected into humans by sandflies as extracellular promastigotes, they bind via a surface glycoprotein, gp63, to the CR3 receptor (specific for C3bi of complement) of macrophages and are quickly phagocytosed (16–18). Although a percentage of the phagocytosed promastigotes are killed, those that survive convert to the intracellular amastigote form within 48 hours (19). The amastigotes are impervious to resting macrophages. There is no attempt to avoid or prevent phagosome/lysosome fusion. The *Leishmania* amastigotes live and multiply within secondary (fused) phagolysosomes containing all of the enzymes and chemicals associated with such organelles (20,21). The cell membranes of *Leishmania* amastigotes contain proteins which are resistant to many proteases (22). Further, they contain molecules, such as a complex glycolipid, lipophosphoglycan (LPG), which are efficient oxygen scavengers (23,24), protecting the amastigotes from the low levels of reactive oxygen and nitrogen intermediates that are produced by resting macrophages. As with *Trypanosoma cruzi* and *Toxoplasma gondii*, *Leishmania* eventually lyse the host macrophage and infect surrounding macrophages. However, macrophages are the only known cells in which the conversion from promastigotes to amastigotes may take place, and in which the amastigotes may grow and divide.

3   Macrophage activation and immunoregulation

In view of such myriad immune evasion mechanisms of parasites described above, one might wonder how it is ever possible for host immunity to contain and resolve parasitic infections. Certainly, the host immune system is so frequently overwhelmed that the parasites listed above, as well as others too numerous to list, are often considered important pathogens. Clinical infection by a number of these organisms may be fatal if left untreated. However, not all individuals exposed to these infectious agents succumb to clinical infection. In studies conducted in an area of Brazil endemic for visceral leishmaniasis (*Leishmania donovani chagasi*), it was found that only 38 per cent of those children exposed to the organism (as determined by antibody positive sera) actually developed classic visceral disease or 'kala-azar' (25,26). Two-thirds of the children exposed to the parasite either remained asymptomatic or developed a subclinical disease which resolved. Both of these latter groups demonstrated antigen-specific immunity (i.e. lymphocyte proliferation *in vitro*).

3.1 Microbicidal activity of activated macrophages

The above indicates that it is possible for the host immune system to circumvent or nullify parasite escape mechanisms. Resolution of infection requires that the host generate an immune response with a cellular (T-cell) component such that activation of macrophages occurs. There exist a number of T-cell derived cytokines with the capacity to activate macrophages (Table 6.1), interferon-gamma (IFNγ) being, perhaps, the most potent (27,28). Activated macrophages are formidable microbicidal cells. They are far more efficient phagocytes in the activated than in the resting state. Furthermore, they can generate a metabolic burst that produces reactive oxygen intermediates, such as hydrogen peroxide, superoxide anion or hydroxyl radical and reactive nitrogen intermediates, especially nitric oxide. These metabolic byproducts are capable of killing parasites (29–36). The activation-boosted production of reactive intermediates is enough to overcome the oxygen scavenging capacity of *Leishmania* amastigotes and effectively kill them (37). Additionally, activation enables macrophage lysosomes to fuse with phagosomes containing *Trypanosoma cruzi*, before the parasites are able to escape into the cytoplasm (38). Likewise, *Toxoplasma gondii* are unable to prevent phagosome–lysosome fusion in activated macrophages (39,40). Thus, the survival mechanisms of parasites, geared for resting macrophages, are nullified if an immune response is initiated and the macrophages are activated.

Until recently, all such protective immune responses were termed 'cell-mediated immunity' (CMI) and were usually associated with delayed type hypersensitivity (DTH), for example, the positive tuberculin skin test reaction. In CMI, antigen-specific CD4+ T-cells (helper-cells) were induced to proliferate and produce macrophage activating factors. It was further thought that in individuals who were susceptible to the infection, antigen-specific CD8+ (suppressor/cytotoxic) T-cells were preferentially stimulated, preventing the development of curative CD4+ cell-mediated immunity (41–45).

3.2   Subsets of CD4$^+$ T-cells determine the presence or absence of macrophage activation

The emerging story, however, appears to be somewhat different. Parasite-specific suppressor T-cells have remained elusive. Additionally, studies with experimental leishmaniasis in mice have shown that in both genetically resistant and genetically susceptible animals, infection with *Leishmania* results in the expansion of CD4$^+$ T-cell populations. In fact, the expansion of such populations in the susceptible animals is greater than in resistant animals (46). It was further shown that both resolution and exacerbation of disease could be attributed to CD4$^+$ T-cells. In vaccinated animals (47–49) as well as in adoptively protected animals (50), cell-mediated resistance to leishmaniasis and DTH in response to *Leishmania* antigens were separate events. Thus, cells capable of adoptively transferring DTH did not transfer resistance and vice versa.

Insight into the immunoregulation of cellular immunity was provided upon the discovery that in mice the CD4$^+$ T-cell population comprises at least two subpopulations, T_H1 and T_H2 (51–53). Both types of CD4$^+$ T-cells are hypothesized to be derived from multifunctional T_H0 CD4$^+$ cells (54) and to respond to stimulation by antigen-presenting (APC) cells, such as macrophages with proliferation and the production of cytokines. However, the profile of cytokine production by these two subpopulations are markedly different (see Table 6.2; for a more complete review of T_H1/T_H2 see reference 52). The T_H1 and T_H2 responses are highly integrated and contra-regulated. Many of the cytokines produced by one or the other subpopulation, in addition to having positive effector functions, negatively regulate

Table 6.2   Characteristics of murine T_H1 and T_H2 CD4$^+$ cells

T_H1		T_H2
	Cellular phenotype	
CD4$^+$, CD8$^-$		CD4$^+$, CD8$^-$
	Cytokine secretion	
IL-2		
IL-3		IL-3
		IL-4
		IL-5
		IL-6
		IL-10
TNFα (cachectin)		TNFα (cachectin)
TNFβ (LT)		
IFNγ		
GM-CSF		

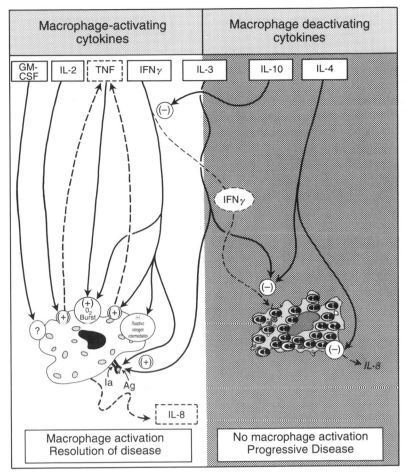

Fig. 6.1 The inter- and contra-regulating activities of cytokines (especially those produced by T_H1 and T_H2 cells) with macrophage-activating and/or deactivating effector functions in mice.

activity of the alternative subgroup. The negative regulation may be at the level of either T-cell expansion or T-cell effector functions, including macrophage activation. (See Figure 6.1)

3.2.1 T_H1 cells

T_H1 cells produce cytokines associated with many aspects of classic cell mediated immunity. In mice, they produce IFNγ, IL-3, GM-CSF, and TNFα and -β, which activate macrophages, and induce a plethora of other effects. As a macrophage-activating factor, IFNγ has a premiere role: it induces an oxygen burst, leading to the production of reactive oxygen intermediates. It also induces the deamination of arginine leading to the production of nitric oxide, NO, which is a very potent microbicidal reactive nitrogen intermediate (55). Moreover, IFNγ has a number of additional immunoregulatory roles. It induces macrophages to express increased levels of surface Ia (56), required for the presentation of antigen to the immune system. Furthermore, it induces B-cells to produce IgG_{2a} antibodies which are important opsonizing antibodies (57). Finally, IFNγ also blocks the proliferative effect of IL-4 on T_H2 cells (58), thus preventing the expansion of this subpopulation. TNFα and -β activate macrophage oxidative metabolism, but although not unanimously agreed (35), they do not seem to induce NO production (55). IL-3 activation of macrophages seems mainly to involve increased antigen processing and presentation, as well as increased Ia expression, but not increased microbicidal activity (59). Additonally, T_H1 cells produce IL-2 which further induces enhanced T_H1 growth. Both induce IFNγ and IL-2, which stimulate macrophages to produce TNFα, which in turn, further helps to activate the macrophage population (60–62). GM-CSF, a cytokine mainly associated with macrophage and neutrophil colony (growth) stimulation (63), has also been shown to activate macrophages to microbicidal levels in concert with other cytokines, especially IFNγ (64,65).

3.2.2 T_H2 cells

This subset of T_H cells produce cytokines that are associated primarily with B-cell responses. IL-4, -5 and -6 are potent stimulatory, maturation, and antibody–isotype switch factors for B-cells (52). IL-5 additionally stimulates the increased production of eosinophils. IL-4 also has several additional immunoregulatory properties. It acts both as a growth factor specific for T_H2 cells as well as an inhibitory factor for both the stimulation of T_H1 cells by IL-2 (preventing the expression of IL-2 receptor), (66). Paradoxically, although IL-4 is able to activate macrophages to a slight degree, including transient surface-Ia expression (67), IL-4 is not only able to induce macrophage microbicidal activity, but effectively inhibits IFNγ activation of macrophages (68,69), especially in conjunction with IL-3. IL-4 further inhibits the production of IL-8, a neutrophil chemotactic and activating cytokine, by macrophages (70). Inhibition of IL-8 synthesis would therefore block induction of the immune system's alternative phagocytic defences. Finally, T_H2 cells produce IL-10, which has a direct inhibitory activity on the production of IFNγ by T_H1 cells (71).

3.2.3   Interaction of T_H1 and T_H2 subsets

The important concept to draw from the above picture of T_H1 and T_H2 cells is one of inter- and contra-regulation. An immune response in which T_H1 cells are stimulated would down-regulate co-stimulation of T_H2 cells. Conversely, an immune response in which T_H2 cells are stimulated would down-regulate both the co-stimulation of T_H1 cells as well as their activity. If an invading parasite which is primarily controlled by the activated macrophages of the host could somehow bias the host's immune response towards T_H2 stimulation, then the resulting immune response would be predominantly antibody-mediated and ineffectual at resolving the infection. The cellular immune response required to limit infection would be absent. In fact, the disease state could be said to have all of the earmarks of a suppressed cellular immune response.

There exists ample evidence that such competition between T_H1 and T_H2 responses does, in fact, follow parasite infection. One very good example of an infection in which this inter-regulation appears to play a role is murine leishmaniasis (for more comprehensive reviews see references 72–75). *Leishmania major* infection of mice is characterized by a similar spectrum of disease as is seen in *L. donovani* infection of humans. At one extreme are susceptible inbred strains such as BALB/c mice. Disease in these mice is comparable to human kala-azar. Curative immunity to the infection never develops; there is eventually visceralization of parasites throughout the reticuloendothelial system and the infection is uniformly fatal. Progressive infection in BALB/c mice is associated with the expansion of *L. major*-specific T_H2 cells capable of producing IL-4 and -5 (75,76). The B-cell bias of the T_H2 response is reflected in the presence of hypergammaglobulinemia, including serum IgE (77). In direct contrast are resistant inbred strains, such as C57BL/6 or C3H/HeN mice. These mice are comparable to the two-thirds of humans exposed to *L. d. chagasi* who develop *Leishmania*-specific immunity. The mice resolve the disease and demonstrate immunity against subsequent infection. The development of resistance in C57BL/6 mice is associated with the expansion of *L. major*-specific T_H1 cells capable of producing IFNγ (75–77).

Evidence has been provided to suggest that a similar immunoregulation between the two pathways exists in other infectious conditions. In *Trichinella spiralis* (78), *Schistosome* (9), and *Plasmodium* (79) infections, susceptibility is associated with T_H2 responses, while resistance is associated with T_H1 responses.

The initial events that bias the immune response towards a T_H1 or T_H2 direction are as yet not clear. Some data suggest particular parasite antigens preferentially stimulate one subpopulation or the other (80), but this does not explain the differences between genetically resistant and susceptible mice. Other possibilities include, but are not limited to, different abilities of host macrophages to process and present protective antigens to the immune system in conjunction with Ia (81), or the preferential or restricted use of T-cell receptors by resistant or susceptible animals (74). What is clear is that the outcome of the competition between stimulation of T_H1 and T_H2 responses following parasite invasion of mice has a profound impact on the ability of the host to activate the appropriate response of macrophages and contain the infection. Elucidation of this immunoregulation is currently the topic of considerable investigation and it is hoped that it will lead to new therapeutic strategies aimed at the regulation of host immunity to parasite infection.

4 Summary

During the co-evolution of mammals and their parasites, the latter have developed many strategies to evade detection and subsequent killing by the host immune system. These include various mechanisms for extracellular avoidance/immune-misdirection and intracellular seclusion. In the final analysis, however, most evasion strategies somehow prevent the activation of host macrophages. Macrophages are responsible both for the killing of most parasites as well as the recruitment and initiation of the anti-parasite immune response. These dual roles of macrophages in parasitic infection are tightly interconnected.

Resting, non-activated macrophages are unable to effect significant anti-parasite activity. Macrophages must properly present parasite antigens in a manner which will elicit a protective immune response in which the macrophage killing systems (reactive oxygen and nitrogen intermediates) are activated to microbicidal levels. The host immune system may respond to macrophage presentation of parasite antigens in one of at least two ways. There may be preferential stimulation of parasite-specific CD4+ T_H1 cells which produce cytokines associated with cell-mediated immunity (IFNγ, IL-2, TNFα, TNFβ, and GM-CSF) that are capable of activating macrophages. Alternatively, there may be preferential stimulation of parasite-specific CD4+ T_H2 cells which produce B-cell-response-associated cytokines (IL-3, IL-4, IL-5 and IL-6). Elucidation of T_H1 and T_H2 responses are highly interdependent. Stimulation and activation of one CD4+ subpopulation appears to preclude and actively prevent the stimulation and activation of the alternative CD4+ subpopulation. Importantly, activation of a T_H2 response to parasite antigens prevents the eventual activation of host macrophages. Thus, an organism capable of preferentially eliciting a T_H2 response is likely to be a successful mammalian parasite, as has been demonstrated for such diverse pathogens as *Leishmania* spp. (72–77), *Trichinella spiralis* (78), *Schistosoma* spp. (9), and *Plasmodia* spp. (79). Although most evidence to date is based upon animal models, the applicability of T_H1 and T_H2 immune responses to human disease is being actively pursued by many laboratory groups. Any future immunotherapy for parasitic infections may well involve the facilitation and stimulation of a parasite-specific T_H1 immune response and the subsequent activation of host macrophages.

References

1 Mackaness, M.B. (1962). Cellular resistance to infection. *J. Exp. Med.*, **116**, 381–406.

2 Nathan, C.F. (1987). Secretory products of macrophages. *J. Clin. Invest.*, **79**, 319–26.

3 Unanue, E.R. (1989). Macrophages, antigen-presenting cells, and the phenomena of antigen handling and presentation. In *Fundamental Immunology*, 2nd edn (ed. W. Paul), pp. 95–115, Raven Press, New York.

4 Murray, H.W. (1982). Pretreatment with phorbol myristate acetate inhibits macrophage activity against intracellular protozoa. *J. Reticulo. Soc.*, **31**, 479–87.

5 Murray, H.W., Masur, H. and Keithly, J.S. (1982). Cell-mediated immune response in experimental visceral leishamaniasis. I. Correlation between resistance to *Leishmania donovani* and lymphokine-generating capacity. *J. Immunol.*, **129**, 344–50.

6 Dempsey, W.L. and Mansfield, J.M. (1983). Lymphocyte function in experimental African trypanosomiasis. V. Role of antibody and the mononuclear phagocyte system in variant specific immunity. *J. Immunol.*, **130**, 405–11.

7 Seed, J.R. and Sechelski, J.B. (1988). Immune response to minor variant antigen types (VATs) in a mixed VAT infection of the African trypanosomes. *Parasite Immunol.*, **10**, 569–79.

8 Colley, D.G. and Colley, M.D. (1989). Protective immunity and vaccines to schistosomiasis. *Parasitol. Today*, **5**, 350–4.

9 Scott, P., Pearce, E., Cheever, A.W., Coffman, R.L., and Sher, A. (1989). Role of cytokines and CD4+ T-cell subsets in the regulation of parasite immunity and disease. *Immunol. Rev.*, **112**, 161–82.

10 Rangachari, K., Dluzewski, A., Wilson, R.J., and Gratzer, W.B. (1986). Control of malarial invasion by phosphorylation of the host cell membrane cytoskeleton. *Nature*, **324**, 364–5.

11 Klotz, F.W., Hudson, D.E., Coon, H.G., and Miller, L.H. (1987). Vaccination-induced variation in the 140 kd merizoite surface antigen of *Plasmodium knowlesi* malaria. *J. Exp. Med.*, **165**, 359–67.

12 Ley, V., Andrews, N.W., Robbins, E.S., and Nussenzweig, V. (1988). Amastigotes of *Trypanosoma cruzi* sustain an infective cycle in mammalian cells. *J. Exp. Med.*, **168**, 649–59.

13 Noguiera, N. and Cohn, Z. (1976). *T. cruzi*: Mechanisms of entry and intracellular fate in mammalian cells. *J. Exp. Med.*, **143**, 1402–11.

14 Joiner, K.A., Fuhrman, S.A., Miettinen, H.M., Kasper, L.H., and Mellman, I. (1990). *Toxoplasma gondii*: Fusion competence of parasitophorous vacuoles in Fc receptor-transfected fibroblasts. *Science*, **249**, 641–9.

15 Jones, T.C. and Hirsch, J.G. (1972). The interaction between

Toxoplasma gondii and mammalian cells. *J. Exp. Med.*, **136**, 1173–80.

16　Russell, D.G. and Wilhelm, H. (1986). The involvement of the major surface glycoprotein (gp63) of *Leishmania* promastigotes in attachment to macrophages. *J. Immunol.*, **136**, 2613–620.

17　Russell, D.G. (1987). The macrophage-attachment glycoprotein gp63 is the predominant C3-acceptor site on *Leishmania mexicana* promastigotes. *Eur. J. Biochem.*, **164**, 213–221.

18　Russell, D.G. and Wright, S.D. (1988). Complement receptor type 3 (CR3) binds to an Arg-Gly-Asp-containing region of the major surface glycoprotein, gp63, of *Leishmania* promastigotes. *J. Exp. Med.*, **168**, 279–92.

19　Lewis, D.H. and Peters, W. (1977). The resistance of intracellular *Leishmania* parasites to digestion with by lysosomal enzymes. *Ann. Trop. Med. Parasitol.*, **71**, 295–312.

20　Prina, E., Antoine, J.C., Wiederanders, B., and Kirschke, H. (1990). Localization and activity of various lysosomal proteases in *Leishmania amazonensis*-infected macrophages. *Infect. Immunol.*, **58**, 1730–7.

21　Antoine, J.C., Prina, E., Jouanne, C., and Bongrand, P. (1990). Parasitophorous vacuoles of *Leishmania amazonensis*-infected macrophages maintain an acidic pH. *Infect. Immunol.*, **58**, 779–87.

22　Handman, E., Mitchell, G.F., and Goding, J.W. (1981). Identification and characterization of protein antigens of *Leishmania tropica* isolates. *J. Immunol.*, **126**, 508–12.

23　Handman, E., Schnur, L.F., Spithill, T.W., and Mitchell, G.F. (1986). Passive transfer of *Leishmania* lipopolysaccharide confers parasite survival in macrophages. *J. Immunol.*, **137**, 3608–13.

24　Chan, J., et al. (1989). Microbial glycolipids: possible virulence factors that scavenge oxygen radicals. *Proc. Natl. Acad. Sci. U.S.A.*, **86**, 2453–7.

25　Badaró, R., et al. (1986). A prospective study of visceral leishmaniasis in an endemic area of Brasil. *J. Infect. Dis.*, **154**, 639–49.

26　Badaró, R., et al. (1986). New perspectives on a subclinical form of visceral leishmaniasis. *J. Infect. Dis.*, **154**, 1003–11.

27　Nathan, C.F., Murray, H.W., Wiebe, M.E., and Rubin, B.Y. (1983). Identification of interferon-gamma as the lymphokine that activates human macrophage oxidative metabolism and antimicrobial activity. *J. Exp. Med.*, **158**, 670–89.

28　Suzuki, Y., Orellana, M.A., Schrieber, R.D., and Remington, J.S. (1988). Interferon-gamma: the major mediator of resistance against *Toxoplasma gondii*. *Science*, **240**, 516–18.

29　Murray, H.W., Stern, J.J., Welte, K., Rubin, B.Y., Carriero, S.M., and Nathan, C.F. (1987). Experimental visceral leishmaniasis: production of interleukin 2 and interferon-gamma, tissue immune reaction, and response to treatment with interleukin 2 and interferon gamma. *J. Immunol.*, **138**, 2290–7.

30 Murray, H.W., Spitalny, G.L., and Nathan, C.F. (1985). Activation of mouse peritoneal macrophages *in vitro* and *in vivo* by interferon-γ. *J. Immunol.*, **134**, 1619–22.

31 Murray, H.W., Rubin, B.Y., and Rothermel, C.D. (1983). Killing of intracellular *Leishmania donovani* by lymphokine-stimulated human mononuclear phagocytes. Evidence that interferon-gamma is the activating lymphokine. *J. Clin. Invest.*, **72**, 1506–12.

32 Hoover, D.L. and Nacy, C.A. (1984). Macrophage activation to kill *Leishmania tropica*: Defective intracellular killing of amastigotes by macrophages elicited with sterile inflammatory agents. *J. Immunol.*, **132**, 1487–93.

33 Belosevic, M. and Nacy, C.A. (1987). Gamma-interferon and other lymphokines cooperate in induction of resistance to *Leishmania major* infection by macrophages. *FASEB*, **46**, 4147.

34 Liew, F.Y., Millot, S., Parkinson, C., Palmer, R.M.J., and Moncada, S. (1990). Macrophage killing of *Leishmania* parasite *in vito* is mediated by nitric oxide from L-arginine. *J. Immunol.*, **144**, 4794–7.

35 Liew, F.Y., Li, Y., and Millot, S. (1990). Tumour necrosis factor (TNFα) in leishmaniasis II. TNFα-induced macrophage leishmaniacidal activity is mediated by nitric oxide from L-arginine. *Immunology*, **71**, 556–9.

36 Green, S.J., Meltzer, M.S., Hibbs, J.B., and Nacy, C.A. (1990). Activated macrophages destroy intracellular *Leishmania major* amastigotes by an L-arginine-dependent killing mechanism. *J. Immunol.*, **144**, 278–83.

37 Nacy, C.A., Meltzer, M.S., Leonard, E.J., and Wyler, D.J. (1981). Intracellular replication and lymphokine-induced destruction of *Leishmania tropica* in C3H/HeN mouse macrophages. *J. Immunol.*, **127**, 2381–6.

38 Noguiera, N. and Cohn, Z.A. (1978). *Trypanosoma cruzi: In vitro* induction of macrophage microbicidal activity. *J. Exp. Med.*, **148**, 258–300.

39 Borges, J.S. and Johnson, W.D. (1975). Inhibition of multiplication of *Toxoplasma gondii* by human monocytes exposed to T-lymphocyte products. *J. Exp. Med.*, **141**, 483–90.

40 Badger, A.M., Hutchman, J.S., Sung, C.P., and Bugelski, P.J. (1987). Activation of rat alveolar macrophages by gamma interferon to inhibit *Toxoplasma gondii in vitro*. *J. Leuc. Biol.* **42**, 447–54.

41 Blackwell, J.M. and Ulczak, O.M. (1984). Immunoregulation of genetically controlled acquired resistance to *Leishmania donovani* infection in mice: demonstration and characterization of suppressor T cells in noncure mice. *Infect. Immunol.*, **44**, 97–102.

42 Hill, J.O., Awwad, M., and North, R.J. (1989). Elimination of CD4+ suppressor T cells from susceptible BALB/c mice releases CD8+ T lymphocytes to mediate protective immunity against *Leishmania*. *J. Exp. Med.*, **169**, 1819–27.

43 Howard, J., Hale, C., and Liew, F. (1981). Immunological regulation of experimental cutaneous leishmaniasis. IV. Prophylactic effect of sublethal irradiation as a result of abrogation of suppressor T cell generation in mice genetically susceptible to *Leishmania tropica*. *J. Exp. Med.*, **153**, 557–68.

44 Liew, F.Y. (1989). Suppressor cells for cell-mediated immunity in infectious disease. *Res. Immunol.*, **140**, 328–33.

45 Petersen, E.A., Neva, F.A., Oster, C.N., and Bogaert-Diaz. H., (1982). Specific inhibition of lymphocyte-proliferation responses by adherent suppressor cells in diffuse cutaneous leishmaniasis. *N. Eng. J. Med.*, **306**, 387–92.

46 Heinzel, F.P., Sadick, M.D., and Locksley, R.M. (1988). *Leishmania major*: Analysis of cellular phenotypes in cutaneous lesions and draining lymph nodes. *Exp. Parasitol.*, **65**, 258–68.

47 Liew, F.Y., Howard, J.G., and Hale, C. (1984). Prophylactic immunization against experimental leishmaniasis. III. Protection against fatal *Leishmania tropica* infection induced by irradiated promastigotes involves Lyt-1$^+$2$^-$cells that do not mediate cutaneous DTH. *J. Immunol.*, **132**, 456–61.

48 Liew, F.Y., Singleton, A., Cillari, E., and Howard, J.G. (1985). Prophylactic immunization against experimental leishmaniasis. V. Mechanism of the anti-protective blocking effect induced by subcutaneous immunization against *Leishmania major* infection. *J. Immunol.*, **135**, 2102–7.

49 Liew, F.Y., Hodson, K., and Lelchuk, R. (1987). Prophylactic immunization against experimental leishmaniasis. VI. Comparison of protective and disease-promoting T cells. *J. Immunol.*, **139**, 3112–17.

50 Titus, R.G., Lima, G.C., Engers, H.D., and Louis, J.A. (1984). Exacerbation of murine cutaneous leishmaniasis by adoptive transfer of parasite-specific helper T cell populations capable of mediating *Leishmania major*-specific delayed-type hypersensitivity. *J. Immunol.*, **133**, 1594–1600.

51 Mosmann, T.R., Cherwinski, H., Bond, M.W., Giedlin, M.A., and Coffman, R.L. (1986). Two types of murine helper T cell clone. I. Definition according to profiles of lymphokine activities and secreted proteins. *J. Immunol.*, **136**, 2348–57.

52 Mosmann, T.R. and Coffman, R.L. (1989). TH1 and TH2 cells: Different patterns of lymphokine secretion lead to different functional properties. *Ann. Rev. Immunol.*, **7**, 145–73.

53 Cherwinski, H.M., Schumacher, J.H., Brown, K.D., and Mosmann, T.R. (1987). Two types of mouse helper T cell clone. III. Further differences in lymphokine synthesis between Th1 and Th2 clones revealed by RNA hybridization, functionally monospecific bioassays and monoclonal antibodies. *J. Exp. Med.*, **166**, 1229–44.

54 Street, N.E., *et al.* (1990). Heterogeneity of mouse helper T cells. Evidence from bulk cultures and limiting dilution cloning for precursors of Th1 and Th2 cells. *J. Immunol.*, **144**, 1629–39.

55 Ding, A.H., Nathan, C.F., and Stuehr, D.J. (1988). Release of reactive nitrogen intermediates and reactive oxygen intermediates from mouse peritoneal macrophages. Comparison of activating cytokines and evidence for independent production. *J. Immunol.*, **141**, 2407–12.

56 King, D.P. and Jones, P.P. (1983). Induction of Ia and H-2 antigens on a macrophage cell line by immune interferon. *J. Immunol.*, **131**, 315–19.

57 Stevens, T.L., *et al.* (1988). Regulation of antibody isotype secretion by subsets of antigen-specific helper T cells. *Nature*, **334**, 255–8.

58 Gajewski, T.F. and Fitch, F.W. (1988). Anti-proliferative effect of IFNγ in immunoregulation. I. IFNγ inhibits the proliferation of Th2 but not Th1 murine helper T lymphocyte clones. *J. Immunol.*, **140**, 4245–52.

59 Frendl, G. and Beller, D.I. (1990). Regulation of macrophage activation by IL-3. I. IL-3 functions as a macrophage-activating factor with unique properties, inducing Ia and lymphocyte function-associated antigen but not cytotoxicity. *J. Immunol.*, **144**, 3392–9.

60 Liew, F.Y., Parkinson, C., Millot, S., Severn, A., and Carrier, M. (1990). Tumour necrosis factor (TNFα) in leishmaniasis. I. TNFα mediated host protection against cutaneous leishmaniasis. *Immunology*, **69**, 570–3.

61 Titus, R.G., Sherry, B., and Cerami, A. (1989). Tumour necrosis factor plays a protective role in experimental cutaneous leishmaniasis. *J. Exp. Med.*, **170**, 2097–104.

62 Wirth, J.J. and Kierszenbaum, F. (1988). Recombinant tumor necrosis factor enhances macrophage destruction of *Trypanosoma cruzi* in the presence of bacterial endotoxin. *J. Immunol.*, **141**, 286–8.

63 Burgess, A.W. and Metcalf, D. (1980). The nature and action of granulocyte-macrophage colony stimulating factor. *Blood*, **56**, 947.

64 Belosevic, M., Davis, C.E., Meltzer, M.S., and Nacy, C.A. (1988). Regulation of activated macrophage antimicrobial activities. Identification of lymphokines that cooperate with IFNγ for induction of resistance to infection. *J. Immunol.*, **141**, 890–6.

65 Weiser, W.Y., Van Niel, A., Clark, S.C., David, J.R., and Remold, H.G. (1987). Recombinant human granulocyte/macrophage colony-stimulating factor activates intracellular killing of *Leishmania donovani* by human monocyte-derived macrophages. *J. Exp. Med.*, **166**, 1436–46.

66 Martinez, O.M., Gibbons, R.S., Garovoy, M.R., and Aranson, F.R. (1990). IL-4 inhibits IL-2 receptor expression and IL-2-dependent proliferation of human T cells. *J. Immunol.*, **144**, 2211–15.

67 Cao, H., Wolff, R.G., Meltzer, M.S., and Crawford, R.M. (1989). Differential regulation of class II MHC determinants on macrophages by IFN-gamma and IL-4. *J. Immunol.*, **143**, 3524–531.

68 Abramson, S.L. and Gallin, J.I. (1990). IL-4 inhibits superoxide production by human mononuclear phagocytes. *J. Immunol.*, **144**, 625–30.

69 Lehn, M., Weisner, W.Y., Englehorn, S., Gillis, S., and Remold, H.G. (1989). IL-4 inhibits H_2O_2 production and antileishmanial capacity of human cultured monocytes mediated by IFNγ. *J. Immunol.*, **143**, 3020–4.

70 Standiford, T.J., Strieter, R.M., Chensue, S.W., Westwick, J., Kasahara, K., and Kunkel, S.L. (1990). IL-4 inhibits the expression of IL-8 from stimulated human monocytes. *J. Immunol.*, **145**, 1436–9.

71 Fiorentino, D.F., Bond, M., and Mosmann, T.R. (1989). Two types of mouse T helper cell. IV. Th2 clones secrete a factor that inhibits cytokine production by Th1 clones. *J. Exp. Med.*, **170**, 2081–95.

72 Bogdan, C., Röllinghoff, M., and Solbach, W. (1990). Evasion strategies of *Leishmania* parasites. *Parasitol. Today*, **6**, 183–7.

73 Liew, F.Y. (1989). Functional heterogeneity of CD4+ T cells in leishmaniasis. *Immunol. Today*, **10**, 40–5.

74 Locksley, R.M. and Scott, P. (1991). T helper subsets in murine leishmaniasis: Induction, expansion and effector function. *Immunol. Today*, **N3**, A58–A61.

75 Scott, P. (1989). The role of TH1 and TH2 cells in experimental cutaneous leishmaniasis. *Exp. Parasitol.*, **68**, 369–72.

76 Heinzel, F.P., Sadick, M.D., Holaday, B.J., Coffman, R.L. and Locksley, R.M. (1989). Reciprocal expression of Interferon-γ or interleukin-4 during the resolution or progression of murine leishmaniasis. Evidence for expansion of distinct helper T cell subsets. *J. Exp. Med.*, **169**, 59–72.

77 Sadick, M.D., Heinzel, F.P., Shigekane, V.M., Fisher, W.L., and Locksley, R.M. (1987). Cellular and humoral immunity to *Leishmania major* is genetically susceptible mice after *in vivo* depletion of L3T4+ T cells. *J. Immunol.*, **139**, 1303–9.

78 Pond, L., Wassom, D.L., and Hayes, C.E. (1989). Evidence for differential induction of helper T cell subsets during *Trichinella spiralis* infection. *J. Immunol.*, **143**, 4232–7.

79 Langhorne, J., Meding, S.J., Eichmann, K., and Gillard, S.S. (1989). The response of CD4+ T cells to *Plasmodium chabaudi chabaudi*. *Immunol. Rev.*, **112**, 71–94.

80 Scott, P., Natovitz, P., Coffman, R.L., Pearce, E., and Sher, A. (1988). Immunoregulation of cutaneous leishmaniasis. T cell lines that transfer protective immunity or exacerbation belong to different T helper subsets and respond to distinct antigens. *J. Exp. Med.*, **168**, 1675–84.

81 Roberts, M., Alexander, J., and Blackwell, J.M. (1989). Influence of Lsh, H-2, and an H-11-linked gene on visceralization and metastasis associated with *Leishmania mexicana* infection in mice. *Infect. Immunol.*, **57**, 875–81.

7 Macrophages in autoimmunity and primary immunodeficiency

S. POLLACK AND A. ETZIONI

1   Introduction

The ability to activate the macrophage for antigen presentation is a crucial factor in the initiation of an immune response. Purified monocytes from peripheral blood and tissue macrophages present antigen (1,2), but alveolar macrophages present antigen only poorly (3). Presentation of self antigen to CD4[+] helper T-cells comprises an autoimmune response which may lead to immunopathology. On the other hand, failure to present and to respond to non-self antigens may lead to immunodeficiency. Most antigens are recognized together with major histocompatibility complex (MHC) Class II (HLA-DR, DP, and DQ) molecules. In humans, 90 per cent of blood monocytes are HLA-DR[+] (4). The relative level of DQ and DR antigens on the surface of macrophages may be one of the factors determining high and low responsiveness to antigens (5).

The activation of macrophages by antigen presentation leads to the production of IL-1 and other molecules which are required for T-cell activation. However, T-cells exposed to antigen liberate interferon-gamma (IFNγ) and other cytokines which augment MHC Class II expression by macrophages. Interaction of the T-cell with the antigen–MHC Class II complex, together with other surface or secreted molecules of the macrophage and T-cells, leads to effector functions of T-cells which are required for the execution of an immune response. The control of immune responses against self antigens, as well as against non-self antigens, is performed at the level of T and B cells. The macrophage plays an important role in these processes: differences in antigen presentation give rise to different types of immune response.

In the present chapter, the role of the macrophage in the immune regulation of autoimmunity, as well as in anti-non-self responses, will be discussed, and the consequences of dysregulation will be described.

2   Immunoregulatory function of macrophages

The immunoregulatory function of monocytes/macrophages may be executed by several mechanisms: (1) mode and type of antigen presentation; (2) direct suppressor effect on other immune cell functions; and (3) induction and activation of other immunoregulatory cells, such as suppressor T-cells. These possibilities will be outlined below.

2.1   Autoantigen processing and presentation

The function of the immune system is to eliminate foreign antigens (non-self) without attacking self. Thus, the immune system should have the ability to discriminate precisely between self and non-self. The mechanism of such discrimination involves thymic positive and negative selection of developing T-cells able to recognize self peptides bound to self-MHC Class II molecules (6). T-cell recognition of self peptide-MHC Class II complexes appears to be the critical event for the induction and maintenance of self-tolerance both in the thymus and in the periphery. Macrophages acting as antigen-presenting cells (APCs) process and present antigens to T-cells. The heterodimeric T-cell receptor on CD4+ T-cells recognizes the bimolecular complex on APCs composed of MHC Class II and antigen. It has been demonstrated that macrophages can process and present self as well as non-self antigens. In rare cases, CD4+ T-cells can recognize self antigens and bring about autoimmune response and tissue damage.

Antigen processing and presentation to CD4+ T-cells by APCs is a prerequisite for the recognition of most antigens by T-cells (7). The antigen is ingested by endocytosis, transported to an acid cellular compartment of APC, and subjected to proteolytic fragmentation. Some of the antigen fragments bind to MHC Class II molecules and are transported to the surface of APCs. Because of the scarcity of MHC Class II molecules expressed in individual cells, each MHC molecule binds many different peptides (8). Accordingly, most peptides capable of binding to a particular MHC molecule share broad structural motifs detectable at the level of primary amino acid sequence (9,10). Given the broad binding capacity of MHC molecules, it is possible that MHC Class II antigens may not distinguish between peptides derived from self and non-self proteins. Indeed, self peptides constitutively occupy the binding site of MHC Class II molecules (11). This has important implications for the development of the T-cell repertoire and the establishment of tolerance to self protein. However, the constitutive occupancy of most MHC-binding sites by self peptides raises the question of how the APC presents non-self antigens. It is suggested that newly synthesized MHC molecules are available for foreign peptide binding (12). Alternatively, during the intracytoplasmic recycling of MHC molecules, peptides can dissociate and be replaced by a competitor protein (13).

MHC Class II molecules have a role in the maintenance of T-cell tolerance. Individuals expressing certain MHC Class II gene products are more likely to be affected with autoimmune diseases (14). Furthermore, susceptibility alleles of MHC Class II genes share regions of allelic hypervariability (15). However, it is not yet clear whether the role of MHC Class II molecules in maintenance of T-cell tolerance lies at the level of self antigen binding to MHC or at the level of other mechanisms. If a self peptide cannot bind to the self Class II molecules then self-tolerance occurs. Not all tolerance can be explained by this mechanism, however, and it has been shown that many self antigens can bind to Class II molecules (16). In this case, tolerance is due to functional or physical deletion of autoreactive T-cells. It should also be noted that through the mechanism of processing self proteins, intracytoplasmic fragments, which are not present on the globular protein's surface, are brought out on to the cell surface in association with MHC molecules and displayed to T-cells, which might be autoreactive (7).

Autoimmune diseases result from the activation of self-reactive T-cells induced by autoantigen. As discussed earlier, these disorders are characterized by an increased frequency of certain MHC Class II alleles in affected individuals. Also, alleles positively associated with a disease share amino acid residues in the hypervariable human leucocyte antigen (HLA) regions involved in peptide binding (17). Thus, it is likely that the development of an autoimmune disease is dependent on the capacity of a disease-associated MHC Class II allele to bind an autoantigen and present it to T-cells. Therefore, by interfering with or blocking the binding of antigenic self-peptides to Class II molecules it may be possible to modulate the activation of autoreactive T-cells and thereby suppress the development of auto-immunity (8).

2.2   Suppressor monocytes/macrophages

Suppressor monocytes are part of the cellular immune network providing physiological control of immune responses. Monocytes/macrophages secrete a number of products which under certain experimental conditions exert an inhibitory effect on T- and B-cell functions, whereas under different culture conditions the same factors may have an enhancing effect. It is not clear whether a monocyte population consists of a mixture of heterogenous cells with differing functions or whether the heterogeneity of function represents differing states of activation/differentiation, or concentrations of homogenous subpopulations. In general, monocyte-mediated suppression is a quantitative phenomenon and increased concentrations of monocytes, even from normal individuals, will result in immune suppression (18). However, suppressive monocytes may be members of a very small subpopulation which is stimulated to increase in certain diseases (19), and the suppressor activity per monocyte may be increased compared to monocytes from normal individuals.

There are several techniques employed to measure monocyte suppressor activity. First, the suppressor activity of monocytes/macrophages removed from mononuclear cell cultures (by adherence to plastic, glass or nylon wool, or by carbonyl iron ingestion) can be examined in one of various forms of bioassay. Secondly, purified populations of macrophages can be added to an assay of normal immune cells and the resulting response is lowered. Thirdly, certain reagents (for example, indomethacin) which inhibit synthesis and secretion of certain macrophage suppressive products (for example, prostaglandin E_2) can be added to mononuclear cell cultures. If the subsequent response induced in the cultures is increased, it can be assumed that the cell culture contained suppressor monocytes. Fourthly, monocytes can be preactivated and the effect of preactivated cells on the immune response of fresh autologous or allogeneic cells measured. If these preactivated monocytes suppress immune function it can be postulated that they act as suppressor cells in network immunity.

Various human diseases, in which impaired immune functions have been reported, are often associated with suppressor macrophage activity. It is not clear, however, whether both B- and T-cells are sensitive directly to suppression by monocytes or whether the effect may be, in part, indirect via the inhibition of CD4[+] helper T-cell function. Monocyte depletion or inhibition experiments offer only circumstantial evidence that the suppression noted is macrophage-mediated. Direct evidence that the macrophage is the suppressor cell is provided by experiments where a certain immune function has been inhibited by the addition of purified populations of macrophages. Suppression by macrophages may be mediated by a number of differing mechanisms which are singled out by a particular assay. It is possible that defective lymphocytes may be more readily suppressed by macrophages. Thus, the suppressive effect of monocytes may sometimes be demonstrated only in autologous culture conditions and not in allogeneic cell combinations.

Monocytes secrete a number of products which act as inhibitors of certain immune functions (for example, TNFα, interferons, and prostaglandins), and other products (for example interleukins 1 and 6) which regulate lymphocyte functions. It should be noted that under certain experimental conditions both PGE_2 and TNFα can also enhance B-cell responses *in vitro* (20,21).

Suppressor effects of macrophages can be mediated by enhanced secretion of inhibiting factors; by decreased secretion of enhancing factors; or by excessive production of a soluble inhibitor of interleukins (ILs). Macrophages are a major source of secreted prostaglandins, in particular PGE_2; the latter can suppress lymphocyte functions by a mechanism which involves stimulation of adenyl cyclase and hence an increase in cAMP (20,22). The suppressive activity of monocytes demonstrated *in vitro* in certain disease states may be the result of stimulation of PGE_2 secretion by various agents used to study mononuclear cell function *in vitro* (23). There is an inverse correlation between PGE_2 secretion and IL-1 secretion by lipopolysaccharide (LPS)-stimulated monocytes (19). Thus, PGE_2 may also suppress lymphocyte function indirectly, by inhibition of IL-1 secretion. Furthermore, PGE_2 may inhibit the expression of MHC Class II antigens and regulate in an autocrine fashion monocyte function (24). PGE_2 may also suppress lymphocyte functions by inducing suppressor T-cells; a possibility which will be discussed later in this chapter.

There are also other mechanisms, in addition to PGE_2, which may be involved in macrophage-mediated suppression. TNFα is secreted by macrophages and induces IL-1 and PGE_2 production by monocytes and thus may regulate lymphocyte functions indirectly through other monocyte products (25,26). TNFα may also inhibit directly CD4[+] T-cell activity and suppress *in vitro* immunoglobulin (Ig) secretion by B-cells (27). There is also evidence for the production by monocytes of factors in response to signals received from T-cells, which suppress T-cell functions (28,29); and for activation of factors, released in a precursor form by T-cells, which become suppressive agents (30). Also, reactive oxygen intermediates may act as suppressive factors and mediate the inhibitory effect of monocytes on natural killer (NK) cell activity (31).

The relationship of macrophage suppressor activity *in vitro* to deficient immune response *in vivo* is not clear. In some cases, in spite of *in vitro* macrophage suppression of lymphoproliferation or Ig production, patients manifest normal delayed hypersensitivity or hypergammaglobulinaemia. Presumably, suppressor macrophages can contribute to *in vivo* immunodeficiency, but whether their role is primary or secondary, the exact mechanisms remain unresolved.

2.3 Monocytes and suppressor T-cells

Monocytes may also act indirectly in regulation of the immune response by inducing suppressor T-cells (32–34). In this regard, monocytes with receptors for the Fc portion of the IgG molecule may play a special role. These monocytes act through CD8[+] T-cells in suppression of antigen and mitogen-induced T-cell poliferation and PWM-stimulated Ig secretion (35–37). Monocytes which are FcγR[+] probably support proliferation and the activation of suppressor T-cells. The exact mechanism by which macrophages induce suppressor T-cells is unknown, but at least in some cases PGE_2 may be involved (24,38). Recently, it has been shown that in PWM-stimulated Ig production there is generation of CD8[+] T cells which, in turn, suppress proliferation of CD4[+] T-cells (34). The differentiation of suppressor T-cells is dependent on the number of monocytes present in culture and on soluble factors derived from T-cells and monocytes which can be replaced by a combination of interferon-gamma (IFNγ) and PGE_2 (39,40). Thus, the induction of suppressor T-cells by macrophages is a complex process dependent partially, but not solely, on PGE_2. This mechanism may play a role particularly in monocyte regulation of Ig production *in vitro*.

3 Macrophages and autoimmunity

The association between MHC Class II antigen and autoimmune diseases has already been discussed (see Section 2.1). This may be due, at least partially, to the role of MHC Class II molecules on macrophages, in determining which epitopes give rise to an immune response (41). Other factors which are associated with macrophage changes may also play a role in the genesis of autoimmune diseases. It should be noted, however, that some monocyte impairments described in autoimmunity are epiphenomena or secondary changes, rather than key factors in the development of the disease. In organ-specific diseases, the activity of peripheral blood monocytes does not always reflect that of activated tissue macrophages. Furthermore, monocytes may be affected by autoantibodies against their surface membrane, the presence of immune complexes and LPS of Gram-negative bacteria. These issues and their relevance in certain autoimmune diseases are reviewed below.

3.1   Rheumatoid arthritis (RA)

RA is an inflammatory joint disease which involves symmetrically the wrists and small joints of the hands and feet, and is more common in women. However, RA is not confined to joint involvement and may present as a system disease with cardiac and lung manifestations, vasculitis, and episcleritis. Rheumatoid nodules often occur on the extensor surface of the forearm. They consist of necrotic material surrounded predominantly by macrophages which often have epitheloid characteristics. The inflammatory process in the joints is synovitis which is often accompanied by destruction of bone and cartilage. Many activated monocytes are found in the peripheral blood.

Macrophages within rheumatoid synovial tissue are believed to participate in the development of RA lesions, both as immunoregulatory cells and as mediators of cartilage and bone destruction (42). Macrophage-like cells which express HLA-DR in RA synovial tissue were found to mediate local T-cell activation (43) as well as suppress local T-cell activation (44). This apparent paradox was resolved in a recent study which outlined the existence of several subpopulations of cells in RA synovial cells fractionated on Percoll density gradients (45). 'Heavy' cells were potent stimulators in the mixed lymphocyte reaction and produced little PGE_2, whereas 'light' cells suppressed the mixed lymphocyte reaction and produced a large quantity of PGE_2 in vitro. It was previously demonstrated that products released by activated T-cells can mediate an increased PGE_2 synthesis by activation of RA adherent cells (46). An increased amount of PGE_2 is produced by monocytes from the blood of RA patients, even in the early stages of the disease (47,48). Thus, macrophage-like cells, should not only be regarded as active in the destructive process in RA joints, but may suppress potentially deleterious immune functions mediated by T-cells. In this regard, it has recently been shown that peripheral blood monocytes from normal subjects could suppress rheumatoid factor production by autologous B-cells (49).

The antigen-presenting capacity of peripheral blood monocytes derived from RA patients is reduced. Rheumatoid macrophages and dendritic cells from synovial membrane and synovial fluid were more potent than blood monocytes as antigen-presenting cells (47,50). This may be related to the fact that RA blood monocytes have a decreased expression of MHC Class II molecules (47). The decreased antigen-presenting capacity of peripheral blood monocytes in RA can be restored to normal levels by exposure to IFNγ *in vitro*.

Monocytes and macrophages are clearly key cells in the inflammatory joint disease of RA, and several changes suggest that they are activated in RA. Neopterin is secreted exclusively by human mononuclear phagocytes. Blood monocytes and synovial macrophages from RA patients secrete high amounts of neopterin (51), and raised levels in urine correlate with the development of disease activity (52). That synovial macrophages also secrete large amounts of IL-1 spontaneously also suggests that these cells may be activated *in vivo* (53). This cytokine activates synovial fibroblasts and chondrocytes to produce large amounts of PGE_2, collagenase, and plasminogen activator. Thus, the existence of IL-1 in synovial fluid is likely to be central in maintaining the inflammation in the rheumatoid joint. Also high levels of IL-6 are found in synovial fluids of patients with active RA (54), which is presumably secreted by local macrophages, as well as B- and T-cells (54). Over-production of IL-6 may play an important role in the pathogenesis of RA and explain both the production of autoantibodies including rheumatoid factor, and the increase in acute phase proteins and fever. Significantly enhanced phagocytosis of opsonized bacteria is also prominent in RA patients (55), together with chemotaxis of blood monocytes (56). This is apparently intrinsic to the cells and not due to serum factors.

3.2   Systemic lupus erythematosus (SLE)

SLE is a complex multisystem disease characterized by inflammation involving many organs, hypergammaglobulinemia, the production of a variety of autoantibodies amongst which anti-DNA is the best characterized. B-cell abnormalities have been identified and the immune disorder is further augmented by poorly functioning suppressor T-cells. Aberrant behaviour of macrophages may amplify the pathological process.

One of the most significant mechanisms leading to inflammation and damage in SLE is the deposition of immune complexes in tissues due to their excessive formation and accumulation in blood. Expression of Fc receptors (FcR) on monocytes is increased in SLE whereas phagocytosis mediated by FcR is markedly impaired. In addition, the defective clearance of IgG anti-Rh(D)-coated erythrocytes has been shown to correlate with disease activity (57). Significant depression of IgG and complement receptor mediated immune complex clearance has been found in lupus nephritis (58).

Recent studies demonstrated decreased MHC Class II expression on monocytes and B-cells in SLE (59,60), and a reduced number of HLA-DR positive monocytes in patients with active SLE (60). The decrease in monocytes expressing HLA-DR in SLE patients seems to be intrinsic and is not induced by corticosteroid treatment, deficient production of IFNγ, or the over-production of prostaglandins (60). However, the presence of antimonocyte antibodies in sera of SLE patients has been implicated in this phenomenon (61). The demonstration of decreased HLA-DR-positive monocytes in human SLE contrasts with findings in autoimmune-prone mice (MRL-lpr/lpr) where Ia-positive macrophages in the peritoneal cavity were markedly increased (62,63). From these murine studies it was suggested that these macrophages might stimulate autologous T- and B-cells by presenting self antigen that might result in autoimmune phenomenon (63). In humans, however, it is not clear whether the decrease in HLA-DR-positive monocytes in SLE is a causal factor or one of the consequences in this form of autoimmunity.

How macrophages help to produce anti-DNA antibodies (64) in active SLE is not known at present (65). This augmentation of anti-DNA antibody production cannot be attributed to increased secretion of IL-1, as IL-1 production by SLE monocytes is low (66). These results of accessory activity for anti-DNA production are at variance with those on PWM-stimulated Ig synthesis *in vitro*, where SLE monocytes showed markedly decreased accessory cell activity (67). Reduced function of monocytes in patients with SLE has been shown also for proliferative responses of T-cells to phytohaemagglutinin (PHA) stimulation (68).

A number of studies have indicated an enhanced suppressive activity of monocytes from SLE patient on PWM-stimulated Ig synthesis (69–71). It is not clear whether the decreased response in these systems is caused by a subset of suppressor monocytes or by an increased secretion of monocyte-derived suppressor factors, and/or increased numbers of monocytes with APC activity. it is suggested that the suppressive activity of monocytes is directed at B-cells and is probably through a prostaglandin-mediated pathway (72). Regarding T-cells in SLE, monocytes may have an impaired ability to activate resting T-cells but are able to assist T-cells activated in SLE (73), which help anti-DNA antibody synthesis (65). It should be noted that alteration of Ia expression on APC might induce stimulation of helper T-cells in the recognition of autoantigens (74), and thereby cause dysregulation of T-cells which results in autoantibody production seen in SLE (75).

In a recent study, the proportion of monocytes in the peripheral blood of SLE patients was found to be significantly higher than in normal individuals (76). This was accompanied by decreased phagocytosis of yeast particles but similar levels of acid phosphatase activity compared to monocytes derived from normal controls. Monocytes in SLE failed to enhance phagocytosis following treatment with LPS. It was suggested that in SLE, monocytes differentiate into a cell with a more limited repertoire than in normal individuals, being less responsive to certain signals but responding to others. Thus, monocytes from SLE patients could stimulate helper T-cells (75) but were deficient in the accessory function necessary for the activation of the suppressor T-cell population (67) thereby promoting the disease.

3.3 Progressive systemic sclerosis (PSS)

Scleroderma is characterized by the widespread and excessive production of collagen in body tissues, most notably in the skin. The aetiological agent(s) is/are unknown, but macrophages may be involved in fibrous tissue formation. The disease is characterized by production of wide range of auto-antibodies which may act directly on fibroblasts (77,78) or indirectly on macrophages (79) and lead to the production of the unknown factor(s) which stimulate collagen production and fibroblast proliferation.

Monocytes from patients with PSS produce normal and even increased amounts of IL-1 (80,81). However, activity of secreted IL-1 is sometimes masked by increased production of a low molecular weight IL-1 inhibitor (82). PSS monocytes demonstrate increased suppressor activity of mitogenic responses *in vitro* (83–85) and decreased stimulatory activity in allogeneic mixed lymphocyte reactions (86). The latter defect could be ascribed to reduced surface expression of Mac 120 antigen whereas HLA-DR expression is normal (87).

It has been suggested that circulating monocytes in PSS may be in a state of activation having undergone an advanced *in vivo* maturation, which may contribute to their increased suppressive activity. Evidence in support of activated circulating monocytes in PSS include low levels of the ectoenzymes 5'-nucleotidase and alkaline phophodiesterase-1, and high levels of leucine aminopeptidase (87). The presence of increased numbers of large, lightly stained esterase-positive monocytes which weakly bind the lectin, peanut agglutinin, and the monoclonal antibody Leu M2, also suggest more advanced differentiation (87). Activated monocytes may represent responses to *in vivo* activation signals, such as IFNγ or immune complexes. In this regard, reactive antimonocyte antibodies, which may contribute to direct activation of circulating monocytes, were found in the majority of patients with PSS (79).

These observations suggest that monocytes in PSS are activated by an immune response and may determine excessive collagen production and fibroblast proliferation. Thus, macrophages may play a role in the immuno-pathogenesis of PSS. It is not clear, however, whether the changes in macrophage functions which take place in PSS are primary or secondary events.

3.4   Autoimmune thyroid disease (ATD)

Thyroid disorders of the autoimmune type occur in two different forms: hyperthyroidism associated with excessive glandular function in Graves' disease; and hypothyroidism associated with deficient thyroid function which characterizes Hashimoto's thyroiditis. Available information regarding the development of autoimmune thyroid disease (ATD) indicates a genetically predisposed imbalance in immunoregulatory mechanisms. It is apparent that the expression of MHC Class II gene products on the surface of monocytes/macrophages is of some significance in the immunopathogenesis of ATD (88). Many investigators have demonstrated that Class II MHC antigens are also expressed on the surface of thyroid epithelial cells (thyrocytes) from patients with Graves' disease, but not on those of normal individuals (89,90). Ectopic expression of MHC Class II antigens by thyrocytes might trigger the immune recognition of thyrocyte-specific surface constituents by self-reactive T-cells with the consequent generation of organ-specific autoimmunity. Indeed, thyrocytes from Graves' patients induced proliferation of both autologous peripheral blood T-cells and thyroid-infiltrating T-cells (91,92). Expression of DR antigens on thyrocytes cannot be induced by thyroid-infiltrating macrophages. However, direct transfer of HLA-DR molecules from antigen-presenting cells to thyrocytes may take place (93). Macrophages and dendritic cells are found in thyroid-infiltrating mononuclear cells in ATD (94). Furthermore, a high percentage of thyroid infiltrating T-cells express HLA-DR (95). Thus, it is possible that cellular interactions between macrophages, T-cells, and thyrocytes within the thyroid gland perpetuate the immune response in ATD.

When thyrocytes from patients with Graves' disease are co-cultured with autologous peripheral blood T-cells, and autologous monocytes are added to the cell mixture, the expression of HLA-DR antigens on both thyrocytes and T-cells significantly increases compared with mixtures incubated in the absence of monocytes (96). Thus, in the presence of monocytes, HLA-DR$^+$ thyrocytes are able to activate T-cells. Moreover, monocytes added to autologous cultures of thyrocytes and T-cells from Graves patients augmented significantly antigen presentation by thyrocytes (97). These findings suggest that monocytes enhance the immune response to antigens resulting from cellular interactions of thyrocytes and T-cells in the thyroid gland. Macrophages may also perpetuate the immune response within the thyroid gland in patients with ATD by providing IL-1 as a second signal which augments antigen presentation by HLA-DR$^+$ thyrocytes.

The above studies suggest an enhancing effect of monocytes in the perpetuation of autoimmune responses in ATD. However, other studies shed a different light on the role of monocytes in ATD. Zeki and co-workers (98) found monocyte/macrophage reactive antibodies (with cytotoxic activity) in the sera of patients with ATD. These antibodies were specific for monocytes but their specificity was different from anti HLA-DR antibodies. Monocytotoxic activities of these antibodies were significantly correlated with levels of antibodies for the receptor for thyroid-stimulating hormone. Thus, it is suggested that in the active stage of ATD, monocyte/macrophage activity is attenuated by monocytotoxic antibodies. Also, in patients with active ATD a decreased proliferative response of T-cells to autologous or allogeneic MHC Class II antigens expressed on monocytes has been reported (99). The defect was ascribed to the T-cell population, whereas DR expression on monocytes was normal and even slightly elevated. Similar results were also reported by other investigators (100,101).

3.5   Multiple sclerosis (MS)

Multiple sclerosis (MS) is a progressive demyelinating disease of the central nervous system. Evidence for multiple abnormalities in the immune status of MS patients has accumulated. Susceptibility to MS appears to be associated with the HLA-DR2 gene products of the major histocompatibility complex (MHC).

In patients with active disease, a decreased proliferative response of T-cells to self MHC Class II gene products (autologous mixed lymphocyte reaction, AMLR) and reduced Con-A-induced suppressor T-cell activity has been reported (102,103). Both T-cell proliferation in AMLR and Con-A-induced T-suppressor function are monocyte-dependent. Indeed, monocyte dysfunction has been found in patients with active MS. Recently, decreased expression of DR antigens on the surface membrane of monocytes from patients with MS has been demonstrated (104). This correlated with low AMLR responses in these patients. T-cells from such cultures expressed deficient suppressor function whereas T-cells obtained from AMLR cultures of patients with inactive disease expressed normal suppressor function (105). Inasmuch as MS is characterized by suppressor cell dysfunction, it could be hypothesized that deficient expression of DR antigens on monocytes causes reduced suppressor function in activated autologous T-cells. This may be a primary abnormality in the immunopathogenesis of MS.

4   Macrophages and primary immunodeficiencies

Monocytes and macrophages take part in inflammatory responses, antigen presentation, and immunoregulatory networks. They have tumouricidal, cytocidal, and microbicidal capacities. Because of this broad range of functions it is not surprising that macrophage dysfunction is involved in a wide variety of immunodeficient conditions. These include both humoral and cellular immunodeficiency disorders. The following sections review the various primary immunodeficiency diseases in which macrophage function was found to be defective and consider the significance of these defects in immunopathogenesis.

4.1   Common variable immunodeficiency (CVID)

CVID encompasses a heterogenous group of familial or sporadic diseases characterized by the aberrant function of B-cells resulting in low levels of serum Ig. This may be due to an intrinsic defect in B-cells and/or an imbalance in the regulatory functions of T-cells. The latter may consist of either the abnormal activity of suppressor T-cells or an absence/defect in helper T-cells (106). T-cell activation requires the macrophage both for antigen presentation and for the production of IL-1, which provides a second activating signal. Various studies have been carried out in an attempt to elucidate the possible role of macrophages in the pathogenesis of CVID (107–111).

Eibl and co-workers (107) reported that 8/9 patients with CVID had a significant defect in macrophage-T cell interactions. In a subsequent study using co-culture techniques the same investigators concluded that macrophages from CVID patients were defective in their antigen-presenting capacity (108). This defective response to antigen was not due to suppression by macrophages (109). Arala-Chaves and co-workers (110) studied two CVID patients with high numbers of monocytes in the peripheral blood, impaired T-cell proliferative responses, and decreased Ig production *in vitro*. Removal of monocytes from cultures of peripheral blood mononuclear cells elicited an increased immunoglobulin secretion and response to T-cell mitogens *in vitro*. A further study (111) has investigated the role of suppressor macrophages in CVID and found that in some patients, peripheral blood monocytes suppressed antigen (SRBC)-stimulated immunoglobulin production *in vitro*. They were able to show that the influence of macrophages was not due to decreased IL-1 secretion. Furthermore, in X-linked infantile agammaglobulinaemia, macrophages may play a role in the development of immunodeficiency (112). A suppressive effect of macrophages on immunoglobulin synthesis could be shown in two brothers with X-linked agammaglobulinaemia. It is suggested that this impairment is secondary to the primary defect in B-cell differentiation. A recent study (113) investigated CVID patients with defects in T-cell activation (expressed as reduced OKT3 stimulated proliferation of T-cells). IL-2 production was decreased and a profound defect in IL-2 receptor expression was demonstrated. Co-culture experiments with T-cells and macrophages suggested that the failure of T-cell activation in CVID patients originated in a macrophage dysfunction. The macrophage defect was not caused by increased secretion of prostaglandin-E. Interestingly, a familial defect in monocyte helper function (resulting in a failure of OKT3 monoclonal antibody to induce lymphocyte mitogenesis but no clinical manifestations) has recently been described (114). Thus it may be concluded that the major role in the pathogenesis of CVID is played by B- and T-cells. However, macrophage dysfunction, whether primary or secondary, appears to play a significant role in this form of immunodeficiency in some patients.

4.2   Chronic granulomatous disease (CGD)

This is a syndrome of defective bacteriocidal activity due to a failure to initiate a respiratory burst in phagocytic cells (neutrophils, monocytes, macrophages, and eosinophils). The largest subgroup of the disease is inherited in an X-linked manner, with affected males and heterozygote carrier females. The molecular basis for the lesion is nearly always the absence of cytochrome b-245, an essential component of the NADPH oxidase which initiates the respiratory burst process (115). Between 20 and 40 per cent of patients have an autosomal recessive pattern of inheritance. In this type of disease, cytochrome b-245 levels and distribution are normal, but the cells are unable to transfer electrons to cytochrome b-245 (116). In both forms, patients suffer from recurrent bacterial and fungal infections.

The failure of the respiratory burst in CGD patients is seen in both neutrophils and monocytes. In several children with the mild form of the disease, in spite of a defect in neutrophils, the phagocytic and bactericidal capacities of monocytes are largely preserved, which accounts for fewer infectious episodes (117). As the oxidative pathways also play an important role in the antigen-presenting process, it was assumed that antigen presentation in CGD patients may be impaired. Indeed, monocytes from patients with CGD can internalize antigen but are defective in presenting the processed antigen to CD4+ T-cells, thereby contributing to the immunodeficiency (118).

4.3   Chronic mucocutaneous candidiasis (CMC)

This disorder is characterized by *Candida* infection of the skin and nucous membranes. A familial occurrence has been reported, suggesting an autosomal recessive inheritance. The disorder is associated with a selective defect in T-cell-mediated immunity, resulting in susceptibility to chronic *Candida* infection. Defective monocyte chemotaxis and *Candida* killing were found in patients with this disease (119). Their monocytes also fail to make IL-1 after stimulation with LPS (120). These defects may play a role in the development and persistence of *Candida* infections.

4.4   Wiskott–Aldrich syndrome (WAS)

This is an X-linked disorder characterized by recurrent infections, eczema of the skin, and abnormalities in the functions of platelets and lymphocytes. It is due to a deficiency in sialophorin (CD43), which normally occurs on lymphocytes, neutrophils, monocytes, and platelets, and may serve to prevent premature senescence and removal of nucleated blood cells by the spleen (121). Sialophorin may also be involved in monocyte activation (122).

Patients with WAS have a variety of immune defects including abnormal monocyte chemotaxis and a defect in monocyte-mediated antibody-dependent cytotoxicity (123,124). The cytotoxicity defect may be due to sialophorin deficiency (125), whereas impaired chemotaxis is probably due to abnormal production of chemotactic cytokines (124).

4.5   Deficiency of MHC Class II antigens

This is an inherited combined immunodeficiency disease characterized by the presence of normal amounts of T- and B-cells, accompanied by profound abnormal cellular and humoral immune responses to foreign antigens. MHC Class II expression is severely defective in both macrophages and lymphocytes (126). All patients have abnormal cellular and humoral responses *in vitro* and suffer from recurrent and severe infections that are frequently the cause of death.

The deficiency of cell surface expression of MHC Class II antigens is the consequence of lack of synthesis of HLA α- and β-chains. There is no gross abnormality of MHC Class II genes, but mRNA for MHC Class II molecules is not detected. Thus, the defect may reside in MHC Class II gene expression and involve transacting regulatory factor (127).

4.6   Deficiency of leucocyte adhesion molecules

These patients share a deficiency in three cell surface molecules, CR3, LFA-1, and CR4, which are expressed on leucocytes. These are heterodimeric glycoproteins composed of a common β-chain of 95 kDA (CD18), associated non-covalently with one of three closely related α-chains, CD11a, 11b, and 11c. The defect is usually in the synthesis of the β-chain and inhibition of cell surface expression of α-chains (128). Clinically, the syndrome is characterized by recurrent cutaneous and deep-seated infections with pyrogenic bacteria, gingivitis, and periodontitis, dystrophic scarring of ulcerated cutaneous infections and delayed separation of the umbilical cord. There is persistent neutrophilia in peripheral blood accompanied by normal or slightly increased monocyte and lymphocyte counts. The syndrome is heterogenous in its severity and this has been correlated with the extent of the deficiency of adhesion molecules (129), which may vary between families affected with this genetic disorder.

The major features of the disease appear to be secondary to neutrophil and monocyte dysfunction, whereas lymphocyte function is preserved.

Monocytes and neutrophils are not able to adhere to endothelial cells and thereafter to migrate from the circulation to sites of inflammation. Monocytes of patients show reduced spreading and anchoring on plastic surfaces, survive poorly during a two-week period in culture, and show defective chemotaxis (130,131). Antibody-dependent monocyte-mediated cytotoxicity is also reduced (132). The degree of the cytotoxic defect correlates with the severity of the deficiency in adhesion molecules.

4.7   Primary familial monocyte disorder

A familial monocyte defect associated with a clinical syndrome of cellular immunodeficiency was reported recently (133). Monocytes derived from family members were found to have reduced cytoskeletal vimentin intermediate filaments. Diminished expression of HLA-DR antigens and the receptors for IgG and C3b were also found. These abnormal macrophages demonstrated impaired phagocytosis and reduced accesory cell function for T-cell activation. IL-1 secretion by macrophages derived from such patients was also found to be defective.

Another primary familial monocyte disorder was described in 1984 by Yamazaki and co-workers (134). Although the clinical features were similar to those of chronic mucocutaneous candidiasis, the primary immunological defect is in the function of macrophage rather than T-cells. In this novel immunodeficiency syndrome, monocytes are abnormal in both their mobility and in their ability to phagocytose. Expression of membrane antigens on macrophages is not impaired. However, IL-1 production by this cell type is markedly suppressed (135).

These primary disorders of macrophages illuminate the role of these cells in the integrated function of immune responses and underline the importance of studying macrophage function in subjects with immunodeficiency.

4.8   Chediak–Higashi syndrome (CHS)

This autosomal recessive disorder is characterized by partial oculocutaneous albinism, neutropenia, and recurrent infections. Monocytes of patients with CHS contain giant lysosomal inclusions, possibly resulting from failure of phagocytic degranulation.

Monocytes from patients wtih CHS have defective chemotaxis (136), and the random migration of monocytes is also decreased. Defective chemotaxis may result from reduced cell mobility due to the large intracellular lysosomal inclusions. Phagocytic cells derived from CHS patients demonstrate a greatly augmented phagocyte capacity, and upon contact with bacteria are able to engulf even autologous blood cells (137).

5 Summary

The macrophage plays an important role in the pathophysiology of human disease. This chapter has focused on the description and analysis of macrophage abnormalities in two groups of disorders: autoimmune diseases and primary immunodeficiencies. Impairment of macrophage function is seen to be predominantly of two types: primary, in which it is the cause of the pathology; and secondary, where it is a consequence of other immune cell dysfunction but may facilitate the development and progression of the disease.

In both autoimmunity and in immunodeficiency, the influence of aberrant macrophages has been described and its relationship to the immuno-pathogenesis of a certain disease. Macrophages may exert their effect on an immune response directly, or indirectly by providing an induction signal for other immune cell types.

Although much is known of the role of monocytes in immunodeficiency and autoimmunity, the exact mechanisms underlying the disrupted immune phenomena observed in these disorders remain unclear. The main defect in autoimmunity lies in the breakdown in self-tolerance at the level of T-cells, whereas in primary immunodeficiency there can be an inherent abnormality of T-and/or B-cells as well as in the macrophage population. The association of processed self-antigens with MHC Class II gene products plays a key role in susceptibility to autoimmune disease. The reduced ability of macrophages to induce suppressor T-cells may also contribute to the breakdown of self-tolerance. Both mechanisms have been reported in SLE, scleroderma, MS, and ATD. In primary immunodeficiencies, enhanced inhibitory activity of macrophages *in vitro* and/or the lack of macrophage accessory functions have been reported and implicated in the pathogenesis of these diseases.

Further studies on human macrophages may provide other insights to the pathogenesis of autoimmunity and immunodeficiency, and possibly facilitate the development of new immune interventions in this group of diseases. In fact, preliminary immunomodulatory treatments involving the use of anti-MHC, anti-TCR, anti-CD4 monoclonal antibodies, and H2-receptor blocking agents with supplementary cytokines are currently underway.

References

1 Becker, S., Johnson, C., Halme, J., and Haskill, S. (1986). Inter-
   leukin-1 production and antigen presentation by normal human
   peritoneal macrophages. *Cell. Immunol.*, **98**, 467–76.
2 Oksenberg, J.R., Mor-Josef, S., Ezra, Y., and Brauthbar, C. (1987).
   Antigen presenting cells in human decidual tissue. II. Accessory cells
   for the development of anti-trinitrophenyl cytotoxic T lymphocytes. *J.
   Reprod. Immunol.*, **10**, 309–18.
3 Holt, P.G. (1986). Down regulation of immune responess in the
   lower respiratory tract: the role of alveolar macrophages. *Clin. Exp.
   Immunol.*, **63**, 261–70.
4 Gonwa, T.A., Grost, J.P., and Karr, R.W. (1987). All human monocytes have the capability of expressing HLA-DQ and HLA-DP
   molecules upon stimulation with interferon-gamma. *J. Immunol.*, **137**,
   519–24.
5 Matsushita, S., Muto, M., Suemura, M., Saito, Y., and Sasuzuki, T.
   (1987). HLA-linked nonresponsiveness to *Cryptomeria japonica*
   pollen antigen. I. Nonresponsiveness is mediated by antigen-specific
   suppressor T cell. *J. Immunol.*, **138**, 109–15.
6 Schwartz, R.H. (1989). Acquisition of immunologic self-tolerance.
   Cell, **57**, 1073–81.
7 Werdelin, O., Mouritsen, S., Petersen, B.L., Sette, A., and Buus, S.
   (1988). Facts on the fragmentation of antigens in presenting cells, on
   the association of antigen fragments with MHC molecules in cell-free
   systems, and speculation on the cell biology of antigen processing.
   Immunol. Rev., **106**, 181–93.
8 Adorini, L. (1990). Antigen presentation and self-nonself discrimination. *Clin. Immunol. Immunopath.*, **55**, 327–36.
9 DeLisi, C. and Berzofsky, J. (1986). T-cell antigenic sites tend to be
   amphipathic structures. *Proc. Natl. Acad. Sci. U.S.A.*, **82**, 7048–52.
10 Sette, A., *et al.* (1989). Prediction of major histocompatibility complex
    binding regions of protein antigens by sequence pattern analysis. *Proc.
    Natl. Acad. Sci. U.S.A.*, **86**, 3296–3300.
11 Bjorkman, P.J., Saper, M.H., Samraoui, B., Bennet, W.S.,
    Strominger, J.L., and Wiley, D.C. (1987). Structure of the human
    class I histocompatibility antigen, HLA-A2. *Nature*, **329**, 506–12.
12 Cresewll, P. (1985). Intracellular class II HLA antigens are accessible
    to transferrin-neuraminidase conjugates internalized by receptor-
    mediated endocytosis. *Proc. Natl. Acad. Sci. U.S.A.*, **82**, 8188–92.
13 Adorini, L., Appella, E., Doria, G., Cardinaux, F., and Nagy, Z.
    (1989). Competition for antigen presentation in living cells involves
    exchange of peptides bound by class II MHC molecules. *Nature*, **342**,
    800–3.

14 Bottazzo, G.F., Todd, I., Mirakian, R., Belfiore, A., and Pujol-Borrell, R. (1986). Organ-specific autoimmunity. *Immunol. Rev.*, **94**, 137–69.

15 Wraith, D.C., McDevitt, H.O., Steinman, L., and Acha-Orbea, H. (1989). T cell recognition as the target for immune intervention in autoimmune disease. *Cell*, **57**, 709–15.

16 Lorenz, R.G. and Allen, P.M. (1988). Processing and presentation of self proteins. *Immunol. Rev.*, **106**, 115–27.

17 Todd, G.A., *et al.* (1988). A molecular basis for MHC class II-associated autoimmunity. *Science*, **240**, 1003–9.

18 Gmelig-Meyling, F. and Waldmann, T.A. (1981). Human B cell activation *in vitro*: augmentation and suppression by monocytes of the immunoglobulin production induced by various B cell stimulators. *J. Immunol.*, **126**, 529–37.

19 Khansari, N., Chou, Y.K., and Fudenberg, H.H. (1985). Human monocyte heterogeneity: interleukin-1 and prostaglandin E2 production by separate subsets. *Eur. J. Immunol.*, **15**, 48–51.

20 Staite, N.D. and Panayi, G.S. (1984). Prostaglandin regulation of B-lymphocyte function. *Immunol. Today*, **5**, 175–8.

21 Jelinek, D.F. and Lipsky, P.E. (1987). Enhancement of human B cell proliferation and differentiation by tumor necrosis factor-α and inter-leukin-1. *J. Immunol.*, **139**, 2970–6.

22 Goodwin, J.S. and Ceuppens, J. (1983). Regulation of the immune response by prostaglandins. *J. Clin. Immunol.*, **3**, 295–315.

23 Shanon, B.T., Finkelstein, S., Hester, J.P., Fudenberg, H.H., and Merler, E. (1983). Altered heterogeneity of monocytes in acute myelomonocytic leukemia. *J. Natl. Cancer. Inst.*, **71**, 1157–63.

24 Steeg, P.S., Johnson, H.M., and Oppenheim, J.J. (1982). Regulation of murine macrophage Ia antigen expression by an immune interferon like lymphokine: inhibitory effect of endotoxin. *J. Immunol.*, **129**, 2402–6.

25 Dayer, J.M., Beutler, B., and Cerami, A. (1985). Cachectin/tumor necrosis factor stimulates collagenase and prostaglandin E2 production by human synovial cells and dermal fibroblasts. *J. Exp. Med.*, **162**, 2163–8.

26 Imamura, K., Spriggs, D., and Kufe, D. (1987). Expression of tumor necrosis factor receptors on human monocytes and internalization of receptor-bound ligand. *J. Immunol.*, **139**, 2989–92.

27 Kashiva, H., Wright, S.C., and Bonavida, B. (1987). Reglation of B cell maturation and differentiation. *J. Immunol.*, **138**, 1383–90.

28 Emilie, D., Crevon, M.C., and Galanaud, P. (1983). Prostaglandin E2 regulation of human specific B cell response: interaction with a mono-cyte product. *Clin. Immunol. Immunopath.*, **29**, 415–23.

29 Warrington, R.J. (1987). Interaction of a lymphokine with normal human macrophages results in release of a suppressor factor for mitogen induced immunoglobulin synthesis. *Scand. J. Immunol.*, **25**, 399–406.

30 Schnaper, H.W., Pierce, C.W., and Aune, T.M. (1984). Identification and initial characterization of concanavalin-A and interferon induced human suppressor factors: evidence for a human equivalent of murine soluble immune response suppressor (SIRS). *J. Immunol.*, **132**, 2429–35.

31 Seaman, W.E., Gindhart, T.D., Blackman, M.A., Dalal, B., Talal, N., and Webb, Z. (1982). Suppression of natural killing *in vitro* by monocytes and polymorphonuclear leukocytes. *J. Clin. Invest.*, **69**, 876–88.

32 Sager, D.S. and Jasin, H.E. (1982). Bacterial lipopolysaccharide induced immunoglobulin synthesis by human blood lymphocytes partially depleted of monocytes. *Clin. Exp. Immunol.*, **47**, 645–52.

33 Zabala, C. and Lipsky, P.E. (1982). Immunomodulatory effect of bacterial lipopolysaccharide on human B lymphocyte activation in vitro. *J. Immunol.*, **129**, 2496–503.

34 Elmasry, M.N., Fox, E.J., and Rich, R.R. (1986). Opposing immuno-regulatory functions of CD8+ lymphocytes: A requirement for monocytes in suppressor cell induction. *J. Immunol.*, **137**, 2468–77.

35 Zembala, M., Uracz, W., Ruggiero, I., Mytar, B., and Pryjma, J. (1984). Isolation and functional characteristics of FcR+ and FcR− human monocyte subsets. *J. Immunol.*, **133**, 1293–9.

36 Ohkawa, S., Martin, L.N., Fukunishi, Y., and Gormus, B.J. (1987). Regulatory role of FcR+ and FcR− monocyte subsets in *Mycobacterium leprae* induced lymphoproliferative response *in vitro*. *Clin. Exp. Immunol.*, **67**, 43–50.

37 Pryjma, J., Flad, H.D., Gruber, M., and Ernst, M. (1986). Monocyte-T cell interactions in the regulation of polyclonal B cell response. *Scand. J. Immunol.*, **24**, 21–8.

38 Lahat, N., Hornstein, L., Moscona, A.R., Kalderon, N., and Pollack, S. (1985). Monocyte suppressor function in burns: T cell monocyte interaction in mediating suppression. *Immunol. Lett.*, **9**, 43–7.

39 Fox, E.J., Cook, R.G., Lewis, D.E., and Rich, R.R. (1986). Proliferative signals for suppressor T cells. *J. Clin. Invest.*, **78**, 214–20.

40 Elmasry, M.N., Fox, E.J., and Rich, R.R. (1987). Sequential effects of prostaglandins and interferon-γ on differentiation of CD8+ suppressor T cells. *J. Immunol.*, **139**, 688–94.

41 Hirayama, S., Matsuhisha, S., Kikuchi, I., Iochi, M., Okta, N., and Sasazuki, T. (1987). HLA-DQ is epistatic to HLA-DR in controlling the immune response to schistosomal antigen in humans. *Nature*, **327**, 426–30.

42 Krane, S., Dayer, J.M., and Goldring, S.R. (1982). Consideration of possible cellular events in the destructive synovial lesion of rheumatoid arthritis. *Adv. Inflamm. Res.*, **3**, 1–15.

43 Klareskog, L., *et al.* (1982). Immune functions of human synovial cells: phenotypic and T cell regulatory properties of macrophage-like cells that express HLA-DR. *Arthr. Rheum.*, **25**, 488–501.

44 Zembala, M. and Lemmel, E.M. (1980). Inhibitory factor(s) of lymphoproliferation produced by synovial fluid mononuclear cells from rheumatoid arthritis patients: the role of monocytes in suppression. *J. Immunol.*, **125**, 1087–92.

45 Klareskog, L., Holmdahl, R., Rubin, K., Victorin, A., and Lindgren, J.A. (1985). Different populations of rheumatoid adherent cells mediate activation versus suppression of T lymphocyte proliferation. *Arthr. Rheum.*, **28**, 863–72.

46 Dayer, J.M., Robinson, D.R., and Krane, S.H. (1977). Prostaglandin production by rheumatoid synovial cells: stimulation by a factor from human mononuclear cells. *J. Exp. Med.*, **145**, 1399–401.

47 Seitz, M. and Hunstein, W. (1985). Enhanced prostanoid release from monocytes of patients with rheumatoid arthritis and active systemic lupus erythematosus. *Ann. Rheum. Dis.*, **44**, 438–45.

48 Bomalaski, J.S., Clark, M.A., and Zurier, R.B. (1986). Enhanced phospolipase activity in peripheral blood monocytes from patients with rheumatoid arthritis. *Arthr. Rheum.*, **29**, 312–18.

49 Okawa-Takatsuji, M., Aotsuka, S., Uwatoko, S., Yokohari, R., and Nagaki, K. (1988). Monocyte-mediated suppression of rheumatoid factor production in normal subjects. *Clin. Immunol. Immunopath.*, **46**, 195–204.

50 Waalen, K., Foree, O., Teigland, J., and Natvig, J.B. (1987). Human rheumatoid synovial and normal blood dendritic cells as antigen presenting cells—comparison with autologous monocytes. *Clin. Exp. Immunol.*, **70**, 1–9.

51 Burmester, G.R., Hahn, G., Kersten, W., Platzer, E., and Kalden, J.R. (1988). T cell regulation and T cell clones in relation to synovial inflammation *Immunobiology*, **178**, 90–91.

52 Reibnegger, G., *et al.* (1986). Urinary neopterin reflects clinical activity in patients with rheumatoid arthritis. *Arthr. Rheum.*, **29**, 1063–70.

53 Baum, W., *et al.* (1988). Prostaglandin E_2, interleukin-1 and gamma interferon production of mononuclear cells of patients with inflammatory and degenerative joint diseases. *Immunobiology.*, **178**, 88–9.

54 Hirano, T., *et al.* (1988). Excessive production of interleukin-6/B cell stimulatory factor-2 in rheumatoid arthritis. *Eur. J. Immunol.*, **18**, 1797–801.

55 Steven, M.M., Lennie, S.E., Sturrock, R.D. and Gemmel, C.G.

(1984). Enhanced bacterial phagocytosis by peripheral blood monocytes in rheumatoid arthritis. *Ann. Rheum Dis.*, **43**, 435–9.

56 Simmons, K.M., Brown, K.A., Kirk, A.P., Perry, J.D. and Dumonde, D.C. (1987). Enhanced chemotaxis of monocytes in rheumatoid arthritis. *Br. J. Rheum.*, **26**, 245–50.

57 Parris, T.M., Kimberly, R.P., Iman, R.D., McDougal, J.S., Gibofsky, A., and Christian, C.L. (1982). Defective Fc receptor-mediated function of the mononuclear phagocyte system in lupus nephritis. *Ann. Intern. Med.*, **9**, 526–32.

58 Kimberly, R.P., Meryhew, N.L., and Runquist, O.A. (1986). Mononuclear phagocyte function in SLE. I. Bipartite Fc and complement-dependent dysfunction. *J. Immunol.*, **137**, 91–6.

59 Sano, H., Compton, L.J., Shiomi, N., Steinberg, A.P., Jackson, R.A., and Sasaki, T. (1985). Low expression of human histocompatibility leukocyte antigen-DR is associated with hypermethylation of human histocompatibility leukocyte antigen-DRα gene regions in B cells from patients with systemic lupus erythematosus. *J. Clin. Invest.*, **76**, 1314–21.

60 Shirakawa, F., Yamashita, U., and Suzuki, H. (1985). Decrease in HLA-DR positive monocytes in patients with systemic lupus erythematosus. *J. Immunol.*, **134**, 3560–2.

61 Brozek, C.M., Hoffmann, C.L., Savage, S.M. and Searles, R.P. (1988). Systemic lupus erythematosus sera inhibit antigen presentation by macrophages to T cells. *Clin. Immunol. Immunopath.*, **46**, 299–313.

62 Kelley, V.E. and Roths, J.B. (1982). Increase in macrophage Ia expression in autoimmune mice: role of the lpr gene. *J. Immunol.*, **129**, 923–7.

63 Lu, C.Y. and Unanue, E.R. (1982). Spontaneous T-cell lymphokine production and enhanced macrophage Ia expression and tumoricidal activity in MRL-lpr mice. *Clin. Immunol. Immunopath.*, **25**, 213–21.

64 Jandal, R.C., George, J.L., Silberstein, D.S., Eaton, R.B., and Shur, P.H. (1987). The effect of adherent cell derived factors on immunoglobulin and anti-DNA synthesis in systemic lupus erythematosus. *Clin. Immunol. Immunopath.*, **42**, 344–52.

65 Sasaki, T., Shibata, S., Hirabayashi, Y., Sekiguchi, Y., and Yoshinaga, K. (1989). Accessory cell activity of monocytes in anti-DNA antibody production in systemic lupus erythematosus. *Clin. Exp. Immunol.*, **77**, 37–42.

66 Alcocer-Varella, J., Laffon, A., and Alarcon-Segovia, D. (1983). Defective monocyte production of, and T. lymphocyte response to, interleukin-1 in the peripheral blood of patients with systemic lupus erythematosus. *Clin. Exp. Immunol.*, **54**, 125–32.

67 Muryoi, I., Sasaki, T., Sekiguchi, Y., Tamate, E., Takai, I., and

Yoshinaga, K. (1989). Impaired accessory cell function of monocytes in systemic lupus erythematosus. *J. Clin. Lab. Immunol.*, **28**, 123–8.

68 Shirakawa, F., Yamashita, Y., and Suzuki, H. (1985). Reduced function of HLA-DR positive monocytes in patients with systemic lupus erythematosus. *J. Clin. Immunol.*, **5**, 396–401.

69 Laughter, A.A., Lidsky, M.D., and Twomey, J.J. (1979). Suppression of immunoglobulin synthesis by monocytes in health and in patients with systemic lupus erythematosus. *Clin. Immunol. Immunopath.*, **14**, 435–44.

70 Joseph, A.M., Michael, D.L., and Laszlo, F. (1980). Suppressor monocytes in patients with systemic lupus erythematosus. Evidence of suppressor activity associated with a cell-free soluble product of monocytes. *J. Lab. Clin. Med.*, **95**, 140–52.

71 Gordon, F.B., Clifford, L.L., and Ian, H.F. (1982). Spontaneous reverse hemolytic plaque formation. III. Monocyte-mediated suppression of elevated plaque formation in autoimmune diseases. *Clin. Immunol. Immunopath.*, **24**, 386–93.

72 Weil, B.J. and Renoux, M.L. (1988). Mononuclear phagocytes from patients with active systemic lupus erythematosus down-regulate the specific *in vitro* reactivity of autologous lymphocytes to double-stranded DNA. *Clin. Exp. Immunol.*, **72**, 43–51.

73 Cohen, P.L., Litvin, D.A., and Winfield, J.B. (1982). Association between endogenously activated T cells and immunoglobulin secreting B cells in patients with active systemic lupus erythematosus. *Arthr. Rheum.*, **25**, 168–75.

74 Van Elven, E.H., Van Der Veenm, F.M., Rolink, A.G., Issa, P., Duin, T.N., and Gleichman, E. (1981). Disease caused by reaction of T. lymphocytes to incompatible structures of the major histocompatibility complex. *J. Immunol.*, **127**, 2435–40.

75 Eisenberg, R.A. and Cohen, P.L. (1983). Class II major histocompatibility antigens and the etiology of systemic lupus erythematosus. *Clin. Immunol. Immunopath.*, **29**, 1–10.

76 Boswell, J. and Schur, P.H. (1989). Monocyte function in systemic lupus erythematosus. *Clin. Immunol. Immunopath.*, **52**, 271–8.

77 Potter, S.R., Bienenstock, J., Lee, P., Wilkinson, S., and Buchanan, W.W. (1984). Clinical associations of fibroblast growth promoting factor in scleroderma. *J. Rheum.*, **11**, 43–7.

78 Kahaleh, M.B. and LeRoy, E.C. (1986). Effect of scleroderma serum on human fibroblast collagen production: possible selection through proliferation. *J. Rheum.*, **13**, 99–102.

79 Pruzanski, W., Lee, P., Willshire, A., (1983). Lymphocytotoxic and phagocytotoxic activity in progressive systemic sclerosis. *J. Rheum.*, **10**, 55–60.

80 Sandborg, C.I., Berman, M.A., Andrews, B.S., and Friou, G.J.

(1985). Interleukin-1 production by mononuclear cells from patients with scleroderma. *Clin. Exp. Immunol.*, **60**, 294–302.

81 Alcocer-Varela, J., Martinez-Cordera, E., and Alarcon-Segovia, D. (1985). Spontaneous production of, and defective response to, interleukin-1 by peripheral blood mononuclear cells from patients with scleroderma. *Clin. Exp. Immunol.*, **59**, 666–72.

82 Berman, M.A., Sandborg, C.I., Calabia, B.S., Andrews, B.S., and Friou, G.J. (1986). Studies of an interleukin-1 inhibitor: characterization and clinical significance. *Clin. Exp. Immunol.*, **64**, 136–45.

83 Krawitt, E.L., Holdstock, G., Bland, J.H., Chastenay, B.F., and Albertini, R.J. (1982). Suppressor cell activity in progressive systemic sclerosis. *J. Rheum.*, **9**, 263–7.

84 Segond, P., Salliere, D., Galanaud, P., Desmottes, R.M., Massios, P., and Flessinger, J.N. (1982). Impaired primary in vitro antibody response in progressive systemic sclerosis patients. Role of suppressor monocytes. *Clin. Exp. Immunol.*, **47**, 147–54.

85 Lockshin, M.D., Markenson, J.A., Fuzesi, L., Kazanjian-Aram, S.. Joachim, C., and Ordene, M. (1983). Monocyte induced inhibition of lymphocyte response to phytohaemagglutinin in progressive systemic sclerosis. *Ann. Rheum. Dis.*, **42**, 40–4.

86 Morse, J.H. and Bodi, B.S. (1982). Autologous and allogeneic mixed lymphocyte reactions in progressive systemic sclerosis. *Arthr. Rheum.*, **25**, 390–5.

87 Andrews, B.S., Friou, G.J., Berman, M.A., Sandborg, C.I., Mirick, G.R., and Cesario, T.C. (1987). Changes in circulating monocytes in patients with progressive systemic sclerosis. *J. Rheum.*, **14**, 930–5.

88 Grumet, F.C. (1983). HLA and disease. *Clin. Immunol. Rev.*, **2**, 123–5.

89 Botazzo, G.F., Pujol-Borell, R., Hanafusa, T., and Feldmann, M. (1983). Role of aberrant HLA-DR expression and antigen presentation in induction of endocrine autoimmunity. *Lancet*, **2**, 1115–18.

90 Jansson, R., Karlsson, A., and Forsum, W. (1984) intrathyroidal HLA-DR expression and T. lymphocyte phenotypes in Grave's thrytoxicosis, Hashimoto's thyroiditis and nodular colloid goiter. *Clin. Exp. Immunol.*, **58**, 264–72.

91 Matsunaga, M., Eguchi, K., Fukuda, T., Ito, K., and Nagataki, S. (1986). Class II major histocampatibility complex antigen expression and cellular interactions in thyroid glands of Grave's diseae. *J. Clin. Endocrinol. Metab.*, **62**, 723–8.

92 Davies. T.F. (1985). Cocultures of human thyroid monolayer cells and autologous T cells: impact of HLA class II antigen expression *J. Clin. Endocrinol. Metab.*, **64**, 418–22.

93 Khoury, E.L., Greenspan, J.S., and Greenspan, F.S. (1988). Ectopic expression of HLA class II antigens on thyriod follicular cells: Induc-

tion and transfer *in vitro* by autologous mononuclear leukocytes. *J. Clin. Endocrinol. Metab.*, **67**, 992–6.

94 Cohen, S.B. and Weetman, A.P. (1988). Activated interstitial and intraepithelial thyroid lymphocytes in autoimmune thyroid disease. *Acta endocrinol.*, **119**, 161–6.

95 Ishikawa, N., Eguchi, K., Otsubo, T., Tezuka, H., Ito, K., and Nagataki, S. (1987). The remarkable reduction in suppressor-inducer T-cell subset and increment in helper T-cell subset in thyroid tissues from patients with Grave's disease. *J. Clin. Endocrinol. Metab.*, **67**, 992–6.

96 Otsubo, T., *et al.* (1988). *In vitro* cellular interactions among patients with Grave's disease. *Acta Endocrinol.*, **117**, 287–8.

97 Eguchi, T., *et al.* (1988). Synergy in antigen presentaton by thyroid epithelial cells and monocytes from patients with Grave's disease. *Clin. Exp. Immunol.*, **72**, 84–90.

98 Zeki, K., *et al.* (1989). Circulating monocyte (macrophage)-specific antibodies in patients with autoimmune thyroid diseases. *Clin. Endocrinol.*, **31**, 1–13.

99 Fournier, C., Chen, H., Leger, A., and Charreire, J. (1983). Immunological studies of autoimmune thyroid disorders: abnormalities in the inducer T-cell subset and proliferative responses to autologous and allogeneic stimulation. *Clin. Exp. Immunol.*, **54**, 539–46.

100 Canonica, G.W., *et al.* (1984). Deficiency of the autologous mixed lymphocyte reaction in patients with autoimmune thyroid disease. *Intl. Arch. Allergy Appl. Immunol.*, **73**, 137–40.

101 Bagnasco, M., Ciprandi, G., Orlandini, A., Torre, G., Canonica, G.W., and Giordano, G. (1985). Autologous mixed lymphocyte reaction in Grave's disease: relationship to clinical status. *Acta Endocrinol.*, **110**, 366–72.

102 Baxevanis, C.N., Reclos, G.J., Sfagos, C., Doufexis, E., Papageorgiou, C., and Papamichail, M. (1987). Multiple sclerosis: I. Monocyte stimulatory defect in mixed lymphocyte reaction is associated with clinical disease activity. *Clin. Exp. Immunol.*, **67**, 362–9.

103 Antel, J.P., Bania, M. B., Reder, A., and Cashman, N. (1986). Activated suppressor cell dysfunction in progressive multiple sclerosis. *J. Immunol.*, **137**, 137–41.

104 Baxevanis, C.N., *et al.* (1989). Decreased expression of HLA-DR antigens on monocytes in patients with multiple sclerosis. *J. Neuroimmunol.*, **22**, 177–83.

105 Baxevanis, C.N., Reclos, G.J., and Papamichail, M. (1990). Decreased HLA-DR antigen expression on monocytes causes impaired suppressor cell activity in multiple sclerosis. *J. Immunol.*, **144**, 4166–71.

106 Waldmann, T.A., Durm, M., Broder, S., Blackman, M., Blaese,

R.M., and Strober, W. (1974). Role of suppressor T cells in pathogenesis of common variable hypogammaglobulinemia. *Lancet*, **2**, 609–13.

107 Eibl, M.M., Mannhalter, J.W., Zielinski, C.C., and Ahmad, R. (1982). Defective macrophage T-cell interaction in common variable immunodeficiency. *Clin. Immunol. Immunopathol.*, **22**, 316–22.

108 Eibl, M.M., *et al.* (1982). Defective macrophage function in a patient with common variable immunodeficiency. *N. Eng. J. Med.*, **307**, 803–6.

109 Eibl, M.M., Zielinski, C.C., and Mannhalter, J.W. (1983). Macrophage function in common variable immunodeficiency. *N. Eng. J. Med.*, **308**, 286–7.

110 Arala-Chaves, M.P., Korn, J.H., Gabraith, G.M.P., Porto, M.T., Smith, C.L., and Fudenberg, H.H. (1982). Effects of thymosin and evidence of monocyte suppression of both T and B cell functions in two cases of common variable immunodeficiency. *Scand. J. Immunol.*, **15**, 97–104.

111 Pollack, S., Reisner, Y., Koziner, B., Good, R.A., and Hoffmann, M.K. (1985). B cell function in common variable immunodeficiency: suppression of *in vitro* anti-sheep erythrocytes antibody production by T cells and monocytes. *Immunology*, **54**, 86–9.

112 Krantman, H.J., Saxon, A., Stevens, R.H., and Stiehm, E.R. (1981). Phenotypic heterogeneity in X-linked infantile agammaglobulinemia with *in vitro* monocyte suppression of immunoglobulin synthesis. *Clin. Immunol. Immunopath.*, **20**, 170–8.

113 Fiedler, W., *et al.* (1987). T cell activation defect in common variable immunodeficiency: Restoration by PMA or allogeneic macrophages. *Clin. Immunol. Immunopath.*, **44**, 206–18.

114 Ceuppens, J.L., Meurs, L., and Van Wauwe, J.P. (1985). Failure of OKT3 monoclonal antibody to induce lymphocyte mitogenesis: A familial defect in monocyte helper function. *J. Immunol.*, **134**, 1498–1502.

115 Segal, A.W., *et al.* (1983). Absence of cytochrome b-245 in chronic granulomatous disease. *N. Eng. J. Med.*, **308**, 245–51.

116 Segal, A.W., Heyworth, P.F., Cockcroft, S., and Barrowman, M.M. (1985). Stimulated neutrophils from patients with autosomal recessive chronic granulomatous disease fail to phosphorylate a Mr-44, **000** Protein. *Nature*, **316**, 547–9.

117 Donowitz, G.R. and Mandell, G.L. (1982). Monocyte function in patients with chronic granulomatous disease of childhood. *Blood*, **60**, 1151–8.

118 Heijnen, C.J., Van der Meer, J.W.M., and Zegers, B.J.M. (1986). Altered antigen presentation in the induction of the *in vitro* antigen

specific helper cell function in patients with chronic granulomatous disease. *Clin. Exp. Immunol.*, **66**, 111–17.

119 Snyderman, R., Alman, L.C., Frankel, A., and Blease, R.M. (1973). Defective mononuclear leukocyte chemotaxis: A previously unrecognized immune dysfunction. *Ann. Int. Med.*, **78**, 509–13.

120 Komiyama, A. *et al.* (1988). Defective interleukin-1 production in a familial monocyte disorder with a combined abnormality of mobility and phagocytosis-killing. *Clin. Exp. Immunol.*, **73**, 500–4.

121 Remold-O'Donnell, E., Zimmerman, C., Kenney, D., and Rosen, F.R. (1987). Expression on blood cells of sialophorin, the surface glycoprotein that is defective in Wiskott–Aldrich syndrome. *Blood*, **70**, 104–9.

122 Nong, Y.H., Remold-O'Donell, E., and Remold, H.G. (1988). Sialophorin, a major surface glycoprotein of human monocytes, is involved in the activation of human monocytes. *FASEB J.*, **2**, A684,

123 Blease, R.M., Muchmore, A.V., Lawrence, E.C., and Poplack, D.G. (1980). The cytolytic effector function of monocytes in immunodeficiency diseases. In *Primary immunodeficiencies* (ed. M. Selligmann and R. Hitzig), pp. 319–98. Elsevier, Amsterdam.

124 Altman, L.C., Snyderman, R., and Blease, R.M. (1974). Abnormalities of chemotactic lymphokine synthesis and monocyte leukocyte chemotaxis in Wiskott–Aldrich syndrome. *J. Clin. Invest.*, **54**, 486–93.

125 Remold-O'Donnell, E. and Rosen, F.S. (1990). Sialophorin (CD43) and the Wiskott–Aldrich syndrome. *Immunodef. Rev.*, **2**, 151–74.

126 Griscelli, C., Lisowska-Grospierre, B., and Mach, B. (1989). Combined immunodeficiency with defective expression in MHC class II genes. *Immunodef. Rev.*, **1**, 135–53.

127 Reith, W., *et al.* (1988). Congenital immunodeficiency with a regulatory defect in MHC class II gene expression lacks a specific HLA-DR promoter binding protein RF-X. *Cell*, **53**, 897–906.

128 Springer, T.A., Thompson, W.S., Schmalsteig, F.C., Miller, L.J., and Anderson, D.C. (1984). Inherited deficiency of the MAC-1, LFA-1, p150,95 glycoprotein family and its molecular basis. *J. Exp. Med.*, **160**, 1901–18.

129 Anderson, D.C., *et al.* (1985). The severe and moderate phenotypes of heritable Mac-1, LFA-1 deficiency: their quantitative definition and relation to leukocyte dysfunction and clinical features. *J. Infect. Dis.*, **152**, 668–89.

130 Bowen, T.J., *et al.* (1982). Severe recurrent bacterial infections associated with defective adherence and chemotaxis in two patients with neutrophils deficient in a cell-associated glycoprotein. *J. Pediat.*, **101**, 932–40.

131 Buescher, E.S., Gaither, T., Nath, J., and Gallin, J.I. (1985). Abnormal adherence-related functions of neutrophils, monocytes, and

Epstein–Barr virus-transformed B cells in a patient with C3bi receptor deficiency. *Blood.*, **65**, 1382–90.

132 Kohl, S., Loo, L.S., Schmalsteig, F.C., and Anderson, D.C. (1986). The genetic deficiency of leukocyte surface glycoprotein Mac-1, LFA-1, p150,95 in humans is associated with defective antibody-dependent cellular cytotoxicity *in vitro* and defective protection against hcrpcs simplcx virus infection *in vivo*. *J. Immunol.*, **137**, 1688–94.

133 Preito, J., Subira, M.L., Castilla, A., Civeira, M.P., and Serrano, M. (1990). Monocyte disorder causing cellular immunodeficiency: a family study. *Clin. Exp. Immunol.*, **79**, 1–6.

134 Yamazaki, M., Yasui, H., Kawai, H., Miyagawa, Y., Komiyama, A., and Akabane, T. (1984). A monocyte disorder in siblings with chronic candidiasis: A combined abnormality of monocyte mobility and phagocytosis-killing ability. *Am. J. Dis. Child.*, **138**, 192–5.

135 Komiyama, A., *et al.* (1988). Defective intcrlcukin-1 production in a familial monocyte disorder with a combined abnormality of motility and phagocytosis-killing. *Clin. Exp. Immunol.*, **73**, 500–4.

136 Gallin, J.I., Klimerman, J.A., Padgett, G.A., and Wolff, S.M. (1975). Defective mononuclear leukocyte chemotaxis in the Chediak–Higashi syndrome of humans, mink, and cattle. *Blood.*, **45**, 863–70.

137 Komiyama, A., Saitoh, H., Yamazaki, M., Kawai, H., and Miyagawa, Y. (1986). Hyperactive phagocytosis by circulating neutrophils and monocytes in Chediak–Higashi syndrome. *Scand. J. Haematol.*, **37**, 162–7.

8 Macrophages in tumour immunity

R.C. REES and H. PARRY

1   Introduction

In attempting to understand the involvement of mononuclear phagocytes in the pathogenesis of malignant disease, it is essential to consider the diversity of phenotypic expression which allows these cells to manifest such a wide variety of biological responses. Cells of the monocyte/macrophage lineage clearly contribute to the generation of antigen-specific immunity, as well as mediating several effector functions using a number of different pathways. Interest in macrophages as antitumour effector cells stems from observations demonstrating their recruitment into tumours, and their capacity to mediate cytotoxic and cytostatic responses towards tumour cells *in vitro*. This, however, is only one facet of their potential influence on tumour growth and survival, and they are now recognized to be important producers of cytokines and growth factors which not only influence immunity, but also provide growth promoting and regulatory signals for cells other than immune effectors, such as stromal cells and the neoplastic cell population itself. Many of the factors produced by mononuclear phagocytes potentiate immunity, whereas other molecules mediate immune suppression. As with other cells possessing multiple functions, monocytes and macrophages are influenced by their micro-environment, their position relative to other cells, and soluble factors which regulate biological function. The tumour melieu provides a unique situation where macrophages potentially have the capacity to influence the pathogenesis and growth/survival of tumours.

In the following sections we will examine the various facets of monocyte/macrophage function likely to be important in their activity during malignant disease, and consider ways in which their potential antitumour properties may be harnessed to combat human malignancy.

2   Origin of mononuclear phagocytic cells

This has already been discussed in full in Chapter 1 and will, therefore, only be described briefly here. Originating from bone marrow stem cells (1) monoblasts and promonocytes differentiate into monocytes which rapidly enter the circulation and extravasate into tissues within a four-day period. The tissue environment predicts the maturation and differentiation sequence, giving rise to phenotypically and morphologically distinct subpopulations (2). Such heterogeneity is illustrated by differences in their ultrastructure and cytochemistry, and particularly peroxidase activity (PA) which is important in determining their activation and maturation status (3,4). During inflammation, for example, PA is detected in the primary lysosomes, whereas mature peritoneal macrophages show PA in the nuclear envelop and rough endoplasmic reticulum. Macrophages colonize the liver (Kupffer cells), lungs (alveolar–interstitial macrophages), spleen, lymph nodes, thymus, gut, marrow, brain, connective tissue, and serous cavities and are clearly capable of mediating diverse biological functions, which are largely dependent on environmental influences.

The relationship of dendritic cells (DC) to monocytes and macrophages is unclear, although evidence suggests that divergence of these cell types occur in bone marrow. Culture of human peripheral blood monocytes in the absence of serum for eight days gives rise to cells which can be identified as DC, whereas in the presence of serum, macrophages are derived. DC are also phentotypically heterogenous, and depending on their location, i.e. blood, tissues or lymph nodes, they may express differing characteristics, some of which are shared with macrophages, for example, the expression of FcR and CR1 on Langerhans cells found in the dermis. Extensive characterization of DC isolated from the tonsils, thymus, synovium, and blood has been undertaken (5–11).

3   Monocyte differentiation and activation: regulation by proto-oncogenes

Activation signals which trigger myeloid cell differentiation appear to be controlled by an orchestrated series of genetically controlled events, some of which have been recently documented. It is interesting to note that the genes we know most about, are the normal cellular counterparts to oncogenes, which are intimately involved in cell transformation.

It is now clear that the transforming viral genes of both DNA and RNA tumour viruses are derived from normal cellular genes (referred to as proto-oncogenes) which regulate, in a systematic way, the normal cellular events during embryogenesis and the differentiation and activation pathways in normal (adult) cells. The abnormal expression of cellular oncogenes occurs

Table 8.1   Oncogenes associated with monocyte differentiation

Oncogene	Encodes for:	Stage of differentiation
c-*fos*	Nuclear-binding protein	Constitutive expression
c-*myc*	Nuclear-binding protein	Transient: early expression
c-*myb*	Nuclear-binding protein	Transient: early expression
c-*sis*	PDGF β-chain	Late events
c-*fms*	M-CSF receptor (membrane-associated tyrosine kinase activity)	Late events
c-*src*	Involved in signal transduction (membrane associated tyrosine kinase activity)	Late events

as a result of translocational or mutational events occurring in the nucleus, the irregular expression of oncogene products being clearly linked with various stages of tumour development. Although progress in oncogene research has been rapid, the dissection of the molecular events leading to oncogenesis remains incomplete. Differentiation of monomyelocytic cells involves the expression of several oncogenes, as demonstrated in studies using established myeloid cell lines. It has been shown that the WEHI 3B murine myeloid leukaemia and the U937 promonocytic cell line undergo macrophage differentiation *in vitro* in response to G-CSF and PMA respectively (12,13), and the human promyelocytic cell line HL-60 can differentiate to granulocyte or monocyte/macrophage lineage depending on the stimulant applied (14).

From studies of these systems it is known that a set of proto-oncogenes (c-*fos*, c-*myc*, c-*myb*) are expressed early in differentiation, whereas other proto-oncogenes (c-*fms*, c-*src*, c-*sis*) are activated later, and related to the acquisition of cellular functions associated with differentiation (Table 8.1).

Although the c-*fos* product is constitutively expressed during differentiation, c-*myc* and c-*myb* are only transiently activated; all three proto-oncogenes encode for nuclear binding proteins of unknown function. These genes are associated with the terminal differentiation of myelmonocytic cells; c-*fos* undergoes rapid activation in cells (HL-60 and U937) exposed to the phorbol ester, PMA, and is involved in cell proliferation in response to growth factors (15,16). With HL-60 differentiation following interferon (IFN) stimulation, c-*fos* and c-*fms* expression occurs later and appears to be associated with markers of maturation (17). Also, in some differentiation studies, c-*fos* activation occurs as an early or late event, depending on the mode of activation. For example, HL-60 cells respond to PMA producing c-*fos* mRNA within 15 minutes, whereas CSF-1 can induce c-*fos* in quiescent, terminally differentiated macrophages. Freshly isolated circulating monocytes and tissue macrophages express high levels of c-*fos*, although differentiation of monocyte precursors can occur in the absence of c-*fos* expression, as shown by the ability of cells to differentiate in the presence of a protein kinase C inhibitor which prevents c-*fos* expression (18).

Activation of monocytes, for example with lipopolysaccharide (LPS), induces a rapid c-*fos* response, after which the cells become refractory to further stimulation with the same agent (19). This also occurs with other cell types, such as natural killer (NK) cells activated with interleukin-2 (IL-2), (20). Despite the available information, we do not, as yet, have a clear understanding, with the possible exception of growth factor receptors encoded by c-*sis* and c-*fms*, of the role of proto-oncogenes and their significance in cell differentiation and activation.

4   Macrophage activation factors and MHC antigen expression

Monocytes and macrophages can become activated to mediate bacteriocidal and tumouricidal effects, as for example, happens during bacterial infection as a result of exposure to LPS and cytokines released by other leucocytes. Monocytes thereafter secrete their own range of cytokines which, in turn, regulate the production of activation molecules by other cell types.

The most widely studied cytokine mediating monocyte activation is interferon-gamma (IFNγ). This is the best characterized of the macrophage-activating factors, possessing, as its name suggests, antiviral as well as immunodulatory activity. This 55 kDa glycoprotein is produced by T-cells and NK cells, and activates monocytes after interaction with its specific receptor site, or when introduced into cells in liposomes or by micro-injection (21,22).

During a period in culture monocytes express IFNγ receptors of two different affinities. Interferon-alpha (IFNα) can compete for the high affinity receptor and thereby inhibit the action of IFNγ (23). Consequences of IFNγ activation of monocytes include the induction of IL-2 receptors (24), Fc RI receptors and the secretion of prostaglandins (25,26). Cultured monocytes also express Fc RIII in response to IFNγ (27). Of particular importance is the selective activation of genes encoding the integrin molecule, LFA-1, (CR3 and p150,95 are not induced), which is principally involved in monocyte adhesion and aggregation, the development of multi-nucleated giant cells, and granuloma formation (28).

The expression of MHC Class I and II molecules at the cell surface is increased by IFNγ and IFNα. These proteins are determining factors in antigen presentation and MHC Class I restricted T-cell cytotoxicity (29–31). Another important consequence of IFNγ activation is the increase in respiratory burst and the production of reactive oxygen radicals, which are capable of mediating cell toxicity. In addition, IL-1, CSF-1, and G-CSF are produced in response to IFNγ.

Several other cytokines have been reported to cause monocyte activation, the best known being GM-CSF, CSF-1, TNFα, and IL-2 (32,37). Monocyte activators, other than these, have been reported, but as yet are not fully characterized (38–40). The tumouricidal activity induced is most probably mediated through the production of TNFα (33–37). Thus, several features of monocyte activation lead some investigators to conclude that positive and negative feedback loops regulate this process. For example, IFNγ, and in some cases GM-CSF and CSF-1, induce the synthesis of TNFα, which results in TNFα further stimulating its own production as well as that of IL-1. IL-1 is capable of inducing the further expression of TNFα, and causing lymphocytes to express IL-2 receptors and to secrete IL-2. Further production of IFNγ by lymphocytes increases monocyte activation, whereas prostaglandin released by monocytes, as a consequence of either TNFα or IL-1 interaction, serves as a negative control signal.

5   Monocyte/macrophage-derived cytokines: production and relevance to tumour biology

Monocytes and macrophages provide important activation signals for the development of immunity and cell growth via the production of a range of cytokines (including various growth factors). Before we address the possible significance of these molecules to tumour growth regulation or cytolysis, consideration will be given to the main factors released by monocytes/ macrophages. Some of the cytokines produced act in an autocrine fashion, and influence monocyte/macrophage responses, while also having an effect on other cells of lymphoid and non-lymphoid origin. The main cytokines produced by mononuclear phagocytic cells are IL-1, IL-6, TNFα, and CSFs (see Chapter 1). Monocytes and macrophages are not the only cells which produce these cytokines, and our discussion below will also include reference to alternative mechanisms of production and action of these molecules.

5.1   IL-1, TNFα, and IL-6

The orchestrated series of events involving IL-1 are primarily responsible for combating the invasion of the body by pathogenic organisms, and prevent the spread of infection. However, many of the properties ascribed to this molecule may be equally important in neoplastic disease.

Two forms of IL-1 exist, and are encoded by genes located on chromosome two. Despite physical and chemical differences between the α and β forms, they mediate similar functions and associate with the same receptor(s). Both IL-1α and IL-1β have been cloned (41,42), and the recombinant proteins found to exhibit the same biological effects as the native molecules; namely, endogenous pyrogen, lymphocyte activation factor activity and the induction of acute phase proteins. Both forms are produced as large molecular weight precursors which are cleaved to a 23 kDa molecule, and secreted in a 17.5 kDa form. IL-1β is the predominant form found in activated moncytes, and up to 5 per cent of the total messenger-RNA of the cell may code for IL-1β; at least 10-fold less IL-1α message is produced in activated monocytes. IL-1β is the major secreted form, whereas IL-1α predominantly functions as a membrane-bound cytokine (43,44). Both a high (80 kDa) and low (67 kDa) affinity receptor for IL-1 exists (45).

Important properties of IL-1 with regard to tumour biology relate to its ability to increase the binding of NK cells to their tumour target cells, and to promote in a synergistic way the biological effects of IL-2, in particular the induction of lymphokine activated killer (LAK) activity, which is mediated through the activation of LGL-NK or T-cell precursors (44,46).

Upon exposure to IL-1, activated T-cells secrete IL-2 and express high affinity IL-2 receptors, which results in cell proliferation, and in the case of antigen-specific T-cells, the clonal expansion of immunoreactive cells. IL-1 is also a potent chemotactic factor for CD3+ T-cells, and if produced within the micro-environment of solid tumours, constitutes a mechanism whereby T-cell infiltration may occur.

Another major cytokine produced by monocytes and macrophages is TNFα, the human form of which is a non-glycosylated 17.3 kDa protein, which occurs naturally as a dimer or trimer, in either secreted or membrane-bound forms (47). Both TNFα and TNFβ (also known as lymphotoxin) genes are located adjacent to the genes encoding for MHC antigens, on chromosome 6 in man and 17 in the mouse (48–51). The TNF genes have been cloned and expressed in *Escherichia coli* (52,53) and this has allowed extensive studies to be conducted into their biological effects.

The production of TNFα by macrophages requires activation (54), and it is able to mediate a wide range of biological activity. TNFα has been linked with septic shock in patients with menningococcal septicaemia (55), although its ability to protect against bacterial, viral, and parasitic infections are clearly situations where TNFα production is beneficial (56), (see also earlier chapters of this volume). TNFα synthesis is positively regulated by several substances, including PMA, LPS, Interleukins 1 and 2, IFNγ, and TNFα itself (54,57–60). Other agents, such as glutocorticoids, prostaglandins, IL-4, TGFβ, and inhibitors of protein kinase C decrease the production of TNFα protein and mRNA. Most cells constitutively express TNFα receptors (usually present at between 10^{-3} to 10^{-4} receptors per cell), but these may be increased on some cells upon IFNγ activation.

A major effect of TNFα is selective toxicity towards certain tumours (61), and studies suggest that the effector pathway for this cytokine is through the activation of protein kinase C, and that GTP-binding proteins may be involved in TNFα cytotoxicity (62,63). TNFα also exhibits growth promoting activity on fibroblasts, T- and B-cells, and melanocytes, and plays an extensive role in the differentiation and activation of cells of the immune system (Table 8.2). An important property of TNFα is its ability to induce MHC Class I antigen expression, and to synergize with IFNγ in the induction of Class I and II MHC products (64–66).

The regulation of MHC antigens is a critical event in the induction and effector phases of the immune response to foreign antigens, regulating antigen presentation to T-cells via Class II determinants, and restricting antigen-specific cytotoxic T-cell killing through MHC Class I molecules. The ability of TNFα to stimulate the production of GM-CSF and IL-6 is indicative of its possible role in haematopoiesis, and other effects include the stimulation of bone resorption, inhibition of new bone formation, the

Table 8.2   Immune responses mediated by TNFα

Proliferation
  T-cells
  B-cells

Activation
  Neutrophils
  Eosinophils
  Macrophages
  Large granular lymphocytes
  Natural killer cells

Growth factor/cytokine induction
  IFNγ
  IFNγ
  IL-1
  GM-CSF
  IL-6
  PDGF

Induction of MHC antigens
  Class I and II

Increases cell adhesion
  Increases inflammatory cell
  adhesion to endothelial cells

induction of collagenases and prostaglandins in rheumatoid joints, and the ability to regulate gelatinase production from human melanoma cells (67–69). Further evidence infers that TNFα mediates tumour cell invasiveness and metastasis *in vivo*, and that cancer cells of epithelial origin produce TNFα (F.R. Balkwill and S. Malik, personal communication). Clearly, TNFα is likely to be at the forefront of the biological consequences of macrophage activation, but the pleiotropic nature of this cytokine has meant that the role played by this factor in the pathogenesis of malignant disease is currently being viewed with caution.

IL-6 is a multifunctional cytokine located on chromosome 7 (70), and is influential in regulating the functions of B- and T-cells and monocytes, as well as other non-lymphoid cells. This 26 kDa protein has previously been termed B-cell-stimulating factor 2, interferon-β2, hybridoma/ plasmocytoma growth factor, and hepatocyte stimulating factor; these biological activities were subsequently shown to be mediated by IL-6 (71,72). G-CSF appears to share sequence homology with IL-6, and both monocytes and macrophages, as well as T- and B-cells and certain tumour cell lines, release IL-6 upon stimulation. Endothelial cells, keratinocytes, fibroblasts, and some tumour and monocyte cell lines constitutively release IL-6. IL-6 acts on B-cells as a differentiation and growth factor, and on T-cells it can act as a co-signal for IL-2 production and promote the proliferation of activated T-cells (73,74). Synergistic effects of IL-6 and IL-2 in the induction of LAK activity have been reported (75), and together with IL-3, IL-6 causes stem cell proliferation and monocyte activation (76,77). The presence of IL-6 may be necessary in the development of antitumour immune responses, and its disregulation may be responsible, in part, for the development of several human disease states (78). It has been shown that IL-6 is an essential autocrine growth factor for human myeloma cells (79), which express both IL-2 and IL-6 receptors.

In vivo, IL-6 may reach appreciable serum levels, and cancer patients may produce excessive amounts during therapy with IL-2 (R.C. Rees, unpublished results). The exact significance of this elevated production of IL-6 has not yet been established.

5.2   Colony-stimulating factors (CSFs)

Many cell types produce CSFs, although monocytes only release these upon activation. For example, IFNγ, GM-CSF, TNFα, and IL-3 cause the release of M-CSF from monocytes, whereas GM-CSF is produced upon activation with LPS (80–84). CSFs promote the growth of myeloid lineage cells in a highly specific and organized manner. Progenitor cells which will eventually differentiate to form monocytes and macrophages are regulated by M-CSF, GM-CSF, and IL-3 (85,86), although other cytokines and growth factors, for example, IL-1,4,6, and TGFβ, act synergistically to enhance the response. M-CSF (CSF-1) is a homodimeric glycoprotein required for mononuclear phagocyte growth, also acting as a survival factor and co-factor in macrophage differentiation. The M-CSF receptor is encoded by the c-*fms* proto-oncogene which has intrinsic tyrosine kinase activity. Alteration in the receptor coding sequences can result in altered activity of the receptor and a persistent signal for cell growth (87).

The response of monocytes and macrophages to activation by M-CSF and GM-CSF is complex, and may be different for these two cell types. Some of the main features of these responses is given in Table 8.3.

5.3   Macrophage-derived growth factors

Tumour cells requiring growth factors for sustained cell division, may obtain these in an autocrine manner, from adjacent tumour cells, or host immune cells. Because of the capacity of mononuclear phagocytes to produce such a wide range of growth-promoting factors, a different, and more sinister role may be ascribed to these cells. It is now clear that macrophages exhibit

Table 8.3 Responses of monocytes and macrophages to CSFs

Response to M-CSF
    Production of cytokines (IFNs, TNFα, G-CSF, IL-1)
    Production of plasminogen activator, ferratin, superoxide anion, acid
    phosphatase
    Enhanced antiviral and antibacterial activity
    Induction of tumouricidal activity and chemotaxis
    Suppression of T-cell mitogen response
    Induces replication of HIV

Response to GM-CSF
    Production of cytokines (TNFα, M-CSF).
    Enhances antimicrobial killing and promotes tumouricidal activity
    Induces replication of HIV
    Inhibits IL-2 receptor expression—possibly by PGE_2 production.

growth control over a variety of different cell types via the secretion of peptide growth factors. In addition to IL-1 and TNFα (which have mitogenic activity for smooth muscle cells and fibroblasts), platelet-derived growth factor (PDGF), transforming growth factor α (TGFα), TGFβ, fibroblast growth factor (FGF), and epidermal growth factor (EGF) are important molecules for the regulation of cell growth and are secreted by activated macrophages under certain conditions. Many have chemotactic as well as growth-promoting properties, which influence fibroblast, smooth muscle cell, and endothelial cell responses, and are important in the process of wound healing. However, their ability to influence the growth of tumour cells must be viewed as a facet of their behaviour which could be potentially detrimental to the host.

Although we know very little about the behaviour of intra-tumour macrophages and the manner in which they may alter tumour cell growth, their capacity to produce factors capable of inducing tumour cell proliferation leads us to speculate on an alternative role for this tumour-infiltrating cell.

Active growth factors are secreted by blood monocytes as well as tissue macrophages upon *in vitro* or *in vivo* stimulation (88–91). Human alveolar macrophages and blood monocytes secrete PDGF when activated, which has similar properties to the platelet-derived form of PDGF, and competes for the same high affinity receptor (92–94). Such macrophages produce a 16 kDa tissue IGF-1-like molecule, which may be used by some tumour cells as one of several factors involved in proliferation. Whereas PDGF and EGF act on cells by increasing the fraction of cells cycling, IGF-1 changes the G1 exit rate. The basic form of fibroblast growth factor (bFGF) is yet another molecule which may be secreted following macrophage activation (95), and is known to be mitogenic for a variety of tumour cells. Cultured macrophages are also able to secrete TGFα which shares 42 per cent homology with human EGF, and competes for the same receptor (96–98).

TGFβ is recognized as being a potent inhibitor of immune responses, and is known to synergize with EGF and PDGF in promoting anchorage independent growth of normal rat kidney cells and smooth muscle cells (99,100). Transcripts for TGFβ are constitutively expressed in resting monocytes and macrophages, but secretion only occurs upon cell activation (101,102). It is not at present clear how many of the several isoforms of the TGFβ family macrophages produce, but they constitute an important mechanism whereby host immunity is suppressed, and it is likely that this contributes to the immunological anergy (relative unresponsiveness) associated with malignant disease.

6   Adhesion molecule interactions: regulation and function

The integrin superfamily include members which are principally involved in the migration of immunocompetent cells, and the expression of these molecules on monocytes is intimately related to the infiltration of these cells into tumours. These molecules are heterodimeric, possessing a common β-chain and a variable α-subunit (103). CR3 and p150,95 are associated with monocytes and all leukocytes (104,105). The expression of LFA-1, together with HLA Class II molecules, is enhanced by IL-4 (106). LFA-1 is especially interesting as it mediates adhesion, chemotaxis, and phagocytosis of monocytes and macrophages, all of which may be blocked by monoclonal antibodies directed against the common β-subunit (107,108). Other integrins also contribute to monocyte adhesion to endothelial cells, and to phagocytosis (109–111). The ligand for LFA-1 is ICAM-1, which is expressed on endothelial cells and melanoma cells, and acts as the target for cell-to-cell adhesion to occur (112). The adhesion of monocytes to tumour cells is likely to involve the interaction of LFA-1 with ICAM-1, and to a lesser extent by CR3 and p150,95 (113).

TNFα and IL-1 induce ICAM-1 expression on endothelial cells (114,115), and illustrates the complex, but organized, manner by which cytokines regulate the expression of adhesion molecules. The up-regulation of MHC Class II molecules and LFA-1 by IL-4 represents a principle mechanism which enhances the interaction between monocytes and T-cells, thereby increasing the magnitude of the immune response. Bacterial *N*-formyl peptides, C5a (derived from complement activation) and thrombin can also influence monocyte migration, as do growth factors and cytokines released from lymphocytes, neutrophils, platelets, and monocytes themselves. These include TGFβ, PDGF, PF4 (platelet factor 4), TNFα, β, lymphocyte-derived chemotactic factor, GM-CSF, natural killer chemotactic factor, neutrophil-derived chemotactic factor, platelet-activating factor, and leukotriene B4. Thus, positive monocyte migration occurs in response to factors released during inflammation, via a process involving cell adhesion.

7   Tumouricidal activity of macrophages

It has long been believed that macrophages represent one of the first lines of defence against neoplastic cell growth, and both monocytes and macrophages have been shown to have cytotoxic effector function towards tumour cells. although the exact mechanisms are still unclear. Killing is thought to occur through a variety of effector pathways including antigen non-specific cytotoxicity, killing by antitumour antibodies via antibody dependent cell mediated cytotoxicity (ADCC), inhibition of DNA synthesis (116) or mitochondrial respiration (117), release of iron (118) and neutral proteases (119), inhibition of tricarboxylic acid cycle enzyme aconitase (120), and the production of reactive oxygen intermediates (ROI), (121), reactive nitrogen intermediates (RNI), (122), and cytostatic and cytolytic cytokines (119).

It has generally been assumed that macrophages need to be activated to display cytoxic effects on tumour cells, but some studies have shown that this assumption is not necessarily true. Itoh and co-workers (123) recently demonstrated cytolytic activity against fresh melanoma targets by unstimulated peripheral blood monocytes, and others have shown human monocytes and alveolar macrophages to be cytotoxic towards tumour cells without deliberate activation (124). It is debatable whether these effector cells were activated naturally *in vivo* or whether the processing of cells *in vitro* causes sufficient stimulation of their tumouricidal activity.

Activation of macrophages for the cytolysis of tumour cells is a multistep pathway in which responsive macrophages sequentially become primed and triggered by a variety of stimuli (125,126). IFNγ, Poly I:C, MAF, SMAF, and the microbial agents LPS, *Corynebacterium parvum* (CP), and *Listeria monocytogenes* (LM) are all putative macrophage-activating agents for tumouricidal effector function (126–133).

One product of macrophage activation is TNFα, which is known to have direct antitumour effects (119,134), and in low concentrations *in vitro* acts synergistically with either IL-1 or IFNα to cause tumour cell cytostasis (119,134). TNFα release can be triggered by recognition of a tumour cell membrane epitope (135,136). These studies showed that the addition of tumour cell membrane vesicles to macrophages stimulated a rapid doubling of TNFα mRNA, and an almost simultaneous release of high levels of TNFα into the supernatant (135). Distinct cell surface molecules on the cell lines, K562 (46–54 kDa), and Jurkat (32–38 kDa), were found to directly induce TNFα mRNA production and TNFα release by human monocytes (136).

Tumour cells resistant to soluble TNFα cytotoxicity may possess a distinct survival advantage and increased invasive capacity. Other cytokines appear to be responsible for inducing tumour cell resistance to TNFα; IL-1 and -6, for example, can promote tumour resistance. However, membrane-associated TNFα may be a mechanism by which human monocytes are able to effect tumour cytotoxicity for target cells insensitive to soluble TNFα (137–9). Adhesion molecules, such as LFA-1, play an important role in tumour cell cytolysis. Monoclonal antibody directed against the LFA-1 chain inhibit monocyte-mediated killing, but although cell adhesion via LFA-1/ICAM-1 is a prerequisite for membrane bound TNFα cytotoxicity, the exact mechanism required for tumour cell killing has yet to be fully established. Recent findings suggest that internalization of TNFα may have an important intracellular biochemical role in promoting cytolysis as micro-injection of TNFα into murine tumour cell lines, resistant to soluble TNFα, resulted in cell death (140).

Monocytes and macrophages from tumour-bearing animals were found to have an increased capacity for TNFα release *in vitro* and some cancer patients have increased levels of serum TNFα and TNFα mRNA transcripts in peripheral blood monocytes (135). In addition, monocytes from the pleural cavity of lung cancer patients were able to produce appreciably higher quantities of TNFα than allogenic blood monocytes (124). Also, tumour-associated macrophages (TAM) from biopsies of human colorectal adenocarcinoma also had elevated levels of TNFα mRNA and protein (135). In some instances at least, enhanced TNFα production is apparent, but its biological effects will depend on the intrinsic properties of tumour cell type, and the level of TNFα inhibitors present. This is an important area which merits further study. Other cytokine pathways, lead-ing to the destruction or inhibited growth of tumour cells have been reported. Low concentrations of TNFα and IL-1 were shown to synergize to inhibit A375 melanoma cell growth (141), and the mastocytoma cell line, P815, which is resistant to the effects of TNFα and IL-1 alone, can be cytolysed by exposure to TNFα with IFNγ. In addition, IFNγ and IL-1 are themselves anti-proliferative agents for tumour cells (142,143).

The main factor responsible for monocyte- and macrophage-mediated cytolysis of P815 cells has been shown to be reactive nitric oxide (NO) produced during metabolism of L-arginine to NO_2^-/NO_3^- (144–6). There does seem to be a role for reactive nitrite intermediates (RNI) in tumour cell killing by activated macrophage *in vitro* or *in vivo* (122). Monocyte-derived RNI have been found to cause cytostasis and mitochondrial respiratory inhibition in lymphoma cells (145,147), and to mediate tumouricidal activity against M-1 and YAC-1 tumour cells (146). The stable products of the L-arginine pathway, NO_2^- and NO_3^-, were found to be incapable of causing cytostasis under culture conditions, NO_2^- only became cytostatic after mild acidification, which would favour its transformation into nitrogen oxides which have greater toxic reactivity (145).

Reactive oxygen intermediates (ROI) are also known to cause cytolysis of tumour cells. Superoxide is formed by the addition of a single electron to oxygen, superoxide dismutes to form peroxide, which, with the addition of another electron, forms two products: the hydroxyl radical and the hydroxyl anion (148,149). Generation of ROI, especially H_2O_2 in the range of concentrations produced by individual macrophages are involved in the induction of DNA strand breaks in tumour cells (150), and represents an important pathway for monocyte/macrophage tumouricidal activity. As discussed below, other factors enhance or activate monocyte function.

M-CSF is known to enhance the antitimour cytotoxicity of murine macrophages *in vitro* (132,133). Their tumouricidal activity against SK-MEL-28 melanoma cells peaked 72–96 hours after exposure to 1000 U/ml M-CSF (132). Munn (133) found that M-CSF induced ADCC against human melanoma and neuroblastoma cell lines in the presence of murine IgG monoclonal antibodies, and which is mediated through epitopes expressed on the surface of tumour cells. MH134 murine hepatoma expresses the MM antigen on its surface, and experimental data suggests that the loss of this antigen results in enhanced growth and metastasis, and appears to be a direct result of a reduced susceptibility to monocyte-mediated ADCC (151). Cytolysis during ADCC is due to the release of ROI. Tumour cells coated with homologous Ig interact with FcRII, expressed on activated macrophages, to trigger an extracellular cytolytic response. Activated mouse peritoneal macrophages become cytolytic to lymphoma cells sensitized with alloantisera (152) through the secretion of ROI (153). Interestingly, ADCC activation of monocytes was found to be significantly higher in cancer patients than normal healthy controls using a murine monoclonal antibody against human colorectal carcinoma cells (154). This effect may only be apparent *in vitro*, and there is no evidence to suggest that appropriate antitumour antibodies are produced *in vivo* against cell surface antigens of solid human tumours.

An important aspect of monocyte-mediated tumour cell killing is the binding of effector monocytes/macrophages to the tumour target through the Gal/GalNAc macrophage lectin (155). A model for this binding suggests that there is an initial Ca^{2+}-independent and trypsin-insensitive low affinity binding step, which changes, in a time-dependent manner, to a Ca^{2+}- and temperature-dependent and trypsin-sensitive high affinity binding (156,157). An 80 kDa LPS-binding protein expressed on murine monocyte and macrophage has been described by Chen (158), and tumouricidal activity can be abrogated by the addition of antibody against this moiety.

A great many studies have reported the cytotoxic effector function of monocytes and macrophages. Recently, investigations in our laboratory have been initiated to establish the regulatory effects of monocytes on the growth of tumour cell lines derived from human carcinomas. HT29 (a colon adenocarcinoma) and T47D (a breast carcinoma) cell lines were co-cultured across a semi-permeable membrane for six days with enriched, unstimulated human peripheral blood monocytes. This resulted in an enhancement and suppression of the growth rate of HT29 or T47D respectively. This effect was evident over a range of monocyte to target cell ratios from $50:1$ to $1:1$, and $100:1$ to $2:1$ for T47D and HT29 respectively. This study infers that similar effector populations of monocytes can differentially regulate carcinoma cells, and that this is likely to depend on signals which monocytes receive from tumour-derived factors. However, after activation with 500 U/ml IFN-α, monocytes elicit a growth suppression of both HT29 and T47D. The factors responsible for this growth modulation are not known, but candidate molecules include RNI, prostaglandin, and various monocyte-derived cytokines (H. Parry and R.C. Rees, unpublished observations).

8   Tumour-associated macrophages

One central dogma surrounding the role of tumour-associated monocytes and macrophages is that cells of the mononuclear phagocyte lineage infiltrate tumours in relatively high proportions (159,160). However, in spite of their tumouricidal potential, these cells are not necessarily able to erradicate the tumour.

The accumulation of monocytes and macrophages into a tumour may be separated into four main stages. Stage one is characterized by the free accumulation and random distribution of macrophages within the micro-tumour mass. With increasing tumour size the relatively high monocyte–tumour cell ratio falls as tumour cell growth increases beyond the rate of macrophage accumulation, representing the second stage of events. Subsequently (stage three), macrophage infiltration is still maintained at a significant rate, and is defined by an almost steady proportion of tumour-associated macrophages (TAM) (161). In the final stage, as tumour growth progresses, the inflammatory response to the tumour is impaired and macrophage content begins to fall compared to the unchecked growth of the tumour cells (161–8). It is evident that although this final stage classification is a convenient model for tumour infiltration, it is also a relatively simplistic view of a rather complicated series of events. The macrophage content of tumours varies greatly, and studies in animal models have provided much information, which serves as a basis for understanding monocyte/macrophage behaviour. Tumours induced with chemical carcinogens can possess up to 55 per cent macrophages (169), and transplantable tumours also have high numbers of macrophages (up to 40 per cent by cell number) which infiltrate rapidly (170,171). However, poorly immunogenic sarcomas of C57BL/6 mice contained a lower proportion of between 15 and 20 per cent TAM (172).

In contrast, the proportion of TAM in human tumours is often much lower. The TAM content of melanomas and breast carcinomas can range between 0 and 30 per cent (173). In thyoma, TAM were uniformly distributed throughout the tumour and did not differ in density from normal thymus (174), and in Bowen's disease, an uncommon intra-epithelial cancer of the skin, contained around 10 per cent TAM (174). In stage III or IV non-mucinous adenocarcinoma of the ovary, 11 per cent TAM have been demonstrated (175), but in a further study, TAM comprised 30 per cent of the total cell population present in ascitic cell suspensions and only 2 per cent in solid ovarian carcinoma (advanced stage III or IV).

There are conflicting reports as to whether the grade of tumour is correlated with TAM content (176,177). In colon cancer (Dukes B and C stage tumour), TAM density was increased above the macrophage content of uninvolved gut tissue (178), and found to be between 15 and 25 per cent and 30 and 40 per cent, respectively (179). A six-fold increase in monocytes in metastasizing Duke C tumours has been reported, but in non-metastasizing Duke B tumours (177,178), monocytes were present in small numbers, or absent (180). In both colon and breast carcinomas, no correlation could be found between the stage of disease and the monocyte/macrophage content (177,181), although higher numbers of TAM were found in malignant, as compared to benign, breast disease (181). In bladder carcinoma, either no significant correlation between macrophage infiltration and tumour stage (182), or an increase in macrophage content with grade (183) has been reported (grade I, 17 per cent; II, 18 per cent; and III, 24 per cent TAM). It is interesting that in many cases, the high grade tumours can have a high macrophage content, and this allows considerable speculation to be made as to the function of these infiltrating host cells. Thus, as the tumour is progressing, and in many cases metastasizing via the lymphatics or the blood, it is unlikely that macrophages are mediating a constraint on tumour growth. It is perhaps more likely that they are contributing to tumour survival and growth through the production of essential growth factors, and suppression of antitumour immunity either at the induction or effector phase.

The discrepancies in the apparent macrophage infiltration of tumours highlight the difficulty of comparing data obtained in different studies. Some of these may be accounted for by a bias in the portion of tumour samples tested, or the use of different methods of identifying TAM, such as non-specific esterase or monoclonal antibody specificity.

TAM numbers are sustained via the recruitment of circulating monocytes by tumour-secreted chemotactic factors found a 10–12 kDa glycopeptide

Table 8.4 Abnormal monocyte/macrophage function in cancer patients

Activity	Response	Details	References
Chemotactic response	→	34% defect in renal cell carcinoma	198–202
		29.8% defect transitional cell and bladder carcinoma and melanoma	
	→	45% defect lung and prostate	197
Fc-receptor	↑	Hodgkin's disease	203, 204
IL-1 production	→	Hepatocellular carcinoma, kidney, cervix, bladder, breast, and colon carcinoma	205–7
	Normal	Hodgkin's disease, lung cancer	
	↑	Lung cancer	
Macrophage attachment to foreign substances	→	Hodgkin's disease	204
Spontaneous cytotoxicity	↑	Colon	207–10
	↑→	Lung	211, 216

Number of peripheral blood monocytes	↑	Hodgkin's disease, lung	203, 204, 207, 208, 212, 213
	Normal	Lung and prostate carcinoma	197
	↓	Head, neck, and colon carcinoma	208
Phagocytosis	↑	Hodgkin's disease	204
PGE_2 production	↑	Hodgkin's disease, head, neck, colon, and bladder carcinoma	211
			204
ADCC	↑	Colon carcinoma	208
IgG surface receptors	Normal	Lung and prostate carcinoma	197
Lysozyme secretion	↑	Malignant melanoma, hypernephroma, breast, head, neck, lung, and colon carcinoma	208, 214
	Normal	Malignant melanoma, breast, lung, and prostate carcinoma	197, 208
Superoxide production	↓	Hodgkin's disease, stomach, oesophagus, and liver carcinoma	204, 215

(184). It has been suggested that significantly more TAM are associated with colorectal adenocarcinomas expressing Class II MHC antigens than class II negative tumours (185), although the significance of this finding remains to be established.

As can be seen from the above, the function of TAM is still unclear. They have been suggested to limit tumour growth by their tumouricidal activity in a specific and non-specific manner (186,187), but conversely to enhance tumour growth by inhibiting anti-tumour immune response and stimulating angiogenesis (187). They are certainly capable of acting as antigen-presenting cells for tumour antigens (186), thereby activating the effector arm of an immune response. Indeed, there is some suggestion that TAM may be sub-optimally activated (185). TAM, like blood monocytes, have procoagulant activity (188), and may play a role in fibrin deposition at the tumour site (189), which could encapsulate malignant cells and make them inaccessible to any immune response mounted by the host. It is now apparent from several studies that, in human cancer, monocyte/macrophage function is altered. For example, tumour cell products can deactivate oxidative metabolic pathways (190,191), alter chemotactic responses (192), and influence the maturation of cells of the myeloid lineage (193,194). In both experimental tumours and human cancers, soluble inhibitors of monocyte/macrophage chemotaxis have been reported (195–197). Table 8.4 summarizes many of the abnormal monocyte/macrophage functions detected in patients with cancer, some of which can be ascribed to tumour cell products.

In addition, the interaction between tumour cells, tumour-derived products (217–220), and monocytes and macrophages has been shown to trigger the production of prostaglandins (PG) which mediate immune suppression (221–224). Patients with cancer often exhibit an increase in serum PGE_2 (225,226), which could potentially suppress lymphocyte function. In tumour-bearing hosts, PG suppression may be mediated by distinct populations of macrophages (223,225,227–230).

9   Monocytes and macrophages in cancer immunotherapy

Approximately one in three people in the Western world will develop a neoplastic disease. With this in mind, research programmes have been directed towards improving on existing surgical radio- and chemotherapy, and much interest has been focused on immune activation as a means of achieving a better clinical response. As discussed previously, monocytes and macrophages often display potent cytostatic and cytotoxic activity towards tumour cells, but these functions are clearly not always expressed by either

peripheral blood monocytes or peritumoural or tumour-infiltrating macrophages. Current approaches to encourage monocytes to induce regression
of malignant disease involve regimes designed to augment monocyte/
macrophage activity, and adoptive immunotherapy (Table 8.5).

Radio- and chemotherapy has been shown in some instances to influence
monocyte behaviour, for example, monocyte cytotoxic activity is augmented by radiotherapy (232), and cisplatin, which is currently used thera-
peutically for ovarian carcinoma, has been shown to have potent antitumour
effects in experimental models (233), enhancing tumour infiltration of
monocytes and lymphocytes. One possible explanation is that administration of this drug increases the immunogenicity of tumours (233), an effect
which may be limited to tumours which express low levels of 'foreign'
antigen.

Interferons are known to modulate the host response to a neoplasm by
activating several immune pathways capable of displaying an effector function against tumour cells (231). IFNα in particular has been shown to exert
direct anti-proliferative effects on ovarian carcinoma cells *in vitro* and *in
vivo* (234,235). Fuith and co-workers (236) have investigated the effect of
IFNα on this form of malignancy in patients previously treated by surgery
and 8–12 cycles of *cis*-platin and epirubicin chemotherapy. IFNα administration was shown to induce T-cells to produce the macrophage-activating
factor IFNγ. Neopterin, which is released by IFNγ-activated macrophages,
was also increased, thus demonstrating that IFNγ indirectly enhanced
macrophage functional status. However, although urinary neopterin levels
increased in all patients receiving this treatment, only one displayed tumour
regression. GM-CSF activates monocyte tumouricidal activity *in vitro*,
Steward and co-workers (237) have investigated the use of GM-CSF for
treatment of solid metastatic tumours. Twenty patients were administered
with GM-CSF daily at doses escalated from 0.3 to 60 µg/kg i.v. for two 10 day
cycles, followed by 20 days of alternate day infusions. Seven patients

Table 8.5 Approaches to augment monocyte-mediated tumour regression

Strategy	Action	Molecules
Active augmentation of the immune response	Non-specific	IFN, GM-CSF
	Specific	Tumour antigen vaccine, MDP, VMTE
Adoptive therapy	Cellular	Monocytes and macrophages
	Antibody	Monoclonal

Adapted from reference 231.

experienced stabilization of previously progressive metastatic disease and one patient with metastatic soft tissue sarcoma, underwent a greater than 50 per cent reduction in tumour volume.

Muramyl dipeptide (MDP) is a potent activator of mouse and human monocyte tumouricidal function, but in a free form is unsuitable for administration to cancer patients and is rapidly cleared from the bloodstream before monocyte activation occurs. To combat this problem, MDP may be encapsulated within multi-lammellar vesicles or liposomes, both of which are effective in rendering mouse monocytes tumouricidal *in vitro* and *in vivo* (232). Murray and co-workers incorporated the more stable synthetic analogue MDP, Muramyl tripeptide phosphatidylethanolamine (MTP-PE), into multi-lamellar vesicles. Twenty-eight patients with metastatic cancer, and refractory to standard treatment protocols, received liposomes containing MTP-PE twice weekly in escalating doses from $0.005-12$ mg/m^2. In this study, there was no evidence of either monocyte activation *in vivo* or tumour regression, although blood monocytes from all patients could be activated *in vitro* to lyse allogenic tumour cells (232).

Recently, adoptive therapy of malignant neoplasms using T-cells and LAK cells has been a focus of attention, but only a small number of studies have been undertaken using autologous activated monocytes to treat patients (238–242). Stevenson and co-workers (240–242) employed monocytes purified to 90 per cent by cytophorisis and countercurrent centrifugal elutriation, and activated *ex vivo* with IFNγ. These monocytes were subsequently re-infused into the peritoneal cavity of patients with peritoneal colorectal carcinomatosis, a metastatic form of colon cancer for which there is no effective therapy. Patients received $4-6 \times 10^8$ cells per week for 16 weeks. On standard therapy, the median disease-free interval for patients is four months, and most relapse within two years. This form of adoptive therapy, however, improved the prognosis of these patients; 4/7 patients were free from local relapse 17 months after therapy and one patient remained free of disease in excess of three years. These activated monocytes were shown to move to the tumour, and to function in at least a cytostatic manner towards the tumour cells. In addition, systemic administration of non-activated or IFNγ-activated monocytes did not allow trafficking to the tumour to occur, and no effect on tumour growth was observed (242).

The established treatments of surgery, radio- and chemotherapy are all too often insufficient to induce regression of a progressive neoplasm. In general, attempts to augment the response rates of patients with immunotherapy has been disappointing. Monocytes and macrophages could prove effective in eradicating tumours once efficient ways of selective activation to tumouricidal function can be achieved. Therapy which consists of administration of relatively high concentration of systemic cytokines may not achieve the local-concentrations required to activate cells of the monocytic lineage. Current regimes are not without their hazards to the patient;

administering comparatively high amounts of IFNα or GM-CSF induces various dose-related toxic side-effects (236,237). Local administration or drug delivery into the tumour tissue may abrogate these effects.

Administration of TNFα to mimic the levels attained by activation of monocytes/macrophages has proved unsuccessful in treating cancer patients (243). This task is hampered by the presence of a variety of TNFα inhibitors, for example, α_2-macroglobulin, anti-TNFα antibodies and possibly soluble TNFα receptors. This highlights the difficulty in using biological response modifiers alone in the treatment of human tumours, and results from experimental studies in animal models have yet to prove readily applicable to human cancer.

Patients with advanced disease are less likely to benefit from cytokine therapy, but there is a need to use immunotherapy protocols after relieving a patient of their tumour burden, when minimal residual disease exists. Another important consideration is the identification of patients at risk, and those who are likely to benefit from immunotherapy. At the present time, markers which identify high risk patients likely to develop secondary metastases are not available. Finding reliable markers for metastasis constitutes one of the most important aims of current cancer research.

An aspect which is crucial to the success of targeted immunotherapy is the inherent susceptibility of tumour subpopulations. It is clear that human tumours are genotypically and phenotypically heterogenous, as exemplified by cytogenetic studies and HLA expression in colon carcinomas (244, 245). Not only are multiple clones identifiable within the primary tumour, but these are, in most cases, constantly diversifying to form new genetic variants. This poses a considerable problem if genetic variation manifests itself phenotypically as populations of cells with varying degrees of resistance and susceptibility to macrophage killing.

10 Summary

It is clear from the evidence presented in this chapter that monocytes and macrophages at various states of differentiation and activation are capable of mediating a plethora of biological responses. Some of these are tumouricidal, but others may benefit tumour cell growth and survival. Although many tumours possess large numbers of macrophages, there is little evidence to suggest that they act to keep tumour cell proliferation in check. Conversely, they may secrete growth factors essential for tumour growth and/or the suppression of the antitumour responses of tumour-infiltrating lymphocytes. Evidence confirming the possibility of this within the tumour has yet to be presented, so tumour biologists are faced with the dilemma of whether macrophages are indeed, friend or foe. Harnessing the tumouricidal potential of mononuclear phagocytes provides the greatest challenge for those involved in their study.

Acknowledgements

We wish to thank the Yorkshire Cancer Research Campaign for their support of our research.

References

1 van Furth, R. and Sluiter, W. (1983). Current views on the ontogeny of macrophages and the humoral regulation of monocytopoiesis. *Trans. R. Soc. Trop. Med. Hyg.*, **77**, 614–19.

2 Hogg, M. (1987). Human mononuclear phagocytic molecules and the use of monoclonal antibodies in their detection. *Clin. Exp. Immunol.*, **69**, 687–94.

3 Beelen, R.H.J., Eestermans, I.L., Dopp, E.A., and Dijkstra, C.D. (1987). Monoclonal antibodies ED1 and ED2, and ED3 against rat macrophages: expression of recognised antigens in different stages of differentiation. *Transplant., Proc.*, **19**, 3166–70.

4 van der Meer, J.W., van de Gevel, J.S., Beelen, R.H., Fluitsma, D., Hoefsmit, E.C., and van Furth, R. (1982). Culture of human bone marrow in the teflon culture bag: identification of the human monoblast. *Reticuloendothel. Soc.*, **32**, 355.

5 Tyndall, A.V., Knight, S.C., Edwards, A.J., and Clarke, J. (1983). Veiled (dendritic) cells in synovial fluid. *Lancet*, **i**, 472–3.

6 Brennan, A., (1987). Dendritic cells from human tissues express receptors for the immunoregulatory vitamin D metabolite, dihydroxycholecalciferol. *Immunology*, **61**, 457–61.

7 Hart, D.N. and McKenzie, J.L. (1988). Isolation and characterisation of human tonsil dendritic cells. *J. Exp. Med.*, **168**, 157–70.

8 King, P.D. and Katz, D.R. (1990). Mechanisms of dendritic cell function. *Immunol. Today*, **11**, 206–11.

9 Knight, S.C. *et al.* (1986). Non-adherent low density cells from human peripheral blood contain dendritic cells and monocytes, both with veiled morphology. *Immunology*, **57**, 595–603.

10 Waalen, K., Forre, O., Linker-Israeli, M., and Thoen, J. (1987). Evidence of an activated T-cell system with augmented turnover of interleukin-2 is rheumatoid arthritis. Stimulation of human T lymphocytes by dendritic cells as a model for rheumatoid T-cell activation. *Scand. J. Immunol.*, **25**, 367–73.

11 Flechner, E.R., Freudenthal, P.S., Kaplan, G., and Steinman, R.M. (1988). Antigen specific T lymphocytes efficiently cluster with dendritic cells in the human primary mixed leukocyte reaction. *Cell Immunol.* **III**, 183–95.

12 Metcalf, D. and Nicola, N.A. (1982). Autoinduction of differentiation in WEHI-3B leukaemia cells. *Int. J. Cancer*, **30**, 773–80.

13 Sundstrom, C. and Nilsson, K. (1976). Establishment and characterisation of a human histiocytic lymphoma cell line (U-937). *Int. J. Cancer*, **17**, 565–77.

14 Collins, S.J. (1987). The HL-60 promyelocytic leukaemic cell line:

proliferation, differentiation, and cellular oncogene expression. *Blood*, **70**, 1233–44.

15 Muller, R. (1986). Cellular and viral *fos* genes: structure, regulation of expression and biological properties of their encoded products. *Biochim. Biophys. Acta*, **823**, 207–25.

16 Mitchell, R.L., Zokas, L., Schreiber, R.D., and Verma, I.M. (1985). Rapid induction of the expression of proto-oncogene *fos* during human monocytic differentiation. *Cell*, **40**, 209–17.

17 Mitchell, T., Griffin, J., and Kufe, D.W. (1987). Effects of interferon-gamma on proto-oncogene expression during induction of human monocytic differentiation. *J. Immunol.*, **138**, **6**, 1954–8.

18 Calabretta, B. (1987). Dissociation of c-*fos* induction from macrophage differentiation in human myeloid leukaemic cell lines. *Mol. Cell. Biol.* **7**, 769–74.

19 Introna, M., Bast, R.C. Jr., Johnston, P.A., Adams, D.O., and Hamilton, T.A. (1987). Homologous and hetrologous densitisation of proto-oncogene c-*fos* expression in murine peritoneal macrophages. *J. Cell Physiol.* **13**, 36–42.

20 Colotta, F., Lampugnani, M.G., Polentarutti, N., Dejana, E., and Mantovani, A. (1988). Interleukin-1 induces c-*fos* proto-oncogene expression in cultured human endothelial cells. *Biochem. Biophys. Res. Commun.*, **152**, 1104–10.

21 Celada, A., Gray, P.W., Rinderknecht, T., and Schreiber, R.D. (1984). Evidence for a gamma-interferon receptor that regulates macrophage tumouricidal activity. *J. Exp. Med.*, **160**, 55–74.

22 Koff, W.C., *et al.* (1985). Monocyte-mediated cytotoxicity against herpes simplex virus-infected cells: activation of cytotoxic monocytes by free and liposome-encapsulated lymphokines. *J. Leuc. Biol.*, **37**, 461–72.

23 Yoshida, R., Murray, H.W., and Nathan, C.F. (1988). Agonist and antagonist effects of interferon alpha and beta on activation of human macrophages. Two classes of interferon gamma receptors and blockade of the high-affinity sites by interferon alpha. *J. Exp. Med.*, **167**, 1171–85.

24 Herrman, F., Cannistra, S.A., Levine, H., and Griffin, J.D. (1985). Expression of interleukin-2 receptors and binding of interleukin-2 by gamma interferon-induced human leukaemic and normal monocytic cells. *J. Exp. Med.*, **162**, 1111–6.

25 Guyre, P.M., Morganelli, P.M., and Miller, R. (1983). Recombinant immune interferon increases immunoglobulin G Fc receptors on cultured human mononuclear phagocytes. *J. Clin. Invest.*, **72**, 393–7.

26 Perussia, B., Dayton, E.T., Lazarus, R., Fanning, V., and Trinchieri, G. (1983). Immune interferon induces the receptor for monomeric

IgG1 on human monocytic and myeloid cells. *J. Exp. Med.*, **158**, 1092–113.

27 Clarkson, S.B. and Ory, P.A. (1988). Developmentally regulated IgGFc receptors on cultured human monocytes. *J. Exp. Med.*, **167**, 408–20.

28 Weinberg, J.B., Hobbs, M.M., and Musukonis, M.A. (1984). Recombinant human interferon-gamma induces human monocytes polykaron formation. *Proc. Natl. Acad. Sci. USA.*, **81**, 4554–7.

29 Basham, T.Y. and Merigan, T.C. (1983). Recombinant interferon-gamma increases HLA-DR synthesis and expression. *J. Immunol.*, **130**, 1492–4.

30 Koeffler, H.P., Ranyard, J., Yelton, L., Billing, R., and Bohman, R. (1984). Gamma-interferon induces expression of the HLA-D antigens on normal and leukaemic human myeloid cells. *Proc. Natl. Acad. Sci. U.S.A.*, **81**, 4080–4.

31 Sztein, M.B., Steeg, P.S., Johnson, H.M., and Oppenheim, J.J. (1984). Regulation of human peripheral blood monocyte DR antigen expression *in vitro* by lymphokines and recombinant interferons. *J. Clin. Invest.*, **73**, 556–65.

32 Reed, S.G. *et al.* (1987). Recombinant granulocyte/macrophage colony-stimulating factor activates macrophages to inhibit *Trypanosoma cruzi* and release hydrogen peroxide. Comparison with interferon gamma. *J. Exp. Med.*, **166**, 1734–46.

33 Grabstein, K.H. *et al.* (1986). Induction of macrophage tumouricidal activity by granulocyte-macrophage colony-stimulating factor. *Science*, **232**, 506–8.

34 Weiser, W.Y., Van Niel, A., Clark, S.C., David, J.R., and Reimold, H.G. (1987). Recombinant human granulocyte/macrophage colony-stimulating factor activates intracellular killing of *Leishmania donovani* by human monocyte-derived macrophages. *J. Exp. Med.*, **166**, 1436–46.

35 Horiguchi, J., Warren, M.K., and Kufe, D. (1987). Expression of the macrophage-specific colony-stimulating factor in human monocytes treated with granulocyte-macrophage colony-stimulating factor. *Blood*, **69**, 1259–61.

36 Warren, M.K. and Ralpha, P. (1986). Macrophage growth factor CSF-1 stimulates human monocyte production and interferon, tumour necrosis factor, and colony stimulating activity. *J. Immunol.*, **137**, 2281–5.

37 Philip, R. (1988). Cytolysis of tumour necrosis factor (TNF)-resistant tumour targets. Differential cytotoxicity of monocytes activated by interferons, IL-2, and TNF. *J. Immunol.*, **140**, 1345–9.

38 Lee, J.C., Rebar, L., Young, P., Ruscetti, F.W., Hanna, N., and Poste, G. (1986). Identification and characterisation of a human T-cell

line-derived lymphokine with MAF-like activity distinct from interferon-gamma. *J. Immunol.*, **136**, 1322–8.

39 Hoover, D.L. *et al.* (1986). A lymphokine distinct from interferon-gamma that activates human monocytes to kill Leishmania donovani *in vitro. J. Immunol.*, **136**, 1329–33.

40 Salata, R.A., Murray, H.W., Rubin, B.Y., and Ravdin, J.I. (1987). The role of gamma interferon in the generation of human macrophages cytotoxic to entamoeba histolytica trophozoites. *Am. J. Trop. Med. Hyg.*, **37**, 72–8.

41 Lomedico, P.T. *et al.* (1984). Cloning and expression of murine interleukin-1 cDNA in *Escerichia coli. Nature*, **312**, 458–62.

42 Auron, P.E. *et al.* (1984). Nucleotide sequence of human monocyte interleukin-1 precursor cDNA. *Proc. Natl. Acad. Sci. U.S.A.*, **81**, 7907–11.

43 Bakouche, O., Brown, D.C., and Lachman, L.B. (1987). Subcellular localisation of human monocyte interleukin-1. Evidence for an inactive precursor molecule and a possible mechanism for IL-1 release. *J. Immunol.*, **138**, 4249–225.

44 Sisson, S.D. and Dinarello, C.A. (1989). Interleukin 1. In *Human monocytes* (ed. M. Zembela and G.L. Asherson), pp. 183–94. Academic Press, London.

45 Sims, J.E. *et al.* (1988). cDNA expression, cloning of the IL-1 receptor, a member of the immunoglobulin superfamily. *Science*, **241**, 585–9.

46 Aribia, M.H.B., *et al.* (1987). rIL-2 induced proliferation of human circulating NK cells and T lymphocytes: synergistic effects of IL-1 and IL-2. *J. Immunol.*, **139**, 43–51.

47 Smith, R.A. and Baglioni, C. (1987). The active form of tumour necrosis factor is a trimer. *J. Biol. Chem.*, **262**, 6951–4.

48 Nedwin, G.E. *et al.* (1985). Human lymphotoxin and tumour necrosis factor genes: structure, homology and chromosomal location. *Nucl. Acids Res.*, **13**, 6361–71.

49 Goeddel, D.V. *et al.* (1986). Tumour necrosis factors: gene structure and biological activities. *Cold Spring Harbor Symp. Quant. Biol.*, **51**, 597–609.

50 Nedospasov, S.A. *et al.* (1986). The genes for tumour necrosis factor (TNF-alpha) and lymphotoxin (TNF-beta) are tandemly arranged on chromosome 17 of the mouse. *Nucl. Acids Res.*, **14**, 7713–25.

51 Nedospasov, S.A. *et al.* (1986). Tandem arrangement of genes coding for tumour necrosis factor alpha (TNFα) and lymphotoxin (TNFβ) in the human genome. *Cold Spring Harbor Symp. Quant. Biol.*, **51**, 611–24.

52 Pennica, D. *et al.* (1984). Human tumour necrosis factor: precursor

structure, expression and homology to lymphotoxin. *Nature*, **312**, 724–9.

53 Gray, P.W., *et al.* (1984). Cloning and expression of cDNA for human lymphotoxin, a lymphokine with tumour necrosis activity. *Nature*, **312**, 721–4.

54 Carswell, E.A., Old, L.J., Kassel, R.L., Green, S., Fiore, N., and Williamson, B. (1975). An endotoxin-induced serum factor that causes necrosis of tumours. *Proc. Natl. Acad. Sci. U.S.A..*, **72**, 3666–70.

55 Waage, A., Halstensen, A., and Espevik, T. (1987). Association between tumour necrosis factor in serum and fatal outcome in patients with meningococcal disease. *Lancet*, **i**, 355–7.

56 Clark, I.A., Cowden, W.B., Butcher, G.A., and Hunt, N.H. (1987). Possible roles of tumour necrosis factor in the pathology of malaria. *Am. J. Path.*, **129**, 192–9.

57 Nedwin, G.E., Svedersky, L.P., Bringman, T.S., Palladino, M.S., and Goeddel, D.V. (1985). The effect of interleukin-2, interferon, and mitogens on the production of tumour necrosis factor α and β. *J. Immunol.*, **135**, 2492–7.

58 Philip, R. and Epstein, L.B. (1986). Tumour necrosis factor as immunomodulator and mediator of monocyte cytotoxicity induced by itself, gamma-interferon and interleukin-1. *Nature*, **323**, 86–9.

59 Pennica, D. *et al.* (1984). Human tumour necrosis factor: precursor structure, expression and homology to lymphotoxin. *Nature*, **312**, 724–9.

60 Pennica, D., Hayflick, J.S., Bringman, T.S., Palladino, M.A., and Goeddel, D.V. (1985). Cloning and expression in *Escherichia coli* of the cDNA for murine tumour necrosis factor. *Proc. Natl. Acad. Sci. U.S.A.*, **82**, 6060–4.

61 Sugarman, B.J., Aggarwal, B.B., Hass, P.E., Figari, J.S. Palladino, M.A., and Shepard, H.M. (1985). Recombinant human tumour necrosis factor-alpha: effects on proliferation of normal and transformed cells *in vitro*. *Science*, **230**, 943–5.

62 Hepburn, A., Boeynaems, J.M., Fiers, W., and Dumont, J.E. (1987). Modulation of tumour necrosis factor-alpha cytotoxicity in L929 cells by bacterial toxins, hydrocortisone and inhibitors of arachidoric acid metabolism *Biochem. Biophys. Res. Commun.*, **149**, 815–22.

63 Holtmann, H. and Wallach, D. (1987). Down regulation of the receptors for tumour necrosis factor by Interleukin-1 and 4 beta-phorbol-12-Myristate-13-acetate. *J. Immunol.*, **139**, 1161–7.

64 Collins, T., Lapierre, L.A., Fiers, W., Strominger, J.L., and Pober, J.S. (1986). Recombinant human tumour necrosis factor increases mRNA levels and surface expression of HLA-A,B antigens in vascular endothelial cells and dermal fibroblasts *in vitro*. *Proc. Natl. Acad. Sci. U.S.A.*, **83**, 446–50.

65 Chang, R.J. and Lee, S.H. (1986). Effects of interferon-gamma and tumour necrosis factor-alpha on the expression of an Ia antigen on a murine macrophage cell line. *J. Immunol.*, **137**, 2853–6.

66 Wong, G.H.W. and Goeddel, D.V., (1989). Tumour necrosis factor. In *Human Monocytes* (ed. M. Zembala and G.L. Asherson), pp. 195–216.

67 Bertolini, D.R., Nedwin, G.E., Bringman, T.S., Smith, D.D., and Mundy, G.R. (1986). Stimulation of bone resorption and inhibition of bone formation *in vitro* by human tumour necrosis factors. *Nature*, **319**, 516–8.

68 Dayer, J.M., Beutler, B., and Cerami, A. (1985). Cochectin/tumour necrosis factor stimulates collogenase and prostaglandin E2 production by human synovial cells and dermal fibroblasts. *J. Exp. Med.*, **162**, 2163–8.

69 Cottam, D. and Rees, R.C. Regulation of melanoma cell gelatinase production by cytokines and growth factors. (Manuscript submitted for publication.)

70 Sehgal, P.B. *et al.* (1986). Human chromosome 7 carries the beta 2 interferon gene. *Proc. Natl. Acad. Sci. U.S.A.*, **83**, 5219–22.

71 Kishimoto, T. and Hirano, T. (1988). Molecular regulation of B lymphocyte response. *Ann. Rev. Immunol.*, **6**, 485–512.

72 Sehgal, P.B., May, L.T., Tamm, I., and Vilcek, J. (1987). Human beta 2 interferon and B-cell differentiation factor BSF-2 are identical. *Science*, **235**, 731–2.

73 Garman, R.D., Jacobs, K.A., Clark, S.C., and Raulet, D.H. (1987). B-cell-stimulating factor 2 (beta 2 interferon) functions as a second signal for interleukin 2 production by mature T cells. *Proc. Natl. Acad. Sci. U.S.A.*, **84**, 7629–33.

74 Lotz, M., *et al.* (1988). B-cell stimulating factor 2/Interleukin-6 is a co-stimulant for human thymocytes and T lymphocytes. *J. Exp. Med.*, **167**, 1253–8.

75 Gallagher, G., Stimpson, W.H., Findley, J., and Al-Azzawi, F. (1990). Interleukin-6 enhances the induction of human lymphokine-activated killer cells. *Cancer Immunol. Immunother.*, **31**, 49–52.

76 Miyaura, C. *et al.* (1988). Recombinant human interleukin-6 (B-cell stimulating factor 2) is a potent inducer of differentiation of mouse myeloid leukaemic cells (M1). *FEBS Lett.*, **234**, 17–21.

77 Ikebuchi, K., Wong, C.G., Clark, S.C., Ihle, J.N., Hirai, Y., and Ogawa, M. (1987). Interleukin-6 enhancement of Interleukin 3-dependent proliferation of multipotential haemopoietic progenitors. *Proc. Natl. Acad. Sci. U.S.A.*, **84**, 9035–9.

78 Hirano, T. *et al.* (1988). Excessive production of interleukin 6/B-cell stimulatory factor-2 in rheumatoid arthritis. *Eur. J. Immunol.*, **18**, 1797–1801.

79 Kawano, M. *et al.* (1988). Autocrine generation and requirement of BSF-2/IL-6 for human multiple myelomas. *Nature*, **322**, 83–5.

80 Rimbaldi, A., Young, D.C., and Griffin, J.D. (1987). Expression of the M-CSF (CSF-1) gene by human monocytes. *Blood*, **69**, 1409–13.

81 Horiguchi, J., Warren, M.K., and Kufe, D. (1987). Expression of the macrophage-specific colony-stimulating factor in human monocytes treated with granulocyte–macrophage colony-stimulating factor. *Blood*, **69**, 1259–61.

82 Oster, W., Lindemann, A., Horn, S., Mertelsmann, R., and Herrmann, F. (1987). Tumour necrosis factor (TNF)-alpha but not TNF-beta induces secretion of colony stimulating factor for macrophages (CSF-1) by human monocytes. *Blood*, **70**, 1700–3.

83 Vellenga, E., Rambaldi, A., Ernst, T.J., and Griffin, J.D. (1988). Independent regulation of M-CSF and G-CSF gene expression in human monocytes. *Blood*, **71**, 1529–32.

84 Lee, F., Yokota, T., Otsuka, T., Arai, K., and Rennick, D. (1985). Isolation of the cDNA for a human granulocyte–macrophage colony-stimulating factor by functional expression in mammalian cells. *Proc. Natl. Acad. Sci. U.S.A.*, **82**, 4360–4.

85 Das, S.K. and Stanley, E.A. (1982). Structure-function studies of a colony stimulating factor (CSF-1). *J. Biol. Chem.*, **257**, 13679–84.

86 Clark, S.C. and Kaman, R. (1987). The human haematopoietic colony-stimulating factors. *Science*, **236**, 1229–37.

87 Sherr, C.J., Roussel, M., and Rettenmier, C.W. (1988). Colony stimulating factor-1 receptor (c-*fms*). In *Growth factors and their receptors* (eds. R. Ross, A.W. Burgess, and T. Hunter), pp. 179–87. Alan R. Liss, New York.

88 Bitterman, P.B., Rennard, S.I., Hunninghake, G.W., and Crystal, R.G. (1982). Human alveolar macrophage growth factor for fibroblasts. Regulation and partial characterisation. *J. Clin. Invest.*, **70**, 806–22.

89 Hamerman, D. *et al.* (1987). Growth factors with heparin binding affinity in human synovial fluid. *Proc. Soc. Exp. Biol. Med.*, **186**, 384–9.

90 Glenn, K.C. and Ross, R. (1981). Human monocyte-derived growth factor(s) for mesenchymal cells: activation of secretion by endotoxin and concanavalin. *Cell*, **25**, 603–15.

91 Dohlman, J.G., Payan, D.G., and Goetzl, E.J. (1984). Generation of a unique fibroblast-activating factor by human monocytes. *Immunology*, **52**, 577–84.

92 Mornex, J.F. *et al.* (1986). Spontaneous expression of the c-*sis* gene and release of a platelet-derived growth factor-like molecule by human alveolar macrophages. *J. Clin. Invest.*, **78**, 61–6.

93 Sariban, E. and Kufe, D. (1988). Expression of platelet-derived

growth factor 1 and 2 genes in human myeloid cell lines and monocytes. *Cancer Res.*, **48**, 4498–4502.

94   Shimokado, K., Raines, E.W., Madtes, D.K., Barrett, T.B., Benditt, E.P., and Ross, R. (1985). A significant part of macrophage-derived growth factor consists of at least 2 forms of PDGF. *Cell*, **43**, 277–86.

95   Baird, A., Mormede, P., and Bohlen, P. (1985). Immunoreactive fibroblast growth factor in cells of peritoneal exudate suggests its identity with macrophage-derived growth factor. *Biochem. Biophys. Res. Comm.*, **126**, 358–64.

96   Madtes, D.K. *et al.* (1988). Induction of transforming growth factor-alpha in activated human alveolar macrophages. *Cell*, **53**, 285–93.

97   Derynck, R., Roberts, A.B., Winkler, M.E., Chen, E.Y., and Goeddel, D.V. (1984). Human transforming growth factor-alpha: precursor structure and expression in *E. coli. Cell*, **38**, 287–97.

98   DeLarco, J.E. and Todaro, G.J. (1980). Sarcoma growth factor (SGF): specific binding to epidermal growth factor (EGF) membrane receptors. *J. Cell. Physiol.*, **102**, 267–77.

99   Wahl, S.M. *et al.* (1987). Transforming growth factor type beta induces monocyte chemotaxis and growth factor production. *Proc. Natl. Acad. Sci. U.S.A.*, **84**, 5788–92.

100 Postlethwaite, A.E., Keski-Oja, J., Moses, H.L., and Hang, A.H. (1987). Stimulation of a chemotactic migration of human fibroblasts by transforming growth factor beta. *J. Exp. Med.*, **165**, 251–6.

101 Assoian, R.K. *et al.* (1987). Expression and secretion of type beta transforming growth factor by activated human macrophages. *Proc. Natl. Acad. Sci. U.S.A.*, **84**, 6020–4.

102 Rappolee, D.A., Mark, D., Banda, M.J., and Werb, Z. (1988). Wound macrophages express TGF-alpha and other growth factors *in vivo*: analysis by mRNA phenotyping. *Science*, **241**, 708–12.

103 Sanchez-Madrid, F., Nagy, J.A., Robbins, E., Simon, P., and Springer, T.A. (1983). A human leukocyte differentiation antigen family with distinct alpha-subunits and a common beta-subunit: the lymphocyte function-associated antigen (LFA-1) the C3bi complement receptor (OKM1/Mac-1) and the p150,95 molecule. *J. Exp. Med.*, **158**, 1785–1803.

104 Hogg, N., Tahacs, L., Palmer, D.G., Selvendran, Y., and Allan, C. (1986). The p150,95 molecule is a marker of human mononuclear phagocytes: comparison with expression of class II molecules. *Eur. J. Immunol.*, **16**, 240–8.

105 Spits, H., Keizer, G., Borst, J., Terhorst, C., Hekman, A., and de Vries, J.E. (1983). Characterisation of monoclonal antibodies against cell surface molecules associated with cytotoxic activity of natural and activated killer cells and cloned CTL lines. *Hybridoma*, **2**, 423–37.

106 Te Velde, A.A., Kemp, J.P.G., Yard, B.A., de Vries, J.E., and

Figdor, C.C. (1988). Modulation of phenotypic and functional properties of human peripheral blood monocytes by IL-4. *J. Immunol.* **140**,
1548–54.

107 Keizer, G.D., Te Velde, A.A., Schwarting, R., Figdor, C.G., and de
Vries, J.E. (1987). Role of p150,95 in adhesion, migration, chemotaxis
and phagocytosis of human monocytes. *Eur. J. Immunol.*, **17**,
1317–22.

108 Hildreth, J. E. and August, J.T. (1985). The human leukocyte
function-associated (HLFA) antigen and a related macrophage differentiation antigen (HMac-1): functional effects of subunit-specific
monoclonal antibodies. *J. Immunol.*, **134**, 3272–80.

109 Yoon, P.S., Boxer, L.A., Mayo, L.A., Yang, A.Y., and Wicha, M.S.
(1987). Human neutrophil lamanin receptors: activation-dependent
receptor expression. *J. Immunol.*, **138**, 259–65.

110 Wright, S.D. and Jong, M.T. (1986). Adhesion-promoting receptors
on human macrophages recognise *Escherichia coli* by binding to
lipopolysaccharide. J. Exp. Med., **164**, 1876–88.

111 Gallatin, M., St. John, T.P., Siegelman, M., Reichert, R., Butcher,
E.C., and Weissman, I.L. (1986). Lymphocyte homing receptors. *Cell*,
44, 673–80.

112 Pober, J.S. *et al.* (1986). Two distinct monokines, Interleukin-1 and
tumour necrosis factor, each independently induce biosynthesis and
transient expression of the same antigen on the surface of cultured
human vascular endothelial cells. *J. Immunol.*, **136**, 1680–7.

113 Te Velde, A.A., Keizzer, G.D., and Figdor, C.G. (1987). Differential
function of LFA-1 family molecules (CD11 and CD18) in adhesion of
human monocytes to melanoma and endothelial cells. *Immunology*,
61, 261–7.

114 Pober, J. S. *et al.* (1986). Overlapping patterns of activation of human
endothelial cells by Interleukin-1, tumour necrosis factor, and immune
interferon. *J. Immunol.*, **137**, 1893–6.

115 Bevilacqua, M.P., Pober, J.S., Mendrick, D.L., Cotran, R.S., and
Grinbrone, Jr. M.A. (1987). Identification of an inducible endothelial-
leukocyte adhesion molecule. *Proc. Natl. Acad. Sci. U.S.A.*, 9238–
42.

116 Keller, R. (1976). Susceptibility of normal and transformed cell lines to
cytostatic and cytocidal effects exerted by activated macrophages.
J.N.C.I., **56**, 369–74.

117 Granger, D., Taintor, R., Cook, J., and Hibbs, J. (1980). Injury of
neoplastic cells by murine macrophages leads to inhibition of
mitochondrial respiration. *J. Clin. Invest.*, **65**, 357–70.

118 Hibbs, J., Taintor, R., and Vavrin, Z. (1984). Iron depletion: possible
causes of tumour cell cytotoxicity induced by activated macrophages.
Biochem. Biophys. Res. Commun., **123**, 716–23.

119 Fidler, I.J. and Ichinose, Y. (1989). Mechanisms of macrophage-mediated tumour cell lysis: role for the monokines tumour necrosis factor and Interleukin-1. *Immunity to Cancer*, **2**, 169–81.

120 Drapier, J. and Hibbs, J. (1986). A conitase, a krebs cycle enzyme with an iron-sulphur centre is inhibited in tumour target cells after cocultivation with cytotoxic activated macrophages. In *Leukocytes and host defense* (ed. J. Oppenheim and D. Jacobs), p. 269. Alan R. Liss, New York.

121 Adams, D.O. and Hamilton, T.A. (1984). The cell biology of macrophage activation. *Ann. Rev. Immunol.*, **2**, 283–318.

122 Keller, R. and Keist, R. (1989). Abilities of activated macrophages to manifest tumouricidal activity and to generate reactive nitrogen intermediates: a comparative study *in vitro* and *ex vivo*. *Biochem, Biophys. Res. Commun.*, **164**, 968–73.

123 Itoh, K., Platsoucas, C.D., and Balch, C.M. (1987). Monocyte- and natural killer cell-mediated spontaneous cytotoxicity against human noncultured solid tumour cells. *Cellular Immunol.*, **108**, 495–500.

124 Kimura, S., Sone, S., Takahashi, K., Uyama, T., Ogura, T., and Monden, Y. (1989). Antitumour potential of pleural cavity macrophages in lung cancer patients without malignant effusion. *Br. J. Cancer*, **59**, 535–9.

125 Uhing, R.J. and Adams, D.O. (1989). Molecular events in the activation of murine macrophages. *Agents and Actions*, **26**, 9–14.

126 Paulnock, D.M. and Lambert, L.E. (1990). Identification and characterization of monoclonal antibodies specific for macrophages at intermediate stages in the tumouricidal activation pathway. *J. Immunol.*, **144**, 765–73.

127 Finbloom, D.S. (1990). The interferon-γ receptor on human monocytes, monocyte-like cell lines and polymorphonuclear leucocytes. *Biochem. Soc. Trans.*, **18**, 222–84.

128 Keller, R., Keist, R., and Schwendener, R.A. (1989). Discrepancy in the abilities of lymphokines and bacteria to mediate tumour protection *in vivo* and/or tumouricidal activity by macrophages *in vitro*. *Int. J. Cancer*, **44**, 512–17.

129 Remels, L., Fransen, L., Huygen, K., and De Baetselier, P. (1990). Poly I:C activated macrophages are tumouricidal for TNFα-resistant 3LL tumour cells. *J. Immunol.*, **144**, 4477–86.

130 Dullens, H.F.J., De Weger, R.A., Van Der Maas, M., Den Besten, P.J., Vandebriel, R.J., and Den Otter, W. (1989). Production of specific macrophage-arming factor precedes cytotoxic T lymphocyte activity *in vivo* during tumour rejection. *Cancer Immunol. Immunoth.*, **30**, 28–33.

131 De Weger, R.A. *et al.* (1989). Initial immunochemical characterization

of specific macrophage-arming factor. *Cancer Immunol. Immunoth.*, **30**, 21–7.

132 Thomassen, M.J., Barna, B.P., Wiedemann, H.P., and Ahmad, M. (1990). Modulation of human alveolar macrophage tumouricidal activity by recombinant macrophage colony-stimulating factor. *J. Biol. Resp. Mod.*, **9**, 87–91.

133 Munn, D.H. and Cheung, N-K.V. (1989). Antibody-dependent anti-tumour cytotoxicity by human monocytes cultured with recombinant macrophage colony-stimulating factor. *J. Exp. Med.*, **170**, 511–26.

134 Feinman, R., Henriksen-De Stefano, D., Tsujimoto, M., and Vilcek, J. (1987). Tumour necrosis factor is an important mediator of tumour cell killing by human monocytes. *J. Immunol.*, **138**, 635–40.

135 Hasday, J.D., Shah, E.M., and Lieberman, A.P. (1990). Macrophage tumour necrosis factor-α release is induced by contact with some tumours. *J. Immunol.*, **145**, 371–9.

136 Janicke, R. and Mannel, D.N. (1990). Distinct tumour cell membrane constituents activate human monocytes for tumour necrosis factor synthesis. *J. Immunol.*, **144**, 1144–50.

137 Peck, R., Brockhaus, M., and Frey, J.R. (1989). Cell surface tumour necrosis factor (TNF) accounts for monocyte and lymphocyte-mediated killing of TNF-resistant target cells. *Cell Immunol.*, **122**, 1–10.

138 Patek, P.Q. and Lin, Y. (1989). Natural cytotoxic activity is not necessarily mediated by the release of tumour necrosis factor. *Immunology*, **67**, 509–13.

139 Klostergaard, J. (1987). Role of tumour necrosis factor in monocyte/macrophage tumour cytotoxicity *in vitro*. *Natl. Immun. Cell Growth Reg.*, **6**, 161–6.

140 Smith, M.R., Munger, W.E., Kung, M-F., Takars, L., and Durum, S.K. (1990). Direct evidence for an intracellular role for tumour necrosis factor α. Microinjection of tumour necrosis factor kills target cells. *J. Immunol.*, **144**, 162–9.

141 Ruggiero, V. and Baglioni, C., (1987). Synergistic anti-proliferative activity of Interleukin-1 and tumour necrosis factor. *J. Immunol.*, **138**, 661–3.

142 Mortarini, R., Belli, F., Parmiani, G., and Anichini, A., (1990). Cytokine-mediated modulation of HLA-Class II, ICAM-1, LFA-3 and tumour-associated antigen profile of melanoma cells. Comparison with anti-proliferative activity by rIL-1, rTNFα, rIFNγ, rIL-4 and their combinations. *Int. J. Cancer*, **45**, 334–41.

143 Nakane, T., Szentendrei, T., Stern, L., Virmani, M., Seely, J., and Kunos, G. (1990). Effects of IL-1 and cortisol on β-adrenergic recep-

tors, cell proliferation, and differentiation in cultured human A549 lung tumour cells. *J. Immunol.*, **145**, 260–6.

144 Higuchi, M., Higachi, N., Taki, H., and Osawa, T. (1990). Cytolytic mechanisms of activated macrophages. Tumour necrosis factor and L-arginine-dependent mechanisms act synergistically as the major cytolytic mechanisms of activated macrophages. *J. Immunol.*, **144**, 1425–31.

145 Stuehr, D.J. and Nathan, C.F. (1989). Nitric oxide. A macrophage product responsible for cytostasis and respiratory inhibition in tumour target cells. *J. Exp. Med.*, **169**, 1543–55.

146 Keller, R., Geiges, M., and Keist, R. (1990). L-Arginine-dependent reactive nitrogen intermediates as mediators of tumour cell killing by activated macrophages. *Cancer Res.*, **50**, 1421–5.

147 Kilbourn, R. and Lopez-Berestein, G. (1990). Protease inhibitors block the macrophage-mediated inhibition of tumour cell mitochondrial respiration. *J. Immunol.*, **144**, 1042–5.

148 Segal, A.W. (1989). The respiratory burst in monocytes and macrophages. In: *Human monocytes* (ed. M. Zembala and G.L. Asherson), pp. 89–100. Academic Press, London.

149 Babior, B.M. (1984). Oxidants from phagocytes: agents of defense and destruction. *Blood*, **64**, 959–966.

150 Chong, Y.C., Heppner, G.H., Paul, L.A., and Fulton, A.M. (1989). Macrophage-mediated induction of DNA strand breaks in target tumour cells. *Cancer Res.*, **49**, 6652–7.

151 Hara, H., Kawase I., Komuta, K., Masuno, T., and Kishimoto, S. (1989). Enhanced tumour growth and metastatic spread of an MH134 variant lacking a part of the MM antigen: a possible role of antibody-dependent cellular cytotoxicity in control of tumour growth and metastasis. *Int. J. Cancer*, **44**, 137–42.

152 Nathan, C.F., Brukner, L., Kaplan, G., Unkeless, J., and Cohn, Z. (1980). Role of activated macrophages in antibody-dependent lysis of tumour cells. *J. Exp. Med.*, **152**, 183–97.

153 Nathan, C.F. and Cohn, Z. (1980). Role of oxygen-dependent mechanisms in antibody-induced lysis of tumour cells by activated macrophages. *J. Exp. Med.*, **152**, 198–208.

154 Takamuku, K., Akiyoshi, T., and Tsuji, M. (1987). Antibody-dependent cell-mediated cytotoxicity using a murine monoclonal antibody against human colorectal cancer in cancer patients. *Cancer Immunol. Immunoth.*, **25**, 137–40.

155 Oda, S., Sato, M., Toyoshima, S., and Osawa, T. (1989). Binding of activated macrophages to tumour cells through a macrophage lectin and its role in macrophage tumouricidal activity. *J. Biochem.*, **105**, 1040–3.

156 Somers, S.D., Mastin, J.P., and Adams, D.O. (1983). The binding of

tumour cells by murine mononuclear phagocytes can be divided into two qualitatively distinct types. *J. Immunol.*, **131**, 2086–93.

157 Somers, S.D., Whisnant, C.C., and Adams, D.O. (1986). Quantification of the strength of cell-cell adhesion: the capture of tumour cells by activated murine macrophages proceeds through two distinct stages. *J. Immunol.*, **136**, 1490–6.

158 Chen, T-Y, Bright, S.W., Pace, J.L., Russell, S.W., and Morrison, B.C. (1990). Induction of macrophage-mediated tumour cytotoxicity by a hamster monoclonal antibody with specificity for lipopoly-saccharide receptor. *J. Immunol.*, **145**, 8–12.

159 McBride, W. H. (1986). Phenotype and functions of intratumoral macrophages. *Biochim. Biophys. Acta*, **865**, 27–41.

160 Aarden, L.A., DeGroot, E.D., Schaap, O.L., and Lansdorp, P.M. (1987). Production of hybridoma growth factor by human monocytes. *Eur. J. Immunol.*, **17**, 1411–16.

161 Whitworth, P.W., Pak, C.C., Esgro, J., Kleinerman, E.S., and Fidler, I.J. (1989). Macrophages and cancer. *Cancer Met. Rev.*, **8**, 319–51.

162 Norman, S.J., Schardt, M.C., and Sorkin, E. (1984). Macrophage inflammatory responses in rats and mice with autochthonous and transplanted tumours induced by 3-methylchloanthrene. *J. Natl. Cancer Inst.*, **72**, 175–84.

163 Norman, S.J., Schardt, M., and Sorkin, E. (1979). Antiinflammatory effect of spontaneous lymphoma in SJL/J mice. *J. Natl. Cancer Inst.*, **63**, 825–33.

164 Norman, S.J., Schardt, M., and Sorkin, E. (1981). Alternation of macrophage function in AKR leukaemia. *J. Natl. Cancer Inst.*, **66**, 157–62.

165 Bernstein, I.D., Zbar, B., and Rapp, H.J. (1972). Impaired inflammatory response in tumour-bearing guinea pigs. *J. Natl. Cancer Inst.*, **49**, 1641–7.

166 Fauve, R.M., Hevin, B., Jacob, M., Gaillard, J.A., and Jacob, F. (1974). Anti-inflammatory effects of murine malignant cells. *Proc. Natl. Acad. Sci. U.S.A.*, **71**, 4052–6.

167 Snyderman, R., Pike, M.C., Blaylock, B.L., and Weinstein, P. (1976). Effect of neoplasms on inflammation: depression of macrophage accumulation after tumour implantation. *J. Immunol.*, **116**, 585–9.

168 Norman, S.J. and Sorkin, E. (1976). Cell-specific defect in monocyte function during tumour-growth. *J. Natl. Cancer Inst.*, **57**, 135–40.

169 Evans, R. (1972). Macrophages in syngenic animal tumours. *Transplantation*, **14**, 468–73.

170 Loeffler, D.A., Keng, P.S., Baggs, R.B., and Lord, E.M. (1990). Lymphocyte infiltration and cytotoxicity under hypoxic conditions in the EMT6 mouse mammary tumour. *Int. J. Cancer*, **45**, 462–7.

171 Wilson, K.M., Siegal, G., and Lord, E.M. (1989). Tumour necrosis factor-mediated cytotoxicity by tumour-associated macrophages. *Cell Immunol.*, **123**, 158–65.

172 Bottazzi, B., Erba, E., Nobili, N., Fazioli, F., Rambaldi, A., and Mantovani, A. (1990). A paracrine circuit in the regulation of the proliferation of macrophages infiltrating murine sarcomas. *J. Immunol.*, **144**, 2409–12.

173 Gauchi, C. L. and Alexander, P. (1975). The macrophage content of some human tumours. *Cancer Lett.*, **1**, 29–32.

174 Ruco, L.P., Rosati, S., Monardo, F., Pescarmona, E., Rendina, E.A., and Baroni, C.D. (1989). Macrophages and interdigitating reticulum cells in normal thymus and in thymona: an immunohistochemical study. *Histopathology*, **14**, 37–45.

175 Lentz, S.S., Mckean, D.J., Kovach, J.S., and Podratz, K.C. (1989). Phenotypic and functional characteristics of mononuclear cells in ovarian carcinoma tumours. *Gynecol. Oncol.*, **34**, 136–40.

176 Koch, B., Giedl, J., Hecnanek, P., and Kalden, J.R. (1985). The analysis of mononuclear cell infiltrations in colorectal adenocarcinoma. *J. Cancer Res. Clin. Oncol.*, **109**, 142–51.

177 Allen, C. and Hogg, N. (1985). Monocytes and other infiltrating cells in human colorectal tumours identified by monoclonal antibodies. *Immunology*, **55**, 289–99.

178 Allen, C. and Hogg, N. (1987). Elevation of infiltrating mononuclear phagocytes in human colorectal tumours. *J.N.C.I.*, **78**, 465–70.

179 Beissert, S. *et al.* (1989). Regulation of tumour necrosis factor gene expression in colorectal adenocarcinoma: *In vivo* analysis by *in situ* hybridization. *Proc. Natl. Acad. Sci. U.S.A.*, **86**, 5064–8.

180 Norazmi, M.N., Hohman, A.W., Skinner, J.M., Jarvis, L.R., and Bradley, J. (1990). Density and phenotype of tumour-associated mononuclear cells in colonic carcinomas determined by computer-assisted video image analysis. *Immunology*, **69**, 282–6.

181 Kelly, P.M.A., Davison, R.S., Bliss, E., and McGee, J.O'D. (1988). Macrophages in human breast disease: a quantitative immunohistochemical study. *Br. J. Cancer*, **57**, 174–7.

182 Tsugihashi, M., Uejima, S., Akiyama, T., and Kurita, T. (1989). Immunohistochemical detection of tissue-infiltrating lymphocytes in bladder tumours. *Urol. Int.*, **44**, 5–9.

183 Hijazi, A., Devonec, M., Brinjuier, P.P., Dutrieux-Berger, N., Derrin, P., and Revillord, J.P. (1989). Flow cytometry analysis of leucocytes infiltrating bladder tumours according to grade and urothelial cell DNA content. *Br. J. Urol.*, **64**, 245–9.

184 Bottazzi, B., Colotta, F., Sica, A., Nobili, N., and Mantovani, A. (1990). A chemoattractant expressed in human sarcoma cells (tumour-derived chemotactic factor, TDCF) is identical to monocyte chemo-

attractant protein-1/monocyte chemotactic and activating factor (MCP-1/MCAF). *Int. J. Cancer*, **43**, 795–7.

185 Allen, C.A. and Hogg, N. (1987). Association of colorectal tumour epithelium expressing HLA-D/DR with CD8-positive T-cells and mononuclear phagocytes. Cancer *Res.*, **47**, 2919–23.

186 Habets, J.M.W., Tank, B., and van Joost, T.L. (1989). Characterization of the mononuclear infiltrate in Bowen's disease (squamous cell carcinoma *in situ*). Evidence for a T cell-mediated anti-tumour immune response. *Vir. Arch. A. Pathol. Anat.*, **415**, 125–30.

187 Martin, M., Chuuffert, B., Caignard, A., Pelletier, H., Hammann, A., and Martin, F. (1989). Histoimmunochemical characterization of the cellular reaction to liver metastasis induced by colon cancer cells in syngeneic rats. *Inv. Metas.*, **9**, 216–30.

188 Adany, Y., Kappelmayer, J., Berenyl, E., Szegedi, A., Fabian, E., and Muszbek, L. (1989). Factors of the extrinsic pathway of blood coagulation in tumour associated macrophages. *Thromb.* and *Haemost.*, **62**, 850–5.

189 Francis, J.L. (1989). Haemostasis and cancer. *Med. Lab. Sci.*, **46**, 331–46.

190 Tsunawaki, S. and Nathan, C.F. (1986). Macrophage deactivation. Altered kinetic properties of superoxide-producing enzyme after exposure to tumour cell-conditioned medium. *J. Exp. Med.*, **164**, 1319–31.

191 Szuro-Sudol, A., Murray, H. W., and Nathan, C.F. (1983). Suppression of macrophage antimicrobial activity by a tumour cell product. *J. Immunol.*, **131**, 384–7.

192 Normann, S.J. and Sorkin, E. (1977). Inhibition of macrophage chemotaxis by neoplastic and other rapidly proliferating cells *in vitro*. *Cancer Res.*, **37**, 705–11.

193 Szuro-Sudol, A. and Nathan, C.F. (1982). Suppression of macrophage oxidative metabolism by products of malignant and nonmalignant cells. *J. Exp. Med.*, **156**, 945–61.

194 Erroi, A., Sironi, M., Chiaffarino, F., Zhen-Guo, C., Mengozzi, M., and Mantovanni, A. (1989). IL-1 and IL-6 release by tumour-associated macrophages from human ovarian carcinoma. *Int. J. Cancer*, **44**, 795–801.

195 Young, M.R., Sundharadas, G., Cantarow, W.D., and Kumar, P.R. (1982). Purification and functional characteristics of a low molecular weight immune modulating factor produced by Lewis lung carcinoma. *Int. J. Cancer*, **30**, 517–24.

196 Cianciolo, G.J., Herberman, R.B., and Snyderman, R. (1980). Depression of murine macrophage accumulation by low-molecular-weight factors derived from spontaneous mammary carcinomas. *J. Natl. Cancer Inst.*, **65**, 829–34.

197 Kjeldsberg, C.R. and Pay, G.D. (1978). A qualitative and quantitative study of monocytes in patients with malignant solid tumours. *Cancer*, **41**, 2236–41.

198 Snyderman, R., Meadows, L., Holder, W., and Wells, S. (1978). Abnormal monocyte chemotasis in patients with breast cancer: evidence for a tumour mediated effect. *J. Natl. Cancer Inst.*, **60**, 737–40.

199 Nielson, H., Bennedsen, J., Larsen, S.O., Dombernowsky, P., and Viskum, K. (1982). A quantitative and qualitative study of blood monocytes in patients with bronchogenic carcinoma. *Cancer Immunol. Immunoth.*, **13**, 93–7.

200 Hausman, M.S., Brosman, S., Snyderman, R., Mickey, M.R., and Fahey, J. (1975). Defective monocyte function in patients with genito-urinary carcinoma. *J. Natl. Cancer Inst.*, **55**, 1047–54.

201 Hausman, M.S. and Brosman, S.A. (1976). Abnormal monocyte function in bladder cancer patients. *J. Urol.*, **115**, 537–41.

202 Boetcher, D.A. and Leonard, E.J. (1974). Abnormal monocyte chemotactic response in cancer patients. *J. Natl. Cancer Inst.*, **52**, 1091–9.

203 Rhodes, J. (1977). Altered expression of human monocyte Fc receptors in malignant disease. *Nature*, **265**, 253–5.

204 Sciborski, R. (1989). Monocytes in Hodgkin's disease. *Folia Haematol.*, **116**, 17–22.

205 Pollack, S., *et al.* (1983). Endotoxin-induced *in vitro* release of Interleukin-1 by cancer patients' monocytes: relation to state of disease. *Int. J. Cancer*, **32**, 733–6.

206 Yokota, M., Sakamoto, S., Koga, S., and Ibayashi, H. (1987). Decreased Interleukin-1 activity in culture supernatants of lipo-polysaccaride stimulated monocytes from patients with liver cirrhosis and hepatocellular carcinoma. *Clin. Exp. Immunol.*, **67**, 335–42.

207 Sone, S., Utsugi, T., Tandon, P., Yanagawa, H., Okabo, A., and Ogura, T. (1990). Tumour cytotoxicity and Interleukin-1 production of blood monocytes of lung cancer patients. *Cancer Immunol. Immunoth.*, **30**, 357–62.

208 Unger, S.W., Bernhard, M.I., Pace, R.C., and Wanebo, H.J. (1983). Monocyte dysfunction in human cancer. *Cancer*, **51**, 669–74.

209 Cameron, D.J. and Stromberg, B.V. (1984). The ability of macrophages from head and neck cancer patients to kill tumour cells. *Cancer*, **54**, 2403–8.

210 Nakata, Y., *et al.* (1985). Decreased monocyte-mediated cytostasis of human cancer cells in patients with lung cancer. *Cancer Immunol. Immunoth.*, **20**, 43–6.

211 Kleinerman, E.S., *et al.* (1980). Defective monocyte killing in patients

with malignancies and restoration of function during chemotherapy. *Lancet*, **2**, 1102–5.

212 Norman, S.J., Schardt, M., and Sorkin, E. (1979). Cancer progression and monocyte inflammatory dysfunction: relationship to tumour excision and metastasis. *Int. J. Cancer*, **23**, 110–13.

213 Wood, G.W., Neff, J.E., and Stephens, R. (1979). Relationship between monocytosis and T-lymphocyte function in human cancer. *J. Natl. Cancer Inst.*, **63**, 587–92.

214 Currie, G.A. (1976). Serum lysozyme as a marker of host resistance. II. Patients with malignant melanoma, hypernephroma or breast carcinoma. *Br. J. Cancer*, **33**, 593–9.

215 Nakagawara, A., Ikeda, K., Inokuchi, K., Kumashiro, R., and Tamada, R. (1984). Deficient superoxide-generating activity and its activation of blood monocytes in cancer patients. *Cancer Lett.*, **22**, 157–62.

216 Peri, G., Polentarutti, N., Sessa, C., Mangioni, C., and Mantovani, A. (1981). Tumouricidal activity of macrophages isolated from human ascitic and solid ovarian carcinomas: augmentation by interferon, lymphokines and endotoxin. *Int. J. Cancer.*, **28**, 143–52.

217 Kennard, J. and Zolla-Pazner, S. (1980). Origin and function of suppressor macrophages in myeloma. *J. Immunol.*, **124**, 268–73.

218 Smith, R.T. and Landy, M. (1970). *Immune surveillance*. Academic Press, New York.

219 Ting, C C. and Rodrigues, D. (1980). Switching on the macrophage-mediated suppressor mechanism by tumour cells to evade lost immune surveillance. *Proc. Natl. Acad. Sci. U.S.A.*, **77**, 4265–9.

220 Young, M.R., Endicott, R.A., Duffie, G.P., and Wepsic, H.T. (1987). Suppressor alveolar macrophages in mice bearing metastatic Lewis lung carcinoma tumours. *J. Leuc. Biol.*, **42**, 682–8.

221 Ting, C. and Hargrove, M.E. (1982). Tumour cell-triggered macrophage-mediated suppression of the T-cell cytotoxic response to tumour-associated antigens. II. Mechanisms for induction of suppression. *J. Natl. Cancer Inst.*, **69**, 873–8.

222 Ting, C. and Rodrigues, D. (1982). Tumour cell-triggered macrophage-mediated suppression of the T-cell cytotoxic response to tumour-associated antigens. I. characterization of the cell components for induction of suppression. *J. Natl. Cancer Inst.*, **69**, 867–72.

223 Yurochko, A.D., Burger, C.J., and Elgert, K.D. (1990). Tumour modulation of autoreactivity: decreased macrophage and autoreactive T cell interactions. *Cell Immunol.*, **127**, 105–19.

224 Fecchio, D., Sirois, P., Russo, M., and Jancer, S. (1990). Studies on inflammatory response induced by ehrlich tumour in mice peritoneal cavity. *Inflammation*, **14**, 125–32.

225 Ikemoto, S., Kishimoto, T., Nishio, S., Wada, S., and Maekawa, M.

(1989). Correlation of tumour necrosis factor and prostaglandin E production of monocytes in bladder cancer patients. *Cancer*, **64**, 2076–80.

226 Nara, K., *et al.* (1987). Increased production of tumour necrosis factor and prostaglandin E by monocytes in cancer patients and its unique modulation by their plasma. *Cancer Immunol. Immunoth.*, **25**, 126–32.

227 Malick, A.P., Elgert, K.D., Garner, R.E., and Adkinson Jr, N.F. (1987). Prostaglandin E production by Mac-2+ macrophages: tumour-induced population shift. *J. Leuc. Biol.*, **42**, 673–81.

228 Garner, R.E., Malick, A.P., Yurochko, A.D., and Elgert, K.D. (1987). Shifts in macrophage (mphi) surface phenotypes during tumour growth: association of Mac-2+ and Mac-3+ Mphi with immunosuppressive activity. *Cell Immunol.*, **108**, 255–68.

229 Yorochko, A.D., Nagarkatti, P.S., Nagarkatti, M., and Elgert, K.D. (1989). Tumour-induced alteration in macrophage accessory cell activity on autoreactive T cells. *Cancer Immunol. Immunoth.*, **30**, 170–6.

230 Yurochko, A.D., Pyle, R.H., and Elgert, K.D. (1989). Changes in macrophage populations: phenotypic differences between normal and tumour-bearing host macrophages. *Immunobiology*, **178**, 416–35.

231 Borden, E.C. and Sondel, P.M. (1990). Lymphokines and cytokines as cancer treatment immunotherapy realized. *Cancer*, **65**, 800–14.

232 Kleinerman, E.S., Murray, J.L., Snyder, J.S., Cunningham, J.E., and Fidler, I.J. (1989). Activation of tumouricidal properties in monocytes from cancer patients following intravenous administration of liposomes containing muramyl tripeptide phosphatidylethanolamine. *Cancer Res.*, **49**, 4665–70.

233 Sarna, S., Bhola, R.K., and Sodhi, A. (1989). Release of protein bound sialic acid from fibrosarcoma cells after *cis*-dichlorodiammine platinum (II) treatment: the possible role in tumour regression. *Pol. J. Pharmacol. Pharm.*, **40**, 295–302.

234 Wilson, A.P. (1984). Characterization of a cell line derived from the ascites of a patient with papillary serous cystadenocarcinoma of the ovary. *J. Natl. Cancer Inst.*, **72**, 513–21.

235 Einhorn, N., Cantell, K., Einhorn, S., and Strander, H. (1982). Human leucocyte interferon therapy for advanced ovarian carcinoma. *Am. J. Clin. Oncol.*, **5**, 167–72.

236 Fuith, L.C., *et al.* (1989). Effects of interferon-alpha on macrophage activation in patients with ovarian carcinoma and cervical dysplasia. *J. Clin. Lab. Immunol.*, **29**, 65–9.

237 Steward, W.P., *et al.*, (1989). Recombinant human granulocyte macrophage colony stimulating factor (rhGM-CSF) given as daily short infusions—a phase I dose-toxicity study. *Br. J. Cancer*, **59**, 142–5.

238 Foon, K.A., *et al.* (1985). A phase I trial of recombinant gamma

interferon in patients with cancer. *Cancer Immunol. Immunoth.*, **20**, 193–7.

239 Poplack, D.G., Bonnard, G.D., Holiman, B.J., and Blaese, R.M. (1976). Monocyte-mediated antibody-dependent cellular cytotoxicity: A clinical test of monocyte function. *Blood*, **48**, 809–16.

240 Stevenson, H.C., Foon, K.A., and Sugarbaker, P.H. (1986). *Ex vivo* activated monocytes and adoptive immunotherapy trials in colon cancer patients. *Prog. Clin. Biol. Res.*, **211**, 75–82.

241 Stevenson, H.C., *et al.* (1987). Analysis of the trafficking of purified activated human monocytes following intra-peritoneal infusion in colon cancer patients. *Cancer Res.*, **47**, 6100–3.

242 Stevenson, H.C., Lacerna, L.V., and Sugarbaker, P.H. (1988). *Ex vivo* activation of killer monocytes (AKM) and their application to the treatment of human cancer. *J. Clin. Apheresis.*, **4**, 118–21.

243 Schaadt, M., Pfreundschuh, M., Loischeidt, G., Peters, K.M., Steinmetz, T., and Diehl, V. (1990). Phase II study of recombinant human tumour necrosis factor in colorectal carcinoma. *J. Biol. Resp. Mod.*, **9**, 247–50.

244 Yaseen, N.Y., Watmore, A.E., Potter, A.M., Potter, C.W., Jacobs, G., and Rees, R.C. (1990). Chromosome studies on eleven colorectal tumours. *Cancer Genet. Cytogenet.*, **44**, 83–97.

245 Rees, R.C., *et al.* (1988). Loss of polymorphic A and B locus HLA antigens in colon carcinoma. *Br. J. Cancer*, **57**, 374–7.

9 Macrophages in cardiovascular disease

D.V. PARUMS

1   Introduction

Cardiovascular disease remains the chief cause of death in the United States and Western Europe, and atherosclerosis, the principal cause of myocardial and cerebral infarction, accounts for the majority of these deaths.

One of the problems inherent to the study of human atherosclerosis is the lack of unanimity concerning the definition of the histopathological structure of the lesion (1). The name 'atheroma' was commonly used by the Greek writers (2) and again by von Haller in 1735 (3) to describe the yellow, intimal plaques or nodules containing 'gruel-like' material. Virchow (4) was not completely satisfied with this name and believed that these intimal nodules not only contained fat but also proliferating cells. Virchow thought these cells were inflammatory and adopted the name *endarteriitis chronica sive nodosa*. However, this did not achieve popular usage because others doubted the inflammatory nature of the disease.

'Arteriosclerosis' was introduced in 1829 by Lobstein (5) as a generic term for all diseases of the artery in which there is thickening of the vessel wall with induration. Turnbull (1915) defined atheroma as follows: 'Atheroma is a degeneration which affects, and is almost confined to the intima. It is found in both the elastic and muscular arteries, but is more common in the large elastic. The degeneration is characterized by the accumulation of debris, which is at first fatty and is later frequently impregnated by calcium.' (6)

The term 'atherosclerosis' was introduced by Marchand in 1904 (7) and was popularized by Aschoff (8). The World Health Organization (9) has provided the following definition of atherosclerosis: 'a variable combination of changes of the intima of arteries consisting of focal accumulations of lipid, complex carbohydrates, blood and blood products, fibrous deposits and calcium deposits associated with medial changes'.

The local complications of the advanced or complicated atheromatous plaque include: ulceration; thrombosis; medial thinning, which leads to aneurysm; haemorrhage into the plaque; and calcification (Figure 9.1 and 9.2). Whatever definition of atherosclerosis one chooses and whatever theory of atherogenesis one believes, the inescapable fact is that it is the local sequelae of the advanced plaque which give rise to the clinical horizon of atherosclerosis. We see atherosclerosis in terms of this clinical horizon, most commonly as ischaemia and infarction.

Thus, in terms of myocardial disease, ischaemia and infarction are consequences of atherosclerosis. Primary myocarditis may result from viral, bacterial or parasitic infection (10). In the absence of atheroma, vasculitis may also result from viral, bacterial or parasitic infection (11). The role of the macrophage in these infectious processes has been reviewed in Chapters 4, 5, and 6. In addition, myocarditis and vasculitis may be seen in association with autoimmune diseases like rheumatoid arthritis (Chapter 7). Current immunohistochemical studies have shown that the 'owl-eye' and Anti-

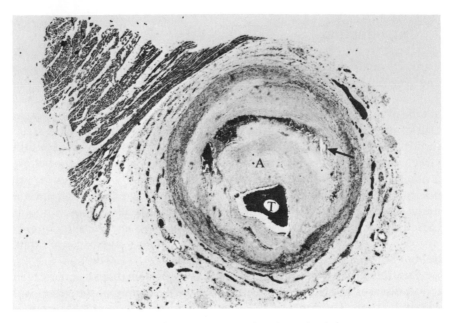

Fig. 9.1 Light micrograph of a transverse section through a human coronary artery showing almost complete occlusion of the vessel lumen with atheroma (A) and organized thrombus (T). Note the angular cholesterol clefts (→) in the atheroma and the dark haemorrhage in the middle of the atheromatous plaque (× 20).

schkow cells of Aschoff bodies in rheumatic carditis are derived from cells of macrophage lineage as are the giant cells in both the idiopathic form of giant cell myocarditis (12) and giant cell arteritis and aortitis (13).

In this chapter, the role of the macrophage in the genesis of the athero-sclerotic plaque will be discussed as this is a unique role of the macrophage in relation to the cardiovascular system. The realization that the macrophage is central to both atherogenesis and the progression of the lesion, has arisen only recently. As will be seen, the pivotal role of the macrophage in atherosclerosis depends not only on its ability to handle lipids but also on its active or physical functions, its passive or secretory functions, and its role as a mediator of inflammation. Chronic inflammatory processes and athe-rosclerosis share many similarities, not least of these being the abundance of macrophages present in these conditions. Chronic inflammation is an im-portant process in the genesis of atherosclerosis, the progression of the lesion and, as this chapter will conclude, chronic inflammation can also be seen as a local complication of atherosclerosis which may give rise to clinical sequelae of its own.

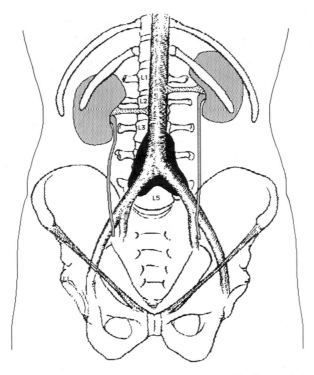

Fig. 9.2   The human aorta and its anatomical relations. The lower abdominal aorta above the aortic bifurcation is the site where atherosclerosis is most apparent. This is also the site where the local complications of atherosclerosis are most apparent. These local complications include stenosis of the aortic lumen, calcification, thrombosis, aneurysm formation, and chronic inflammation (chronic periaortitis).

2   Macrophages, oxidized lipids, and atherosclerosis

2.1   Introduction: macrophages and atherosclerosis

A role for blood-borne mononuclear cells in atherogenesis was first suggested by work on diet-induced lesions in rabbits (14,15). Electron microscopic analysis of spontaneous human atherosclerosis supported this view (16,17), as have both cell marker studies (18) and, more recently, immunohistochemistry using monoclonal antibodies (19–23) (Figure 9.3). Thus, it has been shown that lipid-laden 'foam cells' in early and advanced atherosclerotic plaques are monocyte-derived macrophages rather than smooth muscle cells.

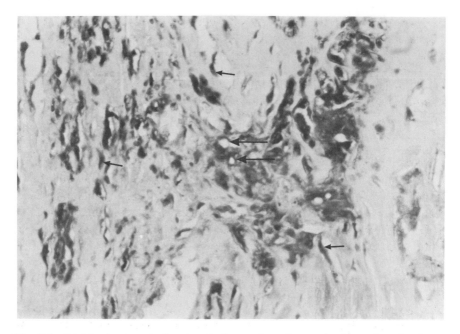

Fig. 9.3   Light micrograph showing the base of an advanced atherosclerotic plaque stained with a mouse monoclonal antibody to human macrophages (KP1), using the indirect immunoperoxidase technique and a dark staining substrate. Note the abundance of both spindle-shaped (small arrows) and 'foamy' macrophages (large arrows) in the lesion. (× 210).

2.2   Modification of low density lipoprotein by macrophages

The recognition that foam cells in human atherosclerotic plaques are macrophages lends credance to studies on lipoprotein uptake. Cholesterol is transported around the body mainly in the form of low density lipoprotein (LDL). Most cell types, including macrophages and smooth muscle cells, take up exogenous cholesterol from LDL for which they have high affinity receptors (see Chapter 1). In times of cholesterol excess, these receptors are down-regulated and thus the cell is prevented from becoming overloaded. In homozygotes with familial hypercholesterolaemia, these receptors are defective and plasma LDL levels are abnormally high (24–26). In this disease, macrophages in a variety of tissues become filled with lipid droplets. The most likely mechanism to account for this phenomenon is uptake of LDL by a low affinity, non-receptor-mediated, non-saturable pathway related to LDL concentration, or by uptake of modified forms of LDL via a 'scavenger receptor pathway'. These scavenger receptors (see Chapter 1) for modified

LDL are present on macrophages and endothelial cells but not other cells. The scavenger receptors for modified LDL are not down-regulated by high cellular cholesterol levels. This leads to the development of the bloated, lipid-laden macrophage foam cell (Figure 9.4).

LDL which has been chemically modified, for example by acetylation or aceto-acetylation, is taken up more readily by macrophages *in vitro* and cleared from the bloodstream *in vivo* than 'native' or unmodified LDL (24,26,27). It has been shown that LDL extracted from the aortic wall is taken up more avidly by mouse peritoneal macrophages than is native LDL (28,29), as is LDL from inflammatory fluid (30).

Acetylation is by no means the only way in which LDL can be modified, leading to increased uptake by macrophages. A variety of artificial treatments have a similar effect (31) and all seem to have in common the ability to make the LDL particle more electro-negative, a property which was shown many years ago to encourage uptake by the macrophage (32).

2.3 Oxidized lipids and atherosclerosis

The mechanism of LDL modification which has recently attracted most attention is oxidation, catalysed by certain ions, including Cu^{2+} (33). The alteration in LDL structure produced by endothelial cells and smooth muscle cells is possibly the result of oxidation (33–5). *In vitro* studies suggest

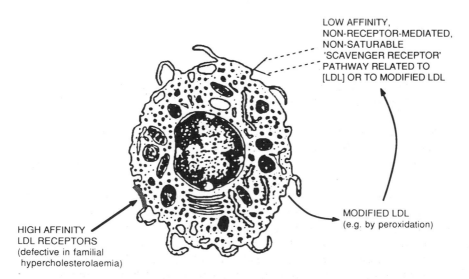

LOW AFFINITY, NON-RECEPTOR-MEDIATED, NON-SATURABLE 'SCAVENGER RECEPTOR' PATHWAY RELATED TO [LDL] OR TO MODIFIED LDL

MODIFIED LDL (e.g. by peroxidation)

HIGH AFFINITY LDL RECEPTORS (defective in familial hypercholesterolaemia)

Fig. 9.4 The role of macrophages in the uptake and modification of low density lipoprotein (LDL). Macrophages have at least two receptors (low and high affinity) for LDL, which are responsible for macrophage involvement in lipid uptake in atheroma (see also Chapter 1).

that LDL modification, perhaps especially oxidation, may occur *in vivo* and that macrophages take up this modified LDL preferentially, much as they phagocytose foreign material in their role as scavenger cells.

In the arterial intima, this role of the macrophage may be crucial to the development of the atherosclerotic plaque. Macrophages are known to release hydrolytic enzymes when they die (36) and they also secrete substances which cause cell proliferation (37). In addition, oxidized lipids have been shown to damage enzymes and membranes, to cause necrosis (38), and to decrease prostacyclin production (39). One other result of LDL modification is that it may be rendered antigenic (40). It is therefore possible that autoallergy to this modified LDL is a factor in the development or the pathogenesis of atherosclerosis.

2.4   Ceroid

Ceroid is the name given to the insoluble yellowish pigment present in mammalian tissues, especially in vitamin E deficiency. It is regularly seen in association with human atherosclerotic plaques and can be regarded as the

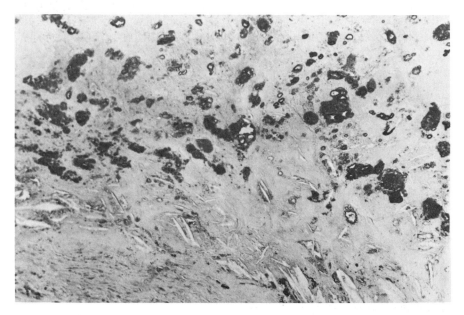

Fig. 9.5 Light micrograph showing an advanced human atherosclerotic plaque which has been stained with a dark lipid stain, oil red O. Note the unstained cholesterol clefts in the lower portion of the photograph. These are sites where soluble cholesterol crystals have dissolved out of the section during routine processing. The dark staining granules and ring forms which remain represent the insoluble lipid, ceroid, which is elaborated in the atheroma by macrophages. (× 125).

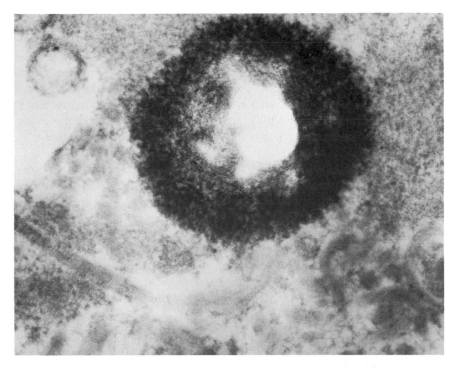

Fig. 9.6 A transmission electron micrograph of the insoluble ceroid fraction of a human atheroma showing the dense granules and the 'fingerprint-like' pattern of the laminations typical of ceroid with alternate electron-dense and electron-lucent areas (× 82 000).

hallmark of the advanced lesion. It is insoluble in lipid solvents and is therefore recognizable in routinely processed tissue sections by lipid stains, such as oil red O (Figure 9.5) and it is autofluorescent. It has a characteristic laminated appearance on electronmicroscopy, with a periodicity to the laminae of 8 nm. (Figure 9.6).

Ceroid is commonly seen in both early and advanced atherosclerotic plaques, both extracellularly and within macrophages, particularly at the necrotic base (41). Ceroid may be regarded as the insoluble, end product of oxidation of LDL in the macrophage and is thought to consist of polymerized products of oxidized lipoproteins. It can be made artificially in the laboratory by oxidizing LDL (29).

2.5 The macrophage hypothesis: a unifying concept of atherogenesis

Until recently, research into atherosclerosis was centred upon the 'response to injury hypothesis' (42). This hypothesis was based on the view that haemodynamic injury to the arterial wall led to endothelial denudation, followed by platelet adhesion and degranulation, which in turn resulted in the release of platelet-derived growth factor (PDGF), causing proliferation of smooth muscle cells. This, along with the accumulation of intracellular and extracellular lipid, basal necrosis and laying down of collagen and connective tissue matrix, led to the development of the lesion. Inherent in this view was the conviction that most, if not all of the cells in the lesion, particularly the lipid-laden 'foam cells', were derived from smooth muscle cells.

It is now apparent that 'foam cells', which are present in fatty streaks and at the edges of most advanced plaques, are macrophages and that macrophages are found in large numbers at the necrotic base of the advanced atherosclerotic plaque. Smooth muscle cells are present in diffuse intimal thickening and are increased in number in larger lesions.

The 'macrophage hypothesis' can be seen as a unifying concept which may shed some light on the mechanisms of atherogenesis but may also permit some understanding of how atherosclerosis causes human disease. Potential roles for the macrophage in the pathogenesis of atherosclerosis include (43):

1. Transport of LDL into the intima from blood borne monocytes.

2. Secretion of cytokines which are chemoattractant for monocytes and smooth muscle cells to the intima.

3. Secretion of growth factors for smooth muscle cells.

4. Secretion of factors which induce phenotypic modulation of smooth muscle cells from a contractile to a secretory state.

5. Secretion of angiogenic factors which stimulate new vessel formation at the base of the plaque.

6. Secretion of neutral proteases, such as collagenases and elastases, which contribute to the formation of the necrotic 'gruel'-like content of the advanced plaque and may be involved in aneurysm formation. Degraded collagen is highly thrombogenic and is also a common site for dystrophic calcification.

7. Production of toxic oxygen radicals which contribute to (6) and which further oxidize free LDL, enhancing its uptake by macrophages.

8. Secretion of lipoprotein lipase which leads to the uptake and degradation of lipoproteins by macrophages.

9. Lipid-laden intimal macrophages may re-emerge into the blood. Although there is no evidence that this occurs in humans, it could be the mechanism for the regression of early lesions.

10. Oxidation of lipid leading to the production of ceroid (See section 2.4).

11. Production of an antigenic stimulus, in the form of oxidized LDL is

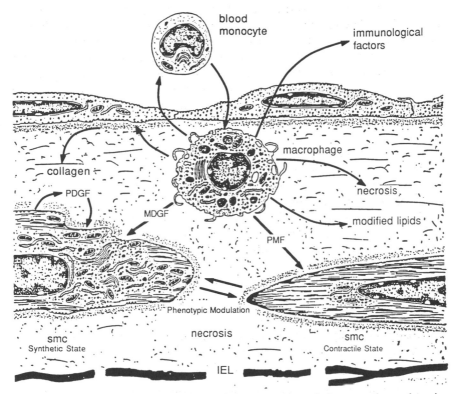

Fig. 9.7 The possible biological roles of the macrophage in human atherosclerosis. smc, smooth muscle cell; IEL, internal elastic lamina; PDGF, platelet-derived growth factor; PMF, phenotypic modulation factors; MDGF, macrophage-derived growth factors.

thought to be due to modification of lysine residues in the apolipo-protein B molecule (see Sections 3.4 and 4.2).

12. Antigen-presentation to cells and secretion of cytokines which recruit lymphocytes to the lesion (see Section 3.5).

When viewed in terms of the development of clinical complications in atherosclerosis, the most important roles of the macrophage most likely include their interactions with lipoproteins; secretion of cytokines which recruit and modulate the behaviour of other cells; release of enzymes; release of oxygen radicals and their ability to modify lipoprotein, rendering it toxic, antigenic, and more amenable to the scavenger receptor pathway (Figure 9.7).

3   Immune mechanisms in atherosclerosis

3.1   Introduction: immune mechanisms in atherogenesis

Chronic inflammatory processes and atherosclerosis share many simil-arities, not least of which is the abundance of macrophages in these conditions. In atherosclerosis, macrophages are numerous in the lipid-rich core. Smooth muscle cells are present particularly in the fibrous plaque. The third major cellular component of the human atherosclerotic plaque is the lymphocyte which is also present, particularly in the fibrous lesion and in the fibrous cap of the advanced lesion. The presence of the macrophage and the smooth muscle cell was identified by light and electron microscopy several years ago. The degree of lymphocytic infiltrate was not apparent until monoclonal antibodies were used for immunohistochemical analysis of the plaque.

3.2   Monocytes and macrophages

One of the major functions of the macrophage is to participate in the immune response by presenting foreign antigen to T-cells. The macrophage does this by internalizing antigen by endocytosis. There then follows a

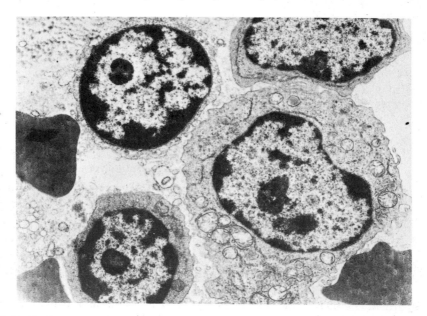

Fig. 9.8   A transmission electron micrograph of the inflammatory cells in the human atherosclerotic plaque showing a macrophage surrounded by smaller lymphocytes (× 4 000).

partial degradation of the antigen within the macrophage lysozomes followed by the transfer of antigen fragments to the macrophage cell surface. The antigen fragments associate with polymorphic cell surface major histocompatibility complex (MHC) proteins and the antigen receptor of the T-cell then binds to this macromolecular complex on the macrophage surface (Figure 9.8).

Monocytes have been shown to bind preferentially to injured endothelium. This is partially due to an interaction between the Fc receptor of the monocyte and IgG which is absorbed on to cytoskeletal intermediate filaments. The binding of IgG also activates the complement cascade, which in turn generates anaphylatoxin C5a, an important chemoattractant for monocytes and granulocytes. Another mechanism for recruitment of monocytes to the vessel is via endothelial expression of specific leucocyte adhesive proteins (Figure 9.9).

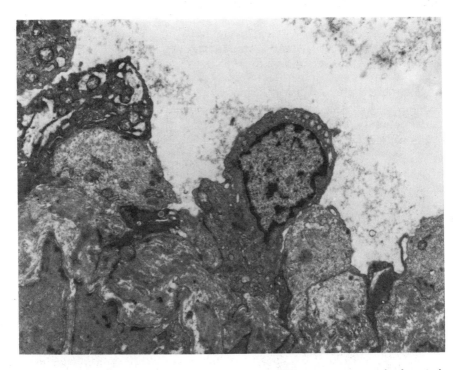

Fig. 9.9   A transmission electron micrograph showing a vasa vasorum in the aortic adventitia of a patient with advanced atherosclerosis. Note the blood mononuclear cell, possibly a lymphocyte, apparently infiltrating between the endothelial cells (× 4400).

3.3   T-cells and Class II MHC antigen expression

Hansson and co-workers (44,45), using immunohistochemical techniques, have detected T-cells and macrophages in atherosclerotic plaques from carotid endarterectomy specimens, but noted that B-cells and natural killer (NK) cells were absent. Macrophages comprised approximately 50 per cent of the cells of the atheromatous plaque. They noted that T-cells, macrophages, and smooth muscle cells were capable of expressing HLA-DR antigen. They also noted that T-cells expressed interleukin-2 (IL-2) receptor and were associated with interferon-gamma (IFNγ) secretion. These findings lead to their suggestion that T-cell–smooth muscle cell interactions may occur during atherogenesis.

More recently, Van der Wahl and co-workers (46), using double immunohistochemical staining, showed that lymphocyte populations in various stages of human atherosclerotic plaques consist of HLA-DR-positive helper and cytotoxic T-cells which express IL-2 receptor molecules. They postulated that local immune-mediated hypersensitivity reactions are associated with atherogenesis.

3.4   Humoral immune mechanisms

Atherosclerotic plaques contain deposits of immunoglobulins that are not present in non-atherosclerotic lesions (47). Complement factors have been found with a similar tissue distribution, suggesting that local complement activation may occur in the plaque (47,48).

Serum sickness has been repeatedly correlated with development or aggravation of the atherosclerotic process (49) and antiendothelial autoantibodies have been shown to correlate with peripheral vascular disease (50). Several micro-organisms, particularly herpes viruses, have been implicated in the pathogenesis of atherosclerosis (51). The local response to these pathogens is likely to be both cell-mediated and antibody-based.

Antibodies to modified lipoproteins have been described, by various workers, in association with complications of atherosclerosis (see Section 4.2), (52,53). How these antibodies may be implicated in the aetiology of human atherosclerosis remains controversial.

3.5   Cytokines

The initiation and propagation of the immune response depends not only on interactions between cell surface molecules but also on humoral factors. Under certain conditions, cells of the immune system may be viewed as wandering endocrine cells, which, when activated, produce substances

Table 9.1   Cytokines of the immune system

Cytokine	Source
IL-1	Monocyte/macrophage, NK cells, endothelial cells, smooth muscle cells
IL-2	T-cells, NK cells
IL-3	T-cells
IL-4	T-cells, NK cells
IL-5	T-cells
IL-6	Many cell types
IFNα	Leucocytes
IFNγ	T-cells, NK cells
Tumour necrosis factor (TNFα)	Monocyte/macrophage, smooth muscle cells, NK cells
Lymphotoxin (TNFβ)	T-cells
Platelet-derived growth factor (PGDF)	Monocyte/macrophage, endothelial cells, smooth muscle cells megakaryocyte/platelet

called cytokines which can act in an autocrine, paracrine and/or endocrine fashion. These molecules have been shown to affect growth and gene expression in vascular cells (Table 9.1).

Monocytes and macrophages, when activated, produce several factors that are important for inflammatory and immune responses. They also produce growth promoters, the best known of which is PDGF (54). Inter-

Table 9.2   Vascular effects of IL-1

Cells and their effect

Endothelial cells
    Induces procoagulant activity
    Induces reorganization of endothelial monolayers
    Stimulates adhesion of granulocytes, monocytes, and lymphocytes by inducing expression of specific adhesive proteins
    Stimulates proliferation
    Increases vascular permeability
    Induces IL-1 release by positive feedback

Smooth muscle cells
    Stimulates proliferation
    Induces platelet-derived growth factor (PDGF) secretion
    Induces IL-1 release by positive feedback

Table 9.3   Vascular effects of TNFα

Cells and their effect

Endothelial cells
    Induces procoagulant activity
    Induces reorganization of endothelial monolayers
    Stimulates adhesion of granulocytes, monocytes, and lymphocyes by inducing
    expression of specific adhesive proteins
    Inhibits proliferation *in vitro*
    Induces angiogenesis
    Induces MHC gene expression

Smooth muscle cells
    Induces Class I MHC genes
    Modulates IFNγ-induced Class II MHC genes

---

leukin -1 (IL-1) is probably the best characterized interleukin (Table 9.2). The activated macrophage also produces a 17 kDa protein, called tumour necrosis factor (TNFα) (Table 9.3). As the lymphocyte makes a structurally related substance, lymphotoxin (TNFβ), it should be emphasized that the macrophage product is TNFα. TNFα can also be produced by vascular smooth muscle cells. It induces vascular and inflammatory responses similar to those of IL-1 but may also cause tumor cell cytotoxicity and cachexia in malignant disease.

The activated T-cell is a rich source of many biologically active proteins, the best characterized of which is IFNγ. IFNγ has three major effects: it induces expression of MHC genes; inhibits cell proliferation; and induces antiviral activity. In addition, it affects expression of a variety of genes in many different cell types including macrophages and vascular cells (Table 9.4).

4   Chronic periaortitis: a local complication of atherosclerosis

4.1   Introduction: inflammation as a local complication of atherosclerosis

In 1915, Allbutt described atherosclerosis as 'a very chronic inflammation' and noted the 'round cell growth' in the adventitia (55). Brief mention of these cellular aggregates, associated with advanced atherosclerotic plaques, have since been made by other workers who have interpreted them in various ways (56,57).

Table 9.4 Vascular effects of IFNγ

Cells and their effect

Endothelial cells
    Induces reorganization of endothelial monolayers
    Induces new surface proteins associated with autoimmune responses
    Inhibits PDGF and IL-1 expression
    Inhibits proliferation
    Increases vascular permeability
    Induces Class I MHC gene expression
    Induces Class II MHC gene expression

Smooth muscle cells
    Induces Class I MHC gene expression
    Induces Class II MHC gene expression
    Inhibits proliferation

Lymphocytes and macrophages in the intima of atherosclerotic arteries have been described by light and electron microscopy. In 1979, an ultrastructural study by Joris and co-workers observed the infiltration of bloodborne mononuclear cells into the intima and proposed that this was in response to a chemical message, perhaps an antigen, originating from the media (58).

In 1962, Schwartz and Mitchell (59) suggested that arterial adventitial infiltrates of small lymphocytes correlated with the severity of the intimal atheromatous lesion and not with the anatomical site of the plaque or with the patient's age or sex. Furthermore, these workers described the predominance of lymphocytes and plasma cells in the adventitia and media. They pointed out that in other conditions in which adventitial cellular changes occur, including polyarteritis nodosa, giant cell arteritis, and disseminated lupus erythematosus, the cellular pattern was different to that found associated with the advanced atherosclerotic plaque. They suggested that these changes were involved in the pathogenesis rather than the aetiology of atherosclerosis and were due to some 'change in immunological tolerance' to a component of the plaque itself.

A spectrum of chronic inflammation is commonly seen in association with advanced atherosclerosis when the aortic media is thinned (57), (Figure 9.10). Chronic periaortitis is a term recently suggested for this condition (56). Chronic periaortitis may be detected only histopathologically, usually at autopsy, or, in its most severe form, may present clinically in the form of 'idiopathic retroperitoneal fibrosis', 'perianeurysmal retroperitoneal fibrosis', or 'inflammatory aneurysm' (56,60).

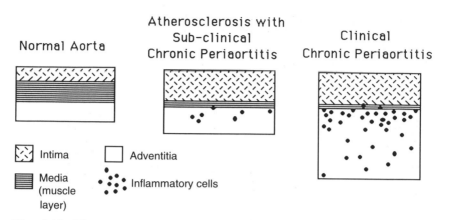

Fig. 9.10 The relative proportions of the intima, media, and adventitia in the normal aorta, subclinical chronic periaortitis and clinical chronic periaortitis. In the latter condition, it is the adventitial inflammation and fibrosis which leads to such symptoms as an obstruction of the ureter and back pain.

Chronic periaortitis is thought to have an autoallergic cause. The allergen is believed to be a component of ceroid, possibly oxidized LDL, elaborated in the human atheroma. This allergen is sequestered from the immune response unless the media is breached; the idea being that the atheromatous plaque acts as an immunologically 'privileged site' (57), (Figure 9.11).

4.2   Antibodies to oxidized LDL and ceroid

Immunoglobulin-secreting plasma cells in the aortic adventitial infiltrate occur in chronic periaortitis. This has been interpreted as evidence that chronic periaortitis is due to an autoallergic reaction to a component of the atherosclerotic plaque (61). The possibility that ceroid, which is produced by macrophages in atheroma, might be antigenic was first suspected when human immunoglobulin was found to localize to ceroid in atherosclerotic plaques from patients which chronic periaortitis (62), (Figure 9.12).

The incidence of human serum antibodies to human LDL, to artificially oxidized LDL, and to ceroid extracted from human atheroma was assessed in 100 subjects using an adaptation of the enzyme-linked immunosorbent assay technique (53). Patients with chronic periaortitis, subclinical chronic periaortitis, ischaemic heart disease, and 'elderly control' individuals were compared with young, healthy adults. Provided that precautions were taken to prevent its oxidation, antibodies were not found to native human LDL. Antibodies to oxidized LDL or ceroid, usually both, were detected in all 20 patients with clinical chronic periaortitis, 17 out of 20 patients with sub-clinical chronic periaortitis, 12 out of 20 patients with ischaemic heart disease, and 10 out of 20 'elderly control' individuals. Binding inhibition

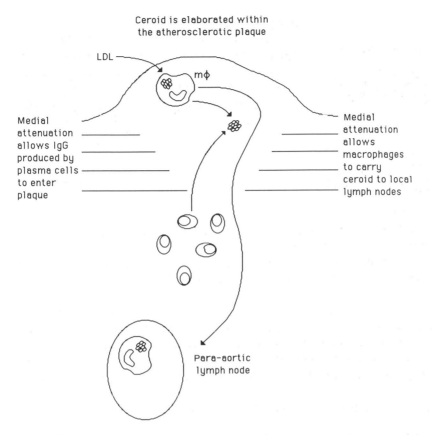

Ceroid is elaborated within
the atherosclerotic plaque

LDL

mø

Medial
attenuation
allows IgG
produced by
plasma cells
to enter
plaque

Medial
attenuation
allows
macrophages
to carry
ceroid to local
lymph nodes

Para-aortic
lymph node

Fig. 9.11   The hypothesis that chronic periaortitis has an autoallergic cause and that the antigen is a component of ceroid elaborated by macrophages (mø) in human atherosclerosis.

studies showed cross-reactions between oxidized LDL and ceroid. Western blotting after sodium dodecyl sulphate polyacrylamide gel electrophoresis showed that in some patients with chronic periaortitis, some of these antibodies were directed against oxidation products of Apo B (53).

The findings in ischaemic heart disease may be due to a relatively high incidence of subclinical chronic periaortitis in this group. Further studies will be necessary to substantiate this.

4.3   Characterization of inflammatory cells in chronic periaortitis

Monoclonal antibodies have been used to study the nature of the inflammatory cell infiltrates in surgical biopsy material from clinical chronic periaortitis (63,64). In each sample, organized lymphoid tissue was observed;

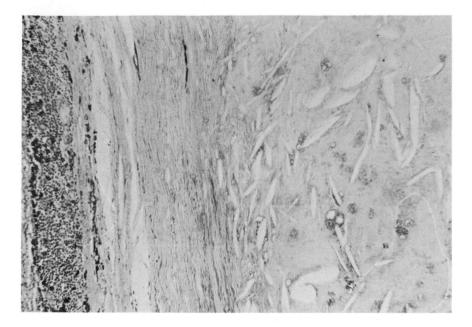

Fig. 9.12 Light micrograph showing a section of human aorta which features advanced atherosclerosis (right) with medial thinning and a dense adventitial chronic inflammatory cell infiltrate which consists of lymphocytes and plasma cell (left). This is chronic periaortitis. The tissue has been stained with a mouse monoclonal antibody to human IgG using the indirect immunoperoxidase technique and a dark substrate. Note the staining for IgG localized to the ceroid rings and granules in the atheroma (right) and to the adventitial plasma cells (left). (× 125).

this was a predominantly plasmacytic response. The infiltrate was composed of approximately 10 per cent macrophages (EBM11 positive), 55 per cent B-cells (CD19/22 positive), 35 per cent T-cells (CD3 positive) with helper T-cells (Th) (CD4 positive), and suppressor T-cells (Tc/s) (CD8 positive) in a ratio of between 3 and 4 to 1. These cells were organized into secondary follicles with germinal centres. The predominance of CD4 over CD8 positive cells was as would be expected in a B-cell response to local extracellular antigen, requiring T-cell help. No polymorphonuclear cells or NK cells were observed.

The expression of MHC Class II antigen was also observed using monoclonal antibodies to the HLA-DR antigen. In the inflamed tissue, 60–80 per cent of the cells expressed in this antigen. The antigen was expressed by macrophages, B-cells, endothelial cells, smooth muscle cells, and by many of the T-cells. This abundant expression indicates a highly immunologically activated site. The MHC Class II molecule is important in antigen presentation and is required for recognition of antigen by helper T-cells and for the subsequent initiation of an immune response. It is, however, unclear if all of these cells are acting as antigen-presenting cells. This abundant, or perhaps aberrant, expression is also seen in other chronic inflammation reactions, as well as in most autoimmune diseases; it may indicate a loss of immunological control.

Proliferating cells have been investigated using the monoclonal antibody

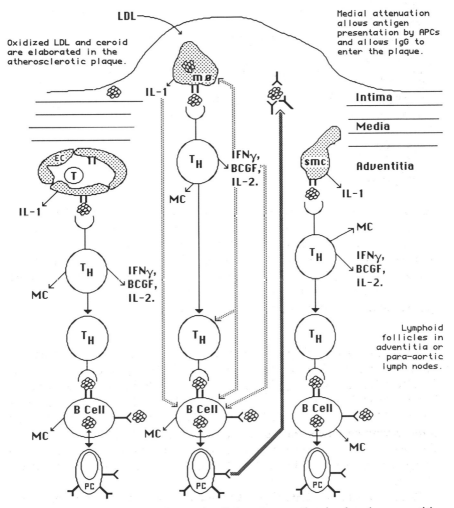

Fig. 9.13 Antigen presentation and cellular co-operation in chronic penaortitis. APCs, Antigen-presenting cells; **mø**, macrophage; **EC**, endothelial cell; **smc**, smooth muscle cell; ⊗, antigen (oxidized LDL/ceroid); **II**, Class II MHC molecule; PC, plasma cell; ⅄, immunoglobulin molecule (IgG); ⊂, T-lymphocyte receptor; T_H, helper T-cell; **IFNγ**, interferon-gamma; **MC**, memory cell; **BCGF**, B-cell growth factor; **IL-1(2)**, interleukin 1(2).

Ki67, which binds a proliferation-associated nuclear antigen (65). The number of proliferating cells appears to correlate with the degree of inflammation. These proliferating cells are found predominantly around the germinal centre within the secondary follicles. They can comprise up to 10 per cent of the lymphocytes. Monoclonal antibodies to the IL-2 receptor revealed a small proportion of the cells, again mostly around germinal centres, to be activated.

Studies have begun to look at the role of cytokines in this chronic inflammatory reaction, as these molecules regulate inflammation and all immune responses. Of special interest are TNFα and IFNγ, which synergize and regulate the expression of the MHC Class II molecule which is so abundant in this tissue (Figure 9.13).

4.4   Clinical implications and future research

The atherosclerotic plaque may represent a site of relative immunological privilege until the muscle layer of the artery (media) is breached or new vessels form in advanced or complicated plaques. Chronic periaortitis may be the end stage of the immune response, directed at antigens elaborated in the atherosclerotic plaque by macrophages during atherogenesis. Functional studies of the lymphocyte populations *in vitro* from atherosclerotic

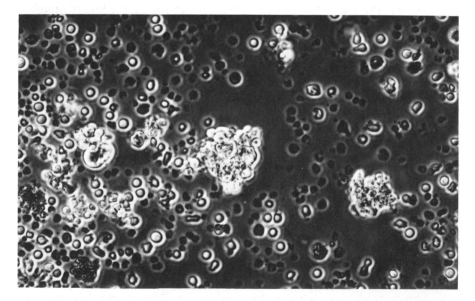

Fig. 9.14 Phase contrast micrograph showing the appearance of lymphocytes in culture from a case of clinical chronic periaortitis. After 1 week in culture, the lymphocytes cluster around macrophages which contain abundant ceroid granules (× 1 080).

plaques in various stages of development, including those with associated chronic periaortitis, would establish whether or not this was the case (Figure 9.14).

The major histopathological changes in chronic periaortitis are medial thinning, fibrosis, and a dense infiltration of mononuclear cells, mainly lymphocytes and plasma cells. These plasma cells are believed to develop from B-cells stimulated by antigen which is locally present in the atheroma, namely a component of ceroid, likely to be oxidized LDL. Isolation and culture of these mature B-cells would allow this hypothesis to be tested and would also allow the isolation and characterization of such antibodies. It is not known whether these antibodies are monoclonal or polyclonal. They are likely to be polyclonal, but still the potential for producing human monoclonal antibodies from such cell cultures exists.

The role of chronic inflammation as a complication of advanced human atherosclerosis remains controversial. Even more controversial is the mechanism of the immunological response to antigens elaborated within the atheromatous plaque. Until now, there has been relatively little experimental work done in this field, especially in the use of human material.

It is now possible to 'capture' human immune responses *in vivo* and investigate them *in vitro*. Perhaps the most exciting aspect of this work lies in the real potential for generating human monoclonal antibodies to components of the atherosclerotic plaque. These may provide a method of imaging human atheroma *in vivo*. At present, the extent of an individual's atherosclerosis is only readily appreciated at autopsy. The time is now right to pursue this research with a view to answering some fundamental questions regarding the pathogenesis of human atherosclerosis.

Successful production of human–human hybridomas secreting monoclonal antibodies has proved difficult. Transformation of human B-cells with Epstein–Barr virus has had some limited success, but such cultures usually secrete low levels of antibody and cease antibody production entirely after a variable period of time. An alternative approach is the fusion of a mouse myeloma with human lymphocytes to produce heterohybridomas. Such immunoglobulin-secreting heterohybridomas with a lifespan of several months have been established by fusing mouse myeloma cells with human B-cells obtained from peripheral blood (66,67), lymph nodes (68), and spleen (69).

Chronic periaortitis is characterized by the presence of adventitial mononuclear cells together with a varied amount of periaortic fibrosis. What determines the degree of fibrosis is unknown, but in its severest form, it is this fibrotic reaction which leads to the clinical manifestations of the disease, such as ureteric obstruction. Cells of the immune system are known to be sources of mediators regulating fibroblast proliferation. The macrophage is a source of fibroblast growth factor, the T-cell is known to produce fibroblast growth factor and collagen synthesis stimulatory factors (70,71). The mechanisms of fibrosis in chronic periaortitis require further examination using *in vitro* techniques.

Chronic periaortitis may not represent a 'classical' autoimmune disease as there is no change in self-tolerance but rather, there is a change in a self protein. It is likely that anyone with oxidized LDL present in their serum could perhaps mount an immune response to this antigen but that in the atheroma the modified LDL is both persistent and abundant and the immune system is unable to clear it. This antibody response may be a 'normal', physiological mechanism to clear harmful oxidized lipid from the serum. Patients with severe, clinical chronic periaortitis may be demonstrating an immunological derangement of a phenomenon commonly seen in those with advanced atherosclerosis.

The findings of these studies may have no relevance to processes occurring in atherogenesis, as they appear to be a consequence rather than a cause of human atherosclerosis. However, they are likely to be of relevance in the progression of the disease.

5   Summary

In summary, this chapter has discussed the role of the macrophage in cardiovascular disease, with particular emphasis on the nature of atherosclerosis and the role of the macrophage in the genesis of the atherosclerotic plaque. The identity of the macrophage as the 'villain of the piece' in term of atherogenesis and the progression of the lesion has been established. Chronic inflammation is thus an important process in the genesis and progression of atherosclerosis and, as this chapter has concluded, chronic inflammation is also a local complication of atherosclerosis which may give rise to clinical sequelae of its own.

The view that in atherosclerosis the macrophage is doing harm to the arterial wall is supported by the inhibition of experimental atherosclerosis by a variety of anti-inflammatory drugs (72). Oxidized lipids elaborated by macrophages are thought to have a cytotoxic and biologically active role.

The role of oxidized lipids derives support from the human epidemiological studies linking vitamin E or selenium deficiency with enhanced risk of the complications of atherosclerosis (73). Furthermore, a number of reports have suggested a beneficial effect of anti-oxidants in experimental atherosclerosis (74). It is possible that the widely canvassed anti-atherogenic effects of the fatty acids of fish oils may be related to their reported inhibition of the oxidative inflammatory activity of phagocytes (75).

If lipid oxidation is important in atherogenesis and the progression of the lesion with its associated clinical sequelae, intervention in the process should be aimed at sites where most of the oxidation occurs. From the research presented in this chapter, it is apparent that the macrophage 'foam cell' is the likely culprit in the production of oxidized lipids. However, there are other possible candidates.

Some foods, such as dehydrated milk and eggs, are susceptible to oxidation on storage and on cooking (76) and some of the oxidation products can be absorbed from the blood (77). Oxidation might also occur in the blood where lipid peroxides are thought to be more common in patients with hyperlipidaemia and atherosclerosis (78).

Endothelial cell mediated oxidation of LDL occurs *in vitro* and if it does occur *in vivo* would result in modified LDL which is taken up more avidly by intimal macrophages. Finally, as discussed above, the macrophage is likely to be a site for LDL oxidation *in vitro*. The relative contributions of all these sites and mechanisms of LDL oxidation *in vivo* are, at present, unknown.

References

1 Pickering, G. (1963). Arteriosclerosis and atherosclerosis; the need for clear thinking. *Am J. Med.*, **34**, 7–18.
2 Long, E.R. (1933). In *Arteriosclerosis* (ed. E.V. Cowdry), Macmillan, New York.
3 Von Haller, A. (1735). *Opuscula pathologica*. Bousquet, Lausanne.
4 Virchow, R. (1862). Gesammelte Abhandlungen z. Wissentschaftlichen Medizin. In *Phlogose und Thrombose in Gefässystem*. Max Hirsch, Berlin.
5 Lobstein, J.G.C.F.M. (1829). *Traité d'anatomie pathologique*. Levrault, Paris.
6 Turnbull, H.M. (1915). Alterations in arterial structure and their relation to syphilis. *Quart. J. Med.*, **8**, 203–10.
7 Marchand, F. (1904). Über Arteriosklerose (Atherosklerose). *Verhandl. Kongr. inn. Med.*, **21**, 23–7.
8 Aschoff, L. (1933). In *Arteriosclerosis*, (ed. E.V. Cowdry). MacMillan, New York.
9 World Health Organization (1958). Report of a study group: Classification of atherosclerotic lesions. *World Health Organization Technical Report Series*, **143**.
10 Aretz, H.T., Billingham, M.E., and Edwards, W.D. (1986). Myocarditis: a histopathological definition and classification. *Am. J. Cardiovasc. Pathol.*, **1**, 3–14.
11 Fauci, A.S., Hayne, B.F., and Katz, P. (1978). The spectrum of vasculitis: Clinical, pathogenic, immunologic and therapeutic considerations. *Ann. Intern. Med.*, **89**, 660–72.
12 Theaker, J.M., Gatter, K.C., Brown, D.C., Heryet, A., and Davies, M.J. (1988). An investigation into the nature of giant cells in cardiac and skeletal muscle. *Hum. Pathol.*, **19**, 974–9.
13 Banks, P.M., Cohen, M.D., Ginsburg, W.W., and Hunder, G.G. (1983). Immunohistologic and cytochemical studies of temporal arteritis. *Arthr. Rheum.*, **265**, 1201–9.
14 Anitschow, E. (1933). Experimental arteriosclerosis in animals. In *Arteriosclerosis* (ed. E.V. Cowdry), pp. 271–322. MacMillan, New York.
15 Leary, T. (1941). The genesis of atherosclerosis. *Arch. Pathol.*, **32**, 507–55.
16 Geer, J.C., McGill, H.C., and Strong, J.P. (1961). The fine structure of human atherosclerotic lesions. *Am. J. Path.*, **34**, 1764–9.
17 Haust, M.D. (1971). The morphogenesis and fate of potential atherosclerotic lesions in man. *Hum. Pathol.*, **2**, 1–29.
18 Scaffner, T., *et al.* (1980). Arterial foam cells with distinctive immuno-

morphological and histochemical features of macrophages. *Am. J. Path.*, **100**, 57–80.

19 Aqel, N.M., Ball, R.Y., Waldmann, H., and Mitchinson, M.J. (1984). Monocytic origin of foam cells in human atherosclerotic plaques. *Atherosclerosis.*, **53**, 265–71.

20 Aqel, N.M., Ball, R.Y., Waldmann, H., and Mitchinson, M.J. (1985). Identification of macrophage and smooth muscle cells in human atherosclerosis using monoclonal antibodies. *J. Path.*, **146**, 197–204.

21 Klurfield, D.M. (1985). Identification of foam cells in human atherosclerotic lesions as macrophages using monoclonal antibodies. *Arch. Pathol.*, **109**, 445–9.

22 Jonasson, L., Holm, J., Skalli, O., Gabbiani, G., and Hansson, G.K. (1985). Expression of Class II transplantation antigen on vascular smooth muscle cells in human atherosclerosis. *J. Clin. Pathol.*, **76**, 125–31.

23 Gown, A.M., Tsukada, T., and Ross, R. (1986). Human atherosclerosis, II. Immunocytochemical analysis of the cellular composition of human atherosclerotic lesions. *Am. J. Pathol.*, **125**, 191–207.

24 Goldstein, J.L., Ho, Y.K., Basu, S.K., and Brown, M.S. (1979). Binding site on macrophages that mediate uptake and degradation of acetylated LDL producing massive cholesterol deposition. *Proc. Natl. Acad. Sci. U.S.A.*, **76**, 333–37.

25 Fogelman, A.M., Seager, J. Haberland, M.E., Hokon, M., Tanaka, R., and Edwards, P.A. (1982). Lymphocyte-conditioned medium protects human monocyte-macrophage from cholesteryl ester accumulation. *Proc. Natl. Acad. Sci. U.S.A.*, **79**, 922–6.

26 Mahley, R.W., Innerarity, T.L., Weisgraber, K.H., and Oh, S.Y. (1979). Altered metabolism (*in vitro* and *in vivo*) of plasma lipoproteins after selective chemical modification of lysine residues of the apoproteins. *J. Clin. Invest.*, **64**, 743–50.

27 Van der Schroeff, J.G., Havekes, L., Emeis, J.J., Wijsman, M., Van der Meer, H., and Vermeer, B.J. (1983). Morphological studies on the binding of low density lipoprotein and acetrylated low density lipoprotein to the plasma membrane of cultured lymphocytes. *Exp. Cell. Res.*, **145**, 95–103.

28 Clevidence, B.A., Morton, R.E., West, G., Dusek, D.M., and Hoff, H.F. (1984). Cholesterol esterification in macrophages, stimulated by lipoproteins containing apo-B isolated from human aortas. *Arteriosclerosis*, **4**, 196–207.

29 Ball, R.Y., Bindman, J.P., Carpenter, K.L.H., and Mitchinson, M.J. (1986). Oxidized low density lipoprotein induces ceroid accumulation by murine peritoneal macrophages *in vitro*. *Atherosclerosis.*, **60**, 173–81.

30 Raymond, T.L. and Reynolds, S.A. (1983). Lipoproteins of the extra-

vascular space; alterations in low density lipoproteins of interstitial inflammatory fluid. *J. Lipid res.*, **24**, 113–18.

31 Brown, M.S. and Goldstein, J.L. (1983). Lipoprotein metabolism in the macrophage; implications for cholesterol deposition in atherosclerosis. *Ann. Rev. Biochem.*, **52**, 223–61.

32 Cohn, Z.A. (1968). The structure and function of monocytes and macrophages. *Adv. Immunol.*, **9**, 163–214.

33 Steinbrecher, U.P., Parthasarathy, S., Leake, D.S., Witztum, J.L., and Steinberg, D. (1984). Modification of low density lipoprotein by endothelial cells involves lipid peroxidation and degradation of low density lipoprotein phospholipids. *Proc. Natl. Acad. Sci. U.S.A.*, **81**, 3883–7.

34 Heinicke, J.W., Baker, L., Rosen, H., and Chait, A. (1984). Superoxide generated by arterial smooth muscle cells mediates metal ion catalyzed by low density lipoprotein modification. *Arteriosclerosis.*, **4**, 551a.

35 Morel, D.W., DiCorletto, P.E., and Chisolm, G.M. (1984). Endothelial and smooth muscle cells alter low density lipoprotein *in vitro* by free radical oxidation. *Atherosclerosis*, **4**, 3557–64.

36 Cookson, F.B. (1971). The origin of foam cells in atherosclerosis. *Br. J. Exp. Pathol.*, **52**, 62–9.

37 Ziats, N.P. and Robertson, A.L. (1981). Effects of peripheral blood monocytes on human vascular cell proliferation. *Atherosclerosis.*, **38**, 401–10.

38 Logani, M.K. and Davies, R.E. (1980). Lipid oxidation; biological effects and anti-oxidants—a review. *Lipids*, **15**, 485–95.

39 Moncada, S., Gryglewski, R.J., Bunting, S., and Vane J.R. (1976). A lipid peroxide inhibits the enzyme in blood vessel microsomes that generates from prostaglandin endoperoxides the substance (prostaglandin X) which prevents platelet aggregation. *Prostaglandins*, **12**, 715–20.

40 Steinbrecher, U.P., Fischer, M., Witztum, J.L., and Curtiss, L.K. (1984). Immunogenicity of homologous low density lipoprotein after methylation, ethylation, acetylation, and carbamylation; generation of antibodies specific for derivatised lysine. *J. Lipid Res.*, **25**, 1109–16.

41 Mitchinson, M.J., Hothersall, D.C., Brooks, P.N., and DeBurbure, C.Y. (1985). The distribution of ceroid in human atherosclerosis. *J. Path.*, **145**, 177–83.

42 Ross, R. (1986). The pathogenesis of atherosclerosis—an update. *N. Engl. J. Med.*, **314**, 488–500.

43 Mitchinson, M.J. and Ball, R.Y. (1987). Macrophages and atherogenesis. *Lancet*, **ii**, 146–8.

44 Hansson, G.K., Jonasson, L., Lojsted, B., Stemme, S., Kocher, O., and Gabbiani, G. (1988). Localization of T lymphocytes and macrophages in fibrous and complicated plaques. *Atherosclerosis*, **72**, 135–40.

45 Hansson, G.K., Holm, J., and Jonasson, L. (1989). Detection of activated T lymphocytes in the human atherosclerotic plaque. *Am. J. Path.*, **135**, 169–75.

46 Van der Wahl, A.C., Das, P.K., Van de Berg, D.B., Van der Loos, C.M., and Becker, A.E. (1989). Atherosclerotic lesions in humans. *In situ* immunophenotypic analysis suggesting an immune mediated response. *Lab. Invest.*, **61**, 166–70.

47 Hansson, G.K., Holm, J., and Kral, J.G. (1984). Accumulation of IgG and complement factor C3 in human arterial endothelium and atherosclerotic lesions. *Acta. Pathol. Microbiol. Immunol. Scand.*, **92A**, 429–35.

48 Pang, A.S., Katz, A., and Minta, J.O. (1979). C3 deposition in cholesterol-induced atherosclerosis in rabbits: a possible etiologic role for complement in atherogenesis. *J. Immunol.*, **123**, 1117–23.

49 Minick, C.R. and Murphy, G.E. (1973). Experimental induction of arteriosclerosis by the synergy of allergic injury to arteries and lipid-rich diet. II. Effect of repeatedly injected foreign protein in rabbits fed a lipid-rich, cholesterol-poor diet. *Am. J. Path.*, **73**, 265–300.

50 Cerilli, J., Brasile, L., and Karmody, A. (1985). Role of the vascular endothelial cell antigen system in the aetiology of atherosclerosis. *Ann. Surg.*, **202**, 329–34.

51 Benditt, E.P., Barrett, T., and McDougal, J.M. (1983). Viruses in the aetiology of atherosclerosis. *Proc. Natl. Acad. Sci. U.S.A.*, **80**, 6386–9.

52 Beaumont, J.L. and Beaumont, V. (1977). Autoimmune hyperlipidaemia. *Atherosclerosis*, **26**, 405–18.

53 Parums, D.V., Brown, D. L., and Mitchinson, M.J. (1990). Serum antibodies to oxidized low density lipoprotein and ceroid in chronic periaortitis. *Arch. Pathol. Lab. Med.*, **114**, 383–7.

54 Shimokado, K., Raines, E.W., Madtes, D.K., Barrett, T.B., Benditt, E.P., and Ross, R. (1985). A significant part of the macrophage-derived growth factor consists of at least two forms of PDGF. *Cell*, **43**, 277–86.

55 Allbutt, C.T. (1915). *Diseases of the arteries*, Vol. 1. MacMillan, London.

56 Mitchinson, M.J. (1984). Chronic periaortitis and periarteritis. *Histopathology*, **8**, 589–600.

57 Parums, D.V. (1990). The spectrum of chronic periaortitis. *Histopathology*, **16**, 423–31.

58 Joris, I., Stetz, E. and Majno, G. (1979). Lymphocytes and monocytes in the aortic intima. An electronmicroscopic study in the rat. *Atherosclerosis*, **34**, 221–31.

59 Schwartz, C.J. and Mitchell, J.R.A. (1962). Cellular infiltration of the human arterial adventitia associated with atheromatous plaques. *Circulation*, **2**, 73–8.

60 Mitchinson, M.J. (1972). Aortic disease in idiopathic retroperitoneal fibrosis. *J. Clin. Pathol.*, **25**, 287–93.
61 Parums, D. and Mitchinson, M.J. (1981). Demonstration of immuno-globulin in the neighbourhood of advanced atherosclerotic plaques. *Atherosclerosis*, **38**, 211–16.
62 Parums, D.V., Chadwick, D.R., and Mitchinson, M.J. (1986). The localization of immunoglobulin in chronic periaortitis. *Atherosclerosis*, **61**, 117–23.
63 Parums, D.V. and Ramshaw, A.L. (1990). Immunohistochemical characterization of inflammatory cells in biopsies from abdominal aortic aneurysms. *J. Pathol.*, **160**, 160A.
64 Ramshaw, A.L. and Parums, D.V. (1990). Immunohistochemical characterization of inflammatory cells associated with advanced atherosclerosis. *Histopathology*, **17**, 543–52.
65 Gerdes, J., Schwab, U., Lemke, H., and Stein, H. (1983). Production of a mouse monoclonal antibody reactive with a human nuclear antigen associated with cell proliferation. *Int. J. Cancer*, **31**, 13–20.
66 Croce, C.M., *et al.* (1979). Chromosomal location of the genes for human immunoglobulin heavy chains. *Proc. Natl. Acad. Sci. U.S.A.*, **76**, 3416–22.
67 Thompson, K.M., Hough, D.W., Maddison, P.J., Melamed, M.D., and Hughes-Jones, N. (1986). The efficient production of stable, human monoclonal antibody-secreting hybridomas from EBV-transformed lymphocytes using the mouse myeloma X63-Ag8.653 as a fusion partner. *J. Immunol. Methods*, **94**, 7–13.
68 Schlom, J., Wunderlich, D., and Teramato, Y.A. (1980). Generation of human monoclonal antibodies reactive with human mammary carcinoma cells. *Proc. Natl. Acad. Sci. U.S.A.*, **77**, 6841–5.
69 Nowinski, R., *et al.* (1980). Human monoclonal antibody against Forssman antigen. *Science*, **210**, 537–42.
70 Freundlich, B., Bomalski, J.S., Neilson, E., and Jiminez, S.A. (1986). Regulation of fibroblast proliferation and collagen synthesis by cytokines. *Immunol. Today*, **7**, 303–7.
71 Leibovich, S.J. and Ross, R.A. (1976). A macrophage-dependent factor that stimulates the proliferation of fibroblasts *in vitro*. *Am. J. Path.*, **84**, 501–9.
72 Bailey, J.M. and Butler, J. (1985). Anti-inflammatory drugs in experimental atherosclerosis. Part 6 (combination therapy with steroid and non-steroid agents). *Atherosclerosis*, **54**, 205–12.
73 Ellis, N.I.A., Lloyd, B., Lloyd, R.S., and Clayton, B.E. (1984). Selenium and vitamin E in relation to risk factors for coronary heart disease. *J. Clin. Pathol.*, **37**, 220–60.
74 Parthasarathy, S.P., Young, S.G., Witztum, J.L., Pittman, R.C., and

Steinberg, D. (1986). Probucol inhibits oxidative modification of LDL. *J. Clin. Invest.*, **77**, 641–4.

75 Leslie, C.A., Gonnermann, W.A., Ullman, M.D., Hayes, K.C., Franzblau, C., and Cathcart, E.S. (1985). Dietary fish oil modulates macrophage fatty acids and decreases arthritis susceptibility in mice. *J. Exp. Med.*, **162**, 1336–49.

76 Taylor, C.B., Peng, S.-K., Werthessen, N.T., Tham, P., and Lee, K.-T. (1979). Spontaneously occurring angiotoxic derivatives of cholesterol. *Am. J. Clin. Nutr* **32**, 40–57.

77 Fornas, E., Martinez-Sales, V., Camanas, A., and Bagnena, J. (1984). Intestinal absorption of cholesterol auto-oxidation products in the rat. *Arch. Pharmacol. Toxicol.*, **10**, 175–82.

78 Goto, Y. (1982). Lipid peroxides as a cause of vascular diseases. In *Lipid peroxides in biology and medicine* (ed. K. Yagi), pp. 295–303. Academic Press, New York.

10 Macrophages in the Central Nervous System

V.H. PERRY and L.J. LAWSON

1 Introduction

A dominant theme in studies on the central nervous system (CNS) is the relationship between structure and function; the wide diversity of neuronal forms is believed to reflect differences in their functions. With the use of immunocytochemistry and antibodies directed against components of the plasma membrane of macrophages it has become clear that tissue macrophages also show a wide diversity of forms (Figure 10.1). These morphological differences not only reflect adaptations of the monocyte to the local micro-environment but also heterogeneity in functional capabilities, expression of membrane receptors, and biosynthetic capacity (1). Adaptation of a

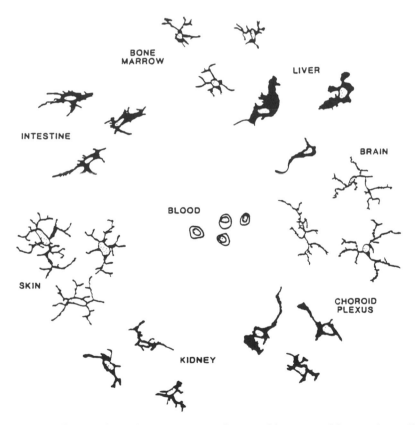

Fig. 10.1 Mononuclear phagocytes can adopt a wide range of forms, depending upon their location in a given tissue. The resident macrophages of the brain, the microglia, provide an extreme example of such specialization (see also Fig. 10.4). (Reproduced from *J. Cell. Sci.*, Suppl., **9**, by permission of The Company of Biologists Ltd.)

monocyte appears to reach its greatest degree of morphological specialization in the microglia, the resident tissue macrophages of the CNS. The highly ramified and complex branching of microglia has possibly played a part in the reluctance of some to believe that these cells were derived from monocytes rather than the neuroectoderm. In recent years, overwhelming evidence has accumulated for the monocytic origin of microglia and some inroads have been made into the biology and possible functions of these cells.

Microglia may form intimate contacts not only with a wide variety of neurons but also several other cell types. The astrocytes and oligodendrocytes are derived from the neuroectoderm and are known collectively as the macroglia. The oligodendrocytes make the myelin sheaths of CNS axons, although they may possess other unknown functions. Astrocytes are a diverse group of cells playing important roles in the development of the CNS, homeostasis, and reaction to injury and infection (2). The vascular supply and fluid environment of the CNS differs significantly from that of other tissues (3). Unlike most other tissues the endothelia of the CNS form tight junctions with each other, limiting the free passage of large molecules from the plasma (4). These tight junctions between the endothelia are induced by contact between a type of astrocyte and endothelial cells (5).

In this chapter we have concentrated on recent studies on microglia and other macrophage populations associated with the CNS of rodents. The reader interested in the historical background to the debate as to the origin of microglia is referred to several earlier reviews (6–8).

2 Microglia

2.1 Origin

It might be expected that the following criteria be fulfilled before accepting that microglia are of monocytic origin: (a) cells of bone marrow origin enter the CNS and adopt the morphology of microglia; (b) that the transition from monocyte to microglia can be documented; and (c) that microglia express antigen(s) known to be partly or wholly restricted to cells of the monocytic lineage.

Radiation chimeras, in which an irradiated host has been reconstituted with bone marrow from a donor bearing a major histocompatibility complex (MHC) antigen different from that of the host, have been used to show that in the adult rodent the brain becomes populated by cells of donor origin (9). Immunocytochemical studies show that small numbers of these donor cells adopt the morphology of microglia within the parenchyma of the CNS (9). The fact that only small numbers of donor cells were found within the parenchyma several months later may reflect the slow turnover of microglia (see Section 2.3) and the fact that MHC Class I antigens are only weakly expressed or absent within the CNS of normal adult rodents (see Section 2.4). These two factors may explain why Matsumoto and co-workers (10) were unable to demonstrate microglia of donor origin following a similar experimental procedure.

Rio Hortega (6) applied a silver staining method to the developing brain and described a class of cell which changes in morphology from a simple rounded or stellate cell to that of microglia. He believed that these cells were of mesodermal origin and, indeed, coined the term 'microglia'. Using a monoclonal antibody directed against the mouse macrophage antigen F4/80 (11), the ontogeny of microglia has been studied in the developing retina and brain (12,13). In the embryonic mouse brain (day 16), the earliest time point studied, F4/80+ macrophages with a rounded or stellate form are found but no microglia. Three to four days later at the time of birth larger numbers of F4/80+ cells are present and many of these have a more ramified appearance (Figure 10.2). In the following postnatal week the F4/80+ cells come to

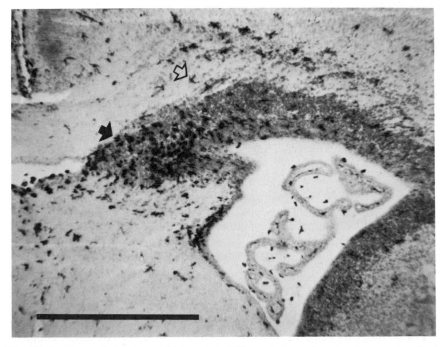

Fig. 10.2 Around the time of birth the differentiation of macrophages recruited into the developing CNS is already underway. In the 1-day-old mouse, ramified F4/80+ cells (open arrow) which resemble adult microglia co-exist with macrophage-like cells (solid arrow). (Immunoperoxidase, counterstained with cresyl violet. Scale bar = 500 μm).

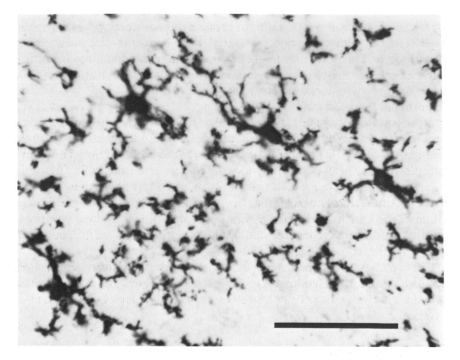

Fig. 10.3 The macrophage-specific antiserum, F4/80, reveals the elaborate morphology of resident microglia in the parietal cortex of the normal adult mouse. (Immunoperoxidase, no counterstain. Scale bar = 50 μm.)

resemble adult microglia (Figure 10.3). Thus, using a specific macrophage marker and antibodies against other plasma membrane antigens known to be present on macrophages, an Fc receptor and the complement type 3 receptor (CR3), it has been possible to follow the differentiation of monocytes to microglia in the developing CNS (13). The time course of the entry of the F4/80+ cells into the CNS was correlated with the increase in naturally occurring cell death in the retina and brain (12,13). Naturally occurring cell death is a major feature of CNS development and as many as 50–70 per cent of the cells generated in the embryo may degenerate during maturation, although this varies considerably from region to region (14). We suggested that cell death may act as a chemotactic stimulus to recruit monocytes into the developing brain although other factors may be involved.

If microglia are derived from monocytes we might expect microglia to share antigens with other tissue macrophages. A number of reports indicating that microglia do not share antigens found on monocytes and macrophages helped fuel the debate concerning the origin of microglia. However, a new, wider range of specific antibodies and improved immunocytochemical procedures with greatly enhanced sensitivity, have resulted in a number of leucocyte or macrophage-restricted antigens being demonstrated on microglia, particularly in rodents. Apart from the macrophage restricted marker F4/80, murine microglia are known to express antigens restricted to leucocytes (the leucocyte common antigen), molecules of known function known to be expressed by monocytes and macrophages (Fc and CR3 receptors), as well as others (15).

Further evidence for the monocytic origin or microglia comes from tissue grafting studies. Retinae from embryonic mice were transplanted into the midbrain region of newborn rats. These retinae develop relatively normal lamination, the axons grow out from the transplant to the host and make specific functional connections with visual centres of the host (16). Microglia in transplanted mouse retinae are only labelled by antibodies directed against bone marrow derived cells of the rat host (17). These transplant studies are analogous to a chimeric CNS with the host bone marrow providing the cells which will enter the tissue graft and differentiate to microglia.

Thus, four lines of evidence leave little room for doubt that microglia are the resident macrophages of the CNS. There is no convincing evidence for a population of cells with the morphology of microglia with neuroectodermal origins.

2.2   Distribution

Macrophages in non-CNS tissues are not usually randomly distributed but commonly found associated with particular tissue elements, frequently vascular endothelium or epithelium. For example, Kupffer cells of the liver line sinusoids and macrophages of the lamina propria of the gut often surround capillaries. Some tissue macrophages may also show overt regular spacing such as the Langerhans cells within the basal layer of the epidermis (1).

The CNS is not a homogeneous organ but has well-defined functionally distinct regions. Within these divisions, neurons differ in their morphology, connections and the type of neurotransmitter employed. The local macroglia may also be markedly different. In the absence of any previous systematic studies of the distribution of microglia within the CNS we undertook such a study of the mouse CNS using a monospecific antiserum to F4/80 (18). We were particularly interested to learn whether the distribution of microglia in the adult CNS reflected the amount of natural cell death that had occurred in a particular structure during development: did regions with high levels of cell death ultimately have more microglia? We also examined whether systematic variations in the morphology and distribution of microglia might exist, and whether these were correlated with other known anatomical or neurochemical differences which might shed light on their function.

We classified microglia into three morphological types. The most complex of these is the *radial* microglia found in the grey matter, that is, those regions containing the cell bodies and processes and synaptic connections of neurons. These cells have from three to five primary processes which branch to give a radial appearance when seen in two-dimensional reconstructions (Figure 10.4). Within this group the cells vary somewhat in the length of the processes. This is partly related to the local density of microglia as smaller, more bushy cells are found in regions of higher cell density.

The second type of microglia is the *longitudinal* microglia found in white matter, the major fibre tracts. These cells are in many respects similar to the radial cells but have their processes oriented along the long axis of the axons within a fibre tract (Figure 10.4).

The third type is the *compact* microglia. They are much simpler in form than the others having few long processes and are sparsely branched (Figure 10.4). These cells are found in those parts of the CNS where the blood–brain barrier is absent and the cells are exposed to plasma proteins. These areas, which include sites such as the median eminence and the subfornical organ, are known collectively as the circumventricular organs. Whether this dramatic difference in form is a direct influence of plasma proteins is at present unclear although it is known that the microglia in these regions express a number of antigens at greater levels than microglia lying within the brain parenchyma (19) (see Section 2.4).

Microglia are ubiquitous but their distribution is heterogeneous. In general there are more microglia in the grey matter than the white matter and there is a trend for phylogenetically and ontogenetically newer structures to contain more microglia than older structures. The microglia are not randomly scattered throughout the CNS but form a quasi-regular distribution with each cell occupying its own territory. A consistent pattern of distribution is found from animal to animal with a more than six-fold difference in density across the CNS. In the cortical white matter, microglia represent about 5 per cent of the total glial population and within the cortical grey matter, they represent about 5 per cent of the total population of neurons and glia. We have found no correlation between the density of microglia and the amount of developmental cell death. The distribution of microglia also does not correlate with functionally distinct subdivisions of the CNS, different neurotransmitter systems, the distribution of non-neuronal cells, or the distribution and density of the vascular network. It is not known how the adult pattern emerges, whether this reflects particular sites of entry of monocytes into the CNS, selective migration pathways, regions of local proliferation or turnover, or some combination of these.

From our quantitative analysis we have estimated that the total number of microglia in the mouse brain is about 3.5×10^6, which on a weight-for-weight basis is similar to the number of Kupffer cells in the liver. However, in addition we have performed image analysis measurements of the total cell surface area of microglia determined from two-dimensional drawings. Our

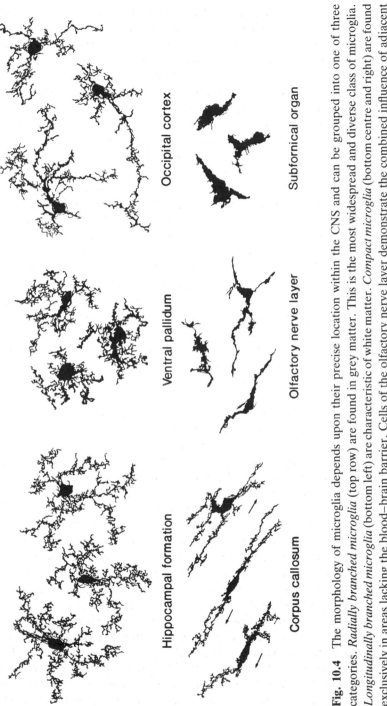

Fig. 10.4 The morphology of microglia depends upon their precise location within the CNS and can be grouped into one of three categories. *Radially branched microglia* (top row) are found in grey matter. This is the most widespread and diverse class of microglia. *Longitudinally branched microglia* (bottom left) are characteristic of white matter. *Compact microglia* (bottom centre and right) are found exclusively in areas lacking the blood–brain barrier. Cells of the olfactory nerve layer demonstrate the combined influence of adjacent nerve fibres and exposure to plasma proteins.

estimates show that radial microglia may have a cell surface area two or more times larger than that of a Kupffer cell. Thus, microglia are not only a significant population of the resident macrophage pool but their large surface area within the CNS suggests that they might be sensitive to changes in the local milieu.

2.3   Kinetics

It is not known at present how long monocytes will live once they have entered the developing CNS and differentiated to microglial cells; whether the cells live for the lifespan of the organism, or whether senescent microglia are replaced by local division and/or incoming monocytes. The extent of monocyte traffic into the normal adult CNS has become of particular interest in view of the possibility that these cells may act as 'Trojan Horses' (20) and carry infectious agents into the CNS. In the adult CNS, neurons are post-mitotic cells and apart from neurons of the olfactory epithelium there is no evidence that they retain a proliferative potential in mammals (21). In contrast, cells of the macroglial lineages may continue to proliferate at low levels throughout life (22,23).

The data on microglia kinetics throughout the CNS is limited, largely due to the fact that, until recently, methods that would allow unambiguous identification of microglia, such as silver staining or electron microscopy, have been tedious to combine with ³H-thymidine autoradiography. A number of studies on the corpus callosum (the major fibre tract joining the two cerebral hemispheres) concluded that following a single pulse of ³H-thymidine or continuous infusion the turnover of microglia or monocyte entry was small or insignificant (24).

As it is relatively straightforward to combine ³H-thymidine autoradiography with immunocytochemistry we have begun a systematic survey of the resident microglia turnover in the mouse CNS using F4/80 to identify the microglia. With a single pulse of ³H-thymidine and a survival time of less than an hour it is possible to determine whether division of the resident cells occurs, and with longer survival times after a single pulse it is possible to estimate whether there is significant monocyte entry (25).

Our results show that following a single pulse of ³H-thymidine and a one hour survival period all types of microglia are labelled with ³H-thymidine, albeit in very small numbers (Figure 10.5). These ³H-thymidine-labelled, F4/80+ microglia are scattered, apparently at random, throughout the brain. The majority of these cells occur in isolation but occasionally several are found together, most commonly they lie within the parenchyma but do not appear to be associated with any particular structures, such as the vascular supply. The percentage of microglia labelled with ³H-thymidine is low, even lower than that reported for other non-lymphoid organs (26,27). After survival times of 24 and 48 hours the numbers of ³H-thymidine labelled

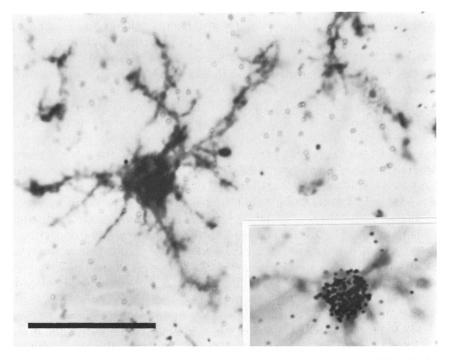

Fig. 10.5 Microglial turnover occurs in the normal adult mouse brain, albeit slowly. One hour after ³H-thymidine administration, a F4/80⁺ cell with normal resident morphology is labelled (immunoperoxidase. Scale bar = 25 μm.) *Inset*: the same cell with the plane of focus altered to display the silver grains over the nucleus.

F4/80⁺ cells is somewhat greater than can be accounted for on the basis of proliferation of the resident cells alone suggesting that there is a low level of monocyte entry into the CNS, as has been described for other organs (27,28). There is clearly much to be learnt about the kinetics of this substantial population of macrophages.

2.4 Functions

Monocytes invade the developing CNS and play a role in the removal of dying neurons and their processes (13,29). There is also evidence that during this period these infiltrating macrophages and/or immature microglia secrete interleukin-1 (IL-1), which may influence both gliogenesis and angiogenesis (30,31) and also specific growth factors promoting astrocyte proliferation (32). Whether the removal of the degenerating neurons and their processes is an important or necessary component in the refinement of CNS connections, or for guiding growing fibres is not yet known. It will be important to devise methods for manipulating the macrophage population in neonates if we are to understand the role of these cells in the developing CNS.

In the adult CNS, the functions of microglia have yet to be elucidated. A striking feature of adult microglia is their apparently inactive appearance. Electron microscopic studies show that these cells have a poorly developed biosynthetic apparatus and the perinuclear cytoplasm lacks the rich complement of organelles normally associated with macrophages (33). This down-regulated quality of the microglia is also apparent in their low expression of a number of antigens typically found on macrophage populations residing in other tissues. For example, in rodents, MHC Class I and II antigens are not expressed on the microglia in the normal CNS (34), and in rat, the leucocyte common antigen and CD4 molecule are only weakly expressed on microglia compared with other tissue macrophages. The nature of the CNS components that influence the microglia in this manner are not understood. There is evidence, however, that the exclusion of plasma proteins may be important. Microglia in the circumventricular organs of the rat, which are exposed to plasma proteins, readily express detectable levels of several antigens only weakly expressed or absent from parenchymal microglia behind the blood–brain barrier (19,35). The nature of these plasma-derived components which possibly influence the microglia phenotype is not known.

Microglia express readily detectable levels of receptors for the Fc portion of IgG1/IgG2b molecules, and complement type 3 (13), although the latter is often down-regulated on other tissue macrophages (36). The significance of this is, however, unclear as both immunoglobulins and complement components are normally excluded from the extracellular fluid of the CNS (3). The expression of other receptors or biosynthesis of secretory products by microglia of the normal CNS has not been reported.

In at least one part of the CNS we have provided evidence that the microglia retain an active and apparently specific role as a phagocytic cell (37). Magnocellular neurons, with their cell bodies in the hypothelamus, terminate in the posterior pituitary where they release the hormones oxytocin and vasopressin into the blood supply. In the rat approximately 20 per cent of the cells in the posterior pituitary (excluding the endothelium) are microglia. Fine processes of microglia surround endings of the magno-cellular axons, in particular those parts of the neuron which have penetrated the basement membrane and lie in the perivascular space. In some instances a sequence of images could be documented showing that the microglia endocytose parts of the neurosecretory axons and digest them in lysosomal bodies. Why microglia should endocytose the terminals of viable neurons is not at all clear but it is unlikely that this is a mode of hormone regulation as the number of terminals being engulfed is a very small fraction of the total. Magnocellular neurones are known to retain the capacity to regenerate and may be constantly growing; a principal function of the microglia could therefore be to 'trim' those parts that have penetrated the basement membrane. Electron microscopic studies of microglia in other parts of the CNS have shown some evidence of phagocytic activity but the origin of the phagocytosed debris is not known. It remains an intriguing possibility that the microglia continually modify the terminals of CNS neurons.

3   Other forms of macrophage in the central nervous system

In addition to the microglia within the parenchyma of the CNS there are several other potentially important macrophage populations at interfaces between the CNS and the blood. These include macrophages associated with the choroid plexus, leptomeninges, and the micro-circulation.

3.1   Choroid plexus

The choroid plexus lies within the ventricles and is responsible for the production of the cerebrospinal fluid (CSF) (3). The endothelium within the choroid plexus is fenestrated but the choroidal epithelial cells have tight junctions between them preventing the free passage of large molecules from the plasma. The CSF is not simply a filtrate of plasma but is actively secreted by the choroidal cells. Macrophages are found to lie both within the stroma of the choroid plexus and also on the apical surface of the epithelium, the latter being known as Kolmer or epiplexus cells (Figure 10.6). In whole-mount preparations of mouse choroid the stromal macrophages are seen to have long processes and lie in a regularly spaced fashion akin to the Langerhans cells in the skin. These stromal macrophages express a wide range of macrophage antigens and, in contrast to the microglia, have high levels of MHC Class II antigen (Matyszak and co-workers, unpublished observations). These macrophages may either play a role in preventing the entry of foreign antigens into the CNS or prevent CNS antigens from being exposed to the peripheral immune system.

The Kolmer cells on the apical surface of the choroid epithelium express a similar spectrum of macrophage antigens as the stromal macrophages and have been shown to be phagocytic cells as are other macrophages found within the ventricles (38,39). These cells may play a role in the removal of debris from the ventricular space.

3.2   Leptomeninges

The surface of the brain is covered by the meninges, made up of several different membranous layers. Immediately beneath the skull there is a tough connective tissue layer, the dura, and immediately beneath the dura lies the arachnoid. Between the arachnoid and the pia there is the subarachnoid

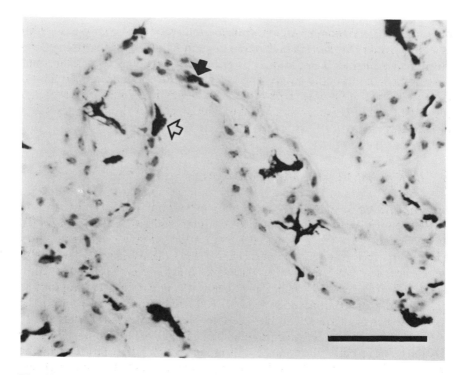

Fig. 10.6   The choroid plexus is an important interface between the CNS and the periphery and has its own distinct macrophage population. F4/80+ cells lie within the stroma (◖) as well as on the apical surface of the choroidal epithelium (◊). Unlike microglia, these cells express MHC Class II antigen. (Immunoperoxidase, counterstained with cresyl violet. Scale bar = 50 µm.)

space and macrophages are found both free within the subarachnoid space and lying on the surface of the pia. These macrophages, again in contrast to the microglia, express a wide range of macrophage antigens and ultrastructurally resemble typical phagocytic macrophages and have been shown to endocytose horseradish peroxidase (40). These cells are well placed to play a role in restricting the movement of antigens from the blood to the CNS compartment and vice versa.

3.3   Perivascular macrophages

Associated with the vasculature of the CNS parenchyma there is a population of macrophages enclosed within the basement membrane and lying adjacent to the endothelium. These cells express macrophage antigens but are morphologically and antigenically distinct from microglia. They lack long ramified processes and express macrophage antigens not expressed on microglia, including MHC Class II (41,42). That these cells are derived from bone marrow cells has been demonstrated in bone marrow chimeras, with donor-derived cells present in this perivascular location within two months after reconstitution. The location of these cells suggests that they could participate in interactions between the CNS and immune system. Studies on graft rejection following transplantation of allogeneic CNS tissue to the CNS suggest that the perivascular cells may play a critical role in the rejection process (43).

4   Response of microglia to injury

In peripheral tissues mononuclear phagocytes play an important part in tissue repair following injury (44). In the peripheral nervous system (PNS) the inflammatory response in a degenerating nerve segment is an important component of nerve degeneration and also involved in the successful regeneration of sensory nerve fibres (45,46). In the CNS it has been repeatedly documented since Rio Hortega (6) that microglia respond to many different forms of injury. However, the relative contributions of recruited monocytes and the resident microglia may vary with the type of lesion and the functional role of mononuclear phagocytes in any possible CNS repair is poorly understood. It should be noted that in the CNS the repair capabilities are restricted since degenerated neurons are not replaced and the capacity for fibre regeneration is very limited. The mononuclear phagocyte response to different types of CNS insult has been recently reviewed (15) and some of the central issues will be considered below.

Following a traumatic wound to the CNS, in which blood vessels and hence the blood–brain barrier are damaged, both polymorphonuclear cells and monocytes are recruited (47). The recruited monocyte population and surrounding microglia may then appear to adopt the morphology of so-called 'activated' microglia. These cells are distinct from the resident microglia with more processes than the normal resident cells (compare Figures 10.3 and 10.7), and a number of macrophage antigens are up-regulated (15). Apart from their obvious role in the removal of the debris these cells may play a role in re-establishing local homeostasis in particular restoration of the blood–brain barrier. Secretion of IL-1 by recruited cells (and possibly the activated resident microglia) may promote restoration of the blood–brain barrier because IL-1 injected into the CNS will promote both angiogenesis and gliogenesis in the CNS (31). *In vivo* administration of chloroquine or colchicine, which have a wide range of effects on many cell types, reduces the number of mononuclear phagocytes at the site of a stab wound and this was in turn found to slow the rate of debris clearance and reduce both astrogliosis and neovascularization (48). It is possible that phagocytosis of degenerating neurons is important as their breakdown products may themselves be neurotoxic (49).

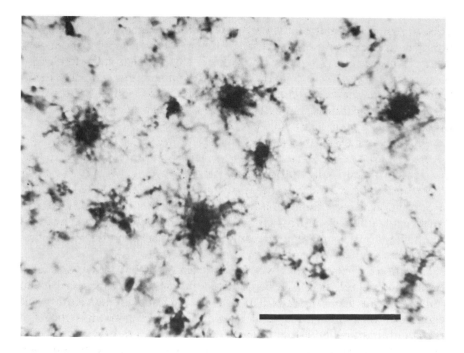

Fig. 10.7 Following an injury, F4/80⁺ cells adopt the morphology of 'activated' microglia. These cells, in the parietal cortex of a mouse injected with kainic acid 5 days previously, are completely unlike normal resident microglia (compare with Figure 10.3). (Immunoperoxidase, no counterstain. Scale bar = 50 μm.)

An important difference between a local lesion to the nervous system and a peripheral tissue is that damage to a fibre tract will result in degeneration at sites distant to the lesion. The segment of a nerve fibre isolated from the cell body will degenerate (Wallerian degeneration) and the parent cell body of a damaged fibre will undergo retrograde degeneration. Both Wallerian and retrograde degeration are accompanied by microglial activation but, in contrast to a traumatic wound, the blood–brain barrier remains intact (50,51) and polymorphonuclear cells are not recruited. The relative contributions made by recruited monocytes and division of resident microglia to the increased numbers of microglia found in these circumstances has yet to be resolved (15). An interesting feature of Wallerian degeneration in the CNS when compared to the PNS is that it is very much slower. In the PNS there is rapid monocyte recruitment and the myelin and axons of the degenerating fibres are rapidly removed over a period of days, but in the CNS recruitment is much slower and the degeneration products may persist for many months (52–54). The response of mononuclear phagocytes in Wallerian degeneration may appear to be an academic question as the isolated segment of axon has no functional relevance. However, recent evidence suggests that the removal of the debris by mononuclear phagocytes may be significant. As was mentioned above there is now evidence that recruited monocytes play a role in successful regeneration of the PNS (46). It has recently been shown that CNS myelin contains several components that inhibit the growth of axons and may thus help to impede any attempts at regrowth by the damaged axons (55). Thus, eliciting an inflammatory response may have beneficial effects, although this may in turn be offset by an enhanced astrogliosis which could impede axon regrowth (56). The mechanisms in the CNS which result in slow recruitment of monocytes and the relatively poor phagocytosis of debris are not understood. The poor phagocytic capacity of mononuclear cells in Wallerian degeneration of the CNS may reflect the observation (Section 2.4) that microglia appear to be down-regulated macrophages within the CNS micro-environment and are thus slow to initiate an inflammatory response when compared to those of other tissues.

Damage to a peripheral nerve results in proliferation of the glial cells surrounding the cell bodies of the damaged axons. Those neurons with cell bodies in the spinal cord retain the capacity to regenerate and do not degenerate after a crush injury. An intriguing observation is that the microglia surrounding these cells interpose their processes between the synaptic contacts and the cell body but do not actually phagocytose the synaptic bouton (57). The functional significance of this process, known as 'synaptic stripping', for restitution of function is not known but may be the overt expression of an ongoing interaction between microglia and neurons in the CNS, in which the former play a role in modifying synaptic connections.

In the normal rodent CNS, microglia do not express MHC Class II antigens but following various forms of injury activated microglia will express these molecules (51,58). It is of interest to know whether these cells might play a role in immune-mediated injury in the CNS. An important difference to note here between the CNS of rodents and man is that in the human CNS the microglia, which express macrophage specific antigens (59), express MHC Class II antigens in the healthy CNS (60). Experimental allergic encephalitis (EAE) has been widely studied as a model of auto-immune disease within the CNS of rodents. It is produced by the administration of myelin basic protein peripherally and can also be induced by the adoptive transfer of sensitized T-cells. EAE is thought to be mediated, at least in part, by sensitized T-cells recognizing CNS antigen in association with a cell expressing MHC Class II antigens. In EAE, microglia express MHC Class II antigens but astrocytes, oligodendrocytes, and endothelial cells do not (61). The perivascular cells which express macrophage antigens and MHC Class II antigens may be cells of particular importance in this respect (9,41).

At the present time our understanding of the functional role of macrophages and microglia in response to CNS injury is very limited. The microglia are, however, an exquisitely sensitive indicator of CNS pathology or disturbances of function. Conspicuous alterations in morphology or antigenic phenotype are readily observed in all forms of degeneration, traumatic wounds, Wallerian, and retrograde degeneration, the cell body response to peripheral nerve injury, neuronal degeneration induced by excitatory neurotoxins (62) and in a model of epilepsy (63).

5   Summary

The resident macrophages of the CNS parenchyma are known as microglia. Monocytes enter the developing CNS and phagocytose degenerating cells and their processes and then differentiate to microglia. Microglia are ubiquitously but heterogeneously distributed throughout the CNS and have a distinct morphology within different regions. In the normal CNS they appear to be quiescent cells as judged by their ultrastructure and antigenic phenotype. However, microglia are exquisitely sensitive to a wide variety of pathological insults and rapidly alter their morphology and phenotype. The functions of these cells in the normal and injured CNS are largely unknown.

Macrophages are also found in association with the CNS vasculature, the chorid plexus, and within the leptomeninges: important interfaces between the vasculature and the CNS. These cells have an antigenic phenotype which is markedly different from microglia. Macrophages at these sites may play an important role in preventing the access of foreign antigens to the CNS or CNS antigens to the peripheral immune system.

Acknowledgements

The work from our own laboratory reported in this review was supported by the MRC, The Wellcome Trust, and Multiple Sclerosis Society. VHP is a Wellcome Senior Research Fellow. We thank Dr S. Gordon for his comments on the manuscript.

References

1 Gordon, S., Perry, V.H., Rabinowitz, S., Chung, L-P., and Rosen, H. (1988). Plasma membrane receptors of the mononuclear phagocyte system. *J. Cell Sci.*, Suppl., **9**, 1–26.
2 Federoff, S. and Vernadakis, A. (1986). *Astrocytes*, Vols 1–3. Academic Press, London.
3 Davson, H., Welch, K., and Segal, M.B. (1987). *The physiology and pathophysiology of the cerebrospinal fluid.* Churchill Livingstone, Edinburgh.
4 Reese, T.A. and Karnovsky, M.J. (1967). Fine structural localization of a blood–brain barrier to exogenous peroxidase. *J. Cell Biol.*, **34**, 207–17.
5 Jazner, R.C. and Raff, M.C. (1987). Astrocytes induce blood–brain barrier properties in endothelial cells. *Nature*, **325**, 253–7.
6 del Rio Hortega, P. (1932). Microglia. In *Cytology and cellular pathology of the nervous system* (ed. W. Penfield), pp. 482–534. Paul B. Hoeber, New York.
7 Ling, E.A. (1981). The origin and nature of microglia. In *Advances in cellular neurobiology*, Vol. 2. (ed. S. Federoff and I. Hertz), pp. 33–82. Academic Press, New York.
8 Jordan, F.L. and Thomas, W.E. (1988). Brain macrophages: Questions of origin and interrelationship. *Brain Res. Rev.*, **13**, 165–78.
9 Hickey, W.F. and Kimura, H. (1988). Perivascular microglial cells of the CNS are bone marrow-derived and present antigen *in vivo*. *Science*, **239**, 290–2.
10 Matsumoto, Y. and Fujiwara, M. (1987). Absence of donor-type major histocompatibility complex class I antigen-bearing microglia in the rat central nervous system of radiation bone marrow chimeras. *J. Neuroimmunol.*, **17**, 71–82.
11 Austyn, J.M. and Gordon, S. (1981). F4/80: a monoclonal antibody directed specifically against the mouse macrophage. *Eur. J. Immunol.*, **11**, 805–11.
12 Hume, D.A., Perry, V.H., and Gordon, S. (1983). Immunohistochemical localization of a macrophage specific antigen in developing mouse retina: phagocytosis of dying neurons and differentiation of microglial cells to form a regular array in the plexiform layers. *J. Cell Biol.*, **97**, 253–7.
13 Perry, V.H., Hume, D.A., and Gordon, S. (1985). Immunohistochemical localization of macrophages and microglia in the adult and developing mouse brain. *Neuroscience*, **15**, 313–26.
14 Oppenheim, R.W. (1981). Neuronal cell death and related regressive phenomenon during neurogenesis: a selective historical review and progress report. In *Studies in developmental neurobiology: Essays in*

honour of Victor Hamburger (ed. W.M. Cowan), pp. 74–133. Oxford University Press.

15 Perry, V.H. and Gordon, S. (1991). Macrophages and the Nervous System. *Int. Rev. Cytol.*, **125**, 203–44.

16 Klassen, H.J. and Lund, R.D. (1987). Retinal transplants can drive a pupillary reflex in host rat brains. *Proc. Natl. Acad. Sci. U.S.A.*, **84**, 6958–60.

17 Perry, V.H. and Lund, R.D. (1989). Microglia in retinae transplanted to the central nervous system. *Neuroscience*, **31**, 453–62.

18 Lawson, L.J., Perry, V.H., Dri, P., and Gordon, S. (1990). Heterogeneity in the distribution and morphology of microglia in the normal adult mouse brain. *Neuroscience*, **39**, 151–70.

19 Perry, V.H. and Gordon, S. (1987). Modulation of the CD4 antigen on macrophages and microglia in rat brain. *J. Exp. Med.*, **166**, 1138–43.

20 Williams, A.E. and Blakemore, W.F. (1990). Monocyte-mediated entry of pathogens into the central nervous system. *Neuropath. Appl. Neurobiol.*, **16**, 377–92.

21 Rakic, P. (1985). Limits of neurogenesis in primates. *Science*, **227**, 1054–6.

22 Schultze, B. and Korr, H. (1981). Cell kinetic studies of different cell types in the developing and adult brain of the rat and the mouse: a review. *Cell Tiss. Kinet.*, **14**, 309–25.

23 ffrench-constant, C. and Raff, M.C. (1986). Proliferating bipotential glial cell progenitor cells in adult rat optic nerve. *Nature*, **319**, 499–502.

24 McCarthy, G.E. and Leblond, C.P. (1988). Radioautographic evidence for slow astrocyte turnover and modest oligodendrocyte production in the corpus callosum of adult mice infused with ^{3}H-thymidine. *J. Comp. Neurol.*, **271**, 589–603.

25 Lawson, L.J., Perry, V.H., Dri, P., and Gordon, S. (1990). Distribution, morphology and turnover of the resident macrophages of the normal adult mouse brain. *Neurosci. Letts.*, **38** (Suppl.), S85.

26 Mackenzie, I.C. (1975). Labelling of murine epidermal Langerhans cells with H3-thymidine. *Am. J. Anat.*, **144**, 127–36.

27 Crofton, R.W., Diesselhoff-den-dulk, M.M.C., and Van Furth, R. (1978). The origin, kinetics and characteristics of the Kupffer cells in the normal steady state. *J. Exp. Med.*, **148**, 1–17.

28 Van Oud Alblas, A.B. and Van Furth, R. (1979). Origin, kinetics and characteristics of pulmonary macrophages in the normal steady state. *J. Exp. Med.*, **149**, 1504–18.

29 Innocenti, G.M., Clarke, S., and Koppel, H. (1983). Transitory macrophages in the white matter of the developing visual cortex. II. Development and relations with axonal pathways. *Dev. Brain Res.*, **11**, 55–66.

30 Giulian, D., Young, D.G., Woodward, J., Brown, D.C. and Lachman,

L.B. (1988). Interleukin-1 is an astroglial growth factor in the developing brain. *J. Neurosci.*, **8**, 709–14.

31 Giulian, D., Woodward, J., Krebs, J.F., and Lachman, L.B. (1988). Interleukin-1 injected into mammalian brain stimulates astrogliosis and neovascularization. *J. Neurosci.*, **8**, 2485–90.

32 Giulian, D. and Young, D.G. (1986). Brain peptides and glial growth. II. Identification of cells that secrete glial promoting factors. *J. Cell Biol.*, **102**, 812–17.

33 Peters, A., Palay, S.L., and Webster, H.D. (1976). In *Fine structure of the nervous system: The neurons and supporting cells* (ed. A. Peters, S.L. Palay, and H.D. Webster). Saunders, Philadelphia.

34 Matsumoto, Y. and Fujiwara, M. (1986). *In situ* detection of Class I and II major histocompatibility complex antigens in the rat central nervous system during experimental allergic encephalitis. *J. Neuroimmunol.*, **12**, 265–77.

35 Perry, V.H. and Gordon, S. (1989). Resident macrophages of the central nervous system: Modulation of phenotype in relation to a specialized microenvironment. In *Neuroimmune networks: Physiology and diseases* (ed. E.J. Goetzl and N.H. Spector). Alan R. Liss, New York.

36 Lee, S.H., Crocker, P., and Gordon, S. (1986). Macrophage plasma membrane and sectretory properties in murine malaria. *J. Exp. Med.*, **163**, 54–74.

37 Pow, D.V., Perry, V.H., Morris, J.F., and Gordon, S. (1989). Microglia in the neurohypophysis associate with and endocytose terminal portions of neurosecretory neurons. *Neuroscience*, **33**, 567–78.

38 Carpenter, S.J., McCarthy, L.E., and Borison, H.I. (1970). Electron microscopic study of the epiplexus (Kolmer) cells of the cat choroid plexus. *Z. Zellforsch. Mikrosk. Anat.*, **110**, 471–86.

39 Blier, R. and Albrecht, R. (1980). Supraependymal macrophages of the third ventricle of hamster: Morphological, functional and histochemical characterization *in situ* and in culture. *J. Comp. Neurol.*, **192**, 489–504.

40 Shabo, A.I. and Maxwell, D.S. (1971). The subarachnoid space following the introduction of a foreign protein: An electron microscopic study with peroxidase. *J. Neuropath. Exp. Neurol.*, **30**, 506–24.

41 Streit, W.J., Graeber, M.B., and Kreutzberg, G.W. (1989). Expression of Ia antigen on perivascular and microglial cells after sublethal and lethal motor neuron injury. *Exp. Neurol.*, **105**, 115–26.

42 Graeber, M.B., Streit, W.J., and Kreutzberg, G.W. (1989). Identity of ED2-positive perivascular cells in rat brain. *J. Neurosci. Res.*, **22**, 103–6.

43 Lawrence, J.M., Morris, R.J., Wilson, D.J., and Raisman, G. (1990). Mechanisms of allograft rejection in the rat brain. *Neuroscience*, **37**, 431–62.

44 Leibovich, S.J. and Ross, R. (1975). The role of macrophages in wound repair. *Am. J. Path.*, **78**, 71–91.

45 Lunn, E.R., Perry, V.H., Brown, M.C., Rosen, H., and Gordon, S. (1989). Absence of Wallerian degeneration does not hinder regeneration in peripheral nerve. *Eur. J. Neurosci.*, **1**, 27–33.

46 Brown, M.C., Lunn, E.R., and Perry, V.H. (1990). Failure of normal Wallerian degeneration results in very poor regeneration of cutaneous afferent fibres in mice. *J. Physiol.*, **422**, 12P.

47 Imamoto, K. and Leblond, C.P. (1974). Presence of labelled monocytes, macrophages and microglia in a stab wound of the brain following an injection of bone marrow cells labelled with ^{3}H-uridine into rats. *J. Comp. Neurol.*, **174**, 255–80.

48 Giulian, D., Chen, J., Ingeman, J.E., George, J.K., and Noponen, M. (1989). The role of mononuclear phagocytes in wound healing after traumatic injury to adult mammalian brain. *J. Neurosci.*, **9**, 4416–29.

49 Nieto-Sampedro, M. and Cotman, C.W. (1985). Growth factor induction and temporal order in central nervous system repair. In *Synaptic plasticity* (ed. C.W. Cotman). The Guilford Press, London and New York.

50 Kiernan, J.A. (1985). Axonal and vascular changes following injury to the rat's optic nerve. *J. Anat.*, **141**, 139–54.

51 Kuono, H., Yamamoto, T., Iwasaki, Y., Suzuki, H., Saito, T., and Terenuma, H. (1989). Wallerian degeneration induces Ia-antigen-expression in rat brain. *J. Neuroimmunol.*, **25**, 151–9.

52 Perry, V.H., Brown, M.C., and Gordon, S. (1987). The macrophage response to central and peripheral nerve injury: a possible role for macrophages in regeneration. *J. Exp. Med.*, **165**, 1218–23.

53 Stoll, G.W., Trapp, B.D., and Griffin, J.W. (1989). Macrophage function during Wallerian degeneration of rat optic nerve: Clearance of degenerating myelin and Ia expression. *J. Neurosci.*, **9**, 2327–35.

54 Stoll, G., Griffin, J.W., Li, C.Y., and Trapp, B.D. (1989). Wallerian degeneration in the peripheral nervous system: participation of both Schwann cells and macrophages in myelin degradation. *J. Neurocytol.*, **18**, 671–83.

55 Caroni, P. and Schwab, M.E. (1988). Two membrane protein fractions from rat central myelin with inhibitory properties for neurite growth and fibroblast spreading. *J. Cell Biol.*, **106**, 1281–8.

56 Reier, P.J. (1986). Gliosis following CNS injury: The anatomy of astrocytic scars and their influences on axonal elongation. In *Astrocytes*, Vol. 3, *Cell biology and pathology of astrocytes* (ed. S. Federoff and A. Vernadakis). Academic Press, London.

57 Blinzinger, K. and Kreutzberg, G.W. (1968). Displacement of synaptic terminals from regenerating motoneurons by microglia. *Z. Zellforsch. Mikrosk. Anat.*, **85**, 145–57.

58 Akiyama, H., Itagaki, S., and McGeer, P.L. (1988). Major histocompatibility complex antigen expression on rat microglia following epidural kainic acid lesions. *J. Neurosci. Res.*, **20**, 147–57.
59 Esiri, M.M. and McGee, J. (1986). Monoclonal antibody to macrophages (EBM/11) labels macrophages and microglial cells in human brain. *J. Clin Pathol.*, **39**, 615–21.
60 Hayes, G.M., Woodroofe, M.N., and Cuzner, M.L. (1987). Microglia are the major cell type expressing MHC Class II in human white matter. *J. Neurol. Sci.*, **80**, 25–37.
61 Vass, K., Lassman, H., Wekerle, H., and Wisniewski, H.M. (1986). The distribution of Ia antigen in the lesions of rat acute experimental allergic encephalomyelitis. *Acta Neuropath.*, **70**, 149–60.
62 Coffey, P.J., Perry, V.H., and Rawlins, J.N.P. (1990). An investigation into the early stages of the inflammatory response following ibotenic acid-induced neuronal degeneration. *Neuroscience*, **35**, 121–32.
63 Shaw, J.A.G., Perry, V.H., and Mellanby, J. (1990). Tetanus toxin-induced seizures cause microglial activation in rat hippocampus. *Neurosci. Lett.*, **120**, 66–9.

Index